Lecture Notes of the Institute for Computer Sciences, Social Informatics and Telecommunications Engineering 281

More information about this series at http://www.springer.com/series/8197

Min Jia · Qing Guo · Weixiao Meng (Eds.)

Wireless and Satellite Systems

10th EAI International Conference, WiSATS 2019 Harbin, China, January 12–13, 2019 Proceedings, Part II

Springer

Editors
Min Jia
Harbin Institute of Technology
Harbin, China

Weixiao Meng
Harbin Institute of Technology
Harbin, China

Qing Guo
Harbin Institute of Technology
Harbin, China

ISSN 1867-8211 ISSN 1867-822X (electronic)
Lecture Notes of the Institute for Computer Sciences, Social Informatics
and Telecommunications Engineering
ISBN 978-3-030-19155-9 ISBN 978-3-030-19156-6 (eBook)
https://doi.org/10.1007/978-3-030-19156-6

This Springer imprint is published by the registered company Springer Nature Switzerland AG
The registered company address is: Gewerbestrasse 11, 6330 Cham, Switzerland

Preface

We are delighted to introduce the proceedings of the 10th edition of the European Alliance for Innovation (EAI) International Conference on Wireless and Satellite Systems (WiSATS 2019). This conference has brought researchers, developers, and practitioners together from around the world who are leveraging and developing wireless and satellite systems. The theme of WiSATS 2019 was "Wireless and Satellite Systems."

The technical program of WiSATS 2019 consisted of 137 full papers. The conference tracks were: Main Track; Workshop 1 - Machine Learning for Satellite-Terrestrial Networks; Workshop 2 - Human–Machine Interactive Sensing, Monitoring, and Communications; Workshop 3 - Integrated Space and Onboard Networks; Workshop 4 - International Workshop Intelligent Signal Processing, Wireless Communications and Networks; Workshop 5 - Vehicular Communications and Networks; Workshop 6 - Intelligent 5G Communication and Digital Image Processing Technology; Workshop 7 - Security, Reliability, and Resilience in Internet of Things; Workshop 8 - Advances in Communications and Computing for Internet of Things.

Aside from the high-quality technical paper presentations, the technical program also featured three keynote speeches. The three keynote speeches were given by Dr. Wei Zhang from the University of New South Wales, Dr. Yi Qian from the University of Nebraska-Lincoln, and Pengren Ding from National Instruments.

Coordination with the steering chairs, Imrich Chlamtac, Kandeepan Sithamparanathan, and Mario Marchese, was essential for the success of the conference. We sincerely appreciate their constant support and guidance. It was also a great pleasure to work with such an excellent Organizing Committee and we than them for their hard work in organizing and supporting the conference. In particular, we also thank the Technical Program Committee, led by our TPC co-chair, Hsiao-Hwa Chen, who completed the peer-review process of technical papers and compiled a high-quality technical program. We are also grateful to the conference manager, Radka Pincakova, for her support and all the authors who submitted their papers to the WISATS 2019 conference and workshops.

We strongly believe that the WISATS 2019 conference provided a good forum for all researchers, developers, and practitioners to discuss all the scientific and technological aspects that are relevant to wireless and satellite systems. We expect that future WISATS conference will be as successful and stimulating as indicated by the contributions presented in this volume.

April 2019

Qing Guo
Weixiao Meng
Min Jia
Hsiao-Hwa Chen

Organization

Steering Committee

Imrich Chlamtac	Bruno Kessler Professor, University of Trento, Italy
Kandeepan Sithamparanathan	RMIT, Australia
Mario Marchese	University of Genoa, Italy

Organizing Committee

General Co-chairs

Qing Guo	Harbin Institute of Technology, China
Weixiao Meng	Harbin Institute of Technology, China
Min Jia	Harbin Institute of Technology, China

TPC Chair

Hsiao-Hwa Chen	National Cheng Kung University, Taiwan

Advisory TPC Chairs

Gengxin Zhang	Nanjing University of Posts and Telecommunications, China
Lidong Zhu	University of Electronic Science and Technology of China, China
Qihui Wu	Nanjing University of Posts and Telecommunications, China
Mugen Peng	Beijing University of Posts and Telecommunications, China
Wei Chen	Tsinghua University, China
Zan Li	Xidian University, China
Shi Jin	Southeast University, China
Feifei Gao	Tsinghua University, China
Xiaoming Tao	Tsinghua University, China
Sheng Zhou	Tsinghua University, China
Caijun Zhong	Zhejiang University, China
Junhui Zhao	East China Jiaotong University, China

Panels Co-chairs

Qinyu Zhang	Harbin Institute of Technology (Shen Zhen), China
Haibo Zhou	Nanjing University, China

Workshops Co-chairs

Xuejun Sha	Harbin Institute of Technology, China
Hongbin Chen	Guilin University of Electronic Technology, China

Publicity and Social Media Chair

Shaochuan Wu	Harbin Institute of Technology, China

Publications Chair

Xin Liu	Dalian University of Technology, China

Sponsorship and Exhibits Co-chairs

Zhutian Yang	Harbin Institute of Technology, China
Wei Wu	Harbin Institute of Technology, China

Local Co-chairs

Xuanli Wu	Harbin Institute of Technology, China
Shuai Han	Harbin Institute of Technology, China

Web Chair

Yanfeng Gu	Harbin Institute of Technology, China

International Advisory Chair

Imrich Chlamtac	University of Trento, Italy

Contents – Part II

International Workshop on Vehicular Communications and Networks

International Workshop on Security, Reliability, and Resilience in Internet of Things

Contents – Part I

Main Track

International Workshop on Machine Learning for Satellite-Terrestrial Networks

International Workshop on Integrated Space and Onboard Networks (ISON)

International Workshop on Vehicular Communications and Networks

Analysis on Merging Collision Probability in TDMA Based VANET

Yuqiang Zhao, Xuan Zhang, Rongping Zheng, and Qi Yang(✉)

Xiamen University, Xiamen 361005, Fujian, China
yangqi@xmu.edu.cn

Abstract. Dynamical channel allocation schemes for TDMA based on Media Access Control (MAC) Protocols usually depend on network topology to allocate slot. However, The nodes in the network are allowed to move freely, which causes dynamic changes in the network topology and merging collisions. As the application of wireless ad hoc network in intelligent traffic system (ITS), vehicle in the network has typical characteristics of high-speed movement. Based on the model of vehicle movement, this paper analyzes the collision problem caused by the mobility of vehicle and it's probability and verifies the correctness of theoretical analysis through simulation. The simulation result shows that a larger access probability or a smaller standard deviation of brings a smaller probability of merging collision.

Keywords: Access protocol · Ad-hoc network · Merging collision

1 Introduction

Vehicular Ad hoc Networks (VANET) is a significant application of wireless ad hoc networks in Intelligence Traffic System (ITS), providing a multitude of services such as security information, traffic management, and infotainment as stated in paper [1] and [2]. Due to the movement of vehicle in network, topology of network changes dynamically, and the speed of vehicle in the network is different which causes the presence of difference of relative speed. It's inevitable that vehicles within different communication sections will enter the communication range of other vehicle. In the protocol based on TDMA, merging collision problem will inevitably occur, exerting a great impact on the performance of the entire network. The problem of merging collision takes the leads in analysis of throughput of network. Due to the particularity and complexity of this problem, the analysis of merging collision is pretty rare, and the relevant research is not taken detailed. And a few articles analyze the issue of probability in practice. The impact of mobility is studied in detail in paper [3]. In paper [4], the problem of merging collision and its cause have been introduced, and a method is proposed to alleviate this. In paper [5], the problem of collision is divided into two types: merging collision and access collision, and the cause is introduced. A novel protocol is proposed in this paper taking the problem of merging collision into consideration. In paper [6], a novel method is proposed to reduce the problem of merging collision. The problem is introduced in detail early in paper [7].

M. Jia et al. (Eds.): WiSATS 2019, LNICST 281, pp. 3–12, 2019.
https://doi.org/10.1007/978-3-030-19156-6_1

Based on the analysis above, this paper analyzes the probability of merging collision based on two model along with the access protocol.

The rest of the paper is organized as follows. The model adopted in this paper is introduced in Sect. 2. A slew of related parameters of the model is described in Sect. 4. The analysis of the merging collision is accomplished in Sect. 4. The simulation and related analysis is presented in Sect. 5. The paper is concluded in Sect. 6.

2 The Model

In the actual circumstance, there are two common traffic road models: one-way unidirectional lane and two-way bidirectional lane, which will be modeled and analyzed in detail. In the saturated state, each vehicle accesses channel based on TDMA protocol with the scheme of dynamic allocation, and the interval between the node allocated to slot and the data sending is *T*.

2.1 One-Way Unidirectional Lane

As shown in Fig. 2, the vehicle is uniformly distributed on road, and the radius of communication is *R* The road is divided into several two-hop sections with length $L = 2R$. As shown in Fig. 1, there are three two-hop sections –TH1, TH2, TH3. The number of nodes in each section is *M*. Each node in the two-hops section is allocated a different slot in a frame while each node in the different two-hop section can be allocated a same slot in a frame.

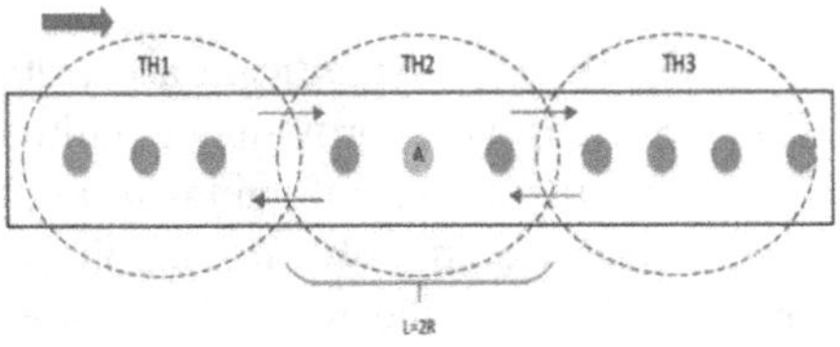

Fig. 1. The vehicle movement model of one-way unidirectional lane.

As mentioned above, the speed of the vehicle follows a special Gaussian distribution $V \sim N(\mu, \sigma^2)$, $V \in [V_{\min}, V_{\max}]$ and the speed is maintained. Thus, the difference of velocity between any two vehicle follows the Gaussian distribution $\Delta V \sim N(0, 2\sigma^2)$, $\Delta V \in [V_{\min} - V_{\max}, V_{\max} - V_{\min}]$. The maximum of distance that a vehicle can reach within time *T* is $S = V_{\max}T$.

2.2 Two-Way Bidirectional Lane

In two-way bidirectional lane, vehicle locates on different roads moving in opposite directions, as shown in Fig. 2. The upper lane is regarded as right lane. Assuming the density of vehicles in two lanes is identical, the nodes in each lane follow uniformly distribution, and the radius of communication of the vehicle is *R*. The section is also divided into two-hop section with the length of $L = 2R$. The total number of nodes in each two-hop section is M, and the number of nodes in unidirectional lane in the two-hop section is $2M$.

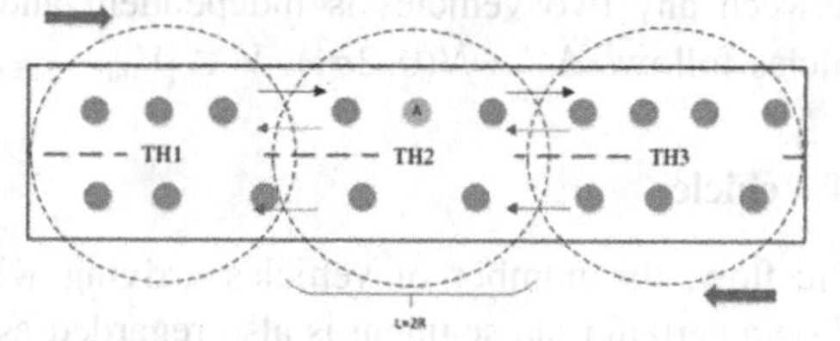

Fig. 2. The vehicle movement model of two way bidirectional lane.

The speed of vehicles in the right direction is considered as positive and follows a special Gaussian distribution $V \sim N(\mu, \sigma^2)$, $V \in [V_{\min}, V_{\max}]$. The speed of the vehicle in the left direction is regarded as negative follows a same distribution. Vehicles travel at a constant speed and their speeds are independent. Consequently, the difference of velocity between any two nodes in the same direction follows the Gaussian distribution $\Delta V \sim N(0, 2\sigma^2)$, $\Delta V \in [V_{\min} - V_{\max}, V_{\max} - V_{\min}]$. The difference of velocity between any two nodes in opposite direction follows the Gaussian distribution $\Delta V_2 \sim N(2u, 2\sigma^2)$, $\Delta V_2 \in [-2V_{\max}, 2V_{\max}]$.

The maximum of difference of speed between any two vehicles is $2V_{\max}$, and the maximum relative distance between any two nodes in time T is $S = 2V_{\max}T$, and it is also satisfy $S < L$.

3 Model Parameters

3.1 The Distribution of Velocity

Previous studies show that speed generally follows the normal distribution on the rural roads and the highway, as shown in Fig. 3.

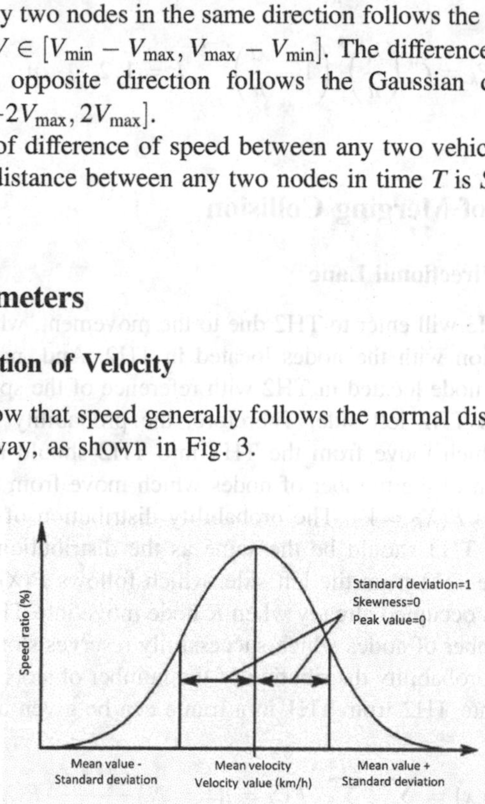

Fig. 3. The speed distribution of nodes on the road.

In the actual scene, the speed of vehicle is bounded, which follows Gaussian distribution. But considering the Gaussian distribution $V \sim N(\mu, \sigma^2)$, the probability close to 0 when vehicle speed is $V < V_{\min}, V > V_{\max}$. Therefore, the distribution of speed of vehicle can be approximately expressed as $V \sim N(\mu, \sigma^2)$, $V \in [V_{\min}, V_{\max}]$. Speed distribution between any two vehicles is independent and the relative speed between any two vehicles follows $\Delta V \sim N(0, 2\sigma^2)$, $V \in [V_{\min-\max}, V_{\max-\min}]$.

3.2 The Arrival of Vehicle

In the theory of traffic flow, the number of vehicles arriving within a certain time interval or distributed on a certain road segment is also regarded as a random variable, and Poisson distribution and binomial distribution are usually used to describe the statistical law of such random variables. And the Poisson distribution and binomial distribution, depicting the movement of vehicle in different scenarios, can be given as following:

$$P_k = \frac{(\lambda t)^k}{k!} e^{-\lambda t}, k = 1, 2, \cdots n \tag{1}$$

$$P_k = C_n^k \left(\frac{\lambda t}{n}\right)^k \left(1 - \frac{\lambda t}{n}\right)^{n-k}, k = 1, 2, \cdots, n \tag{2}$$

4 The Analysis of Merging Collision

4.1 One-Way Unidirectional Lane

Nodes in TH1 and TH3 will enter to TH2 due to the movement, which will be subject to the merging collision with the nodes located in TH2. And, node in TH1 have a higher speed than the node located in TH2 with reference of the speed of node A will move into TH2 from TH2 left side. Therefore, the probability distribution of the number of vehicle which move from the TH1 into TH2 should be the same as the probability distribution of the number of nodes which move from the TH1 into TH2, both of which follows $P(X_R = \mathrm{k})$. The probability distribution of the number which move into TH2 from TH3 should be the same as the distribution of the number of nodes which leave the TH2 from the left side, which follows $P(X_L = \mathrm{k})$.

If there are X slots occupied already when K node move into TH2 from TH1 in the condition that the number of nodes which successfully reserves slot is no less than x in one frame. Thus, the probability distribution of the number of slots which occupied by the node that move into TH2 from TH1 in a frame can be given as

$$P(X_{IN1} = x) = \sum_{j=x}^{N} \sum_{k=x}^{M-j+x} P(S = j | T = N) \frac{C_k^x C_{M-x}^{j-x}}{C_M^j} P(X_R = k) \tag{3}$$

where $x = 0, 1...N$. The number of nodes moving into TH2 and occupying slot is the sum of the number of nodes moving into TH2 from TH1 and TH3, namely:

$$P(X_{IN} = l) = \sum_{i=0}^{l} P(X_{IN1} = i)P(X_{IN3} = l - i) \tag{4}$$

where $L = 0, 1...N$. The probability that there are still X_{STAY} nodes in TH after one frame time is

$$P(X_{STAY} = y) = P(X_{OUT} = M - y) \tag{5}$$

Then the probability that there is still m node within TH is

$$P(X_{TH} = m) = \sum_{j=m}^{N} \sum_{k=m}^{M-j+m} P(S = j|T = N) \frac{C_k^m C_{M-m}^{j-m}}{C_M^j} P(X_{STAY} = k) \tag{6}$$

where $m = 0, 1...N$. The number of nodes entering into TH2 and occupying the slot in TH2 is $X_{IN} = y$ and the number of nodes occupying the slot in TH2 is k. k and y satisfy $0 \leq k, y \leq N$, where N is the number of slots in a frame, as shown in Fig. 4. The probability that there are i slots is exposed to merging collision is expressed as $P(C = i; y, k)$.

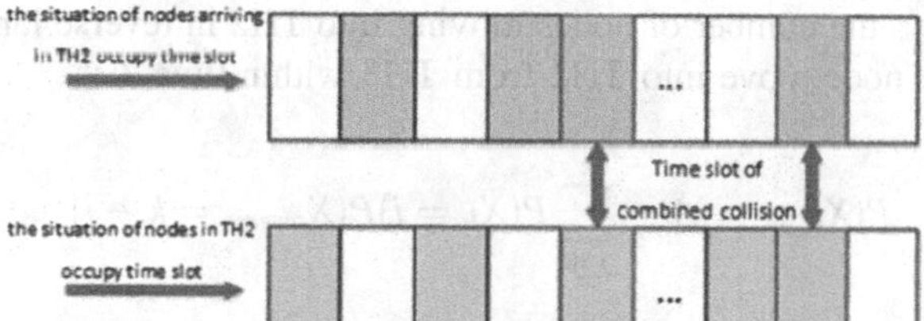

Fig. 4. The illustration of merging collision.

(1) when $y + k \leq N$

$$P(C = i; y, k) = \begin{cases} \dfrac{C_k^i C_{N-k}^{y-i}}{C_N^y} & i \leq \min(y, k) \\ 0 & i > \min(y, k) \end{cases} \tag{7}$$

(2) when $y + k > N$, the number of slots which expose to merging collision is no less than $x = k + y - N$

$$P(C=i;y,k)=\begin{cases}0 & i<y+k-N \text{或} i>\min(y,k)\\ \frac{C_k^i C_{N-k}^{y-i}}{C_N^y} & y+k-N<i\leq\min(y,k)\end{cases} \tag{8}$$

As stated above:

$$P(C=i;y,k)=\begin{cases}\frac{C_k^i C_{N-k}^{y-i}}{C_N^y} & \max(y+k-N,0)\leq i\leq\min(y,k)\\ 0 & i<\max(y+k-N,0) \text{ or } i>\min(y,k)\end{cases} \tag{9}$$

Thus, the probability distribution of the number of occurrences of merging collision in time T can be given as

$$P(C=i)=\sum_{k=1}^{N}\sum_{y=1}^{N}P(X_{TH}=k)\,P(X_{IN}=y)\,P(C=i;k,y) \tag{10}$$

4.2 Two-Way Bidirectional Lane

In two-way bidirectional lane, vehicles located in reverse lane in TH1 travel at opposite speed with reference of node A, and nodes in this section will not enter TH2. Thus the number of nodes that move into TH2 from TH3 in T time is $X_{3\_in}=X_L+X_{reverse}$, where X_L represents the number of nodes moving into TH2 in the same direction lane of TH3 and $X_{reverse}$ the number of nodes moving into TH2 in reverse lane of TH3. The probability that k node move into TH2 from TH3 within time T is

$$P(X_{3\_in}=k)=\sum_{j=0}^{k}P(X_L=j)P(X_{reverse}=k-j) \tag{11}$$

where $k=0,1\ldots 2M$. Thus, the probability distribution of the result of slot allocation in the saturated state is $P(S=j|T=N)$, and the probability distribution of m node occupying slot move into TH2 from TH3 within time T is

$$P(X_{3\_IN}=m)=\sum_{j=m}^{N}\sum_{k=m}^{2M-j+m}P(S=j|T=N)\frac{C_k^m C_{2M-m}^{j-m}}{C_{2M}^j}P(X_{3\_in}=k) \tag{12}$$

where $m=0,1\ldots,N$. The probability distribution of m node occupying slot move into TH2 from TH1 within time T is

$$P(X_{1\_IN}=m)=\sum_{j=m}^{N}\sum_{k=m}^{2M-j+m}P(S=j|T=N)\frac{C_k^m C_{2M-m}^{j-m}}{C_{2M}^j}P(X_R=k) \tag{13}$$

Thus, the probability distribution of the number of nodes occupying slots in TH2 within time T can be obtained as

$$P(X_{double\_IN} = l) = \sum_{i=0}^{l} P(X_{IN1} = i) P(X_{IN3} = l - i) \tag{14}$$

where $l = 0, 1 \ldots, N$. Then, the probability that there are still X_{STAY} nodes in the TH2 after one frame can be given is $X_{STAY} = M - X_{OUT}$

$$P(X_{double\_STAY} = y) = P(X_{double\_OUT} = 2M - y) \tag{15}$$

Then, the probability that there are still m nodes occupying a slot in the TH2 is as follows:

$$P(X_{double\_TH} = m) = \sum_{j=m}^{N} \sum_{k=m}^{2M-j+m} P(S = j | T = N) \frac{C_k^m C_{2M-m}^{j-m}}{C_{2M}^{j}} P(X_{double\_STAY} = k) \tag{16}$$

where $m = 0, 1, \cdots, N$. Finally, the probability distribution of occurrences of merging collision within time T is i can be given as:

$$P(C_{double} = i) = \sum_{k=1}^{M} \sum_{y=1}^{M} P(X_{double\_TH} = k)\, P(X_{double\_IN} = y)\, P(C = i; k, y) \tag{17}$$

5 Simulation and Analysis

Assuming that the node B in the two hop Sect. 1 and the node E in the two hop Sect. 2 use same slot, and the node B and the node E move in opposite directions. When the Node B enters the range of the two-hop Sect. 2, the Node B and the node E become two-hop neighbors, as shown in Fig. 5. And no other factors are considered and there is no interference caused by the communication of other nodes. Moreover, it transmits signals at its same maximum transmit power.

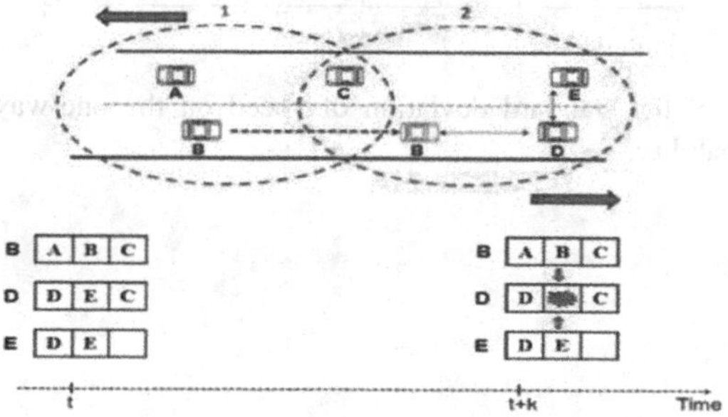

Fig. 5. The scene of merging collision.

5.1 Simulation Scenario

5.1.1 One-Way Unidirectional Lane

Supposing the nodes are uniformly distributed on a one-way unidirectional and their speed follows a Gaussian distribution $V \sim N(\mu, \sigma^2)$, where $V \in [V_{\min}, V_{\max}] > 0$, $\mu = (V_{\min} + V_{\max})/2 > 0$, $\sigma^2 = (V_{\max} - V_{\min})^2/12$, and the speed is constant. Moreover, the communication radius is R = 10 m.

There are three two-hop section: TH1, TH2 and TH3, which are disjoint. Their range is TH1 = [0 m, 20 m], TH2 = [20 m, 40 m], TH3 = [40 m, 60 m], and the number of nodes in TH1, TH2 and TH3 all are $M = 10$.

5.1.2 Two-Way Bidirectional Lane

In the same condition, the speed of the vehicle nodes traveling in the right lane follows the Gaussian distribution $V_1 \sim N(\mu, \sigma^2)$, $V_1 \in [V_{\min}, V_{\max}]$. And the Gaussian distribution is parameterized by $\mu = (V_{\min} + V_{\max})/2$, $\sigma^2 = (V_{\max} - V_{\min})^2/12$. The speed of the nodes traveling in the opposite lane follows a Gaussian distribution $V_2 \sim N(-\mu, \sigma^2)$ and $V_1 \in [-V_{\max}, -V_{\min}]$, $\mu = -(V_{\min} + V_{\max})/2$, $\sigma^2 = (V_{\max} - V_{\min})^2/12$ and the speed is constant. Other parameters are the same as mentioned above in on 4 way unidirectional lane.

5.2 Simulation

Next, the simulation is completed with 1000 iteration and the average value is taken as final result.

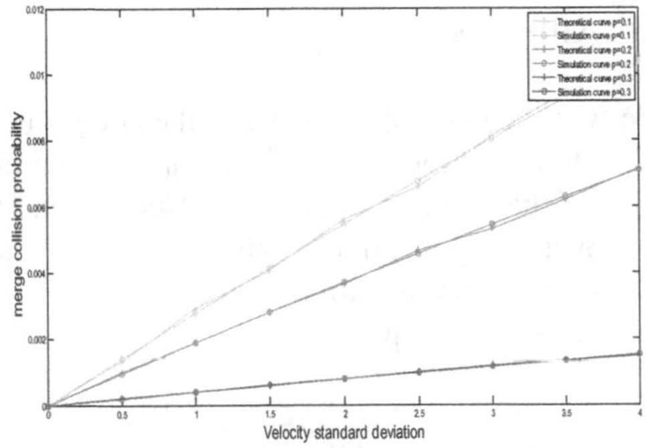

Fig. 6. The influence of the standard deviation of speed on the one-way single lane on the merging collision probability.

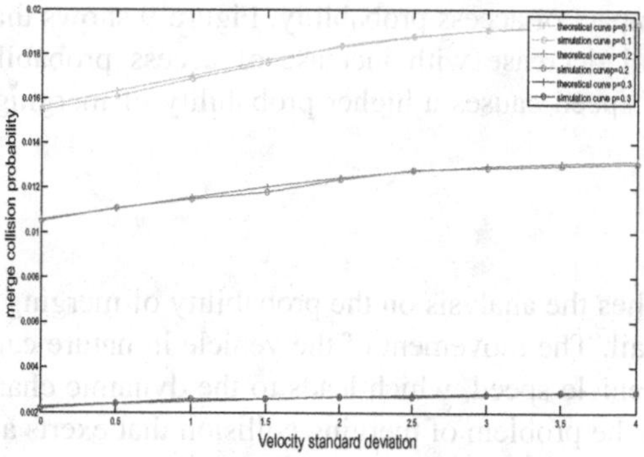

Fig. 7. The influence of the standard deviation of the speed on the two-way dual lane on the merging collision probability.

Figures 6 and 7 present influence of standard deviation of speed. Simulation shows that probability of merging collision increases with increasing of it. Further, it's evident that the difference of simulation in two model is enormous.

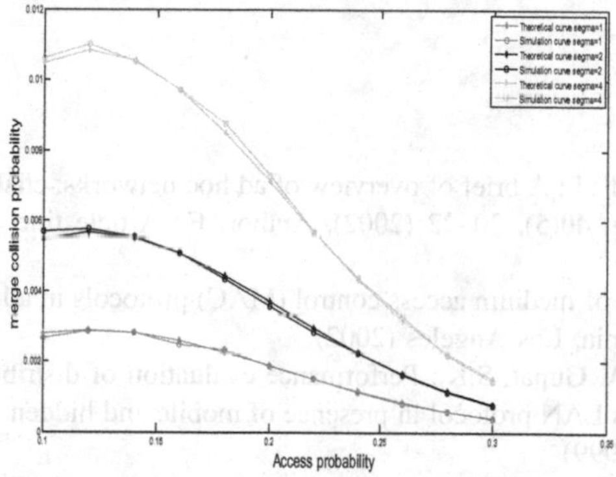

Fig. 8. The influence of the access probability on the one-way single lane on the merging collision probability.

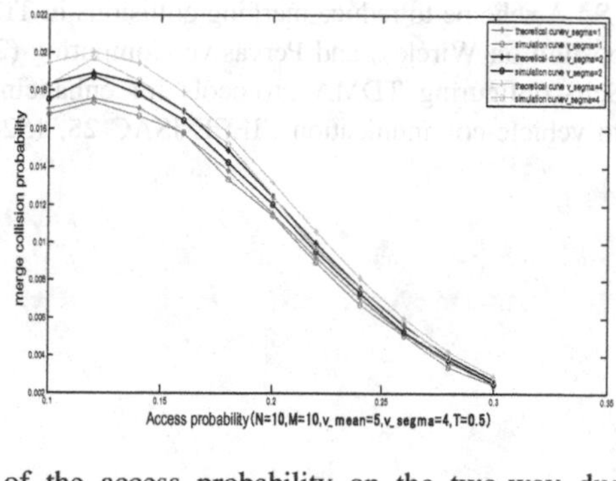

Fig. 9. The influence of the access probability on the two-way dual lane on the merging collision probability.

Figure 8 shows impact of access probability. Figure 9 shows that the probability of merging collision will decrease with increase of access probability. And a greater standard deviation of speed causes a higher probability of merging collision.

6 Conclusion

This paper accomplishes the analysis on the probability of merging collision in TDMA based VANET in detail. The movement of the vehicle in nature causes the appearance of the difference of vehicle speed, which leads to the dynamic changes in the network topology, resulting in the problem of merging collision that exerts a tremendous impact on the performance of the whole network. Two model of vehicular movement is established in this paper–one way unidirectional lane and two-way bidirectional lane. Then, the probability of merging collision is derived in two models of vehicular movement respectively and the analytic result has been given in this paper. Finally, the simulations verify the theoretical derivation results in two scenarios. It is found that a greater standard deviation of velocity leads to a greater probability of merging collision and a larger probability of access brings a excellent consequence about problem merging collision in two scenarios, namely a smaller probability of merging collision.

References

1. Ramanatham, R., Redi, J.: A brief of overview of ad hoc networks: challenges and directions. IEEE Commun. Mag. **40**(5), 20–22 (2002). Author, F.: Article title. Journal **2**(5), 99–110 (2016)
2. Tang, K.: Challenges of medium access control (MAC) protocols in ad hoc mobile networks. University of California, Los Angeles (2002)
3. Khurana, S, Kahol, A, Gupat, S.K.: Performance evaluation of distributed co-ordination for IEEE 802.11 wireless LAN protocol in presence of mobile and hidden terminals, p. 40. IEEE Computer Society (1999)
4. Huang, J.-J., Chiu, Y.-S..: A scheme to reduce merging collisions in TDMA-based VANETs. IEEE Commun. Mag. 20–22 (2013)
5. Hassan, A.O., Weihua, Z.: VeMAC: a TDMA-based MAC protocol for reliable broadcast in VANETS. IEEE Trans. Mob. Comput. **12**, 1724–1736 (2013)
6. Huang, J.-J., Chiu, Y.-S.: A scheme to reduce merging collisions in TDMA-Based VANTEs. In: International Symposium on Wireless and Pervasive Computing (2013)
7. Yu, F., Biswas, S.: Self-configuring TDMA protocols for enhancing vehicle safety with DSRC based vehicle-to-vehicle communications. IEEE JSAC **25**, 1526–1537 (2007)

Industry Research and Standardization Progress in Cellular Communication Solution for Unmanned Aerial Vehicle Application

Pei Guo(✉) and Zhao Cheng

Institute of Manned Space System Engineering,
China Academy of Space Technology, Beijing 100094, China
guopei923@163.com

Abstract. Unmanned Aerial Vehicles have been widely used in many scenarios, and several kinds of wireless communication methods are adopted for UAV monitoring and remote control, e.g. satellite communication, WiFi communication and cellular communication. During the wireless communication solutions mentioned above cellular method is considered as a potentially dominant solution due to the wide deployment and low cost advantage. In this paper we present the latest industry research and standardization progress in cellular communication solution for UAV application from 3GPP. Two technical issues are observed, i.e. high neighbour cell interference and frequent handover, and based on the analysis three kinds of enhancement for current cellular network are proposed, i.e. flight path information reporting, virtual cell solution and dedicated base station.

Keywords: UAV · Neighbour cell interference · Cell fragmentation

1 Introduction

Small UAVs, also called drones, and other low altitude aircrafts, have many current or future applications, including network tower inspection, search and rescue, small package delivery, mapping and surveying, etc. During these applications, the data types for transmission are telemetry data, command and control data, application data [1]. Telemetry refers to data from the UAV reporting various status messages and sensor results. Examples are position, velocity/airspeed, attitude and heading, fuel/power status, communication link quality, etc. For command and control, two-way links that enable sending commands to the drones and receiving responses are required. This data link supports messages such as navigation commands, waypoint entry, configuration adjustments, information requests and safety commands. Application data usually refer to image data or video data especially for inspection and mapping applications.

Considering the requirements of wireless communications, telemetry data, command and control data need high reliable links both for uplink and downlink, and image and video data need high speed uplink link.

M. Jia et al. (Eds.): WiSATS 2019, LNICST 281, pp. 13–22, 2019.
https://doi.org/10.1007/978-3-030-19156-6_2

In 3GPP the study item on enhanced support of aerial vehicles began in March 2017 and the first version of release, i.e. Rel-15, including UAV feature was frozen in September 2018.

The 3GPP working group considers adopting the requirements listed in the following table for the connectivity services for UAV [2] (Table 1).

Table 1. Requirements of connectivity services for UAV.

Requirement items	Value
Data type	Command and Control (C&C) This includes telemetry, waypoint update for autonomous UAV operation, real time piloting, identity, flight authorization, navigation database update, etc. Application data This includes video (streaming), images, other sensors data, etc.
Heights	Target up to 300 m AGL
Speeds	Horizontal: up to 160 km/h for all the scenarios (Urban, Rural)
Latency	C&C: 50 ms (one way from eNB to UAV) Application data: similar to LTE UE (ground user)
DL/UL data rate	C&C: [60–100] kbps for UL/DL Application data: up to 50 Mbps for UL
C&C reliability	Up to 10-3 Packet Error Loss Rate

Aiming to fulfill the requirements above, some research work has been done to identify the issues which exist in current cellular network and several candidate solutions have been proposed to solve them.

The following sections are organized as follows, Sect. 2 presents the identified issues in cellular network performance, and several candidate solutions are provided in Sect. 3, we conclude the paper in Sect. 4.

2 Technical Issue

2.1 High Neighbour Cell Inference

In the intra-frequency network deployment UEs often suffer from intra-frequency interference from neighbour cells, especially for UE in cell edges. For UAVs flying at a relatively high altitude above base stations they will "see" more base stations than that on the ground, and at the same time they can receive more downlink signals from these base stations, which means more downlink interference. Besides of more interfering neighbour cell, another factor that influence signal strength is side lobes. Current cellular network are focused on terrestrial user equipments, and the antennas are usually down tilted to adjust the main lobes to aim to ground users. When the UAV flies at a high altitude, the serving lobe of the serving antenna changes from main lobe to side lobe illustrated as the following figure [3]. In this case the antenna gain provided by side lobe is reduced heavily compared to that from main lobe. So when the signal strength from serving cell decreases and the interference comes from more neighbour cells, the downlink neighbour cell interference is more severe for UAVs than UEs on ground (Fig. 1).

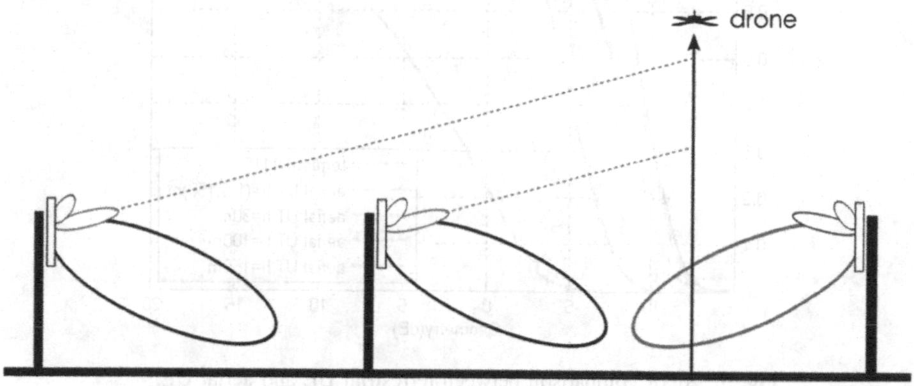

Fig. 1. Serving lobe changes from main lobe to side lobe when UAV's height increases.

Some simulation results related to downlink coupling loss and SINR are also provided in [4] as follows (Figs. 2 and 3).

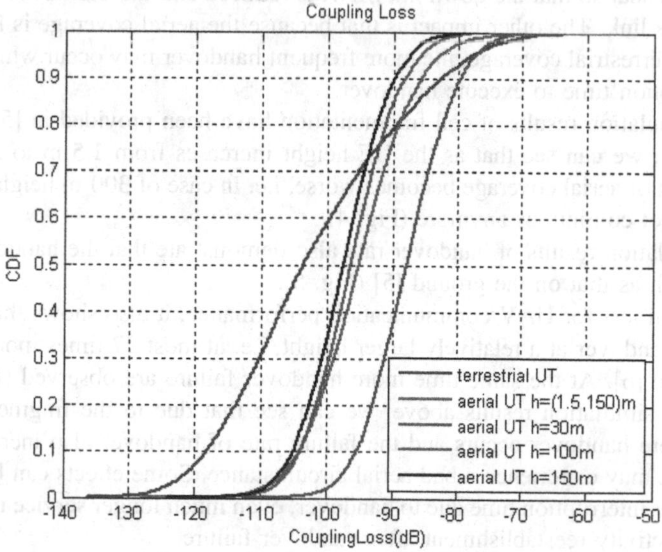

Fig. 2. Coupling loss comparison between terrestrial UE and aerial UE.

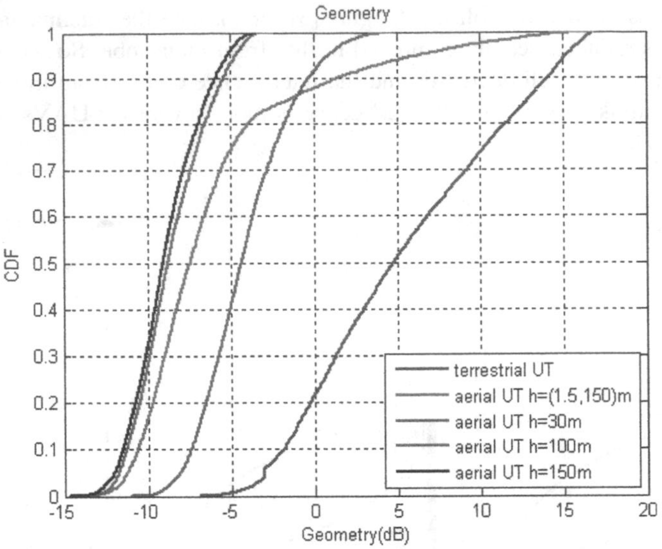

Fig. 3. SINR comparison between terrestrial UE and aerial UE.

2.2 Frequent Handover

When the UAV flies from ground up to sky, the serving lobe changes from main lobe to side lobe of base station antenna, one impact is that the serving signal strength is weaken than usual so that the downlink SINR is reduced and the UE has to experience a bad wireless link. The other impact is that because the aerial coverage is fragmented compared to terrestrial coverage, the more frequent handover may occur which leads to more interruption time to execute handover.

Some simulation results of cell fragmentation have been provided in [5], from the figures below, we can see that as the UE height increases from 1.5 m to 300 m, the fragmentation of aerial coverage becomes worse, i.e. in case of 300 m height the aerial coverage is not continuous anymore (Fig. 4).

The simulation results of handover rate also demonstrate that the handover occurs twice as much as that on the ground [5] (Fig. 5).

In the field test for UAV communication performance, it also shows that there are much more handover at a relatively larger height, i.e. at most 27 times more than that on the ground [6]. At the same time more handover failure are observed (Fig. 6).

From the simulation results above, we can see that due to the fragmented aerial coverage, more handover occurs and the failure rate of handover also increases, consequently UE may experience a bad aerial circumstance. Some effects can be foreseen such as longer interruption time due to handover, even much longer service interruption due to connectivity reestablishment after handover failure.

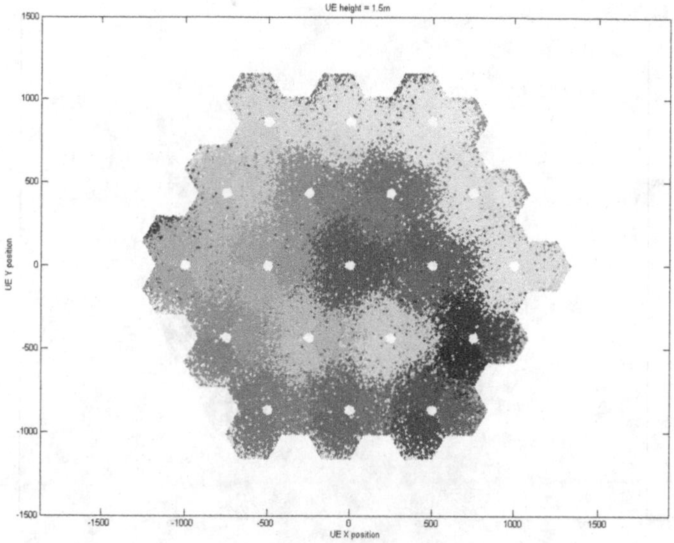

(a). Cell coverage at 1.5m height.

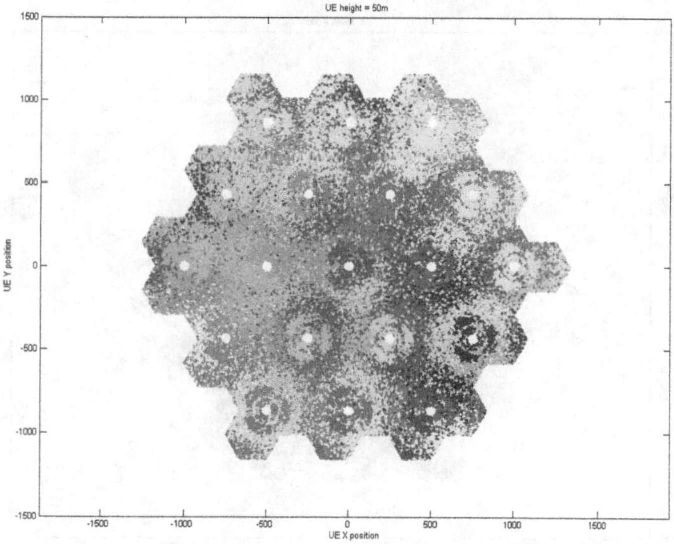

(b). Cell coverage at 50m height.

Fig. 4. Cell coverage variation in different heights.

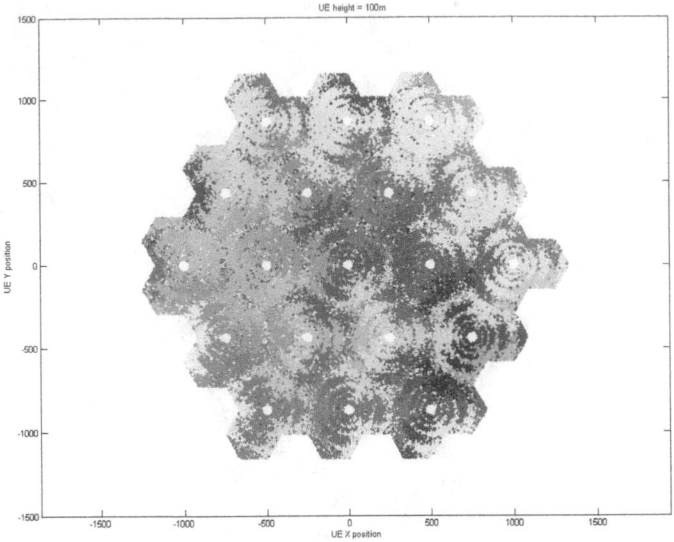

(c). Cell coverage at 100m height.

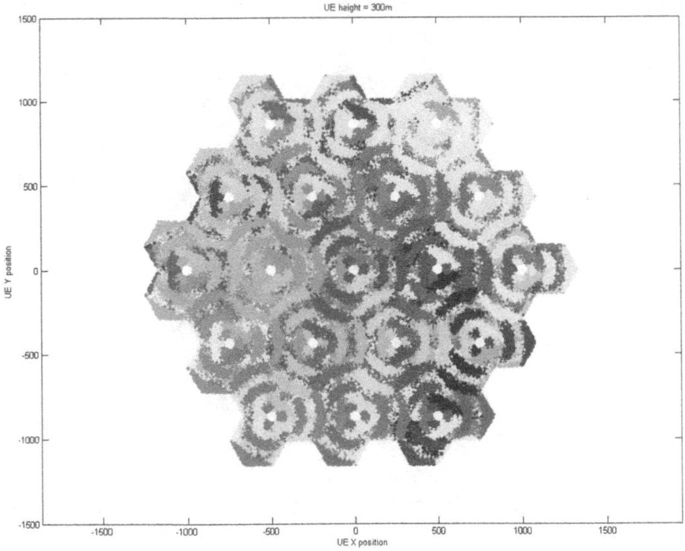

(d). Cell coverage at 300m height.

Fig. 4. (*continued*)

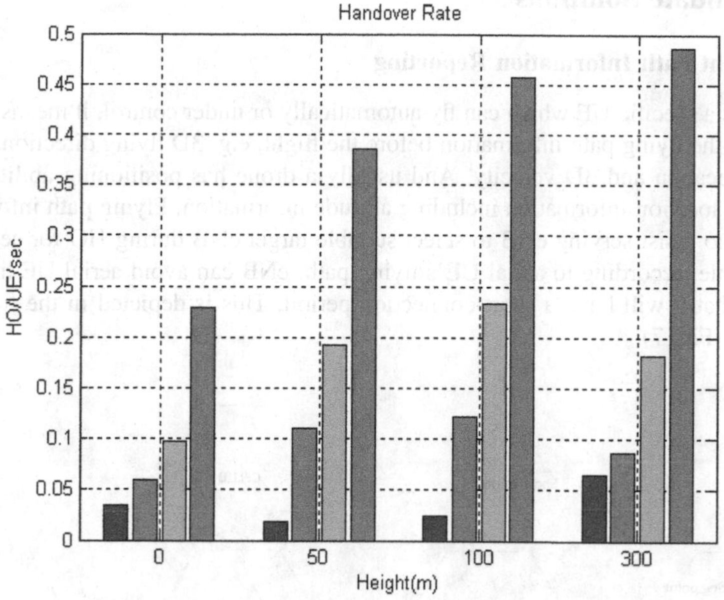

Fig. 5. Comparison of handover results in different height.

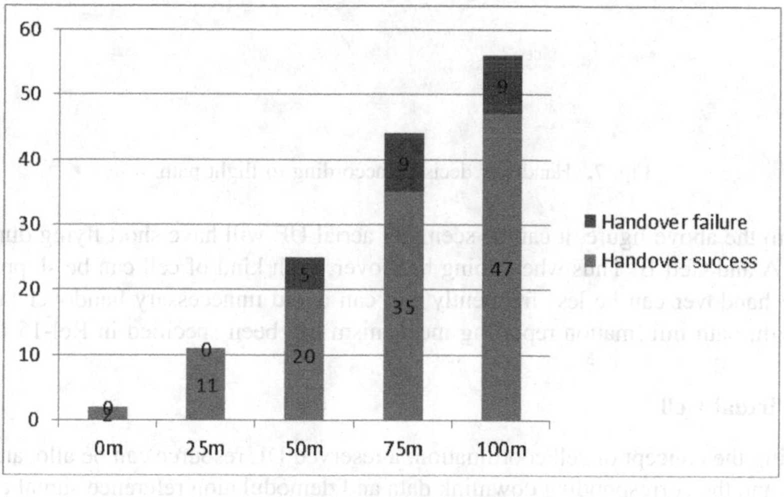

Fig. 6. Field test result of handover success and failure.

3 Candidate Solutions

3.1 Flight Path Information Reporting

A drone is a specific UE which can fly automatically or under control, it means a drone can know the flying path information before the flight, e.g. 3D flying direction, critical midway location and 3D velocity. And usually a drone has positioning ability and it can report location information including altitude information. Flying path information is helpful to assist serving eNB to select suitable target eNB during HO for aerial UE. For example, according to aerial UE's flying path, eNB can avoid aerial UE handover to a cell that it will have a short connection period. This is depicted in the following figure [7] (Fig. 7).

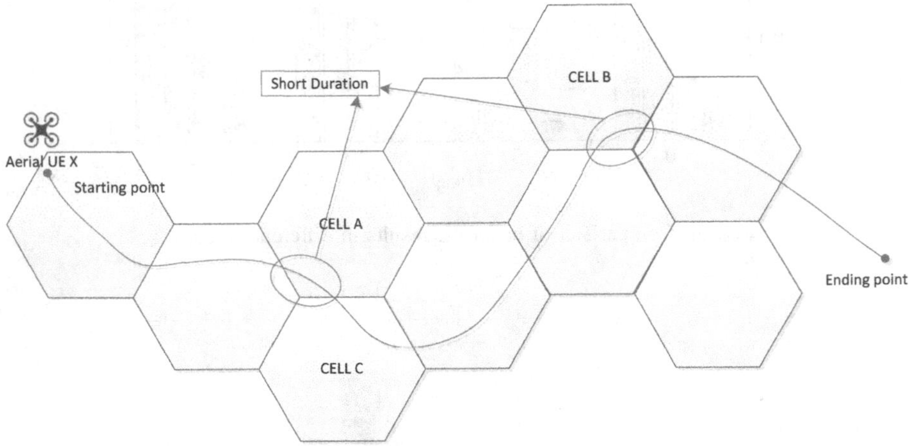

Fig. 7. Handover decision according to flight path.

From the above figure, it can be seen that aerial UE will have short flying duration in Cell A and Cell B. Thus when doing handover, such kind of cell can be skipped so that the handover can be less frequently and can avoid unnecessary handover failure. This flight path information reporting mechanism has been specified in Rel-15 LTE.

3.2 Virtual Cell

Following the concept of cell coordination, a reserved DL resource can be allocated for drones, and the corresponding downlink data and demodulation reference signal can be jointly transmitted by multiple eNBs. As this reserved resource is specific for drones, it is named as Virtual Drone Cell (VDC) [8]. As a VDC is the composition of several neighbour cells, the VDC has a more large coverage area, so the handover rate can be declined. And this solution also changes interference from the neighbour cells into useful signals, the DL SINR can be improved obviously. This solution has been discussed in 3GPP, due to potential deployment complexity some other enhancements may be considered (Fig. 8).

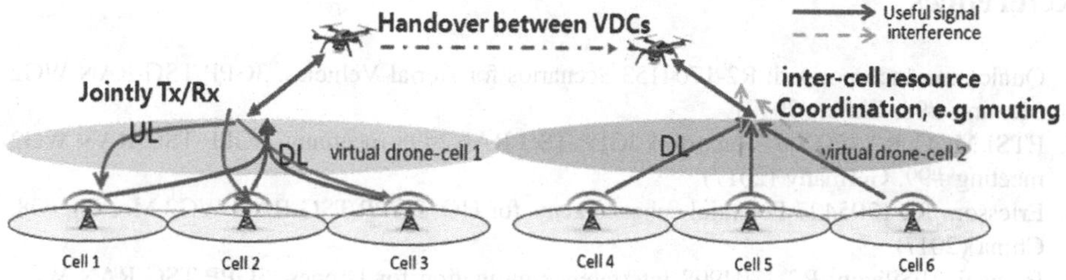

Fig. 8. Virtual Drone Cell.

3.3 Dedicated Base Station

Another solution is that the base station is a dedicated only for drones, which has a specific antenna elevation angle to serve flying UEs above an altitude as illustrated in Fig. 9. So a drone UE is supposed to be served by theses dedicated eNBs for better signal quality [9]. but there are still some technical issues that need to be done further, e.g. signal interference with satellite communications in the same frequency band.

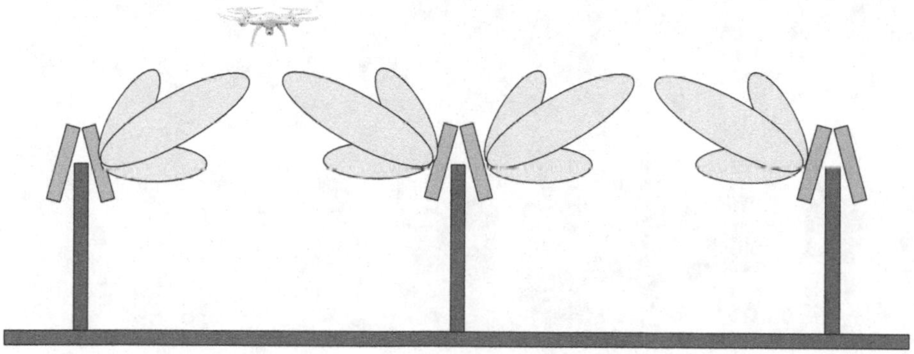

Fig. 9. Dedicated UAV base stations.

4 Conclusion

UAVs have many current or future applications, but current cellular network cannot support UAV type UE perfectly. Some technical issues have been identified in 3GPP, e.g. high neighbour cell interference and frequent handover, and several candidate solutions have been proposed to solve the problems. One of them, i.e. flight path information reporting has been specified in 3GPP Rel-15, other solutions such as virtual drone cell and dedicated base station still need further study.

References

1. Qualcomm Incorporated: R2-1704153 Scenarios for Aerial Vehicles. 3GPP TSG-RAN WG2 Meeting #98, China (2017)
2. ETSI MCC: R2-1707601 Report of 3GPP TSG RAN2#98 meetinng. 3GPP TSG-RAN WG2 meeting #99, Germany (2017)
3. Ericsson: R2-1705427 Potential enhancements for HO. 3GPP TSG-RAN WG2 Meeting #98, China (2017)
4. Huawei, HiSilicon: R2-1704998 Interference mitigation for Drones. 3GPP TSG-RAN WG2 Meeting #98, China (2017)
5. Huawei, HiSilicon: Simulation Results of Mobility Issues for Drones. 3GPP TSG-RAN WG2 Meeting #99bis, Czech (2017)
6. KDDI: R2-1705669 Proposal of potential LTE enhancements for Aerial Vehicles. 3GPP TSG-RAN WG2 Meeting #98, China (2017)
7. Lenovo, Motorola Mobility: R2-1805190 Discussion on potential mobility enhancement for aerial UE. 3GPP TSG-RAN WG2 Meeting #101bis, China (2018)
8. Huawei, HiSilicon: R2-1710406 Discussion on Virtual drone cell. 3GPP TSG-RAN WG2 Meeting #99bis, Czech (2017)
9. Huawei, HiSilicon: R2-1710409 Potential enhancements for drones in idle state. 3GPP TSG-RAN WG2 Meeting #99bis, Czech (2017)

Radio Resource Allocation for V2X Communications Based on Hybrid Multiple Access Technology

Tong Xue, Wei Wu(✉), Qie Wang, and Xuanli Wu

Communication Research Center, Harbin Institute of Technology,
Harbin 150080, China
{17s105154,18S005082}@stu.hit.edu.cn,
{kevinking,xlwu2002}@hit.edu.cn

Abstract. With the increasing number of vehicles, many road accidents have occurred. To solve this problem, this paper investigates a security application in vehicle communications where all links require high reliability. We consider that each vehicle-to-infrastructure (V2I) communication shares spectrum resource with multiple vehicle-to-vehicle (V2V) communications. Firstly, we aim to maximize the successful transmission probability (STP) of V2V communications while guaranteeing the reliability of all V2I communications. Then, we formulate the above resource allocation problem as a combinatorial double resource auction (CDRA) problem. In the auction, radio resources occupied by V2I communications are considered as bidders competing for V2V packages. We propose an algorithm to solve the resource allocation algorithm. Finally, simulation results indicate that the proposed scheme outperforms the traditional resource allocations in terms of the reliability.

Keywords: V2X · Hybrid multiple access · Resource allocation · Combinatorial double auction

1 Introduction

Recently, road accidents and traffic congestion have become global issues [1]. With the development of the information technology, safe and efficient automatic driving technology becomes the key to solve the above traffic problems. In general, autonomous driving capability of vehicles greatly rests with timely collecting and sharing of critical information by leveraging vehicular communications. Consequently, it is essential to research high reliable vehicular communications in future intelligent transportation systems (ITS).

High reliability and low latency are the requirements of vehicular communication in ITS. Vehicular communications refer to achieve information exchange via vehicle-to-everything (V2X) communications which including V2V communications, V2I communications, vehicle-to-pedestrian (V2P) communications and so on. There are two technologies to achieve V2X communications: dedicated short-range communications (DSRC) and cellular V2X (C-V2X). DSRC based on the IEEE 802.11p standard. However, the DSRC has been weakened by recent studies that it is lack of quality

M. Jia et al. (Eds.): WiSATS 2019, LNICST 281, pp. 23–35, 2019.
https://doi.org/10.1007/978-3-030-19156-6_3

of services guarantees in congested road and is difficult to deal with non-line of sight scenarios. In contrast, C-V2X makes up for the shortcomings of DSRC and has the advantage of wide coverage, the quality of services can be guaranteed and low latency in non-line of sight [2].

The research of Device-to-Device (D2D) communications are focus on how to improve the energy efficiency. Since the D2D users are handheld equipment with limited battery life [3]. However, unlike the traditional D2D underlay cellular network, V2V underlay cellular network requires stringently low latency and high reliability in terms of security applications, which poses new challenges to the C-V2X. The main existing C-V2X communications utilize the orthogonal multiple access (OMA), and limited spectrum resource have not been fully and efficiently utilized [4–6]. With the development of wireless communication technology, non-orthogonal multiple access (NOMA) scheme has been introduced as a potential solution for the 5th generation wireless systems (5G), which allows users to access the channel non-orthogonally by code-domain multiplexing, i.e. sparse code multiple access (SCMA) or power-domain multiplexing, i.e. NOMA. Nonetheless, the complex interference caused by reusing the same resources may significantly deteriorate the performance of the system. Recently, the study of multiple access are concentrate on the power-domain NOMA [7, 8]. Di et al. investigated the NOMA for V2X communication to improve the packet reception probability, formulated the centralized scheduling and resource allocation problem as a multi-dimensional stable roommate matching problem [7]. Qian et al. presented the joint optimization of cell association and power control to reduce the handover rate, transform it into a weighted sum rate maximization and proposed the hierarchical power control algorithm [8]. But some studies have shown that the spectral efficiency and the number of users by NOMA is not as good as SCMA [9] and few works have discussed how to improve the performance of the safety critical applications from a SCMA-based perspective in vehicular communications.

Since the requirement of the security application, this paper considering the number of V2I communications are less than V2V communications and the former are higher priority over the latter. We aim to maximize STP of V2V communications while ensuring reliability guarantee for each V2I communication. The multiple access scheme of V2V communications are implemented by SCMA while V2I communications are carried out by OMA. More specifically, each codebook of SCMA can be occupied by more than one V2V communication and shares the same resource block with OMA in order to improve spectral efficiency. However, there are complex interference caused by hybrid multiple access scheme. Consequently, we further research the radio resource allocation to reduce the interference of V2X communications and propose the CDRA algorithm where we combine the orthogonal resource blocks and V2V links separately.

The rest of this paper is organized as follows. Section 2 is system model, including V2V underlay cellular network and hybrid SCMA-OMA scheme. The problem formulation is proposed in Sect. 3. To solve the spectrum sharing problem, we propose the detail of the CDRA algorithm in Sect. 4. Section 5 presents and analyzes the simulation results of algorithm performance, and finally, we conclude the paper in Sect. 6.

2 System Model

In this section, we present a V2V underlay cellular network and propose a mixed SCMA-OMA scheme in a single cell.

2.1 Scenario Description

As shown in Fig. 1, we consider a Manhattan model, which consists of N vehicles requiring V2I communications, denoted as V2I users (CUEs), and M pairs of vehicles to V2V communications, denoted as V2V users (VUEs). The set of $\mathbf{C} = \{C_1, C_2, \ldots, C_N\}$ is denoted as CUEs, i.e. red vehicles, and the set of $\mathbf{V} = \{V_1, V_2, \ldots, V_M\}$ as VUEs, i.e. green vehicles. Each of neighboring vehicles transmit safety-critical information to central vehicle in every time slot. The central vehicles always act as CUEs who feed back to eNodeB whether there is an emergency message. The message is denoted as a binary variable $\zeta_j^{(t)}$. $\zeta_j^{(t)} = 1$ indicates that a security incident occurred in the neighboring vehicle of the center vehicle j in time slot t, otherwise, $\zeta_j^{(t)} = 0$. The system will establish V2V communications to allow more vehicles to receive this urgent message when $\zeta_j^{(t)} = 1$.

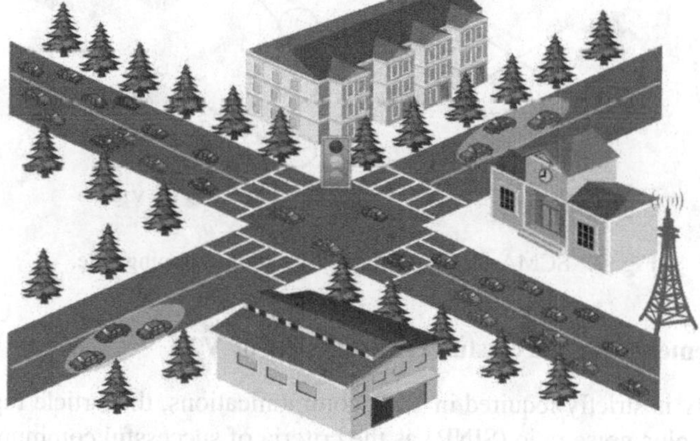

Fig. 1. Manhattan model. (Color figure online)

In order to simply the scenario model, we assume that the interference of users only exist in single cell and eNodeB could obtain the channel state information (CSI) of all vehicles. The detail multiple access scheme and interference analysis are as shown in Sect. 2.2.

2.2 SCMA-OMA Scheme

Because the shortage of radio spectrum resource, the number of users is limited. In order to increase the number of access vehicle users in the system and improve STP of vehicle users, this paper proposes SCMA that one codebook can be occupied by more than one vehicle user simultaneously.

From the above scenario description, it is not difficult to conclude that V2I communications are higher priority over V2V communications and the number of VUEs is far more than CUEs in model, the multiple access scheme of V2V communications are implemented by SCMA while V2I communications are carried out by OMA. Each codebook of SCMA shares the same resource blocks with OMA in order to improve spectral efficiency. Figure 2 illustrates the hybrid SCMA-OMA resource allocation mapping rule, noted (J, K, L). L $(1 \leq L \leq K)$ represents the number of RBs of every SCMA user. J represents the maximum number of codebooks. In Fig. 2, $L = 2$, $K = 4$ and $J = 6$.

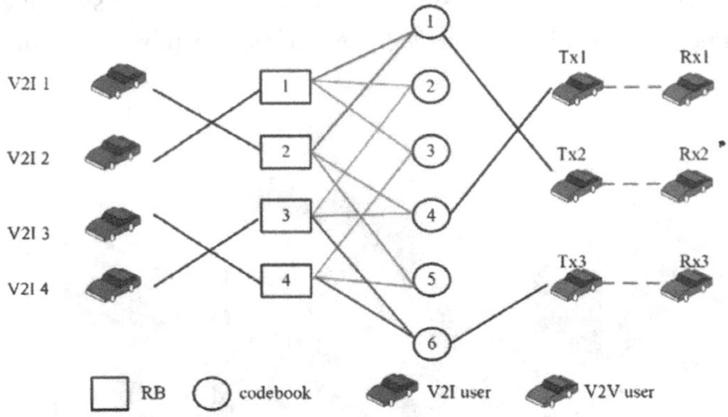

Fig. 2. SCMA-OMA resource allocation mapping rule.

2.3 Requirements for Successful Transmission of V2X

Since reliability is strictly required in V2X communications, this article regards signal to interference plus noise ratio (SINR) as the criteria of successful communication. We note the $SINR_{th}^{C}$ and $SINR_{th}^{V}$ as successful transmission of V2I and V2V communications threshold value, respectively. We define that the SINR of V2I links C_n over the resource block k and the SINR of V2V links V_m over the codebook j in time t should not less than $SINR_{th}^{C}$ and $SINR_{th}^{V}$, separately. As shown in following inequations

$$\mu_{Cn,k}(t) = \frac{P_{Cn}(t)H_{Cn,bs}(t)S_{Cn,k}(t)}{\sum_{m=1}^{M}\sum_{j=1}^{J}\frac{1}{\omega}P_{Vm}(t)H_{V_{m,Tx},Cn}(t)B_{Vm,j}(t)L_{j,k}(t)+N_0} \geq SINR_{th}^{C} \tag{1}$$

$$\mu_{Vm,j}(t) = \frac{P_{Vm}(t)H_{V_{m,Tx},V_{m,Rx}}(t)B_{Vm,j}(t)}{\sum_{k=1}^{K}\sum_{n=1}^{N}\frac{1}{\sigma}P_{Cn}(t)H_{Cn,V_{m,Rx}}(t)S_{Cn,k}(t)L_{k,j}(t) + \rho_{Vm,j}(t) + N_0} \geq SINR_{th}^{V} \quad (2)$$

$$\rho_{Vm,j}(t) = \sum_{k=1}^{K}\sum_{m'=1,m'\neq m}^{M} P_{Vm'}(t)H_{V_{m',Tx},V_{m,Rx}}(t)B_{Vm',j}(t) \quad (3)$$

Where, $P_{Vm}(t)$ and $P_{Cn}(t)$ are the transmit power of VUEs and CUEs, correspondingly. $N_0 \sim CN(0, \sigma_{\mathrm{n}}^2)$ is additive white Gaussian noise (AWGN). $H_{V_{m,Tx},V_{m,Rx}}(t)$ and $H_{V_{m,Tx},Cn}(t)$ are the channel gain of the same resource block from V2V transmitter $V_{m,Tx,}$ to its receiver $V_{m,Rx}$ and CUEs C_n in time t, separately. $H_{V_{m',Tx},V_{m,Rx}}(t)$ and $H_{Cn,V_{m,Rx}}(t)$ denote the channel gain of the same resource block from other V2V transmitter $V_{m',Tx,}$ and CUEs C_n to V2V receiver $V_{m,Rx}$ in time t, receptively. $\rho_{Vm,j}(t)$ represents the interference from other V2V transmitters $V_{m',Tx,}$ to V2V receivers $V_{m,Rx}$ over the codebook j in time t. ω is the number of subcarrier for a codebook. However, σ is the number of codebooks for a subcarrier.

The achievable rate obtained from VUEs V_m over the codebook j in time t can be formally presented

$$R_{Vm,j}(t) = \log_2(1 + \mu_{Vm,j}(t)) \quad (4)$$

Similarly, the achievable rate obtained from CUEs C_n over the resource block k in time t can be denoted

$$R_{Cn,k}(t) = \log_2(1 + \mu_{Cn,k}(t)) \quad (5)$$

3 Problem Formulation

3.1 Problem Description

In this paper, high reliability is explicitly considered, which is essential since the vehicular communications are required to transmit security information about vehicles. Our research focuses on V2V communications and V2I communications in V2V underlay cellular network. The eNodeB allocates frequency resource to V2V communications and V2I communications. More specifically, this paper formulates high-reliable problem as the maximum STP of V2V links while ensuring reliability guarantee for each V2I link.

We transform the problem as a combinatorial double resource auction game, in which the orthogonal radio resources used by the V2I links need to be considered as bidders while V2V links are goods and eNodeB is auctioneer.

3.2 Utility Function

There are M V2V links (goods) and N orthogonal radio resources (bidders). The goods are combined to form D V2V packages $G_m, m = 1, 2, \ldots, D$ and the bidders are formed to E packages $G_n, n = 1, 2, \ldots, E$. For the sake of fairness, each package is non-empty subset.

We denote by $U_p(G_n, G_m)$ the private valuation of the bidder n who obtains the package G_m, and $U_c(G_n, G_m)$ the cost for obtaining the package G_m. Therefore, the utility function of the bidder, denoted by U_u, can be expressed as $U_u(G_n, G_m) = U_p(G_n, G_m) - U_c(G_n, G_m)$, and we have

$$U_p(G_n, G_m) = \sum_{j=1}^{j\max} \sum_{i=1}^{i\max} \mu_{G_{m,i}, G_{n,j}} \tag{6}$$

$$U_c(G_n, G_m) = \rho \cdot \sum_{j=1}^{j\max} \begin{cases} 0, \mu_{G_{n,j}} \geq SINR_{th}^{C} \\ SINR_{th}^{C} - \mu_{G_{n,j}}, \mu_{G_{n,j}} < SINR_{th}^{C} \end{cases}, \forall G_{n,j} \in G_n \tag{7}$$

Here $\mu_{G_{m,i}, G_{n,j}}$ is the SINR of user i who is the member of package G_m over the resource block $G_{n,j}$. Because the reliability of V2I links will decrease when V2V links who share the same resource blocks obtain high SINR. We consider the extent to which V2I communications unsuccessfully as cost. In this paper, to simplify this problem, we use the linear anonymous prices. The unit price ρ of the cost is asked by the auctioneer.

We define a set of binary variable $\{S_{G_n, G_m}\}$ in which $S_{G_n, G_m} = 1$ indicates that bidder G_n gets the package G_m, otherwise, $S_{G_n, G_m} = 0$. Meanwhile, considering the self-interested of bidders, we maximize the overall utility of bidders as follows

$$\max \sum_{n=1}^{E} \sum_{m=1}^{D} S_{G_n, G_m} \cdot U_u(G_n, G_m) \tag{8}$$

Subject to

$$\sum_{m=1}^{D} S_{G_n, G_m} \leq 1, \forall G_n \in G_N \tag{8a}$$

The V2I links which can be transmitted successfully is a higher priority to obtain good package. Meanwhile, Eq. (8) pursues to the maximum SINR of V2V links. The constraint ensures that a bidder can at most buy one good package. What is more, the following CDRA algorithm can solve the problem of Sect. 3.1. j^* and i^* are denoted as the package and the bidder which are successful auction in Table 2, receptively. The V2V links will be considered as transmission information successfully when the constraints $\mu_{i^*, j^*} \geq SINR_{th}^{v}$ and $\mu_{i^*} \geq SINR_{th}^{c}$ are satisified. Consequently, the STP γ of V2V links is

$$\gamma = \sum_{n=1}^{E}\sum_{m=1}^{D}\frac{S_{G_n,G_m}}{M} \tag{9}$$

4 Combinatorial Double Resource Auction Algorithm

4.1 Combination Scheme

Considering the number of V2V links are far more than V2I links in Manhattan model and the codebook mapping rules of SCMA, we propose a combinational double resource auction mechanism. The groups of V2I links are combinational bidders and groups of V2V links are combinational goods in the proposed auction mechanism. We then propose a combination scheme, as listed in detail in Table 1.

Table 1. Double combination scheme

1: Initialization:

· Ungrouped goods set: $\varphi = \{1,2,\ldots,N\}$, Grouped goods set: *match*= $\varnothing$

2: Bidders grouping stage:

· The adjacent four bidders as one group according to the SCMA codebook mapping rules. There are G_n groups, marked as $\{G_1, G_2,\ldots,G_N\}$ in which $G_n \in \{1,2,\ldots,N\}$.

· Calculate total of bidders' SNR in every groups, noted as: $SNR\_n, n \in \{G_1, G_2,\ldots,G_N\}$

· The sum of SNR in the group is sorted in descending order, set $SNR\_Gn\_sorted(i)$, $i \in \{G_1, G_2,\ldots,G_N\}$

3: Goods grouping stage:

· **while** $\varphi \neq \varnothing$ which is exist unmatched goods

for $SNR\_Gn\_sorted(G_1) : SNR\_Gn\_sorted(G_N)$

for *i*=1:*M*

for *j*=1:*J*

◆ according to codebooks mapping rules: $j \rightarrow l, l \in 1,\ldots,N$

◆ calculate the interference value of *i* to *l*: $I_{i,l}$

end for

end for

⅄ average value *ave_I_i* (*i=1:M*) of the interference of the *SNR_Gn*

⅄ $SNR\_Gn\_sorted(i) = \arg\max_{i} \; ave\_I\_i(i=1:M)$

end for

end while

In combinational auction, the orthogonal radio resources will be interested in sorting all V2V links considering factors such as minimum interference and access fairness before the auction. Firstly, the adjacent four orthogonal radio resources (bidders) are as one group according to the SCMA codebook mapping rules. Secondly, we sort the sum of Signal Noise Ratio (SNR) within the group in descending order, as $SNR\_Gn\_sorted(i)$. Thirdly, we collect the interference value of goods i over the codebooks j and calculate the average value ave_I_i for $SNR\_Gn\_sorted(G_i)$. Finally, the corresponding goods are placed in the ith combination when the average value ave_I_i is the minimize value.

4.2 Combinatorial Double Resource Auction Algorithm

We proposed auction is round-based reverse iterative combinatorial double auction. Firstly, the auctioneer announces an initial price ρ^0, dutch price reduction rule α and the auctioneer would update prices and the number of iteration τ whose initial value is 0 in every round. Secondly, the bidders calculate bidders private value attribute M_c and utility $U_c(G_m, G_n)$ of the combinational goods. Bidders should collect all bids and determine a bid for every combinational good package in the current round price ρ. The auctioneer will auction when the maximum bid is non-negative. Otherwise, the bidder will not bid for the package. Finally, the price will be decreased and the combinational auction will move to the next round. Our detail double auction algorithm is summarized in Table 2.

The proof of convergence of the CDRA algorithm is given. From (6), we know that revenue valuations are non-negative functions. Thus, the utility satisfies

$$U_u(G_n, G_m) \geq -U_c(G_n, G_m) = -\rho \cdot \sum_{j=1}^{j\max} \begin{cases} 0, \mu_{G_{n,j}} \geq SINR_{th}^C \\ SINR_{th}^C - \mu_{G_{n,j}}, \mu_{G_{n,j}} < SINR_{th}^C \end{cases} \tag{10}$$

The $\rho^\tau = \rho^0 - \tau\alpha$ is a linear monotonically decreasing function of the time τ. We can find when $\tau > \rho^0/\alpha$, i.e. $\rho^\tau > 0$, $U_u(G_n, G_m) \geq -U_c(G_n, G_m) \geq 0$. What is more, subjects to constraints in (8), there is not a loop in the auction. When $\tau > \rho^0/\alpha$, it takes no more than another finite rounds to end the auction, as there are D packages and during each round, at least one package will be sold since all the utility functions are non-negative. The auction can be concluded no more than $\rho^0/\alpha + D$ rounds [10].

Table 2. Combinational double resource auction algorithm

```
1. Initialization Stage:
· Map radio subcarrier resource of V2I links to codebooks in SCMA;
· The auctioneer determined initial prices ρ = ρ^0 ;
· Initialize the number of iterations τ = 0 ;
· Dutch price reduction step α > 0 ;
· Unsuccessful auction goods sets φ = {1,2,. . . ,N}
2. Auction Stage:
· for group number ϑ = SINR_G_n_sorted(G_1) : SINR_G_n_sorted(G_N)
   while ϑ^th : SNR_Gn_sorted ≠ ∅
    for i=1:4 (bidder sort in ϑ^th )
     for j=SNR_Gn_sorted
      Calculate private value attribute M_c and utility function U_c(G_m, G_n) according to (8)
     end for;
    end for;
     set κ = max U_c(G_m, G_n);
     j* = arg max_m U_c(G_m, G_n) and i* = arg max_n U_c(G_m, G_n);
     if κ ≥ 0 (successful auction)
       allocate codebooks i* to goods j*;
       update sets φ = φ \ {j*};
     else
       do not allocate;
       ρ^(τ+1) = ρ^(τ) - α;
       τ = τ + 1;
    end if
   end while
· end for
```

5 Performance Simulation

In this section, we provide the hybrid SCMA-OMA scheme for Manhattan urban model in V2X communications, as shown in Fig. 1. In this scenario, the average inter-vehicle distance in the same lane is 2.5 s × speed [3]. The mapping rule is (6, 4, 2) in SCMA. Furthermore, we set the shadowing standard deviations as 8 dB for VUEs and CUEs, the SINR requirements of VUEs and CUEs 0 dB and 10 dB, respectively, the noise spectral density −174 dBm/HZ, the vehicle speeds are different from 15 km/h to 60 km/h and the channel model of this article is UMi model [11]. The other parameters are listed in Table 3.

Table 3. Simulation parameters and values

Parameter	Value
Transmit power of V2I links	20 dBm
Transmit power of V2V links	17 dBm
System bandwidth	20 MHz
Cell radius	250 m

In Fig. 3, we compare the performance of the proposed hybrid SMCA-OMA CDAA scheme in Table 2 and the OMA CDAA scheme in which the orthogonal radio resources are used by the V2I and V2V links. Figure 3 indicates the trend of system total STP for V2V links with the gradual increase of the number of V2V links. We consider a STP only when the SINR $\mu_{Cn,k}(t)$ and $\mu_{Vm,j}(t)$ should be more than $SINR_{th}^{C}$ and $SINR_{th}^{V}$ in the simulation. Success reception probability has a significant decrease as the increasing number of V2V communications. It is obviously that the hybrid SCMA-OMA CDAA scheme is superior to the OMA CDAA. That is because the interference in SCMA-OMA scheme is lower than that in OMA scheme, due to the sparse property of SCMA. However, the performance of OMA CDAA will be better when V2V links are more than 95. Since one SCMA user can interfere two orthogonal V2I users and the interference by V2V users will increase exponentially.

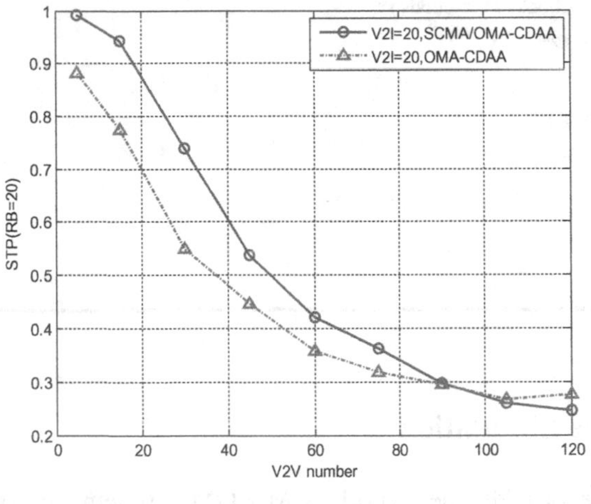

Fig. 3. Successful transmission probability v.s. the number of V2V links in different multiple access

Figure 4 evaluates the performance of hybrid SCMA-OMA combinational double resource auction algorithm compared with the hybrid SCMA-OMA greedy algorithm (SCMA-OMA GA) and a traditional method for hybrid SCMA-OMA random resource algorithm (SCMA-OMA RRA). In RRA, SCMA codebooks are randomly allocated to V2V links after V2I links use OMA. When the number of V2V links is larger, the success reception probability by SCMA-OMA CDAA is higher than other algorithms.

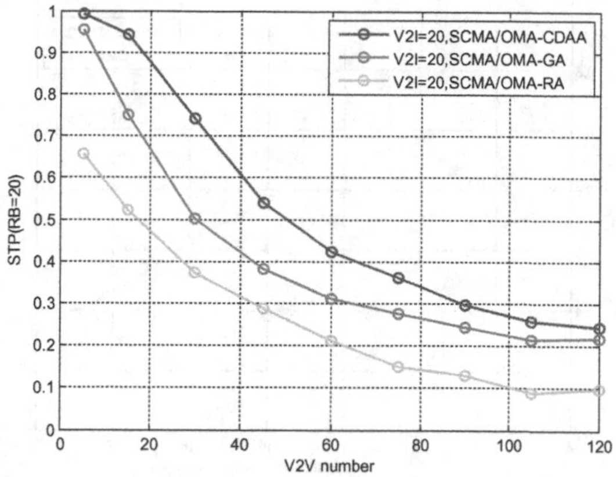

Fig. 4. Successful transmission probability v.s. the number of V2V links in different algorithms

In Fig. 5, we illustrate the STP of V2V links with different number of V2V links and different V2I communication links. Since the number of resource blocks in the system is limited, in order to improve spectral efficiency, the remaining spectrum resources are allocated to the V2V link when the V2I user does not fully occupy all orthogonal resources. As shown in Fig. 5, there are 8 V2V links using orthogonal resources while the number of V2I communication links is 12. In other words, it is equivalent to reducing the number of users of SCMA and the interference among them is also decreased. Consequently, the performance of V2I communication links which is 12 is better than the V2I communication links which is 20. Figure 6 presents the STP with the difference of the SINR threshold. It is clearly that the higher the threshold is, the harder the requirements of threshold are to be satisfied.

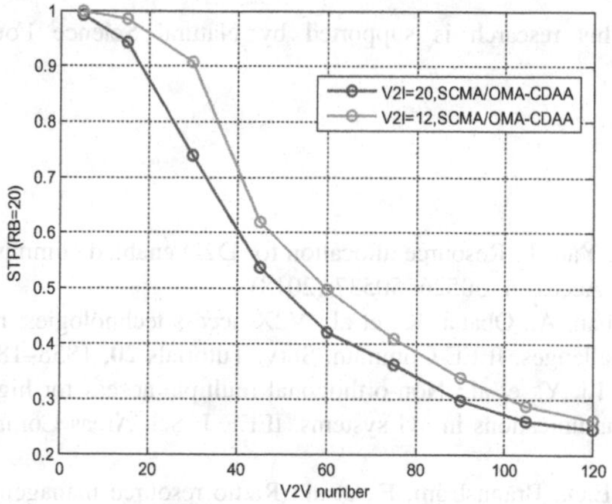

Fig. 5. Successful transmission probability v.s. the number of V2V links in different V2I links

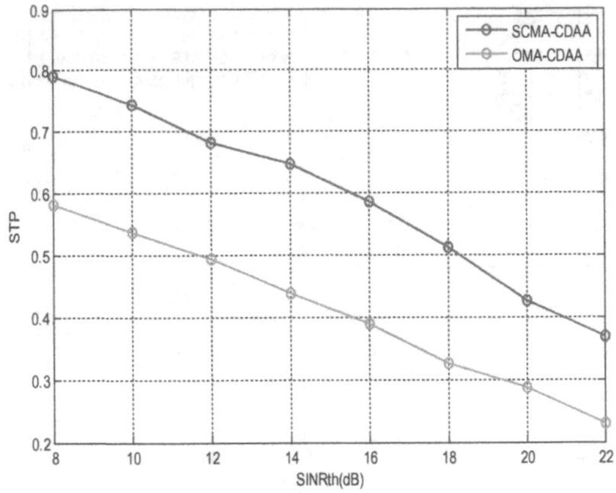

Fig. 6. Successful transmission probability v.s. SINR threshold in different multiple access

6 Conclusions

In this paper, we have investigated the radio resource allocation in a hybrid SCMA-OMA V2X system model. To reduce the interference and improve the reliability of the V2X communications, we have proposed mixed SCMA-OMA scheme, in which V2I links use OMA and V2V links use SCMA reuse V2I links RBs. What is more, to solve the complex interference caused by the introduction of resource reuse strategy, we proposed the combinatorial double auction algorithm based on game theory. Simulation results prove that our proposed the mixed SCMA-OMA CDAA scheme can significantly improve the system performance in terms of the STP for V2X communications. The current work is limited to radio resource management in a single cell. In the future work, we will extend our work to improved STP during the handover.

Acknowledgment. This research is supported by Natural Science Foundation of China (No. 61501136).

References

1. Wang, R., Wu, J., Yan, J.: Resource allocation for D2D-enabled communications in vehicle platooning. IEEE Access **6**, 50526–50537 (2018)
2. MacHardy, Z., Khan, A., Obana, K., et al.: V2X access technologies: regulation, research, and remaining challenges. IEEE Commun. Surv. Tutorials **20**, 1858–1877 (2018)
3. Di, B., Song, L., Li, Y., et al.: Non-orthogonal multiple access for high-reliable and low-latency V2X communications in 5G systems. IEEE J. Sel. Areas Commun. **35**(10), 2383–2397 (2017)
4. Sun, W., Ström, E.G., Brännström, F., et al.: Radio resource management for D2D-based V2V communication. IEEE Trans. Veh. Technol. **65**(8), 6636–6650 (2016)

5. Peng, H., Li, D., Ye, Q., et al.: Resource allocation for D2D-enabled inter-vehicle communications in multiplatoons. In: 2017 IEEE International Conference on Communication, pp. 1–6 (2017)
6. Liang, L., Li, G.Y., Xu, W.: Resource allocation for D2D-enabled vehicular communications. IEEE Trans. Commun. **65**(7), 3186–3197 (2017)
7. Di, B., Song, L., Li, Y., et al.: NOMA-based low-latency and high-reliable broadcast communications for 5G V2X services. In: GLOBECOM 2017-2017 IEEE Global Communications Conference, pp. 1–6 (2017)
8. Qian, L., Wu, Y., Zhou, H., et al.: Dynamic cell association for non-orthogonal multiple-access V2S networks. IEEE J. Sel. Areas Commun. **35**(10), 2342–2356 (2017)
9. Wang, Y., Ren, B., Sun, S., et al.: Analysis of non-orthogonal multiple access for 5G. China Commun. **13**(2), 52–66 (2016)
10. Wang, F., Xu, C., Song, L., et al.: Energy-efficient resource allocation for device-to-device underlay communication. IEEE Trans. Wireless Commun. **14**(4), 2082–2092 (2015)
11. ITU-R: Guidelines for evaluation of radio interface technologies for IMT-advanced. Report ITU-R M.2135 (2008)

Power Control Based on Kalman Filter for Uplink Transmission in Two-Tier Heterogeneous Networks

Kai Sun(✉), Yongze Cao, Anqi Shen, Xiaojun Yue, and Wei Huang

College of Electronic Information Engineering, Inner Mongolia University, Huhhot 010021, China
sunkai1501@gmail.com

Abstract. The problem of interference management and power control in two-tier heterogeneous network is investigated in this paper. Due to the time-varying characteristics of channels, the optimal transmit power changes with time. A hierarchical power control based on Kalman filter is proposed. Using Kalman filter, the current uplink transmit power under the influence of time varying channel gains due to the shadow fading effect is obtained by estimating the power of the last moment. This proposed method follows the slowly varying channel characteristics under the influence of the shadow fading effect in order to obtain an accurate power allocation. The proposed power control method is verified by computer simulations.

Keywords: Heterogeneous networks · Time-varying channel · Kalman filter · Power control

1 Introduction

Recently, the amount of traffic created in cellular systems increased rapidly. According to the estimation, most of the data traffic and the calls come from indoor scenarios [1]. The small cell/femtocell is a promising solution for the indoor scenario, which can increase the capacity and coverage [2]. However, due to the limit of licensed bands, co-channel deployment is inevitable for femtocells, which raises a critical issue on interference. Co-tier interference is generated between adjacent femtocells, besides, cross-tier interference between femtocells and microcells will greatly degrade the system performance [3]. Power control is a particularly critical issue for the auto-configuration of femtocells, especially in the cochannel deployment since it determines the interference and thus further affects coverage, handover, and drop-call-rate [4]. In uplink, the cross-tier interference from femtocell users (FUEs) has to be maintained in a reasonable range or below a certain threshold, in order to ensure the quality of transmissions in microcell [5].

There are many prior works on power control in heterogeneous networks. The authors in [6] propose a distributed power allocation scheme based on game theory which can adjust the signal to interference plus noise ratio (SINR) at femtocells so that the cross-tier interference from the co-channel femtocells can be reduced. In [7], the

M. Jia et al. (Eds.): WiSATS 2019, LNICST 281, pp. 36–46, 2019.
https://doi.org/10.1007/978-3-030-19156-6_4

macrocell base station (MBS) first decides the power of macrocell users (MUEs) and the interference allowance according to the average uplink power budget. Then FUEs adjust their transmitting power below the interference allowance based on the broadcasted message from MBS. In [8], an interference estimation method based on Kalman is proposed to increase the handshaking success rate in IEEE 802.11. Given channel uncertainty, a robust hierarchical game is formulated and solved with distributed algorithms in [9].

On the basis of the above, we propose a new distributed uplink power control method for MUEs and FUEs based on Kalman filter. The shadow fading is considered and the maximum likelihood estimation is used to obtain the mean value of the shadow fading effect between users and their serving base stations. Then we use Kalman filter to estimate user's current powers. This method can reduce measurement errors when the MBS measures the channel gain due to the shadow fading effect.

The remainder of this paper is organized as follows. The system model is presented in Sect. 2. Section 3 gives the details of our proposed power control scheme based on Kalman filter. Section 4 analyses the simulation results. Section 5 concludes the works done in this paper.

2 System Model

It assumed that the system is consisted of a single central macrocell with a coverage radius R_{m}, and N_{f} co-channel femtocells with each providing a coverage radius R_{f}, as shown in Fig. 1. FUEs are located in a small region, which are served by femtocell APs. We assume one scheduled user in each wireless resource block for the macrocell, as well as for each femtocell. Let $i \in \{0, 1, \ldots, N\}$ be the index of the user who connected to its BS B_i, and let P_i denote its transmission power. Without loss of generality, the index 0 represent the MBS/MUE, the other indexes denote FBSs/FUEs. It assumed that the number of the active FUEs is K. The received SINR at B_i can be written as

$$\gamma_i = \frac{P_i \cdot g_{i,i}}{\sum_{j \neq i} P_j \cdot g_{i,j} + \sigma^2} \geq \Gamma_i \tag{1}$$

where Γ_i is the minimum target SINR of user i at B_i, σ^2 is the power of additive white Gaussian noise (AWGN) at B_i. The term $g_{i,i}$ and $g_{i,j}$ denote the channel gain between user i, user j and B_i, respectively. In this paper we just consider the large-scale path loss and shadow fading effect. The fast fading is ignored because power control can effectively compensate for the slowly variations of channel shadow fading. The term $g_{i,j}$ can be expressed as

$$g_{i,j} = r_{i,j}^{-\alpha_{i,j}} e^{k\xi_{i,j}} \tag{2}$$

where $r_{i,j}^{-\alpha_{i,j}}$ denotes the path loss between user j and B_i, $e^{k\xi_{i,j}}$ models the shadow fading effect, $\alpha_{i,j}$ is the path loss factor, $\xi_{i,j}$ is a Gaussian r.v., k equals $\ln 10/10$.

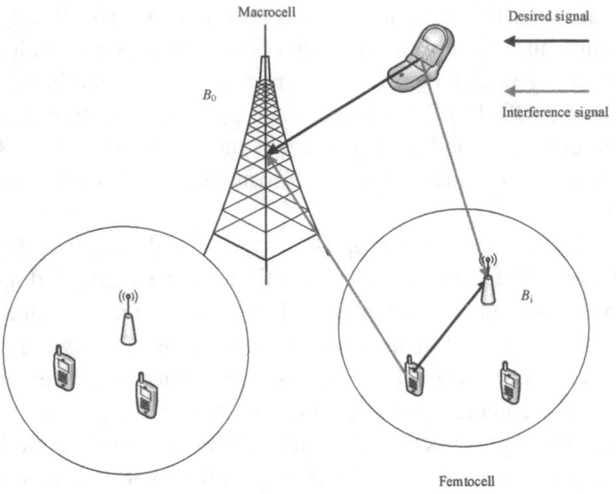

Fig. 1. A macrocell underlaid with co-channel femtocells

3 Proposed Algorithm

In this paper, the MUE is considered as a primary user. This means that the transmissions from macrocell users should reach the target SINR at the MBS's side by limiting the aggregate interference from active femtocells. FUEs adjust their power ensuring that the sum of their power is within the budget of aggregate interference power. User's signal will suffer from propagation loss including distance-dependence path loss and shadow fading effect. It is assumed that the base station can obtain the accurate path loss between its user and itself. B_0 estimates the mean of its serving user's channel gain due to the shadow fading effect by maximum likelihood estimators

$$\widehat{E}_{0,0} = e^{\hat{\mu}_{0,0} + \frac{\hat{\sigma}^2_{0,0}}{2}} \tag{3}$$

Here $\widehat{\mu}_{0,0}$ and $\widehat{\sigma}^2_{0,0}$ are given by

$$\widehat{\mu}_{0,0} = \frac{1}{N}\sum_{i=1}^{N} \ln x_{i,0} \tag{4}$$

and

$$\widehat{\sigma}^2_{0,0} = \frac{1}{N}\sum_{i=1}^{N}\left(\ln x_{i,0} - \frac{1}{N}\sum_{i=1}^{N}\ln x_{i,0}\right)^2 \tag{5}$$

where $x_{i,0}$, $i = 1,\ldots,N$, are the samples which can be obtain from the pilot information. Similarly, the maximum likelihood estimators of mean of the channel gain from the FUE to B_0 are

$$\widehat{E}_{0,j} = e^{\widehat{\mu}_{0,j} + \frac{\widehat{\sigma}^2_{0,j}}{2}}, j = 1,\ldots,N \tag{6}$$

where $\widehat{\mu}_{0,j}$ and $\widehat{\sigma}^2_{0,j}$ can be derived as

$$\widehat{\mu}_{0,j} = \frac{1}{N}\sum_{i=1}^{N} \ln x_{i,j} \tag{7}$$

$$\widehat{\sigma}^2_{0,j} = \frac{1}{N}\sum_{i=1}^{N}\left(\ln x_{s,j} - \frac{1}{N}\sum_{i=1}^{N}\ln x_{s,j}\right)^2 \tag{8}$$

3.1 MUE Power Allocation

The minimum target SINR should be guaranteed for the MUE, given its primary role in two-tier heterogeneous networks. B_0 first decides L_0 called the uplink power allocation reference. L_0 can be formulated as

$$L_0 = P_{\max,m}\widehat{E}_{0,0}r_m^{-\alpha_m} \tag{9}$$

where $P_{\max,m}$ is the maximum transmission power, $\widehat{E}_{0,0}$ is the estimated mean value of shadow fading effects, and $r_m^{-\alpha_m}$ is the channel gain from the MUE located on the cell edge to B_0. Then the transmitting power of MUE can be obtained for the first time with the power constraint $P_{\max,m}$ as follows

$$P_0 = \min\left(P_{\max,m}, \frac{L_0}{r_0^{-\alpha_m}\cdot\widehat{E}_{0,0}}\right) \tag{10}$$

where $r_0^{-\alpha_m}$ is the channel gain between the MUE and B_0. The minimum target SINR can be expressed as

$$(1+\delta)\Gamma_0 = \frac{L_0}{P_{\text{AGGI}} + \sigma^2} \tag{11}$$

where σ^2 is AWGN and P_{AGGI} represents the interference allowance of the MUE in the uplink transmission. Let $1+\delta$ be the protection margin, which provides extra SINR to cushion the aggregate interference from all active FUEs. The interference allowance of the MUE can be determined as

$$P_{\mathrm{AGGI}} = \frac{L_0}{(1+\delta)\Gamma_0} - \sigma_n^2 \tag{12}$$

The uplink transmitting power of each FUE is allocated for the first time according to (12), which can be given under the maximum transmitting power constraint $P_{\mathrm{max,f}}$ by

$$P_j = \min\left\{P_{\mathrm{max,f}}, \frac{P_{\mathrm{AGGI}}}{K \cdot r_j^{-\alpha_{\mathrm{f}}} \cdot \widehat{E}_{0,j}}, j = 0, 1, \ldots, K\right\} \tag{13}$$

where K represents all active FUEs, $r_j^{-\alpha_{\mathrm{f}}}$ is the path loss from the FUE to B_0, and $\widehat{E}_{0,j}$ is mean value of shadow fading effects between B_0 and FUEs.

Kalman filtering is a linear quadratic estimator for unknown variables according to the measurement values with the statistical noise or other inaccuracies. In our work, the base station uses a Kalman filter to reduce measurement errors when measuring the received power under the influence of time-varying channel gains due to the shadow fading effect.

The uplink power P_0 can be formulated as

$$P_0 \cdot e^{k\xi_{0,0}} \cdot r_0^{-\alpha_{\mathrm{m}}} = L_0 \tag{14}$$

Take logarithm on both sides of (14), and then divide $k\widehat{\xi}_{0,0}$ into two parts $k\widehat{\mu}_{0,0}$ and $k^2\widehat{\sigma}_{0,0}^2\tau$, we can get

$$\ln\left(P_0 \cdot r_0^{-\alpha_{\mathrm{m}}}\right) + k\widehat{\mu}_{0,0} + k^2\widehat{\sigma}_{0,0}^2\tau = \ln L_0 \tag{15}$$

where $k\widehat{\xi}_{0,0}$ is a Gaussian r.v. with mean $k\widehat{\mu}_{0,0}$ and standard deviation $k\widehat{\sigma}_{0,0}$, τ is a Gaussian r.v. with zero mean and unit standard deviation, k is a constant equals to $\ln 10/10$.

Let $P_L = \ln\left(P_0 \cdot r_0^{-\alpha_{\mathrm{m}}}\right) + k\widehat{\mu}_{0,0}$, which is known as the process in Kalman filter and is to be estimated according to (7). The dynamics of P_L can be described as

$$P_L(t) = P_L(t-1) - W(t-1) \tag{16}$$

where $W(t-1)$ represents the fluctuation of P_L as the MUE start a new transmission and/or adjust its transmission. In the terminology of Kalman filtering, $W(t-1)$ is the "process noise", which obeys the Gaussian r.v. with zero mean and variance $Q = k^2\widehat{\sigma}_{0,0}^2$. Let $Z(t)$ be the measured power P_L for slot t. Then

$$Z(t) = P_L(t) - V(t) \tag{17}$$

where $V(t)$ is called as measurement noise and is a Gaussian r.v. with zero mean and variance R. Based on Kalman filter theory, the update equations for P_L are [10]

$$\begin{cases} \widetilde{P}_L(t+1) = \widehat{P}_L(t) \\ \widetilde{P}(t+1) = \widehat{P}(t) + Q \\ K(t+1) = \frac{\widetilde{P}(t+1)}{\widetilde{P}(t+1)+R} \\ \widehat{P}_L(t+1) = \widetilde{P}_L(t+1) + K(t+1)\varepsilon(t+1) \\ \varepsilon(t+1) = Z(t+1) - \widetilde{P}_L(t+1) \\ \widehat{P}(t+1) = [1 - K(t+1)]\widetilde{P}(t+1) \end{cases} \tag{18}$$

where $\widehat{P}_L(t)$ and $\widehat{P}(t)$ are the updated filter estimate of P_L and error variance associated with the filter estimate $\widehat{P}_L(t)$ at time t, and $\widetilde{P}_L(t+1)$ is the predictive estimate of P_L at time $(t+1)$ given all the measurements through t, $\widetilde{P}(t+1)$ is the error covariance associated with the predictive estimate $\widetilde{P}_L(t+1)$, $K(t+1)$ is the Kalman gain, and Q and R are the variances for the process voice $W(t-1)$ and measurement noise $V(t)$, respectively. We need the initial conditions when using the Kalman filter for the first time. From the problem statement we can say

$$\widehat{P}_L(t_1) = \ln(L_0) \tag{19}$$

Otherwise, the previous updated filter estimate is input to the filter to obtain the current updated estimate. The uplink transmitting power of MUE can be obtained from the above filtering result under the power constraint $P_{\max,m}$ by

$$P_0(t+1) = \min\left(P_{\max,m}, \frac{\exp\left(\widehat{P}_L(t+1) - \frac{\ln 10}{10} \cdot \widehat{\mu}_{0,0}\right)}{r_0^{-\alpha_m}}\right) \tag{20}$$

3.2 FUE Power Allocation

The uplink transmit power of FUE can be determined for the first time subject to the power constraint $P_{\max,f}$ according to (13). The interference allowance of the MUE can also be formulated as

$$P_{AGGI} = \sum_{j=1}^{K} P_j \cdot r_j^{-\alpha_f} \cdot e^{k\hat{\xi}_{0,j}} \tag{21}$$

where $r_j^{-\alpha_f}$ is the path loss from the FUE to B_0, $k\hat{\xi}_{0,j}$ is a Gaussian r.v. with mean $k\widehat{\mu}_{0,j}$ and standard deviation $k\widehat{\sigma}_{0,j}$, and k is a constant equals to $\ln 10/10$. The uplink power P_j can be formulated as

$$P_j \cdot r_j^{-\alpha_f} \cdot e^{k\hat{\xi}_{0,j}} = \frac{P_{AGGI}}{K}, j = 0, 1, \ldots, K \tag{22}$$

Take logarithm on both sides of (22), and then divide $k\widehat{\xi}_{0,j}$ into two parts $k\widehat{\mu}_{0,j}$ and $k^2\widehat{\sigma}_{0,j}^2\tau$, we can get

$$\ln\left(P_j \cdot r_j^{-\alpha_f}\right) + k\widehat{\mu}_{0,j} + k^2\widehat{\sigma}_{0,j}^2\tau = \ln\frac{P_{\mathrm{AGGI}}}{K} \tag{23}$$

where τ is a standard normal r.v.

Let $P_f = \ln\left(P_j \cdot r_j^{-\alpha_f}\right) + k\widehat{\mu}_{0,j}$ be the estimated process state by the Kalman filter. Using the similar analysis procedure of MUE in the above section, the uplink transmit power of each FUE subject to maximal power constraint $P_{\max,f}$ can be determined

$$P_j'(t+1) = \min\left(P_{\max,f}, \frac{\exp\left(\widehat{P}_f(t+1) - \frac{\ln 10}{10}\cdot\widehat{\mu}_{0,j}\right)}{r_j^{-\alpha_f}}\right) \tag{24}$$

4 Performance Evaluation

In this section, we evaluate the performance of our proposed power control scheme through Monte Carlo simulation. We consider a simulation scenario referring to [6]. The simulation scenario is shown in Fig. 2. The main system parameters are given in Table 1.

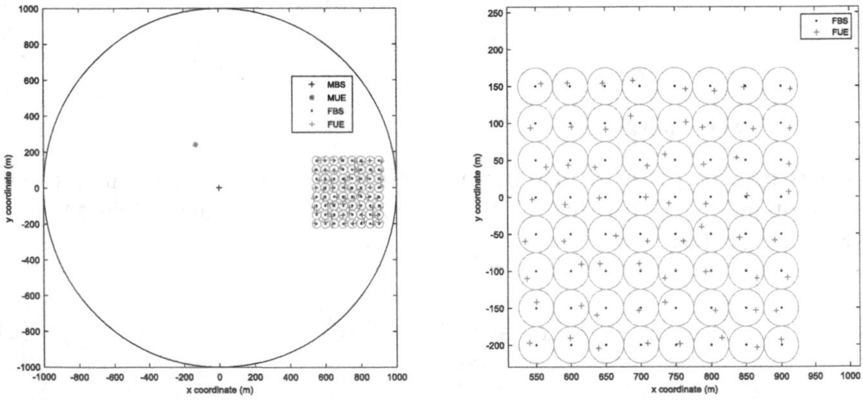

Fig. 2. Simulated two-tier heterogeneous network

Table 1. System parameters

Variable	Parameter	Value
R_{m}	Macrocell radius	1000 m
R_{f}	Femtocell radius	30 m
$P_{\max,\mathrm{m}}$	Max transmission power of MUE	30 dBm
$P_{\max,\mathrm{f}}$	Max transmission power per FUE	25 dBm
Γ_0	Max cellular SINR target	10
$\alpha_{\mathrm{m}}, \alpha_{\mathrm{f}}$	Path loss exponents	4, 4

Figure 3 shows the estimated power performance of MUE through Kalman filter. The true power of MUE means MUEs optimal transmit power which makes MUE reach its minimum target SINR, mitigating the shadow fading effect to a large extent. The MBS measures its received power transmitted by MUE at time t and determines the transmit power of MUE at time $(t + 1)$ without Kalman filter. We call this transmit power as the measured power of MUE. If the MBS determines the transmit power of MUE at time $(t + 1)$ with Kalman filter, we will call this power as the estimated power of MUE based on Kalman filter. Using Kalman filter we can effectively reduce the measurement errors.

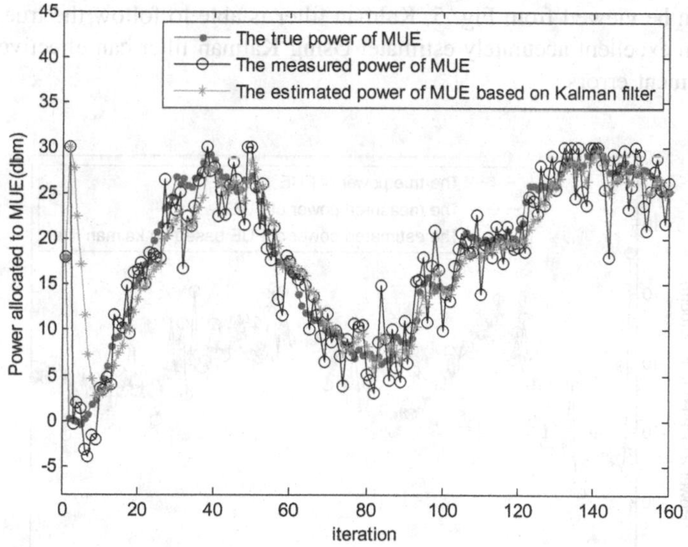

Fig. 3. Power allocated to MUE

Figure 4 compares the measured deviation and estimated deviation. As can be viewed from Fig. 4, the estimated deviation is smaller than the measured deviation.

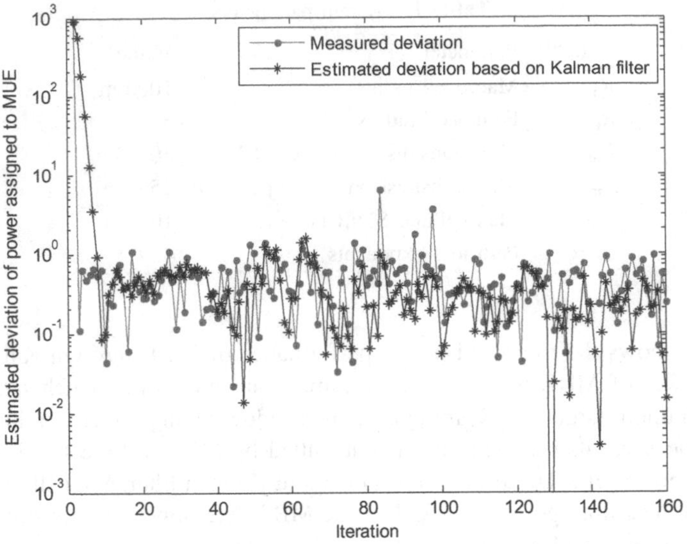

Fig. 4. Estimated deviation of power allocated to MUE

Figure 5 shows the estimated power performance of a certain FUE through Kalman filter. As can be viewed from Fig. 5, Kalman filter is able to follow the true power of FUE with an excellent accurately estimate. Using Kalman filter can effectively reduce the measurement errors.

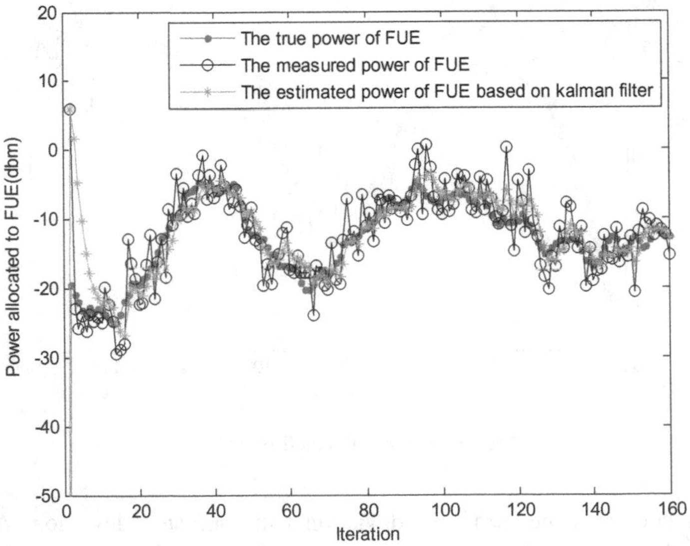

Fig. 5. Power allocated to FUE

Figure 6 compares the measured deviation and estimated deviation based on Kalman filter. As can be viewed from Fig. 6, the estimated deviation is smaller than the measured deviation.

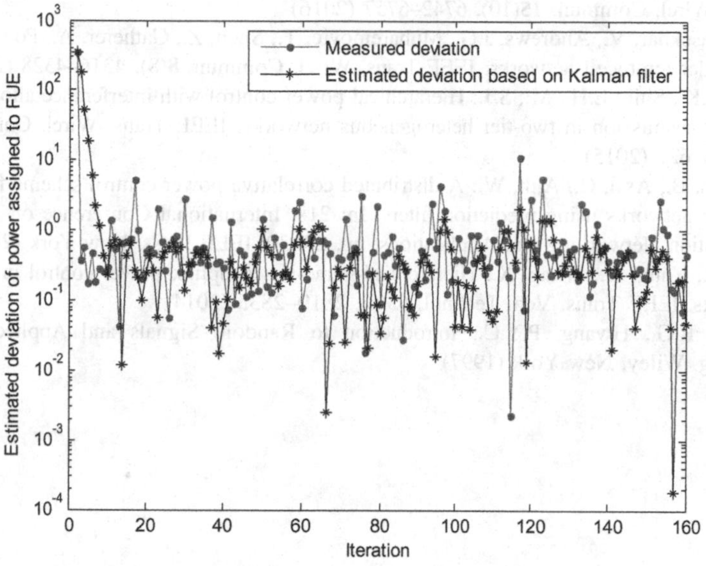

Fig. 6. Estimated deviation of power allocated to FUE

5 Conclusion

In this paper, we have proposed a hierarchical power control scheme based on Kalman filter in two-tier heterogeneous networks. Kalman filter is used to estimate the power P_L and P_f. Then user's transmit power P_0 and P_j can be determined according to P_L and P_f respectively. Through simulations we have proved that using Kalman filter can effectively reduce the measurement errors.

Acknowledgment. This research was supported by the National Natural Science Foundation of China (61861034, 61461035), the Natural Science Foundation of Inner Mongolia (2018MS06004).

References

1. Chandrasekhar, V., Andrews, J.G., Gatherer, A.: Femtocell networks: a survey. IEEE Commun. Mag. **46**(9), 59–67 (2008)
2. Ghosh, A., Mangalvedhe, N., Ratasuk, R., et al.: Heterogeneous cellular networks: from theory to practice. IEEE Commun. Mag. **50**(6), 54–64 (2012)
3. Zhang, H., Dong, Y., Cheng, J., Hossain, Md.J., Leung, V.C.M.: Fronthauling for 5G LTE-U ultra dense cloud small cell networks. IEEE Wirel. Commun. **23**(5), 48–53 (2016)

4. Zhang, L., Nie, W., Feng, G., Zheng, F.C., Qin, S.: Uplink performance improvement by decoupling uplink/downlink access in HetNets. IEEE Trans. Veh. Technol. **66**(8), 6862–6876 (2017)
5. Martin-Vega, F.J., Gomez, G., Aguayo-Torres, M.C., Di Renzo, M.: Analytical modeling of interference aware power control for the uplink of heterogeneous cellular networks. IEEE Trans. Wirel. Commun. **15**(10), 6742–6757 (2016)
6. Chandrasekhar, V., Andrews, J.G., Muharemovic, T., Shen, Z., Gatherer, A.: Power control in two-tier femtocell networks. IEEE Trans. Wirel. Commun. **8**(8), 4316–4328 (2009)
7. Dong, I.K., Shin, E.H., Mi, S.J.: Hierarchical power control with interference allowance for uplink transmission in two-tier heterogeneous networks. IEEE Trans. Wirel. Commun. **14** (2), 616–627 (2015)
8. Alawieh, B., Assi, C., Ajib, W.: A distributed correlative power control scheme for mobile Ad Hoc networks using prediction filters. In: 21st International Conference on Advanced Information Networking and Applications, pp. 23–30. IEEE Press, New York (2007)
9. Han, Q., Yang, B., Wang, X.: Hierarchical-game-based uplink power control in femtocell networks. IEEE Trans. Veh. Technol. **63**(6), 2819–2835 (2014)
10. Brown, R.G., Hwang, P.Y.C.: Introduction to Random Signals and Applied Kalman Filtering. Wiley, New York (1997)

A 3-D Migration Imaging Algorithm Suitable for Expressway Detection

Yiming Pu(✉), Jiayan Zhang, Yongkui Ma, Xu Bai, and Shuai Wang

Harbin Institute of Technology, Harbin 150001, China
yillming@163.com, x_bai@hit.edu.cn

Abstract. The imaging technology is an important part of the ground penetrating radar (GPR) technology research. Traditional ground penetrating radar imaging technology mostly stays in two-dimensional (2-D) imaging. However, when the line of the 2-D section is inclined obliquely to the underground target, the 2-D section will be inconsistent with the actual underground structure, which makes the 2-D imaging technology have inherent defects. Therefore, the research of the 3-D imaging technology has become a hot and difficult problem in current research. In this paper, a 3-D prestack time migration imaging algorithm for expressway detection is proposed. In order to better realize the 3-D migration imaging display, it is necessary to do some preliminary processing on the 3-D ground penetrating radar reflected echo data, including data preprocessing and data processing. Then the 3-D prestack migration imaging technique is applied to the process of the 3-D ground penetrating radar reflected echo data after pre-processing. By rearranging the amplitude of the collected reflected echo signals, the reflected echo energy can be homing to the real position of the space where the initial reflection point is located, thereby the horizontal resolution of the detection area is improved and finally the true outline of the measured target can be reconstructed. The simulation results verify the effectiveness and superiority of the proposed algorithm.

Keywords: GPR · Data processing · 3-D prestack time migration imaging

1 Introduction

In the traditional expressway roadbed detection, it is generally to use the punch coring excavating the sample to obtain the sample first, and then pass the soil test. This method not only has low efficiency, low accuracy, but also damages the roadbed and increases the cost of roadbed quality inspection. The advanced ground penetrating radar solution has the advantages of fast detection, no damage to the roadbed and high detection accuracy. As early as the late 1980s, Europe and the United States began to apply advanced ground penetrating radar technology, and it was not introduced to China until the 1990s. In recent years, the community has become more and more concerned about road maintenance, and the ground penetrating radar with non-destructive detection features has become one of the dark horses.

Ground penetrating radar provides a non-destructive detection solution for underground target detection, which is used more and more widely in engineering. For the

M. Jia et al. (Eds.): WiSATS 2019, LNICST 281, pp. 47–55, 2019.
https://doi.org/10.1007/978-3-030-19156-6_5

research of ground penetrating radar imaging methods, it is generally concentrated on 2-D imaging. Commercial ground penetrating radar products generally do not have 3-D imaging functions. However, for the 2-D image of ground penetrating radar, when the line of the 2-D section is inclined obliquely to the underground target, the reflected signal from the target interface directly below the line is not within the section, but for the reflection point not in the section can be recorded, causing the 2-D section to be inconsistent with the actual underground structure. On the one hand, the use of 3-D imaging of ground penetrating radar can solve the above-mentioned shortcomings of 2-D imaging section. On the other hand, 3-D image facilitates a more detailed understanding of the distribution of underground targets, so 3-D imaging technology has been extensively studied [1].

In the research of 3-D imaging technology, imaging migration can improve the resolution of target detection and restore the original shape of the target. Therefore, to some extent, the development level of imaging migration technology indicates the development level of detection technology. Imaging migration techniques can be divided into two categories: one is the polarization method based on the Huygens principle, and the method is based on the geometric principle of electromagnetic waves propagating in the medium. The other type is based on physical optics, starting from the solution of the wave equation, which is collectively referred to as the wave equation migration method. The common wave equation migration method mainly includes: Kichhoff integral migration method, finite difference migration method, F-K migration method, finite element migration method [2], etc.

In 1972, Claerbout introduced a finite difference migration method based on the parabolic equation [3]. In 1978, Stolt and Gazdag first performed the F-K transformation on the data, then solved the wave equation and extrapolated the electromagnetic wave field in reverse. This method is called the F-K migration method [4]. In 1978, Schneider used the Kichhoff integral equation solved by the wave equation to perform the migration imaging process [5]. In 1996, Grasmuck used the phase shift method to migration the common migration data [6]. In 1987, Lee et al. used the one-way acoustic equation to implement the finite difference method [7]. In 1992, Fisher et al. applied a split Fourier migration method to transform data for single migration data. In the same year, Fisher applied the inverse time migration method for migration processing for multi-migration data post-profiles [8]. In 1993, Deng et al. researched the Kichhoff integral migration method in depth [9]. In 2003, Chen et al. applied the hybrid domain one-way wave propagation operator to the migration imaging technique [10]. In 2011, Qu et al. applied compressive sensing theory to frequency stepped ground penetrating radar migration imaging [11]. In 2013, Huang conducted a study on the least squares migration imaging method for carbonate fractured reservoirs [12]. In 2015, Zheng et al. proposed a data autocorrelation multiple-wave migration imaging technique [13]. In 2016, Lu Yuting gave an analysis of the migration imaging method based on regularization of multi-source mixed mining data [14]. In 2017, He et al. carried out research on high-order generalized screen migration imaging based on particle swarm optimization algorithm [5].

In recent years, migration imaging technology has become a key technology in the development of ground penetrating radar technology. The use of migration imaging technology can improve the horizontal resolution of the system at the data processing level and analyze the distribution of underground media more accurately.

In this paper, the proposed 3-D prestack migration imaging algorithm combines the advantages of prestack migration imaging technology and time migration imaging technology. The prestack migration imaging technique performs the migration processing on the common midpoint (CMP) gather of ground penetrating radar. Then the algorithm extracts signal gather, which has the same reflection point. Finally, it stacks the common reflection point (CRP) gathers [15]. This algorithm has high precision and can improve the signal to noise ratio. The time migration imaging algorithm is implemented based on the summation of the diffraction curves, and the result is placed at the apex of the diffraction curve [16]. This algorithm is simple, the calculation speed is fast, the efficiency is high, and the actual engineering is widely used. The 3-D prestack migration imaging technique is applied to the echo data processing of the ground penetrating radar system. By rearranging the amplitude of the collected reflected echo signals, the reflected echo energy can be homing to the real position of the space where the initial reflection point is located, and finally the true outline of the measured target can be reconstructed [17].

At the same time, in order to better realize the 3-D migration imaging display, it is necessary to do some preliminary processing on the three-dimensional ground penetrating radar reflected echo data, including data preprocessing and data processing [18]. The preprocessing algorithm includes processing for removing bad sectors, zero correction, gain control, and the data processing algorithm includes background elimination, band pass filtering, and wavelet domain filtering [19].

2 3D Ground Penetrating Radar Data Processing Scheme

When studying the 3-D migration imaging technology, in order to obtain a better migration imaging effect, it is necessary to do some preliminary processing on the three-dimensional ground penetrating radar reflected echo data, including data preprocessing and data processing, and the 3-D data processing can be converted into multiple 2-D data processing. In the data processing part of this paper, the 2-D data preprocessing algorithm is given first, including the processing of removing bad track, zero correction, gain control and so on. The algorithm of removing bad track is used to estimate the effective echo data corresponding to the bad track and replace it, so as to reduce the influence of the bad track on the subsequent data processing; use the algorithm of zero correction to adjust the same axis to the same horizontal line, and reduce the effect of the up and down jitter on the detection in the actual detection in ground penetrating radar system; the gain control algorithm is used to amplify the echo signal data generated by the deep target, thereby making the deep target easier to be identified1. Then a 2-D data processing algorithm is provided, including background elimination, band pass filtering, wavelet domain filtering. The algorithm of background elimination is used to reduce the influence of standing wave interference, and highlight the detection target located at the standing wave position; the algorithm of band-pass filtering is used to improve the signal-to-noise ratio of the reflected echo signal, and reduce the interference of high-frequency clutter on the target detection; the algorithm of wavelet domain filtering is performed aimed at the non-stationary characteristics of the reflecting echo, achieving a better filtering effect. Finally, using the migration imaging algorithm, the 2-D prestack time migration imaging algorithm and the 3-D prestack time migration algorithm proposed in this paper are used respectively. By rearranging the amplitude of the collected reflected echo signals, the reflected echo energy can be homing to the real position of the space where the initial reflection point is located, finally the true outline of the measured target can be reconstructed. The entire data processing flow chart is shown in Fig. 1.

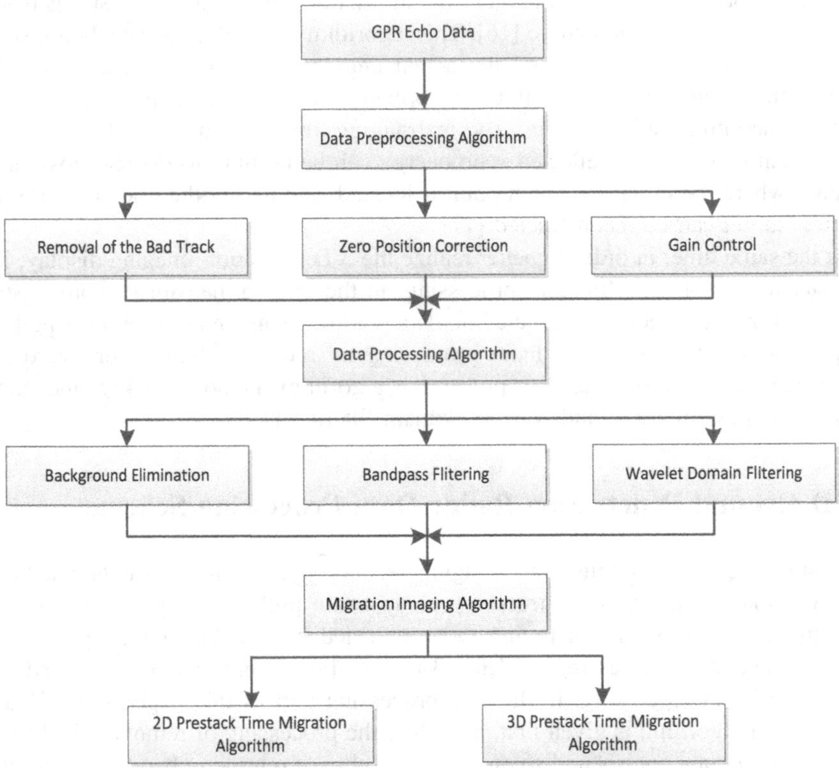

Fig. 1. Flowchart of the data processing

3 The Principle of 3-D Prestack Time Migration Imaging Algorithm

First the following assumptions are given: a coordinate system is given for the measured area, assuming that the z-axis is vertically downward, and the ground penetrating radar moves in the positive direction of the x-axis, where the positive direction of the y-axis conforms to the left-handed criterion. Also assume that the velocity of electromagnetic waves propagating in a lossy medium is constant, $u(x, y, z, 0)$ represents the true restoring section after using the migration algorithm, and $u(x, y, 0, t)$ is the superimposed section before using migration algorithm. By using half speed instead of the average propagation velocity of electromagnetic waves in a lossy medium, then the scalar wave equation in 3-D space can be expressed as

$$\frac{\partial^2 u}{\partial t^2} - \frac{v^2}{4}\left(\frac{\partial^2 u}{\partial x^2} + \frac{\partial^2 u}{\partial y^2} + \frac{\partial^2 u}{\partial z^2}\right) = 0 \tag{1}$$

First, the basic Fourier transform pairs used is given as follows:

$$\left.\begin{array}{l} u(x,y,z,t) \Leftrightarrow \tilde{u}(k_x,k_y,k_z,\omega) \\ \frac{\partial^2 u}{\partial t^2} \Leftrightarrow -\omega^2 \tilde{u} \\ \frac{\partial^2 u}{\partial y^2} \Leftrightarrow -k_y^2 \tilde{u} \\ \frac{\partial^2 u}{\partial x^2} \Leftrightarrow -k_x^2 \tilde{u} \\ \frac{\partial^2 u}{\partial z^2} \Leftrightarrow -k_z^2 \tilde{u} \end{array}\right\} \tag{2}$$

The Stolt-migration method is used for derivation. Let $\tilde{u}(k_x,k_y,k_z,t)$ is the 3-D - FT of $u(x,y,z,t)$, 3-D - FT is performed on the Eq. (1), and substituting the (2) into the above (1), Then we can obtain:

$$\left\{\begin{array}{l} \omega^2 \tilde{u} - \frac{v^2}{4}\left(k_x^2 + k_y^2 + k_z^2\right)\tilde{u} = 0 \\ \frac{\partial^2 \tilde{u}}{\partial t^2} + \frac{v^2}{4}\left(k_x^2 + k_y^2 + k_z^2\right)\tilde{u} = 0 \end{array}\right. \tag{3}$$

Hence:

$$\frac{\partial^2 \tilde{u}}{\partial t^2} + \omega^2 \tilde{u} = 0 \tag{4}$$

Solve the differential equation and take the up-going wave to get the positive value:

$$\tilde{u}(k_x,k_y,k_z,t) = A(k_x,k_y,k_z)e^{i\omega t} \tag{5}$$

We can see that $A(k_x,k_y,k_z)$ is unrelated to t. Assume that $t = 0$ in Eq. (5). Hence:

$$\tilde{u}(k_x,k_y,k_z,0) = A(k_x,k_y,k_z) \tag{6}$$

It is easy to see that $A(k_x,k_y,k_z)$ is the FT of the migration section $u(x,y,z,0)$ to be sought.

Next, we will discuss how to use the horizontal stacking section $u(x,y,0,t)$ to solve $A(k_x,k_y,k_z)$. Inverse FT is performed on $\tilde{u}(k_x,k_y,k_z,t)$. Hence:

$$u(x,y,z,t) = \frac{1}{8\pi^3}\int_{-\infty}^{\infty} dk_x \int_{-\infty}^{\infty} dk_y \int_{-\infty}^{\infty} A(k_x,k_y,k_z)e^{i\omega t} \cdot e^{-i(k_x x + k_y y + k_z z)} dk_z \tag{7}$$

Assume that $z = 0$. Equation (7) can be written as

$$u(x, y, 0, t) = \frac{1}{8\pi^3} \int_{-\infty}^{\infty} dk_x \int_{-\infty}^{\infty} dk_y \int_{-\infty}^{\infty} A(k_x, k_y, k_z) e^{i(\omega t - k_x x - k_y y)} dk_z \tag{8}$$

Assume that $B(k_x, k_y, \omega)$ is the 3-D - FT of the horizontal stacking section $u(x, y, 0, t)$. Then:

$$B(k_x, k_y, \omega) = \int_{-\infty}^{\infty} dx \int_{-\infty}^{\infty} dy \int_{-\infty}^{\infty} u(x, y, 0, t) e^{-i(\omega t - k_x x - k_y y)} dt \tag{9}$$

Inverse transform is performed on Eq. (9). Then:

$$u(x, y, 0, t) = \frac{1}{8\pi^3} \int_{-\infty}^{\infty} dk_x \int_{-\infty}^{\infty} dk_y \int_{-\infty}^{\infty} B(k_x, k_y, \omega) e^{i(\omega t - k_x x - k_y y)} d\omega \tag{10}$$

Compare Eq. (8) with Eq. (10), implies

$$A(k_x, k_y, k_z) dk_z = B(k_x, k_y, \omega) d\omega \tag{11}$$

Hence:

$$A(k_x, k_y, k_z) = B(k_x, k_y, \omega) \frac{d\omega}{dk_z} \tag{12}$$

Solve by the up-going wave, where ω takes a positive sign and differentiate k_z, then we can get

$$A(k_x, k_y, k_z) = B\left(k_x, k_y, \frac{v}{2} k_z \cdot \sqrt{1 + k_x^2/k_z^2 + k_y^2/k_z^2}\right) \cdot \frac{v}{2 \cdot \sqrt{1 + k_x^2/k_z^2 + k_y^2/k_z^2}} \tag{13}$$

Inverse 3-D - FT is performed on the $A(k_x, k_y, k_z)$, hence

$$u(x, y, z, 0) = \frac{1}{8\pi^3} \int_{-\infty}^{\infty} \int_{-\infty}^{\infty} \int_{-\infty}^{\infty} A(k_x, k_y, k_z) e^{-i(k_x x + k_y y + k_z z)} dk_x dk_y dk_z \tag{14}$$

Where $u(x, y, z, 0)$ is the solution of the migration section.

In summary, the flowchart of the 3D prestack time migration imaging algorithm is shown in Fig. 2.

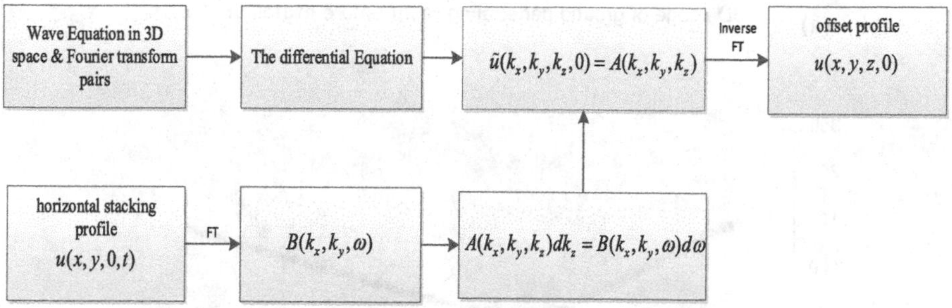

Fig. 2. Flowchart of the 3D prestack time migration imaging algorithm

4 Simulation Results

Figure 3 shows the 2-D image of the ground penetrating radar after the migration. Figure 4(a) shows the 3-D image of the ground penetrating radar before migration, Fig. 4(b) shows the 3-D image of the ground penetrating radar after migration. It can be seen that the diffraction wave in the form of a hyperbola after the Stolt migration is homing, which improves the lateral resolution, and proves the superiority of the algorithm.

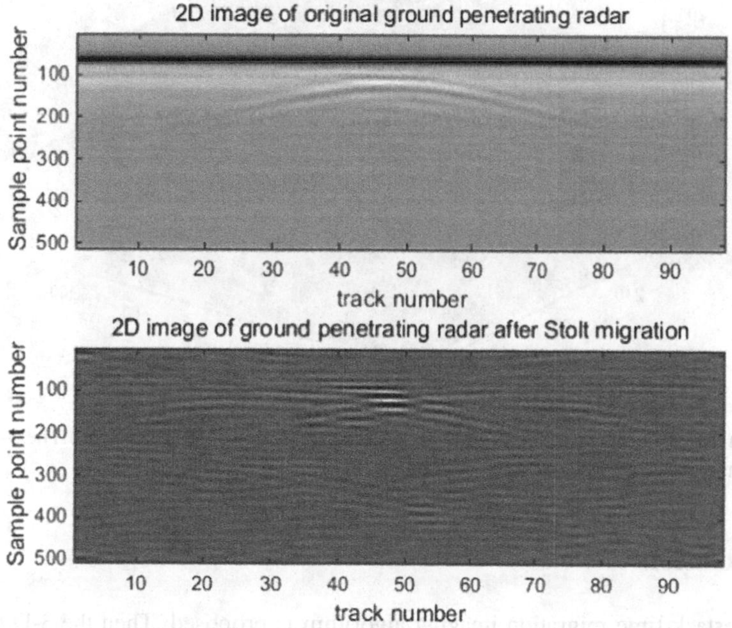

Fig. 3. The 2D prestack time migration imaging result

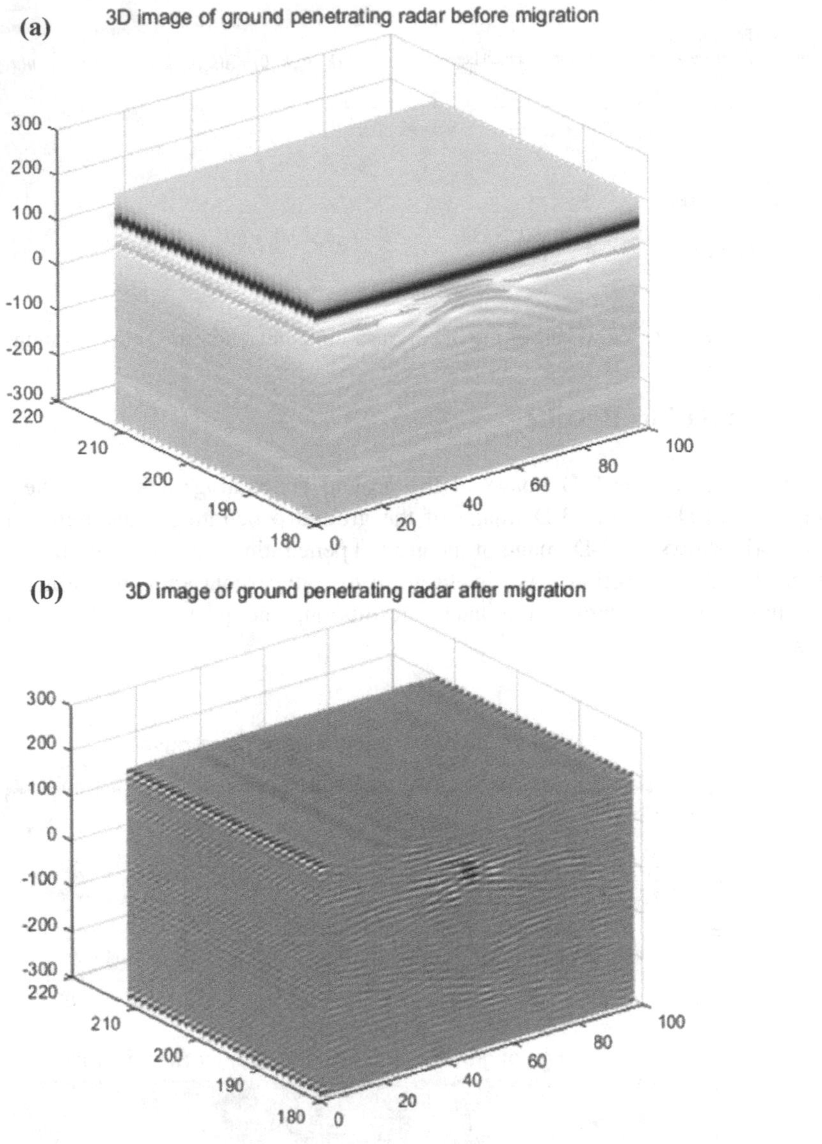

Fig. 4. (a) The 3-D image of the ground penetrating radar before migration. (b) The 3-D image of the ground penetrating radar after migration

5 Conclusion

A 3-D prestack time migration imaging algorithm is proposed. Then the 3-D prestack migration imaging technique is applied to the process of the 3-D ground penetrating radar reflected echo data after pre-processing. By rearranging the amplitude of the collected reflected echo signals, the reflected echo energy can be homing to the real position of the space where the initial reflection point is located, thereby the horizontal resolution of the detection area is improved and finally the true outline of the measured target can be reconstructed Simulation results verify the effectiveness and superiority of the proposed algorithm.

Acknowledgement. This work was supported in part by the National Key R&D Program of China under grant No. 2017YFC1500601.

References

1. Zhao, J., Guo, Y., Tang, P.: Application research of ground penetrating radar in highway subgrade quality inspection. **19**(1), 25–30 (2003)
2. Zhang, A., Jiang, Y., Wang, W., Wang, C.: Three-dimensional imaging method of ground-penetrating radar sweeping frequency. (03), 313–316 (2000)
3. Liu, Z.: Application of offset technology in data processing of ground penetrating radar. **19** (6), 118–121 (2007)
4. Wu, L.: Wave equation migration algorithm for large dip angle formations. (1), 35–41 (1979)
5. Stolt, R.H.: Migration by Fourier transform. Geophysics **43**(1), 23–48 (1978)
6. Gazdag, J.: Wave equation migration with the phase-shift method. Geophysics **43**(43), 1342–1351 (2012)
7. Zhou, H., Qiu, D.: Current status and prospects of data processing for geological radar. **8**(2), 234–234 (2001)
8. Fisher, E., McMechan, G.A., Annan, A.P.: Examples of reverse-time migration of single-channel, ground-penetrating radar profiles. Geophysics **57**(4), 577–586 (1992)
9. Deng, S.: Application of Kirchhoff integral shift method in image processing of ground penetrating radar. (3), 303–309 (1993)
10. Chen, S., Cao, J., Ma, Z.: Mixed-domain one-way wave propagation operator and its application in migration imaging. **18**(02), 210–217 (2003)
11. Qu, L., Fang, G., Yang, T.: Application of compressed sensing theory in frequency stepping ground penetrating radar migration imaging. **33**(1), 21–26 (2011)
12. Huang, J., Li, Z., Kong, X., et al.: Research on least squares migration imaging method for fractured reservoirs of carbonate rocks. **56**(05), 1716–1725 (2013)
13. Zheng, Y., Wang, Y., Xu, J.: Data autocorrelation multiple-wave migration imaging. **58**(03), 993–1001 (2015)
14. He, R., You, J., Liu, B.: High-order generalized screen migration imaging based on particle swarm optimization algorithm. (1), 64–72 (2017)
15. Wang, Y., Chen, W.: Research on detection of parallel underground pipeline with small intervals. (3), 22–25 (2011)
16. Li, X.B., Hong, L.B.: Development and application of urban underground pipe-line detection and management technology. (4), 5–11 (2010)
17. Liu, Y.Y., Yang, L.: Application of ground penetrating radar in underground pipe-line detection. (3), 73–76 (2015)
18. Jol, H.: Ground Penetrating Radar: Theory and Applications. Elsevier Science, Amsterdam (2009)
19. Neal, A.: Ground-penetrating radar and its use in sedimentology: principles, problems and progress. Earth Sci. Rev. **66**(3), 261–330 (2004)

Narrowband-IoT as an Effective Developmental Strategy for Internet of Things in Sub-Saharan Africa: Nigerian Case Study

Oluwaseun Ologun, Shaochuan Wu(✉), Yulong Gao, and Xiaokang Zhou

School of Electronics and Information Engineering, Harbin Institute of Technology, Harbin, China
oluwaseunologun@yahoo.com, {scwu,ylgao}@hit.edu.cn, kangsenneo@sina.com

Abstract. With the recent standardization of Narrow-Band Internet of Things (NB-IoT) as a category of Low Power Wide Area (LPWA) technology by the 3GPP, the endless possibilities it brings for IoT development cannot be overemphasized. Nigeria as a developing nation, has continued to struggle in the development and deployment of Internet of Things (IoT) technology. The approach of this paper is basically to critically analyze the current state and the technological deficiencies of IoT development in Sub-Saharan Africa by using Nigeria as a case study, and to show how the emergence of NB-IoT can help to significantly improve the penetration and optimal development of this relatively modern technology in Nigeria and consequently in Africa, as it is in developed nations. Relevant features of NB-IoT are enumerated, we propose possible NB-IoT use cases that are suitable for the Nigerian eco-system and finally, we give a summarized developmental plan for the mobile network operators (MNOs) in Nigeria.

Keywords: Development strategy · Internet of Things · Low Power Wide Area · NB-IoT · Nigeria

1 Introduction

The nations in Sub Saharan Africa has continue to take the back seat when it comes to technological advancements and innovations. However, in recent years, sub-Saharan African countries such as Nigeria, South Africa, Kenya and Angola has witnessed a tremendous increase in technological advancements. Specifically, the mobile internet penetration and tele-density has continued to be on the rise in the last five years. Nigeria which is unarguably by far the most populous country in Africa with an estimated population of over one hundred and ninety million has an approximate fifty one percent (51%) internet penetration with an average increase of rate 2.5% every year [1]. One of the most recent technological innovations currently shaping the connected world of humans and objects is the Internet of Things (IoT). Nigeria and few other sub-Saharan African countries lead the pack in the deployment and development of IoT.

M. Jia et al. (Eds.): WiSATS 2019, LNICST 281, pp. 56–69, 2019.
https://doi.org/10.1007/978-3-030-19156-6_6

The acclaimed discovery of Internet of Things (IoT) in 1999 by Kevin Ashton might be one of the greatest technological innovations of mankind. It is a technology that is currently revolutionizing wireless communications by allowing connectivity between humans, machines and objects. Machines, appliances, buildings, healthcare, transport systems, energy systems, agricultural systems are some of the few aspects that will be significantly transformed when IoT has been fully and effectively developed. IoT seeks to create a world where everything and everyone becomes relatively smarter and are all connected via the internet.

The Internet of Things works by embedding highly intelligent sensors and chips on physical things around us, these sensors can transmit useful data of how these physical things not only work, but also how they can seamlessly work together. The useful data are securely transferred to a common IoT platform that allows connectivity between devices/physical things and apps, and at same time perform real time data analytics that are shared with industries to address their specific needs.

It is estimated that by the year 2025, the number of connected devices around the world would have risen to about 75 Billion (see Fig. 1), out of this enormous amount, it is expected that the entire sub-Saharan Africa would only be able to account for about 2% by projection and analytics [2]. Although, sub-Saharan African nations are mostly developing, but we believe that they should contribute meaningfully to this number especially because they are about 14% of the world's population.

There are instances where there is need for deployment of internet of things devices in areas where coverage is significantly low. NB-IoT has a wide coverage area because it was designed to have an extra coverage range of 20 dB. The coupling pathloss for GSM is estimated to be 144 dB, with an increment of 20 dB extra, the maximal coupling path loss for NB-IoT is given as 164 dB. In addition, the devices can be able to transmit and acquire data irrespective of environments that they are installed.

For scalability, easy development and deployment, and to cater for the growing number of connected devices in IoT, different wireless technologies are developed. These wireless technologies are broadly classified into two; short range radio connectivity such as Bluetooth, ZigBee, NFC/RFID and the long-range radio connectivity, which is generally referred to as Low Power Wide Area (LPWA).

Low Power Wide Area (LPWA) is a standardized 3GPP wireless and mobile technology that is used to describe a wide range of all IoT devices that are low powered, cost effective, wide/long range of network coverage, data transmission efficient and highly secured. With an increased requirement and diverse application scenarios for IoT, there is need to introduce a technology that will cater for the transmission of minute amount of information over a long distance. Furthermore, LPWA can also be grouped into authorized and unauthorized spectral usage depending on the licensed spectrum used. The unauthorized spectral usage is basically customized or proprietary based, examples are LoRa and SigFox, while the authorized spectral usage are standardized by 3GPP; 2G cellular network, LTE network and the NB-IoT are in this category [3]. The NB-IOT which this paper will critically analyze, is a LPWA technology that is key to the optimal development and deployment of IoT because it is known to support massive number of connections, it has very low power consumption rate and supports a wide coverage area.

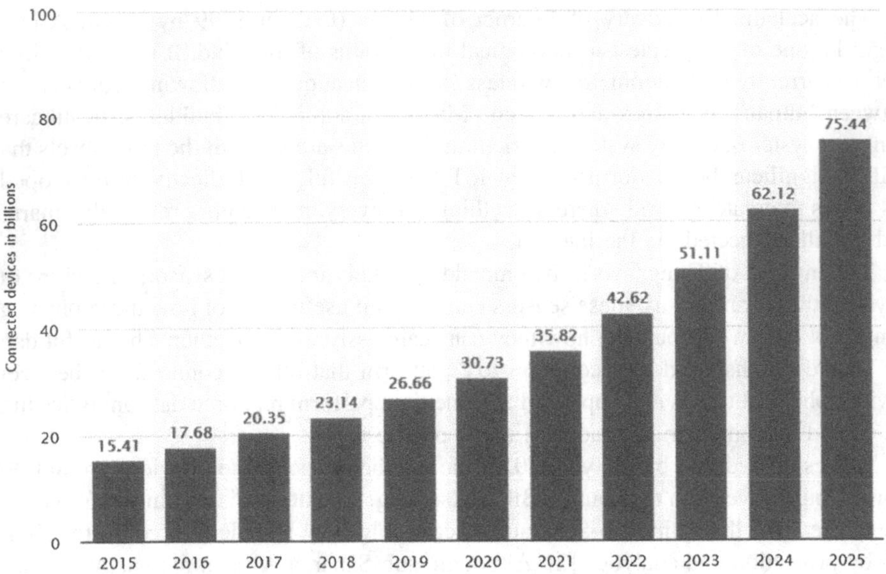

Fig. 1. Internet of Things projected installed base worldwide [2].

The traditional cellular network and short-range network technologies as shown in Fig. 2 are known to be unable to address the growing demands, deployment and penetration of IoT, this is particularly prevalent in the African market where cost and power consumption are key. In Nigeria, where power supply is at an all-time low and cost of living is very high, it is necessary for IoT operators to deploy technologies that is accessible by the bulk of the population and at the same time profitable. It is estimated that approximately one fourth of the over 30 billion projected IoT devices in 2020 are to be connected to the Internet using LPWA [4]. With a ready ecosystem and its population, we expect that Nigeria to significantly contribute to this number.

Therefore, in this paper, we first highlight the status of IoT in Nigeria and identify the main socio-economic and technical problems preventing penetration and development of IoT in the Nation. Furthermore, we explore the usefulness of NB-IOT as a key enabler for the development of IoT in Nigeria, we do this by objectively considering the technical specifications/features and use cases that makes NB-IoT suitable for IoT development in the Nigerian ecosystem. In addition, a developmental plan is summarized, and finally, we present our conclusion.

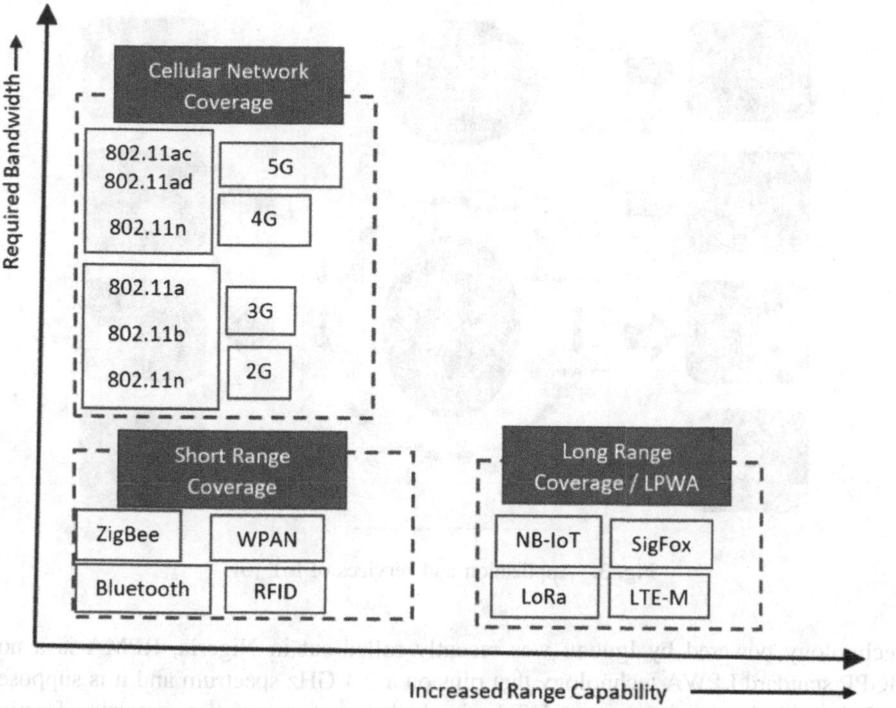

Fig. 2. Bandwidth required vs increase range of capability of short range, long range and cellular networks [5].

2 Internet of Things in Nigeria

Nigeria has continued to consistently remain relevant in the sub-Saharan Information and Communications technology sphere. With increased digitization of systems and technological innovations around the globe, Nigeria is always one of the first nation in sub-Saharan Africa to have a feel of these innovations and this is largely due to its population and tele density. With five mobile network operators and huge presence of mobile, telecom and IT servicing companies such as Huawei, Ericsson, Nokia, Microsoft, Cisco etc., there is a constant awareness to improve the IoT development and deployment in the ecosystem.

2.1 Current Developmental Trend

Radio Frequency Identification (RFID) and Unmanned Aerial vehicles also known as drones are two of the first Internet of Things technology to be developed in Nigeria. The former was used largely in the detection of controlled substances and in card readers while the latter was used by the Nigerian military for easy combat of terrorism [3]. More recently, with the availability of scalable technologies for deploying IoT, innovative solutions are beginning to surface. Random Phase Multiple Access (RPMA)

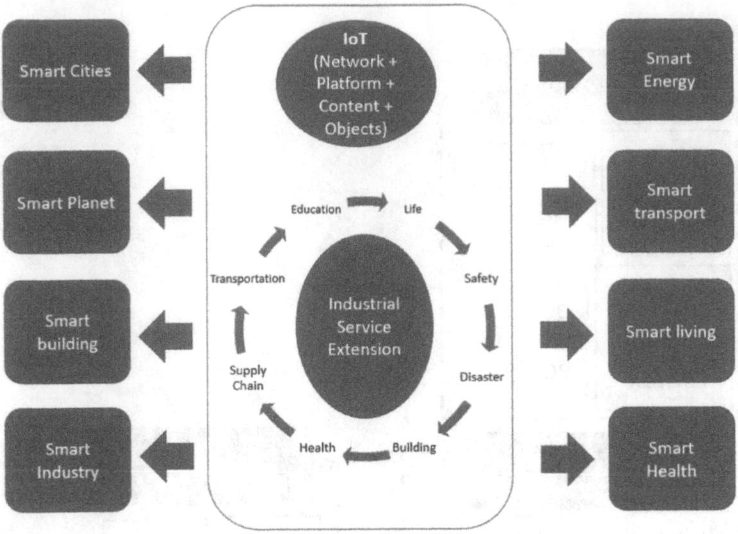

Fig. 3. Application and services of IoT [6]

technology powered by Iguenu was recently rolled-out in Nigeria, RPMA is a non 3GPP standard LPWA technology that runs on a 2.4 GHz spectrum and it is supposed to help with the development of IoT by its deployment in logistics, precision farming and smart grid [4]. Also, Smart metering is an IoT based service that is gradually gaining in-road in Nigeria, recently, Huawei technologies partnered with one of the electricity distribution companies to provide smart power meters for its customers. Huawei is also in the forefront of providing a cloud- based platform called the GLOCAL; the target of this system is to provide IoT as a service directly to verticals. MTN Nigeria is the biggest MNO in Nigeria and is collaborating with Huawei to improve the penetration of IoT by providing NB-IoT based services such as user-based insurance (UBI), smart metering and smart refrigerator [5]. SMS for Life 2.0 is an IoT based technology for smart health, the platform has already been deployed by Vodacom in a Northern state in Nigeria.

At the stake holders meeting of International Telecommunications Union on IoT for Sub-Saharan African countries, it was generally agreed that key areas shown in Fig. 3 are the areas that need urgent development.

Although, Nigeria has witnessed somewhat increased development in the last one year, but it still faces some challenges to the development and deployment of IoT.

Please note that the first paragraph of a section or subsection is not indented. The first paragraphs that follows a table, figure, equation etc. does not have an indent, either.

2.2 Technical Challenges

Broadband connectivity is a major bottleneck for the deployment of IoT. Presently in Nigeria, broadband penetration is estimated to be less than 50%, deploying an IoT system that involves massive connectivity between machines, objects and humans becomes a herculean task. *Cost* of modules and related sensors for IoT is also another issue. A solution such as precision farming needs farmers to be able to buy and pay for services, but most of these farmers are peasants and paying for the IoT service becomes difficult. Total cost of ownership is a problem network operator face in the deployment of IoT. *Power* is a threat to the development of IoT in Nigeria, IoT devices need to constantly have power to be able to send and receive data, electricity supply in Nigeria is currently rated one of the worst in the world. *Scalability of MNOs equipment* is also impeding the development of IoT, the current architecture of is not suitable for the growth pattern of IoT.

Interoperability, security, privacy and regulatory standards are some other challenges facing the development of Internet of Things.

In the next part of our paper, we present a NB-IoT approach of how IoT can be effectively developed and deployed.

3 The Narrow-Band Internet of Things Approach

NB-IoT is a recently standardized protocol by the 3GPP that is used for cellular communication. It is a low bandwidth protocol that is basically intended to optimize the needs of Internet of things (IoT) applications, and consequently help in the easy deployment and development of IoT. Smart metering, precision agriculture, smart parking, smart health, industrial controls are few of the numerous IoT applications that has been found suitable for the African or Nigerian ecosystem. The flexibility of using existing telecom infrastructure like GSM and LTE for NB-IoT deployment, makes it particularly useful in Nigeria, considering that GSM coverage in Nigeria is over 75%.

A review of historical development and standardization process of NB-IoT by 3GPP indicates that it is created to optimize all Machine Type Communication (MTC) services. MTCs are generally classified into; firstly, services such as video surveillance and fleet tracking that require an enormous amount of data for uplink while they are unmovable and a minute amount of data during handovers, and secondly, services which require meter reading for water and power usage. Devices used to achieve the latter services are considered to always remain stationary and handover is always required. Furthermore, the amount of data transferred is usually small and the devices have the tendency of increasing geometrically. The first specification released by 3GPP was mainly focused on these devices. In June 2016, 3GPP introduced R13 which clearly standardized the NB-IoT technology and set five (5) objectives for MTC, these includes; flexibility to support various latency features, support massive number of devices and connections, enhance indoor coverage, optimized energy efficiency and finally, lower cost and reduced terminal complexity [7].

3.1 NB-IoT Network Architecture

With eNodeB upgrade and deploying of NB-IoT core integrated into the existing LTE system architecture, operators can deploy the NB-IoT system. However, it should be noted that interoperability and integration with other network elements such as HSS, PCRF, Customer IT etc., will be dependent on lifecycle of the equipment (Fig. 4).

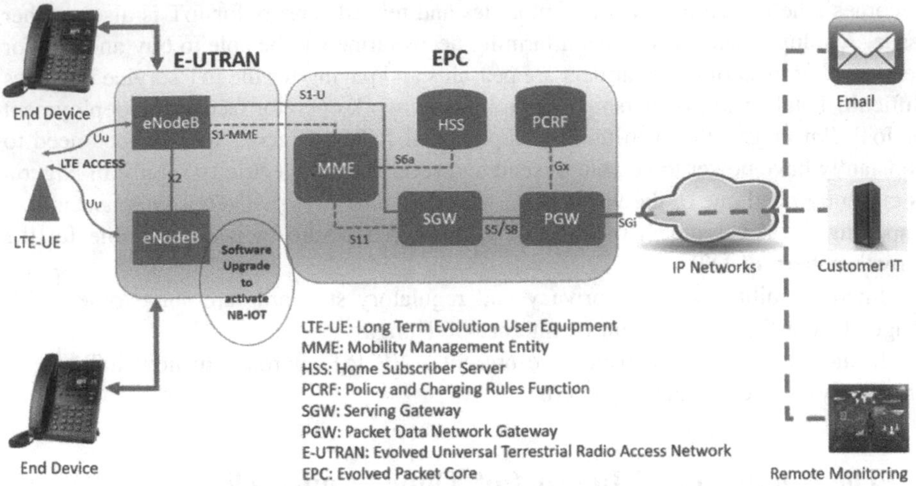

Fig. 4. The network architecture of NB-IoT (I)

In the access network of the NB-IoT architecture, data packets and messages sent from the NB-IoT User equipment are transferred to eNodeB via the air interface, and subsequently transferred to SGW and MME via the S1 interface. At the core network, the CIoT EPS (Cellular Internet of Things Evolved Packet Switch) carries out optimization processes for both the user plane and the control plane. The optimization of the control plane CIoT occurs when non-IP data packets are transferred to the SCEF or PGW via the SGW before been finally forwarded to the cellular internet of things (CIoT) services. This is particularly useful for transmission of minute data packets that are inconsistent. The SCEF is designed to be able to handle only delivery of non-IP data packets. On the other hand, user plane optimization occurs when IP data or non-IP data transferred over radio bearers are sent to the cellular internet of things (CIoT) services via the PGW and SGW. This optimization is more useful for exchange of data between the CIoT platform server and the customer end device (Fig. 5).

3.2 Features of NB-IoT

The unique physical or technical features of NB-IoT technology has made it a superb and future oriented technology that helps for the deployment of IoT services around the globe. In Nigeria, some of these features are key for the development and actualization of Internet of things services. They are highlighted here.

Flexibility in Deployment. The available options required for deploying the NB-IoT technology makes it a suitable way for the development of internet of things in Nigeria. Telecom operators are currently facing a huge challenge deploying modern technologies such as IoT because of the currency devaluation in Nigeria. However, this challenge can be surmounted with deployment flexibility available using NB-IoT. Operators already have existing infrastructure that can be used, they can either use the

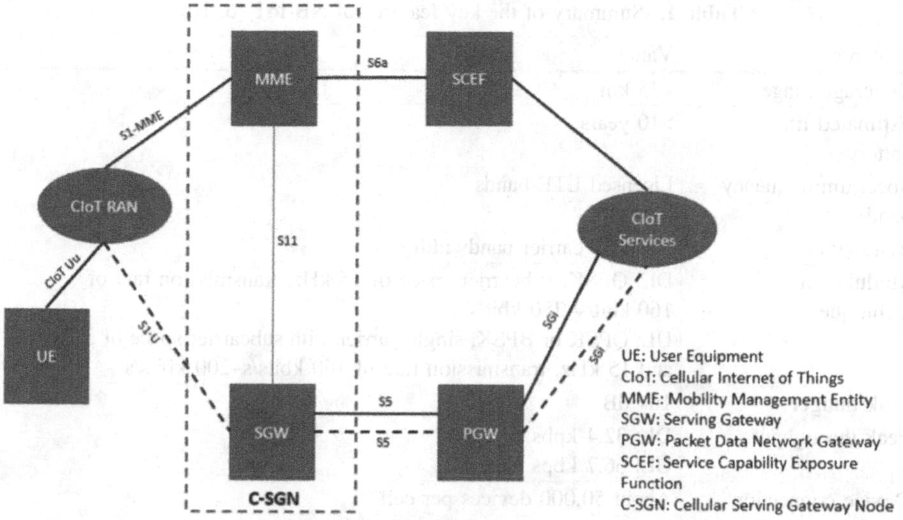

Fig. 5. The network architecture of NB-IoT (II) [8].

well-established GSM architecture or the recently deployed LTE network. Deployment options shown in the latter part of this paper.

Excellent Power Consumption of Devices. The power consumption design of NB-IoT modules makes it a commercially viable technology, especially in places where provision of stable power supply is a challenge. These devices have a battery lifetime of 10 years. Nigeria is generally known for the erratic power supply and deploying IoT services that rely solely on power from the national grid becomes a huge burden for telecom operators. NB-IoT devices are built to last and operate for years, they can do this because the modules for data communication save energy by activating the sleep mode when in idle state [9] (Table 1).

Cost of Device and High Capacity of Device Connection. The Internet of things technology is a cost-effective technology that requires high capital for it to be fully deployed, investment by operators will have a negative effect on the consumers and return on investment is not guaranteed. However, the cost of deploying NB-IoT service is minimal and average the cost of a device is about $5. The technology behind the design of NB-IoT modules makes it cheap. Furthermore, NB-IoT technology has the capability to massively support up to 50K simultaneous device connections in a single cell.

Significant Network Coverage. There are instances where there is need for deployment of internet of things devices in areas where coverage is significantly low. NB-IoT has a wide coverage area because it was designed to have an extra coverage range of 20 dB. The coupling pathloss for GSM is estimated to be 144 dB, with an increment of 20 dB extra, the maximal coupling path loss for NB-IoT is given as 164 dB. In addition, the devices can be able to transmit and acquire data irrespective of environments that they are installed.

Table 1. Summary of the key features of NB-IoT [6, 10]

Features	Value
Coverage range	<35 km
Estimated life of battery	>10 years
Spectrum/frequency bands	Licensed LTE bands
Bandwidth	200 kHz carrier bandwidth
Modulation technique	DL: QPSK, subcarrier space of 15 kHz, transmission rate of 160 kbit/s–250 kbit/s UL: QPSK or BPSK, single carrier with subcarrier space of 3.75 kHz and 15 kHz, transmission rate of 160 kbits/s–200 kbits/s
Link budget	164 dB
Peak throughput	DL: 32.4 kpbs UL: 66.7 kbps
Device connection capability	About 50,000 devices per cell

3.3 Deployment Strategy

As explained in the introductory part of our paper, Nigeria has over 75% nationwide coverage of GSM. Also, three out of the five telecom operators have deployed the LTE infrastructure. Therefore, leveraging on the existing infrastructure and with little or no CAPEX, operators can deploy NB-IoT using any of the following 3GPP standardized methods;

Using GSM Band. This is a deployment done as a standalone or independently using the available GSM band with the help of GSM channel re-farming technique. Spectrum re-farming is a worldwide recognized technology used to reassign available frequency bands for other purposes to save cost in deployment of new services. NB-IoT can make use of GSM frequency with bandwidth of 200 kHz between guard bands of 10 kHz for a stand-alone operation [11] (Fig. 6).

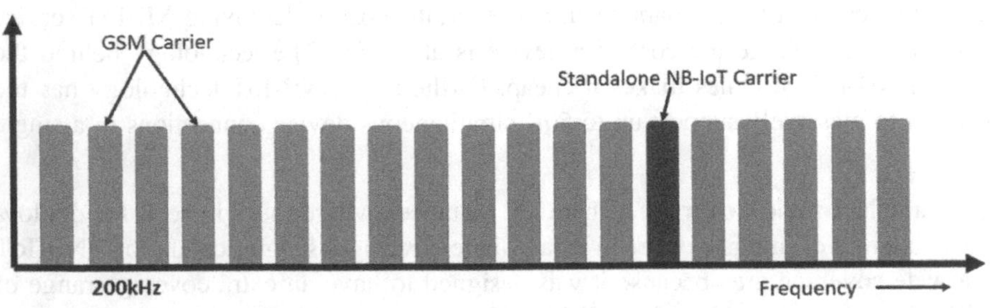

Fig. 6. The stand alone operational mode

Using LTE Band. As the name same implies; it simply involves making use of the existing LTE infrastructure for deployment. The deployment method can either be guard-band mode or in-band mode. Guard-band operational mode is based on unused resource block within a LTE carrier's guard band, while the In-band operational mode is based on using the resource blocks within a normal LTE carrier.

There are 12 subcarriers of 15 kHz interval in the downlink using Orthogonal Frequency Division Multiple Access (OFDMA) with a transmission rate of 160 kbit/s–250 kbit/s and 3.75 kHz & 15 kHz subscriber interval in the uplink using Single Carrier Frequency Division Multiple Access (SC-FDMA) (Figs. 7 and 8).

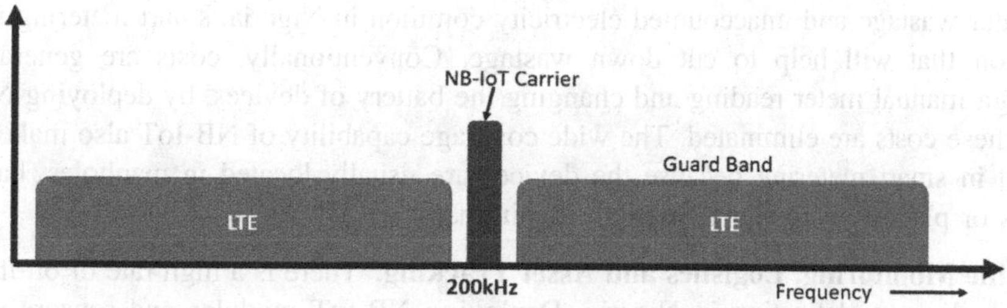

Fig. 7. The guard band operational mode

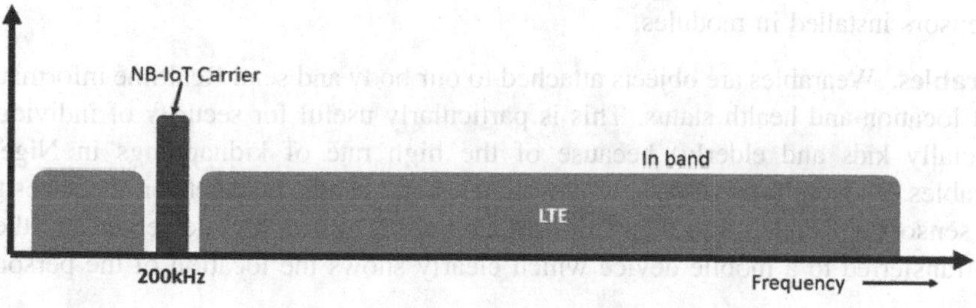

Fig. 8. The In band operational mode

3.4 Proposed NB-IoT Use Cases for Nigeria

There are several use cases that have been deployed by different operators around the world, but the cases enumerated below have been carefully selected considering the current available infrastructure in Nigeria, and how commercially viable these cases are. Also, for the deployment and easy development of internet of things, these NB-IoT use cases are most suitable.

Smart Agriculture. The alternative to the current over-dependence on oil and gas is Agriculture, and the government of Nigeria recently started investing heavily in this sector. The incorporation of NB-IoT in agriculture will be to increase productivity and save cost for farmers. Possible areas are Animal or livestock monitoring, precision farming, smart greenhouse, aquaponics, smart irrigation etc. Animal monitoring is achieved by installing NB-IoT sensors on the animals, this can be in the form of neck tags and ear tags, these sensors are able to store and transmit data with regards to the health and location of the animals. This will help to save labor cost and easy identification of sick animal. Furthermore, NB-IoT modules can help in the control of water usage in smart irrigation, sensing of soil moisture and nutrients in precision farming and allow farmers have minimal supervision and cultivation of crops in smart greenhouse [12]. Overall, deploying NB-IoT in Agriculture helps to eliminate operational inefficiency.

Smart Metering. The smart metering system works by using highly smart meters which have been pre-installed with NB-IoT modules to remotely monitor and transfer data on usage of water, electricity and gas over a cellular network. With a high amount of water wastage and unaccounted electricity common in Nigeria, smart metering is a solution that will help to cut down wastage. Conventionally, costs are generated through manual meter reading and changing the battery of devices, by deploying NB-IoT, these costs are eliminated. The wide coverage capability of NB-IoT also makes it useful in smart metering because the devices are usually located in manholes, basements or places where signal strength is minimal.

Pipeline Monitoring, Logistics and Asset Tracking. There is a high rate of oil theft and pipeline vandalization in Nigeria. Deploying NB-IoT modules and sensors will help to alert relevant authorities when there is a leakage, or a pipeline has been vandalized. Sensors can send data to a monitoring center, and swift action can be taken. Assets can also be monitored by asset owners through broadcasting of asset location by the sensors installed in modules.

Wearables. Wearables are objects attached to our body and send Realtime information about location and health status. This is particularly useful for security of individuals (especially kids and elderly) because of the high rate of kidnappings in Nigeria. Wearables can be in form of tags, wristwatches, hand bands, bracelets or necklaces that have sensors embedded into them. Information are sent to a remote server and thereafter transferred to a mobile device which clearly shows the location of the person.

Smart Parking. The smart parking services are useful in urban areas where traffic congestion caused by lack of parking space is an issue. This service works by providing parking information to drivers via a geomagnetic NB-IoT sensor installed under the car [8]. Presentation of information is usually through a mobile device.

4 Proposed Developmental Plan

In the earlier part of our paper, we have briefly outlined the standardized deployment options that are available to mobile network operators (MNOs). In this part of our paper, we propose a summarized developmental plan by looking at the available frequency bands standardized by 3GPP, deployment bands possible for MNOs in Nigeria and the possible impact on their network.

In Release 13, 3GPP already proposed a set of frequency bands that can be used by NB-IoT. They include; 1, 2, 3, 5, 8, 12, 13, 17, 18, 19, 20, 26, 28, 66 and Release 14 which will include; 11, 25, 31 and 70.

Nigerian MNOs currently have frequency spectrum of Band 3 and Band 8 for Global System for Mobile Communication (GSM), however, some also have Band 1 deployed for 3G. In Sub-Saharan Africa, which Nigeria belongs to, the frequency bands supported are B3 (900) and B8 (1800) [13].

From Table 2, NB-IoT offers a wide range of supportive bands for MNOs depending on the available spectrum.

Table 2. E-UTRA operating bands as specified by 3GPP [13].

Operating Band	Uplink Operating Band BS Receive UE Transmit $F_{UL_{Low}} - F_{UL_{High}}$	Downlink Operating Band BS Transmit UE Receive $F_{DL_{Low}} - F_{DL_{High}}$	Duplex Mode
1	1920 MHz – 1980 MHz	2110 MHz – 2170 MHz	*FDD*
2	1850 MHz – 1910 MHz	1930 MHz – 1990 MHz	*FDD*
3	**1710 MHz – 1785 MHz**	**1805 MHz – 1880 MHz**	***FDD***
5	824 MHz – 849 MHz	869 MHz – 894 MHz	*FDD*
8	**880 MHz – 915 MHz**	**925 MHz – 960 MHz**	***FDD***
12	699 MHz – 716 MHz	729 MHz – 746 MHz	*FDD*
13	777 MHz – 787 MHz	746 MHz – 756 MHz	*FDD*
17	704 MHz – 716 MHz	734 MHz – 746 MHz	*FDD*
18	815 MHz – 830 MHz	860 MHz – 875 MHz	*FDD*
19	830 MHz – 845 MHz	875 MHz – 890 MHz	*FDD*
20	832 MHz – 862 MHz	791 MHz – 821 MHz	*FDD*
26	814 MHz – 849 MHz	859 MHz – 894 MHz	*FDD*
28	703 MHz – 748 MHz	758 MHz – 803 MHz	*FDD*
66	1710 MHz – 1780 MHz	2110 MHz – 2200 MHz	*FDD*

Although, there would be need for MNOs to take few steps before they can deploy NB-IoT, but these steps are worth taking for the development of IoT. A summarized developmental strategy is shown in Table 3 below.

Table 3. Proposed initial use cases for MNOs in Nigeria [14].

Mobile network operator	Available frequency spectrum	Mobile market share (%)	Proposed deployment mode	Proposed use cases to start deployment	Possible impact on network
MTN	**GSM900** Tx: 950 MHz–955 MHz Rx: 905 MHz–910 MHz **GSM1800** Tx: 1835 MHz–1850 MHz Rx: 1740 MHz–1755 MHz	40	Stand-alone deployment by GSM Re-farming	Smart metering, Smart Agriculture, Wearables, Logistics	Upgrade of Baseband unit, New RF Modules, Upgrade antenna systems, Frequency planning
GLO	**GSM900** Tx: 945 MHz–950 MHz Rx: 900 MHz–905 MHz **GSM1800** Tx: 1820 MHz–1835 MHz Rx: 1725 MHz–1740 MHz	25	Stand-alone deployment by GSM Re-farming	Smart parking, Smart agriculture, wearables	Upgrade of Baseband unit, New RF Modules, Upgrade antenna systems, Frequency planning
AIRTEL	**GSM900** Tx: 955 MHz–960 MHz Rx: 910 MHz–915 MHz **GSM1800** Tx: 1850 MHz–1865 MHz Rx: 1755 MHz–1770 MHz	23	Stand-alone deployment by GSM Re-farming	Smart parking	Upgrade of Baseband unit, New RF Modules, Upgrade antenna systems, Frequency planning
9MOBILE	**GSM900** Tx: 935 MHz–940 MHz Rx: 890 MHz–895 MHz **GSM1800** Tx: 1865 MHz–1880 MHz Rx: 1770 MHz–1785 MHz	13	Stand-alone deployment by GSM Re-farming	Smart parking, Smart metering	Upgrade of Baseband unit, New RF Modules, Upgrade antenna systems, Frequency planning
NTEL	**LTE** Tx: 940 MHz–945 MHz Rx: 895 MHz–900 MHz **LTE** Tx: 1805 MHz–1820 MHz Rx: 1710 MHz–1725 MHz	Relatively new comer, recently lunch LTE-A and VoLTE	In-band, Guard-band deployments	Smart parking	Upgrade eNodeB, Reuse RF modules and Antenna system, No

5 Conclusion

The Narrow-band Internet of Things technology remains the most effective and efficient way to develop internet of things in Nigeria. In this paper, we have carefully reviewed the current state of Internet of things technology in Nigeria, and the factors that prevents the development of the technology. We have identified NB-IoT as the most cost-effective technology that can help to improve the penetration of IoT. Specifically, we looked at the unique features of NB-IoT that makes it suitable for the eco-system, in addition, we explained the different deployment modes possible. Finally, we gave a summary of use cases that can be deployed by each operator based on their infrastructure.

Acknowledgement. This work was supported by the Nation Science Foundation of China (Under Grant: 61671173).

References

1. Nigerian Bureau of Statistics: Nigerian telecommunication sector report. http://www.nigeriastat.gov.ng/elibrary. Accessed 01 Sept 2018
2. The statistics portal: Internet of Things. https://www.statista.com/statistics/471264/iot-number-of-connected-devices-worldwide/. Accessed 05 Sept 2018
3. Ndubuaku, M., Okereafor, D.: State of Internet of Things deployment in Africa and its future: the Nigerian scenario. Afr. J. Inf. Commun. (AJIC) 154–163 (2015)
4. SmartCitiesWorld IoT Network Rolls out in Nigeria. https://www.smartcitiesworld.net/IoT. Accessed 10 Sept 2018
5. Guardian Technology: Huawei NB-IoT in Nigeria. http://www.guardian.ng/technology. Accessed 25 July 2018
6. Kunle, O.J., Olubunmi, O.A., Sani, S.: Internet of Things prospect in Nigeria: challenges and solutions. In: 3rd International Conference on Electro-Technology for National Development NIGERCONFERENCE 2017, pp. 736–745. IEEE, Owerri (2017)
7. Chen, M., Miao, Y., Hao, Y., Hwang, K.: Narrow band Internet of Things. IEEE Access **5**, 20557–20577 (2017). IEEE Access on Key Technologies for Smart Factory of Industry
8. Rhode & Schwarz: Narrow Band Internet of Things white paper. https://cdn.rohde-schwarz.com/pws/dl_downloads/dl_application/application_notes/1ma266/1MA266_0e_NB_IoT.pdf. Accessed 25 Sept 2018
9. Rakić, A., Popović, I., Petruševski, I., Begenišić, Đ., Spajić, V., Rakić, M.: Key aspects of narrow band Internet of Things communication technology driving future IoT applications. In: 25th Telecommunication Forum, TELFOR, Belgrade, pp. 1–4 (2017)
10. Sinha, R.S., Wei, Y., Hwang, S.-H.: A survey on LPWA technology: LoRa and NB-IoT. ICT Express **3**, 14–21 (2017)
11. T Mobile White Paper: Narrowband IOT; Groundbreaking in the Internet of Things. https://warpaccelerator.com/nb-iot/whitepaper.pdf. Accessed 22 July 2018
12. Huawei Technologies: Narrowband IOT; Wide Range of Opportunities. MWC (2016). http://www-file.huawei.com/-/media/CORPORATE/minisite/mwc2016/pdf/NarrowBand-IoT-Wide-Range-of-Opportunities-en.pdf?la=en. Accessed 24 May 2018
13. GSMA Mobile IoT, NB-IoT Deployment Guide to Basic Feature set Requirements (2016). https://www.gsma.com/iot/wp-content/uploads/2017/08/CLP.28-v1.0.pdf. Accessed 24 July 2018
14. Nigeria Communications Commission: Frequency assignment tables (2018). https://www.ncc.gv.ng/technonoly/spectrum. Accessed 15 Mar 2018

Automatic Identification of Underground Pipeline Based on Ground Penetrating Radar

Xu Bai, Weile An, Bin Wang, Jianyu Jiang, Yanjia Zhang, and Jiayan Zhang(✉)

Communication Research Center, Harbin Institute of Technology, Harbin 150000, China
{x_bai,JYZhang}@hit.edu.cn

Abstract. The underground pipelines of cities are complex and diverse, and they are responsible for important functions such as energy transportation and information transmission. In urban life and construction, it is necessary to grasp the location and depth of underground pipelines. Ground Penetrating Radar (GPR) is a real-time and efficient non-destructive detection technology. It has the advantages of fast detection speed, high resolution, easy operation and wide detection range. Therefore, it is the preferred method for urban underground pipeline detection. Based on the electromagnetic wave reflection mechanism of GPR detection underground pipeline, this paper proposes a new method of non-excavation and non-destructive on-site detection to identify underground pipe diameter, determine the position and radius of underground circular pipeline, and realize the automatic identification to underground pipeline.

Keywords: Underground pipelines · GPR · Automatic identification

1 Introduction

There are many types of underground pipelines in the city, including wire and cable for electrical signal transmission, pipes of various materials for water and oil gas transmission, and pipes for complex underground drainage systems. Underground pipelines play a major role in information transmission and energy transmission, providing convenience and guarantee for urban life [1, 2]. However, due to the imperfect and unsatisfactory information of underground space in the early stage of urban construction, underground pipelines often face problems such as aging, diversion and error mining during the continuous construction of the city. These problems will not only affect normal city life, but also cause accidents such as fires, water cuts, and power outages. In order to avoid such a situation, comprehensive investigation, recording and system management of underground pipelines are required [3].

Ground Penetrating Radar (GPR) is a highly efficient shallow stratigraphic geophysical detection technology with the advantages of fast detection speed, high resolution, flexible operation, non-destructive detection, and low cost [4, 5]. The preferred tool for pipeline detection. In the process of actually detecting underground pipelines, the radar image generated by ground penetrating radar mostly relies on manual discrimination, which has high dependence on the operator's experience. It can only judge

M. Jia et al. (Eds.): WiSATS 2019, LNICST 281, pp. 70–78, 2019.
https://doi.org/10.1007/978-3-030-19156-6_7

the position and depth of the pipeline, and lacks the identification of the pipe diameter information.

Based on GPR to detect the electromagnetic wave reflection mechanism of underground pipelines and the special circular shape of underground pipelines, after the operations of noise reduction and edge extraction on the acquired images, this paper uses the idea of "three-point rounding" to calculate the position of pipelines and the diameter of pipelines.

2 Underground Pipeline Echo Signal Characteristics

In the process of the ground penetrating radar advancing along the ground in the direction perpendicular to the pipeline, the transmitting antenna emits high-frequency pulsed electromagnetic waves to the underground, and when the local lower pipeline is within the detection depth range of the antenna wave, the echo signal of the target can be received. Figure 1 shows the schematic diagram of transmitting and receiving the co-located antenna ground penetrating radar to the underground pipeline. In the figure, the horizontal axis is the horizontal position of the antenna at the time of detection, and the vertical axis corresponds to the depth of the ground.

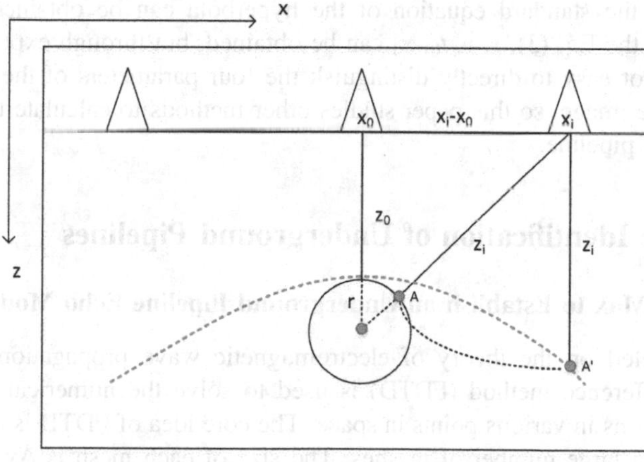

Fig. 1. Circular pipeline echo characteristics

If the echo received by the radar during the advancement of the ground penetrating radar along the surface of the earth is regarded as the signal returned from the point directly below the antenna, the virtual point targets are arranged according to the position to be illuminated, and the dotted line in Fig. 1 is obtained. That is to say, when the ground penetrating radar appears at the x_i position, the reflected wave at the point A of the pipe will appear at the point A' on the captured image. As can be seen from Fig. 1, the antenna can form a triangle at two points x_i and x_0 and three points in the center of the pipeline, and the three sides follow the Pythagorean theorem, i.e.

$$(x_i - x_0)^2 + (z_0 + r)^2 = (z_i + r)^2 \tag{1}$$

Where r is the radius of the pipeline, z_0 is the buried depth at the top of the pipeline, z_i is the distance between the antenna and the outer wall of the pipeline when the antenna is in the x_i position, and is also the distance from the echo signal received by point x_i. In the actual acquired image, the vertical axis of the image reflects not the distance z, but the two-way travel time t (reception delay) of the echo, and the delay and distance satisfy the relationship $z_i = vt_i/2$. Substituting the above equation

$$(x_i - x_0)^2 + \left(\frac{vt_0}{2} + r\right)^2 = \left(\frac{vt_i}{2} + r\right)^2 \tag{2}$$

Further conversion equation

$$\frac{(t_i + 2r/v)^2}{(t_0 + 2r/v)^2} - \frac{(x_i - x_0)^2}{(vt_0/2 + R)^2} = 1 \tag{3}$$

Each raw data pair (x_i, t_i) of the underground pipeline satisfies this equation. From this equation, it can be seen that the echo edge of the pipeline is a hyperbolic equation with (x_0, t_0) as a vertex. In order to solve the pipe radius r and the pipe depth position z_0, theoretically, the standard equation of the hyperbola can be obtained first, and corresponding to the Eq. (3), r, v, t_0, x_0 can be obtained, but through experiment It is found that it is not easy to directly distinguish the four parameters of the hyperbolic equation from the image, so this paper studies other methods to calculate the position and radius of the pipeline.

3 Automatic Identification of Underground Pipelines

3.1 Using gprMax to Establish an Underground Pipeline Echo Model

gprMax is modeled on the theory of electromagnetic wave propagation. The time domain finite difference method (FDTD) is used to solve the numerical solution of Maxwell's equations in various points in space. The core idea of FDTD is to discretize a 3D space into a large number of meshes. The size of each mesh is $\Delta x \times \Delta y \times \Delta z$, calculate the electric field strength and magnetic field strength in each mesh. Figure 2 shows an 8-space discrete space model.

The Maxwell relationship between the electric and magnetic fields in different directions within the grid is as follows

$$\frac{\partial E_x}{\partial t} = \frac{1}{\varepsilon}\left(\frac{\partial H_z}{\partial y} - \frac{\partial H_y}{\partial z} - J_{S_x} - \sigma E_x\right) \tag{4}$$

$$\frac{\partial E_y}{\partial t} = \frac{1}{\varepsilon}\left(\frac{\partial H_x}{\partial z} - \frac{\partial H_z}{\partial x} - J_{S_y} - \sigma E_y\right) \tag{5}$$

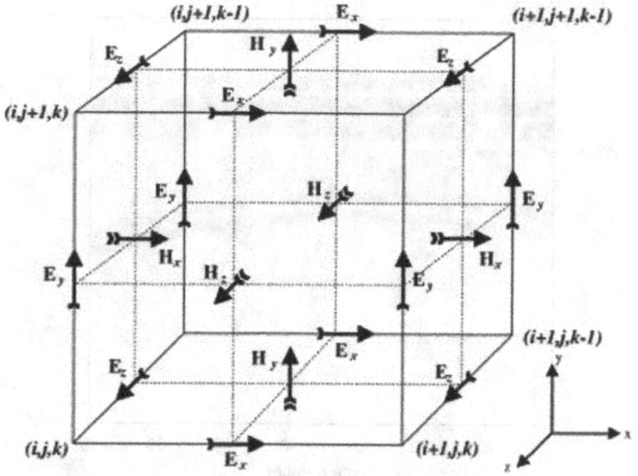

Fig. 2. FDTD discrete space

$$\frac{\partial E_z}{\partial t} = \frac{1}{\varepsilon}\left(\frac{\partial H_y}{\partial x} - \frac{\partial H_x}{\partial y} - J_{S_z} - \sigma E_z\right) \tag{6}$$

$$\frac{\partial H_x}{\partial t} = \frac{1}{\mu}\left(\frac{\partial E_y}{\partial z} - \frac{\partial E_z}{\partial y} - M_{S_x} - \sigma^* H_x\right) \tag{7}$$

$$\frac{\partial H_y}{\partial t} = \frac{1}{\mu}\left(\frac{\partial E_z}{\partial x} - \frac{\partial E_x}{\partial z} - M_{S_y} - \sigma^* H_y\right) \tag{8}$$

$$\frac{\partial H_z}{\partial t} = \frac{1}{\mu}\left(\frac{\partial E_x}{\partial y} - \frac{\partial E_y}{\partial x} - M_{S_z} - \sigma^* H_z\right) \tag{9}$$

These equations are discrete in both time and space and can be solved in an iterative manner in the time domain. At each iteration, the electromagnetic field goes one step further in the grid, which simulates the field strength at each point in space.

The basic conditions to be set by gprMax modeling include: the size of the detection area, spatial resolution, time window, underground environment, excitation and boundary conditions.

Figures 3 and 4 are a B-scan diagram of the underground pipeline when the center frequencies of the two excitation sources are 1.5 GHz and 900 MHz, respectively. The horizontal axis of the B-scan shows the number of tracks scanned, and the horizontal axis represents the echo time. The horizontal stripes appearing when the echo time is small in the figure are ground echoes. After the echo time increases, the curve that appears is the echo of the underground pipeline.

As can be seen from the figure, the higher the center frequency, the higher the spatial resolution, which is consistent with the theory, indicating that gprMax is more accurate in calculating the reflected echo.

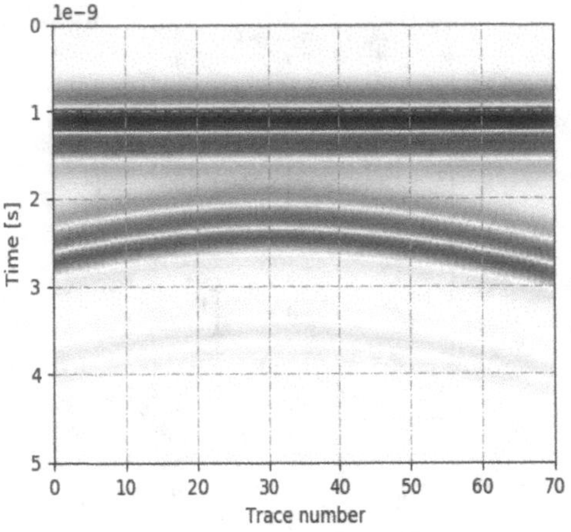

Fig. 3. B-scan map at center frequency of 1.5 GHz

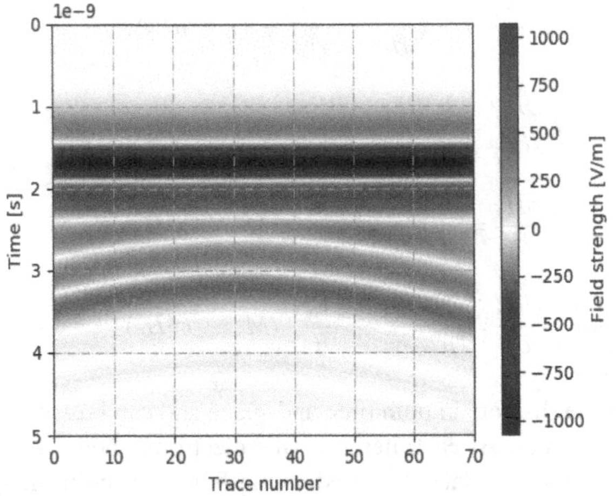

Fig. 4. B-scan map with center frequency of 900 MHz

3.2 Pipeline Identification Method

Both the tube depth and the tube diameter are estimated based on the acquired image, and the echo of the tube in the image has a hyperbolic characteristic. It is relatively easy to find the hyperbolic vertices to estimate the depth of the pipeline, even if it is judged by hand, there will not be too much error. At present, the application of ground penetrating radar in pipeline identification is mainly used to estimate the location of underground pipelines. It is not possible to directly determine the diameter of the pipe from the image, because the echo hyperbola is not a linear correspondence with the pipe cross-section circle.

In this paper, the method of "three-point rounding" is used in the research of pipe-pipe deep automatic identification. The traditional three-point circle method is to determine the center position and radius of the circle by three points on the circle. Here we determine the center and radius by reflecting three points on the hyperbola of the echo edge. It has been analyzed before. From Eq. (2), we can see the relationship between the position and delay of the measuring point and the coordinates and radius r of the vertex. In order to calculate the vertex coordinates and the radius r, three measuring points are selected and recorded. The position and time delay of these three measuring points can list three equations consistent with Eq. (1). With these three equations, the three variables of vertex coordinates and radius can be determined. Point to circle method, the equation is

$$\begin{aligned}(x_1-m)^2+(n+r)^2&=\left(\frac{vt_1}{2}+r\right)^2\\(x_2-m)^2+(n+r)^2&=\left(\frac{vt_2}{2}+r\right)^2\\(x_3-m)^2+(n+r)^2&=\left(\frac{vt_3}{2}+r\right)^2\end{aligned}\tag{10}$$

Where (x_1, t_1), (x_2, t_2), and (x_3, t_3) are the coordinates of the three points on the edge, respectively, and m and n are the horizontal and vertical coordinates of the vertices of the pipeline, respectively. In a picture to be processed, the number of tracks x' is often expressed in abscissa and the number of samples y' is plotted on the vertical axis. Their relationship with the horizontal distance x and the delay t is

$$x = ax' \tag{11}$$

$$t = \Delta t \bullet y' = \frac{T}{N}y' \tag{12}$$

Where a represents the track pitch, T represents the time window, and N represents the number of sample points. These values can be set in one sample, so they are known quantities. Substituting Eqs. (11) and (12) into Eq. (10), x' and y' are represented by x, y, which can be obtained.

$$\begin{aligned}(a(x_1-m))^2+(bn+r)^2&=(by_1+r)^2\\(a(x_2-m))^2+(bn+r)^2&=(by_2+r)^2\\(a(x_3-m))^2+(bn+r)^2&=(by_3+r)^2\end{aligned}\tag{13}$$

Here $b = \frac{T}{N} \bullet \frac{v}{2}$ is a constant. The Canny operator obtains three different positions on the extracted edge. It is worth noting that before substituting the three coordinate points into the above equations, the ordinate should be subtracted from the position of the road surface. Because the road surface position in the image is not on the x-axis, and the equation is based on setting the road surface position to the x-axis.

4 Simulation Result

In the verification of the effect of the "three-point rounding" method to identify the position and radius of the pipeline, the influence of the selected three edge points on the recognition effect is studied. The error is analyzed by comparing with the real value.

In the model established by gprMax, the antenna center frequency is 900 MHz, the transmission and reception pitch is 0.01 m; the relative dielectric constant of the underground medium is 10, and the conductivity is 0.01; the interval between each channel is 0.01 m, the number of collection points per channel is 2545, and the time window is 30 ns; The pipe radius is 0.4 m and the pipe depth is 0.6 m. From the above-determined conditions, a = 5.5915e−04 and b = 0.01 in the Eq. (13) can be calculated.

Select points (30, 1375), (70, 1121), (130, 1214) on the extracted edges to test, determine the depth and radius of the pipeline, and draw the circular section of the pipeline into the edge extraction map, such as Fig. 5 shows.

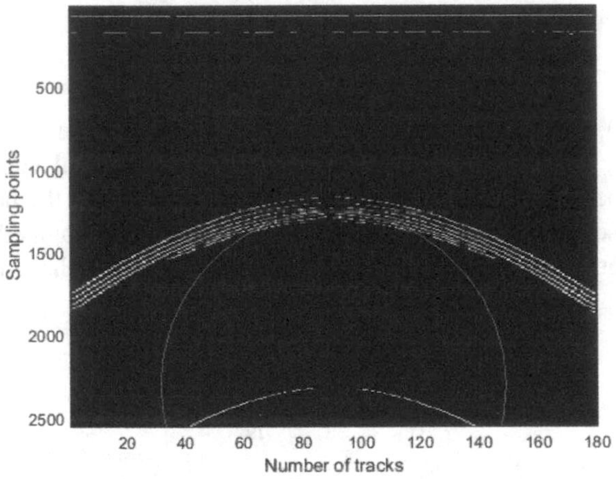

Fig. 5. Pipeline section

The cross-sectional view shows that the pipeline vertices are tangent to the hyperbolic vertices, which is consistent with the theory. This model was tested several times, and the three edge points selected for each test were positioned differently. Table 1 shows the tube depth and diameter and their errors measured at different points.

The rule for selecting coordinates in the table is to select a point close to the vertex of the hyperbola, and the other two points are symmetric about the vertex and closer to the hyperbolic vertex.

In order to facilitate the observation of the relationship between radius error, depth error and selected points, the error line graph is used to analyze the error trend, as shown in Fig. 6.

Table 1. Pipe diameter and pipe depth error when selecting different edge points

Edge point 1	Edge point 2	Edge point 3	Radius/m	Depth/m	Radius error	Depth error
(15, 1640)	(82, 1238)	(165, 1640)	0.4945	0.6273	0.2362	0.0455
(20, 1589)	(82, 1238)	(160, 1588)	0.5003	0.6270	0.2506	0.0451
(25, 1540)	(82, 1238)	(155, 1540)	0.5175	0.6274	0.2937	0.0456
(30, 1495)	(82, 1238)	(150, 1495)	0.5238	0.6268	0.3096	0.0447
(35, 1453)	(82, 1238)	(145, 1454)	0.5385	0.6271	0.3464	0.0452
(40, 1418)	(82, 1238)	(140, 1419)	0.5230	0.6271	0.3075	0.0452
(45, 1394)	(82, 1238)	(135, 1394)	0.4541	0.6272	0.1352	0.0453
(50, 1364)	(82, 1238)	(130, 1364)	0.4164	0.6265	0.0410	0.0442
(55, 1337)	(82, 1238)	(125, 1337)	0.3932	0.6267	0.0169	0.0445
(60, 1311)	(82, 1238)	(120, 1330)	0.3336	0.6254	0.1659	0.0424
(65, 1282)	(82, 1238)	(115, 1282)	0.4853	0.6267	0.2132	0.0445
(70, 1269)	(82, 1238)	(110, 1269)	0.2681	0.6255	0.3299	0.0425
(75, 1254)	(82, 1238)	(105, 1254)	0.2244	0.6260	0.4391	0.0433

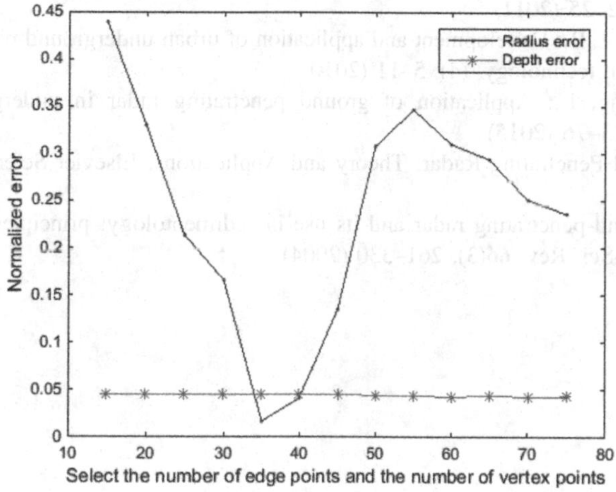

Fig. 6. The influence of the selection of edge points on the error

5 Conclusion

The error of the pipe diameter identified by the "three-point rounding" method is controlled within 0.45, and the error at the lowest time can reach about 0.01, so it is feasible to use this method for pipeline identification. The depth estimation is more accurate and the selection of the three edge points has little effect on the depth estimation. The selection of the three edge points has a great influence on the estimation of the pipe diameter. If the edge point is too far or too close to the pipeline, it will cause a relatively large error, and a minimum error will occur at a certain position in the middle.

In a position too close to the center, the curvature of the hyperbola is large, and the small change of the coordinate value of the selected point will have a great influence on the shape of the whole curve, so it is easy to cause errors. In the position far away from the pipeline, the reflection point of the antenna wave on the pipeline surface is not necessarily on the connection line between the center of the pipeline and the measurement position, that is, the condition that does not completely conform to the Pythagorean theorem, so the use of "three points" Large errors occur when the circle method is used.

Acknowledgement. This work was supported by the National Key R&D Program of China with Grant 2017YFC1500601.

References

1. Wang, Y., Chen, W.: Research on detection of parallel underground pipeline with small intervals, (3), 22–25 (2011)
2. Li, X.B., Hong, L.B.: Development and application of urban underground pipeline detection and management technology, (4), 5–11 (2010)
3. Liu, Y.Y., Yang, L.: Application of ground penetrating radar in underground pipeline detection, (3), 73–76 (2015)
4. Jol, H.: Ground Penetrating Radar: Theory and Applications. Elsevier Science, Amsterdam (2009)
5. Neal, A.: Ground-penetrating radar and its use in sedimentology: principles, problems and progress. Earth-Sci. Rev. **66**(3), 261–330 (2004)

Analysis of the Impact of Communication Link Outage on Throughput of VANETs Based on TDMA

Guiting Li, Xuan Zhang, Junyu Guo, and Qi Yang(✉)

Xiamen University, Xiamen 361005, Fujian, China
yangqi@xmu.edu.cn

Abstract. In vehicular ad hoc network, the random movement of nodes leads to constant changes in the network topology, in turn causing communication link outage (others is not consider in this paper). This paper will analyze the link outage caused by vehicular motion and the impact on the overall network throughput based on the vehicular movement model and the TDMA dynamic allocation access protocol. And the simulation results show that the increase of velocity standard deviation and the decrease of access probability will increase the probability of vehicle communication link outage, resulting in a decrease in the network throughput.

Keywords: Dynamic allocation TDMA · VANET · Link outage

1 Introduction

Vehicular Ad hoc Networks (VANET) in the paper [1] is an important part of the Intelligent Transport System (ITS), providing security for vehicles on the road and entertainment service for in-vehicle personnel. At the same time, the velocity of nodes are different, there is a velocity difference between nodes making communication link outage, that is the question we discussed in this paper. A large velocity difference will have a great distance between nodes, causing the problem of link outage. The influence on its performance in the entire network will be very high. Therefore, this problem has to be considered in the practical application of VANET. However, due to the particularity of this problem, the analysis of link outage problem in the actual research work is very small and the research is not deep enough.

The mobility of nodes will have different effects on the performance of the MAC protocol. Paper [2] shows that with the node moving faster, the delivery rate of network packets is gradually reduced and the transmission delay is gradually increased. Paper [3] analyzes the impact of nodes' mobility and the problem of hidden terminal on the performance of IEEE 802.11 protocol. Paper [4] analyzed the effects of different motion models on the throughput of IEEE 802.11 protocol.

M. Jia et al. (Eds.): WiSATS 2019, LNICST 281, pp. 79–88, 2019.
https://doi.org/10.1007/978-3-030-19156-6_8

Based on the above analysis, this paper analyzes the problem of link outage and its probability caused by the node's movement in the network, and the impact of the whole network throughput based on two common vehicular motion models under the dynamic allocation of TDMA channel access protocol mechanism.

2 The Dynamic Allocation of TDMA Access Protocol

The time is divided into frames, frames are divided into slots of equal length. One frame is divided into a RF (reserved frame) and *K* IF (information frames). In RF, the node with data to be sent competes for a slot in IF with an access probability *p* by using the slotted-ALOHA random access method. If there is only one node in RF contends to access in the *ith* slot, the node must successfully subscribe to the slot. Otherwise it will causes a collision. Then these nodes will continue to compete for other slots. After the end of RF, nodes can transmit data in IF in the corresponding slot that the node successfully subscribes to in RF. After one frame, the process will repeat in a new frame. Therefore, the analysis of the number of slots successfully accessed in the RF also reflects the number of slots successfully occupied in each IF (Fig. 1).

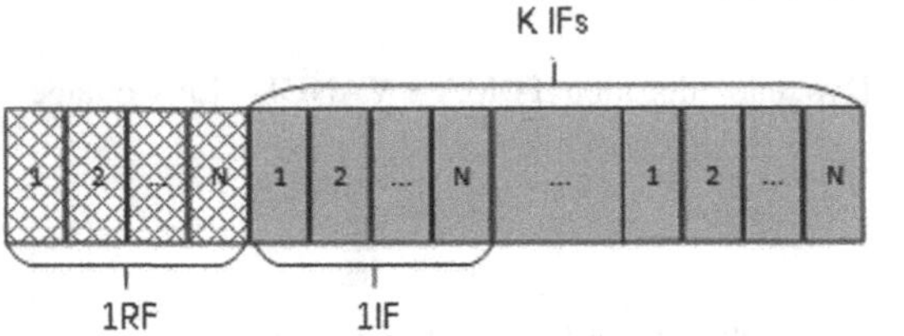

Fig. 1. The structure of a frame based on dynamic allocation with TDMA access protocol.

3 Model Description

One-way unidirectional and two-way bidirectional lane are two common traffic models. Assuming that nodes are evenly distributed in the lane, the road is divided into many two-hop regions with length $L = 2R$, the communication radius of vehicles is R. Vehicles travel at a constant velocity and their velocities are independent of each other. In the saturated state, each vehicle accesses the channel based on TDMA protocol with dynamically allocated, the interval between nodes from allocating slot to sending data packet is T.

3.1 One-Way Unidirectional Lane

The number of nodes in each region is M. The velocity of nodes follow a special Gaussian distribution: $V \sim N(\mu, \sigma^2)$. Thus the difference of velocity between any two nodes should be subject to the Gaussian distribution $\Delta V \sim N(0, 2\sigma^2)$ and $\Delta V \in [V_{\min} - V_{\max}, V_{\max} - V_{\min}]$.

The maximum distance which a vehicle can travel within time T is $S = V_{\max}T$. Given the time value is small and the maximum velocity of a vehicle is bounded, generally, the maximum distance of a vehicle can reach within time T is smaller than the length of the two-hop region (Fig. 3).

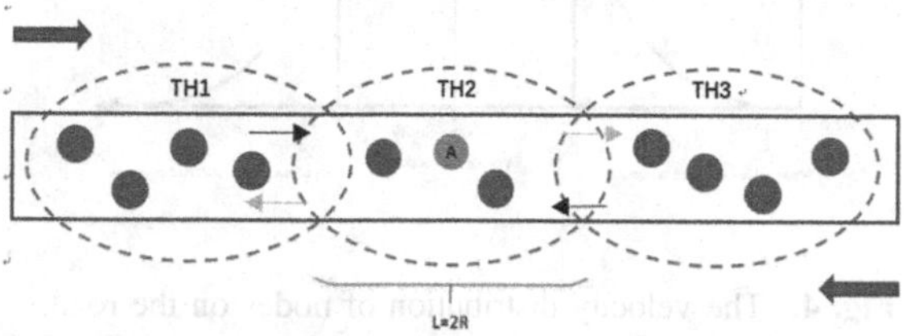

Fig. 2. The vehicle movement model in One-way unidirectional lane.

3.2 Two-Way Bidirectional Lane

The total number of nodes in each two-hop region is $2M$, the number of nodes in one lane in the two-hop section is M.

The moving velocity of a vehicle in the upper lane (i.e. the rightward direction) considered as positive, follows a special Gaussian distribution: $V \sim N(\mu, \sigma^2)$, $V \in [V_{\min}, V_{\max}]$. The other lane follows distribution $V \sim N(-\mu, \sigma^2)$, $V \in [V_{\min}, V_{\max}]$.

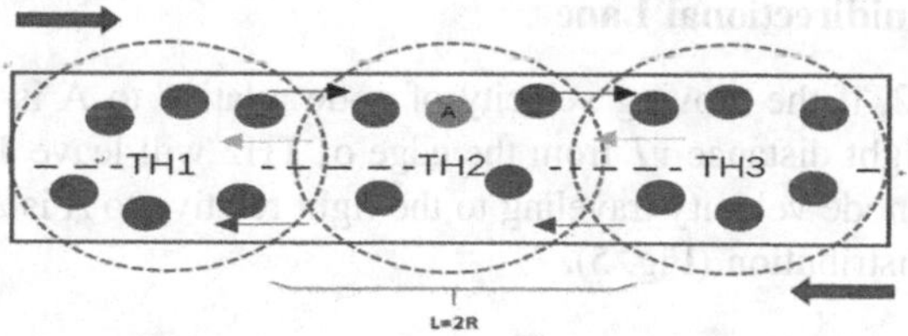

Fig. 3. The vehicle movement model of Two-way bidirectional lane.

3.3 System Parameter

3.3.1 The Distribution of Velocity

A number of related studies show that the driving velocities on the rural roads and the highway generally follow the normal distribution as stated in the paper [5].

Considering the actual scene, velocity of a vehicle is bounded, approximately following the special Gaussian distribution. Therefore, velocity distribution of vehicles can be approximately expressed as $V \sim N(\mu, \sigma^2)$, $V \in [V_{\min}, V_{\max}]$ (Fig. 4).

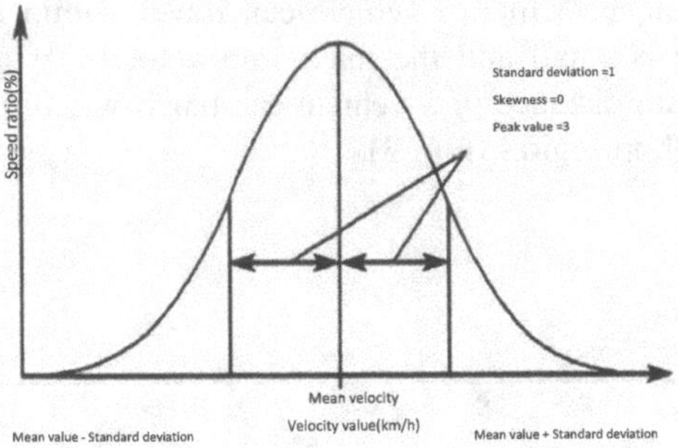

Fig. 4. The velocity distribution of nodes on the road.

3.3.2 The Arrival of Vehicle

Based on the existing knowledge of traffic flow theory, the number of vehicles' arrival within a certain interval or distributed on a certain road segment is also regarded as a random variable. Poisson distribution and binomial distribution are usually used to describe the statistical law of such random variable as stated in the paper [6]. The discrete distribution should be adopted to describe the process of nodes' arrival in this paper.

4 The Analysis of Communication Link Outage

4.1 One-Way Unidirectional Lane

As shown in Fig. 2, if the moving velocity of node relative to A is v, only the node distributed at the right distance vT from the edge of TH2 will leave TH2 after T time. Assuming that the node velocity traveling to the right relative to A is ΔV_R, obeying the special Gaussian distribution (Fig. 5).

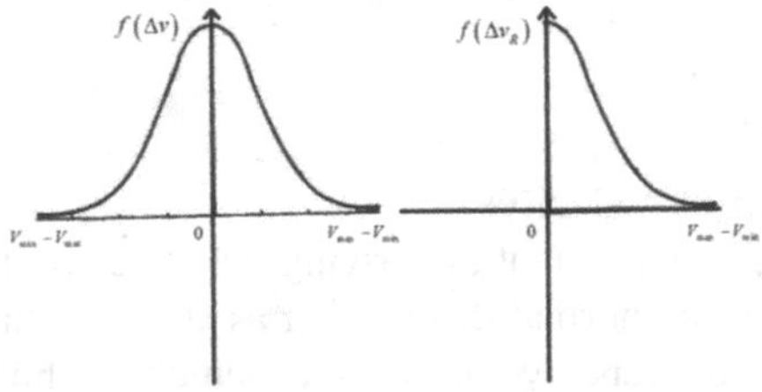

Fig. 5. The probability density map of velocity.

Based on the analysis before, considering the limited number of nodes in the TH2, this paper uses the binomial distribution to analyze the nodes' distribution from TH2 to

TH3 and TH1. In summary, after the period of one frame T, the number of nodes leaving TH2 should be $X_{OUT} = X_L + X_R$.

Since the link outage problem occurs in nodes occupying slots, the number of nodes who have link outages is equivalent to the number of nodes occupying the slots among the nodes leaving from the TH2 range after time T. The probability distribution of the slot allocation result is $P(S = i|T = N)$, where N is the number of slots.

4.2 Two-Way Bidirectional Lane

Compared with the one-way unidirectional lane, the total number of nodes left from TH2 during T time, in addition to the number of nodes discussed above on the one-way unidirectional lane, should also add the number of nodes in TH2 leaving from the left side of the lane on the left-travel lane. And the velocity of nodes on the left-travel lane relative to A following the Gaussian distribution $\Delta V_2 \sim N(2u, 2\sigma^2)$, $\Delta V_2 \in [-2V_{\max}, 2V_{\max}]$. Then, the number of nodes in the two-way lane that driving out of the TH2 during time T is $X_{double\_OUT} = X_{OUT} + X_{reverse}$.

5 The Throughput Based on Dynamic Allocation TDMA

Assuming that when the kth slot of an RF, there have been successfully allocated i slots. If the access is successful, status i is transferred to the next status j. If the access fails, status i is transferred to itself. If the current slot is the last slot in the RF, then the next slot corresponds to the first slot of the next RF. Since at the beginning of a frame, all nodes will release the original occupied slots and reschedule the slots, each state can only be transferred to state 0 or state 1 (Fig. 6).

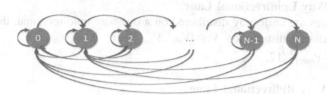

Fig. 6. First-order Markov process state transition diagram.

Based on the above analysis, the throughput of network can be determined as:

$$Throughput = \frac{c \cdot \sum_{i=0}^{N} iP(S = i|T = N)}{N} \tag{1}$$

where $c = L_{packet}/t_{slot}$ is the number of bits sent per unit time, L_{packet} is the length of the packet sent at a slot, t_{slot} is a slot's length.

Due to the space reasons, the formula detailed analysis will be discussed in other place.

6 Simulation

6.1 Simulation Scenario

Node 2 and node 3 who are the neighbor nodes of node 1 leave the communication radius of node 1 over a period of time. So that the link between node 1 and node 2 or node 1 and node 3 is invalid (Fig. 7).

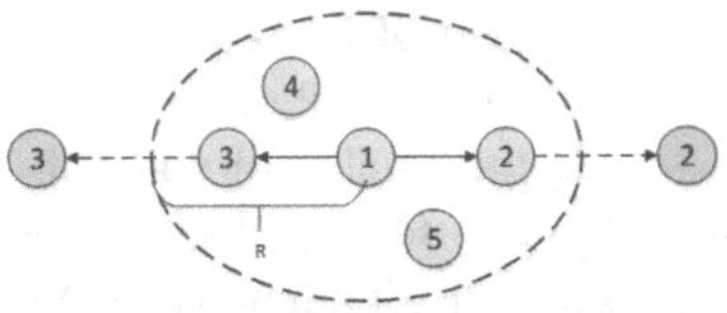

Fig. 7. The problem of communication link outage.

Assuming that in the actual scenes, the communication between nodes in the network is in the ideal channel. Since the actual two-hop communication range is limited, when each node is communicating, the signal is transmitted at its maximum transmission power (all nodes are the same). Then the velocity difference between nodes, the problem of link outage is inevitable when nodes move on the road. Moreover, based on the dynamically allocated TDMA channel access protocol, this paper analyze the problem of link outage, only two nodes are communicating at a specific time in the two-hop communication range, and there is no interference problem caused by other nodes communicating at the same time (combine Sect. 3).

6.1.1 One-Way Unidirectional Lane

Assuming nodes are uniformly distributed on a one-way unidirectional, their velocity follows a Gaussian distribution $V \in [V_{\min}, V_{\max}] > 0$, $\mu = (V_{\min} + V_{\max})/2 > 0$ and $\sigma^2 = (V_{\max} - V_{\min})^2/12$.

6.1.2 Two-Way Bidirectional Lane

Supposing that nodes are uniformly distributed on a two-way bidirectional. The velocity distribution of nodes on the right-travel lane are the same as the one-way unidirectional lane. The velocity of nodes travelings in the other lane follow the Gaussian distribution $V \in [-V_{\min}, -V_{\max}] < 0$, $\mu = (-V_{\min} + V_{\max})/2$ and $\sigma^2 = (V_{\max} - V_{\min})^2/12$.

6.2 Simulation Results and Analysis

There are three two-hop disjoint section, the parameters satisfy the following conditions: $R = 10$ m, $T = 0.5$ s, $M = 10$. Their range is TH1 = [0 m, 20 m], TH2 = [20 m, 40 m], TH3 = [40 m, 60 m]. The number of slots in one frame is $N = 10$, and average vehicles' velocity are $v = 5$ m/s.

The simulation is performed 10000 iteration in different scenarios, then the average of the simulation results is taken as 10,000. The final result is compared with the theoretical derivation value, and the relationship between the standard deviation of the vehicle velocity and the access probability to the link outage probability is observed.

Figures 8 and 9 both show that as the standard deviation of velocity increases, the probability of link outage increases. The shorter the link is, the greater the probability of link outage is. The link outage probability curve with a small access probability is higher than the curve with a large-access probability. The probability of link outage in Fig. 9 is significantly higher than the probability in Fig. 8.

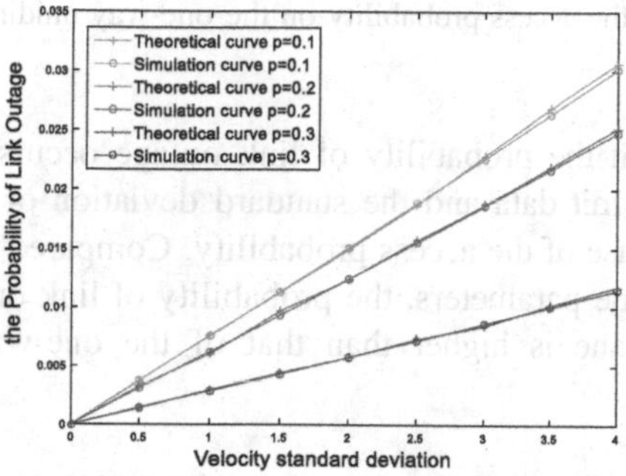

Fig. 8. The influence of the standard deviation of velocity on the one-way unidirectional lane on the link outage probability.

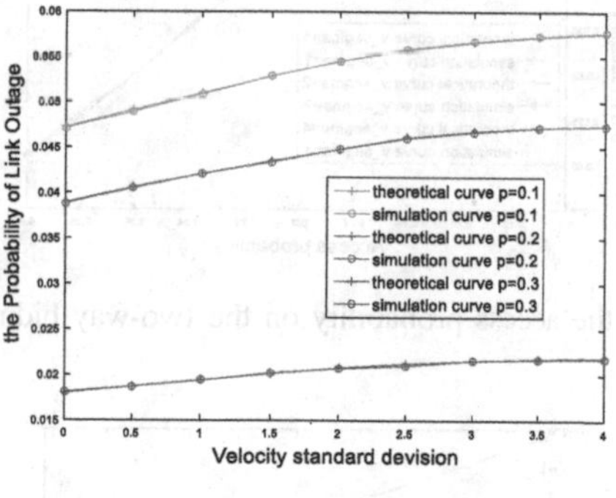

Fig. 9. The influence of the standard deviation of velocity on the two-way bidirectional lane on the link outage probability.

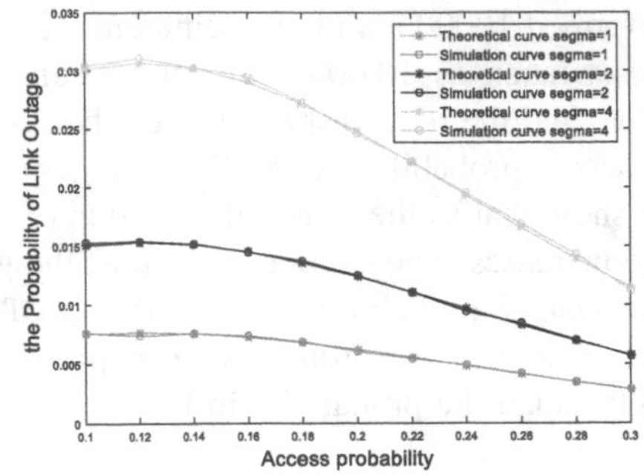

Fig. 10. The influence of the access probability on the one-way unidirectional lane on the link outage probability.

Figure 11 shows that the probability of link outage occurs when the number of nodes that want to transmit data and the standard deviation of velocity are constant, decreases with the increase of the access probability. Compared with Fig. 10, it can be found that under the same parameters, the probability of link outage occurring on the two-way bidirectional lane is higher than that of the one-way unidirectional lane (Figs. 12 and 13).

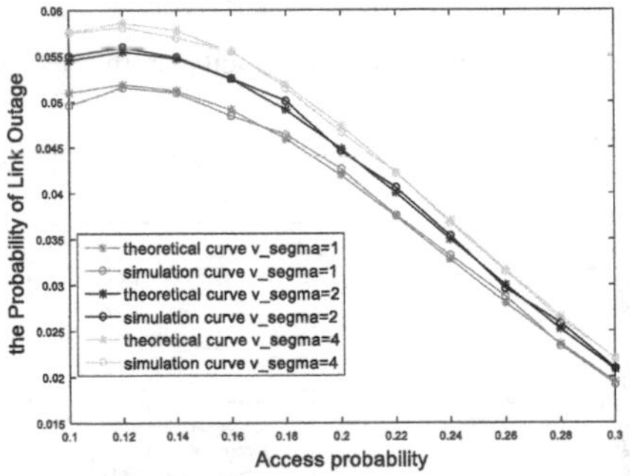

Fig. 11. The influence of the access probability on the two-way bidirectional lane on the link outage probability.

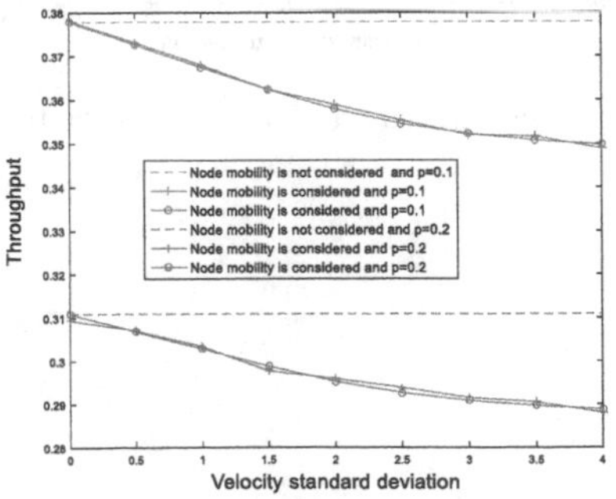

Fig. 12. The influence of the velocity standard deviation on the one-way unidirectional lane on the probability of link outage.

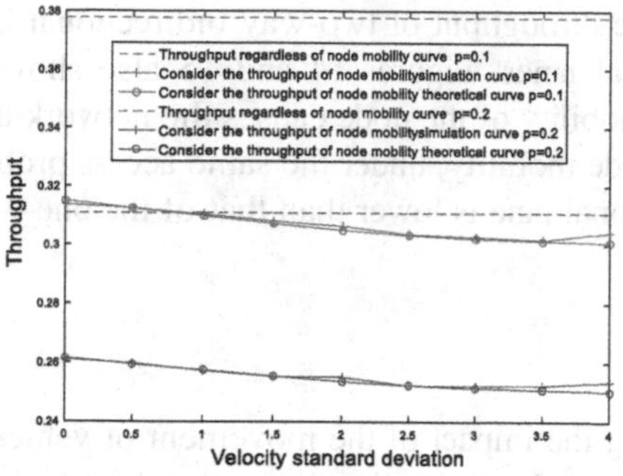

Fig. 13. The influence of the velocity standard deviation on the two-way bidirectional lane on the probability of link outage.

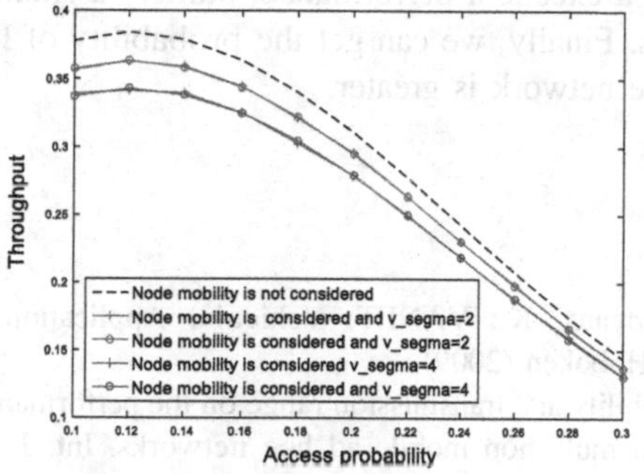

Fig. 14. The influence of the access probability on the one-way unidirectional lane on the probability of link outage.

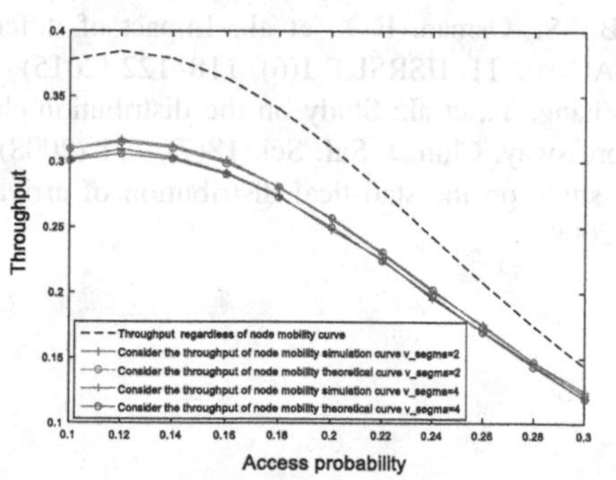

Fig. 15. The influence of the access probability on the two-way bidirectional lane on the probability of link outage.

When the node mobility is not considered, the network throughput on a one-way unidirectional lane is the same as that of a two-way bidirectional lane. When other parameters are equal, the throughput of two-way bidirectional lanes is lower than that of one-way unidirectional lanes. Figures 14 and 15 also shows that under the same access probability, the mobility of the node causes the network throughput to decrease; when considering the node mobility, under the same access probability, the throughput of the two-way bidirectional lane is lower than that of the one-way unidirectional lane.

7 Conclusion

In this paper, considering the impact of the movement of vehicles in the media access protocol with the scheme of dynamic allocation, namely the problem of link outage is taken into consideration, the throughput of the network is analyzed in this paper with the manifest of the simulation in two scenarios. It is noticeable that a greater standard deviation of velocity leads to a greater probability of link outage, and a larger probability of access brings a excellent performance, namely a smaller probability of link outage in two scenarios. Finally, we can get the probability of link outage is smaller, the throughput of whole network is greater.

References

1. Hartenstein, H., Laberteaux, K.: VANET: Vehicular Applications and Inter-Networking Technologies. Wiley, Hoboken (2009)
2. Saini, P.: Impact of mobility and transmission range on the performance of backoff algorithms for IEEE 802.11-based multi-hop mobile ad hoc networks. Int. J. Adv. Technol. **1**(1), 26 (2010)
3. Khurana, S., Kahol, A., Gupta, S.K.S., et al.: Performance evaluation of distributed co-ordination function for IEEE 802.11 wireless LAN protocol in presence of mobile and hidden terminals. In: International Symposium on Modeling, Analysis and Simulation of Computer and Telecommunication Systems, p. 40. IEEE Computer Society (1999)
4. Ahmed, E.S.A., Ali, B.E.S., Osman, E.O., et al.: Impact of different mobility models in MANETs based on MAC 802.11. IJSRSET **1**(6), 118–122 (2015)
5. Geng, Y., Wang, X., Zhang, Y., et al.: Study on the distribution characteristics of speed of section running on expressway. Chin. J. Saf. Sci. **18**(7), 171 (2008)
6. Hu, M.: An empirical study on the statistical distribution of arrival at intersections. Road Traffic Saf. **2**, 10–15 (2009)

International Workshop on Security, Reliability, and Resilience in Internet of Things

Research on Image Static Target Recognition and Extraction Based on Space Intelligent System

Yufei Huang(✉), Jia Xu, Xiangyu Lin, Xiongwen He, Ran Zhang, and Wenjie Li

Beijing Institute of Spacecraft System Engineering, Beijing, China
billyyufei@sina.com

Abstract. With the continuous development of remote sensing technology, remote sensing images and other multimedia information in the civil field has become more and more widely used. Unmanned aerial vehicle (UAV)/satellite image recognition and extraction of ground targets has become one of the important means of information acquisition in the civil field. At the same time, intelligent systems (such as mobile phones) have gradually become the core of UAV/nano-satellites. In this paper, through JAVA, the recognition and extraction of static targets in remote sensing images are realized. This method provides a theoretical basis for future image processing in remote sensing applications.

Keywords: Space intelligent system · Remote sensing image · Static target recognition and extraction

1 Introduction

Space smart platforms, such as smart phones, are becoming the core of UAVs/nano satellites. Since April 2013, NASA has used Orbital Science's Antares rocket to launch mobile satellites into space and explore their applications. This paper discusses the application of target recognition and extraction in remote sensing image in intelligent platform, analyzes the method of static target recognition and extraction in remote sensing image based on intelligent system platform, and finally demonstrates the method by using JAVA to verify the vehicle in parking lot, which provides theoretical basis for remote sensing satellite image acquisition and processing in the future. The foundation.

2 Principles

The core principles of static target recognition and extraction based on intelligent system platform are: imaging a certain area of the ground by satellite or unmanned aerial vehicle (UAV) camera; focusing on the scale problem in static target extraction based on satellite image after pre-processing, the scale conversion of vehicle satellite image in parking lot is carried out. In the evaluation and analysis of scale effect, the

M. Jia et al. (Eds.): WiSATS 2019, LNICST 281, pp. 91–99, 2019.
https://doi.org/10.1007/978-3-030-19156-6_9

correlation between scale and object extraction is used to extract static objects, and all the static objects identified in the image are numbered in order. The specific task flow chart is as follows (Fig. 1):

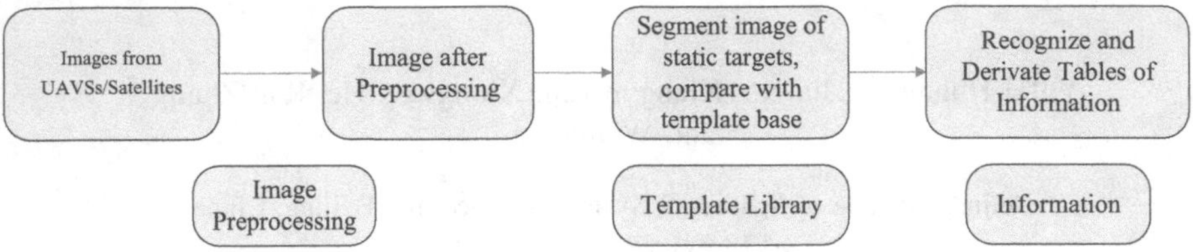

Fig. 1. Task process diagram.

2.1 Image Preprocessing

Image Enhancement

Image distortion often occurs in the process of acquiring images, which makes the obtained image different from the original image to some extent. For some imaging conditions, the weak signal is highlighted to make it easier to distinguish. The methods of image enhancement are divided into frequency domain method and spatial domain method. Spatial filtering is based on the relationship between pixels and adjacent pixels. Neighborhood processing method in spatial domain is used to highlight some features of the image. In each transform domain, the transformed coefficients, such as the coefficients of Fourier transform, DCT transform and so on, are modified to manipulate the image, and then inversely transformed to obtain the processed image.

(1) Enhancement of Grayscale Transformation

In case of $x = f(i,j)$ as the gray value of the original image, $y = F(i,j)$ as the gray value of the transformed image, the relationship of the function $y = h(x)$ as follows:

$$y = h(x) = \begin{cases} \frac{y_1}{x_1} x, 0 \leq x < x_1 \\ \frac{y_2 - y_1}{x_2 - x_1}(x - x_1) + y_1, x_1 < x < x_2 \\ \frac{255 - y_1}{255 - x_1}(x - x_2) + y_2, x_2 < x \leq 255 \end{cases} \quad (1)$$

(x_1, y_1) and (x_2, y_2) are the two turning points. These two turning points determine the slope of three straight lines.

(2) Histogram Transformation Enhancement

The cumulative distribution function is used in histogram equalization because the cumulative distribution function is a monotone increasing function (control size relationship) and the range is 0 to 1 (control crossing problem), so the cumulative distribution function is used in histogram equalization.

In case of the area of the image $f(i,j)$ is A, and there are L gray levels. n_i is used to represent the pixel list of the grayscale r_i. Histogram equalization is to establish a transformation T, that is, to construct a monotone increasing function is as follows:

$$r' = T(r), r \in [f_{\min}, f_{\max}] \tag{2}$$

The gray value r of the original image $f(i,j)$ is transformed into the gray $r' \in [g_{\min}, g_{\max}]$ of the output image $g(i,j)$.

The formula for histogram equalization is as follows:

$$r' = \left\lfloor \frac{L-1}{A} \sum_{k=0}^{i} n_k + 0.5 \right\rfloor, (i = 0, 1, \ldots, L-1) \tag{3}$$

(3) Smoothing Filtering

There are two types of smoothing filtering: one is fuzzy; the other is noise cancellation. Smoothing filtering in spatial domain usually uses simple averaging method, which is to find the average brightness of adjacent pixels. The size of the neighborhood is directly related to the smoothing effect. The mean filtering formula for setting A is as follows:

$$F(i,j) = \frac{1}{M} \sum_{(i',j') \subset A} f(i',j') \tag{4}$$

(4) Median Filtering

The basic principle of median filtering is to replace the value of a point in a digital image or sequence with the median value of each point in a neighborhood of the point, so that the value of the surrounding pixels close to the true value, thereby eliminating isolated noise points. It uses a neighborhood A containing odd points, which is called a sliding window, and replaces the gray value of the pixel in the center of the window with the median gray value of each point in the window.

(5) High Pass Template Filtering

The high pass filter can smooth the high-frequency components and weaken the low frequency. The edge and detail of the image are mainly located in the high frequency part, and the blur of the image is caused by the weak high frequency component. High pass filter can be used to sharpen the image, in order to eliminate blurring and highlight edges. Therefore, high-pass filter is used to let the high-frequency component pass through, so that the low-frequency component is weakened. The 5 convolution templates commonly used for high pass filters are sometimes referred to as convolution kernels.

$$H_1 = \begin{bmatrix} 0 & -1 & 0 \\ -1 & 5 & -1 \\ 0 & -1 & 0 \end{bmatrix}, H_2 = \begin{bmatrix} -1 & -1 & -1 \\ -1 & 9 & -1 \\ -1 & -1 & -1 \end{bmatrix}, H_3 = \begin{bmatrix} 1 & -2 & 1 \\ -2 & 5 & -2 \\ 1 & -2 & 1 \end{bmatrix},$$
$$H_4 = \frac{1}{7}\begin{bmatrix} -1 & -2 & -1 \\ -2 & 19 & -2 \\ -1 & -2 & -1 \end{bmatrix}, H_5 = \frac{1}{2}\begin{bmatrix} -2 & 1 & -2 \\ 1 & 6 & 1 \\ -2 & 1 & -2 \end{bmatrix} \quad (5)$$

Simulation takes H_5 as an example.

Target Edge Detection

In this paper, Roberts operator is used, which uses the difference between two adjacent pixels in diagonal direction to approximate the gradient amplitude to detect the edge, so it is also called four-point difference method. Vertical edge detection is better than oblique edge detection. It has high positioning accuracy and is sensitive to noise and cannot suppress the influence of noise. The formula for the Roberts operator is as follows:

$$|gradf(x,y)| = \sqrt{(f(x+1,y+1) - f(x,y))^2 + (f(x+1,y) - f(x,y+1))^2} \quad (6)$$

$$|gradf(x,y)| = |f(x+1,y+1) - f(x,y)| + |f(x+1,y) - f(x,y+1)| \quad (7)$$

Image Morphology Design

This section is mainly reflected in noise filtering, area filling, expansion and corrosion, to a certain extent, can eliminate the resulting contour loss and other phenomena. The algorithm used in noise filtering is first open operation, then closed operation; region filling operation first assigns 1 to the point within the boundary as seed point, and then fills it by iterative method; expansion and corrosion operations are defined as follows:

$$\begin{cases} (f \oplus b)(s,t) = \max\{f(s-x,t-y) + b(x,y) \,|\, (s-x,t-y) \in D_f, (x,y) \in D_b\} \\ (f \odot b)(s,t) = \max\{f(s+x,t+y) + b(x,y) \,|\, (s+x,t+y) \in D_f, (x,y) \in D_b\} \end{cases} \quad (8)$$

D_f and D_b are the definitions of image f and structure element b, which are determined by the width and height of the image.

2.2 Image Segmentation

In this paper, a threshold based image segmentation method is used in image segmentation and initial recognition. The aim is to divide the pixel set according to the gray level, and each subset is formed into a region corresponding to the real scene. Each region has the same attributes, while the adjacent regions do not have the same attributes. The basic principle is to divide pixels into several classes by setting characteristic thresholds. Common features include gray or color features directly from the original image, and features transformed from the original gray or color values. In this paper, we use the best threshold segmentation iterative algorithm. The steps are as follows:

The steps are as follows:

1. The maximum and minimum gray values of the image are calculated by $P_{\max}$ and $P_{\min}$, respectively. The initial value of the threshold T is as follows:

$$T_0 = (P_{\max} + P_{\min})/2 \tag{9}$$

2. Then, according to the threshold $T_k(k = 0, 1, \ldots, k)$, the image is divided into two parts: the target and the background, and the average gray value P_O and P_B of the two parts are calculated, as follows:

$$\begin{cases} P_O = \dfrac{\sum_{p(i,j) < T_k} p(i,j)\omega(i,j)}{\sum_{p(i,j) < T_k} \omega(i,j)} \\ P_B = \dfrac{\sum_{p(i,j) > T_k} p(i,j)\omega(i,j)}{\sum_{p(i,j) > T_k} \omega(i,j)} \end{cases} \tag{10}$$

In the upper form, $p(i,j)$ is the gray value of the image at (i,j), and $\omega(i,j)$ is the weight coefficient of the gray value $p(i,j)$, usually taking $\omega(i,j) = 1.0$.

3. The new threshold is calculated as follows:

$$T_{k+1} = (P_O + P_B)/2 \tag{11}$$

4. If $T_k = T_{k+1}$, then the program ends, and the final T_k is the best threshold T. Otherwise, $k \leftarrow k + 1$ returns to step 2.

2.3 Image Recognition and Extraction

The method of image recognition is based on template matching algorithm. A commonly used measure for template matching is the sum of squares of errors in the corresponding regions of the template and the source image, which measures the difference between the blocks and templates in the original image, i.e. the square error measure. If $f(x, y)$ is the source image of $M \times N$ and $t(j, k)$ is the template image of $J \times K(J \leq M, K \leq N)$, the error square sum measure is defined as follows:

$$D(x, y) = \sum_{j=0}^{J-1} \sum_{k=0}^{K-1} [f(x + j, y + k) - t(j, k)]^2 \tag{12}$$

For upper type expansion, the following formula can be obtained.

$$D(x,y) = \sum_{j=0}^{J-1}\sum_{k=0}^{K-1}[f(x+j,y+k)]^2 - 2\sum_{j}^{J-1}\sum_{k}^{K-1}t(j,k)\bullet f(x+j,y+k) + \sum_{j=0}^{J-1}\sum_{k=0}^{K-1}[t(j,k)]^2 \quad (13)$$

If:

$$\begin{cases} DS(x,y) = \sum_{j=0}^{J-1}\sum_{k=0}^{K-1}[f(x+j,y+k)]^2 \\ DST(x,y) = 2\sum_{j=0}^{J-1}\sum_{k=0}^{K-1}t(j,k)\bullet f(x+j,y+k) \\ DT(x,y) = \sum_{j=0}^{J-1}\sum_{k=0}^{K-1}[t(j,k)]^2 \end{cases} \quad (14)$$

In the above formula, $DS(x,y)$ denotes the energy of the corresponding area of the template in the source image. It is related to the pixel position (x,y), but the change of $DS(x,y)$ is slow with the change of the pixel position (x,y). $DST(x,y)$ template and the corresponding region of the source image are correlated, which changes with the change of the pixel position (x,y). When the template $t(j,k)$ matches the corresponding region of the source image, the maximum value is obtained. $DT(x,y)$ represents the energy of the template, which is independent of the pixel position (x,y) of the image, and can be calculated only once, which reduces the amount of calculation. After the comparison of all pixels, finding the smallest error is the result of matching (Fig. 2).

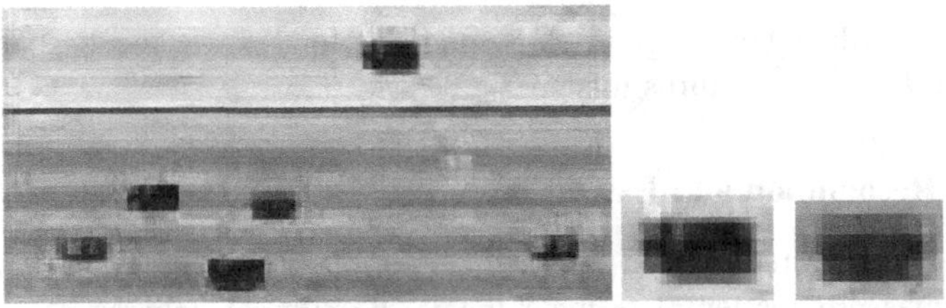

Fig. 2. Source images and partial template images

3 Simulation

This section mainly compiles and implements the above contents. The parking lot is used as the setting scene. The contrast expansion parameters are set as follows: X1 = 50, Y1 = 30, x2 = 200, y2 = 210. The template of high-pass template filtering is H5. The simulation results are as follows (Figs. 3, 4, 5, 6 and 7):

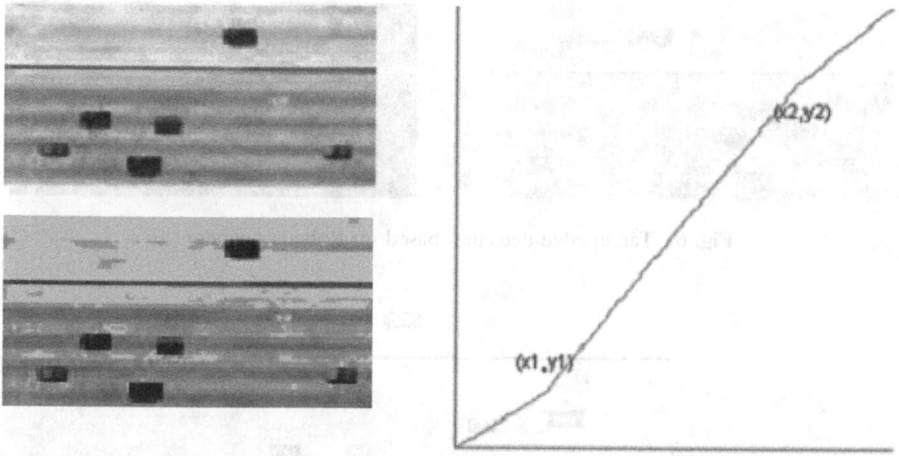

Fig. 3. Visual preview of the original image and contrast extension, as well as comparison of effects (top-left picture is the original one, bottom-left picture is the processed one, as contrast extension)

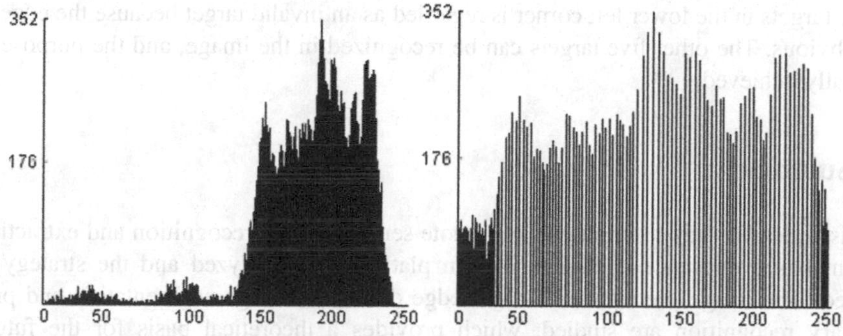

Fig. 4. Histogram comparison before and after homogenization

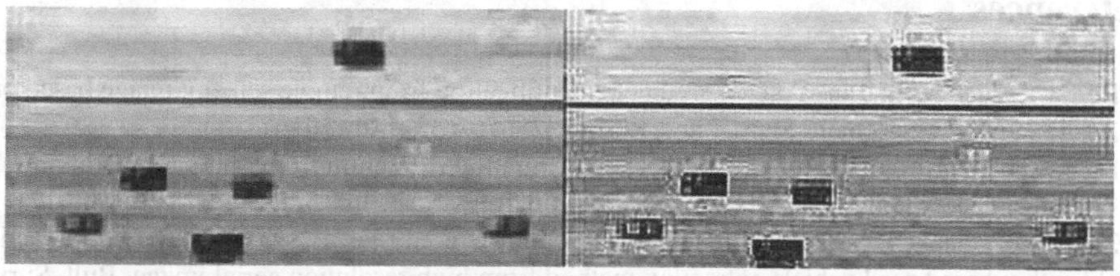

Fig. 5. Template selection and effect comparison of high pass template filtering

Fig. 6. Target edge detection based on Roberts operator

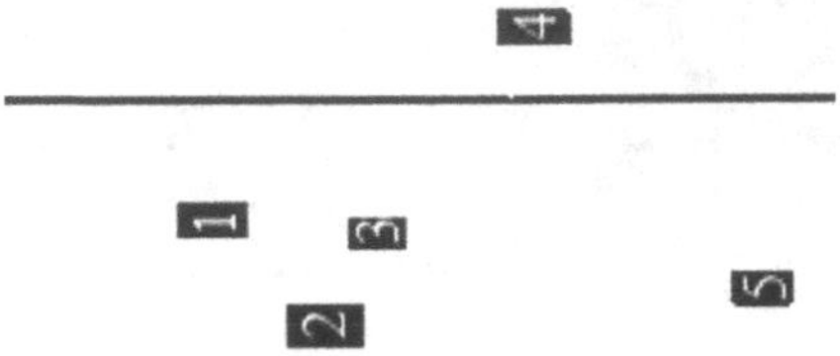

Fig. 7. The example of image morphology and image segmentation and recognition algorithm.

There are six target vehicles in the source image. After a series of processing, one of the targets in the lower left corner is regarded as an invalid target because the edge is not obvious. The other five targets can be recognized in the image, and the purpose is basically achieved.

4 Summary

In this paper, the key technologies of remote sensing image recognition and extraction system based on space intelligent system platform are analyzed and the strategy is studied. The image pretreatment, target edge detection, image segmentation and preliminary recognition are studied, which provides a theoretical basis for the future remote sensing satellite image acquisition and processing.

References

1. Ren, C., Huang, H., Tan, Y., et al.: Vehicle identification from remote sensing image based on image symmetry. Remote Sens. Land Resour. **28**(4), 135–140 (2016)
2. Mishra, R.K.: Automatic moving vehicle's information extraction from one-pass worldview-2 satellite imagery. Int. Arch. Photogram. Remote Sens. Spat. Inf. Sci. **39**, 323–328 (2012)
3. Zhao, Q., Chang, B., Wang, Y., Huang, H., Tan, Y., et al.: Fuzzy segmentation and genetic algorithm based road vehicle extraction method from high resolution aerial image. Bull. Surv. Mapp. (8), 62–66 (2017)
4. Cao, T., Shen, L.: A method for vehicles detection method based on traffic remote sensing. In: The Eighth China Intelligent Transportation Annual Meeting, pp. 389–394 (2013)

5. Wu, D., Liu, D., Puskas, Z., et al.: A learning based deformable template matching method for automatic rib centerline extraction and labeling in CT images. In: Proceedings of the IEEE Computer Society Conference on Computer Vision and Pattern Recognition, Providence, pp. 980–987. IEEE (2012)
6. Li, S., Xu, Y., Sun, W., et al.: Remote sensing image recognition for vehicles based on self-feedback template extraction. J. South China Univ. Technol. (Nat. Sci. Ed.) **42**(5), 97–102 (2014)
7. Chen, X., Xiang, S., Liu, C.L., et al.: Vehicle detection in satellite images by hybrid deep convolutional neural networks. IEEE Geosci. Remote Sens. Lett. **11**(10), 1797–1801 (2014)

Design of a All-CMOS Second-Order Temperature Compensated Bandgap Reference

Jianhai Yu(✉), Guojin Peng, Kuikui Wang, and Meini Lv

Wuzhou University, Wuzhou 543002, China
40802622@qq.com

Abstract. In this paper, a second-order temperature compensated bandgap voltage source based on 0.18 μm standard COMS process with low temperature coefficient (TC) and high power supply rejection ratio (PSRR) was presented. The core structure of the circuit was the improvement of the traditional bandgap reference. The cascade structure was adopted to improve the PSRR and the line sensitivity, and the square of the proportional to absolute temperature current I_{PTAT2} was utilized to compensate the first order circuit. This circuit constitutes of all-CMOS transistors in order to save the power consumption. The simulation results show that TC of the bandgap reference source in the −25 °C–125 °C temperature range, is 4.5 ppm/°C. At low frequency, the PSRR reaches −45.63 dB@100 Hz, and the power consumption is only 287.2 μW.

Keywords: Bandgap reference source · Second-order compensation · Temperature coefficient · Power supply rejection ratio

1 Introduction

Bandgap reference (BGR) is an essential basic block in VLSI and many electronic systems. It is widely used in many analog, digital and mixed signal IC, such as A/D converter, DRAM and flash control module, so its performance will have an impact on the performance index of the whole signal processing system [1]. Bandgap voltage reference is widely used in analog and digital circuits and is an important part of the system [2].

Due to high precision and temperature independence, high precision BGR is an indispensable module in many applications, Like data and power converters. However, due to the non-linearity of base-emitter voltage of BJT, the temperature characteristics of first order temperature compensation BGR are limited. Through the study found that usually the temperature coefficient of first order compensation BGR range between 20 and 100 ppm/°C [3]. In addition, the reference voltage source provides a high-precision voltage reference for other functional modules in the circuit system, or is converted into a high-precision current reference. For analog circuit systems, the performance of reference voltage source directly affects the accuracy and performance of the whole system [4, 5]. Therefore, in order to achieve better temperature independence and

M. Jia et al. (Eds.): WiSATS 2019, LNICST 281, pp. 100–108, 2019.
https://doi.org/10.1007/978-3-030-19156-6_10

provide a stable reference voltage for the system, we need to add a high-price compensation circuit to compensate the first-order bandgap reference circuit.

In the CMOS second-order temperature compensated bandgap reference source proposed in this paper, the structure of the first-order bandgap reference circuit adopts the standard CMOS process, which is improved in the traditional bandgap reference voltage source structure [6], the original resistance is replaced by PMOS tube, reduces the power consumption of the circuit. Not only the cascode structure can not only improve the power rejection ratio of the circuit, but also enhance the stability of the whole circuit. The second order temperature compensation circuit adopts IPTAT2 circuit to compensate the first order circuit. The circuit has the advantages of simple structure, low temperature coefficient and high power rejection ratio.

2 First-Order Compensating Bandgap Reference Voltage Source

Since the idea of bandgap reference source has been proposed, many researchers have improved and optimized this structure, a wide variety of bandgap reference source core circuits based on bipolar transistors are designed. But many structures cannot be implemented by using standard CMOS processes, since the collector of the triode PNP of the traditional Kujik structure is directly grounded, the standard CMOS process can be used to realize it [7]. Therefore, this design adopts Kujik structure as the core structure of the first-order bandgap reference voltage source.

In this paper, the first-order bandgap reference source circuit is improved by using the basic structure of Kujik, as shown in Fig. 1. Different from the traditional bandgap reference, the original resistance is replaced by the line of PMOS tube M14-M18, which helps to reduce the power consumption. On the basis of single-row PMOS tube, a layer of PMOS tube M19–M23 is connected in series. In this way, two rows of P tubes form a common source and common gate structure, which can not only improve the power rejection ratio of the circuit, but also enhance the stability of the whole circuit. Bipolar transistor Q1–Q5 will produce a positive and negative temperature coefficient, the voltage of the zero temperature coefficient can be obtained by adding the appropriate specific gravity. The resulting current is then copied to Q5 through the current mirror, and the output voltage of the first-order bandgap reference is finally obtained.

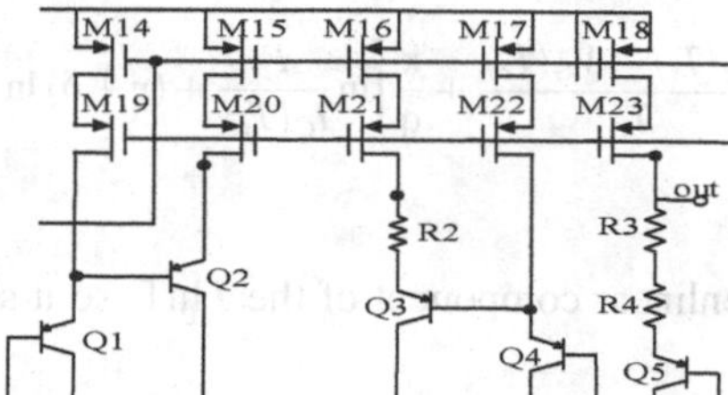

Fig. 1. First-order bandgap reference with cascade structure

Second, the PNP bipolar triode Q3 and Q4 are connected to Q1 and Q2 in series, reducing the effect of the misalignment voltage of the operational amplifier on the reference output. The collector electrodes for transistors Q1, Q2, Q3, and Q4 are all connected to the ground, and this structure is guaranteed to be implemented under standard CMOS processes. Through analysis, the output expression of the band gap reference source core circuit designed in this paper is shown in Eq. (1) by

$$V_{REF}=V_{\mathrm{be5}}+\frac{(2V_t\ln \mathrm{N}-V_{OS})(R3+R4)}{R2} \tag{1}$$

Since the base and emitter voltage V_{be} of Eq. (1) Q5 has a positive temperature coefficient and $2V_t$lnN has a negative temperature coefficient, V_{OS} is the misaligned voltage, and the output voltage V_{REF} is basically unchanged, so the effect of misaligned voltage on the bandgap reference source can be reduced through the base-emitter connection of bipolar transistors. It is also possible to adjust the ratio of R3 + R4 to R2 to obtain the first-order bandgap reference output voltage.

3 Second-Order Temperature Compensated Bandgap Reference Voltage Source

In fact, only the first order temperature coefficient of the output voltage can be eliminated by the first order compensated reference source, then the voltage independent of temperature is obtained, but the high voltage component that cannot be compensated is not eliminated, so high compensation is needed [8]. V_T is proportional to the absolute temperature and the value is small, which is the voltage of the first-order temperature coefficient, so the higher order temperature term introduced from V_T is basically negligible. High order temperature coefficient is mainly determined by the temperature characteristics of bipolar transistors V_{BE}, so it can be obtained:

$$V_{BE}(T)=V_G(T)+\left(\frac{T}{T_{\mathrm{r}}}\right)[V_{BE}(T_{\mathrm{r}})-V_G(T_r)]-\eta\left(\frac{kT}{q}\right)\ln\left(\frac{T}{T_r}\right)+\left(\frac{kT}{q}\right)\ln\left[\frac{I_c}{I_c(T_r)}\right] \tag{2}$$

Where V_G is the bandgap voltage of silicon at 0 K, η is the electric field factor, T_r is a given constant temperature. Since I_C is related to temperature, it can be set $I_C(T)=FT^{\delta}$, δ is a coefficient introduced by resistance, bring it into the above formula:

$$V_{BE}(T)=V_G(T)+T\left\{\frac{V_{BE}(T_{\mathrm{r}})-V_G(T_{\mathrm{r}})}{T_{\mathrm{r}}}+\frac{\mathrm{k}}{\mathrm{q}}\left[\ln\frac{F}{I_C(T_{\mathrm{r}})}+(\eta+\delta)\ln T_{\mathrm{r}}\right]\right\}-T\mathrm{lnT}\frac{(\eta-\delta)\mathrm{k}}{\mathrm{q}} \tag{3}$$

The last term is the nonlinear component of the TlnT, so it still exists after the first order compensation [9].

The I_{PTAT}^2 second order temperature compensation circuit is introduced in this paper. As shown in Fig. 2, the overall circuit structure is shown in Fig. 3. The second-order temperature compensation circuit consists of M24-M33, M24 is the voltage supplied by the output of the previous amplifier as the conduction voltage, which then produces the bias current I_{PTAT}. The conduction voltage of M25 and M26 is provided by the previous bias circuit, M25 and M26 themselves constitute the bias circuit, which can provide the bias voltage for the second-order compensation circuit. M26, M27 and M29, M30, and M33 can produce a current with a negative temperature coefficient, which is squared with the offset current of M24. The conduction voltage of M31 and M32 is provided by the bias voltage generated by M25 and M26, and they are proportional. The resulting I_{PTAT}^2 current is compensated to the output end through the first-order bandgap reference via M32.

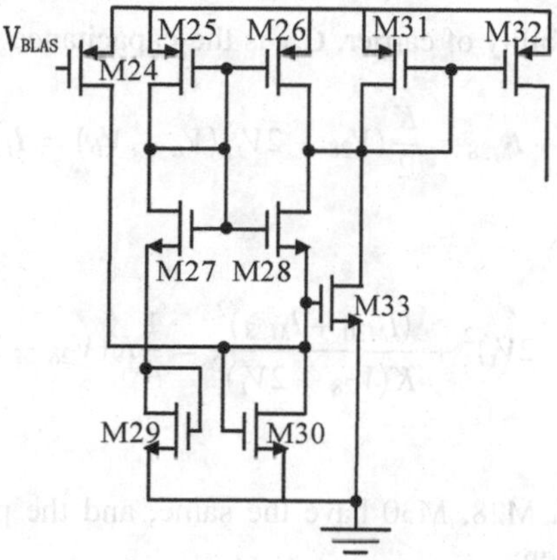

Fig. 2. I_{PTAT}^2 second-order temperature compensation circuit

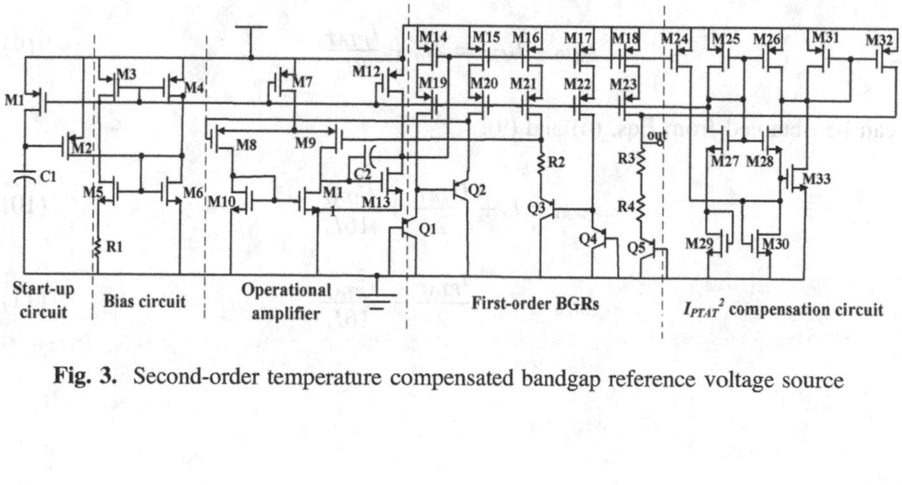

Fig. 3. Second-order temperature compensated bandgap reference voltage source

Analyzed in Fig. 3, V_{BLAS} is the bias voltage of the second-order compensation circuit, which is the output voltage of the operational amplifier. Set the aspect ratio of M25 and M26 to work in the saturation area, the width/length ratio of the pipe M26 is twice that of M25, so the current flowing through M26 is twice that of M25. If the circuit of M25 is, then the current of M26 is $2I_a$. Let $V_{GS28} = V_b$, $V_{GS30} = V_a$, $V_{28} = V_a + V_b$, Set M28 to have the same aspect ratio as M30. It is assumed that all MOS tubes work in the saturated zone and the back gate effect is ignored. If the open voltage of M28 and M30 is set as V_t, it can be obtained through analysis:

$$I_{M28} = \frac{K}{2}(V_b - V_t)^2 \tag{4}$$

$$I_{M30} = \frac{K}{2}(V_a - V_t)^2 \tag{5}$$

$K = \mu_n C_{ox}$, μ_n is the mobility of carrier, C_{ox} is the capacitance of gate oxide layer, so:

$$I_{M30} - I_{M28} = \frac{K}{2}(V_{28} - 2V_t)(V_a - V_b) = I_{PTAT} \tag{6}$$

Then, it can be obtained:

$$I_{M30} + I_{M28} = \frac{1}{4}K(V_{28} - 2V_t)^2 + \frac{(I_{M30} + I_{M28})^2}{K(V_{28} - 2V_t)^2} = \frac{1}{4}K(V_{28} - 2V)^2 + \frac{I_{PTAT}^2}{K(V_{28} - 2V_t)^2} \tag{7}$$

Suppose M27, M29 and M28, M30 have the same, and the parameters of M27 and M29 match perfectly, then:

$$\frac{1}{4}K(V_{28} - V_t)^2 = 2I_a \tag{8}$$

$$I_{M30} + I_{M28} = 2I_a + \frac{I_{PTAT}^2}{8I_a} \tag{9}$$

It can be obtained from Eqs. (6) and (9):

$$I_{M30} = I_a + \frac{I_{PTAT}}{2} + \frac{I_{PTAT}^2}{16I_a} \tag{10}$$

$$I_{M28} = I_a - \frac{I_{PTAT}}{2} + \frac{I_{PTAT}^2}{16I_a} \tag{11}$$

Set the aspect ratio of M33 equal to M30, then:

$$I_{M33} = I_{M30} = I_{\mathrm{a}} + \frac{I_{PTAT}}{2} + \frac{I_{PTAT}^2}{16I_{\mathrm{a}}} \tag{12}$$

Suppose the aspect ratios of M31 and M32 is A, simultaneous Eqs. (10) and (12), the current flowing through M32 can be expressed as:

$$I_{M32} = AI_{31} = I_{M33} + I_{M28} - I_{M26} = A\frac{I_{PTAT}^2}{8I_a} = KI_{PTAT}^2 \tag{13}$$

Among them $K = \frac{A}{8I_a}$, in order to make the tube work in the right area, it need $I_{M28} \geq 0$, so we can be obtained from formula (13). The leakage current of M32 is in a second-order positive temperature relationship, herefore, in the case that all the MOS tubes of this circuit are working in the saturated zone, the aspect ratios of M31 and M32 can be adjusted and set I_a to adjust the leakage current of M32. Finally, the current is introduced to the output end. Finally, the temperature coefficient of the output voltage of the bandgap reference source is corrected.

Analyzed by Fig. 3, this second order temperature compensation reference voltage is including starting circuit, biasing circuit, operational amplifier. Startingup circuit: when it power on, the voltage of C1 can't change suddenly, it amount to break, the grid voltage's absolute value of M2 is power voltage, M2 breakover, the output current will break the original balance of the bias circuit, and get rid of degeneracy point, the circuit starts working normally. Then the power supply began to charge C1, when the voltage of C1 rises to a certain point, the M2 tube stops working, the reference voltage source circuit starts working normally, the starting circuit is off. Biasing circuit: M3 and M4 are constituting the PMOS current mirror, copy the offset current to M7 and M12, provides offset current for two-stage operational amplifiers. M8 and M9 are differential input stage, their grid electrodes are connected to a first-order compensation circuit to clamp the voltage on a bipolar transistor. M10 and M11 are constitute the NMOS current mirror, and Copy the generated current to the output. M7's gird connects biasing circuit, provide stable bias current for the entire operational amplifier. Output stage is constituting by M12 and M13, M13 is common-source amplifier, M12 is output load of the second stage, and also provide the constant current for M13. Miller's capacitor C2 compensates the frequency of the operational amplifier circuit, to prevent the output shock when it works.

4 Simulation Results and Comparison

The design of all the circuits was completed by 0.18 μm standard COMS technology. The simulation of the whole circuit was performed by using Spectre tool. Under the 1.8 V power supply voltage process, the power consumption of the whole circuit was

287.2 μW. At −25 °C–125 °C temperature range, temperature coefficient of the first-order compensation is 9.7 ppm/°C, the power rejection ratio at low frequency is −33.29 dB; Temperature coefficient of the second order compensation is 4.5 PPM/°C, the low frequency power supply rejection ratio reaches 45.63 dB, It is shown that the temperature coefficient and power rejection ratio of the first order bandgap reference are improved obviously after the second order compensation, performance is enhanced. The simulation results are respectively shown in Figs. 4, 5, 6 and 7.

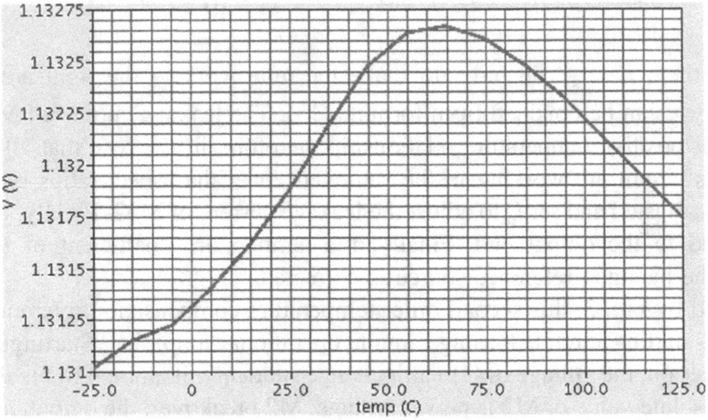

Fig. 4. The first-order compensated BGR voltage versus temperature

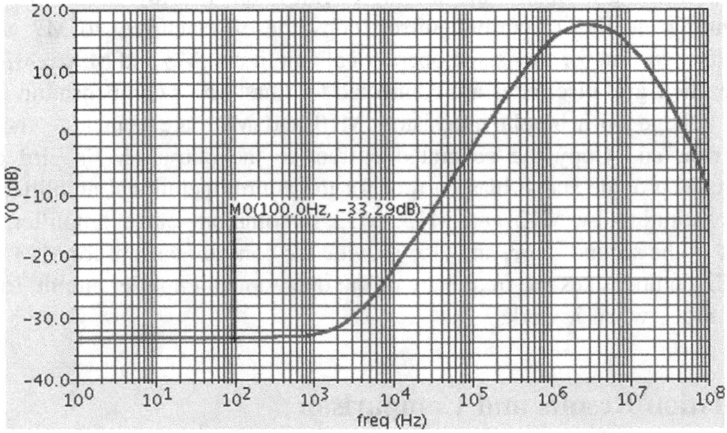

Fig. 5. The PSRR of first-order compensated BGR

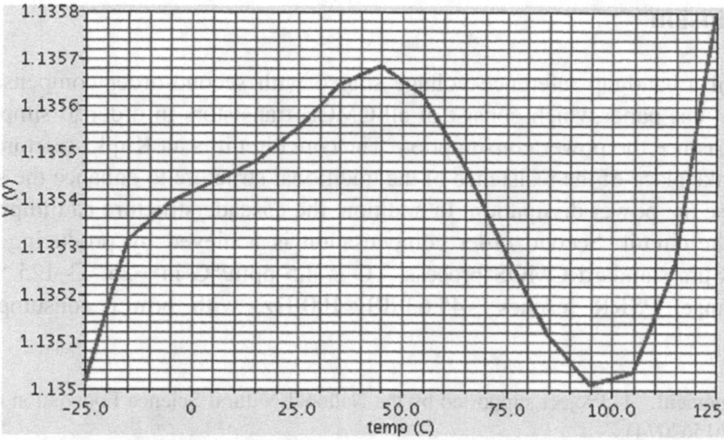

Fig. 6. The second-order compensated BGR voltage versus temperature

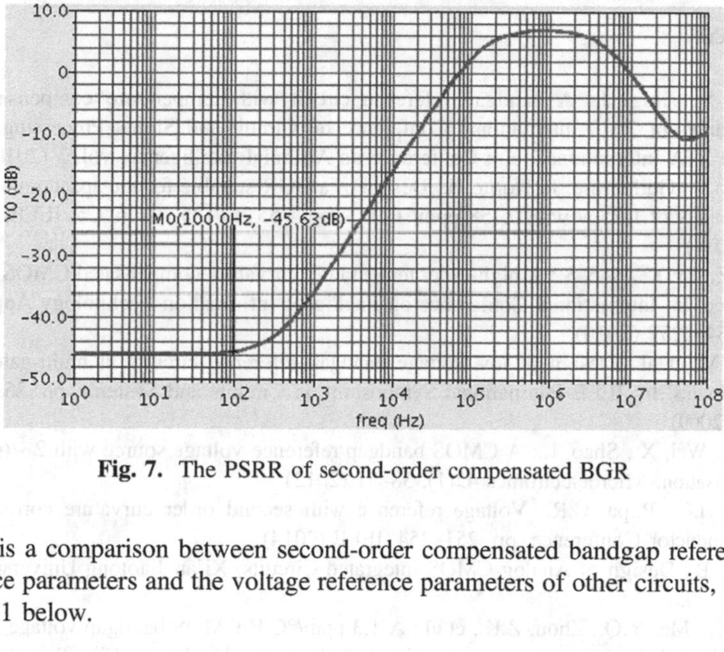

Fig. 7. The PSRR of second-order compensated BGR

This is a comparison between second-order compensated bandgap reference voltage source parameters and the voltage reference parameters of other circuits, as shown in Table 1 below.

Table 1. Comparison of reported second-order compensated BGR

	This work	The literature [5]	The literature [10]	The literature [11]
Process	0.18 μm, CMOS	0.5 μm, CMOS	0.13 μm, CMOS	0.5 μm, CMOS
Temperature range (°C)	−25–125	−50–125	−40–125	−30–130
The power supply voltage	1.2 V–1.8 V	1.24 V–5 V	3 V–3.6 V	2.4 V–5 V
Power consumption	287.2 μW	860 μW	370.37 μW	62.28 μW
Temperature coefficient (ppm/°C)	4.5	14.2	6.2	3.4
PSRR@100 Hz	−45.63 dB	−86.3 dB	−85.4 dB	−43 dB

5 Conclusion

A design of a bandgap reference voltage source with second-order compensation is proposed in this paper,which consist of all-CMOS transistors in order to simplify the circuit and reduce the power consumption. The core circuit is an Kujik structure, using PMOS to take place of the resistance of the traditional structure to enhance the stability and decrease the power dissipation. In addition, the cascade structure can improve the PSRR of the circuit. Second order compensation is achieved by producing I_{PTAT2}. Using 0.18 μm standard CMOS process, TC is 4.5 ppm/°C in −25 °C–125 °C temperature range. PSRR reaches −45.63 dB@100 Hz, with power consumption is 287.2 μW.

Acknowledgement. 1. Project supported by the National Natural Science Foundation of China (Grant No. 61562074).

2. Project supported by the Guangxi University Science and Technology Research Project (Grant No. KY2015ZD123).

References

1. Wang, S., Xing, J.: A bandgap reference circuit with temperature compensation. In: Proceedings of 2010 International Conference on Circuit and Signal Processing & 2010 Second IITA International Joint Conference on Artificial Intelligence, vol. 3 (2010)
2. Calvillo, J., Guilherme, J., Horta, N.: Design of a BGR suitable for the space industry with performance of 1.25 V with 0.758 ppm/°C TC from - 55° to 125 °C. In: Cas IEEE, pp. 197–200 (2017)
3. Peng, Z., Lv, C., She, S.: A high-order temperature curvature compensated CMOS bandgap reference. In: International Conference on Intelligent Information Technology Application, pp. 2254–2257 (2010)
4. Fulde, M, et al.: Design of low-voltage bandgap reference circuits in multi-gate CMOS technologies. In: IEEE International Symposium on Circuits and Systems, pp. 2537–2540. IEEE (2009)
5. Liu, Y., Wei, X., Shao, L.: A CMOS bandgap reference voltage source with 2∼(nd)-order compensation. Microelectronics **42**(1), 38–41 (2012)
6. Necula, I.C., Popa, C.R.: Voltage reference with second order curvature correction. In: Semiconductor Conference, pp. 251–254. IEEE (2014)
7. Razavi, B.: Design of Analog CMOS integrated Circuits. Xi'an Jiaotong University Press, Xi'an (2003)
8. Ming, X., Ma, Y.Q., Zhou, Z.K., et al.: A 1.3 ppm/°C BiCMOS bandgap voltage reference using piecewise-exponential compensation technique. Analog Integr. Circ. Sig. Process. **66** (2), 171–176 (2011)
9. He, L., Wang, Y.: Analog integrated circuit design and simulation. Beijing: Science Press (2008)
10. Zhuo, M., Xiaoqiang, T., Lunguo, X., et al.: A curvature calibrated bandgap reference with base-emitter current compensating in a 0.13 μm CMOS process. J. Semicond. **31**(11), 82–87 (2010)
11. Yu, J.H., Dong, C.C.: A new design of CMOS bandgap reference based on genetic algorithm. Adv. Mater. Res. **712–715**, 1780–1786 (2013)

Coverage of Hotspot Region with Small Satellite Constellation Design and Optimization

Anlin Xu[1], Xiaoen Feng[2(✉)], Yuqing Li[2], Huaifeng Li[3], and Donglei He[3]

[1] Beijing Institute of Tracking and Telecommunications Technology, Beijing 100094, China

[2] Deep Space Exploration Research Center, Harbin Institute of Technology, Harbin 150001, China

fengxiaoen0923@163.com

[3] Institute of Spacecraft System Engineering, Beijing 100094, China

Abstract. In the face of increasingly frequent regional emergency missions, the use of small satellites to obtain spatial information in hotspots has important practical needs. Under the premise of avoiding the short coverage of single satellites and limited access to information, this paper aims at research on the design and optimization of multi-satellite network orbits covered by hotspots regions. Firstly, based on the analysis of satellite coverage characteristics, the satellite coverage model is established, and the coverage calculation and coverage judgment conditions are discussed. Then a genetic algorithm based regional coverage satellite network design and optimization algorithm is proposed, which is designed the coding method, algorithm flow and corresponding constraint test rules in detail. The rationality, feasibility and effectiveness of the algorithm are finally verified by simulation examples. are provided, which provides a useful reference for regional space missions and its certain theoretical significance.

Keywords: Space-to-earth observation · Regional coverage · Orbit design · Network design · Genetic algorithm

1 Introduction

In recent years, the development of space technology, especially the rapid advancement and application of small satellite technology, has provided fast and timely information support for people to cope with and solve regional emergency space missions, such as war conflicts in hot sensitive areas and sudden major natural disasters [1]. Compared with traditional spacecraft, which mainly performs global tasks, large mass, high cost, long design life and long launch period, small satellites can be launched on demand, light in weight, low in cost, short in development time, and relatively simple maintenance on carriers and ground. Therefore, these are more suitable for deployment in low-Earth orbit to complete specific tasks for regional targets [2]. So the research on the design and optimization of small satellite network coverage for regional targets has urgent practical significance and is also the focus of scholars at home and abroad.

M. Jia et al. (Eds.): WiSATS 2019, LNICST 281, pp. 109–119, 2019.
https://doi.org/10.1007/978-3-030-19156-6_11

Chao [3] based on an improved grid point simulation method, proposed a corresponding coverage performance index calculation method; Larrimore [4] analyzed the advantages of the constellation of inclined orbit in covering local areas, and designed the pair. The ground area realizes continuous coverage of the oblique orbit satellite constellation; Weng [5] studied the mathematical model of satellite ground cover, constraints and decision algorithms; Vtipil [6] comprehensively compared the existing three repeated ground track designs. In his paper, an initial optimization method for quickly determining the initial value of the solution is proposed, and then the improved optimization design method is proposed. The advantages of the method in solving accuracy and calculation time are also analyzed.

Based on the research results at home and abroad, the current satellite orbit design has not been related to regional coverage tasks, especially the coverage of hotspots, and it is difficult to achieve better regional coverage. Therefore, in the design of satellite orbits, it is necessary to carry out research on coverage characteristics of regional targets and orbital design research for regional coverage, with a focus on improving spatial information acquisition capabilities for regional targets.

In this regard, this paper takes the spatial information support of hotspots as the research background, and studies the design and optimization of small satellite networks for hotspot regional targets, focusing on satellite coverage characteristics analysis, satellite network orbit design and optimization. Based on the analysis of satellite coverage characteristics, the regional complete coverage judgment method is established, and the satellite-to-ground coverage model is established. Also a genetic algorithm-based regional coverage satellite network orbit optimization method is proposed. The simulation method is used to verify the method, proving that it is feasible and effective to cover satellite network optimization calculations for hotspots.

2 Satellite Grounding Characteristics Analysis and Modeling

To study the satellite coverage problem, we must first understand the coverage characteristics of the satellite. Coverage performance metrics are the basic requirement that must be addressed in track design. In this paper, based on the spatial geometric constraint relationship between satellite and ground, the satellite-to-ground coverage model is established, and the coverage performance index is proposed. The coverage analysis is carried out and the coverage judgment conditions are proposed to provide reference for the subsequent orbit design.

2.1 Coverage Problem Description

When the satellite performs the Earth observation mission, it generally carries the sensor as a payload to observe the ground target. The satellite observation area is a cone field of view, and the ground coverage area is a circular area centered on the star point. When entering the coverage area, it means that the satellite can cover the ground target. The satellite sensor sweeps across the surface of the Earth as shown in Fig. 1, which is a strip-like area.

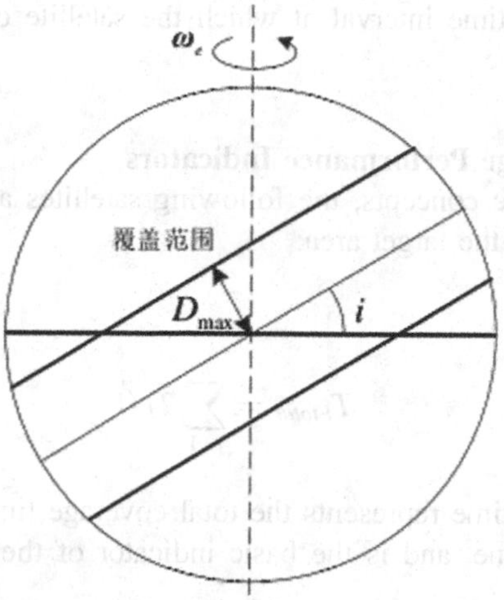

Fig. 1. Schematic diagram of satellite coverage

2.2 Ground Coverage Performance Indicators

The satellite coverage characteristics are an important basis for the satellite to complete related tasks. It is mainly determined by the orbit parameters of the satellite, the performance of the satellite platform itself, and the sensor performance. The satellite coverage characteristics mainly include basic performance indicators and evaluation indicators.

2.2.1 Ground Coverage Performance Indicators

Set in the simulation time T, the satellite covers the target n times. When the target is covered for the i-th time, the coverage start time is $t_{start}(i)$, and the coverage end time is $t_{stop}(i)$. The following coverage performance basic indicators are defined in this design:

(1) Single coverage time

$$T_F(i) = t_{stop}(i) - t_{start}(i)$$

$T_F(i)$ Indicates the duration of a single coverage, in seconds.

(2) Interval

$$T_G(i) = t_{start}(i+1) - t_{stop}(i)$$

$T_G(i)$ Indicates the interval between the start of the i + 1th overlay and the end of the i-th overlay.

(3) Revisiting time

$$T_C(i) = t_{start}(i+1) - t_{start}(i)$$

$T_C(i)$ Indicates the time interval at which the satellite continuously covers the target start time twice.

2.2.2 Ground Coverage Performance Indicators

Based on the above basic concepts, the following satellites are used to evaluate the coverage performance of the target area:

(1) Total coverage time

$$T_{Ftotal} = \sum_{i=1}^{n} T_F(i)$$

The total coverage time represents the total coverage time of the satellite to the target in a given time, and is the basic indicator of the satellite coverage time characteristics.

(2) Average coverage time

$$T_{Fmean} = \frac{1}{n} T_{Ftotal}$$

The average coverage time is the average of each coverage time, which represents the average of the satellite's single-to-ground coverage time, and the average level of satellite-to-ground coverage.

(3) Maximum coverage time

$$T_{F\max} = \max\{T_F(i)\}$$

The maximum coverage time is the maximum of a single coverage time, reflecting the ability of the satellite to cover the ground. The larger the maximum coverage time, the more sufficient the coverage time is, and the more favorable it is to complete the reconnaissance observation and other tasks.

(4) Minimum coverage time

$$T_{F\min} = \min\{T_F(i)\}$$

The minimum coverage time is the minimum of a single coverage time, reflecting the worst case scenario of satellite coverage. The smaller the minimum coverage time, the shorter the coverage time, and the more difficult it is to complete the reconnaissance observation of the target.

(5) Average revisit time

$$T_{Cmean} = \frac{1}{n} \sum_{i=1}^{n} T_c(i)$$

The average revisit time is the average of the satellite's single revisit time, indicating the ability of the satellite to continuously cover the ground. The smaller the average revisit time, the stronger the ability of the satellite to continuously cover the ground.

For regional targets, it is also necessary to consider the relevant time characteristics of a complete coverage. Suppose that in the kth complete coverage, the definition of the coverage start time is, and the end time is, then the following time coverage characteristic indicators are proposed:

(6) Time required for complete coverage of the area

$$T_{stop}(k) - T_{start}(k)$$

(7) Regional full coverage revisit time

$$T_{start}(k+1) - T_{stop}(k)$$

The spatial coverage characteristic mainly refers to the distance between the satellite and the target when the satellite covers the ground target. Since the target is not necessarily in the orbital plane every time the satellite covers the target, even if the target is in the orbital plane, the satellite is not always above the target, so the distance from the satellite to the target is generally greater than the orbital altitude of the satellite. For satellites with orbital parameters and sensor parameters, the distance between the satellite and the ground target will affect the resolution of the satellite to the target, and the resolution is an important performance parameter of the remote sensing satellite. The spatial coverage characteristics mainly include: the average distance between the satellite and the target; the maximum distance between the satellite and the target; the minimum distance between the satellite and the target.

2.3 Coverage Calculation Process

Set the S′ latitude and longitude of the satellite star point at a certain time (λ_s, φ_s), the latitude and longitude of the target point (λ_0, φ_0), and calculate the geocentric angle of the target point and the sub-satellite point ψ. If so $\psi < \beta$, the target is in the instantaneous coverage area of the spacecraft, otherwise, it is not in the coverage area. If the initial time t_0 is given, the appropriate step size Δt is selected. By judging whether the target is within the satellite coverage area after each step of time advancement, the start time t_1 and the end time t_2 of the satellite coverage target can be obtained, and the difference T_F between the two can be obtained. The coverage time of the satellite to the target. The specific judgment process is shown in Fig. 2.

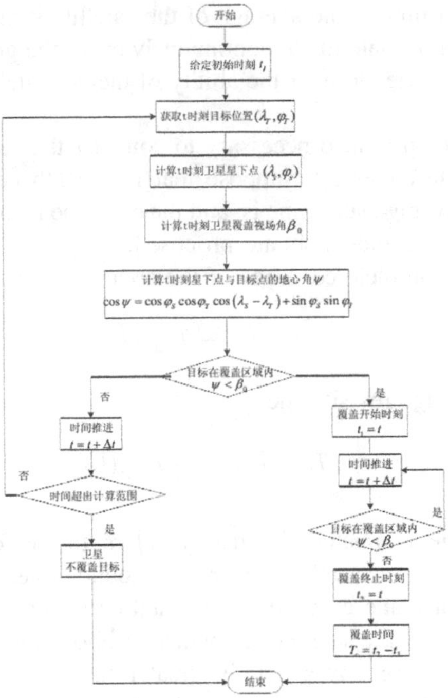

Fig. 2. Calculation process of the coverage time of the ground

3 Design and Optimization of Satellite Area Coverage Network Based on Genetic Algorithm

The problem of regional coverage satellite network optimization is a multi-parameter optimization problem under complex constraints [7]. The problem is to meet the requirements of coverage, coverage time performance and space performance under the premise of system tasks. Excellent networking parameters.

3.1 Network Track Design Optimization Variables

For the hot spot coverage observation problem, the satellite orbital height, orbital inclination, ascending node and the near-earth angle can affect the coverage performance of the network orbit to a certain extent. Therefore, in the orbit optimization process, the orbital parameters of each satellite in the networking system, namely the orbital height, the orbital inclination, the ascending point, the ascension, the initial latitude and the angle, are used as design variables, respectively a_j, i_j, Ω_j, u_j ($1 \leq j \leq n$, n is the number of satellites) said. Since the system cost determines the number of satellites in the constellation, the satellite number n is not used as an optimization variable.

3.2 Regional Coverage Network Optimization Mathematical Model

The regional coverage network optimization problem in this paper refers to the reasonable selection of the orbit parameters and networking parameters of the networked satellites in the case of the number of satellites required for a given network, the orbital type of the satellite, and the geographic location of the network coverage target, to achieve the best possible coverage performance of the constellation formed by the networking.

3.2.1 Constraints

The following constraints must be met during the satellite network coverage optimization process:

(1) In order for the satellite to achieve continuous coverage of the target, the satellite orbital inclination i is constrained by the target latitude φ:

$$\varphi \leq i \leq \varphi + 5^{\circ}$$

(2) The orbital planes in the constellation are arranged in order:

$$0^{\circ} \leq \Omega_1 < \Omega_2 < \cdots < \Omega_n < 360^{\circ}$$

(3) Need to meet the lighting conditions, the sun's elevation angle meets the constraints:

$$\delta \geq 5^{\circ}$$

3.2.2 Optimization Objectives

Considering that the average revisiting time can affect the satellite's ability to quickly revisit the target to a certain extent, generally, the shorter the average revisiting time, the stronger the satellite's ability to quickly revisit the target, so the average revisiting time is minimized to optimize. The target, its mathematical expression is as follows (2–5).

$$Q_2 = \min\left(\frac{\sum_{i=1}^{n} InT_i}{n}\right)$$

Where InT_i is the interval between two observations of the satellite adjacent to the target area.

3.3 Genetic Algorithm Based on Continuous Optimization Variables

Genetic algorithms (GA) are a kind of random search algorithm based on biological evolution mechanism. The main steps are as follows:

(1) Encoding method. The orbital parameters of each satellite in the network system, namely the orbital height, the orbital inclination, the ascending node and the initial

latitude, are expressed as a_k, i_k, Ω_k, u_k ($1 \le k \le n$, n is the number of satellites). A pool of population genes with a population of m can be expressed as:

$$\left.\begin{array}{c} a_{11}, i_{11}, \Omega_{11}, u_{11}, a_{12}, i_{12}, \Omega_{12}, u_{12}, \cdots a_{1n}, i_{1n}, \Omega_{1n}, u_{1n} \\ a_{21}, i_{21}, \Omega_{21}, u_{21}, a_{22}, i_{22}, \Omega_{22}, u_{22}, \cdots a_{2n}, i_{2n}, \Omega_{2n}, u_{2n} \\ \vdots \\ a_{m1}, i_{m1}, \Omega_{m1}, u_{m1}, a_{m2}, i_{m2}, \Omega_{m2}, u_{m2}, \cdots a_{mn}, i_{mn}, \Omega_{mn}, u_{mn} \end{array}\right\} m$$

(2) The initial population is randomly generated. This paper uses a random method to generate chromosome strings from the initial population.
(3) Evaluation of fitness value. This paper directly uses the objective function in Sect. 2.2.2 as the fitness function.
(4) Genetic operators, including selection operators, crossover operators, and mutation operators. For the selection operator, the higher the fitness function value, the higher the probability of being selected to pass to the next generation; using the single-point crossover operator, that is, arbitrarily selecting two individuals after the selection operator operation, randomly generating a cross Point position, the two-part gene code with the intersection point as the boundary is exchanged to form two new sub-individual replacement individuals; the basic bit mutation operator is used to realize the probability replacement of the gene code, and provide opportunities for the generation of new individuals to maintain the diversity of the population.
(5) Termination conditions. The search is terminated when the genetic algebra is greater than a certain set algebra or the fitness value of the current population is less than the fitness limit. The chromosome with the greatest fitness after termination of the search is an approximate optimal solution, and the networking parameters are obtained by decoding the chromosome to determine the optimal networking scheme.

4 Simulation Examples and Analysis

4.1 Simulation Environment and Conditions

In the test simulation, all algorithms and programs are implemented with MATLABR2012a programming software. The target and satellite model establishment and time window calculation are all implemented by STK9.2 simulation software (Fig. 3).

Fig. 3. GUI operation diagram

4.2 Analysis of Simulation Results

The number of satellites is set to one to four, the orbital inclination angle range is (20°, 30°), and the orbital height range is (500 km, 1000 km). The range of the ascending node and the initial latitude of the satellite in the constellation are both varied in (1°, 360°). The optimized orbital parameter values are shown in Table 1. The relationship between the average revisit time optimization result and the number of satellites is shown in Fig. 4.

Table 1. Optimize the orbit parameters and optimization results.

Number of satellites	Orbital height/km	Orbital inclination/deg	Ascending node right ascension/deg	Initial latitude angle/deg	Average revisit time/s
1	6960.24384	23.8432884	332.6851722	101.0735087	9782.17271
2	6918.79902	20.4639945	339.5476814	94.78888381	6448.15512
	6909.52367	20.1011046	291.7468287	71.36647551	
3	6960.56384	23.8413242	332.6553142	102.0735087	4252.26223
	6938.05164	21.1285090	184.3200334	37.31650155	
	6950.81939	23.6590556	332.6875425	316.0013522	
4	6960.24272	23.8767674	333.7576766	101.8524243	3025.15413
	6909.52243	20.1243893	291.7689667	71.27389724	
	6938.05776	21.7676676	184.3376764	37.85675242	
	6950.82339	23.6572722	332.6727865	316.0212352	

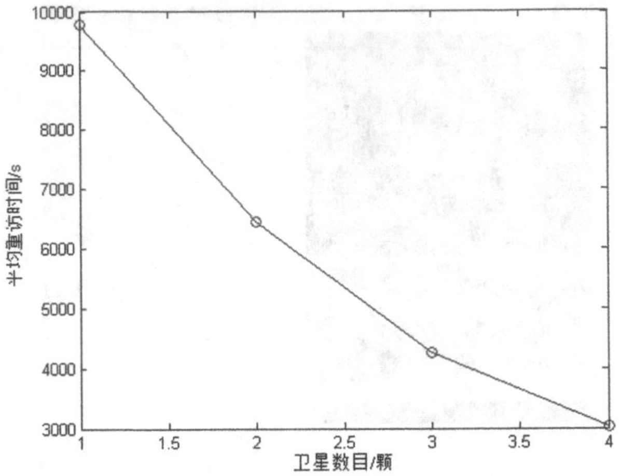

Fig. 4. Relationship between the average revisit time and the number of satellites

As can be seen from the above figure, the number of satellites has increased from 1 to 3, and the rate of decline is relatively fast, 3 to 4, and the average revisiting time has slowed down significantly. Since then, increasing the number of satellites will lead to an increase in system cost line type. However, coverage performance optimization benefits are reduced, so consider using four satellites to form a networking solution.

On the other hand, from the coverage of the target area, the optimization results obtained under the respective satellite numbers are brought into the STK for simulation verification, and the regional coverage results are shown in Table 2.

Table 2. Relationship between coverage of target area and number of satellites.

Number of satellites	Target area coverage
1	64.43%
2	100%
3	100%
4	100%

It can be seen from the above table that by increasing the number of satellites, the average revisit time of the satellite to the target area is shortened, and the coverage of the target area can be improved. When the number of satellites reaches two, full coverage of the target area can be achieved within the simulation period, and the number of satellites continues to increase, and only the average revisit time is shortened.

5 Conclusion

In this paper, based on the design and optimization of small satellite network for hotspot target, a genetic algorithm based design and optimization method for regional coverage satellite network orbit is proposed: (1) Based on the analysis of satellite coverage characteristics, a satellite coverage model is established. This model gives the satellite coverage performance index including time characteristics and spatial characteristics, and discusses coverage calculation and coverage judgment conditions. (2) Research on satellite orbit design and optimization for area coverage is launched, and this paper proposes a genetic algorithm which covers the satellite network design and optimization algorithm. Also the algorithm flow and corresponding constraint checking rules are designed in detail. (3) The rationality, feasibility and effectiveness of the algorithm are verified by simulation examples, which provides a useful solution reference and technical ideas for regional space mission.

References

1. Sandau, R.: Status and trends of small satellite missions for Earth observation. Acta Astronaut. **66**, 1–12 (2010)
2. Doyne, T., Wegner, P., Riddle, R.: A TacSat and ORS update including TacSat-4. In: 4th Responsive Space Conference. Los Angeles, CA (2006)
3. Chao, H., Li, D., Jia, X.: Improved grid simulation for constellation coverage performance evalution. Comput. Simul. **22**(12), 21–23, 56 (2005)
4. Larrimore, S.C.: Partially continuous earth coverage from a responsive space constellation. In: 5th Responsive Space Conference. Los Angeles, CA (2007)
5. Weng, H.: Ground coverage analysis and simulation of remote. Information Engineering University (2006)
6. Vtipil, S.D., Newman, B.: Determining an earth observation repeat-ground-track orbit for an optimization methodology. J. Spacecr. Rocket. **49**(1), 157–164 (2012)
7. Yu, X., Ding, Y.: Application of genetic algorithms to structural optimization with mixed continuous/discrete design variables. J. Nanjing Univ. Aeronaut. Astronaut. **05**, 564–568 (1999)

Design of a 200-nW 0.8-V Voltage Reference Circuit in All-CMOS Technology

Jianhai Yu(✉) and Hui Guo

Wuzhou University, Wuzhou 543002, China
40802622@qq.com

Abstract. Based on the negative temperature characteristics of threshold voltage and positive temperature characteristics of a multiple of thermal voltage, adding them with proper weight coefficient A voltage reference circuit was proposed with a zero temperature coefficient (TC). The device consists of pure MOSFET operated in subthreshold region and uses no resistors and bipolar transistors. The triple-branch current reference structure is adopted for independence of supply voltage instead of cascade structure and embedded operational amplifier structure with the merit of chip area and power consumption. Simulation results showed that based on standard CMOS 0.18 um process, the circuit can operate at 0.75 V supply voltage with the output voltage only 563 mV. The TC of the voltage was 17.5 ppm/°C in a range from −40 °C–125 °C. The line sensitivity was 569.5 ppm/V in a supply voltage range of 1.2 V–1.8 V, and the power supply rejection ratio (PSRR) was 66.5 dB at 100 Hz. The power dissipation was only 187.4 nW.

Keywords: Low power · All-CMOS · Subthreshold · Current reference

1 Introduction

Voltage reference and current reference are the important part in analog and mixed signal integrated circuits, e.g. sensors, portable mobile devices and biomedical chip [1]. It can provide reference for other blocks so its characteristics directly affect the performance of all the system [2]. Traditional bandgap reference (BGR) circuit [3, 4] got the zero TC by weighting the negative temperature characteristics of base-emitter voltage of NPN bipolar transistor and positive temperature characteristics of thermal voltage [5], which produces a voltage that is basically independent of power supply voltage, process and temperature [6]. While the traditional circuit invoked operation amplifier structure or cascade structure to stabilize the voltage for improving the PSRR with the drawback of power dissipation and chip area, and also the noise and speed of the op-amp can affect the output voltage [7].

To solve above problems, a low power voltage reference circuit is proposed in this paper with all the MOSFETs working in the subthreshold region. To provide bias for the voltage reference a triple-branch current reference is developed with high PSRR. The circuit consists of all-CMOS devices without resistors and bipolar transistors so as to save the chip area and power consumption. Simulation results shows the benefits of the circuit.

M. Jia et al. (Eds.): WiSATS 2019, LNICST 281, pp. 120–130, 2019.
https://doi.org/10.1007/978-3-030-19156-6_12

2 A Traditional Current Source

A typical circuit for generating the bias current independent of the power voltage is shown in Fig. 1 [7]. When the circuit is powered on, M5 provides the access from VDD to the ground through M3 and M1. The M5 can be turned off after the circuit was started up in order to avoid degenerate on the condition that $V_{TH1} + V_{TH5} + |V_{TH3}| < V_{DD}$ and $V_{GS1} + V_{TH5} + |V_{GS3}| > V_{DD}$. The output current of the circuit can be expressed as

$$I_2 = \frac{2}{u_n C_{ox} (\mathrm{W/L})_n} \frac{1}{R_S} \left(1 - \frac{1}{\sqrt{K}}\right)^2 \tag{1}$$

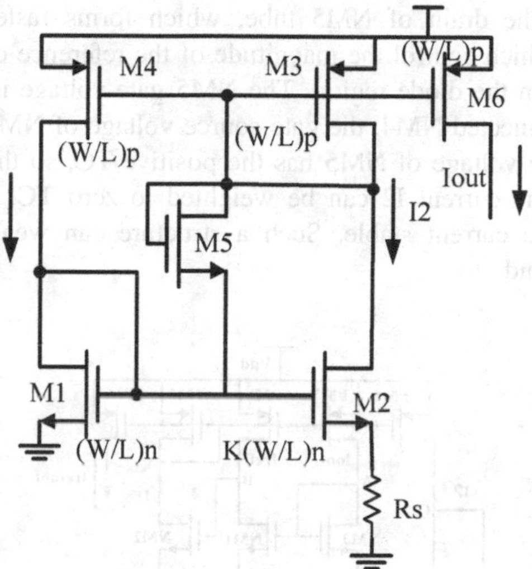

Fig. 1. Traditional supply voltage independent current source

Thus the reference current independent of the supply voltage is produced. In this block, with the fluctuating of power supply voltage, the drain voltages of M1 and M2 will change in opposite direction. So the transistors M3, M4, M1 and M2 constitute a positive feedback, and resistor Rs acts as the negative feedback of the circuit. On the whole this circuit presents a weak positive feedback loop, so the PSRR of the block will be relatively poor. In order to weaken the sensitivity of the reference current to the power supply voltage, a triple-branch current reference structure was proposed in literature [8] and [9], which constitute a negative feedback loop. In this circuit resistors was used to control the bias current, so the silicon area would be increased in order to get nanoampere current. In standard CMOS technology, not only the resistor model may be unavailable or unreliable, but also the resistors increase susceptibility of the reference to substrate noise coupling [10].

3 Improved Triple-Branch Current Reference

A novel current reference circuit which can increase the PSRR and weaken the sensitivity of the temperature is shown in Fig. 2. The triple-branch structure was adopted and the negative feedback loop was formed to restrain the variation of the power supply. When the power supply voltage V_{DD} increases, the voltage V_X decreases at the same time, and the voltage V_B increases under the operation of NM2 as common-source amplifier. For the same reason, under the action of common-source NM1, the voltage of A point drops consequently. Thus, a negative feedback loop $V_X \rightarrow V_B \rightarrow V_A \rightarrow V_X$ is formed, so the PSRR of the circuit together with linear sensitivity are relatively high. When the voltage at X point increases, the current of *I1*, *I2*, *Iout*, *Iref* decreases, $V_Y = (I1 + I2 + Iout)R_{NM5} + (I1 + I2 + Iout + Iref)R_{NM6}$ the voltage at Y point decreases rapidly, which makes the voltage at X point drop rapidly. The source of NM2 is connected with the drain of NM5 tube, which forms faster negative feedback loop. The resistor which control the magnitude of the reference current is replaced by NM5 that operates in the diode region. The NM5 gate-voltage is biased by the drain voltage of diode-connected NM4, the gate-source voltage of NM4 has a negative TC, and the drain-source voltage of NM5 has the positive TC, so the voltage of point Q which determines the current I2 can be weighted to zero TC. NM6 is used as big resistor to make the current stable. Such a structure can weaken the influence of temperature in the end.

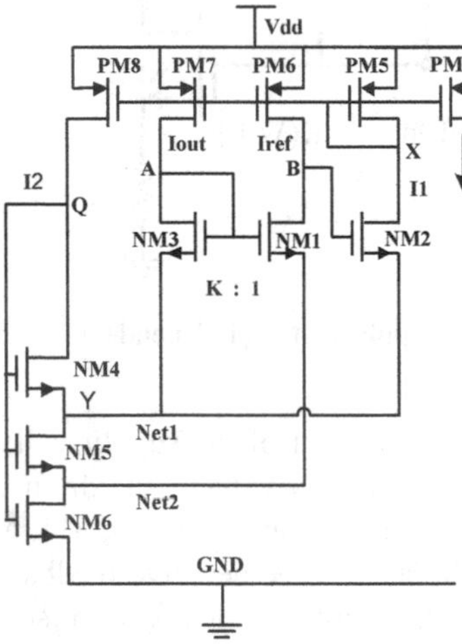

Fig. 2. Proposed current source subcircuit

In order to reduce the power consumption of the circuit, MOSFET is generally used to work in the subthreshold region in the nanoampere current reference. When $V_{GS} \approx V_{TH}$ or V_{GS} slightly smaller than V_{TH}, the current is expressed as follows [7]:

$$I_D = SI_0 \exp\left(\frac{V_{GS} - V_{TH}}{\zeta V_T}\right)\left[1 - \exp\left(-\frac{V_{DS}}{V_T}\right)\right] \tag{2}$$

S is the aspect ratio of the transistor, I_O is the characteristic current, ξ represents the subthreshold slope factor, C_{ox} is the gate-oxide capacitance, $V_T = KT/q$ is the thermal voltage, K is the Boltzmann constant, T is the absolute temperature, q is the elementary charge Vth is the threshold voltage of a MOSFET [11]. For $V_{DS} > 0.1$ V, current Id is almost independent of V_{DS} and given by

$$I_D = SI_0 \exp\left(\frac{V_{GS} - V_{TH}}{\xi V_T}\right) \tag{3}$$

NM1, NM2 and NM3 operate in the subthreshold region. According to the equation above, the current of NM1 and NM3 can be obtained:

$$I_{\text{out}} = S_{NM3} I_0 \exp\left(\frac{V_{GS,NM3} - V_{\text{th}}}{\zeta V_T}\right) \tag{4}$$

$$I_{\text{ref}} = S_{NM1} I_0 \exp\left(\frac{V_{GS,NM1} - V_{\text{th}}}{\zeta V_T}\right) \tag{5}$$

PM6 and PM7 constitute a pair of current mirror structures, PM6 and PM7 have the same size, so $I_{out} = I_{ref}$, the aspect ratios of NM3 is K times that of NM1, that is $S_{\text{NM3}} = KS_{NM1}$, we get the formula:

$$I_{out} = KS_{NM1} I_0 \exp\left(\frac{V_{GS,NM3} - V_{th}}{\zeta V_T}\right) \tag{6}$$

According to the formula (4) and (6) can be obtained:

$$\ln K = \frac{V_{GS,NM1} - V_{GS,NM3}}{\zeta V_T} = \frac{I_{\text{ref}} R_{NM5}}{\zeta V_T} \tag{7}$$

transistor NM5 operates in deep-triode region, so its resistance is given by

$$R_{NM5} = \frac{1}{S_{NM5} \mu C_{OX} (V_{GS,NM5} - V_{\text{th}})} \tag{8}$$

So the current reference can by written as

$$I_{\text{ref}} = \zeta V_T \ln(K) \bullet S_{NM5} \mu C_{OX} (V_{GS,NM5} - V_{\text{th}}) \tag{9}$$

It can be seen from the above equation the output current depends on the aspect ratio of NM5. The voltage of Q point is easy to change with the temperature, and the current of I2 will also change accordingly. It can be obtained I_{out}, the voltage I_{ref}

changes with the temperature. Only if the voltage at the Q point is stable, the current I_{ref} not change with the temperature be produced. According to the formula (6) and (7), we get:

$$I_{out} = I_{ref}\frac{S_{PM7}}{S_{PM6}} \tag{10}$$

$$V_{DS,NM5} = V_{net1} - V_{net2} = \xi V_T \ln\left(\frac{S_{NM3}}{S_{NM1}}\right) \tag{11}$$

$$V_Q = V_{GS4} + V_{DS,NM5} + V_{DS6} \tag{12}$$

$$V_Q = \xi V_T \ln\left(\frac{I_2}{S_{NM4}I_0}\right) + V_{th} + \xi V_T \ln\left(\frac{S_{NM3}}{S_{NM1}}\right) + V_{DS6} \tag{13}$$

$$V_Q = \xi V_T \ln\left(\frac{I_2 K}{S_{NM4}I_0}\right) + V_{th} + V_{DS6} \tag{14}$$

From Eq. (14) it can be seen that the first term is the multiple of the thermal voltage which has the positive TC, and the second term is the threshold voltage of MOSFET which has a negative TC. Properly weighting, the V_Q with zero TC can be derived, and the temperature effect on the reference current is weakened.

At the corner of ttssff, the output current varies versus supply voltage is shown in Fig. 3 and the temperature characteristic of output current is shown in Fig. 4. It can be seen that output current has slightly positive *TC*, and it can work normally when power supply is 0.75 V.

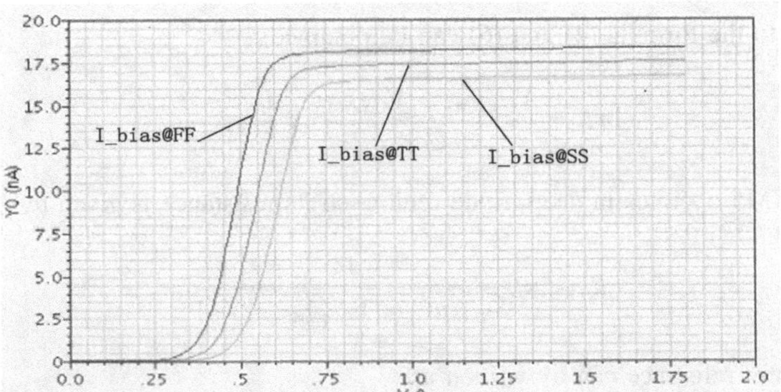

Fig. 3. Output current versus supply voltage under different corner

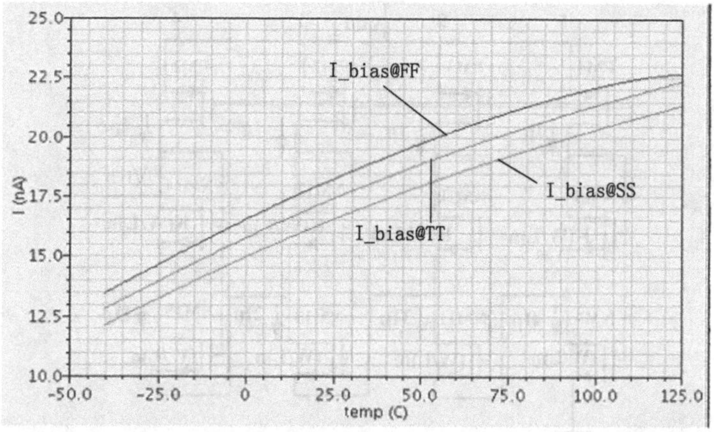

Fig. 4. Output current versus temperature under different corner

4 Voltage Reference Circuit

The bias voltage circuit is shown in Fig. 5. PM4, PM3, PM2, PM1 have the same aspect ratio and all work in saturation region in order to guarantee the same drain current (I_P) of them. It can be seen that the gate-source voltage (from V_{GS8} to V_{GS15}) of the transistors form a closed loop, and the current in M9, M11 and M13 are $4I_P$, $3I_P$ and $2I_P$ respectively. Therefore, we find that output voltage V_{REF} of the circuit is given by

$$V_{ref} = V_{GS9} - V_{GS8} + V_{GS11} - V_{GS10} + V_{GS13} - V_{GS12} + V_{GS15} \tag{15}$$

according to Eq. (3)

$$V_{GS} = V_{TH} + \xi V_T \ln\left(\frac{I_D}{SI_0}\right), \ (I_D = aIp) \tag{16}$$

And Eq. (15) can be rewritten as:

$$\begin{aligned} V_{ref} &= V_{GS9} + \xi V_T \ln\left(\frac{6S_8S_{10}S_{12}}{S_{11}S_{13}S_{15}}\right) = V_{GS9} + \xi V_T \ln\left(6K^3\right) \\ &= V_{TH} + \xi V_T \ln\left(\frac{4Ip}{S_9I_0}\right) + \xi V_T \ln\left(6K^3\right) \end{aligned} \tag{17}$$

where we assumed that the mismatch between the threshold voltage of the transistors can be ignored. Equation (17) shows that V_{REF} can be expressed as a sum of the gate-source voltage V_{GS9} and thermal voltage V_T scaled by the transistor sizes. Because V_{TH} has a negative *TC* and V_T has a positive *TC*, output voltage V_{REF} with a zero TC can be obtained by adjusting the size of the transistors.

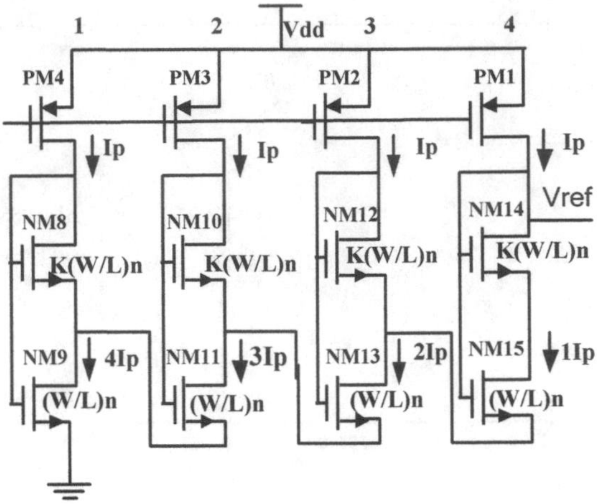

Fig. 5. The proposed zero TC voltage circuit

The entire circuit is illustrated in Fig. 6. It is composed of three blocks, which are start-up circuit, current source subcircuit and bias voltage subcircuit. A start-up circuit is used to avoid the stable state in the zero bias condition. When the power is on, PM10 works in the conducting state. *Iin* injects into the main circuit. At the same time, PM9 is on and MOS capacitor NM7 is charged, the voltage of PM10 gate increases gradually. At last PM10 cuts off and the start-up circuit separates from the main circuit.

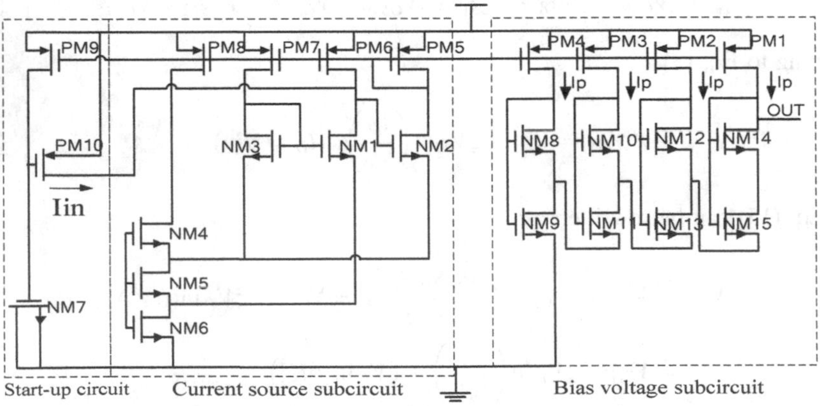

Fig. 6. The whole schematic of our voltage reference circuit

5 Simulation Results and Comparison

The performance of our proposed circuit is verified with the aid of SPECTRE simulation using a set of 0.18 um standard CMOS press with 1.8 V power supply.

The TC of output voltage under different corner are shown in Fig. 7 respectively. It can be seen under corner of FF, the TC is 48.88 ppm/°C, with the mean output voltage 506.242 mV; under the corner of TT, the TC is 17.25 ppm/°C, with the mean output voltage 564.39 mV; under the SS corner, the TC is 23.48 ppm/°C, with the output voltage 626.516 mV. It is easy to see that output voltage varies greatly with different corner. Because the threshold voltage changes evidently under different corner, and output voltage of proposed circuit under zero TC is equal to the threshold voltage of the MOSFET at 0 K temperature. So more accurate process should be used in order to achieve excellent reference.

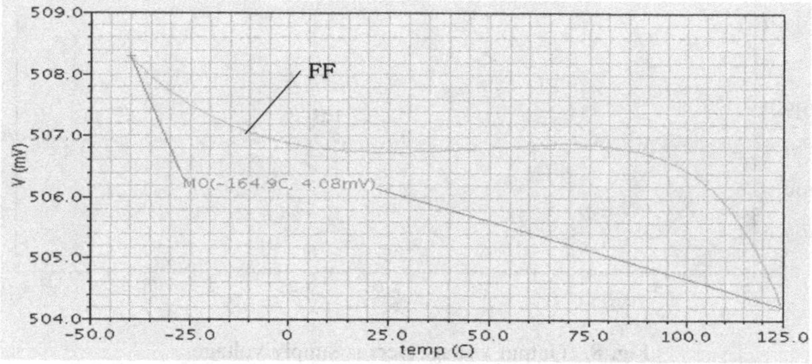

A FF corner

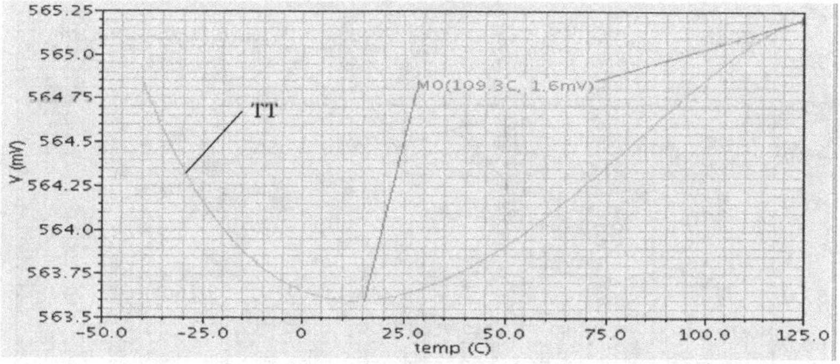

B TT corner

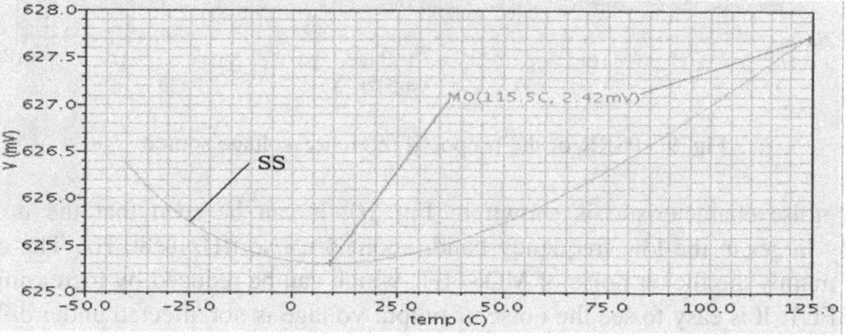

C SS corner

Fig. 7. Output voltage VREF as a function of temperature under various corner

The output voltage exhibits good power independence. Figure 8 shows output voltage V_{REF} at room temperature as a function of supply voltage under different corner. The circuit operates properly when supply voltage is higher than 0.75 V. The line sensitivity is 596.5 ppm/V in the power range of 1.2 V to 1.8 V under TT corner. Figure 9 shows the PSRR at room temperature with 1.8 V power supply. The PSRR is −66 dB@100 Hz, and the worst is −29 dB@63 kHz. At different corner, maximum deviation is less than 2 dB. Thus the voltage reference which is almost independent of temperature and supply voltage is achieved.

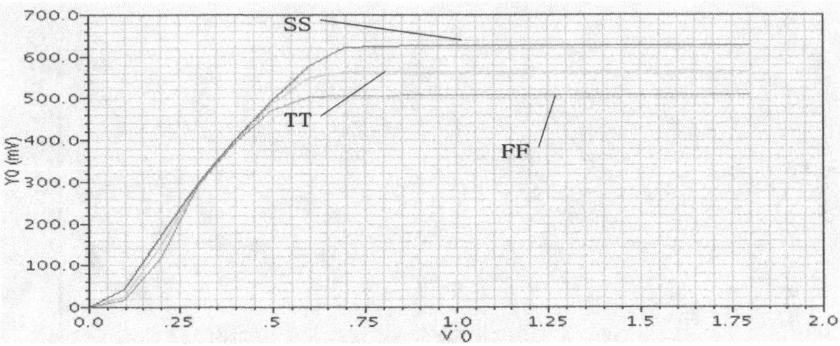

Fig. 8. Output voltage versus supply voltage

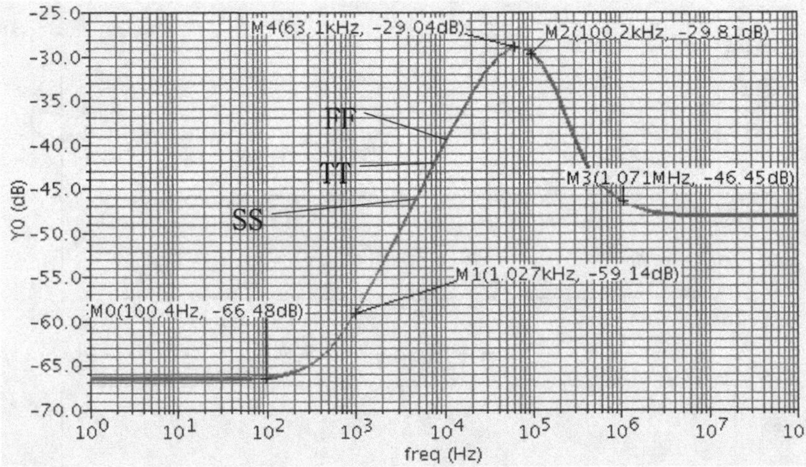

Fig. 9. PSRR of the proposed reference voltage source

The noise characteristic is shown in Fig. 10. It can be seen that the noise is relatively larger in the low frequency band, about 4 uV/sqrt(Hz)@80 Hz. The circuit noise is mainly the flicker noise of MOSFET, which can be reduced by increasing size of MOSFET. It is easy to see the noise of output voltage is not affected under different corner.

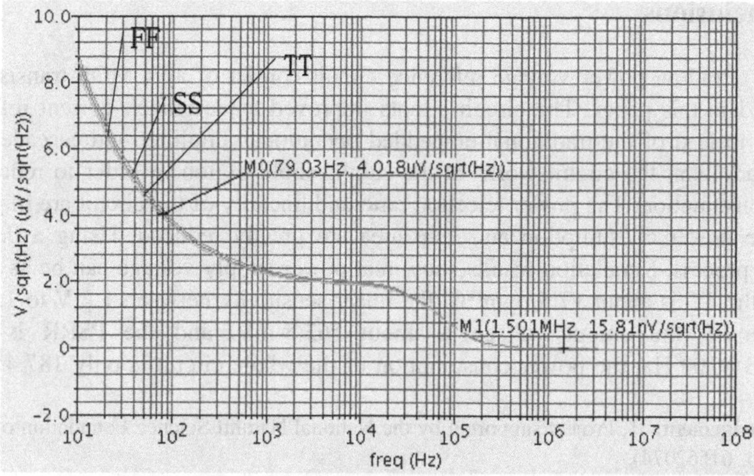

Fig. 10. Output noise versus frequency

Table 1 summarizes the characteristics of our circuit in comparison with other triple-branch structure CMOS voltage references reported in [7, 8, 12]. Our device is comparable to other circuits in PSRR, line sensitivity, and it is superior to other in TC and power consumption. Our circuit gives new improvement to the triple-branch structure circuits, so it is useful as a voltage reference for low power design.

Table 1. Comparison of reported low power CMOS voltage reference circuits

	This work	[7]	[8]	[12]
Process	0.18 um, CMOS	0.5 um, CMOS	0.18 um, CMOS	0.35 um, CMOS
Temperature range (°C)	−40–125	−40–130	−40–100	−20–80
VDD	0.75–1.8 V	2–6 V	0.7–3 V	1.4–3 V
V_{ref}	563.5 mV	1.2–3.5 V	700 mV	745 mV
Power	187.4 nW	*N.A.*	1.5 uW	0.3 uW (@.4 V)
TC (ppm/°C)	17.25	20	80	7
Line sensitivity (ppm/V)	569.5	*N.A.*	*N.A.*	20
PSRR@100 Hz	−66.5 dB	−50 dB@1 kHz	−62 dB	45 dB
Noise@80 Hz	4 uV/sqrt (Hz)	*N.A.*	4.9 uV/sqrt (Hz)	*N.A.*

6 Conclusions

A novel ultra-low power voltage reference circuit consist of all-CMOS transistors is developed in this paper. The circuit adopts improved triple-branch current reference structure instead of the traditional embedded operational amplifier and cascade structure. In addition, the circuit works at the subthreshold region in order to reduce the power consumption. The power rejection ratio and linearity of the circuit are improved while the power consumption and chip area are greatly reduced. Using a 0.18 um standard process, Simulation results show that power supply voltage can be as low as 0.75 V, the TC is about 17.5 ppm/°C, the linear sensitivity between 1.2 V to 1.8 V is 569.5 ppm/V, the output voltage is about 563.5 mV, and the PSRR is about −66.5 dB@100 Hz, the power consumption of the whole circuit is only 187.4 nW.

Acknowledgement. 1. Project supported by the National Natural Science Foundation of China (Grant No. 61562074).

2. Project supported by the Guangxi University Science and Technology Research Project (Grant No. KY2015ZD123).

3. Guangxi Innovation Driven Development Special Fund Project.

References

1. Lee, E.K.F.: Low voltage CMOS bandgap references with temperature compensated reference current output. In: IEEE International Symposium on Circuits and Systems, pp. 1643–1646. IEEE (2010)
2. Yue, M.: A 46.468 μW low-power bandgap voltage reference. In: IEEE International Conference on Computer Science and Information Technology, pp. 256–258. IEEE (2010)
3. Hua, L., Lüjian, Yadong, J.: A curvature-compensated CMOS bandgap voltage reference for high precision applications. Microelectronics **39**(1), 38–41 (2009)
4. Wang, N., Wei, L.: A low-power high PSRR OMOS bandgap voltage reference. Microelectronics **34**(3), 330–333 (2004)
5. Zhou, Q., et al.: High-PSRR high-order curvature-compensated CMOS bandgap voltage reference. J. Harbin Inst. Technol. **5**, 116–124 (2015)
6. Wadhwa, S.K., Chaudhry, N.: High accuracy, multi-output bandgap reference circuit in 16 nm FinFet. In: International Conference on VLSI Design and 2017, International Conference on Embedded Systems, pp. 259–262. IEEE (2017)
7. Razavi, B.: Design of Analog CMOS Integrated Circuits. Xi'an Jiaotong University Press (2003)
8. Yi, W., He, L., Xiaolang, A.Y.: A 30 nA temperature-independent CMOS current reference and its application in an LDO. Chin. J. Semicond. **27**(9), 1657–1662 (2006)
9. Xu, Y., Hu, W.: Design of a novel All-CMOS low power voltage reference source. Microelectronics **43**(6), 742–746 (2013)
10. Buck, A.E., et al.: A CMOS bandgap reference without resistors. IEEE J. Solid-State Circ. **37**(1), 81–83 (2002)
11. Wang, A., Calhoun, B.H., Chandrakasan, A.P.: Sub-threshold Design for Ultra Low-Power Systems. Series on Integrated Circuits & Systems. Springer, Heidelberg (2006). https://doi.org/10.1007/978-0-387-34501-7
12. Ueno, K., et al.: A 300 nW, 15 ppm/°C, 20 ppm/V CMOS voltage reference circuit consisting of subthreshold MOSFETs. IEEE J. Solid-State Circ. **44**(7), 2047–2054 (2009)

RSSI-Fading-Based Localization Approach in BLE5.0 Indoor Environments

Bo Xu, Xiaorong Zhu, and Hongbo Zhu(✉)

Nanjing, China
zhuhb@njupt.edu.cn

Abstract. How to filter fluctuant RSSI signal has always been a difficult problem in an indoor localization system. This paper provides an efficient indoor localization algorithm in a BLE5.0 based scan-broadcast network by building RSSI path-loss model without a great deal of fingerprints. This method builds a RSSI-Distance fading model between one position node (PN) and one markup node (MN) by maximum likelihood estimation (MLE) based on Gauss distribution of RSSI data. Then the rough fading model about RSSI in data collecting intervals of 1 m will be get. In this paper we reduce the distance intervals in 0.1 m by fitting of path loss model and making discrete samples of confidence intervals to improve the accuracy of localization. Finally, the whole fading regularly will be fixed and the location errors of PN will be determined by centroid model (CM). The results show that sampling interval with high precision can benefit the accuracy performance in an indoor localization environment.

Keywords: RSSI · BLE5.0 · Maximum likelihood estimation (MLE) · Centroid model (CM) · Indoor localization

1 Introduction

With the development of wireless network, Internet of Things (IOT) has realized extensive service provisions and high quality of communication guarantees in our life [1]. In many application scenes, localization based services (LBS) [2] make the interaction between millions people. Two main scenes of the localization are open outdoor environment and indoor environment. Global Navigation Satellite System (GNSS) is the main implementation scheme in outdoor environments where scenes have low effect for transmission path. The density of outdoor

This work was supported by Foundation Items: National Natural Science Foundation of China (61871237), Natural Science Foundation of China under Grant 61871446, National Science and Technology Major Project (2017ZX03001008), and Natural Science Foundation of the Higher Education Institutions of Jiangsu Province (16KJA510005).

M. Jia et al. (Eds.): WiSATS 2019, LNICST 281, pp. 131–144, 2019.
https://doi.org/10.1007/978-3-030-19156-6_13

objects is low, and in many scenes, determining an abbreviated distance is completely enough for LBS. The maximum precision of outdoor localization is 10 m [3]. However, GPS or other outdoor localization technologies have their limits in indoor environment [4]. Object blocking is complex in each specific scene where satellite signal will be weakened by roofs or walls and meter scale precise is no conformity for indoor environments. To solve the problem, scientists have promoted many coping strategies for indoor localization and their improved methods focus on two aspects: indoor communication technologies and localization algorithms.

Indoor communication technologies include widely used technology such as WLAN, Zigbee, Bluetooth (BLE), Zigbee and Radio Frequency Identification (RFID) [5]. Some special technologies for indoor localization are also born such as iBeacon (a technique for ios7 system mobile phone location by BLE) [6] and Ultra Wideband (UWB) [7]. They are all effective methods to make localization and there have no absolute superiorities or disadvantages among them, so they should be chosen according to the emphasis of the study.

In aspect to localization algorithms, according to the features from the localization network, can be divided into Angle of Arrival (AOA), Time difference of Arrival (TDOA), Time of arrival (TOA) and Received signal Strength (RSSI) [8]. No matter which methods be used, fluctuation of the collected features is difficult to clear up and even when we get the results of indoor localization, the amid coordination itself is still fluctuated. As a result, in a model of an indoor localization system needs consider the measures both in front filter and back filter [9]. In this paper, we just innovate the front filter algorithm and use RSSI as our features. Recent researches of revising RSSI will be displayed later.

1.1 Related Researches

Inventing a more advanced wireless technology or designing a more ingenious algorithm is the research direction in indoor localization. Advanced wireless technology such as UWB which mentioned above can transmit data from nanosecond to microsecond non sinusoidal pulse and many people think it as the mainstream technology of near field communication in the future. Ingenious algorithms such as neutral network which is hot spots of current research and is remarkable in many ways. The platform of our research is BLE5.0, and the algorithm purpose is to build a filter model of RSSI when the PN collects broadcast packets from MNs.

1.1.1 BLE5.0

BLE5.0: Why we choose BLE5.0 as our PN and MNs? The main consideration is its low power waste and the capacity of large deployment. BlE5.0 is a Bluetooth technology standard proposed by Bluetooth Technology Alliance in 2016.12. BLE5.0 can improve and optimize the speed of low-power devices and it has a wider coverage and 4 times faster speed for low-power devices. The upper limit of transmission speed is 24 Mbps, which is 2 times the previous version of

BLE4.2. The effective working distance can reach 300 m, which is 4 times that of the previous BLE4.2 version [10]. Although BLE5.0 has been optimized, the limitations of BLE5.0 is still exits. BlE5.0 only has penetration capacity within 10 m and the BLE5.0 chip can't collect precise time difference so that RSSI is almost the only feature to utilize [11]. BLE5.0 has the advantages of lower power consumption and transmission capacity. The localization of BLE5.0 is not particularly prominent, but in reality scenes, decimeter grade accuracy is enough for users and with the optimization of algorithm, location performance will become better and better.

1.1.2 RSSI in Indoor Localization

In most of the wireless system, RSSI is the value which without extra hardware for auxiliary measurement. Many researches of indoor localization use RSSI as their location parameters no matter which wireless technology they choose. The basic usage of RSSI in indoor localization is a three point centroid model [12]. This method detection RSSI in the PN surrounded by at least three MNs and through the junction point of RSSI, the PN will be located. Fingerprints based positioning strategy is another common strategy by collecting large amount of fingerprints and build a neural network based multi classification model to find the coordinate of PN [13]. Front filtering and back filtering are in [14] and [15], constantly changing RSSI sequence will be mapped to a particular distribution. In methods [16], Kalman filter, - filter and particle swarm are effective methods to reduce the jump of location results. Different indoor environments affect the performance of algorithm and a localization algorithm based on RSSI in specific indoor map can be found in [17]. Data filtering from a large number of MNs to find the most reliable RSSI is another thinking when the PN is in a dense MNs network [18]. RSSI maybe mutual interference when the network is concentrated and keeping the independence of RSSI is significant [19]. In this paper we examines the front filter algorithm to find the fading regularity between RSSI fading, and this regularity will realizes a convenient localization in non specific environments.

1.2 Mathematical Formulation: Centroid Model (CM)

One of the significant advantage in our method is that we discard the process of fingerprints collecting. Combining the RSSI-Distance model and centroid model will easily calculation the coordinate of PN. In weighted centroid model, we assume that the number of MN is 3 and the following function is formed:

$$f(x,y,t)=\begin{cases}(x_1-x)^2+(y_1-y)^2=r_1(x_1,y_1,d_1,t)\\(x_2-x)^2+(y_2-y)^2=r_2(x_2,y_2,d_2,t)\\(x_3-x)^2+(y_3-y)^2=r_3(x_3,y_3,d_3,t)\end{cases}\tag{1}$$

where (x_1,y_1), (x_2,y_2), (x_3,y_3) are the coordinates of the nearest three MNs. $r(x,y,d,t)$ is the RSSI from MNs to PN at the linear distance d, t time. By calculating each d of MNs, PN coordinate (x,y) will be get. Because of RSSI fluctuation, (x, y) will jump in a certain range at different time. Within the time interval of T, if estimated by Gauss distribution, RSSI from MN_i can be defined as follows:

$$r_i(x_i, y_i, d_i, T) \sim \frac{1}{\sqrt{2\pi\sigma^2(d_i)}} e^{-\frac{(r-\mu(d_i))^2}{2\sigma^2(d_i)}} \tag{2}$$

where T is the time interval of RSSI samplings. d_i represents the distance from PN to MN_i and its constantly changing when the PN is moving. $\mu(d_i)$ and $\sigma(d_i)$ are parameters based on the distance from PN to ith MN and in a certain localization scene. In Fig. 1, we present CM model where radiation of RSSI is simplified from 3-D spherical radiation to a 2-D plane.

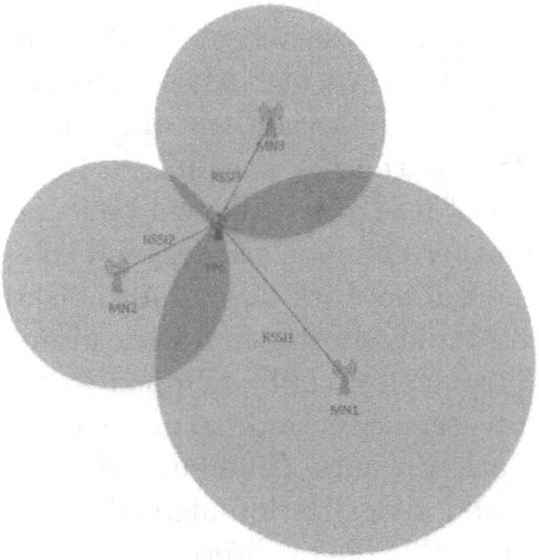

Fig. 1. Mathematical formulation: weighted centroid model based on RSSI

1.3 Problems: How to Make a Rapid Positioning

In a new indoor environment, the scenery is always specific. The method based on the fingerprints usually needs training data which are collected from the well divided train coordinates. With powerful classification ability of neural network, in a specific home, this method is effective. However, the process of collecting fingerprints is complex, in some exceptional case, such as military and fire rescue, localization of soldiers is hard to collect the fingerprints because of the limited time. We put forward a rapid measurement model which circumvent fingerprints collecting, and by build RSSI-Distance model, the accuracy of our method is reliable.

The remainder of this paper is organized as follow. Section 2 outlines the BLE5.0 scan-broadcast network and the preparation of features. The RSSI-Distance model based on MLE are discussed and we will know approximately trends of RSSI fading in interval of 1 m in Sect. 3, followed by a more precise evaluation model which makes fitting of path loss model and realizes discrete sampling of confidence interval in distance interval of 0.1 m. Experiments and results are in Sect. 4, followed by conclusion in Sect. 5. Measurements are carried out in Communications Technology Research Institute of Nanjing University of Posts and Telecommunications.

2 BLE5.0 Scan-Broadcasting Network

The scan-broadcast network includes the deployment of MNs and settings of transmission mechanism. MNs determine the localization of PN and when the PN moves out the area, the RSSI sequence will be eliminated that because RSSI will generate terrible amplitude twitter as the distance widening. Considering of the transmission capacity of BLE5.0, the maximum PN to MN distance should be within 10 m and if the number of PNs is enough, the density of PNs can be raised. In our research, transmission mechanism is based on the process of broadcasting and scanning. When the localization starts, MNs will in the state of fasting broadcast and the identification of the MNs is its MAC address. When the PN scans on the broadcast packets, it will analysis the MAC field of MNs and RSSI can be perceived. To make the MNs are unique in nearby BLE equipment, MAC addresses of PNs usually have its naming rules. The BLE5.0 scan-broadcasting network is shown in Fig. 2.

RSSI and MAC information will form the data sequence in (1) and (2). Usually a serial communication model (Lora or WIFI) assistants the PN to send the sequence to server where calculating the RSSI-Distance function. In addition, Mesh network by BLE5.0 [26] is another networking mode which realise the pressure of MN, however in our research, simplifying deployment process is our aim, so we will use a low complexity network. To say the least, BLE5.0 Mesh is nothing with the localization accuracy theoretically.

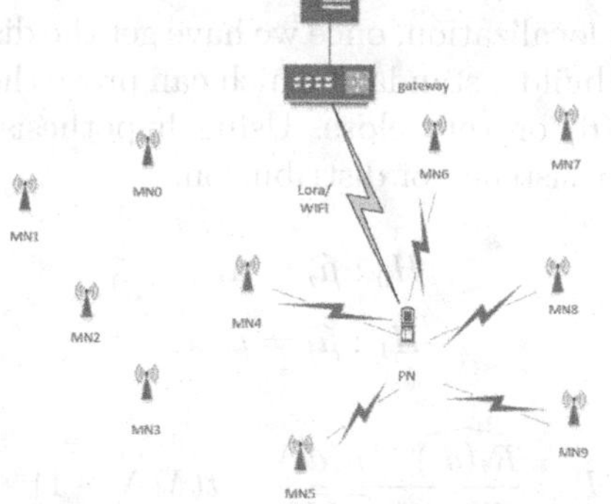

Fig. 2. The BLE5.0 scan-broadcasting network

2.1 Approximately RSSI Fading Model in Interval of 1 m

To make the current model can best reflect the real RSSI propagation, we need figure out μ and σ in (2) and make error analysis. We record RSSI sequence of MNs in a short time interval. The transmission speed of BLE5.0 is fast enough to divide the sequence into more groups where each group has independent and identical distribution. The RSSI sequence from MN_i in group j can be set as $\{R_{i-j-1}, R_{i-j-2}, \ldots, R_{i-j-N}\}$, where the N is the number of RSSI in each group. We set the number of groups is M. Each group separately calculate μ and σ in (2) by MLE. Finally, averaging the results of every group, the RSSI-Distance model of MN_i is formed. The formula as follows:

$$L\{\mu, \sigma^2\} = \prod_{n=1}^{N} \frac{1}{\sqrt{2\pi\sigma^2(d_i)}} e^{-\frac{(R_{i-j-n}-\mu(d_i))^2}{2\sigma^2(d_i)}} \tag{3}$$

Using the MLE to get the value of $\mu(d_i)$ and $\sigma(d_i)$.

$$\begin{cases} \frac{\partial \log L(\mu(d_i),\sigma^2(d_i))}{\partial \mu} = \frac{1}{\sigma^2(d_i)} \sum_{n=1}^{N} (R_{i-j-n} - \mu(d_i)) = 0 \\ \frac{\partial \log L(\mu(d_i),\sigma^2(d_i))}{\partial \sigma} = -\frac{n}{2\sigma^2} + \frac{1}{2\sigma^4(d_i)} \sum_{n=1}^{N} (R_{i-j-n} - \mu(d_i)) = 0 \end{cases} \tag{4}$$

The result of μ and σ are as follows:

$$\mu(d_i) = \frac{1}{M}\frac{1}{N}\sum_{j=1}^{M}\sum_{n=1}^{N} R_{i-j-n} \tag{5}$$

$$\sigma^2(d_i) = \frac{1}{M}\frac{1}{N}\sum_{j=1}^{M}\sum_{n=1}^{N}(R_{i-j-n} - \overline{R_{i-j-n}})^2 \tag{6}$$

In the process of indoor localization, once we have get the distribution of $RSSI$ in (5) and (6), we need to build a standard which can prove the current distribution is the same with (5)–(6) or very close. Using hypothesis test is the common method to prove the consistency of distribution.
Assumption:

$$H_0 : \widehat{\mu_i} = \mu_i$$

$$H_1 : \widehat{\mu_i} \neq \mu_i$$

and test statistics:

$$T = \frac{\widehat{R_i(d_i)} - \mu(d_i)}{S(d_i)/\sqrt{MN}} \sim t(MN-1) \tag{7}$$

Reject region:

$$|T| \geq t_{\frac{\alpha}{2}(MN-1)}$$

where $\widehat{R_i(d_i)}$ is the $RSSI$ sample mean of MN_i and we keep the number of $RSSI$ received is MN which is same as that in (5), (6). $s(d_i)$ is sample variance of raw data. α is the significance level, usually $\alpha = 0.05$. Similarity, we also test $\sigma^2(d_i)$.

Assumption:

$$H_0 : \widehat{\mu_i} = \mu_i$$
$$H_1 : \widehat{\sigma_i} \neq \sigma_i$$

and test statistics:

$$F = \frac{max(S^2(d_i) - \widehat{S^2(d_i)})}{min(S^2(d_i) - \widehat{S^2(d_i)})} \sim F(M-1, M-1) \quad (8)$$

Reject region:

$$F \geq F_\alpha$$

where $\widehat{S^2(d_i)}$ is sample variance of current data. When all of the MNs are working together, the value of $RSSI$ which we choose is a normal value. For example, in time interval T, PN has scanned broadcast packets of MN_1, MN_2, MN_3. Other MNs maybe scanned yet, but we can easily calculate that $\mu(d_i)$ of them are too low and they will be excluded. The straight distances between three MNs shouldn't be too long or too short and according to our experiment, the range of the value is [1 m, 5 m]. In Fig. 3, we show RSSI-Distance model in distance difference of 1 m. Figure 4 is the verification environment of our experiments.

In Fig. 3, PN is collecting RSSI from MN_1. We set the PN moving in a specific route and equal distance cutting is carried out in this line. It is worth noting that MN_1, MN_2 and MN_3 build a right angle. The reason for this arrangement is that almost each house has a right angle of the roof, so when we use us indoor localization method in a new scene, we can realize rapid assembly of our system based on this structure without temporary test. In Fig. 4, means of RSSI-distance model indicates that when we uniform increase the distance between PN and MN_i, the attenuation of $RSSI$ will slow down and that is because the power of BLE5.0 is limited and the sensitivity of $RSSI$ detection can only work in a short range. Variances show the stability of the system and we find that variances are erratic. As a result, we will use means of $RSSI$ as our localization feature. The localization range of three MN_s should be limited less than $4 \times 4\,\text{m}^2$.

Complements about confidence intervals of means are shown in Fig. 5 where we calculate in distance of 1 m, 2 m, 3 m and 4 m (5 m is excluded and we use opposite number to represent confidence intervals). The confidence interval in d_i is written as (PL_i, PH_i). Similarly as the conclusion in Fig. 4, in the distance of 4 m, the complement has a more board range in which we will have more difficulties in detecting whether a certain gauss distribution could be recognized as happened. We can imagine that with the distance increased, distribution between different length will be indistinct. As a conclusion, the range of localization must be limited in a area where statistical parameters have obvious discrepancy. The next work for us is to make evaluation model in which we will map gauss distribution into specific distance and we will try to narrow the intervals of distance.

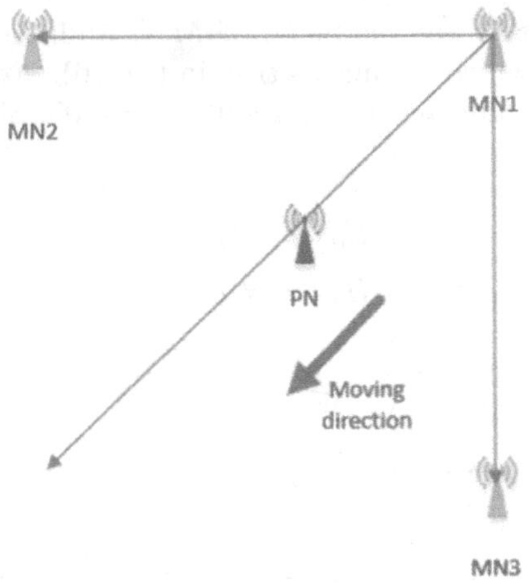

Fig. 3. RSSI collecting environment for RSSI-Distance model

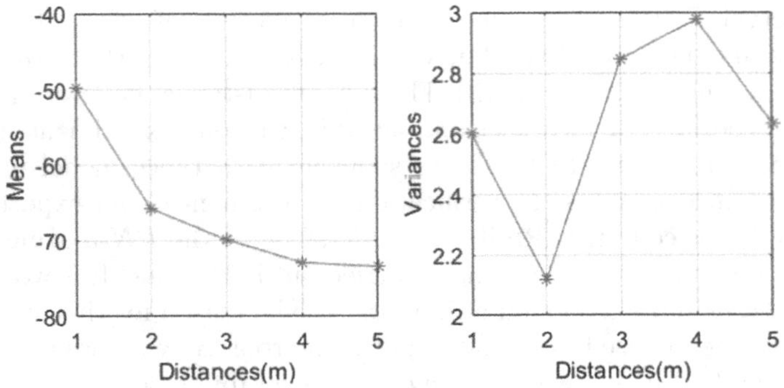

Fig. 4. Means and Variances of RSSI-Distance model

3 More Precise Evaluation Model in Interval of 0.1 m

Confidence intervals in Fig. 4 delimit appropriate mapping regularity when we know the current data distribution. In this paper, minimum unit of distance must be more precise and if we want to exclude interference caused by similar confidence intervals, the strategy of setting interval distance is the key. When we have a ideal partition strategy, the evaluation model will be more effectively to map *RSSI* distribution to its adjacent straight distance.

3.1 Strategy of Making More Precise Interval

In real application, propagation model based on exponential decline is often used in *RSSI* fading.

$$p_{d_i} = p_0 - 10\eta Log(d_i/d_0) + \varepsilon \tag{9}$$

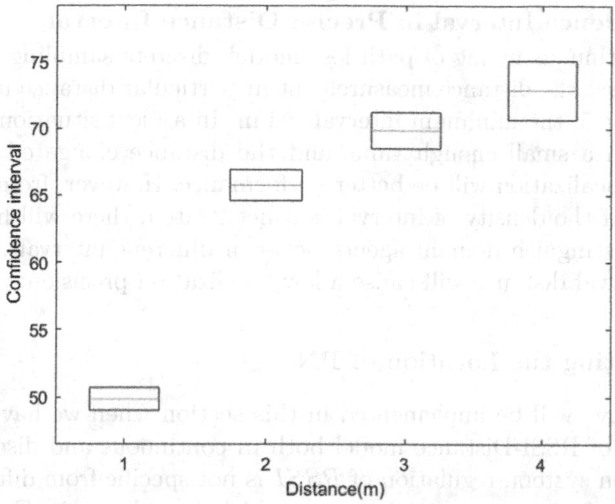

Fig. 5. Complements about confidence interval

where η is the path-loss exponent and ε represents the measurement error. Combined with Figs. 4 and 5, this logarithmic distribution is measured in real measurements. In this paper, we put forward two ways about mapping.

3.1.1 Fitting of Path Loss Model

Assuming that PN is in the process like in Fig. 3. According to interval T in one sampling and advanced partition distance, the RSSI-Distance sequence about PN and MN_i can be setted as

$$Q_i = \{R_{d_i1}, d_{i1}; R_{d_i2}, d_{i2}; \ldots; R_{d_iH}, d_{iH}\}$$

where R_{d_ih} is the aggregates of all groups of R_{i-j-n} where the distance is h which has been defined in part III. This two-dimension array will be fitted in the trend of function (9). We set function (10) is another form of expression about (9)

$$R_{d_ih} = R_0 + 10\eta log(d_{ih}) + \varepsilon \tag{10}$$

According to least square method fitting target is

$$\min \sum_{h=1}^{H} (R_{d_ih} - (R_0 + 10\eta log(d_{ih}) + \varepsilon))^2 \tag{11}$$

Once function of (11) is determined, distribution regularity of $RSSI$ from MN_i in limited transmission distance is fixed. The form of expression is a smooth logarithmic curve in which the input variables are $RSSI$ calculated in (5) and the reject region is nothing with this mapping process because the results of distance are continuous.

3.1.2 Confidence Interval in Precise Distance Interval

Unlike the continuous fitting of path loss model, discrete sampling about confidence interval set the distance measurement in particular distance intervals. For instance, in Fig. 5, the minimum interval is 1 m. In a ideal situation, if intervals could be set in a small enough value and the distance elongated can also be detected, the localization will be better performance. However, from the conclusion in Fig. 5, if the density of interval is concentrated, there will have the risk of failing to distinguish domain agents between different intervals. Conversely, extending interval distance will cause a low localization precision.

3.2 Calculating the Location of PN

CM talked above will be implemented in this section when we have researched the regulation of RSSI-Distance model both in continuous and discrete formal. In a localization system, regulation of $RSSI$ is not specific from different MNs, even the original power sets is the same which has shown in Fig. 4 and this characteristic is reflect in $r_1(x_1, y_1, d_1, t)$ in (1). As a result, combined with (1) and continues sampling algorithm or discrete sampling algorithm, the location of PN will be easily detected.

4 Results and Analysis

Figure 6 shows the experiment environment in our laboratory where the shaded areas are computer tables or other equipments. We set four MNs and they are

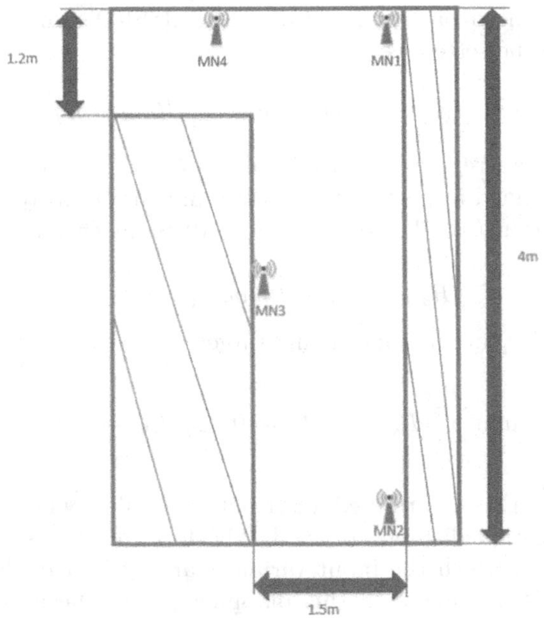

Fig. 6. Indoor location environment of experiment

fixed. We choose MN_i as the object node for RSSI-Distance research and the results are shown in Fig. 7(a) and (b).

We can compare Fig. 7(a) with Fig. 4 where the distance ranging is decreased from 4 m to 1 m and combined with two pictures, the regularity of *RSSI-Distance* model will be found. With the distance increased, the growth trend approach gentle, because the RSSI detection ability of BLE5.0 model is limited when the signal power is undersize. Another influence of distance increasing is shown in Fig. 7(b). The range of box shows the receive of means in a specific distance. We repeat doing two experiment in the same scenes. When the distance is 0.1 m, 0.2 m, 0.3 m, there are no overlap between boxes and with the distance increased, if we choose 0.1 m as the interval of discrete sampling, the phenomenon of overlapping in receive areas is serious.

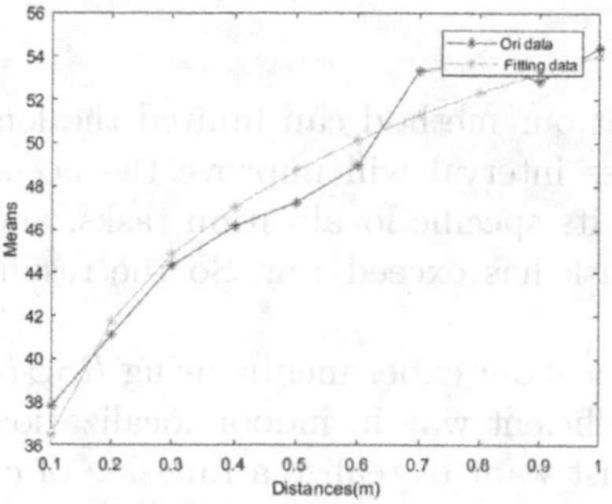

(a) Means of RSSI in fitting of path loss model

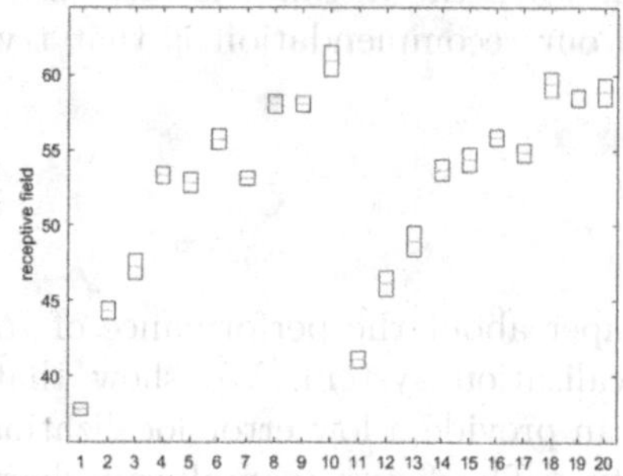

(b) Confidence intervals in sampling interval of 0.1m (1-10 and 11-20 are results of the first and the second experiments in 1m)

Fig. 7. RSSI-Distance model interval of 0.1 m

The results of localization are shown in Table 1, we choose 10 coordinates as localization targets and errors are linear distances between calculation locations and 10 coordinates. The solution method is based on RSSI-Distance model and the CM algorithm which we have built above. In practice, solving the function of (1) is hard and in many situations the function is unsolvable, so we just give the minimum error distances, this value also can represent the accuracy of the BLE5.0 indoor localization system. Coordinates from MN_1 to MN_4 are follows: [0, 0], [0, 4], [1.5, 2], [1, 0].

Table 1. The comparison between accuracy in different sampling intervals

Coordinates (m)	[0.4, 0.4]	[0.8, 0.8]	[0.4, 1.4]	[0.4, 2.6]	[0, 2.6]
Errors (m) (interval of 0.1 m)	0.68	0.48	0.32	0.59	0.53
Errors (m) (interval of 1 m)	1.78	1.14	0.67	1.14	0.97
Coordinates (m)	[0.8, 2.8]	[0.8, 3.2]	[0.3, 3.2]	[0.4, 3.6]	[0.2, 3.8]
Errors (m) (interval of 0.1 m)	0.64	0.73	0.71	0.79	0.81
Errors (m) (interval of 1 m)	1.08	0.92	0.87	1.05	0.96

The results show that our method can limited the localization error in 1 m and using a more precise interval will improve the accuracy. In practice, the target point usually has its specific localization tasks, and in many scenes, the density of positioning task has exceed 1 m. So the result of our experience is reliable.

Concerning the results of our experiments, using *RSSI-Distance* model with the CM function is an efficient way in indoor localization. As shown in Fig. 7, we observe that if you just want to realize a function of close range perception, BLE5.0 is a dependable equipment which can distinguish the distance in 1 m. The only problem is that when the distance is increased, it's hard to make a precise measurement, so our recommendation is that trying to chose a more precise interval.

5 Conclusion

We investigate in this paper about the performance of *RSSI-Distance* model in a BLE5.0 indoor localization system. We show that building a reliable *RSSI-Distance* model can provide a low error localization accuracy without a mass of fingerprint collecting. The discrete sampling in short distance shows good performance and this regulation is suitable in a equipment perception system when the people approach the devices. Continue sampling is a feasible scheme when we need to know the specific coordinates in room, if the precise needed to be improved, tedious method of fingerprint collecting can only be used. Using the methods in this paper, user just need to associate the BLE5.0 module with its *RSSI-Distance* model, then the function of indoor localization will be realized. Of course, the next work for us is to consider of more complex features in the room and apply the indoor location in more scenes.

References

1. Abouzar, P., Michelson, D.G., Hamdi, M.: RSSI-based distributed self-localization for wireless sensor networks used in precision agriculture. IEEE Trans. Wirel. Commun. **15**(10), 6638–6650 (2016)
2. Ahmed, R., Edwards, M.G., Lamine, S., Huisman, B.A.H., Pal, M.: Three-dimensional control-volume distributed multi-point flux approximation coupled with a lower-dimensional surface fracture model. J. Comput. Phys. **303**, 470–497 (2015)
3. Bouet, M., Dos Santos, A.L.: RFID tags: positioning principles and localization techniques. In: 1st IFIP Wireless Days, WD 2008, pp. 1–5. IEEE (2008)
4. Chen, Z., Zou, H., Jiang, H., Zhu, Q., Soh, Y.C., Xie, L.: Fusion of WiFi, smartphone sensors and landmarks using the Kalman filter for indoor localization. Sensors **15**(1), 715–732 (2015)
5. Cho, S.Y.: Adaptive wireless localization filter containing NLOS error mitigation function. J. Position. Navig. Timing **5**(1), 1–9 (2016)
6. Gubbi, J., Buyya, R., Marusic, S., Palaniswami, M.: Internet of Things (IOT): a vision, architectural elements, and future directions. Future Gener. Comput. Syst. **29**(7), 1645–1660 (2013)
7. Hofmann-Wellenhof, B., Lichtenegger, H., Wasle, E.: GNSS-Global Navigation Satellite Systems: GPS, GLONASS, Galileo, and More. Springer, Heidelberg (2007). https://doi.org/10.1007/978-3-211-73017-1
8. Jiang, Q., Ma, Y., Liu, K., Dou, Z.: A probabilistic radio map construction scheme for crowdsourcing-based fingerprinting localization. IEEE Sens. J. **16**(10), 3764–3774 (2016)
9. Jourdan, D.B., Dardari, D., Win, M.Z.: Position error bound for UWB localization in dense cluttered environments. IEEE Trans. Aerosp. Electron. Syst. **44**(2), 613 628 (2008)
10. Junglas, I.A., Watson, R.T.: Location-based services. Commun. ACM **51**(3), 65–69 (2008)
11. Liu, K., Liu, X., Li, X.: Guoguo: enabling fine-grained indoor localization via smartphone. In: Proceeding of the 11th Annual International Conference on Mobile Systems, Applications, and Services, pp. 235–248. ACM (2013)
12. Liu, K., Mulky, R.: Enabling autonomous navigation for affordable scooters. Sensors (Basel) **18**(6), s18061829–s18061829 (2018)
13. Mazuelas, S., et al.: Robust indoor positioning provided by real-time RSSI values in unmodified WLAN networks. IEEE J. Sel. Top. Signal Process. **3**(5), 821–831 (2009)
14. Pak, J.M., Ahn, C.K., Shmaliy, Y.S., Lim, M.T.: Improving reliability of particle filter-based localization in wireless sensor networks via hybrid particle/FIR filtering. IEEE Trans. Ind. Inform. **11**(5), 1089–1098 (2015)
15. Selvaraju, R.R., Cogswell, M., Das, A., Vedantam, R., Parikh, D., Batra, D., et al.: Grad-CAM: visual explanations from deep networks via gradient-based localization. In: ICCV, pp. 618–626 (2017)
16. Stoleru, R., He, T., Stankovic, J.A.: Walking GPS: a practical solution for localization in manually deployed wireless sensor networks. In: 29th Annual IEEE International Conference on Local Computer Networks, pp. 480–489. IEEE (2004)
17. Wang, X., et al.: A 0.9–1.2 V supplied, 2.4 GHZ Bluetooth Low Energy 4.0/4.2 and 802.15. 4 transceiver SoC optimized for battery life. In: 42nd European Solid-State Circuits Conference, ESSCIRC Conference 2016, pp. 125–128. IEEE (2016)

18. Xiao, H., Zhang, H., Wang, Z., Gulliver, T.A.: An RSSI based DV-hop algorithm for wireless sensor networks. In: 2017 IEEE Pacific Rim Conference on Communications, Computers and Signal Processing, PACRIM, pp. 1–6. IEEE (2017)
19. Zanca, G., Zorzi, F., Zanella, A., Zorzi, M.: Experimental comparison of RSSI-based localization algorithms for indoor wireless sensor networks. In: Proceedings of the Workshop on Real-World Wireless Sensor Networks, pp. 1–5. ACM (2008)

Real-Time System Fault-Tolerant Scheme Based on Improved Chaotic Genetic Algorithm

Jie Wang[1,2](✉), Junjie Kang[1,2], and Gang Hou[1,2]

[1] School of Software Technology,
Dalian University of Technology, Dalian 116620, China
wangjie1003@163.com
[2] Ubiquitous Network and Service Software Laboratory in Liaoning,
Dalian 116620, China

Abstract. Traditional evolutionary fault-tolerant scheme can effectively repair circuit faults, but for large-scale integrated circuits, the evolution process consumes a lot of time and it is difficult to meet the real-time requirements. In this paper, a real-time system fault-tolerant scheme based on improved chaotic genetic algorithm is proposed. The scheme uses a built-in test detection mechanism with feedback to detect the running state of the circuit in real time. When a fault occurs, normal system operation is maintained by the fault compensation mechanism. At the same time, the system uses the evolution repair mechanism to repair the faulty circuit. Evolution process uses an improved chaotic genetic algorithm, which can quickly converge to obtain a repair circuit through adaptive chaotic crossover and mutation. This paper builds a fault-tolerant system on the FPGA. In the experiment, the fault is randomly injected into circuit so that to simulate the actual circuit fault. The proposed algorithm and fault-tolerant scheme are used to verify the self-repairing ability of the system. The experimental results show that under real-time constraints, the repair rate of the fault circuit reaches 94%.

Keywords: Fault-tolerant · Evolution hardware · Chaotic genetic algorithm

1 Introduction

With the continuous development of electronic information technology, integrated circuits are widely used in aerospace and communications. Due to the increasing size and complexity of integrated circuits, microelectronic systems may malfunction in complex and variable environments. For example, in areas such as aerospace and deep-sea exploration where reliability is critical, if faults occur and the electronic system do not have self-healing capabilities, the entire electronic system will face a serious situation [1]. Therefore, it is very important to design a circuit system with fault tolerance.

According to different implementation methods, the fault tolerance of electronic systems is divided into active fault-tolerant control and passive fault-tolerant control [2]. Passive fault-tolerant control utilizes redundant hardware resources to implement fault repair, such as three-mode redundancy. However, for large scale integrated

M. Jia et al. (Eds.): WiSATS 2019, LNICST 281, pp. 145–156, 2019.
https://doi.org/10.1007/978-3-030-19156-6_14

circuits, hardware redundancy is difficult to implement in many practical circuit systems and fault tolerance is limited. Active fault-tolerant control has better fault tolerance than passive fault-tolerant control. Active fault-tolerant control completes fault repair by fault adjustment or signal reconstruction online adjustment to ensure system stability and reliability after faults occur [3]. Evolution hardware technology is an effective active fault-tolerant control. The adaptive and self-repairing features of the evolution hardware can make the fault circuit automatically adjust the circuit structure to achieve self-repair [4]. However, because the evolution process consumes a lot of time and the evolution efficiency is not high, it cannot complete the evolution operation of the entire electronic system. Considering the real-time requirements of system fault tolerance, after fault occurs, if the fault circuit cannot complete the self-repair in real time, normal operation of the system will be affected a lot.

Aiming at the above problems, this paper proposes a real-time system fault-tolerant scheme based on improved chaotic genetic algorithm. The fault-tolerant scheme uses the Built-in Test technology to monitor the circuit system in real time. When the system detects the fault, the faulty circuit is differentiated through the Built-in Test to quickly find the fault source. After the fault source isolation is completed, the system uses the fault compensation mechanism to maintain the normal operation of the circuit, and adopts an efficient chaotic genetic algorithm to quickly obtain the repair circuit, so as to realize the online real-time repair.

2 Related Work

Programmable logic devices such as FPGAs are widely used in integrated circuit design due to the features of high integration and flexible design. However, due to the complex environmental changes, programmable logic devices used in aerospace are susceptible to radiation, then faults may occur in the circuit system. Therefore, fault-tolerant research on programmable logic devices has been widely concerned by researchers.

The most common fault-tolerant method used in FPGAs is the Triple Modular Redundancy technology (TMR) [5]. TMR does not require an additional fault detection circuit, and the correct output of the system is determined only by voting, thereby quickly completing the fault repair. Sari et al. combined TMR with scrubbing technology to improve system reliability by reducing the execution time of configuration memory scrubbing [6]. But it was difficult to utilize redundant resources for the entire electronic system. And for the problem of on-chip embedded memory failure, Patil et al. [7] proposed a scheme for detecting and repairing faults in multi-port memories by using built-in self test, thereby reducing resource area consumption. Similar to redundancy technology, another popular fault-tolerant technology is reconstruction technology. The reconstruction technology pre-stores the configuration circuit of the original system. After detecting the fault, it reconstructs the fault circuit with the saved configuration information, so that the circuit resumes normal operation [8, 9]. However, the reconstruction technology needs to reconfigure the entire electronic system. Every time a small fault occurs, the entire system will be reconfigured, which will generate a lot of time overhead. In order to meet real-time constraints, Nazar [10] proposed a partial reconfiguration scheme to repair circuit faults and reduce repair time consumption. But this scheme relies on fine-grained fault detection, which is difficult to meet complex circuit systems.

Evolution fault-tolerant technology does not require a large amount of additional redundant resources, nor does it require pre-stored system configuration information. It can adjust the circuit structure to adaptively repair faulty circuits, significantly reducing hardware resource consumption and repair time consumption. Yang et al. [11] proposed a three-module redundancy architecture based on evolution mechanism. This scheme evolves the system circuit into a redundant module with different structures through an interactive two-stage mutation evolution strategy, which can effectively solve the common mode fault problem, but the hardware resources are more expensive. Zhang et al. [12, 13] proposed a new self-repair technology based on evolution hardware and compensation balance technology, which can realize fault self-repair of various circuits and devices through dynamic configuration. However, if the same problem occurs multiple times in different time periods, the system will repeat the evolution repair, which takes time. In response to this problem, Liu et al. [14, 15] proposed a real-time system fault-tolerant strategy based on evolutionary hardware, which accesses the configuration library when multiple faults occur in the same circuit, and reduces the repair time by combining the configuration library and the similarity evolution algorithm. However, the problem is that the repair constraint duration of the system circuit cannot be accurately predicted, and maintaining the configuration library also adds extra time and resource consumption.

The above fault-tolerant schemes have good fault tolerance after experimental verification. But since the specific fault repair constraint period cannot be obtained, the real-time performance is relative. If the repair circuit cannot be obtained within the constraint period, even if the repair circuit is finally generated, fault tolerance fails too, so a fault-tolerant scheme with efficient real-time and fault tolerance must be designed.

3 Real-Time Fault Tolerant System

Since different circuit systems have different complex structures, each circuit unit has different repair constraint time after a circuit failure occurs. In the case that the constraint time cannot be obtained, it must be ensured that the normal operation of the circuit cannot be stopped when the system is repaired, and the repair should be as fast as possible. This paper presents an online real-time repair scheme. This scheme detects circuit faults through built-in test. After the fault occurs, the detection mechanism finely locates and isolates the fault source. Then it uses the fault compensation mechanism to maintain the normal operation of the system. At the same time, it runs the evolution repair mechanism to quickly generate the repair circuit, and finally realizes the online real-time repair of the system and improves the reliability of the system.

3.1 Fault Detection Mechanism

The premise of fault tolerance is that after the circuit fails, the system can quickly detect the fault area and take corresponding repair measures. This paper proposes a detection mechanism of Built-in test (BIT) with feedback. By running the BIT, the system periodically detects the working conditions of the various components during the operation of the circuit. As shown in Fig. 1, the input parameter is used to compare and analyze with the truth table. The system records the circuit results of each cycle for the feedback mechanism. If there is no fault, the system runs normally. If a fault occurs, the system generates a feedback signal, and the circuit re-runs and get the result, and compares the two running results with the truth table to determine whether it is a transient fault. If the fault is a transient fault, the system is operating normally. If it is not a transient fault, the system generates a fault signal and isolates the fault source.

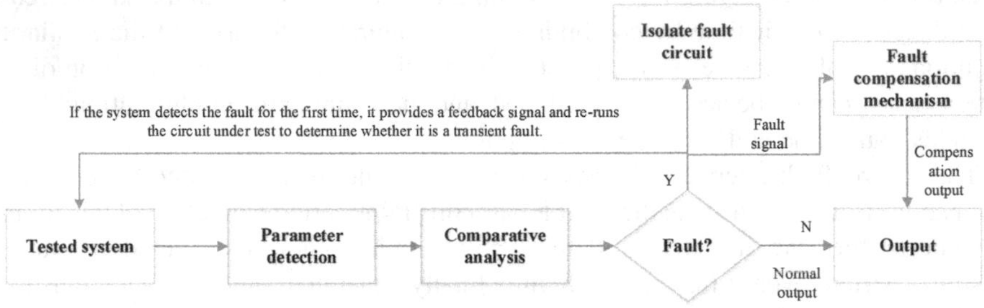

Fig. 1. BIT fault detection mechanism with feedback

BIT technology has circuit status detection and fault detection to improve the accuracy of fault diagnosis and locate fault sources. However, there are defects in the detection of transient faults. The BIT detection mechanism with feedback proposed in this paper can effectively deal with transient faults, and reduce the diagnosis and repair time.

3.2 Fault Compensation Mechanism

After fault detection locates the fault source circuit, it is necessary to isolate the fault circuit. At this time, the system still needs normal operation. Due to the complicated structure of the circuit system, it is impossible to predict the repair constraint period of the faulty circuit. If the fault repair cannot be completed within the constraint period, the operation of the system is directly affected, and even leads to serious consequences.

Based on the above reasons, this paper proposes a fault compensation mechanism. After receiving the fault signal, the system uses the fault compensation mechanism to maintain the normal operation of the circuit, and then uses the BIT to isolate the fault circuit to provide security for fault repair. Figure 2 shows the fault compensation mechanism. The system uses the truth table for fault detection and fault compensation. When the fault occurs, the fault detection mechanism sends a signal C1 to the multi-channel analog switch MUX. Then BIT isolates the faulty circuit. Signal C0 triggers the fault compensation mechanism. Truth table provides the correct output data, and the compensation mechanism outputs the correct data through the MUX to ensure the normal operation of the system.

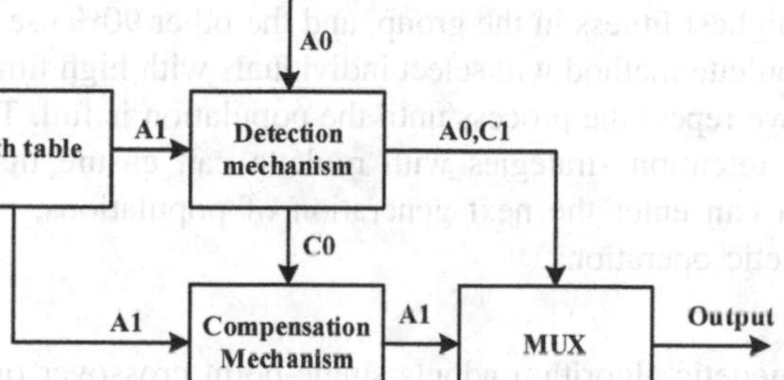

Fig. 2. Fault compensation mechanism

While the repair mechanism is running, the system can operate normally. It is not necessary to predict the repair constraint duration of the circuit, and the faulty circuit can be reconfigured after the rapid evolution, so that the online real-time repair of the fault can be realized.

3.3 Evolution Repair Mechanism

System fault tolerance is a real-time process. If the evolution mechanism cannot obtain the repair circuit under the real-time constraints, the system function will be directly affected. For the evolution hardware fault tolerance technology, it is necessary to obtain a repair circuit within the fault repair time of the system. In the case of unknown problems, running evolution algorithms occupies most of the repair time, so a good evolution algorithm plays a key in improving the real-time performance of the evolution hardware fault-tolerant technology. Genetic algorithms are the most commonly used algorithms for evolution hardware. It uses the fitness value to guide the search process without requiring the target function to be continuous. And its search process starts from the solution group, not from the point. However, the population of the genetic algorithm is randomized at the time of initialization, and the quality of the individual cannot be guaranteed. A large part of the population is far away from the optimal solution. And because the crossover and mutation operations of genetic algorithms are random, the performance of individuals after hybridization and mutation cannot be guaranteed to be better than the original. Finally, the convergence speed and accuracy of the algorithm may be affected. Based on the above reasons, this paper proposes an improved chaotic genetic algorithm (ICGA). ICGA improves the evolution rate and local search ability of the algorithm by improving the process of selection, intersection and mutation of genetic algorithm, thereby improving the efficiency of evolution repair.

Selection

The initial group determines the search efficiency of the optimal solution to some extent. The genetic algorithm usually randomly generates the initial population within a given range, and the randomly generated population has discrete, random and irregular characteristic. In order to improve the ergodicity of the initial population and increase the diversity of the population, The elite retention mechanism is adopted for the 10% group with the highest fitness in the group, and the other 90% use roulette to make the selection. The roulette method will select individuals with high fitness from 90% of the population and we repeat the process until the population is full. The selection method combining elite retention strategies with roulette can ensure that each generation's optimal solution can enter the next generation of populations, accelerating the convergence of genetic operations.

Intersection

The traditional genetic algorithm adopts single-point crossover or uniform crossover, which leads to slow convergence in the early stage of evolution, and it is easy to destroy the excellent mode of chromosomes and reduce the evolution efficiency. To improve algorithm efficiency, ICGA uses adaptive chaotic crossover. The crossover operator is continuously adjusted according to the change in chromosome fitness of the individual. As shown in Eq. 1, the number of individual intersections individuals is obtained by calculating individual fitness values and population fitness values. As shown in Eq. 2, then we use the Tent chaotic map with strong traversal uniformity to generate intersections that are evenly distributed across chromosomes. The 10% of individuals with large initial chromosome adaptation values need to be judged. If the offspring fitness value is smaller than the parental fitness value, the parental chromosome is still retained.

$$Pc = \begin{cases} k_1, f \leq f_{avg} \\ k_2(f_{\max} - f)/(f_{\max} - f_{avg}), f > f_{avg} \end{cases} \tag{1}$$

$$x^{n+1} = \begin{cases} 2x^n, 0 \leq x^n \leq 0.5 \\ 2(1 - x^n), 0.5 \leq x^n \leq 1 \end{cases} \tag{2}$$

K_1 and k_2 are constants, f is the current fitness value of the chromosome, f_{max} is the current maximum fitness value of the population, and f_{avg} is the average fitness value of the population, and x is a random number in the interval [0, 1], and the repeated operation generates a uniform random number. Then we map the random numbers to the feasible range of the chromosome length to get the intersection position of the chromosome.

Mutation

In the later stage of evolution, the average fitness of the population is close to the optimal chromosome fitness. At this time, we need to fine-tune the population chromosomes through the mutation operation to solve the local optimal problem. Similar to the crossover process, ICGA uses adaptive chaotic mutation. By comparing the fitness of the population's optimal chromosome with the current chromosome's, the mutation numbers of the current individual is calculated. ICGA continuously searches the surrounding area of the chromosome and gradually reaches the optimal chromosome fitness. The mutation number is calculated by the following formulas, where N is the length of the chromosome, F_{max} is the maximum fitness specified by the user, F_i is the fitness of the ith chromosome, P_{max} is the maximum mutation rate specified by the user, L_{max} is the maximum mutation number, and N_i is the mutation number of the ith chromosome. From formulas (3) and (4), we first calculate the difference between the fitness of the ith chromosome and the maximum fitness, and then obtain the proportion of the difference. Finally, we combine the proportion and the mutation rate to obtain the mutation number of the ith chromosome. It can be seen that the greater the proportion is, the smaller the chromosome fitness is, and the more the mutation number will be.

$$L_{\max} = N * P_{\max} \tag{3}$$

$$N_i = L_{\max} * \frac{F_{\max} - F_i}{F_{\max}} \tag{4}$$

When the variant numbers are obtained, ICGA generates random mutation positions through the Tent chaotic map and maps the random numbers to the feasible region of the chromosome length. In the early stage of evolution, ICGA quickly achieves a higher level of average fitness of the population through crossover and mutation operations. Later, since the individual's chromosome fitness is close to the maximum fitness value, the number of variants is also reduced. In this way, the optimal solution is searched in the solution space, and each variation only retains high-quality individuals, which can make the algorithm break through the limitation of the local optimal solution. The algorithm flow of ICGA is as follows.

ICGA

```
begin
  Initialize P(g);
  Fitness(g)←CalculateFit(P(g));
  if (get the solution) break;
  while g< gmax do
    begin
     P'(g)← Select(P(g), Fitness(g));
     CrossoverNum(g)← CalCossover[P'(g)];
    CrossoverPosition(g): get crossover positions through Tent chaotic map;
      P''(g)← Crossover(P'(g), CrossoverPosition(g));
     Fitness(g)←CalculateFit(P(g));
      while i <N do
       begin
       CurrentFit ← calFit(chrom[i]);
       MutationRate(i) ← MutRatemax *(Fitmax -CurrentFit)/ Fitmax;;
       MutationNum(i) ← MutationRate(i)*N;
       while j < MutationNum(i)
       begin
         MutationPosition(i):Get mutation positons through Tent chaotic map;
       end
       P'''(g)← Mutation(P''(g), MutationPosition(i));
         if(CalculateFit(P''(g)) < CalculateFit(P'''(g)))
           P''(g)← P'''(g);
         i ← i+1;
       end
     Fitness(g)←CalculateFit(P''(g));
     if (get the solution) break;
     g← g+1;
    end
 end
```

4 Implementation

The experiment uses Xilinx's Zynq UltraScale zcu102 development board. We use 2-bit multiplier and 8-bit parity checker as experimental objects for fault-tolerant evolution. In this experiment, the fitness evaluation of the evolution hardware uses the internal evolution method, that is, each chromosome in the group is downloaded to FPGA for fitness evaluation, thereby accelerating the calculation speed of the fitness and reducing the time consumption caused by the fitness calculation. Considering the reconfiguration time of chromosomes and the computational cost of fitness, this experiment uses Virtual Reconfigurable Circuits (VRC) [16], which implements more efficient chromosome coding operations, simplifies the complexity of the evolution target circuit, and reduces computing costs. The important parameters of the algorithm and circuit in the experiment are shown in Table 1. It can be seen that virtual reconfigurable circuit of the 8-bit parity checker uses an 8 * 4 matrix with a total of 32 configuration function blocks (CFB). Each CFB contains two inputs and one output. The inputs of column 0 are from the circuit input, and the outputs are used as the inputs of the column 1. After the calculations are completed in the column 3, we can get the final circuit results based on the outputs of the last column. Therefore, after configuring the chromosome as VRC, we can calculate all the circuit inputs and get all the actual outputs. By comparing the actual outputs with the theoretical outputs in the truth table, we can finally get the fitness value of the chromosome.

Table 1. Algorithm and circuit structure parameters

Parameters	8-bit parity checker	2-bit multiplier
VRC scale	8 * 4	8 * 4
Chromosome length, bit	291	300
Population size	30	30
Maximum fitness	256	64
Largest generation	4000	10000

In order to make full use of the software and hardware cooperation characteristics of ZYNQ, in the programmable logic part, we configure the VRC module of the experimental circuit, and build the fault detection module and fault compensation module; then in the processing system, we execute various evolution algorithms to get chromosomes of each generation; finally we transmit the chromosomes to the VRC module in the programmable logic part through the AXI bus to complete the fitness calculation.

We use a fixed fault injection to simulate an actual circuit fault. In the experiment, we keep the inputs of some CFBs in the virtual reconfigurable circuit at 0 or 1 to achieve the effects of circuit failure, resulting in circuit failure. After replacing the fault location repeatedly, the experimental process is as similar as possible to the failure caused by environmental problems, which improves the credibility of the experiment.

When the fault occurs, system determines the fault circuit through the BIT detection mechanism with feedback, and then uses the fault compensation mechanism to maintain the normal operation of the circuit, and simultaneously stimulates the evolution repair mechanism to generate the repair circuit, and finally realizes the online fault repair. We use particle swarm optimization (PSO), simulated annealing (SA), standard genetic algorithm (SGA), adaptive genetic algorithm (AGA) and improved chaotic genetic algorithm (ICGA) as the evolution algorithms to repair the proposed fault-tolerant system. The experimental results are shown in Figs. 3 and 4.

It can be seen from the figure that the fault-tolerant scheme proposed in this paper can repair circuit faults well, but different repair algorithms have different efficiency. With the increase of generations, ICGA can change the crossover operator and mutation operator according to the fitness of the chromosome. In the early stage of evolution, the average fitness of the population is quickly reached a higher level. In the

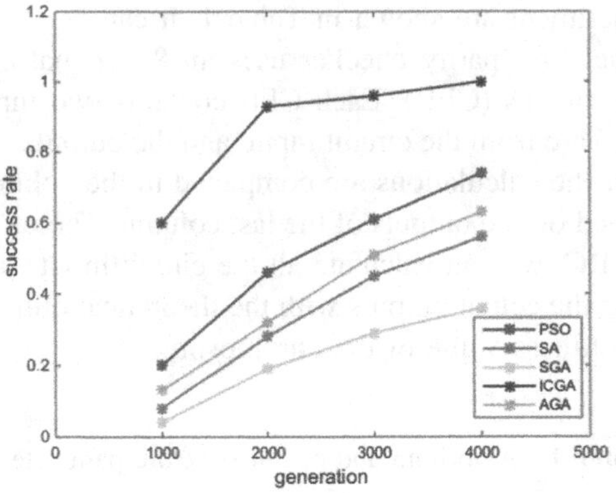

Fig. 3. Results of 8-bit parity

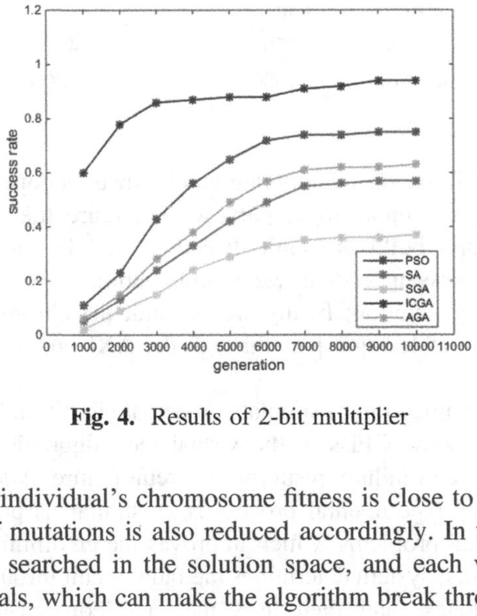

Fig. 4. Results of 2-bit multiplier

later stage, since the individual's chromosome fitness is close to the maximum fitness value, the number of mutations is also reduced accordingly. In this way, the optimal solution is gradually searched in the solution space, and each variation only retains high-quality individuals, which can make the algorithm break through the limitation of the local optimal solution. Figure 3 shows the repair results of the 8-bit parity checker. We performed 30 fault injections on the 8-bit parity circuit. The best repair result is ICGA, and the repair success rate can reach 93% within 2000 generations. Figure 4 shows the experimental results of a 2-bit multiplier. For a more complex 2-bit multiplier, ICGA can complete 60% fault repair within 1000 generations and 90% repair rate within 4000 generations. Compared with other algorithms, ICGA improves the real-time performance of fault-tolerant schemes most obviously.

Figure 5 shows the repair circuit and chromosome coding structure of 8-bit parity checker. Due to the randomness of the evolution hardware repair technology, the optimal chromosome may not be obtained in the end, but the adaptive value of the iterative local optimal chromosome is very different from the optimal chromosome, which can satisfy most of the circuit functions. Therefore, the local optimal chromosome can still be used to configure the repair circuit, and if the fault is detected again, the evolution repair is performed again.

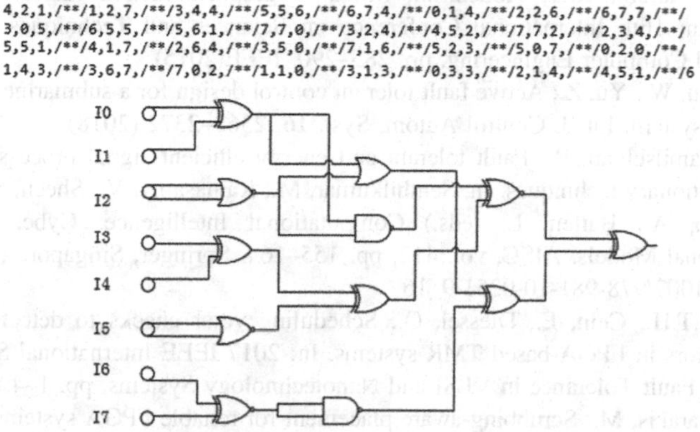

Fig. 5. The repair circuit of 8-bit parity checker

5 Conclusion

Evolution fault-tolerant technology can adjust the circuit structure of the programmable logic device to adaptively repair circuit faults, but the evolution process takes a lot of repair time. Aiming at the real-time problem of evolution repair, this paper proposes a real-time system fault-tolerant scheme based on improved chaotic genetic algorithm. The scheme detects the state of the circuit in real time through the BIT detection mechanism with feedback. When the fault occurs, the system uses the fault compensation mechanism to maintain the normal operation of the circuit, at the same time, stimulate the evolutionary repair mechanism. Through the improved chaotic genetic algorithm, the scheme greatly improves the rate and success rate of evolution repair. Ultimate, the solution realizes online repair of fault circuits, which improves the reliability and stability of the system.

Funding. This work was supported by the National Nature Science Foundation of China (No.61472100) and Fundamental Research Funds for the Central Universities, China (No. DUT17JC26).

References

1. Jamshidpour, E., Poure, P., Saadate, S.: Photovoltaic systems reliability improvement by real-time FPGA-based switch failure diagnosis and fault-tolerant DC-DC converter. IEEE Trans. Industr. Electron. **62**(11), 7247–7255 (2015)
2. Najari, H., Harabi, R.E., Abdelkrim, M.N.: A graphical active fault tolerant control approach. In: 16th International Conference on Sciences and Techniques of Automatic Control and Computer Engineering, pp. 285–290. IEEE(2015)
3. Liu, L.J., Yu, W., Yu, Z.: Active fault-tolerant control design for a submarine semi-physical simulation system. Int. J. Control Autom. Syst. **16**, 2363–2372 (2018)
4. Jose, D., Tamilselvan, R.: Fault tolerant and energy efficient signal processing on FPGA using evolutionary techniques. In: Senthilkumar, M., Ramasamy, V., Sheen, S., Veeramani, C., Bonato, A., Batten, L. (eds.) Computational Intelligence, Cyber Security and Computational Models. AISC, vol. 412, pp. 155–164. Springer, Singapore (2016). https://doi.org/10.1007/978-981-10-0251-9_16
5. Nguyen, N.T.H., Cein, E., Diessel, O.: Scheduling voter checks to detect configuration memory errors in FPGA-based TMR systems. In: 2017 IEEE International Symposium on Defect and Fault Tolerance in VLSI and Nanotechnology Systems, pp. 1–4. IEEE (2017)
6. Sari, A., Psarakis, M.: Scrubbing-aware placement for reliable FPGA systems. IEEE Trans. Emerg. Top. Comput. (2017)
7. Patil, S.R., Musle, D.B.: Implementation of BIST technology for fault detection and repair of the multiported memory using FPGA. In: Proceedings of the International Conference on Electronics, Communication and Aerospace Technology, pp. 43–47. IEEE (2017)
8. Chatterjee, N., Mukherjee, P., Chattopadhyay, S.: A strategy for fault tolerant reconfigurable Network-on-Chip design. In: 2016 20th International Symposium on VLSI Design and Test. IEEE (2016)
9. Walker, J.A., Trefzer, M.A., Bale, S.J., Tyrrel, A.M.: PAnDA: a reconfigurable architecture that adapts to physical substrate variations. IEEE Trans. Comput. **62**(8), 1584–1596 (2013)
10. Nazar, G.L.: Improving FPGA repair under real-time constraints. Microelectron. Reliab. **55**(7), 1109–1119 (2015)
11. Yang, X., Li, Y., Fang, C., Nie, C., Ni, F.: Research on evolution mechanism in different-structure module redundancy fault-tolerant system. In: Li, K., Li, J., Liu, Y., Castiglione, A. (eds.) ISICA 2015. CCIS, vol. 575, pp. 171–180. Springer, Singapore (2016). https://doi.org/10.1007/978-981-10-0356-1_17
12. Zhang, J.B., Cai, J.Y., Meng, Y.F.: Fault self-repair strategy based on evolvable hardware and reparation balance technology. Chin. J. Aeronaut. **27**(5), 1211–1222 (2014)
13. Zhang, J.B., Cai, J.Y., Meng, Y.F.: Performance analysis of circuit fault self-repair strategy based on EHW and RBT. Beijing Hangkong Hangtian Daxue Xuebao/J. Beijing Univ. Aeronaut. Astronaut. **42**(11), 2423–2435 (2016)
14. Wang, J., Liu, J.W., Feng, B., Hou, G.: The dynamic evaluation strategy for evolvable hardware. In: Proceedings of the 2015 9th International Conference on Frontier of Computer Science and Technology, pp. 91–95. IEEE (2015)
15. Wang, J., Liu, J.W.: Fault-tolerant strategy for real-time system based on evolvable hardware. J. Circ. Syst. Comput. **26**(7) (2017)
16. Srivastava, A.K., Gupta, A., Chaturvedi, S., Rastogi, V.: Design and simulation of virtual reconfigurable circuit for a Fault Tolerant System. In: International Conference on Recent Advances and Innovations in Engineering. IEEE (2014)

International Workshop on Intelligent 5G Communication and Digital Image Processing Technology

A Transfer Learning Method for CT Image Classification of Pulmonary Nodules

Ran Wang[1,2(✉)], Huadong Sun[1,2], Jialin Zhang[1], and Zhijie Zhao[1,2]

[1] School of Computer and Information Engineering, Harbin University of Commerce, Harbin 150028, China
wr0905@sina.com

[2] Provincial Key Laboratory of Electronic Commerce and Information Processing, Harbin University of Commerce, Harbin 150028, China

Abstract. A pulmonary nodule classification method of Computer Tomography (CT) images based on transfer learning of deep convolutional neural network (CNN) is proposed. Lung CT images with labels are quite limited compared with the large scale image database such as ImageNet. It is easy to produce over-fitting problem when using the limited data to train the deep CNN for classification task. In this paper, in order to overcome this difficulty, the deep CNNs GoogleNet and ResNet are pre-trained on the large scale database ImageNet. The fully connected layers and the classifiers of the pre-trained networks are replaced to complete the classification of CT images of pulmonary nodules. A sub set of the Lung Image Database Consortium image collection (LIDC-IDRI) is used to fine-tune the network and validate the classification accuracy. This is the process of transfer learning. It solves the problem of the deficiency of lung CT images as labeled training data for CNNs. By the knowledge obtained from the pre-trained CNNs which have been trained on ImageNet, the network is easier to converge and the training time is greatly reduced. The classification accuracy of Pulmonary Nodules can be reached up to 71.88% by using the proposed method.

Keywords: Transfer learning · Convolutional neural network · Computer tomography image · Pulmonary nodule

1 Introduction

In recent years, with the increase of environmental pollution, the incidence of lung cancer is on the rise. According to the published 2017 Chinese Cancer Annual Report, morbidity and mortality of lung cancer are both in the first place, seriously harm the health of Chinese people. The survey report of American Cancer Society (ACS) shows, at present the 5-years survival rate of lung cancer patients is only 17%, but the survival rate can be increased to 55% as long as early treatment is obtained [1]. Therefore, the early diagnosis of lung cancer is of great significance to patients. Early lung cancer is mainly characterized by pulmonary nodules. Therefore, early detection of pulmonary nodules is important for increasing the survival rate of lung cancer patients.

M. Jia et al. (Eds.): WiSATS 2019, LNICST 281, pp. 159–166, 2019.
https://doi.org/10.1007/978-3-030-19156-6_15

For the detection of pulmonary nodules, the currently widely accepted method which is safe and effective is Computer Tomography (CT). The advantage of CT images is that its resolution is high, and organ slices can be seen at different locations. By analyzing the CT image, it is not only possible to check whether there is a pulmonary nodule and locate the nodule, but also to analyze the size, density, morphology, internal structure and edge characteristics of the nodule [2]. However, the amount of CT images is large, one patient's lung CT images can reach more than 100 sheets. For doctors, viewing CT images of patients requires a large amount of time.

The emergence of the computer-aided diagnosis based on image processing and convolutional neural network (CNN) has reduced the workload of doctors for reading CT images [3]. The CNN can be used to classify the CT images when being successfully trained. Image classification based on CNN overcomes some shortcomings of traditional image classification methods. There is no need to manually design features, the network can extract image features and classify the images when having trained on a large data set. The CNN is going deeper and larger to increase its expression ability. However, if the training data is limited, it is easy to produce over-fitting and network degradation problems [4, 6]. In order to solve these problems, the GoogleNet [5], ResNet [6] architecture and the concept of transfer learning have been proposed [7–9].

Using these methods, we start with the concept of transfer learning. Then the steps of transfer learning of CNN and the medical image database we use to train the networks are shown. Finally, the experimental results and analysis are given to prove the validity of the presented method.

2 The Transfer Learning of Convolutional Neural Network

Transfer learning is a machine learning method that solves different but related domain problems by using existing knowledge [7]. The basic idea of transfer learning is to learn a representation that is shared across related tasks. In transfer learning the higher the correlation between the source and target fields, the better the learning results will be [8]. Different levels of features have different transfer learning abilities; higher-level features have better transfer learning ability than lower-level features [9]. In transfer learning, the common features can be learned by solving an optimization problem, given as follows:

$$J(\Theta, U) = \underset{\Theta, U}{\arg\min} \left[\sum_{t \in \{T,S\}} \sum_{i=1}^{n_t} L\left(y_{t,t}, \left\langle \theta_t, U^T x_{t,t} \right\rangle\right) + \gamma \|\Theta\|_{2,1}^2 \right] \quad (1)$$

In Eq. (1), S and T denote the tasks in the source domain and target domain, x and y denote the feature vectors and the labels, respectively. $\Theta = [\theta_s, \theta_t] \in R^{d \times 2}$ is a matrix of parameters. γ is the regularization parameter. U is a $d \times d$ orthogonal matrix (mapping function) for mapping the original high-dimensional data to low-dimensional representations. The (r, p)-norm of Θ is defined as:

$$\|\Theta\|_{r,p} = \left(\sum\nolimits_{i=1}^{d} \|\theta^i\|_r^p\right)^{1/p} \tag{2}$$

The optimization problem (1) estimates both of the low-dimensional representations $U^T X_T$, $U^T X_S$ and the parameters Θ of the model at the same time.

The transfer learning flow chart of CNN is shown in Fig. 1:

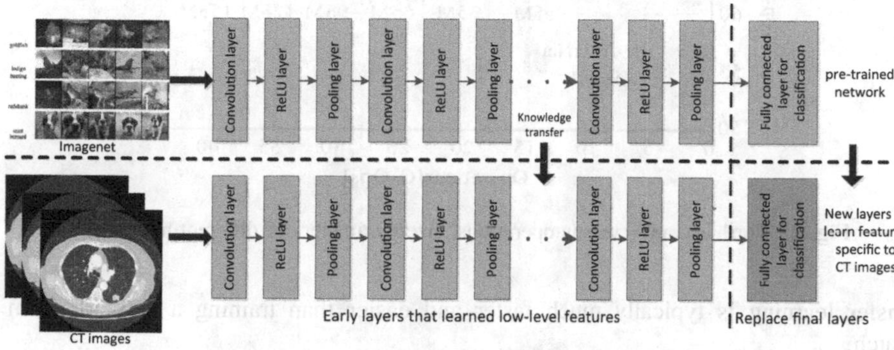

Fig. 1. The transfer learning flow chart of CNN.

First, a pre-trained CNN is loaded, it may have been trained on a large scale data set such as ImageNet; then, the last few layers of the loaded network are replaced by new layers to learn features specific to the dataset of new field; finally, the new dataset and training parameters are used to fine-tuning the network.

2.1 The Pre-trained CNNs for Transfer Learning

Different CNNs have different characteristics. The most important characteristics are network accuracy, speed, and size. Choosing a network is generally a tradeoff between these characteristics. A good network has high accuracy and is fast. Figure 2 shows the top1 accuracy versus operations, size/parameters of different CNNs [11].

Top-1 one-crop accuracy versus amount of operations required for a single forward pass is shown in Fig. 2. The size of the blobs is proportional to the number of network parameters. A legend is reported in the bottom right corner, spanning from 5×10^6 to 155×10^6 parameters. In general, GoogleNet and its derivative inception series have the characteristics of lower resource consumption and medium accuracy. ResNet series have the characteristics of medium resource consumption and higher accuracy. These two types of CNN architectures have the best comprehensive performance.

In this paper, GoogleNet and ResNet are chosen for transfer learning. The pre-trained GoogleNet and ResNet we used in this paper have been trained on more than one million images and can classify images into 1000 object categories. The training images are a subset of the ImageNet database [10], which is used in ImageNet Large-Scale Visual Recognition Challenge (ILSVRC). Using a pre-trained network with

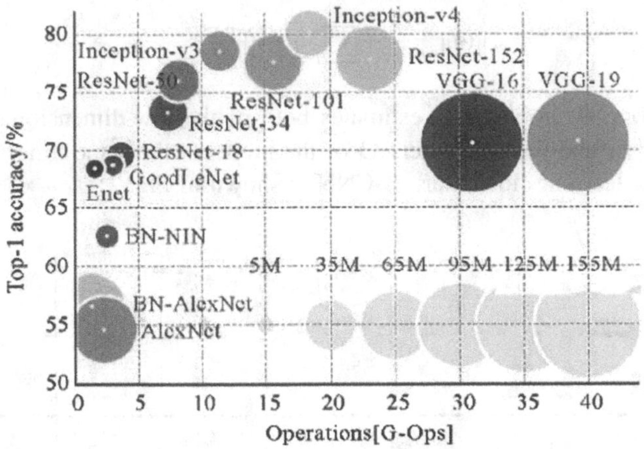

Fig. 2. Top1 accuracy versus operations, size/parameters of different networks

transfer learning is typically much faster and easier than training a network from scratch.

2.2 Fine-Tuning of the CNNs

For large scale CNNs as GoogleNet and ResNet, the lower level features show the color or edge feature of the image, well the higher level features show the texture feature, the more class-specific features and the entire objects with significant pose variation successively [8]. The effects of transfer learning of different levels of CNNs have been studied: high-level features of CNNs have better transfer learning ability than lower-level features [12]. In this paper, all the parameters and structure of the pre-trained networks are preserved besides the last three layers to obtain the higher level features before the fine-tuning of the networks.

The last three layers of the pre-trained CNNs are replaced by three new layers to complete classification of CT images of pulmonary nodules. The new layers are one fully connect layer, one softmax layer and one classifier of three categories. A sub set of CT images of the Lung Image Database Consortium image collection (LIDC-IDRI) is divided into training set and test set. After the replacement of the last three layers, the training set is used to fine-tune the network. When the fine-tuning is finished, the test set is used to validate the classification accuracy of the network.

GoogleNet can be iterated quickly and try out different parameter settings such as data preprocessing steps and training options. From that we may find which parameters are fit for our problem. Then a more accurate network: ResNet will be tried to see if the predict accuracy is improved.

3 The Lung Image Database Consortium Image Collection

In this paper, a sub set of the Lung Image Database Consortium image collection (LIDC-IDRI) is used for classifying the pulmonary nodules. LIDC-IDRI consists of diagnostic and lung cancer screening thoracic computed tomography (CT) scans with marked-up annotated lesions [13]. It is a web-accessible international resource for development, training, and evaluation of computer-assisted diagnostic (CAD) methods for lung cancer detection and diagnosis. It initiated by the National Cancer Institute (NCI), further advanced by the Foundation for the National Institutes of Health (FNIH). The data set contains 1018 cases. Each subject includes images from a clinical thoracic CT scan and an associated XML file that records the results of a two-phase image annotation process performed by four experienced thoracic radiologists.

Figure 3 shows Lung CT images of a patient in LIDC-IDRI. All the images are in the format of bitmap, they have three channels and the resolution of them is 512 × 512. Figure 3(a) shows CT images with pulmonary nodules, the edge of the nodule is marked with a red line. Figure 3(b) shows CT images without nodules. Figure 3(c) shows CT images with a suspected nodule which is marked with a green line.

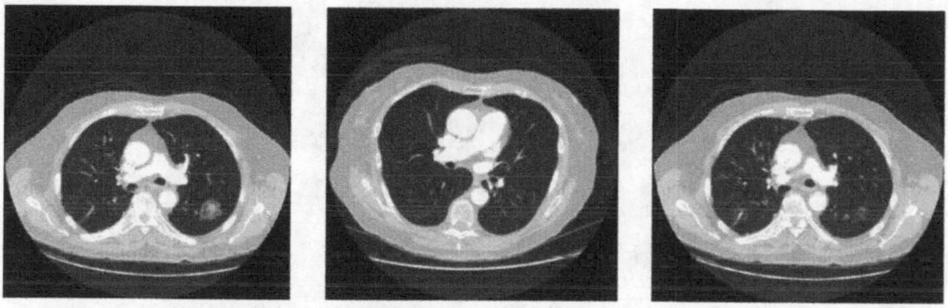

(a) Pulmonary nodule (b) Without nodule (c) Suspected nodules

Fig. 3. Lung CT images of a patient in LIDC-IDRI (Color figure online)

4 Experimental Results and Analysis

The experimental environment is Windows 7 operating system and Matlab R2017b with deep learning toolbox.

Table 1. Training options for fine-tuning

Training options	GoogleNet	ResNet
Mini Batch Size	28	28
Epochs	7	7
Initial Learn Rate	1.4×10^{-4}	10^{-4}
Verbose Frequency	1	1
Network Depth	22	50

We choose 213 CT images of three patients in LIDC-IDRI which are divided into 3 categories: 73 CT images of lung tissue without nodules, 68 CT images of pulmonary nodules and 72 CT images of suspected nodules. 149 of 213 (70%) CT images are chosen stochastically from all 3 categories as training data and the rest 64 CT images are defined as validating data. All the images are resized to the resolution of 224 × 224 to fit the input size of the networks. Then the pre-trained GoogleNet or ResNet is loaded directly by googlenet and resnet50 function of Matlab. The last three layers: fully connected layer, softmax layer and classification layer are replaced by new ones which can be seen as a classifier of 3 classes. Then we use the CT images to fine-tune the network. The training options we use for fine-tuning GoogleNet and ResNet are shown in Table 1. For 149 training images and the Mini Batch Size of 28, there are 5 iterations per epoch and 35 iterations in total. Figure 4 shows the Classification accuracy of the two networks:

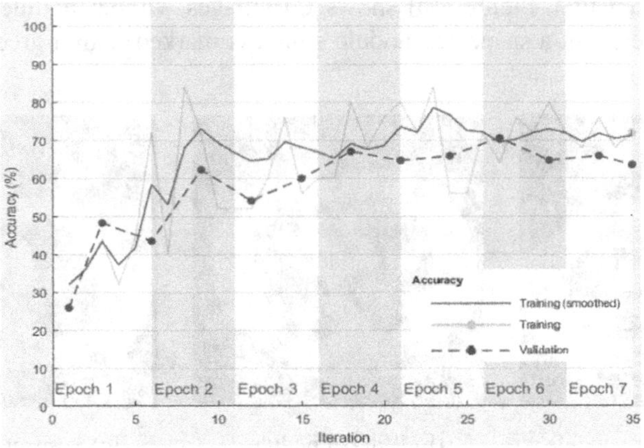

(a) Classification accuracy of GoogleNet

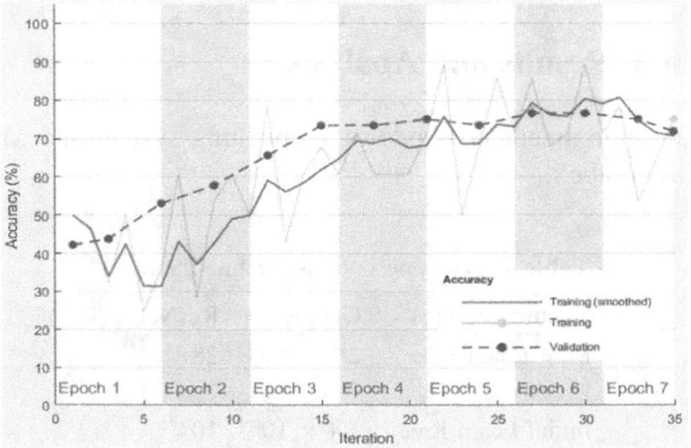

(b) Classification accuracy of ResNet

Fig. 4. Classification accuracy of the two networks

Figure 4(a) and (b) is the classification accuracy of GoogleNet and ResNet, respectively. In Fig. 4, training accuracy means the classification accuracy on each individual mini-batch. Smoothed training accuracy is obtained by applying a smoothing algorithm to the training accuracy. It is less noisy than the unsmoothed accuracy, making it easier to spot trends. Validation accuracy is the classification accuracy on the entire validation set. As shown in Fig. 4, the validation accuracy of the ResNet is higher than the GoogleNet. The validation accuracy of the GoogleNet has larger variation in the initial 3 epochs because of the larger Initial Learn Rate. It becomes smoother in the last 4 epochs. The final results of validation accuracy of the GoogleNet and the ResNet are 63.53% and 71.88%, respectively.

5 Conclusion

In this paper we presented a pulmonary nodule classification method in CT images based on transfer learning of CNN. The application of transfer learning solved the problem of the insufficiency of training data of CT images for training the network. By using transfer learning, we need only about two hundreds CT images in total to finish fine-tuning and validating the pre-trained GoogleNet or ResNet. Compared with training from scratch, the training time is greatly reduced when using transfer learning.

Two architectures of deep CNNs GoogleNet and ResNet have been pre-trained on a subset of ImageNet which contains millions of images in 1000 categories. By the replacement of last few layers and fine-tuning of the network, the knowledge which the networks learned from ImageNet by pre-training was transferred to pulmonary nodule CT images classification task.

It has been shown in our experiments that GoogleNet is iterated quickly, while ResNet is more accurate. The classification accuracy of the GoogleNet and the ResNet reaches up to 63.53% and 71.88% respectively, and the computing resource requirement is quite small.

Acknowledgment. This work is supported by the Basic Scientific Research Operating Expense Project of Provincial Institutions of Higher Education in Heilongjiang (17XN003); the Doctoral Research Startup Project of Harbin University of Commerce (2016BS28); and the Humanities and Social Sciences Research Projects of the Ministry of Education (18YJAZH128).

References

1. American Cancer Society: Cancer Facts and Figures 2016. American Cancer Society, Atlanta (2016)
2. Diciotti, S., Picozzi, G., Falchini, M., Mascalchi, M., Villari, N.: 3-D segmentation algorithm of small lung nodules in spiral CT Images. IEEE Trans. Inf. Technol. Biomed. **12**(1), 7–19 (2008)
3. Wang, Y., Zhou, T., Lu, H., Wu, C., Yang, P.: Computer aided diagnosis model for lung tumor based on ensemble convolutional neural network. J. Biomed. Eng. **4**(34), 543–551 (2017)

4. Hinton, G.E., Srivastava, N., Krizhevsky, A.: Improving neural networks by preventing co-adaption of feature detectors, pp. 1–18. arXiv:1207.0580 [cs.NE] (2012)
5. Szegedy, C., Liu, W., Jia, Y.: Going deeper with convolutions. In: Proceedings of the 2015 IEEE Conference on Computer Vision and Pattern Recognition, pp. 1–8. IEEE Computer Society, Washington (2015)
6. He, K., Zhang, X., Ren, S.: Deep residual learning for image recognition. In: 2016 IEEE Conference on Computer Vision and Pattern Recognition, Las Vegas, NV, United States, pp. 770–778 (2016)
7. Zhuang, F., Luo, P., He, Q., Shi, Z.: Survey on transfer learning research. J. Softw. **26**(1), 26–39 (2015)
8. Zeiler, M.D., Fergus, R.: Visualizing and understanding convolutional networks. In: Fleet, D., Pajdla, T., Schiele, B., Tuytelaars, T. (eds.) ECCV 2014. LNCS, vol. 8689, pp. 818–833. Springer, Cham (2014). https://doi.org/10.1007/978-3-319-10590-1_53
9. Zhou, B., Lapedriza, A., Xiao, J.: Learning deep features for scene recognition using places database. In: Proceedings of Advances in Neural Information Processing Systems, pp. 487–495. MIT Press, Cambridge (2014)
10. ImageNet Homepage. http://www.image-net.org. Accessed 8 July 2018
11. Canziani, A., Paszke, A., Culurciello, E.: An analysis of deep neural network models for practical applications, pp. 1–7. arXiv:1605.07678 [cs.CV] (2016)
12. Razavian, S., Azizpor, H., Sullivan, J.: CNN features off-the-shelf: an astounding baseline for recognition, pp. 1–8. arXiv:1403.6382 [cs.CV] (2014)
13. LIDC-IDRI Collection. https://wiki.cancerimagingarchive.net/display/Public/LIDC-IDRI. Accessed 4 Aug 2018

Depth Recovery from Focus-Defocus Cue by Entropy of DCT Coefficient

Huadong Sun[1,2(✉)], Zhijie Zhao[1,2], Xiaowei Han[1,2], and Lizhi Zhang[1,2]

[1] School of Computer and Information Engineering, Harbin University of Commerce, Harbin 150028, China
kof97_sun@163.com

[2] Heilongjiang Provincial Key Laboratory of Electronic Commerce and Information Processing, Harbin University of Commerce, Harbin 150028, China

Abstract. Depth recovery for single image is very important to 2D-3D image conversion, which is a challenging problem in computer vision. The focus-defocus as an effective pictorial cue, has been paid more and more attention. In this paper, we reveal the relationship between entropy of DCT coefficient and scale parameter of PSF. Then, a new method to depth recovery for single images using focus-defocus cue is proposed, in which the entropy of DCT coefficient is regarded as the measure of blur, and linear operation mapping the level of blur to depth is adopted. The proposed method, which can generate pixel-level depth map, is unnecessary to select threshold. The experimental results indicate that the new method is reliable and effective.

Keywords: Depth · Entropy of DCT coefficient · Focus-defocus cue · Measure of blur

1 Introduction

Three-Dimension display is an important form of expression to image information in future. Compared with traditional media, it provides outstanding intuitive and real scene feeling, diversified and comprehensive media interaction ability for the audience. Recently, Depth-image-based- rendering (DIBR) technique is applied to some advanced 3D TV system, in which a new 3D data representation, including tradition 2D image and its associated depth map, is adopted [1], which is efficient for rendering, transmission and coding [2]. But how to realize the depth information extraction from 2D image is a key problem.

In traditional image-forming system, 3D scene lost its depth information after projected by 2D image sensors. The efficient solution is to utilize signal processing or computer vision techniques to extract the lost depth information through employing various cues, such as linear perspective, motion parallax, texture gradient, atmospheric scattering, etc. [3]. In recent years, as an important pictorial cue, focus-defocus has been paid more and more attention.

In 1994, Gokstorp presented multi-resolution local frequency algorithm which needs two images of a scene obtained from the same view-point but using different

M. Jia et al. (Eds.): WiSATS 2019, LNICST 281, pp. 167–176, 2019.
https://doi.org/10.1007/978-3-030-19156-6_16

aperture settings, where the difference in defocused blur between two images can be calculated by local frequency representations of the two images and the sub-sampled scale-space pyramids [4]. In 2001, polynomial system identification method was presented by Rayala, which modeling the underlying phenomenon of defocusing as a linear system and a two-dimensional equation error algorithm is developed to calculate the coefficient of parametric transfer function [5]. In 2009, Mendapara introduced the exponentially decaying algorithm based on SUSAN operator, where a sequence of images acquired at varying focus is necessary [6]. In 2012, a formulation of unscented Kalman filter for depth estimation was designed, which is suitable to both motion and defocusing blur without constraining the PSF as Gaussian function [7]. In 2016, an iterative feedback method is presented which is for the simultaneous estimation of depth by joint spatiotemporal optimization, which needs all-in-focus videos from a defocused video pair [8]. In the same year, Xiao presented a method of multi-focus image fusion based on the depth recover, where the optical imaging of two multi-focus images can be simulated as the heat equations of positive regions, and the scene depth information is calculated by inhomogeneous diffusion equations [9]. Although providing good depth estimation, it is too restrictive that these algorithms require several images or videos to the same or similar scene screened by the different optical parameters.

Because of the multi-scale and multi-resolution characteristics, wavelet transform is used to estimate the level of blur in 2003, in which wavelet decomposition of macro-blocks within an image was carried on to analyze the high frequency information of that macro-block and the number of high-value wavelet coefficients was defined as the measure of blur [10]. However, how to select the threshold of wavelet coefficients was not mentioned in this method.

In this paper, a novel method is proposed, where the entropy of DCT coefficient is adopted as the measure of blur. In contrast to count number of high-value wavelet coefficients as a measure of blur in [10], entropy of DCT coefficient is unnecessary to select threshold and more effective.

2 Background

Focus-defocus is a significant cue to extract depth information for the single picture. Normally, the defocus phenomenon will happen when the object is not in the focal plane of the scene. The longer the distance between the focal plane and objects is, the worse the blurring is, and more smoothed objects' texture is. So, the level of blur is correlative to the depth of the objects.

The blur diameter can be referred as the intuitional measure to the level of blur. Suppose the background object defocus while the foreground object focus, the optical image-forming model of camera can be illustrated as Fig. 1. The parameters are defined as follows: f is the focus length, L is the optical lens aperture, p is the distance between focal plane and lens, q is the distance between imaging plane and lens, z is the distance between object and lens which is equivalent to the true depth value, and v is the image distance of object. The point object located at p will focus as one point in the imaging plane. But the point object which located at z will defocus as a blur circle in the image-forming plane. Apparently, larger diameter d of blur circle is, more seriously blur phenomenon happens.

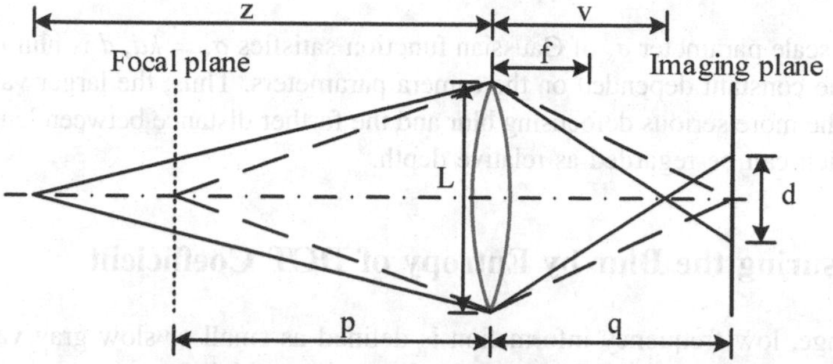

Fig. 1. The optical imaging model of camera.

The following equations can be obtained from the theory of optical lens image-forming and geometry relationship:

$$\frac{1}{p}+\frac{1}{q}=\frac{1}{f},\frac{1}{z}+\frac{1}{v}=\frac{1}{f},\frac{d}{L}=\frac{q-v}{v} \tag{1}$$

Through (1), the relationship between blur diameter (blur circle's diameter d) and true depth value z, can be calculated as

$$d=\frac{Lpf}{p-f}\left(\frac{1}{p}-\frac{1}{z}\right) \tag{2}$$

Obviously, when the true depth z increases, the blur diameter d will augment which indicates the blur phenomenon becomes worse.

Generally speaking, when the picture is not calibrated, the true depth can't be got because parameters $l, p.f$ are unknown. But the relative location between object and lens can be recovered, which means the relative depth. The relative depth is also enough to 2D-to-3D image conversion.

The mean square deviation of point spread function (PSF) can be regarded as the other measure to the level of blur. A 2D image point of a given object point can be regarded as the sum of the contributions of each point belonging to the surface in the neighbour of that 3D point which reflects light to the camera. 2D convolution operation can model above process. The observed defocused image $I'(x,y)$ can be described as the 2D convolution between PSF $g(x,y)$ and the ideal focused image $I(x,y)$.

$$I'(x,y)=I(x,y)\otimes g(x,y) \tag{3}$$

The PSF, which is determined by camera parameters and blur diameter, can be modeled as a 2D Gaussian function approximately,

$$g(x,y) = \frac{1}{2\pi\sigma_s^2}\exp(-\frac{x^2+y^2}{2\sigma_s^2}) \tag{4}$$

where the scale parameter σ_s of Gaussian function satisfies $\sigma_s = kd$, d is blur diameter, and k is the constant depended on the camera parameters. Thus, the larger value of σ_s indicates the more serious defocusing blur and the farther distance between lens and the object which can be regarded as relative depth.

3 Measuring the Blur by Entropy of DCT Coefficient

To an image, low frequency information is defined as small or slow gray value variation, such as the plain area of images. On the contrary, high frequency information is considered as a transient section which contains sharp or fast amplitude variation, such as edge and texture of images. Intuitively, to the same texture or edge, the focused image will have more high frequency component and less low frequency component than the defocused image. So, the more serious blur indicates less high frequency information and more low frequency information. It suggests that the frequency spectrum can be adopted to measure the level of blur.

3.1 Entropy of DCT Coefficient

Discrete Cosine Transform, especially type-II DCT, is widely used in signal processing and image compression. It profits from the strong characteristic, which most energy of natural signals (including sound and image) is concentrated at the low-frequency coefficients of DCT.

Let $f(m,n)$ denotes a pixel's gray value of the image, it's size is $N \times N$, then the type-II DCT of image can be described as.

$$A(k,l) = \sum_{m=0}^{N-1}\sum_{n=0}^{N-1} f(m,n)[a(m)cos\frac{\pi(2m+1)k}{2N}][a(n)cos\frac{\pi(2n+1)l}{2N}] \tag{5}$$

where

$$a(n) = \begin{cases} \sqrt{\frac{1}{N}}, & n = 0 \\ \sqrt{\frac{2}{N}}, & 1 \le n \le N-1 \end{cases}.$$

The frequency of corresponding cosine kernel will rise with the increase of k, l, and the DCT coefficient $A(k,l)$ can be considered as the map of image signal to the cosine kernel whose frequency increases. Therefore, the DCT coefficient can reflect the spectrum of image from low frequency to high frequency which can be used to measure the level of blur.

On the other hand, we can observe that $A(k,l)$ is the cosine weighted summation of $f(m,n)$ from (5). Suppose all $f(m,n)$ submit the identical distribution in different m, n, then as the weighted sum of random variables with the identical distribution, $A(k,l)$ can approximately submit to Gaussian distribution according to the central limit theorem. Although each $f(m,n)$ are spatial correlated, the central limit theorem can apply as long as the magnitude of correlation is less than 1. The correlation of typical image, is not too large and there are enough pixels to obtain a good approximation to Gaussian distribution. Moreover, because of the unitary nature of DCT, the mean of Gaussian distribution is zero. So, the DCT coefficient $A(k,l)$ submits a zero-mean Gaussian as follows.

$$p(A) = \frac{1}{\sqrt{2\pi\sigma}} exp(-\frac{A^2}{2\sigma^2}) \tag{6}$$

where σ^2 is variance, and A is $A(k,l)$ for short. Some examples about the distribution of DCT coefficient are shown in Fig. 2.

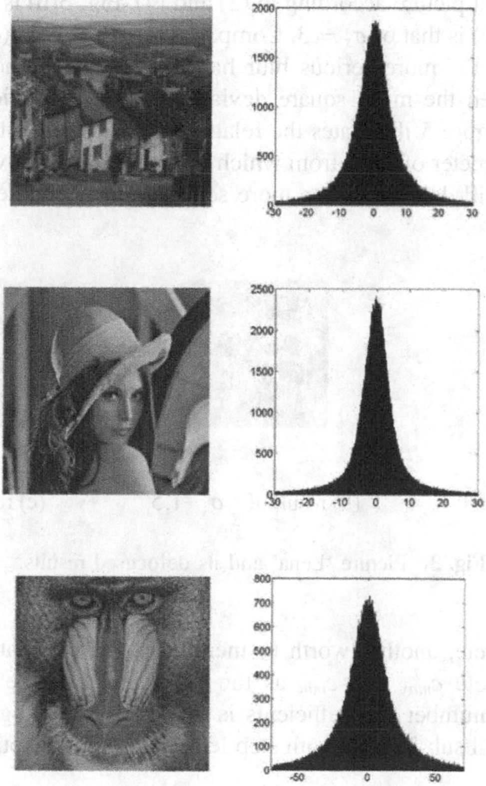

Fig. 2. Some standard images and their DCT coefficient histograms.

Thus, entropy of DCT coefficient can be obtained by

$$\begin{aligned} H &= -\int_{-\infty}^{+\infty} p(A)ln\,p(A)dA = -\int_{-\infty}^{+\infty} \frac{1}{\sqrt{2\pi}\sigma} exp(-\frac{A^2}{2\sigma^2}) \cdot [-ln(\sqrt{2\pi}\sigma) - \frac{A^2}{2\sigma^2}]dA \\ &= [\frac{1}{2} + ln(\sqrt{2\pi}\sigma)] \cdot \int_{-\infty}^{+\infty} \frac{1}{\sqrt{2\pi}\sigma} exp(-\frac{A^2}{2\sigma^2})dA + \frac{1}{\sqrt{2\pi}\sigma} \cdot \frac{A}{2} \cdot exp(-\frac{A^2}{2\sigma^2})|_{-\infty}^{+\infty} \\ &= ln(\sqrt{2\pi e} \cdot \sigma) \end{aligned} \tag{7}$$

It can be seen obviously that the entropy of DCT coefficient is decided by σ only. The following proof will indicate the decreasing relationship between mean square deviation σ of DCT coefficient and the scale parameter σ_s of Gaussian PSF.

3.2 Relationship Between Entropy of DCT Coefficient and Level of Blur

The relationship between the level of blur and entropy of DCT coefficient can also be verified by the following simulations. Figure 3(a) is the original focused picture. After defocusing the original picture according to (3) and (4), Fig. 3(b) is defocused result of $\sigma_s = 1.5$, and Fig. 3(c) is that of $\sigma_s = 3$. Compared Fig. 3(b) with (c), it shows that the more value of σ_s is, the more serious blur happens. Figure 4 shows the decreasing characteristics between the mean square deviation of DCT coefficient and the scale parameter of PSF. Figure 5 illustrates the relationship between entropy of DCT coefficient and scale parameter of PSF, from which it can be shown obviously that entropy of DCT coefficient will decrease when more serious blur phenomenon happens.

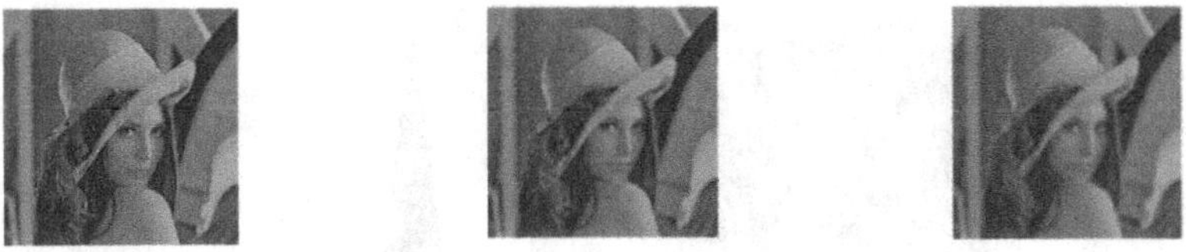

(a) original picture (b) result of σ_s=1.5 (c) result of σ_s=3

Fig. 3. Picture 'Lena' and its defocused results.

As the data discrete, another worth to mention is the calculation of DCT coefficient's entropy. Denote c_{max} and c_{min} as the maximum and the minimum of DCT coefficients, and the number of coefficients is K. Firstly, dividing the whole interval $[c_{min}, c_{max}]$ into several sub-interval with step length 0.1, and denoting all sub-intervals with order number *i*. Secondly, calculating the number K_i of coefficients whose values locate at the ith sub-interval. Thus, the entropy of DCT coefficient can be obtained by

$$H = -\sum_i P_i \cdot log\, P_i = -\sum_i \frac{K_i}{K} \cdot log(\frac{K_i}{K}) \quad (8)$$

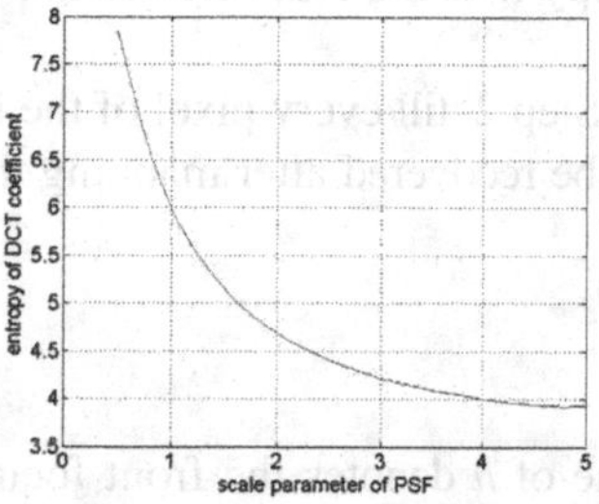

Fig. 4. Relationship between mean square deviation of DCT coefficient and scale parameter of PSF.

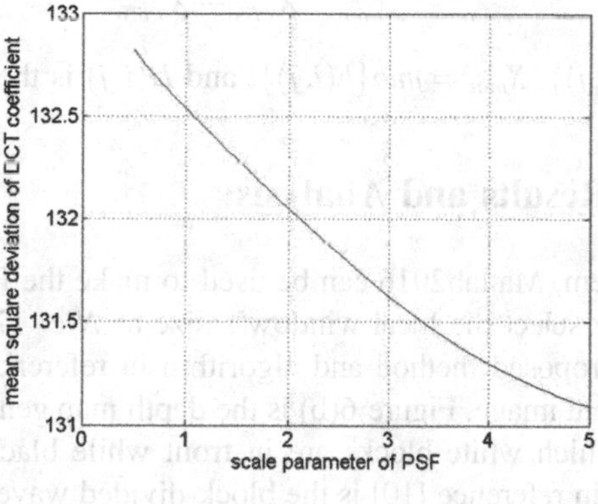

Fig. 5. Relationship between entropy of DCT coefficient and scale parameter of PSF.

4 Proposed Method for Depth Recovery

In this section, the proposed method will employ the entropy of DCT coefficient as the measure of blur, and adopt the linear operation mapping the blur into the depth. The algorithm flowing and linear mapping will be discussed in detail.

4.1 Outline of Algorithm

The entropy of DCT coefficient is adopted as the measure of blur in the presented method, whose flow is as follows.

Step 1: To each pixel (i,j), select the local window with size $N \times N$ from its neighbourhood, then carry on 2D DCT to this local window whose center is pixel (i,j). Generally, N is odd number.
Step 2: Calculate the entropy h of DCT coefficient according to (8) as the measure of blur in the pixel (i,j).
Step 3: Repeat Step 1 and Step 2, till every pixel of the image is traversed. Then the pixel-level depth map can be recovered after mapping the entropy h into depth with linear operation.

4.2 Linear Mapping

In our method, the large value of h denotes the front focused objects while the small value represents the defocused background. In order to generate the depth map with 256 gray-level, linear operation is necessary, which can be described as

$$D(i,j) = 255 \cdot \frac{h(i,j) - X_{min}}{X_{max} - X_{min}} \tag{9}$$

where $X_{max} = max\{h(i,j)\}$, $X_{min} = min\{h(i,j)\}$, and $D(i,j)$ is the depth of pixel (i,j).

5 Experimental Results and Analysis

In the Windows 7 system, Matlab2016 can be used to make the following experience. In our experiments, we select the local window's size as $N = 17$. Comparison of the depth maps between proposed method and algorithm in reference [10] is carried on. Figure 6(a) is the original image. Figure 6(b) is the depth map generated by the method in reference [10], in which white blocks are in front while black blocks are behind. Because the algorithm in reference [10] is the block-divided wavelet method, its initial depth map is blocky. Figure 6(c) is that of proposed method. We can observe distinctly that the depth map adopting thc proposed pixel-level algorithm preserves more details.

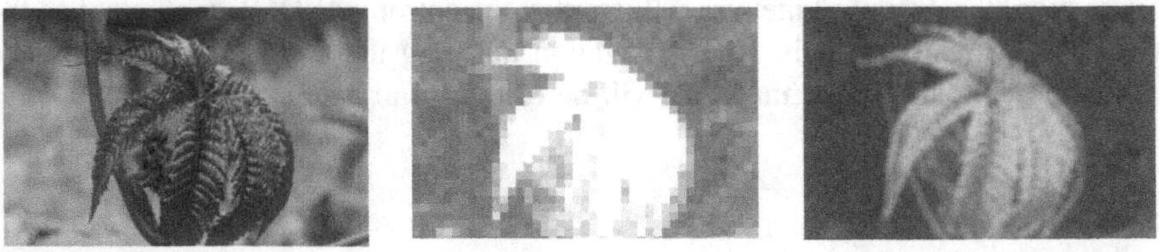

(a) original picture (b) depth map of [10] (c) depth map of our method

Fig. 6. Picture 'leaf' and its depth map.

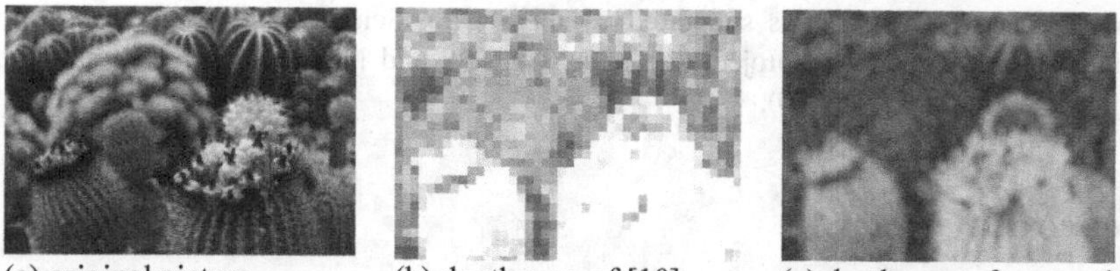

(a) original picture (b) depth map of [10] (c) depth map of our method

Fig. 7. Picture 'cactuses' and its depth map.

Another comparison is shown in Fig. 7. From Fig. 7(b), it can be seen that the cactuses can hardly be identified because of the series blocky effect.

Figure 8 illustrates other images and there depth maps generated by proposed algorithm in this paper. The left column shows the original images while the right column shows the corresponding depth maps, which demonstrate that the method presented here is reliable and robust.

Fig. 8. Other pictures and their depth maps.

6 Conclusion

In this paper, we propose a depth recovery algorithm for single images based on focus-defocus cue, which is enough for 3D rendering and stereo applications. Because of the decreasing relationship between entropy of DCT coefficient and scale parameter of PSF, this proposed algorithm employs the entropy of DCT coefficient as the amount of blur, and adopts the linear process mapping the blur into depth. The experimental result shows that this reliable method does a good job in depth recovery. The further work is to improve the accuracy of depth recovery combined with other monocular cues for single image.

Acknowledgement. This work is supported by the Harbin Science and Technology Bureau outstanding subject leader fund project (2017RAXXJ055), and Nature Science Foundation of Heilongjiang Province (F2018020).

References

1. Fehn, C.: A 3D-TV approach using depth-image-based rendering (DIBR). In: Image Process, pp. 482–487 (2003)
2. Liu, Y., Wang, J., Zhang, H.: Depth image-based temporal error concealment for 3-D video transmission. Circuits Syst. Video Technol. **20**, 600–604 (2010)
3. Zhang, L., Knorr, S.: 3D-TV content creation: automatic 2D-to-3D video conversion. Broadcasting 1–12 (2011)
4. Gokstorp, M.: Computing depth from out-of-focus blur using a local frequency representation. In: Pattern Recognition-Conference A: Computer Vision & Image Processing, vol. 1, pp. 153–158 (1994)
5. Rayala, J., Gupta, S., Mullick, S.K.: Estimation of depth from defocus as polynomial system identification. Image Signal Process. **148**, 356–362 (2001)
6. Mendapara, P., Minhas, R., Wu, Q.M.J.: Depth map estimation using exponentially decaying focus measure based on SUSAN operator. In: Systems, Man and Cybernetics, pp. 3705–3708 (2009)
7. Paramanand, C., Rajagopalan, A.N.: Depth from motion and optical blur with an unscented Kalman filter. IEEE Trans. Image Process. **21**, 2798–2811 (2012)
8. Lin, X., Suo, J., Dai, Q.: Extracting depth and radiance from a defocused video pair. IEEE J. Mag. **25**(4), 557–569 (2016)
9. Xiao, J., Liu, T., Zhang, Y., Zou, B., Lei, J., Li, Q.: Multi-focus image fusion based on depth extraction with inhomogeneous diffusion equation. Signal Process. **14**(1), 1–30 (2016)
10. Valenecia, S.A., Rodriguez-Dagnino, R.M.: Synthesizing stereo 3D views from focus cues in monoscopic 2D images. In: Proceedings of SPIE-IS&T Electronic Imaging, vol. 5006, pp. 377–388 (2003)

Research on Diabetes Management Strategy Based on Deep Belief Network

Yang Liu[1,2](✉), Zhijie Zhao[1,2], Jiaying Wang[1,2], Ang Li[1,2], and Jialin Zhang[1,2]

[1] School of Computer and Information Engineering, Harbin University of Commerce, Harbin 150028, China
1249182744@qq.com

[2] Heilongjiang Provincial Key Laboratory of Electronic Commerce and Information Processing, Harbin University of Commerce, Harbin 150028, China

Abstract. Diabetes is a chronic disease that seriously endangers human health. Early detection, early diagnosis and early treatment can reduce the possibility of diabetic complications and mortality, which can be solved effectively by prediction model, assisting doctors to make more comprehensive and reliable diagnosis and treatment decisions, and improving diabetes management strategies. Thus, a diabetes prediction model based on Deep Belief Network (DBN) is proposed. Based on the Pima Indians Diabetes data set, the relative strength between the input attributes and the output targets of the model is calculated by using the weight matrix among the layers of the DBN diabetes prediction model. The results showed that plasma glucose concentration, body mass index, diabetic pedigree function, gestational frequency and age are important indexes for diabetes diagnosis. Then, this paper proposes three management strategies, including diabetes prevention education, diabetes individual prevention and diabetes community prevention to improve the management and control of diabetes in China.

Keywords: Diabetes mellitus · Deep learning · DBN model · Diabetes prediction · Diabetes management strategy

1 Introduction

Diabetes is one of the most serious and critical health problems facing the world in the twenty-first Century. Data provided by the International Diabetes Federation in 2017 showed that 424.9 million people suffer from diabetes in the world, and that by 2045, the number of diabetics in the world could increase by 48% to 628.6 million [1].

Diabetes is highly correlated with various factors such as age, sex, obesity and heredity, most of which is hidden and likely to cause acute or severe long-term complications. Now it is very important to develop predictive models for assisting doctors to make more comprehensive and reliable diagnosis and treatment decisions [2]. Many kinds of models have been established for predicting the risk of Diabetes mellitus. Thirteen classification models are evaluated and Random Forest is confirmed to be the best performance, which is used to create a web application for predicting

M. Jia et al. (Eds.): WiSATS 2019, LNICST 281, pp. 177–186, 2019.
https://doi.org/10.1007/978-3-030-19156-6_17

disease risk classification [3]. The Cox proportional hazards regression method is used to construct a prediction model for type 2 diabetes mellitus [4]. Some researchers set up a prediction model from the perspective of drug failure. An efficient and effective ensemble of SVMs is proposed for the anti-diabetic drug failure prediction problem, which is confirmed that the prediction model is suitability and the accuracy is about 80% [5]. However, most of these articles use statistical methods or machine learning methods for modeling, whose ability to express complex functions is limited, and there are relatively few articles on factor analysis and pertinent suggestions. This paper combining the characteristics of diabetes diagnosis and data, constructs the diabetes prediction model by using DBN, which can identify complex patterns in data, to assist doctors to make more comprehensive and reliable diagnosis and treatment decisions. The relative strength between the input attributes (factors) and the output targets (diabetes) of the model is calculated by using the weight matrix among the layers of the DBN diabetes prediction model, and comprehensively analyzes the results to put forward and consummate diabetes management strategies for improving the status of managing and controlling diabetes in China.

2 DBN Prediction Modeling and Simulation Experiment

The DBN diabetes prediction model, the theoretical basis for its establishment is mainly based on literature [6–9].

The data is divided into two parts: training set and test set. For training set, the prediction model of diabetes based on DBN is established, combined with empirical formula, setting and adjusting the parameters to determine the optimal network structure of DBN. For test set, The DBN diabetes prediction model is validated by it. The establishment process is shown in Fig. 1.

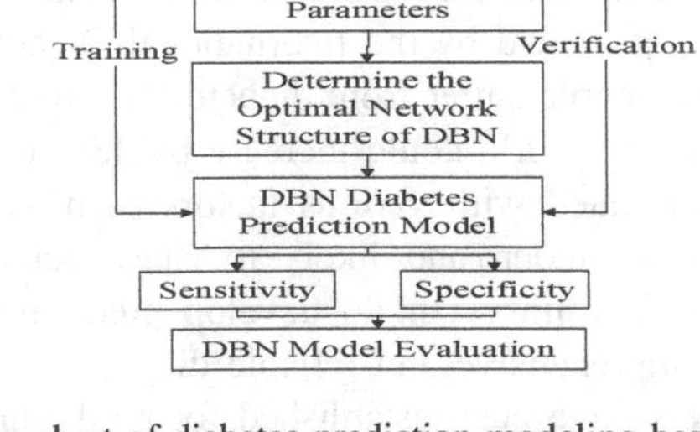

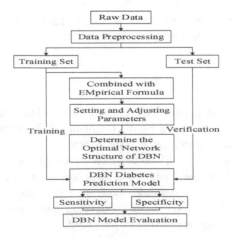

Fig. 1. Flow chart of diabetes prediction modeling based on DBN.

2.1 Data Source

The Data is about diabetes diagnosis information of native American women from Pima Indian heritage near phoenix, Arizona. They are above the age of 21 per capita. Eight risk factors related to diabetes are extracted, including six quantitative and continuous features, composed of a variety of clinical trial results, the remaining two quantitative and discrete features. The 9 features and sample data, including the classification codes, are shown in Tables 1 and 2 respectively. In Table 1, Body Mass Index (BMI) is calculated by formula, being recorded as $BMI = wei \div hei^2$, where *wei* represents weight, unit kg and *hei* represents height, unit m. In Table 2, Column 1 is the patient number. Columns 2–9 are the eigenvalues of the diabetes checking, as the attribute of the input data. The last column shows whether a given individual will suffer from diabetes within five years: 1 represents the positive in diabetes, that is, the individual will have diabetes in five years, a total of 268 cases. 0 represents the negative in diabetes, that is, the individual will not have diabetes within five years, a total of 500 cases. The Pima Indians Diabetes data set can be achieved in the UCI machine learning database.

Table 1. Data feature list (including category).

Feature number	Feature descriptions
Feature 1	Number of times pregnant
Feature 2	Plasma glucose concentration
Feature 3	Diastolic blood pressure (mm Hg)
Feature 4	Triceps skin fold thickness (mm)
Feature 5	2-Hour serum insulin (mu U/ml)
Feature 6	Body mass index
Feature 7	Diabetes pedigree function
Feature 8	Age in years
Classification codes	Binary class variable

Table 2. Original data sample (including category).

Number	Feature 1	Feature 2	Feature 3	Feature 4	Feature 5	Feature 6	Feature 7	Feature 8	Classification codes
1	6	148	72	35	0	33.6	0.627	50	1
2	8	183	64	0	0	23.3	0.672	32	1
3	1	85	66	29	0	26.6	0.351	31	0
4	1	89	66	23	94	28.1	0.167	21	0
…	…	…	…	…	…	…	…	…	…

2.2 Training Set and Test Set

After considering the problem about the number of diabetes data sets and model training, this paper adopts K-fold Cross Validation method to determine the training set and test set, so as to avoid over-learning and under-learning effectively. The basic idea of K-fold Cross Validation is to divide the available data into K parts (K $\geq$ 3), each representing a subset. Arbitrary K-1 subset is combined into a training set, and the remaining subset is used as a test set [10]. Thus, different training sets and corresponding test sets of K groups could be obtained. In the implementation, making K = 3, 768 pieces of input data, which are normalized by [0, 1] of the interval normalization method, are divided into three parts. 256 pieces of each part represent a subset, and three groups of training sets and corresponding test sets are obtained.

2.3 DBN Network Structure

Only four important parameters including the number of input layer nodes, hidden layer nodes, hidden layer nodes and output layer nodes are identified to determine the DBN network structure before the prediction model can be established. The number of input layer nodes is the attribute number of the dataset and the number of output layer nodes is equal to the class number in the dataset. The empirical formula for selecting the number of hidden layers and nodes is adopted to determine its approximate range, which can avoid the blindness and increase the effectiveness of selection [11]:

$$S = \sqrt{mn} + \mathrm{k}/2 \tag{1}$$

Here, S is the number of nodes in the hidden layer, m is the number of nodes in the input layer and n is the number of nodes in the output layer. K is constant belonging to 1–10.

Under the condition that m, n, k are known, the number of nodes in the first hidden layer S_1 can be calculated to have p values according to formula (1), which are recorded as $S_1 = [S_{11}, S_{12}, S_{13}, \cdots, S_{1P}]$. Assuming that the number of nodes in the first hidden layer has been determined, the number of nodes in the first hidden layer is equal to the number of nodes in the input layer, for example, if $S_1 = S_{1P}$, then $m = S_{1P}$, and the number of nodes in the output layer n remains unchanged. According to formula (1), the number of nodes in the second hidden layer S_2 can be calculated to have q values, which are recorded as $S_2 = \left[S_{21}, S_{22}, S_{23}, \cdots, S_{2q}\right]$. By analogy, under the different values of the number of nodes in the first hidden layer S_1, the number of nodes in the second hidden layer S_2 can be calculated respectively, which should be merged, and are recorded as $S_2 = \left[S_{21}, S_{22}, S_{23}, \cdots, S_{2q}, \cdots, S_{2(q+a)}\right]$. This calculation idea of simultaneously determining the number of hidden layers and the number of corresponding hidden layer nodes can be continued and determined experimentally.

2.4 DBN Network Parameters

In the process of training DBN model, parameters need to be set and adjusted to improve the classification accuracy of it. The sigmoid function is set as the hidden layer and the output layer neuron activation function. The maximum number of network cycles is 1000 times and the training data per batch is 128. The value of learning rate is set to 1 and the value of momentum factor is set to 0, which are contained in the RBM training parameters. BP training parameters include learning rate, the value of which is set to 2, and momentum factor, the value of which is set to 0.9.

2.5 DBN Network Training

Under the same training parameters, it is necessary to combine the p value of S_1 with the $q+a$ value of S_2, and K-time DBN training should be carried out by using the K-group training set and test set, totaling $K * p * (q+a)$ experiments. The average accuracy of each classification under K-time DBN training is calculated as the final classification accuracy. The higher the classification accuracy rate, the better the prediction effect of DBN model.

2.6 DBN Experiment Results and Analysis

Seeing the data characteristics of Pima Indians Diabetes, it is known that the number of input nodes m is 8 and the number of output categories n is 2. Using the formula (1) and the idea of the corresponding algorithm, which are mentioned in Sect. 2.3, experiments are conducted to determine that the number of hidden layers is 2 layers. The number of nodes in the first hidden layer S_1 has 6 values, recorded as $S_1 = [4, 5, 6, 7, 8, 9]$, and the number of nodes in the second hidden layer S_2 has 9 values, recorded as $S_2 = [2, 3, 4, 5, 6, 7, 8, 9, 10]$. Three DBN network training are conducted for three groups of training sets, and 6 values of S_1 and 9 values of S_2 are combined in two to conduct each DBN training, in total of 3 * 6 * 9 experiments. The experimental results are shown in Table 3.

Table 3. DBN experiment results.

S2	S1					
	4	5	6	7	8	9
2	0.7591	0.7630	0.7721	0.7669	0.7697	0.7656
3	0.7630	0.7630	0.7565	0.7552	0.7578	0.7682
4	0.7734	0.7682	0.7318	0.7617	0.7642	0.6966
5	0.7708	0.7643	0.7617	0.7617	0.7513	0.7656
6	0.7656	0.7747	0.7396	0.7669	0.7708	0.6862
7	0.7565	0.7096	0.7357	0.7552	0.7695	0.7318
8	**0.7760**	0.7617	0.7591	0.7669	0.7305	0.7708
9	0.7734	0.7656	0.7620	0.7539	0.7539	0.7500
10	0.7565	0.7396	0.7591	0.7578	0.7669	0.7305

Table 3 shows that under the same training parameters, the number of nodes in two hidden layers is different, resulting in different classification accuracy of DBN, but the overall effect of the model is better than 65%, and the classification accuracy of some DBN network structures is as high as 80%. When the number of nodes in the input layer is 8, the number of nodes in the first hidden layer is 4, the number of nodes in the second hidden layer is 8, and the number of nodes in the output layer is 2, the diabetes prediction model is best and the accuracy is 77.60%.

For verifying the accuracy of DBN model prediction, BP Neural Network and Support Vector Machine (SVM) are used to comparative experiments. The experimental results are shown in Table 4, which can be seen that the accuracy of the three diabetes prediction models is above 75%, indicating that they can predict diabetes accurately for the experimental data. The accuracy of DBN model is the highest, reaching 77.60%, which shows that it performs better than the other two models in the term of prediction accuracy.

Table 4. Accuracy comparison results of several models.

Model	Acc (%)
DBN	77.60
BP	76.3
SVM	76.56

3 Diabetes Prevention and Management Strategies

Diabetes is a complex lifelong disease, with the continuous development of artificial intelligence and in-depth learning technology, prediction accuracy of which could be improved, leading to be diagnosed more effectively and treated earlier. According to the experimental results of the DBN prediction model in Sect. 2, this paper discusses the effect of the input attributes on the output goals, analyzes the influencing factors of diabetes mellitus, and improves the prevention and management strategies of diabetes mellitus on the basics of the final analysis results.

Since DBN is a deep neural network, this paper evaluates the relationship between input attributes and output targets by the following formula [12]:

$$Y_{ji} = \frac{\sum_{h=0}^{n} (W_{hi} \times W_{jh})}{\sum_{i=0}^{m} \sum_{h=0}^{n} |W_{hi} \times W_{jh}|} \tag{2}$$

Here, W_{hi} represents the weights between the hth hidden nodes and the ith input nodes. W_{jh} represents the weights between the jth output nodes and the hth hidden nodes. Y_{ji} is the relative strength between the ith input and the jth output variable, representing the ratio of the relationship strength between the ith input and the jth output variable to the total relationship strength of all input and output variables.

Obtaining the weight matrix of each layer in the DBN-based diabetes prediction model, and combining with the formula (2), the relative strength between the eight influencing factors and diabetes mellitus was calculated. The results are shown in Table 5.

From Table 5, we can see that the relative strength values of the factors influencing diabetes are plasma glucose concentration, body mass index, diabetes pedigree function, pregnancy frequency and age in turn. The strongest effect on diabetes is plasma glucose concentration, with a relative strength of 0.3407, suggesting that in glucose testing, the higher the plasma glucose concentration 2 h after oral administration, the greater the likelihood of diabetes. The relative effect of BMI on diabetes is 0.2637, which suggests that people with high BMI, or obesity, are more likely to suffer from diabetes. Relative strength values of the two factors to diabetes are large, indicating that they are important factors for diabetes, which need to be controlled by personal daily living habits and self-management ability, so as to delay the onset of diabetes. Among the 8 attributes, the correlation strength of diabetes pedigree function is 0.1332, which is in the third place, indicating that diabetes is related to heredity. The relative intensity of pregnancy frequency and age are not more than 0.1, indicating that they are not the main cause of diabetes, but also have a certain impact on it. The three factors are almost uncontrollable, but also closely related to diabetes, which need persons to increase the knowledge of diabetes and improve self-prevention awareness. Although the relative strength values of the other three factors are all negative, it does not mean that they had no effect on diabetes. It may be affected and limit by the data itself, which didn't reflect. All the above analyses are based on the Pima Indians Diabetes dataset. According to the analysis, the paper proposes management strategies of diabetes prevention and treatment besides basic drug treatment, which are summarized from the following aspects: diabetes prevention education management strategy, diabetes individual prevention and treatment management strategy, diabetes community prevention and treatment management strategy.

Table 5. Relative strength values.

Feature	Diabetes
Number of times pregnant	0.0904
Plasma glucose concentration	0.3407
Diastolic blood pressure (mm Hg)	−0.0549
Triceps skin fold thickness (mm)	−0.0261
2-Hour serum insulin (mu U/ml)	−0.0021
Body mass index	0.2637
Diabetes pedigree function	0.1332
Age in years	0.0534

(1) Diabetes prevention education management strategy

Studies have shown that diabetes is very common in clinical practice. Strengthening health education for diabetic patients is not only conducive to promoting patients' awareness of the disease, improving patients' compliance with treatment, but also can avoid wasting medical resources and lighten the social burden [13–15]. The strategies of diabetes prevention education management are mainly targeted at three kinds of people. For the non-diabetic patients, introduce the basic knowledge of diabetes to them, helping them strengthen awareness of prevention. For diabetics, they not only need to master basic knowledge of diabetes, but also need to know how to control it. Considering the signs on recession of understanding and memory in elderly diabetic patients, family members or primary caregivers should be included to play a role of supervision and reminder, who have a direct impact on the rehabilitation effect of patients [16]. For medical professionals, education and training should be planned to enhance the professional knowledge and skills of diabetes.

(2) Diabetes individual prevention and treatment management strategy

Good living habits and self-management ability are the basis of diabetes treatment, throughout the entire diabetes treatment process. Studies at home and abroad have confirmed that increasing physical activities, diet control and weight loss can reduce or delay the onset of diabetes [17, 18]. Diabetes personal prevention and treatment management strategies are proposed for the details of daily life of diabetic patients, including self-blood glucose testing, diet therapy and exercise intervention. Firstly, small and fast blood glucose meters are gradually popularized, which can be used for blood glucose detection. Secondly, reasonable and effective diet treatment and control are conducive to weight loss, so as to preventing and treating diabetes. The last but not the least, regular and appropriate exercise intervention is also an important method, long-term exercise is an example, which can reduce weight, enhance physical fitness, and improve the body's disease resistance, so as to prevent and control the occurrence and process of diabetes.

(3) Diabetes community prevention and treatment management strategy

As a chronic and lifelong disease, diabetes patients need to return to family and society when their condition is stable, if they can't be effectively managed after discharge, they will increase the risk of readmission and the incidence of complications, which means that community plays an important role in the prevention and treatment of chronic diseases [19, 20]. There are many forms of diabetes prevention and management activities available in the community. Firstly, regular lectures on diabetes health education and publicity brochures are given to improve the level of awareness of diabetes. Secondly, the hospital-community integration model should be established by taking advantages of hospitals to provide professional training for community hospitals and diagnose, treat, guide patients, and making use of community to establish community prevention and monitoring websites to the registration, follow-up and various intervention activities, which is evaluated systematically to prove that it could enhance the awareness and reduce the incidence of diabetes [21]. Thirdly, the DBN-based diabetes prediction model can be embedded into the diabetes community prevention and monitoring website to strengthen the real-time prediction function for improving the management. Finally, according to the predicted results of model, a primary warning is given to the population with a disease probability of less than 30%, an intermediate warning is given to the population with a disease probability of more than 30% and less than 60%, and a severe warning is given to the population with a disease probability of more than 60%. Then, different strategies for prevention and treatment are proposed for different early-warning groups.

4 Conclusion

Diabetes is a complex lifelong disease, which could be predicted effectively by DBN. Based on the Pima Indians Diabetes dataset, the DBN prediction model is established and the accuracy is 77.60%. BP and SVM are used to establish model for comparison experiments, the results of which show that DBN is superior to the other two algorithms in predicting diabetes. Furthermore, the weight matrix of each layer of DBN prediction model is used to calculate the relative strength between each influencing factor and diabetes mellitus, and they are analyzed. The results showed that the relative strength values of plasma glucose concentration, body mass index, diabetic pedigree function, gestational frequency and age are 0.3407, 0.2637, 0.1332, 0.0904 and 0.0534 respectively, and on the basis of it, three management strategies, namely, diabetes education, personal prevention and community control, are put forward and improved.

Acknowledgements. This research is supported by the Harbin Science and Technology Bureau outstanding subject leader fund project (2017RAXXJ055) and the Humanities and social sciences research projects of the Ministry of Education (18YJAZH128).

References

1. International Diabetes Federation (IDF) Diabetes Atlas Eighth Edition poster Homepage. http://diabetesatlas.org/resources/2017-atlas.html. Accessed 24 Sept 2018
2. Kandhasamy, J.P., Balamurali, S.: Performance analysis of classifier models to predict diabetes mellitus. Proc. Comput. Sci. **47**, 45–51 (2015)
3. Nai-Arun, N., Moungmai, R.: Comparison of classifiers for the risk of diabetes prediction. Proc. Comput. Sci. **69**, 132–142 (2015)
4. Su, P., Yang, Y., Yang, Y., et al.: Prediction models on the onset risks of type 2 diabetes among the health management population. J. Shandong Univ. (Health Sci.) **55**(6), 82–86 (2017)
5. Kang, S., Kang, P., Ko, T., et al.: An efficient and effective ensemble of support vector machines for anti-diabetic drug failure prediction. Expert Syst. Appl. **42**(9), 4265–4273 (2015)
6. Hinton, G.E., Osindero, S., Teh, Y.W.: A fast learning algorithm for deep belief nets. Neural Comput. **18**(7), 1527–1554 (2006)
7. Li, H., Li, X., Ramanathan, M., et al.: Identifying informative risk factors and predicting bone disease progression via deep belief networks. Methods **69**(3), 257–265 (2014)
8. Lim, K., Lee, B.M., Kang, U., et al.: An optimized DBN-based coronary heart disease risk prediction. Int. J. Comput. Commun. Control **13**(4), 492–502 (2018)
9. Sun, Z., Xue, L., Xu, Y., et al.: Overview of deep learning. Appl. Res. Comput. **29**(8), 2806–2810 (2012)
10. Hu, J., Zhang, G.: K-fold cross-validation based selected ensemble classification algorithm. Bull. Sci. Technol. **29**(12), 115–117 (2013)
11. Yang, X.: Study of early warning for cerebrovascular risk based on deep beliefs networks. Beijing Jiaotong University (2016)
12. Lee, S., Choeh, J.Y.: Predicting the helpfulness of online reviews using multilayer perceptron neural networks. Expert Syst. Appl. **41**(6), 3041–3046 (2014)

13. Gao, Y., Hu, Y.: Influence of different health education modes on self-management level of diabetic patients. Jilin Med. J. **35**(3), 616 (2014)
14. Wu, S.: Application effect of health education in clinical nursing of diabetic patients. J. Tradit. Chin. Med. Manag. **25**(11), 1948–1949 (2014)
15. Zhao, F., Luo, J., Wang, Y., et al.: Analysis of the influencing on clinical health education management effect of diabetes. Int. J. Nurs. **35**(24), 3387–3392 (2016)
16. Scollan-Koliopoulos, M., O'Connell, K.A., Walker, E.A.: The first diabetes educator is the family: using illness representation to recognize a multigenerational legacy of diabetes. Clin. Nurse Spec. **19**(6), 302–307 (2005)
17. Li, G., Zhang, P., Wang, J., et al.: The long-term effect of lifestyle interventions to prevent diabetes in the China Da Qing Diabetes Prevention Study: a 20-year follow-up study. Lancet **371**(9626), 1783–1789 (2008)
18. Saaristo, T., Moilanen, L., Korpihyövälti, E., et al.: Lifestyle intervention for prevention of type 2 diabetes in primary health care. One-year follow-up of the Finnish National Diabetes Prevention Program (FIN-D2D). Diabetes Care **33**(10), 2146–2151 (2010)
19. Xu, L., Liu, S., Chen, S., et al.: Readiness for hospital discharge and its influencing factors among diabetes patients. J. Nurs. Sci. **33**(10), 12–15 (2018)
20. Fang, W., Li, Y.: Correlation analysis between the readiness for hospital discharge and social support status in diabetic patients. Chin. J. Mod. Nurs. **22**(25), 3558–3561 (2016)
21. Fang, R., Xia, X.: Effect evaluation of whole course diabetes health education in hospital community integration. Chin. Community Doct.: Med. Spec. **11**(18), 251 (2009)

HMM Static Hand Gesture Recognition Based on Combination of Shape Features and Wavelet Texture Features

Lizhi Zhang[1,4(✉)], Yingrui Zhang[2], Lianding Niu[3], Zhijie Zhao[1,4], and Xiaowei Han[1,4]

[1] School of Computer and Information Engineering, Harbin University of Commerce, Harbin 150028, China
zhanglizhi58@163.com
[2] School of Information and Communication Engineering, Harbin Engineering University, Harbin 150001, China
[3] Network and Educational Technology Center, Harbin University of Commerce, Harbin 150028, China
[4] Heilongjiang Provincial Key Laboratory of Electronic Commerce and Information Processing, Harbin University of Commerce, Harbin 150028, China

Abstract. Gesture recognition is one of the key technologies in the field of computer vision, and hand gesture recognition can be divided into static hand gesture recognition and the dynamic hand gesture recognition. This paper presents a new static gesture recognition algorithm based on hidden markov model. It uses two kinds of new shape features, the specific angle shape entropy feature and the upper side contour feature. They are firstly used for parameters training of hidden makov model, and then identify gesture categories hierarchically. In order to further improve the recognition effect for those small shape differences gesture, this paper adopts wavelet texture energy feature which can reflect the internal details of the gesture image, and makes the final correction estimation based on minimum total error probability. The experimental results show that the method has good recognition effects for gestures no matter the shape differences are big or not, and it has good real time performance as well.

Keywords: Static gesture recognition · Shape entropy feature · Texture energy feature · Minimum total error probability · HMM

1 Introduction

Hand gesture recognition is one of the important technologies in the field of computer vision, it has many applications such as: Motion Simulation Games, Sign Language Communication, Virtual Reality and so on. Hand gesture recognition can be divided into static hand gesture recognition and the dynamic hand gesture recognition, and static hand gesture recognition is the recognition from a single image. So far, there are many works on static hand gesture recognition, and various classification methods have been adopted [1, 2].

M. Jia et al. (Eds.): WiSATS 2019, LNICST 281, pp. 187–197, 2019.
https://doi.org/10.1007/978-3-030-19156-6_18

Ren et al. [3] used depth threshold to remove simple background, extracted finger distance as feature, and used template matching to identify 10 kinds of gestures. Singh et al. [4] used Radon transform to recognize the skeletal representation of gestures, extracted features in the transform domain, and then used K-means clustering algorithm to classify gestures. Jiang et al. [5] set up a standard sample base of gestures based on the model of hand geometric relationship and data glove, and then they implemented the gesture recognition based on BP neural network. Dardas et al. [6] used subtraction, skin color detection and contour comparison to track and detect gestures in complex background, they used HSV space to segment gestures, extracted features, and then used multiclass SVM to recognize gestures.

HMM classifier is a successful classifier for gesture recognition. It has flexible and efficient training and recognition algorithm. Xu et al. [7] established the HMM model for ten Arabic numerals (0–9) gestures, and implemented the real-time recognition system of gesture trajectory. In this paper, we present a HMM static hand gesture recognition method based on combination of shape features and wavelet texture features. The algorithm has good recognition effects for gestures with big shape differences and slight shape differences.

2 Static Hand Gesture Feature Extraction

2.1 Preprocessing

Preprocessing is the first stage for our algorithm which mainly contains ROI (region of interest) detection and denoising. The skin color is firstly detected by histogram statistics and threshold setting, and the denoising can be effectively processed by the mathematical morphology method. Figure 1 shows the preprocessed static hand gesture images.

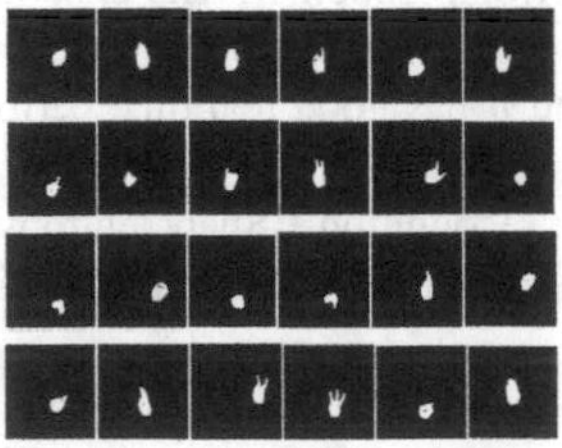

Fig. 1. Preprocessed static hand gesture images.

2.2 The Shape Feature Extraction

The Specific Angle Shape Entropy Feature Extraction of Hand Gesture. For this feature extraction method, the hand gesture edge should be firstly detected. We adopt the Pretty differential operator method to detect the hand gesture edge, and then calculate the centroid pixel coordinate $O(O_X, O_Y)$ of the hand gesture region as shown by the Eq. (1).

$$O_x = \frac{\sum_{i=0}^{sum} x_i}{sum}, O_y = \frac{\sum_{j=0}^{sum} y_i}{sum} \tag{1}$$

Where (x_i, y_i) denotes the coordinate of the pixel on the hand gesture contour, sum denotes total number of the pixels on the hand gesture contour, and the hand gesture region can be divided n parts with uniform angle division as shown Fig. 2.

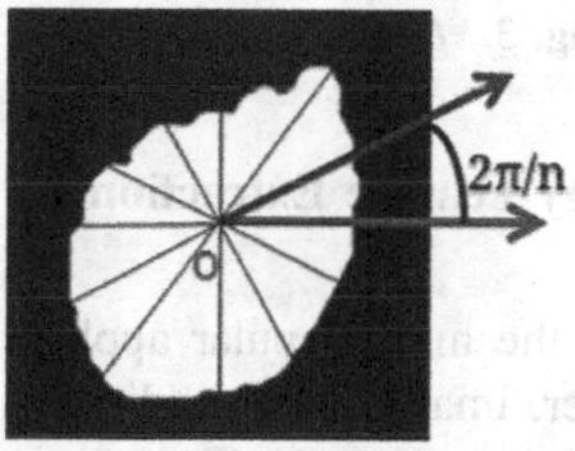

Fig. 2. The specific angle contour illustration.

Based on these processing, we define the specific angle shapc cntropy to describe the uncertainty of the hand gesture contour so as to distinguish the different hand gesture. We firstly define a probability measurement regarding the specific angle shape of the hand gesture contour as the Eq. (2).

$$p_{ij} = \frac{d_{ij}}{\sum_{(i,j)\subset L_C} d_{ij}} \tag{2}$$

Where L_c denotes the set of the pixels on the on the hand gesture contour within the specific angle divided part, and d_{ij} denotes the distance between the pixels on the contour of the specific angle part and the centroid of the whole contour. With this probability measurement, the specific angle shape entropy can be naturally defined as Eq. (3). The specific angle shape entropy of every part of the whole contour can be put together to form an n dimensional feature vector. For instance, we divide the whole hand gesture contour with every 30° in our experiment, we then obtain 12 dimensional feature vector for a hand gesture.

$$H_{Lc} = -\sum_{(i,j)\subset L_c} p_{ij} \log_a p_{ij} \tag{3}$$

Upper Side Contour Feature Extraction of Hand Gesture. The upper side contour of the hand refers to the contour above the horizontal line through the centroid pixel, and experiment shows that the hand gesture difference mainly depends on the upper side contour of the hand. We can calculate the vertical distance between a specific pixel on the upper side contour and the centroid pixel D_y as shown in Fig. 3. Considering the width of the hand contour, a 42-dimensional feature vector can be properly formed.

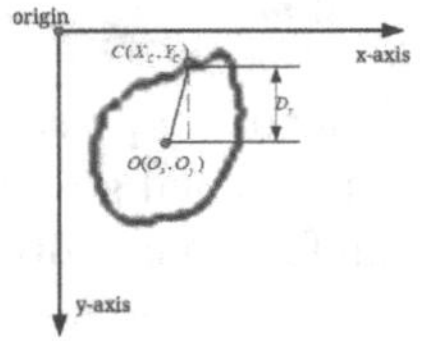

Fig. 3. D_y distance illustration

2.3 Wavelet Texture Energy Feature Extraction

Wavelet Transform. One of the most popular application of wavelets has been to image decomposition. However, images are two-dimensional and decomposition can be illustrated as Fig. 4. The Discrete Wavelet Transform decomposes an image into a multi-resolution expression and it can be shown in Fig. 5. The spatial subbands LL1, HL1, LH1 and HH1 can be got with a two-dimensional image wavelet decomposition. The first subband contains the main information of the image and the other three subbands are the additional information of the image in the horizontal, diagonal and vertical directions. And the spatial subbands LL2, HL2, LH2 and HH2 can be got after a further two-dimensional image wavelet decomposition to LL1. When LL2 is further decomposed, a growing quad-tree can be got [8].

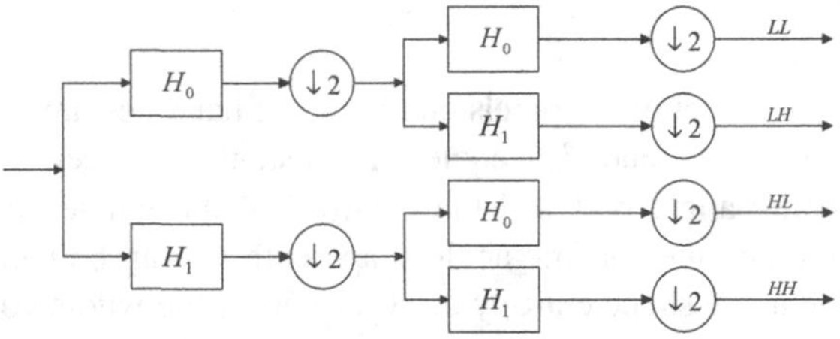

Fig. 4. Subband decomposition of an image.

Wavelet Texture Energy Feature Extraction. Many research works show that the wavelet energy feature is an effective feature in gesture recognition, it can be defined by the coefficients of wavelet decomposition to a cutting gesture image. A cutting gesture image is a part of an image cut off from an image containing a gesture. According to the characteristics of the gesture, Images containing gesture are grouped to several groups

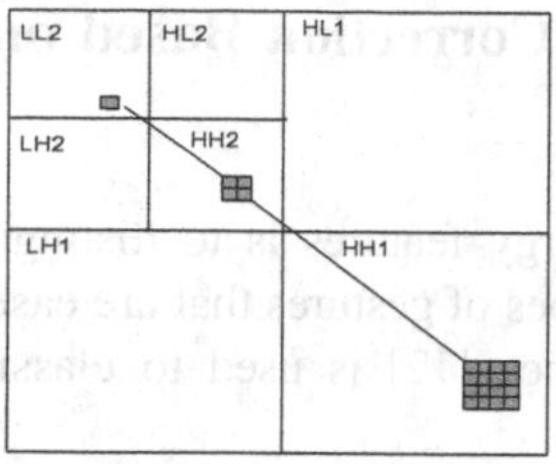

Fig. 5. The subband structure of image.

by the similarity, for instance, gesture g and gesture t, gesture n and gesture q, gesture u and gesture r for editing and cutting, so that most of the resulting cutting gesture image can have differences. The i_{th} level of the wavelet energy in the horizontal, vertical and diagonal directions of a cutting gesture image can be expressed as the Eq. (4) [9, 10]:

$$E_i^h = \sum_{x=1}^{M}\sum_{y=1}^{N}[H_i(x,y)]^2$$
$$E_i^v = \sum_{x=1}^{M}\sum_{y=1}^{N}[V_i(x,y)]^2 \quad (4)$$
$$E_i^d = \sum_{x=1}^{M}\sum_{y=1}^{N}[D_i(x,y)]^2$$

Where H_i, V_i, D_i is the i_{th} level wavelet decomposition of the cutting gesture image in three directions. Considering the size of the cutting gesture, the cutting gesture is applied to 5-layer haar wavelet transform. In this way, each cutting gesture image can get $1 * 15$ dimensional texture feature vector.

3 Static Hand Gesture Recognition Algorithm

The Hidden Markov process is a double stochastic process as shown in Fig. 6, one is hidden, and another is observation sequence. The notation $\lambda = (\pi, A, B)$ denotes the parameter set of the model [11], where π indicates the initial probability distribution of the hidden state, A indicates the state transition probability distribution, and B indicates the observation symbol probability distribution at given state. The HMM model can be trained using empirical data, and this leads to the model parameters achievement.

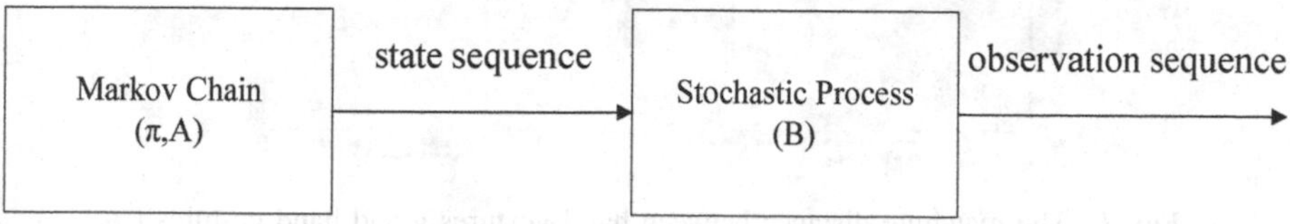

Fig. 6. A hidden Markov process.

4 Gesture Recognition Correction Based on Minimum Total Error Rate

The extraction of wavelet energy features is to distinguish the gesture groups with similar contour. For the two types of gestures that are easily confused with the contour, the weighted city block distance [12] is used to classify the gesture based on the minimum total error rate.

Let V and U be the wavelet energy features of the two gesture images, M be the total levels of wavelet decomposition, and the i_{th} level wavelet energy features of V and U are the weights of the i_{th} level wavelet energy features. Then the definition of wavelet energy features similarity measurement based on the weighted city block distance is given by the formula (5)

$$D(V,U) = \sum_{i=1}^{M} \left(c_i \sum_{j=1}^{3} \left| V_{\underset{(j)}{i}} - U_{\underset{(j)}{i}} \right| \right) \tag{5}$$

The weighted city block distance calculation mainly depends on the influence to the recognition results by the wavelet energy features at each level. The larger the influence of the wavelet energy features is, the larger the corresponding weight c_i is chosen. In the experiment, we extracted the energy features with 5 levels wavelet transform. Figure 7 shows the matching distance of each wavelet transform level of gesture g and gesture t. It can be seen that the 5th-level energy features can most obviously distinguish these two types of gestures, so its weight is set to be the maximum value.

Considering the gesture *g* and the gesture *t*, the gesture n and the gesture *q*, the gesture u and the gesture r, we calculate the reciprocal of the intersecting graphic area

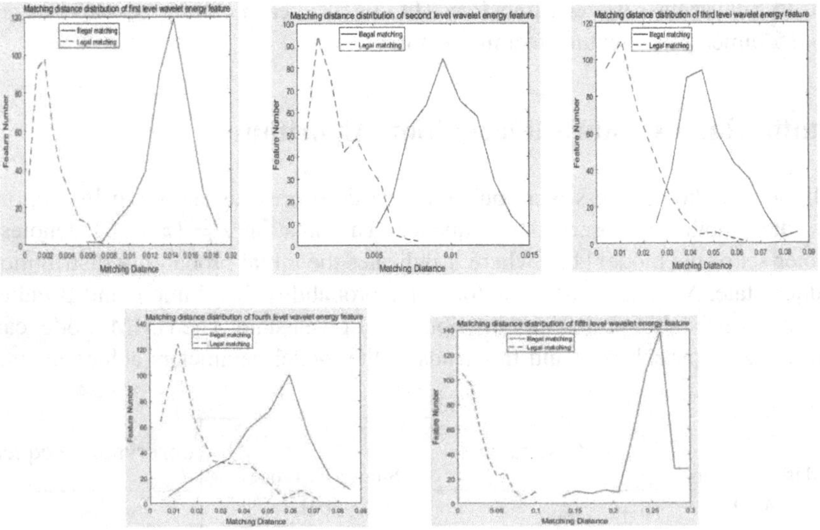

Fig. 7. The matching distance between hand gestures g and hand gestures t

of each wavelet transform levels matching distances curve, and the c_i values can be obtained as shown in Table 1. With the determined weights, we can recognize the gesture in the corresponding gesture group with the following steps. We firstly calculate the wavelet energy features of the gesture, and the matching distance D can be then calculated according to the similarity formula (5). Finally based on the criterion of the minimum overall error rate, the gesture class can be determined as the class with the smaller D value.

Table 1. Gesture group weights at all levels.

Gesture group	c_1	c_2	c_3	c_4	c_5
Gesture g & gesture t	0.3764	0.5388	0.0024	0.0020	0.0804
Gesture n & gesture q	0.5787	0.0692	0.0817	0.0933	0.1771
Gesture u & gesture r	0.8977	0.0645	0.0277	0.0036	0.0065

5 Experimental Results and Analysis

The gesture database used in the experiment was derived from the Thomas Moeslund gesture recognition database of the Aalborg University, Denmark. The gesture recognition database images are TIF format, resolution 248 * 256, the gestures are in different scales and different rotation plane, and it contains small contour differences but belongs to different classes of gestures. So, it is suitable for gesture recognition. 24 kinds of original images are shown in Fig. 8. There are 40 images in each class of gesture A–F and 100 images in each class of gesture G–Y. We select the first 20 groups of images in 24 kinds of gestures as training samples, and the rest of the images are used for recognition test. All experiments take matlab.2012a as an experimental platform.

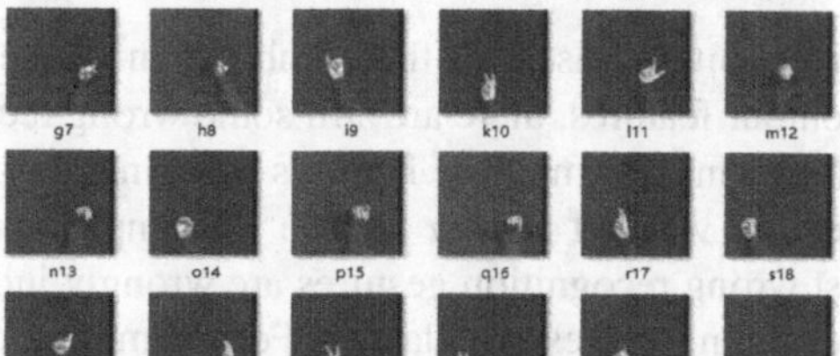

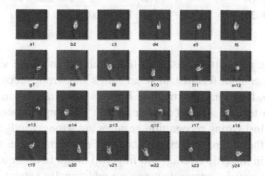

Fig. 8. 24 groups of original gesture images

Table 2. Recognition results using the specific angle shape entropy feature

Gesture group	Recognition rate (%)					
1–6	95	100	100	100	95	85
7–12	80	100	100	100	100	100
13–18	100	100	100	100	85	95
19–24	100	100	85	95	100	100

When HMM statistical model is used as classifier, the computation complexity is its drawback. For the two kinds of shape features extracted before, it is desirable that the specific angle shape entropy features can have an advantage in recognition, or a single feature can get a good recognition result. Therefore, without considering the combination of features, HMM is trained using specific angle contour entropy features and upper contour features separately. Tables 2 and 3 shows the results of the recognition rate respectively, and it illustrates that the special angle contour entropy features outperform the upper contour features in terms of the recognition rate. However, the recognition failure will not occur using the upper contour feature when it fails using the special angle contour entropy features.

So, in order to improve the recognition effect, the shape entropy features and upper side contour features are combined. The former recognition is firstly implemented using shape entropy features, and then we judge whether the recognition rate can be increased further using upper side contour features. Finally, the secondary recognition is implemented if necessary.

Table 3. Recognition results using upper side contour feature.

Gesture group number	Recognition rate (%)					
1–6	95	95	95	100	70	100
7–12	85	100	100	100	80	100
13–18	100	95	85	35	100	85
19–24	100	100	100	100	55	50

After the gesture recognition based on the combination of the shape entropy features and upper side contour features, there are still some wrong recognition gestures as shown in Fig. 9. So, following the multiple features combination strategy, recognition correction based on texture wavelet energy feature was implemented by the steps as shown in Fig. 10. Most wrong recognition gestures are wrongly judged as gestures that are very similar to the outline of gesture classes. For example, gesture *r* and gesture *u* are different only in fingertip overlap and fingertip tiling. In order to distinguish such gestures, the texture wavelet energy features are additionally extracted, and finally the recognition results are corrected according to the similarity of the texture wavelet energy features. The correction results are shown in Table 4, it can be seen that only two gesture recognition failures after the correction based on the principle of minimum total error rate of texture wavelet energy for the gesture n, gesture t and gesture u with

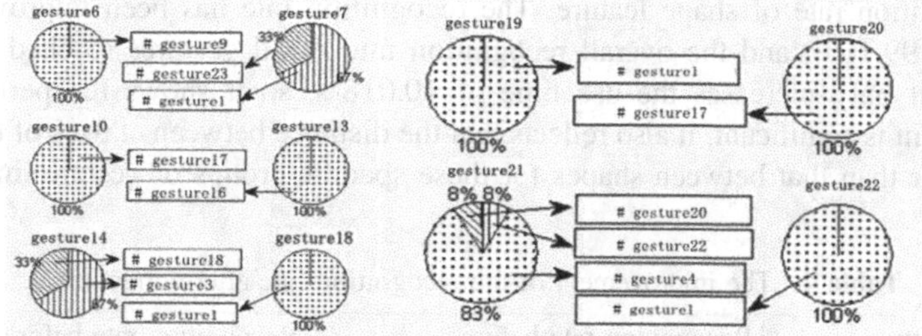

Fig. 9. Wrong gesture recognition distribution (# gesture number means misrecognition as the number).

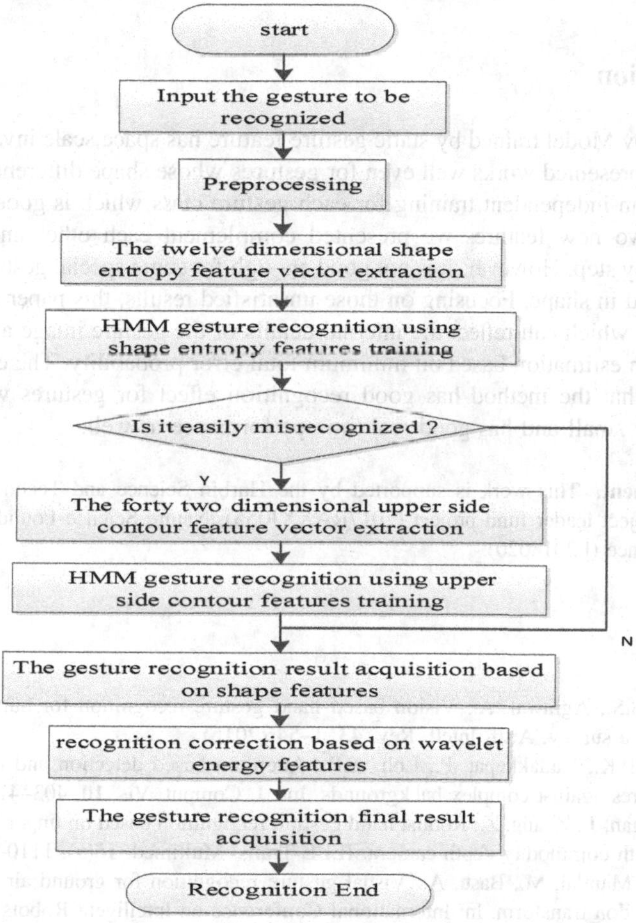

Fig. 10. Static gesture recognition flow chart based on shape features and wavelet texture features.

low recognition rate of shape feature. The recognition rate has been improved from 80.83% to 99.16%, and the overall recognition rate of all gestures reached 98.78%. However, it only increases the use time of 10.018 s, so it shows the performance improvement is significant. It also reflects that the distance between classes of texture is much larger than that between shapes for these specific groups of gesture images.

Table 4. The improvement of the recognition rate after correction.

Gesture group number	Recognition rate before correction	Recognition rate before correction
13%	72.5%	100%
19%	76.25%	97.5%
20%	93.75%	100%

6 Conclusion

Hidden Markov Model trained by static gesture feature has space scale invariance. The algorithm we presented works well even for gestures whose shape difference is not big and provides an independent training for each gesture class which is good for system expansion. Two new features we presented complement each other and recognize gestures step by step. However, it is not good enough for some special gestures who are easily confused in shape. Focusing on those unsatisfied results, this paper adds texture energy feature which can reflect the internal details of the gesture image and make his final correction estimation based on minimum total error probability. The experimental results show that the method has good recognition effect for gestures whose shape differences are small and has good real time performance as well.

Acknowledgement. This work is supported by the Harbin Science and Technology Bureau outstanding subject leader fund project (2017RAXXJ055), Nature Science Foundation of Heilongjiang Province (F2018020).

References

1. Rautaray, S.S., Agrawal, A.: Vision based hand gesture recognition for human computer interaction: a survey. Artif. Intell. Rev. **43**, 1–54 (2015)
2. Pisharady, P.K., Vadakkepat, P., Loh, A.P.: Attention based detection and recognition of hand postures against complex backgrounds. Int. J. Comput. Vis. **10**, 403–419 (2013)
3. Ren, Z., Yuan, J., Zhang, Z.: Robust hand gesture recognition based on finger-earth mover's distance with commodity depth camera. IEEE Trans. Multimed. **15**(5), 1110–1120 (2013)
4. Singh, M., Mandal, M., Basu, A.: Visual gesture recognition for ground air traffic control using the radon transform. In: International Conference on Intelligent Robots and Systems, pp. 2586–2591 (2005)
5. Jiang, L.: Research of Gesture Recognition Based on CAS-Glove. Jiaotong University, Beijing (2006)

6. Dardas, N.H., Georganas, N.D.: Real-time hand gesture detection and recognition using bag-of-features and support vector machine techniques. IEEE Trans. Instrum. Meas. **60**(11), 3592–3607 (2011)
7. Xu, X.: Hand Gesture Recognition based on Hidden Markov Module. University of Technology, Guangzhou (2011)
8. Wainwright, M.J., Simoncelli, E.P., Willsky, A.S.: Random cascades on wavelet trees and their use in analyzing and modeling natural images. Appl. Comput. Harmonic Anal. **11**(1), 89–123 (2001)
9. Wu, X., Wang, K., Zhang, D.: Wavelet energy features extraction and matching for palmprint recognition. J. Comput. Sci. Technol. **20**(5), 411–418 (2005)
10. Wu, X., Wang, K., Zhang, D.: Wavelet based palmprint recognition. In: IEEE Proceedings of the International Conference on Machine Learning Cybernetics, USA, pp. 1253–1257 (2002)
11. Rabiner, L.R.: A tutorial on hidden Markov models and selected applications in speech recognition. Proc. IEEE **77**, 257–286 (1989)
12. Wu, X., Zhang, D., Wang, D.: Palmprint recognition. Science Press (2006)

An Algorithm of Single Image Depth Estimation Based on MRF Model

Lizhi Zhang[1,3(✉)], Yongchao Chen[1,3], Lianding Niu[2], Zhijie Zhao[1,3], and Xiaowei Han[1,3]

[1] School of Computer and Information Engineering, Harbin University of Commerce, Harbin 150028, China
zhanglizhi58@163.com
[2] Network and Educational Technology Center, Harbin University of Commerce, Harbin 150028, China
[3] Heilongjiang Provincial Key Laboratory of Electronic Commerce and Information Processing, Harbin University of Commerce, Harbin 150028, China

Abstract. The image depth estimation problem is the basic issue of computer vision, and extracting the depth information from the two-dimensional image information is a challenge work. Focusing on the issue of extracting the depth information, an algorithm based on Markov Random Field (MRF) model has been proposed to estimate depth from single image. It includes calculating multi-scale texture features using Laws filers to the two-dimensional image, and calculating the probability relationship between texture clues and scene depth according to the texture features at different scales. Then, it establishes MRF probabilistic model and estimate parameters of MRF to get the initial depth image using the least squares method. Finally, an iterating algorithm depending on neighborhood mixing depth information is adopted to further improve the estimation accuracy. The experimental results show that the method performs well both in areas with small range of depth and areas with large range of depth when the texture feature is obvious.

Keywords: Least-square method · Laws filer · Multi-scale texture feature · MRF · Depth estimation

1 Introduction

The image depth estimation problem is the basic issue of computer vision. After the success of 3D movies, more and more researchers are devoted to study 2D to 3D conversion technologies [1, 2]. The reconstruction of 3D image information not only brings new vitality to some industries such as TV movie, but also gradually affects agriculture development. More and more researchers study the depth information of plants as an important plant feature in the agriculture field, and the works such as simulation, design and measurement are becoming easy to do due to the depth information study applied in the second industry. However, extracting the depth information from the two-dimensional image information is a challenge work, many early researchers such as [3–5] studied extracting image depth information from two or more

M. Jia et al. (Eds.): WiSATS 2019, LNICST 281, pp. 198–207, 2019.
https://doi.org/10.1007/978-3-030-19156-6_19

images which captured the geometrical differences of the images. In fact, there are many important useful depth clues in single image, such as texture change, color, gradient, focus and haze etc., these depth clues can also be used to extract the depth information. Compared with extracting depth information from multiple images, the depth information is very vague regarding the local features of the single image, so it is necessary to firstly investigate the global information of the single image, then establish the prior knowledge of the features and depth in the scene, and finally estimate the local depth value.

In this paper, the image depth estimation is considered as a supervised learning problem. The Laws' filters is used to capture multi-scale texture energy of an image from the edge, point and gradient directions. Based on the statistical relationship between texture features and scales, the probability relation between texture clue and depth is calculated, and we then establish MRF probability model. Taking the image and its true depth as training samples, the model parameters are obtained through training with the least square method. The initial depth map of the test image is calculated according to the MAP criterion. Finally, to further improve the accuracy of depth estimation, we adopt an iterate algorithm to re-estimate the depth values based on the mixed depth information in the single image field.

2 Multi-scale Texture Feature Extraction

Image texture is a kind of depth clues often used in depth information extraction technologies because the surface texture of an object changes obviously with depth in the image. With the atmospheric scattering, the farther away the scene becomes more blurred, and the color of the image becomes more and more blue. Haze is also helpful to judge depth, especially in the outdoor scene. So, texture changes, texture gradients and haze can be chosen as clues to extract depth information in the image.

2.1 Texture Energy Analysis Method

Laws filter is a typical texture analysis method [6]. Texture energy analysis is one of the effective methods of image analysis. Through the texture energy analysis, many features of the image can be obtained, such as texture changes, texture gradient, haze and so on. Laws originally defined a vector-form template, which he later did convolution calculation to these vectors, so the template can be extended to obtain a series of templates with one-dimensional vector and two-dimensional matrices. These templates can describe and measure the texture's structural information, the three different one-dimensional filter templates with 3 components chosen by Laws are:

$$\begin{aligned} L_3 &= [1 \quad 2 \quad 1] \\ E_3 &= [-1 \quad 0 \quad 1] \\ S_3 &= [-1 \quad 2 \quad -1] \end{aligned} \tag{1}$$

Where L (Gray Levels) is grayscale; E (Edge) is the edge feature; and S is the point feature. Applying the convolution calculation to the L, E, S with one another respectively, a vector filter template of 5 components can be obtained as shown in formula (2):

$$\begin{aligned} L_5 = L_3 * L_3 &= [\ 1 \quad 4 \quad 6 \quad 4 \quad 1] \\ E_5 = E_3 * L_3 &= [-1 \quad -2 \quad 0 \quad 2 \quad 1] \\ S_5 = L_3 * S_3 &= [-1 \quad 0 \quad 2 \quad 0 \quad -1] \\ R_5 = S_3 * S_3 &= [\ 1 \quad -4 \quad 6 \quad -4 \quad 1] \\ W_5 = L_3 * E_3 &= [-1 \quad 2 \quad 0 \quad -2 \quad 1] \end{aligned} \tag{2}$$

Applying the convolution calculation with a selected above 5 components template vector as a row vector and another one as column vectors, we can obtain 25 two-dimensional Laws filter templates with 5 × 5 components $F_{(p,q)}$, $1 \le p \le 5, 1 \le q \le 5$. The image is divided into multiple fixed macroblocks, and each macroblock may have 1 × 25 texture energy matrix. Applying the convolution calculation with these 25 filters $F_{(p,q)}$ and image $I(x,y)$, the texture energy feature for any macroblock $B_{(i,j)}$ of the image can then be obtained as shown in the Eq. (3):

$$E_{B_{(i,j)}}(p,q) = \frac{1}{25}\sum_{p=1}^{5}\sum_{q=1}^{5}\sum_{(x,y)\in link} I(x,y) * F_{(p,q)} \tag{3}$$

Where $(x,y) \in link$ denotes the position of the pixel in the block, and this texture energy feature of the image macroblock is the result of filtering the macroblock by using the Laws filters.

2.2 Multi-scale Texture Energy Analysis Method

Two-dimensional scene image is the projection of the three-dimensional scene in the two-dimensional plane. Therefore, the two-dimensional scene images we obtained will lose a large amount of three-dimensional information. The lost information includes not only the depth information of the scene, but also geometric information such as the shape of the object in the scene, for instance, the occlusion, the shading. In order to restore stereoscopic information in a two-dimensional scene image, clues can only be extracted from the remaining two-dimensional scene images for judgment and recovery.

The depth value of an image macroblock in the scene object cannot be exactly estimated only from the local texture feature, so it is necessary to introduce other local or global features. Based on the multi-scale space concept, the MRF first-order neighborhood is considered as the global feature. The texture energy of the neighborhood of the specific macro-block is also considered and used as the texture energy feature of the macro-block in terms of multi-scale. The four adjacent macroblocks' features, including the upper, the lower, the left and the right, are used as the first-scale features of the specific macroblock to retain the dependencies between adjacent macroblocks. Applying this multi-scale procedure further, the different scales of texture features of a specific macroblock can be obtained. In this way, the depth features of each macroblock should include four neighborhood features, self-block features and vertical features on three scales.

The concept of scale space was first proposed in 1962, and it gradually attracted more attention and developed rapidly in the 1980s [7]. Multi-scale spatial analysis is a dynamic analysis framework that introduces variable scale parameters into single scale image processing technology, so it is easier to obtain the essential features of images. As shown in Fig. 1(a), (b) and (c) are a macroblock at the respective three scales in the image. For an image macroblock (a), it is not possible to estimate its depth information only by its own features. While (b) and (c) provide image features at different scales, the depth information of the macroblock (a) can be estimated easily by overall investigating these global informations.

(a)Scale one (b)Scale two (c)Scale three

Fig. 1. Image expressions at different scales.

3 Image Depth Estimation Based on Markov Random Field Model

The flow chart of image depth information extraction algorithm based on texture feature probability model is shown in Fig. 2.

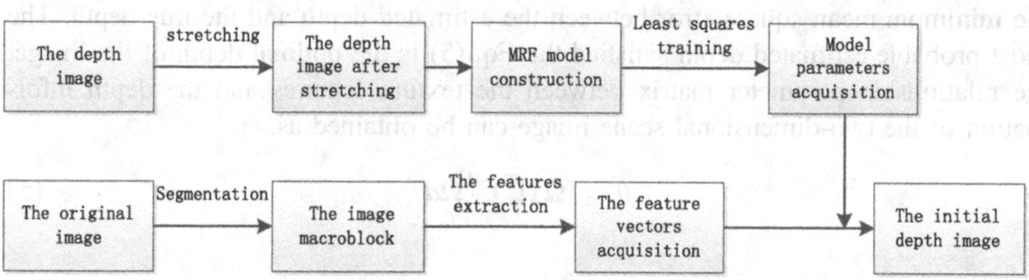

Fig. 2. Flow chart of image depth information extraction Algorithm.

3.1 Texture Feature Probability Model

The pattern recognition classification method is used to supervise and train the existing true depth images and two-dimensional scene images. In this paper, the mathematical model of Saxena [8] is used to divide the training sample image into $M \times N$ macro-block units. Selecting three scale texture as the texture feature of the training sample set, the texture features of the 400 training samples are combined to form the feature vector to study the relationship between the depth of the scene image and the texture energy in the sample set. Based on the equivalence of MRF and Gibbs distribution, MRF model can be established as:

$$P(d|\Omega;\theta,\sigma) = \frac{1}{Z}\exp(-\sum_{i=1}^{n}\frac{(d_i - \psi_i^T\theta_r)^2}{2\sigma_r^2}) \tag{4}$$

The algorithm can determine the class which the depth value of a specific macroblock should belong to in terms of probability as shown in Eq. (4). Where Ω is the texture features, $Z = \sum_{\psi\in\Omega}\exp[-\frac{1}{T}U(\psi)]$ is a normalization constant. For different scenes in different layout of the same image, the training row parameters are not same. using θ_r to denote the parameter matrix of each row, θ_r can be estimated by the maximum likelihood estimation of $l(d) = \log^{P(d|\Omega;\theta_r)}$. Assuming the other parameters as known parameters, the maximum likelihood estimation of θ_r is a linear least squares solution problem. ψ_i denotes the feature vector of the i_{th} macroblock. d_i is the true depth value of the i_{th} macroblock in the training set. σ_r denotes the variance of true depth, which is used to measure the uncertainty of depth for texture energy features.

3.2 MRF Parameters Estimation

The optimal estimation plays an important role in the field of image processing because it can properly handles the problem related to the uncertainty. For many optimal estimation methods using to solve image problem, the problem is often described as an optimal estimation to an objective function. In this paper, the parameter vector θ in the MRF model can be used to solve the problem of trade-off between the maximum depth probability and the minimum error obtained by the model. Therefore, we use the optimization method to train the model parameters and define an objective function as the minimum least square form. We estimate the optimal parameter vector θ_r based on the minimum mean square error between the estimated depth and the true depth. The most probable estimated depth satisfied the Eq. (5) is the optimal depth of the image, the relationship parameter matrix between the texture features and the depth information of the two-dimensional scene image can be obtained as.

$$\theta = (\Omega\Omega^T)^{-1}\Omega d \tag{5}$$

3.3 Image Depth Estimation

The Eq. (6) shows that the parameter matrix θ_r is related to the texture feature Ω. So, it can be considered that the depth d_i is a non-linear combination of the texture feature matrices, and the parameter matrix θ_r is a combination of different weights. The weight is the degree to which the corresponding texture feature affects the depth, and thus the depth value can be calculated as:

$$d_i \approx \psi_i\theta_r \tag{6}$$

4 Iterative Update Algorithm Based on Neighborhood Mixed Depth Information

Although the depth map estimation obtained by the Eq. (6) is of good effect, it is limited for the area with relatively small depth difference in the image. It can be improved further through an iterative update algorithm based on the analysis of the texture energy different changes varies with the scale for the far and near scenes.

4.1 Depth Revaluation Function

Based on the depth values of the neighborhoods for a specific macroblock, we construct a depth revaluation function to compare the multi-scale texture values of specific macroblock with its neighborhoods. The probability of whether the macroblock depth is adjusted and the adjustment parameter values are linked to the multi-scale texture of each neighborhood. Taking the probabilities as the affecting degree weights for those the depths of the different neighboring macroblocks affects the specific macroblock depth, the algorithm extracts 5-scale texture energy for each macroblock. Based on the energy statistics of far and near texture as shown in Fig. 3 [9], the depth re-estimation functions are designed as follows:

(1) if $E_s \leq E_{s+1}, 1 \leq s \leq 4$ and $E_s^{link} \leq E_{s+1}^{link}, 1 \leq s \leq 4$, it illustrates that the specific block is in the a, b scale interval, then the depth re-estimation switching function is designed as:

$$f''_{(s,link)} = \begin{pmatrix} 1 & E_s \leq E_s^{link} \\ 0 & E_s > E_s^{link} \end{pmatrix}$$

(2) if $\max(E_s^{link})$ and $\max(E_s)$ are in the scales s^{link} and s^{link} respectively, then the depth re-estimation switching function is designed as:

$$f''_{(s,link)} = \begin{pmatrix} 1 & s^E \geq s^{link} \\ 0 & s^E < s^{link} \end{pmatrix}.$$

(3) if $E_s \geq E_{s+1}, 1 \leq s \leq 4$ and $E_s^{link} \geq E_{s+1}^{link}, 1 \leq s \leq 4$, it illustrates that the specific block is in the c, d scale interval, then the depth re-estimation switching function is designed as:

$$f''_{(s,link)} = \begin{pmatrix} 1 & E_s \geq E_s^{link} \\ 0 & E_s < E_s^{link} \end{pmatrix}.$$

E_s denotes the texture energy value of any macroblock B at the s_{th} scale, and E_s^{link} denotes the texture energy value of the $link_{\mathrm{th}}$ neighborhood macroblock at the s_{th} scale. Based on these notations, we compare the texture energies of the specific macroblock and its neighboring macroblocks in terms of multiple scales, and the switching functions are designed aiming to establish the depth update iteration algorithm.

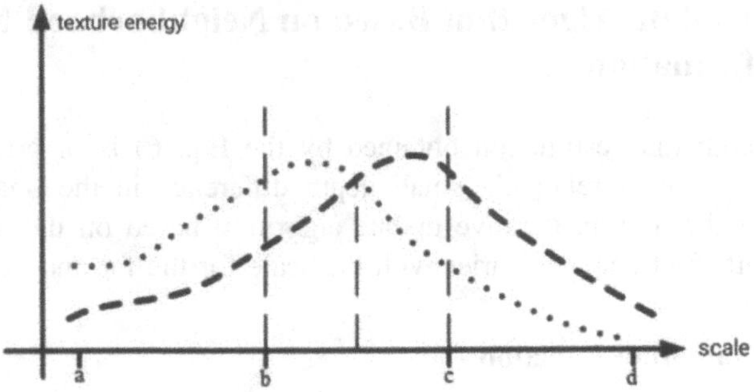

Fig. 3. Far and near texture energy statistic characteristic.

4.2 The Depth Estimation Iteration Criteria

Based on the designed switching functions, we next design an iteration criterion of the depth re-estimation algorithm as follows:

$$d^{(n+1)} = d^{(n)} + \lambda \times \sum_{link=1}^{l} \left(\frac{1}{5} \sum_{s=1}^{5} f''_{(s,link)} \times \left(d_{link} - d^{(n)} \right) \right) \tag{7}$$

Where d_{link} is the depth value of the $link_{\text{th}}$ neighbor macroblock, $f''_{(s,link)}$ is a probability value reflecting the relative position relationship between the specific macroblock and its $link_{\text{th}}$ neighbor macroblock on the s_{th} scale, l denotes the number of neighbor macroblocks for the specific macroblock, and λ is an adjusting factor which can be either chosen as a fixed value or as a flexible value with respect to the edge features of the image.

4.3 The Depth Update Iteration Steps

The depth of a whole image is further re-estimated by the iteration method as the depth value of each macroblock is iterative updated. The $dep^{n}_{(i,j)}$ in Eq. (8) is the depth value of the macroblock at *i* row and *j* column obtained by the by the n_{th} update and the depth values of all macroblocks forms the whole image depth values. The iterative steps are as follows:

(1) Depth value initialization: For selecting the depth of a specific macro-block $d^{(0)}$, we use the experimental results obtained by the least square method as the initial depth [10].
(2) Depth update: The depth value of any macroblock is adjusted according to the depth iteration criterion Eq. (7) to obtain the depth value $d^{(n)}$ of the macroblock.
(3) The iterative convergence condition: The global average depth variation after every iteration is considered as the convergence condition, and the expected global average depth variation after the nth iteration is calculated as shown in Eq. (8).

$$\tau_n = \frac{1}{M \times N} \sum_{i=1}^{M} \sum_{j=1}^{N} dep_{(i,j)}^{n} \tag{8}$$

When $\tau_n^2 - \tau_{n-1}^2 \leq \Delta$, the iteration ends, where Δ is a setting constant. It means that the change of the global variable has reached a steady state. Otherwise taking $n = n + 1$, go to step (2).

5 Experimental Results and Analysis

In order to test the performance of the proposed depth estimation algorithm, we carried out the experiment using the images from the Cornell University's two-dimensional scene images database. It includes scene images and their corresponding true depth

(a)The original images (b) The true depth images (c) The depth images of proposed algorithm

Fig. 4. The experimental results.

images about some artificial environments (buildings, streets, etc.) and natural environments (forests, bushes, etc.). We take 400 images with the pixels of 1704 $\times$ 2272 as training sample sets and 133 other images were used as test sample sets, and the experiment was carried out using the matlab.2011b platform.

In order to achieve good performance and cost less training time, we divided the scene image into 17 $\times$ 32 pixel fixed macroblocks, and the adjusting factor was selected as $\lambda = 0.05$, the iterative convergence threshold Δ was set to 1. The experimental results are shown in Fig. 4, the original images (a) include buildings, trees, sky, etc., the depth images (b) are the true depth images obtained by the laser scanning device, the depth images (c) are the results of the depth images obtained by the proposed algorithm.

The experimental results show that the proposed depth estimation algorithm performs well for regions with large texture differences and clear contour no matter whether the depth differences are large or not. However, for those relatively smooth regions with small texture differences and small depth differences, the estimated depth is not very accurate.

6 Conclusion

This paper focuses on the problem of single image depth estimation, the MRF probability model is firstly established. The model parameters are estimated by the maximum likelihood criterion, so the relationship between parameter and depth is obtained, with that we then generate the initial depth image. Finally, in order to improve the depth estimation accuracy, the initial depth image is re-estimated by an iterative algorithm based on the mixed depth information in the single image. The proposed algorithm can effectively estimate the image depth using the texture clues in both natural and artificial scenery. However, the depth estimation accuracy needs to be further improved in the smooth texture regions. In addition, reducing the algorithm complexity and improving the algorithm calculating speed will also be our important research work in the future.

Acknowledgement. This work is supported by the Harbin Science and Technology Bureau outstanding subject leader fund project (2017RAXXJ055), Nature Science Foundation of Heilongjiang Province (F2018020).

References

1. Liu, F., Shen, C., Lin, G.: Deep convolutional neural fields for depth estimation from a single image. In: Conference on Computer Vision and Pattern Recognition (2015)
2. Zhou, W., Dai, Y., He, R.: Efficient depth estimation from single image. In: IEEE China Summit & International Conference on Signal and Information Processing (2014)
3. Scharstein, D., Szeliski, R.: A taxonomy and evaluation of dense two-frame stereo correspondence algorithms. Int. J. Comput. Vis. **47**(1), 7–42 (2002)
4. Forsyth, D.A., Ponce, J.: Computer Vision: A Modern Approach. Prentice Hall, New York (2003)

5. Das, S., Ahuja, N.: Performance analysis of stereo, vergence, and focus as depth cues for active vision. IEEE Trans. Pattern Anal. Mach. Intell. **17**(12), 1213–1219 (1995)
6. Ge, L., Zhu, Q., Fu, S.: Application of laws' masks to stereo matching. Acta Optica Sinica **29**(9), 2507–2508 (2009)
7. Sun, J., Xu, Z.: A review on scale method in computer vision. Chin. J. Eng. Math. **22**(6), 951–960 (2005)
8. Saxena, A., Sun, M., Ng, A.Y.: Make3D: learning 3D scene structure from a single still image. IEEE Trans. Pattern Anal. Mach. Intell. (PAMI) **30**(5), 824–840 (2009)
9. Lan, J., Ding, Y., Huang, D.: Depth estimation of single image based on multi-scale texture energy measure. Comput. Eng. Des. **32**(1), 224–231 (2011)
10. Davies, E.R.: Laws texture energy in TEXTURE. In: Machine Vision: Theory, Algorithms, Practicalities, 3rd edn., pp. 756–799 (2005)

FPGA-Based High Definition Image Processing System

Xinxin He and Linbo Tang(✉)

Beijing Key Laboratory of Embedded Real-Time Information Processing Technology, Beijing Institute of Technology, Beijing, China
hxx9418@163.com, tanglinbo@bit.edu.cn

Abstract. With the continuous development of mobile communication and the Internet, people's requirements for the speed and quality of digital image processing are increasingly improved. A large amount of high-speed, parallel video stream data needs to be processed in real time, especially in video image processing. The author presents a method of high-definition image transmission and processing system based on FPGA. The system uses FPGA as the main controller, consisting of front-end HDMI video receiving module, image fast median filtering processing module, image ping pong Storage module and HD-SDI video display module through hardware description language programming, effectively realizing real-time video capture, transmission and display. It has been verified that the processing and transmission of digital video signals in this system is stable and reliable. The system also has a series of advantages such as low power consumption, low cost, flexible design, and easy expansion and has been applied in practical engineering.

Keywords: FPGA · HDMI · SDI · Advanced median filtering

1 Introduction

Digital image processing technology has developed rapidly in contemporary society and plays an irreplaceable role and has been widely used in aerospace, communications, medical and industrial production. With the continuous development of mobile communication and the Internet, people's requirements for the speed and quality of digital image processing are increasingly improved. A large amount of high-speed, parallel video stream data needs to be processed in real time, especially in video image processing, and FPGA can exert its unique advantages.

As the amount of image data grows, the computation of algorithm that is implemented in FPGA becomes increasingly large. The traditional method of increasing the clock frequency is difficult to solve the system power consumption problem and the cache speed problem, which are caused by the large computation. Because of the structural characteristics and design rules of FPGA in image processing, there are many common design ideas and techniques can be used: serial-to-parallel conversion, pipeline operation, Ping-Pong operation. These design techniques increases not only the efficiency of code execution, but also the speed of code calculations and the stability of the design. In this paper, these design ideas have been all applied in the system [1].

M. Jia et al. (Eds.): WiSATS 2019, LNICST 281, pp. 208–219, 2019.
https://doi.org/10.1007/978-3-030-19156-6_20

(1) Serial and parallel conversion. Spatial parallelism based on image processing divides the image into several parts, and the same algorithm is used for each part at the same time. The calculation time of all data processing is long, and processing at the same time saves a lot of calculation time, but the storage resources required for spatial parallel processing are large. Changing serial data to parallel data processing is done by increasing the consumption of logic resources in exchange for processing speed, which can reduce processing time and improve design performance. Conversely, changing parallel data to serial can save logic resources [2].
(2) Ping Pong Cache. The Ping-Pong cache caches data into two different spaces, buffers data in one space, and reads data in another space, usually used in the processing of high-speed data streams. The most important thing to achieve Ping-Pong cache is the mutual cooperation of the two spaces to achieve seamless switching.
(3) Pipeline operation. Time parallelism is a pipeline idea that divides image processing into different modules, each of which runs separately and is irrelevant in terms of computation time. When processing video stream image data, the data is pipelined to the FPGA and the image processing through a multi-stage pipeline greatly increases data throughput.

Due to the characteristics of video images, the characteristics of image processing algorithms and the processing techniques of FPGA, FPGA become the fastest and best performing hardware platform for real-time video image processing [3].

In this paper, an FPGA-based high-definition digital image transmission and processing system is designed, which can convert the HD video with resolution of 1080P60 received by the front-end HDMI receiving module. It can also use DDR3 to Ping-Pong the image data and display the processed video in real time on the terminal device supporting the SDI interface. At the same time, in order to meet the image quality and speed requirements, a fast median filtering process is added to the system to ensure the image clarity and real-time processing. The system has the advantages of low cost, flexibility, and ease of expansion.

2 System Structure Design

The high-definition video transmission system proposed in this paper uses XILINX's A7 series FPGA as the core device. First, the video is sent to the FPGA through the HDMI interface for decoding, and 24-bit RGB image data and the horizontal and field synchronizing signal are extracted therefrom. Then, the fast median filtering algorithm is used to denoise the video signal, and the SRAM is used for the Ping-Pong buffer. Finally, the SDI data stream is generated and displayed through the SDI output.

The entire structure framework of the system is shown in the Fig. 1.

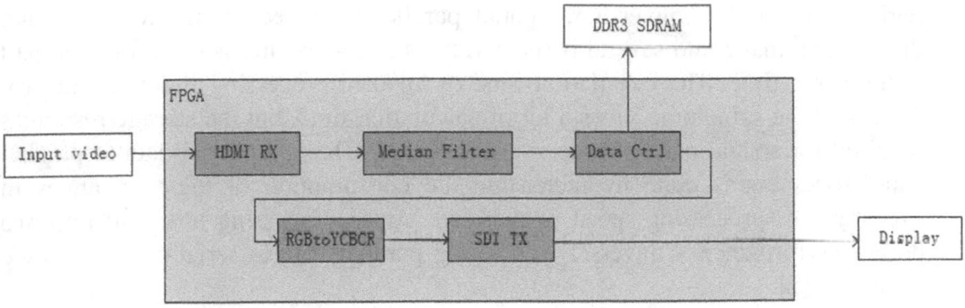

Fig. 1. The entire structure framework of the system

The entire design of the system can be divided into the following modules:

(1) HDMI receiving module: This module will extract valid 24-bit RGB image signal and horizontal and field synchronizing signal from the received HDMI format video;
(2) Median filter module: Image preprocessing module, which can effectively remove noise and smooth the image. Using the fast median filtering algorithm can remove the noise without degrading the edges of the image, better maintain the clarity of the image, and meet the real-time requirements;
(3) Storage module: In the real-time video processing system, since the video processing code execution process is variable speed, it is necessary to provide a certain buffer circuit between the input and output of the image.
(4) SDI output module: This module is mainly divided into two parts: image format conversion and SDI data stream generation. Since the SDI interface has its specific output standard, the RGB format needs to be converted to the YCbCr format, and the SDI data stream output is generated according to the interface protocol.

3 Core Module Introduction

3.1 HDMI Receiving Module

High Definition Multimedia Interface (HDMI) is a dedicated digital video/audio interface technology suitable for image transmission, which can transmit audio and video signals at the same time. The maximum data transmission speed of HDMI is 2.25 GB/s and a 1080p video requirement is less than 0.5 GB/s. Therefore, HDMI can be used as a receiving interface for HD video [4].

HDMI uses the Time Minimized Differential Signal (TMDS) transmission technology. TMDS, also known as a transiently modulated differential signal, is a differential signaling mechanism that uses a differential transmission. When HDMI is encoded by TMDS technology, the video signal is divided into R, G, and B data signals and two horizontal and field control signals H and V. These five signals are transmitted in four channels. Each of R, G, and B uses one channel. The horizontal and field control signal is transmitted in the B signal channel, and the audio signal is transmitted in the R and G signal channels. There is also a separate channel for transmitting clock data. One TMDS channel can transmit 10 bits of data per clock cycle.

Therefore, it is necessary to decode the video transmitted through the HDMI interface to generate a data stream in the VGA format. The timing diagram of the video decoding module is illustrated in the Fig. 2.

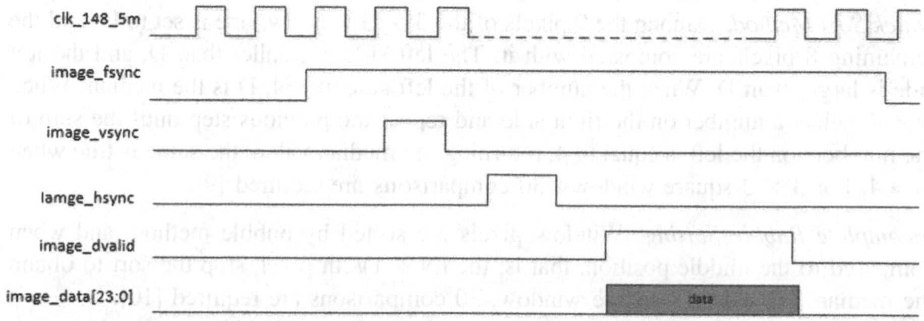

Fig. 2. The timing diagram of the video decoding module

There are three processes in the HDMI transmission process: video data period, data island period, and control period. Each stage transmits different data and has different functions. When HDMI works in the video data period, the three TMDS data channels transmit video data; when HDMI works in the data island period, the TMDS channel transmits audio data and auxiliary data in the form of data packets; when HDMI works during thc control period, it transmits the boot information, indicating that no valid data is currently transmitted [5].

3.2 Image Processing Module

Median filtering is a common image preprocessing method that effectively removes noise and smoothes the image. Compared with the mean filter and other linear filters, it can denoise without degrading the edges of the image and better maintain the clarity of the image [6].

Median Filtering Principle

The basic principle of median filtering: the gray value of each pixel is set to the median value of the gray value of all pixels in its neighborhood window [7]. The two-dimensional median filtering is based on a two-dimensional sliding window, which in turn slides from left to right and top to bottom at the pixel points of the image. At each pixel, the gray values in the window are sorted to produce a monotone grayscale sequence with the median value as the output of this pixel:

$$g(x,y) = Med\{f(x-i,\ y-j)\};\ subject\, to(i,j) \in s \tag{1}$$

where $f\ (x,\ y)$ is the original image, $g\ (x,\ y)$ is the processed image, s is the two-dimensional template [8].

Typical Median Filtering Optimization Algorithm

The core of median filtering is sorting, and the sorting algorithm uses the most traditional bubbling method. A square filter window with N × N pixels is subjected to about $N^2 * (N^2-1)/2$ comparisons every time it is run. The algorithm complexity is o (N^4), and the commonly used 3 × 3 filter window needs to be sorted 36 times. Up to now, there are some mature optimization algorithms at home and abroad.

Quick Sort Method. Among the 9 pixels of the 3 × 3 window, one is set to D, and the remaining 8 pixels are compared with it. The left side is smaller than D, and the left side is larger than D. When the number of the left side m = 4, D is the median. When m < 4, select a number on the right side and repeat the previous step until the sum of the numbers on the left is equal to 4, returning the median value; the same is true when m > 4. For 3 × 3 square windows, 30 comparisons are required [9].

Incomplete Bubble Sorting. Window pixels are sorted by bubble method, and when compared to the middle position, that is, the (N + 1)/2th pixel, stop the sort to obtain the median. For a 3 × 3 square window, 30 comparisons are required [10].

Compared to the 36 binary comparisons of the traditional bubbling method, the two optimization algorithms are reduced by 6 times. However, the above algorithm is not stable enough and the number of comparisons is still too much. The advanced algorithm of this paper overcomes the above shortcomings, that is, the comparison times are the least and the stability is better.

Implementation Methodology of the Advanced Median Filtering Algorithm

The advanced median filtering algorithm has three main steps:

(1) Sort 3 pixels of each row in the 3 × 3 window in ascending order and respectively obtain 3 ordered sequences;
(2) Sort the three ordered sequences in ascending order according to their median sizes;
(3) Compare the minimum value in the max row, the maximum value in the min row, and all the three values in the mid row. And the median of them is the required median.

The sorting process is shown in the Fig. 3.

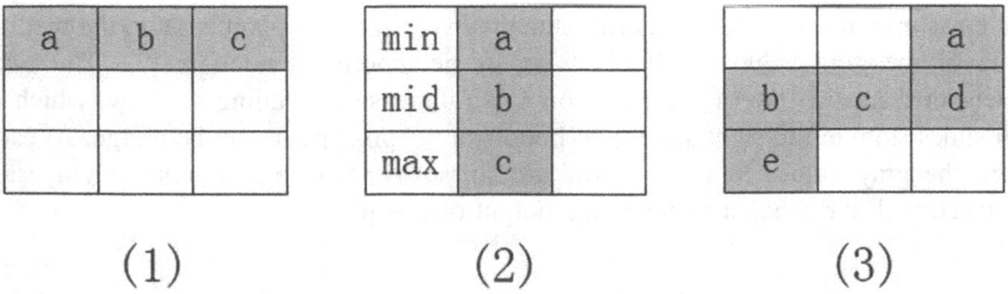

Fig. 3. The sorting process of the advanced median filtering algorithm

Implementing the advanced median filtering algorithm on an FPGA requires three main modules: a 3 × 3 window generation module, a median filter module, and a row and column counting module. The implementation scheme is illustrated in Fig. 4.

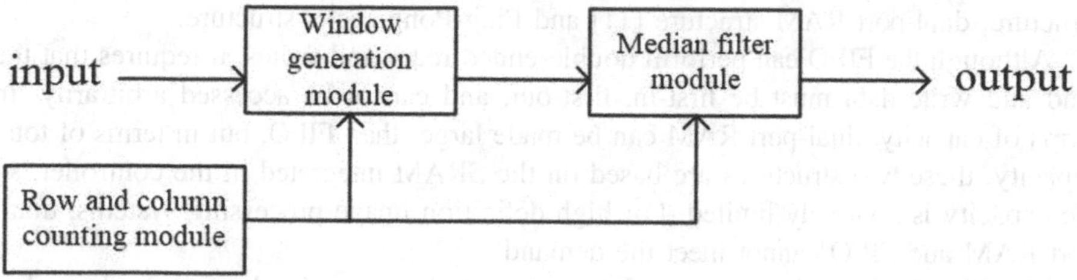

Fig. 4. The implementation scheme of the advanced median filtering algorithm

The function of the 3 × 3 window generation module is to generate a 3 × 3 scan window. When the window passes through the image, a 3 × 3 pixel value is read and passed to the system for subsequent data processing. The window scans from left to right, from top to bottom, until the entire frame is read.

The function of the median filtering module is to process the pixels collected by the 3 × 3 window according to the advanced median filtering algorithm proposed in this paper, and output the processed pixels.

The function of the row and column counting module is to determine whether the center pixel is located at the edge of the image. For the edge portion, the image cannot be covered with a 3 × 3 window, and the filtered output is meaningless. The usual processing method is to output the pixel values of the edge to "0".

Therefore, the system in this paper is designed with the advanced median filtering algorithm, which utilizes parallel and pipeline processing methods, and requires 19 comparisons to complete a median filter. After a latency of 9 clocks, a result is calculated for each clock, which greatly speeds up the calculation of the median filter. The calculation principle is shown in Fig. 5.

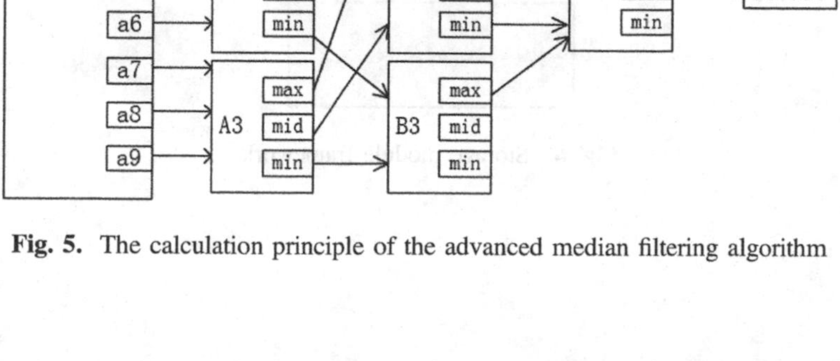

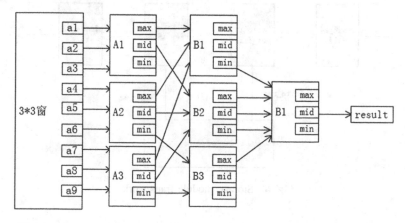

Fig. 5. The calculation principle of the advanced median filtering algorithm

3.3 Storage Module

In a real-time video processing system, since the video processing code execution process is variable, it is necessary to provide a certain buffer circuit between the input and output of the image. The more commonly used cache circuits include: FIFO structure, dual-port RAM structure [11] and Ping-Pong cache structure.

Although the FIFO can perform double-ended reads and writes, it requires that the read and write data must be first-in, first-out, and cannot be accessed arbitrarily. In terms of capacity, dual-port RAM can be made larger than FIFO, but in terms of total capacity, these two structures are based on the SRAM integrated in the controller, so the capacity is relatively limited. For high-definition image processing systems, dual-port RAM and FIFO cannot meet the demand.

The Ping-Pong cache allocates data to two cache units simultaneously through a cache switching unit. The write data is buffered to cache unit 1 during the first read and write cycle. At the beginning of the second read/write cycle, the write data is buffered to the cache unit 2 by the cache switch. At the same time, the data of the first read/write cycle of the cache unit 1 is selected by the output switch and read, and then sent to the processor operation unit for processing. In the third read/write cycle, the cached read unit is switched again, so that the cycle is repeated.

Because the speed of RAM reading is much faster than the speed of writing, the Ping-Pong cache can not only meet the real-time requirements of high-speed video streams, but also give the CPU enough time to process data, which solves the synchronization between data modules effectively. Storage module framework is illustrated in Fig. 6.

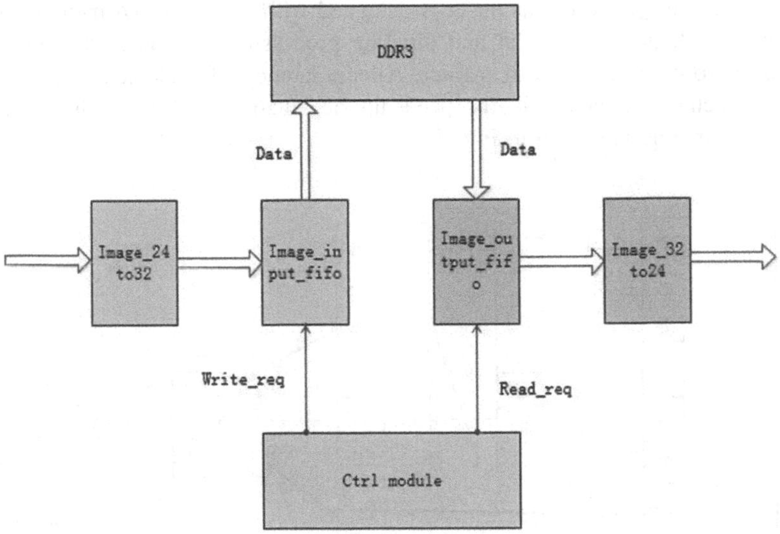

Fig. 6. Storage module framework

3.4 SDI Output

Serial Digital Interface (SDI) is a video standard interface defined by the Society of Motion Picture and Television Engineers (SMPTE) for serial transmission of uncompressed digital video and audio signals over a single coaxial cable. SDI video is divided into standard definition (SD), high definition (HD) and 3G.

The HD-SDI interface has a transfer rate of 1.485/1.4835 Gbps or higher and is compliant with the SMPTE 292M standard. It transmits a 4:2:2 serial uncompressed digital component signal (YCrCb signal) with a transmission rate of 270 Mbps and a maximum transmission distance of 300 m [12].

The SMPTE 292M video standard is an image transmission standard for internal synchronization, which refers to embedding the image horizontal and field synchronizing signal in the image data, and no external synchronizing signal is needed. There are two types of image timing reference codes. One is at the start of the image valid data block (SAV) for the start control of the active image, and the other is at the end of the valid data block (EAV), which is also the starting position of the digital horizontal blanking. Two timing references are used to control the start and end of a line of the image [13]. The 1080P SDI image data format is shown in Fig. 7.

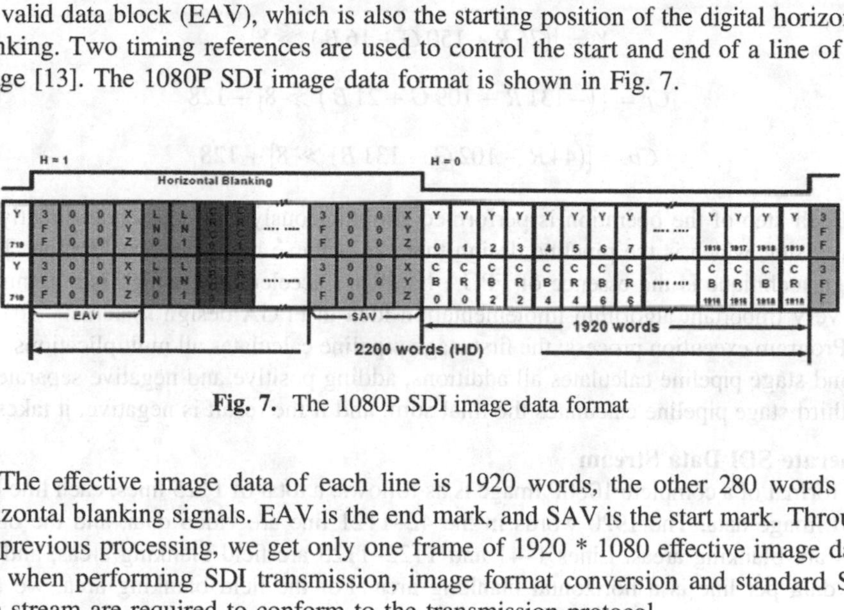

Fig. 7. The 1080P SDI image data format

The effective image data of each line is 1920 words, the other 280 words are horizontal blanking signals. EAV is the end mark, and SAV is the start mark. Through the previous processing, we get only one frame of 1920 * 1080 effective image data. But when performing SDI transmission, image format conversion and standard SDI data stream are required to conform to the transmission protocol.

RGB to YCBCR

YCbCr, a type of color space, is often used for continuous image processing in movies or digital photography systems. Where Y is the brightness, which is the gray level value. "Brightness" is established by RGB input signals by superimposing specific parts of the RGB signal. Cb reflects the difference between the blue portion of the RGB input signal and the luminance value of the RGB signal. Cr reflects the difference between the red portion of the RGB input signal and the luminance value of the RGB signal [14].

The conversion formula is shown as follows:

$$Y = (0.299\,R + 0.587\,G + 0.114\,B) \tag{2}$$

$$Cr = (0.511\,R - 0.428\,G - 0.083\,B) + 128 \tag{3}$$

$$Cb = (-0.172\,R - 0.399\,G + 0.511\,B) + 128 \tag{4}$$

In the process of RGB to YCb Cr algorithm, since the FPGA cannot perform floating-point operations, it is necessary to first expand the right end of the whole equation by 256 times and then shift the right side by 8 bits, so that it can be processed by multiplication and addition operations suitable for FPGA.

$$Y = [(76\,R + 150\,G + 16\,B) \gg 8] \tag{5}$$

$$Cr = [(-131\,R - 109\,G + 21\,B) \gg 8] + 128 \tag{6}$$

$$Cb = [(44\,R - 102\,G - 131\,B) \gg 8] + 128 \tag{7}$$

Each step of the operation is performed simultaneously and calculated directly in the register, which is the pipeline design that can achieve hardware acceleration. This design technique is the essence of FPGA hardware acceleration, which is a common and very important algorithm implementation idea in FPGA design systems.

Program execution process: the first stage pipeline calculates all multiplications; the second stage pipeline calculates all additions, adding positive and negative separately; the third stage pipeline calculates the final sum, and if the result is negative, it takes 0.

Generate SDI Data Stream

The format of a complete 1080P image is as follows: a total of 1125 lines, each line has 2200 image data. The 1920 words in the 42–1121 line are video data, and the other parts are blanking areas. Lines 1–41 and 1122–1125 are field blanking areas, and 1–280 data per line is a horizontal blanking area. For the field blanking area, we can directly output white. For the horizontal blanking area, we need to meet the format of Fig. 7, adding the start signal of frame, end signal of frame, line count signal and other signals [15]. The structure of one frame image is shown in Fig. 8, where the color portion represents video data.

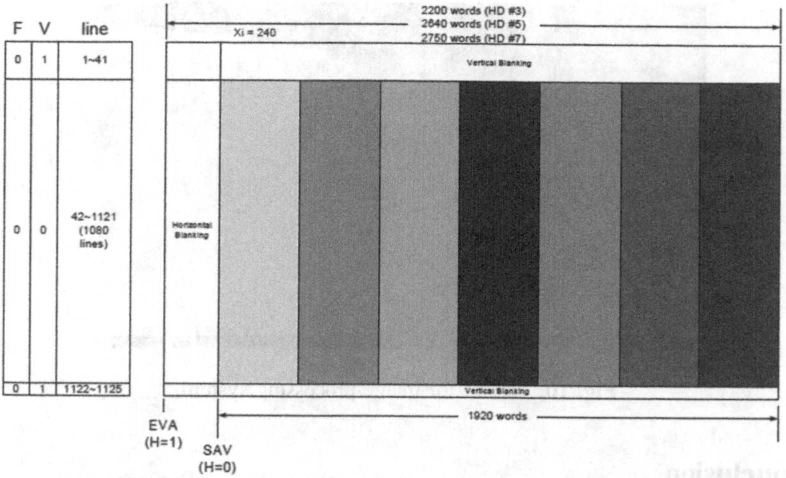

Fig. 8. The structure of one frame image (Color figure online)

4 Practical Application and Testing

This design uses ADLINK's SDI video capture card for image display testing. After testing, the system can send 1080P HD SDI video images of 60 frames per second and display the video correctly on the PC (Fig. 9). It can be seen from the test results Fig. 10 that the image is clear and stable, and the display effect is good.

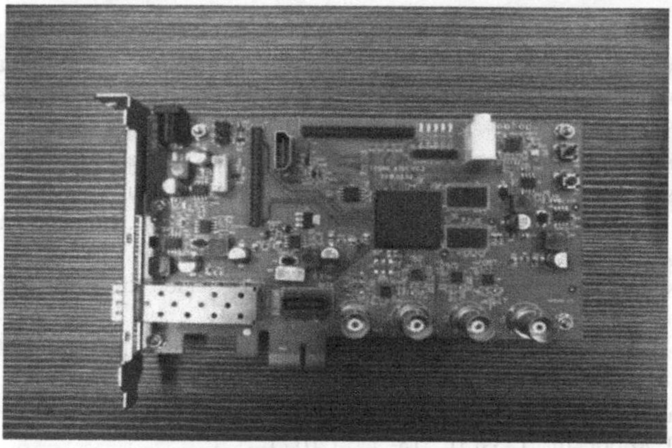

Fig. 9. Experiment environment

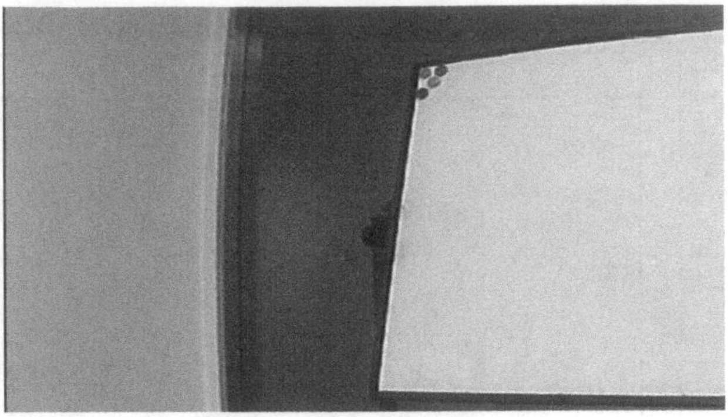

Fig. 10. Result for image processing system

5 Conclusion

In this paper, an FPGA-based high-definition digital image transmission and processing system is designed and implemented. The system realizes the conversion of HDMI to HD-SDI, and the advanced median filtering and DDR buffer are added, which not only improves the processing speed and quality of image, but also provides a foundation for implementing image processing in FPGA later. Through the experiment verification, the system has a series of advantages, such as low power consumption, low cost, flexible design, and easy expansion, which can output clear and stable processed video. Currently, the system has been applied to practical engineering.

References

1. Sun, J.: Research on high speed image compression technology based on parallel pipeline structure. Doctor Thesis, Graduate School of the Chinese Academy of Sciences, Beijing, China (2015)
2. Hu, X.: Research of hardware design for video compression algorithm based on FPGA. Master Thesis, Xidian University, Xi'an, Shaanxi, China (2013)
3. Yu, J.: FPGA realization of video compression-related problems. Comput. Knowl. Technol. **5**(24), 6771–6773 (2009)
4. Pan, L.: Design of image processing system for HDMI's video stream based on FPGA. Res. Explor. Lab. **34**(10), 77–78 (2015)
5. Xiao, J.: Design of video data codec based on HDMI. Electron. Des. Eng. **24**(13), 190–193 (2016)
6. Xu, Y.: Real-time image capturing and processing of seam and pool during robotic welding process. Ind. Robot: Int. J. **39**(5), 513–523 (2012)
7. Xu, F.: Feature extraction of acoustic emission signals based on median filter-singular value decomposition and empirical mode decomposition. Chin. J. Sci. Instrum. **32**(11), 2712–2719 (2011)
8. Shen, X.: Research of the advanced median filtering algorithm based on FPGA. Microelectron. Comput. **31**(1), 21–24 (2014)

9. Hou, F.: Image median filter algorithm and FPGA implementation. Microcomput. Inf. **27**(1), 69–71 (2011)
10. Huang, H.: Road recognition and tracking for intelligent vehicle based on SOPC. Chin. J. Sci. Instrum. **33**(2), 321–326 (2012)
11. Zhang, S.: Design and implementation of HDMI high-definition video editing based on Leonardo DaVinci. Microelectron. Comput. **34**(6), 54–57 (2017)
12. Interface for digital component video signals in 525-line and 625-line television systems operating at the 4:2:2 Level of Recommendation ITURBT.601 (ITU-RBT.656) (2010)
13. Television 10bit 4:2:2 component and 4FSC composite digital signal serial interface (SMPTE-259M) (2011)
14. Gonzalez, R., Woods, R., Stevenl, E.D.: Digital Image Processing Using Matlab, 2nd edn. Tsinghua University Press, Beijing (2013)
15. Liu, L.: FPGA-based SD-SDI transmission system design. Electron. Des. Eng. **25**(23), 94–97 (2017)

Research on Image Classification Method Based on Adaboost-DBN

Huadong Sun[1,2(✉)], Wuchao Tao[1,2], Ran Wang[1,2], Cong Ren[1,2], and Zhijie Zhao[1,2]

[1] School of Computer and Information Engineering, Harbin University of Commerce, Harbin 150028, China
kof97_sun@163.com

[2] Heilongjiang Provincial Key Laboratory of Electronic Commerce and Information Processing, Harbin University of Commerce, Harbin 150028, China

Abstract. Image classification has been applied in many fields, which is an important branch of computer vision and pattern recognition. The boosting algorithm which is belong to ensemble learning can integrate several homogeneous classifiers, and combine the output layer's result of every classifier to improve the final classification accuracy. In this paper, the Adaboost-DBN algorithm is used to combine the four weak classifiers (DBN) and construct a strong classifier. The Adaboost-DBN algorithm is based on the Adaboost M1 algorithm and is used to achieve higher classification accuracy. The proposed algorithm is tested on the Corel-1K data set, and the result of classification is significantly improved comparing to other classifiers.

Keywords: Image classification · Adaboost-DBN

1 Introduction

Image classification is composed of feature extraction and feature classification. The most common feature of the image is the underlying visual features [1], including color features, texture features and shape features. Texture features are not based on pixel points, they need to be statistically calculated in regions containing multiple pixels. There are many methods to extract [2], such as the co-occurrence matrix, the local binary pattern (LBP), wavelet transform and so on. At present, texture features are widely used in image retrieval, face recognition and other fields. In this paper, the local neighborhood rotation right-angle pattern [3] is used to extract the texture features of the image. The method decomposes the image into R, G, B three-channel, and arranges them into spatial stereo in order, centering on the central pixel of the middle layer, and extracting features according to local neighborhood rotation. Finally, the feature value is dimension-reduced and expressed in the form of LBP.

Among the classification methods, the primitive method [4] has Naive Bayesian, K-Nearest Neighbor, Fisher Linear Discrimination and so on. With the rise of machine learning algorithms [5], classification algorithms such as Ensemble Learning, Convolutional Neural Networks, Deep Belief Networks, and Back Propagation Neural Networks have emerged, and the accuracy of classification of classifiers have been greatly

M. Jia et al. (Eds.): WiSATS 2019, LNICST 281, pp. 220–228, 2019.
https://doi.org/10.1007/978-3-030-19156-6_21

improved. Also it is suitable for large quantities and high levels of complexity. Many algorithms in machine learning are implemented in image classification. The Neural Networks can achieve non-linear fitting of images according to its complex network structure. Therefore, Neural Networks have been widely used. As a kind of boost algorithm for ensemble learning, Boosting algorithm combines several homogeneous classifiers into a strong classifier by linear weighting. The most widely used algorithm is the Adaptive Boost algorithm [6]. The Deep Belief Network (DBN) is composed of several restricted Boltzmann machines (RBM) and a layer of BP. The neural network contains many neurons and parameters (weights and offsets), so it has the strong ability of fitting. This article combines Adaboost and DBN to classify images. The traditional multi-classification method of boosting is based on the binary-class of "one-to-one" and "one-to-many" [7]. But the algorithm structure is cumbersome and the implementation of program wastes a lot of time. Therefore, this paper adopts the improved version of the Adaboost-DBN algorithm. It can output multi-classification directly and avoids complex computational processes. The algorithm is tested on the Corel-1K data set, and the classification accuracy show that it is greatly improved compared with the single classifier.

2 Feature Extraction

2.1 LBP

The LBP is a method for describing local texture features. The 3 * 3 local pixels are extracted to construct a local binary pattern, which is composed of a central pixel and a neighborhood pixel. LBP [3] uses a binary code in which each neighborhood pixel gray value is compared to the center pixel gray value to be converted into a binary coded form. The formula is as shown in (1) and (2):

$$LBP_{P,R} = \sum_{P=1}^{P} 2^{(P-1)} \cdot f_1(g_p - g_c) \quad (1)$$

$$f_1(x) = \begin{cases} 1, & x \geq 0 \\ 0, & x < 0 \end{cases} \quad (2)$$

Where g_p is the gray value of the neighborhood pixel, g_c is the gray value of the center pixel, and P is the number of neighboring pixels. R is the radius of the neighborhood. Figure 1 shows the working process of LBP.

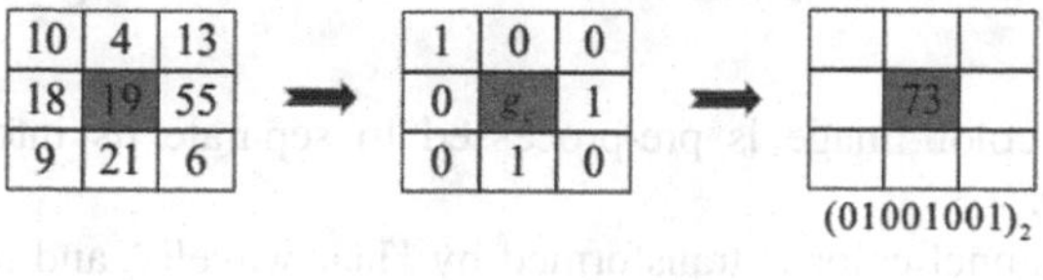

Fig. 1. LBP pattern.

2.2 VLBP

VLBP [8] is based on the dynamic texture change of adjacent frames in the video sequence. The dynamic texture of the image is calculated according to the gray value of the central pixel $g_{t_c,c}$ and the gray value of it's neighborhood pixel $g_{t,p}(t = t - L, t_c, t_c + L; P = 0, \cdots p - 1)$, p represents the number of neighboring pixels of the image center pixel. The formula can be expressed as:

$$VLBP_{L,P,R} = \sum_{q=0}^{3P+1} v_p 2^q. \tag{3}$$

The Fig. 2 shows the process of collecting samples of VLBP:

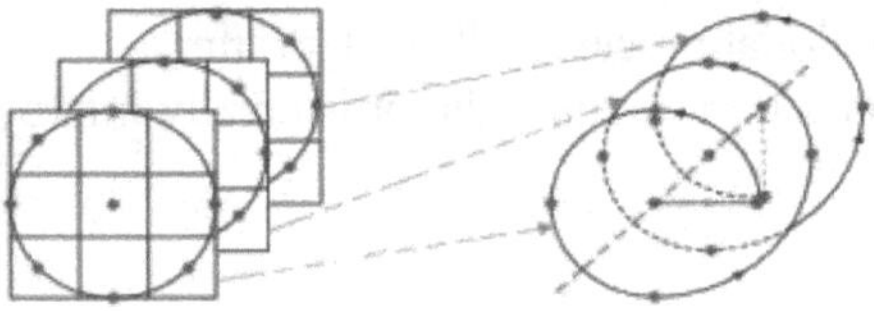

Fig. 2. The process of collecting samples of VLBP.

According to the collected samples obtained by VLBP (as shown in the Fig. 1), the central pixel is used as the reference point, and the local pattern values in the five directions are extracted showing in the Fig. 3:

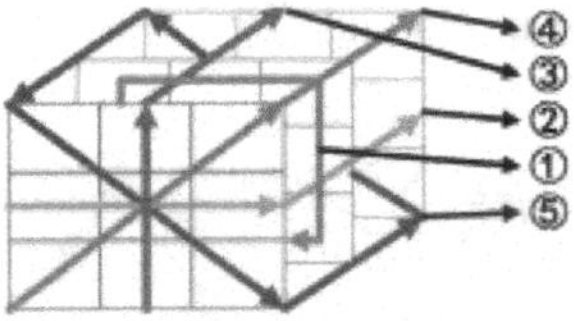

Fig. 3. The local pattern values in the five directions.

Feature extraction is the expression of images in a abstract fashion, which is the basis of image processing. Texture features characterize image information by analyzing the distribution of central pixels and their neighboring pixels. There are many methods for extracting texture features. In this paper, local neighborhood rotation right-angle patterns [3] are used to extract texture features. The algorithm steps are as follows:

(1) The original color image is pre-processed to separate its into R, G, B three-channel color;
(2) The single channel color is transformed by Haar wavelet, and the low frequency band is extracted as contour information;

(3) Based on the VLBP pattern, the three low frequency sub-bands are arranged in the order of R, G, B;
(4) The local neighborhood rotation right-angle patterns are used to extract feature extraction and it is represented into histogram form;
(5) The LBP pattern is used to reduce the dimension.

3 Adaboost-DBN Algorithm

3.1 Deep Brief Network

Belief in the Deep Belief Network refers to probability, so Deep Belief Network refers to a kind of neural network that can learn by probability. DBN is a probability generation model that aims to establish a joint distribution between data and labels. The DBN is composed of multiple restricted Boltzmann machine and an output layer. The data is putted into the neural network from the input layer. First, unsupervised training is performed by the restricted Boltzmann machine, and then supervised training is performed by the BP algorithm. The DBN can exploit the nonlinear relationship fully between the input data and labels, and finally get the weight and offset in the neural network.

Restricted Boltzmann Machine. The restricted Boltzmann machine is generated stochastic neural network proposed by Hinton and Sejnowski in 1986. The RBM model is consisted of a visible layer (v) and a hidden layer (h). The neurons between the layers are connected to each other, and the neurons in the layer are not connected. The restricted Boltzmann machine is used to perform unsupervised training between layer-by-layer on the neural network. The parameters obtained by training are used as the initial parameters of the neurons in each layer of the neural network, which are in a better location for space. RBM [9] is an energy-based model whose energy of the joint distribution of the visible variable (v) and the hidden variable (h) is:

$$E(\mathrm{v}, \mathrm{h}; \theta) = -\sum_{i,j} W_{i,j} v_i h_j - \sum_i b_i v_i - \sum_j a_j b_j \quad (4)$$

In (4) θ is the parameter $\{w, a, b\}$ of RBM, w is the weight of between the visible unit and the hidden unit, b and a is the bias of the visible unit and the hidden unit. With the energy of the joint distribution of v and h in (1), we can get the joint probability of v and h:

$$P_\theta(v, h) = \frac{1}{Z(\theta)} \exp\left(\sum_{i=1}^{D}\sum_{j=1}^{F} W_{ij} v_i h_j + \sum_{i=1}^{D} v_i b_j + \sum_{j=1}^{F} h_j a_j\right) \quad (5)$$

Where Z(θ) is a normalization factor, also known as a partition function in (5), and $p_\theta(v,h)$ is find to get the edge distribution of h to get $p_\theta(v)$, and $p_\theta(v)$ is processed to get the parameters θ^* of RBM:

$$\theta^* = \arg\max L(\theta) = \arg\max \sum_{t=1}^{T} \log\, p(v^t|\theta) \tag{6}$$

After the parameters are acquired, they are updated according to the contrastive divergence algorithm proposed by Hinton. The expression is as follows:

$$\begin{aligned} \Delta\omega_{ij} &= \varepsilon(<v_ih_j>_{data} - <v_ih_j>_{recon}) \\ \Delta a_i &= \varepsilon(<v_i>_{data} - <v_i>_{recon}) \\ \Delta b_i &= \varepsilon(<h_j>_{data} - <h_j>_{recon}) \end{aligned} \tag{7}$$

Where ε is the learning rate of pre-training, $< >_{data}$ is the mathematical expectation of the training data set, and $< >_{recon}$ is the reconstructed mathematical expectation.

BP neural Network. BP neural network is a multi-layer feed forward neural network. Its main characteristic is: the signal is forward propagating, and the error is back propagating. In this thesis, The neural network is trained by BP algorithm, and the parameters of the network will eventually converge in a good position. The process of BP neural network is divided into two phases. The first phase is the forward propagation of the signal, the signal from the input layer through the hidden layer, and finally get to the output layer. The second phase is the back propagation of the error, there is an error between the output layer and the hidden layer, from the output layer and finally get to the input layer, which adjusts the weight and offset of the output layer to the hidden layer, and the weight and offset of the hidden layer to the input layer.

The BP algorithm [10] updates the parameters as follows, assuming that the number of nodes of the input layer is n, the number of nodes of the hidden layer is l, the number of nodes of the output layer is m, and the weight of the input layer to the hidden layer is ω_{ij}, implied the layer-to-output layer weight is ω_{jk}, the offset between input layer and the hidden layer is a_j, the offset between hidden layer and the output layer is b_k, and H_j is the output of the hidden layer. The learning rate is η, the excitation function is $g(x)$. The error between the expected output and the actual output is:

$$E = \frac{1}{2}\sum_{k=1}^{m} (Y_K - O_K)^2 \tag{8}$$

In (8) Y_k is the expected output and O_k is the actual output, as $Y_k - O_K = e_k$. An update formula for the weights and offsets obtained by E-derivation using the gradient descent method:

$$\begin{aligned} \omega_{ij} &= \omega_{ij} + \eta H_j(1-H)x_i \sum_{k=1}^{m} \omega_{jk} e_k \\ \omega_{jk} &= \omega_{jk} + \eta H_j e_k \\ a_j &= a_j + \eta H_j(1-H_j) \sum_{k=1}^{m} \omega_{jk} e_k \\ b_k &= b_k + \eta e_k \end{aligned} \tag{9}$$

3.2 The Proposed Adaboost-DBN Algorithm

The Adaboost algorithm is the most widely used in the boosting algorithm, and its central idea has not changed. That is, some weak classifiers are trained, the weight of the wrong samples in each training will become larger in the next training, and the weight of the correct samples will be reduced. The traditional algorithm is based on the two-category "one-to-one" and "one-to-many", dealing with multiple classifications. Because two methods have great redundancy in algorithm design and program implementation, this thesis uses the Adaboost M1algorithm [11] and made some improvements on this basis. The flow chart of the improved algorithm is:

(1) Initialize the weight distribution of the sample: $D1 = (\frac{1}{N}, \frac{1}{N}, \cdots, \frac{1}{N})$;
(2) $t = 1, 2, 3 \cdots T$;
   (1) Training the weak classifier DBN using the initialized weight samples;
   (2) The error of classifier: $\varepsilon_t = \sum_{i=1}^{m} D_i^t[h_t(x_i) \neq y_i], h_t(x_i)$ is the final value of the output layer, and its value is composed of 0 and 1, and is the same as $h_t(x_i)$ in step (4);
   (3) Weight of the classifier: $\alpha = \frac{1}{2}\lg\frac{1-\varepsilon^{(t)}}{\varepsilon^{(t)}} + \lg(K-1)$;
   (4) The updated weight of sample: $D_i^{t+i} = D_i^t \cdot \exp(\alpha_t \cdot [h_t(x_i) \neq y_i])$;
   (5) Normalized the weight of D_i^{t+i};
(3) Obtained the strong classifier: $H(x) = \sum_{t=1}^{T} \alpha(t)h'(x), h'(x)$ represents the proportion of each sample in different class before the output layer output classification results, usually a decimal.

The Proposed Algorithm Analysis. There are two improvements between the proposed algorithm and the Adaboost M1 algorithm, the first improvement is step (3) the weight of the classifier, it is added a positive term $\lg(K-1)$ [12] on the basis of the original. The term brings a great improvement to the performance of the algorithm. The original Adaboost M1 algorithm is asked that the correct rate of the classifier is greater than 1/2. It is difficult for the general classifier to meet this requirement. It is known from the improved classifier that the error of classifier meets $\varepsilon(t) < 1 - 1/K$. In other words, as the number of iterations increases, the accuracy of the classifier is reduced.

The second improvement is step (6). The original is $H(x) = \arg\max_k \sum_{t=1}^{T} \alpha^{(t)}[h(x) = k]$, in the formula: $[h(x) = k]$ can be interpreted as, when the logical expression is true, then $[h(x) = k] = 1$, otherwise $[h(x) = k] = 0$, therefore the output form of $[h(x) = k]$ is a matrix consisting of 0 and 1. 1 means the result of classification is correct, 0 means the result of classification is error (the representation is the final value of the DBN output), then the α weights the value of the output layer. The improvement in this paper is $H(x) = \sum_{t=1}^{T} \alpha(t)h(x)$. The biggest difference compared with the original one is that $h(x)$ replaces the original $[h(x) = k]$, and $h(x)$ represents the proportion of each sample in the various types, usually it's a decimal. The $h(x)$ is weighted by the classifier weights, which can reflects the essential characteristics of each sample. The test has shown that improved algorithms can achieve better accuracy.

4 Experimental Results and Analysis

This experiment is compiled in the Matlab R2016b, using Corel-1K data set including 10 categories of 1000 pictures, which are divided into training set and testing set. In the proposed algorithm, the integrated weak classifiers are consisted of 4 DBNs, the number of input neurons and output neurons of are both 580 and 10, and the number of hidden layers are as: [100 100], [110 100], [90 90], [140 140]. The classifiers are Adaboost M1, DBN, and the proposed algorithm.

In order to fully exploit the classification ability of the classifier, the experimental data set is divided into 9 groups. The number of training set and testing set are (100, 900), (200, 800)…(900, 100). The classification result of the classifier is shown in the Fig. 4, in which the classification accuracy of the DBN takes the maximum value of the four results in each training (that is, the accuracy of DBN shown in the figure does not refer to a certain DBN). It can be seen from the figure that the classification curve of the classifier DBN coincides with the classification curve of Adaboost M1, which shows that the advantage of integrated learning that it can integrate the classification capabilities of classifiers to achieve higher performance. In the comparison of the data of the first to third groups and the ninth group, the classification ability of the Adaboost M1 algorithm is superior to the proposed algorithm in this paper. In the third to eighth groups, the proposed algorithm has the highest correct rate and reaches the maximum value (81.6%) in the test. The three classifiers achieved the best performance in the data (500, 500), which shown that the DBN has the best fitting capacity at this time. In the first four data sets, due to there are fewer training sets, the under-fitting of neural network leads to poor classification. Similarly, in the last four data sets, due to there are many training sets, the over-fitting of neural network also leads to poor results of classification.

The following table shows the classification accuracy of the three classifiers in the 9 data sets (%):

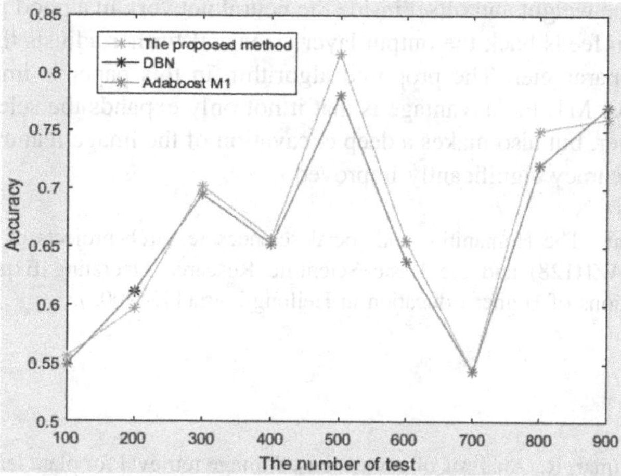

Fig. 4. The accuracy of three classifiers.

Table 1. The accuracy of three classifiers.

Train data	Test data	The proposed algorithm	DBN	Adaboost M1
100	900	0.556	0.5489	0.5489
200	800	0.5963	0.6112	0.6113
300	700	0.7014	0.6943	0.6943
400	600	0.6567	0.6517	0.6517
500	500	0.816	0.78	0.78
600	400	0.655	0.6375	0.6375
700	300	0.5433	0.5433	0.5433
800	200	0.75	0.72	0.72
900	100	0.76	0.77	0.77

It can be seen from the Table 1. that the accuracy of the proposed algorithm is significantly improved compared with the traditional classification. There are two reasons for this. Firstly, ensemble learning can integrate multiple classifiers, which fully exploits the classification capacity of each classifier; Furthermore, the traditional ensemble learning is improved which can get better performance.

5 Conclusion

Adaboost algorithm belongs to the category of decision-level fusion, it can superimposes the classification results of several weak classifiers to obtain a stronger classification effect. In this paper, the texture features of the image are extracted by the local neighborhood rotation right-angle pattern, and then these features are classified by DBN. The training process of DBN is divided into two steps: First, the RBM training process makes the weight and offset inside the neural network in a good position. Then, the BP algorithm feeds back the output layer error and further adjusts the value of the neural network parameter. The proposed algorithm in this paper is improved on the basis of Adaboost M1, the advantage is that it not only expands the selection range of the weak classifier, but also makes a deep excavation of the image features to make the classification accuracy significantly improved.

Acknowledgement. The Humanities and social sciences research projects of the Ministry of Education (18YJAZH128) and the Basic Scientific Research Operating Expense Project of Provincial Institutions of Higher Education in Heilongjiang (17XN003).

References

1. Patil, J.K., Kumar, R.: Analysis of content based image retrieval for plant leaf diseases using color, shape and texture features. Eng. Agric. Environ. Food **10**, 69–78 (2016)
2. Srivastava, P., Khare, A.: Integration of wavelet transform, local binary patterns and moments for content-based image retrieval. J. Vis. Commun. Image Represent. **42**, 78–103 (2017)
3. Hong, T.: Image retrieval technology research based on local neighborhood rotation right-angle pattern. Harbin University of Commerce (2017)
4. Cui, B., Ma, X., Xie, X., Ren, G., Ma, Y.: Classification of visible and infrared hyperspectral images based on image segmentation and edge-preserving filtering. Infrared Phys. Technol. **81**, 79–88 (2017)
5. Al-Mudhafar, W.J.: Integrating well log interpretations for lithofacies classification and permeability modeling through advanced machine learning algorithms. J. Petrol. Explor. Prod. Technol. **7**(4), 1023–1033 (2017)
6. Hassan, A.R., Bhuiyan, M.I.H.: An automated method for sleep staging from EEG signals using normal inverse Gaussian parameters and adaptive boosting. Neurocomputing **219**, 76–87 (2017)
7. Lv, Y., Hou, Z., Zhang, K.: Study of multi-class BP-AdaBoost and its application. High Technol. Lett. **25**(05), 437–444 (2015)
8. Kong, J., Zhan, Y., Chen, Y.: Expression recognition based on VLBP and optical flow mixed features. In: Fifth International Conference on Image and Graphics, ICIG (2009)
9. Probst, M., Rothlauf, F., Grahl, J.: Scalability of using restricted Boltzmann machines for combinatorial optimization. Eur. J. Oper. Res. **256**(2), 368–383 (2017)
10. Ding, W., Zhang, J., Leung, Y.: Prediction of air pollutant concentration based on sparse response back-propagation training feedforward neural networks. Environ. Sci. Pollut. Res. **23**(19), 19481–19494 (2016)
11. Zhang, Z.: The improvement and application of Adaboostalgorithm. Lanzhou University (2017)
12. Hu, J., Luo, G., Li, Y., Wang, C., Yu, X.: An AdaBoost algorithm for multi-class classification based on exponential loss function and its application. Acta Aeronaut. ET Astronaut. Sin. (04), 811–816 (2008)

Research on Diabetes Aided Diagnosis Model Based on Deep Belief Network

Zhijie Zhao[1,2(✉)], Yang Liu[1,2], Huadong Sun[1,2], Xiaowei Han[1,2], and Ran Wang[1,2]

[1] School of Computer and Information Engineering, Harbin University of Commerce, Harbin 150028, China
1249182744@qq.com

[2] Heilongjiang Provincial Key Laboratory of Electronic Commerce and Information Processing, Harbin University of Commerce, Harbin 150028, China

Abstract. Diabetes is a chronic disease that seriously endangers human health, which should be early detection, early diagnosis and early treatment by establishing prediction model. With the help of disease auxiliary diagnosis based on machine learning, the process of early diagnosis could be more reliable. Then, the patients have more chances of early treatment. Deep learning technology can take advantage of its own powerful feature learning ability to the application of disease auxiliary diagnosis, and has gained good results. This paper proposes a diabetes prediction model based on Deep Belief Network (DBN). The model is established by using Pima Indians Diabetes data set, combined with cross-validation, setting DBN structure and adjusting DBN network parameters. The experimental results show that the accuracy of the model is as high as 77.60% and the performance is good.

Keywords: Deep learning · DBN model · Auxiliary diagnosis · Diabetes prediction model

1 Introduction

Diabetes is one of the most serious and critical health problems facing the world in the twenty-first Century [1]. Traditionally, physicians mainly take years of accumulated personal experience and laboratory or instrumental indicators as the basis for diabetes mellitus diagnosis. Many subjective factors are in doping and easily misdiagnosed [2]. Prediction of diabetes mellitus can effectively solve the drawbacks of traditional methods and assist doctors in more comprehensive and reliable disease diagnosis by establishing a deep learning model [3, 4].

Establishing diabetes prediction model needs to consider the non-linear effect between the various pathogenic factors. Modeling methods such as statistics and machine learning, which are commonly used at home and abroad, are limited in the ability of expressing complex functions, and are more or less restricted [5]. Deep learning takes advantage of its own powerful feature learning ability, which is applied to the application of disease auxiliary diagnosis, has achieved good results. A deep belief networks model framework based on the heterogeneous electronic health records (EHRs) has been developed for identifying informative risk factors and predicting

M. Jia et al. (Eds.): WiSATS 2019, LNICST 281, pp. 229–240, 2019.
https://doi.org/10.1007/978-3-030-19156-6_22

osteoporosis, which performances well [6]. Chen and others have constructed a prediction model of thyroid nodules based on DBN, which has high accuracy in both non-sparse and sparse data sets, reaching 94% and 88.84% respectively [7]. Combined with genetic algorithm, an improved DBN model is proposed to predict coronary artery disease, which the prediction result of is good and the accuracy is as high as 89.24% [8]. Therefore, according to the diagnostic and data characteristics of diabetes mellitus, this paper constructs a diabetes prediction model by using DBN technology, and achieves a higher accuracy.

2 Deep Belief Network

In 2006, Hinton proposed a DBN structure and showed that each layer can perform unsupervised training again on the basis of the output of training results on the previous level, which clearly pointed out the effectiveness of unsupervised learning at all levels of training [9]. The typical DBN model is stacked by a series of Restricted Boltzmann Machine (RBM), which can solve the problem of slow convergence rate and easy to fall into local optimum, when the traditional back-propagation algorithm trains multilayer neural networks [10].

2.1 Restricted Boltzmann Machine

As the core of DBN model, RBM has a powerful architecture, which has two layers of network structure, namely visual layer and hidden layer. As shown in Fig. 1. According to the graph, the lower level $v = (v_1, v_2, \cdots, v_m)$ represents the visual layer formed by m visible nodes and the upper layer $h = (h_1, h_2, \cdots, h_n)$ represents the hidden layer formed by n hidden nodes. There is a weight connection between the visible layer node and the hidden layer node and there is no connection between the visible layer and the hidden layer unit. That is to say, each visual node is only affected by the n hidden nodes and independent of other visual nodes, which means that each visual node has only two states {0, 1}. The same is true for hidden nodes. The architecture features make RBM training easier. RBM training uses Contrastive Divergence (CD) algorithm, which is a fast learning algorithm of RBM proposed by Hinton in 2002. The training process is as follows [11–14].

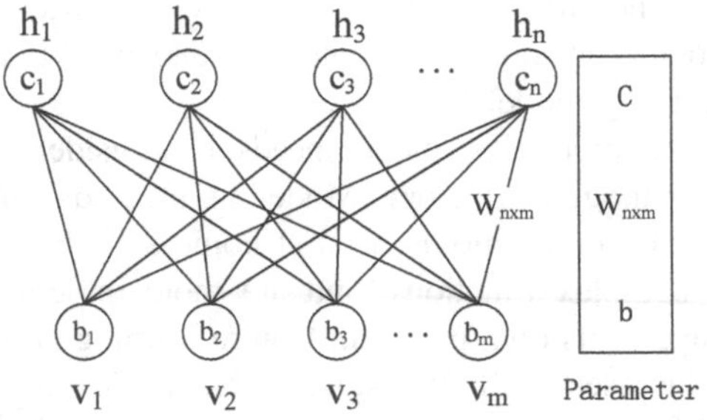

Fig. 1. Schematic diagram of RBM network structure.

Input: Training Sample x_0, Hidden Layer Node Number n, Learning Rate λ, Maximum Training Period T.

Output: Link Weight Matrix W, Visible Layer Bias Vector b, Hidden Layer Bias Vector c.

Training Phase: The state of initializing visible layer nodes is $v_1 = x_0$, and W, b 和 c are small random number.

For $t = 1{:}T$

For $j = 1{:}n$ # For All Hidden Nodes

$$P(h_{1j} = 1|v_1) = \text{sigmoid}\ (c_j\ +\ \text{sum\_}i(v_{1i} * W_{ij})) \tag{1}$$

For $i = 1{:}m$ # For All Visible Nodes

$$P(v_{2i} = 1|h_1) = \text{sigmoid}(b_i\ +\ \text{sum\_}j(W_{ij} * h_{1j})) \tag{2}$$

For $j = 1{:}n$ # For All Hidden Nodes

$$P(h_{2j} = 1|v_2) = \text{sigmoid}\ (c_j\ +\ \text{sum\_}i(v_{2i} * W_{ij})) \tag{3}$$

Update Weight and Bias

$$W = W + \lambda * (P(h_1 = 1|v_2) * v_1 - P(h_2 = 1|v_2) * v_2) \tag{4}$$

$$b = b + \lambda * (v_1 - v_2) \tag{5}$$

$$c = c + \lambda * (P(h_1 = 1|v_1) - P(h_2 = 1|v_2)) \tag{6}$$

2.2 DBN Structure and Training

DBN is a deep neural network composed of multi-layer RBM and a BP neural network. The basic structure is shown in Fig. 2. The DBN model is based on the joint distribution of data and features, the basic idea of it is to use the layer-by-layer greedy algorithm for hierarchical unsupervised learning of DBN, and then take advantage of the tagged data at the top level to conduct supervised learning and adjustment of the network. The training process is as follows [11–14].

(1) The method of unsupervised greedy layer by layer is used to pre train to obtain the weights of generated models. Unsupervised training for each layer of RBM is carried out. At this stage, the visual layer produces a vector v_1, which is mapped to the hidden layer vector value h_1, and uses the hidden layer vector value h_1 to reconstruct the vector value of the visual layer v_1 to get v_2, then the reconstructed v_2 mapping h_2 is used again, the process of which is called Gibbs sampling. This method can ensure that feature information is retained as much as possible when feature vectors are mapped to different feature spaces. The difference between the visible layer vector value and the hidden layer vector value is used to update the weight.

(2) After pre-training, the top layer associates the output of the lower layer with its memory. Each layer of RBM training can only ensure that the weight of its own layer achieves the best mapping of the layer feature vector. Therefore, the whole DBN needs to be adjusted from top to bottom according to the difference between the network output and the expected output. The BP network is added to the top layer of DBN, and the output vector of the last layer RBM is used as the input vector of BP network, then according to tagged data, the discriminative performance is adjusted through supervised training of the classifier by using BP algorithm.

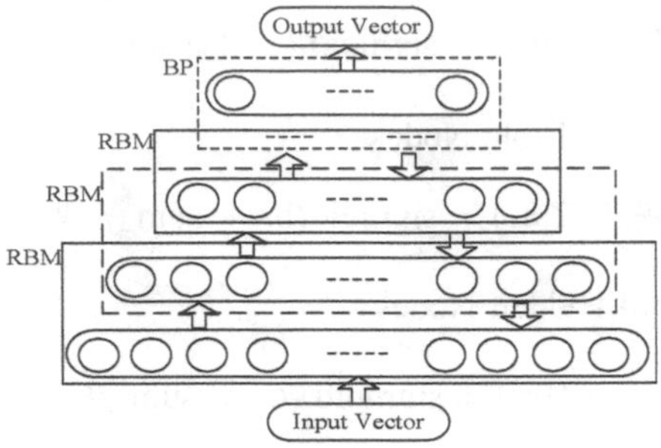

Fig. 2. Schematic diagram of DBN basic structure.

3 Prediction Modeling Process Based on Deep Belief Network

The data is divided into two parts: training set and test set. For training set, the prediction model of diabetes based on DBN is established, combined with empirical formula, setting and adjusting the parameters to determine the optimal network structure of DBN. For test set, The DBN diabetes prediction model is validated by it. The sensitivity and specificity are used to evaluate the performance of the model. They complement each other and complete the construction of DBN diabetes prediction model. The establishment process is shown in Fig. 3.

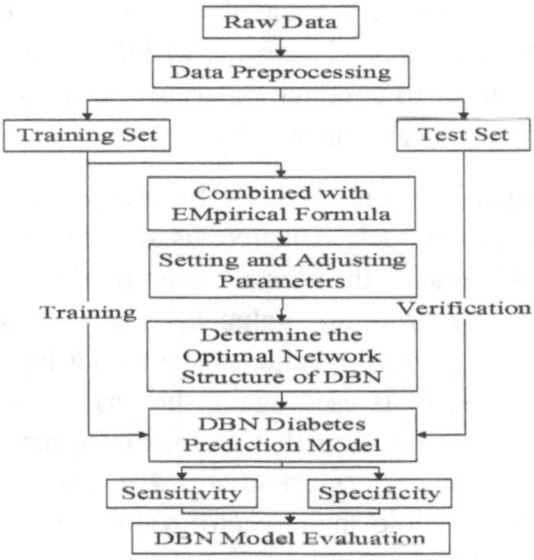

Fig. 3. Flow chart of diabetes prediction modeling based on DBN.

3.1 Training Set and Test Set

After considering the problem about the number of diabetes data sets and model training, this paper adopts K-fold Cross Validation method to determine the training set and test set, so as to avoid over-learning and under-learning effectively. The basic idea of K-fold Cross Validation is to divide the available data into K parts ($K \geq 3$), each representing a subset. Arbitrary K-1 subset is combined into a training set, and the remaining subset is used as a test set [15]. Thus, different training sets and corresponding test sets of K groups could be obtained.

3.2 DBN Network Structure

Only four important parameters including the number of input layer nodes, hidden layer nodes, hidden layer nodes and output layer nodes are identified to determine the DBN network structure before the prediction model can be established.

The number of input layer nodes is the attribute number of the dataset and the number of output layer nodes is equal to the class number in the dataset. What we need to pay attention to is the choice of DBN hidden layer and node number. A DBN model with multiple hidden layers performs better, but it doesn't mean that the more layers there are, the better [16]. Hidden layer nodes are the knowledge acquired by the DBN model through the data set, which can show the complex nonlinear relationship among them. The appropriate number of nodes should be selected to maximize the performance of DBN [17]. The empirical formula for selecting the number of hidden layers and nodes is adopted to determine its approximate range, which can avoid the blindness and increase the effectiveness of selection [12]:

$$S = \sqrt{mn} + \mathrm{k}/2 \tag{7}$$

Here, S is the number of nodes in the hidden layer, m is the number of nodes in the input layer and n is the number of nodes in the output layer. K is constant belonging to 1–10.

Under the condition that m, n, k are known, the number of nodes in the first hidden layer S_1 can be calculated to have p values according to formula (7), which are recorded as $S_1 = [S_{11}, S_{12}, S_{13}, \cdots, S_{1P}]$. Assuming that the number of nodes in the first hidden layer has been determined, the number of nodes in the first hidden layer is equal to the number of nodes in the input layer, for example, if $S_1 = S_{1P}$, then $m = S_{1P}$, and the number of nodes in the output layer n remains unchanged. According to formula (7), the number of nodes in the second hidden layer S_2 can be calculated to have q values, which are recorded as $S_2 = \left[S_{21}, S_{22}, S_{23}, \cdots, S_{2q}\right]$. By analogy, under the different values of the number of nodes in the first hidden layer S_1, the number of nodes in the second hidden layer S_2 can be calculated respectively, which should be merged, and are recorded as $S_2 = \left[S_{21}, S_{22}, S_{23}, \cdots, S_{2q}, \cdots, S_{2\,(q+a)}\right]$. This calculation idea of simultaneously determining the number of hidden layers and the number of corresponding hidden layer nodes can be continued and determined experimentally.

3.3 DBN Network Parameters

In the process of training DBN model, parameters need to be set and adjusted to improve the classification accuracy of it. On the basis of DBN network structure, hidden layer and output layer neuron activation function need to be set, and not only RBM training parameters, but also BP training parameters should be set up. DBN can be trained in batches, which is determined by the number of training set samples and each batch of training data. In addition, the setting of parameters including maximum number of network cycles, learning rate and momentum factor are also crucial.

3.4 DBN Network Training

Under the same training parameters, it is necessary to combine the p value of S_1 with the $q+a$ value of S_2, and K-time DBN training should be carried out by using the K-group training set and test set, totaling $K * p * (q+a)$ experiments. The average accuracy of each classification under K-time DBN training is calculated as the final classification accuracy. The higher the classification accuracy rate, the better the prediction effect of DBN model.

3.5 DBN Model Evaluating

The performance of DBN prediction model was evaluated by accuracy, specificity and sensitivity. The calculation of specificity and sensitivity needs to draw on the confusion matrix, as shown in Table 1. For a specific example, there will be four cases if the disease is positive class and no disease is negative class. If a positive class is predicted to be a positive class, it is True Positive. If a negative class is actually predicted to be a positive class, it is False Positive. If a negative class is predicted to be a negative class, it is True Negative. If a positive class is predicted to be a negative class, it is False Negative [18].

Table 1. Confusion matrix.

	Predict disease	Predict no disease
Actual disease	True Positive (TP)	False Negative (FN)
Actual no disease	False Positive (FP)	True Negative (TN)

The accuracy is the classification accuracy of the DBN optimal prediction model, expressed in Acc.

The specificity is the ratio of the actual uninfected people number in the predicted number of uninfected people to the total number of actual uninfected people, representing the generalization ability of the model, expressed in Spe.

$$Spe = \frac{TN}{TN + FP} \tag{8}$$

The sensitivity is the ratio of the actual infected people number in the predicted number of infected people to the total number of actual infected people, representing the accuracy of the model classification, expressed in Sen.

$$Sen = \frac{TP}{FN + TP} \tag{9}$$

In the medical diagnosis of diabetes mellitus, it is the primary task to diagnose patients with diabetes mellitus, that is, the greater the value of Sen, the better. The number of times that the normal person without diabetes is misdiagnosed as the disease, that is, the smaller the value of Spe, the better. Jointly evaluating the performance of the DBN diabetes prediction model by the above indicators is more comprehensive and objective.

4 Diabetes Prediction Simulation Experiment

4.1 Data Sources

The Data is about diabetes diagnosis information of native American women from Pima Indian heritage near phoenix, Arizona. They are above the age of 21 per capita. Eight risk factors related to diabetes are extracted, including six quantitative and continuous features, composed of a variety of clinical trial results, the remaining two quantitative and discrete features. The 9 features and sample data, including the classification codes, are shown in Tables 2 and 3 respectively. In Table 2, Body Mass Index (BMI) is calculated by formula, being recorded as $BMI = wei \div hei^2$, where wei represents weight, unit kg and hei represents height, unit m. In Table 3, Column 1 is the patient number. Columns 2–9 are the eigenvalues of the diabetes checking, as the attribute of the input data. The last column shows whether a given individual will suffer from diabetes within five years: 1 represents the positive in diabetes, that is, the individual will have diabetes in five years, a total of 268 cases. 0 represents the negative in diabetes, that is, the individual will not have diabetes within five years, a total of 500 cases. The Pima Indians Diabetes data set can be achieved in the UCI machine learning database.

Table 2. Data feature list (including category).

Feature number	Feature descriptions
Feature 1	Number of times pregnant
Feature 2	Plasma glucose concentration
Feature 3	Diastolic blood pressure (mm Hg)
Feature 4	Triceps skin fold thickness (mm)
Feature 5	2-h serum insulin (mu U/ml)
Feature 6	Body mass index
Feature 7	Diabetes pedigree function
Feature 8	Age in years
Classification codes	Binary class variable

Table 3. Original data sample (including category).

Number	Feature1	Feature2	Feature3	Feature4	Feature5	Feature6	Feature7	Feature8	Classification codes
1	6	148	72	35	0	33.6	0.627	50	1
2	8	183	64	0	0	23.3	0.672	32	1
3	1	85	66	29	0	26.6	0.351	31	0
4	1	89	66	23	94	28.1	0.167	21	0
...	...	...	...	...	...	...	...	...	...

4.2 Experiment Results and Analysis

The Referring to the Sect. 3 and making K = 3, 768 pieces of input data, which are normalized by [0, 1] of the interval normalization method, are divided into three parts. 256 pieces of each part represent a subset, and three groups of training sets and corresponding test sets are obtained.

Seeing the data characteristics of Pima Indians Diabetes, it is known that the number of input nodes m is 8 and the number of output categories n is 2. Using the formula (7) and the idea of the corresponding algorithm, which are mentioned in Sect. 3.2, experiments are conducted to determine that the number of hidden layers is 2 layers. The number of nodes in the first hidden layer S_1 has 6 values, recorded as $S_1 = [4, 5, 6, 7, 8, 9]$, and the number of nodes in the second hidden layer S_2 has 9 values, recorded as $S_2 = [2, 3, 4, 5, 6, 7, 8, 9, 10]$. The sigmoid function is set as the hidden layer and the output layer neuron activation function. The maximum number of network cycles is 1000 times and the training data per batch is 128. The value of learning rate is set to 1 and the value of momentum factor is set to 0, which are contained in the RBM training parameters. BP training parameters include learning rate, the value of which is set to 2, and momentum factor, the value of which is set to 0.9. Three DBN network training are conducted for three groups of training sets, and 6 values of S_1 and 9 values of S_2 are combined in two to conduct each DBN training, in total of 3 * 6 * 9 experiments. The experimental results are shown in Table 4.

Table 4. DBN experiment results.

S2	S1					
	4	5	6	7	8	9
2	0.7591	0.7630	0.7721	0.7669	0.7697	0.7656
3	0.7630	0.7630	0.7565	0.7552	0.7578	0.7682
4	0.7734	0.7682	0.7318	0.7617	0.7642	0.6966
5	0.7708	0.7643	0.7617	0.7617	0.7513	0.7656
6	0.7656	0.7747	0.7396	0.7669	0.7708	0.6862
7	0.7565	0.7096	0.7357	0.7552	0.7695	0.7318
8	**0.7760**	0.7617	0.7591	0.7669	0.7305	0.7708
9	0.7734	0.7656	0.7620	0.7539	0.7539	0.7500
10	0.7565	0.7396	0.7591	0.7578	0.7669	0.7305

Table 4 shows that under the same training parameters, the number of nodes in two hidden layers is different, resulting in different classification accuracy of DBN, but the overall effect of the model is better than 65%, and the classification accuracy of some DBN network structures is as high as 80%. When the number of nodes in the input layer is 8, the number of nodes in the first hidden layer is 4, the number of nodes in the second hidden layer is 8, and the number of nodes in the output layer is 2, the diabetes prediction model is best and the accuracy is 77.60%.

In the training process of DBN model, a training times-error graph is generated. As shown in Fig. 4. The horizontal axis represents the times of training, the vertical axis represents the reconstruction error generated by each training, and the three different colored curves represent training process of different training sets under 3 fold cross validation. It can be seen from Fig. 4 that the directions of three curves are roughly the same, indicating that the essential characteristics of different training data represented by the three curves are similar. With the increase of training times, each curve decreases sharply, and tends to be stable after the inflection point appears around the fiftieth training, which shows that the reconstruction error decreases rapidly before the inflection point and it still decreases, but the decrease is small after the inflection point.

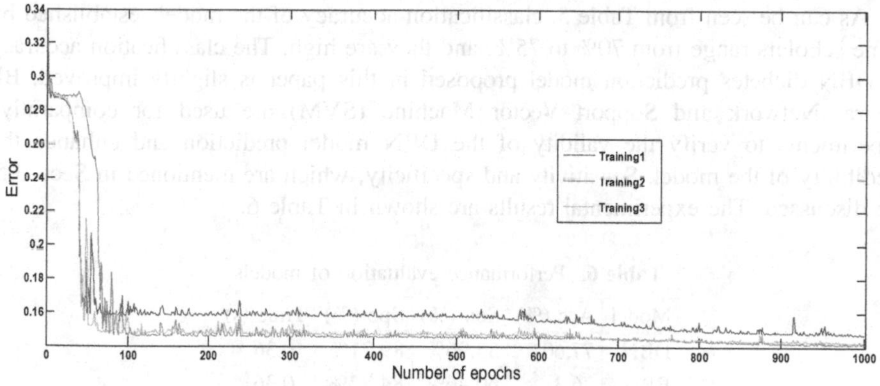

Fig. 4. Training times-error graph of DBN model.

4.3 Comprehensive Comparisons of Testing Results

For Pima Indians Diabetes data set of UCI machine learning database, some scholars also established classification models to predict diabetes, and compared it with the DBN prediction model built in this paper. As shown in Table 5.

Table 5. Accuracy comparison results of several models.

Authors	Year	Data size & class	Classification model	Accuracy (%)
Eggermont et al. [19]	2004	768 Controls: 500 Diabetes: 268	C4.5	71.60
Karthikeyani et al. [20]	2012	768 Controls: 500 Diabetes: 268	SVM	74.80
Karthikeyani et al. [21]	2013	768 Controls: 500 Diabetes: 268	LDA	74.40
Bozkurt et al. [22]	2015	768 Controls: 500 Diabetes: 268	AIS, ANN	76.00
Iyer et al. [23]	2015	768 Controls: 500 Diabetes: 268	DT, NB	74.79

As can be seen from Table 5, classification accuracy of the models established by some scholars range from 70% to 75%, and they are high. The classification accuracy of DBN diabetes prediction model proposed in this paper is slightly improved. BP Neural Network and Support Vector Machine (SVM) are used for comparative experiments to verify the validity of the DBN model prediction and enhance the credibility of the model. Sensitivity and specificity, which are mentioned in Sect. 3.5, are discussed. The experimental results are shown in Table 6.

Table 6. Performance evaluation of models.

Model	Acc (%)	Sen (%)	Spe (%)	Time (s)
DBN	77.60	55.96%	89.21%	0.36
BP	76.3	60.46%	84.82%	0.36
SVM	76.56	54.11%	89.28%	62.57

It can be seen from Table 6 that the accuracy of the three diabetes prediction models is above 75%, indicating that they can predict diabetes accurately for the experimental data. The accuracy of DBN model is the highest, reaching 77.60%, which shows that it performs better than the other two models in the term of prediction accuracy. Compared with sensitivity and specificity index, DBN diabetes prediction model is at a moderate level among them. The running time of DBN model is 0.36 s, which is greatly shortened comparing with SVM. The feature makes it more conducive to practical application in the field of diabetes auxiliary diagnosis. Overall, the DBN diabetes prediction model based on Pima Indians Diabetes data set is the best, with high prediction accuracy, good model effect and fast running time. The experimental results show that the modeling process of DBN on diabetes is feasible, and the established DBN model can predict diabetes effectively and perform well.

5 Conclusion

Using Pima Indians Diabetes data set, a DBN-based diabetes prediction model is established, the optimal network structure of it is 8-4-8-2, the accuracy of it is 77.60%, the sensitivity of it is 55.96%, the specificity of it is 89.21%, and the running time of it is 0.36 s. Compared with BP and SVM, DBN diabetes prediction model has the best prediction accuracy and running time, and has a moderate level among them in terms of sensitivity and specificity index. The test results are better. This study shows that the application of DBN model in the auxiliary diagnosis of diabetes mellitus is good, and it can provide a reference for the application of similar methods in China.

Acknowledgements. This research is supported by the Harbin Science and Technology Bureau outstanding subject leader fund project (2017RAXXJ055), the Nature Science Foundation of Heilongjiang Province (F2018020) and the Humanities and social sciences research projects of the Ministry of Education (18YJAZH128).

References

1. IDF Diabetes Atlas Eighth Edition poster Homepage. http://diabetesatlas.org/resources/2017-atlas.html. Accessed 24 Sept 2018
2. Liu, X., Jia, H., Li, A., et al.: Common methods and standards for screening and diagnosing diabetes mellitus. Med. Recapitul. **11**(12), 1104–1106 (2005)
3. Pérez-Gandía, C., Facchinetti, A., Sparacino, G., et al.: Artificial neural network algorithm for online glucose prediction from continuous glucose monitoring. Diabetes Technol. Therap. **12**(1), 81–88 (2010)
4. Gao, W., Wang, S., Wang, Z., et al.: Study on the application of artificial neural network in analysing the risk factors of diabetes mellitus. Chin. J. Epidemiol. **25**(8), 715–718 (2004)
5. Zhu, M., Wu, Y.: Research on image processing based on deep network. Electron. Technol. Softw. Eng. (5), 101–102 (2014)
6. Li, H., Li, X., Ramanathan, M., et al.: Identifying informative risk factors and predicting bone disease progression via deep belief networks. Methods **69**(3), 257–265 (2014)
7. Chen, D., Zhou, D., Le, J.: Thyroid nodule benign and malignant prediction based on deep learning. Softw. Algorithms **36**(12), 13–15 (2017)
8. Lim, K., Lee, B.M., Kang, U., et al.: An optimized DBN-based coronary heart disease risk prediction. Int. J. Comput. Commun. Control **13**(4), 492–502 (2018)
9. Hinton, G.E., Osindero, S., The, Y.W.: A fast learning algorithm for deep belief nets. Neural Comput. **18**(7), 1527–1554 (2006)
10. Wang, Z., Li, Y., Feng, X., et al.: Personalized information recommendation based on deep belief network. Computer Engineering **42**(10), 201–206 (2016)
11. Wang, F., Li, Q.: Research on face recognition algorithm based on improved deep belief networks. J. Lanzhou Jiaotong Univ. **35**(1), 42–48 (2016)
12. Yang, X.: Study of early warning for cerebrovascular risk based on deep beliefs networks. Beijing Jiaotong University (2016)
13. Sun, Z., Xue, L., Xu, Y., et al.: Overview of deep learning. Appl. Res. Comput. **29**(8), 2806–2810 (2012)
14. Yang, X.H., Zhong, N.Y.: Forecasting of hospital outpatient based on deep belief network. Comput. Sci. **43**(11A), 26–30 (2016)

15. Hu, J., Zhang, G.: K-fold cross-validation based selected ensemble classification algorithm. Bull. Sci. Technol. **29**(12), 115–117 (2013)
16. Gao, Q., Ma, Y.-M.: Research and application of the level of the deep belief network (DBN). Sci. Technol. Eng. **16**(23), 234–238 (2016)
17. Liao, Q., Zhang, J.: Optimization of DBN network structure based on information entropy. Inf. Commun. **1**, 44–48 (2018)
18. Ma, L.: Analyzing risk factors for multi-diseases with decision tree, logistic regression and improved neural network. Software **12**, 58–65 (2014)
19. Eggermont, J., Kok, J.N., Kosters, W.A., et al.: Genetic programming for data classification: partitioning the search space. In: ACM Symposium on Applied Computing, pp. 1001–1005 (2004)
20. Karthikeyani, V., Begum, I.P., Tajudin, K., et al.: Comparative of data mining classification algorithm (CDMCA) in diabetes disease prediction. Int. J. Comput. Appl. **60**(12), 26–31 (2012)
21. Karthikeyani, D.V., Begum, I.P.: Comparison a performance of data mining algorithms (CPDMA) in prediction of diabetes disease. Int. J. Comput. Sci. Eng. **5**(3), 205 (2013)
22. Bozkurt, M.R., Yurtay, N., Yilmaz, Z., et al.: Comparison of different methods for determining diabetes. Turk. J. Electr. Eng. Comput. Sci. **22**(4), 1044–1055 (2015)
23. Iyer, A., Jeyalatha, S., Sumbaly, R.: Diagnosis of diabetes using classification mining techniques. Int. J. Data Min. Knowl. Manage. Process **5**(1), 1–14 (2015)

Research on Fourier Descriptor Image Retrieval Technology Based on Minimum Inertia Axis

Zhijie Zhao[1,2], Ze Gao[1,2(✉)], Huadong Sun[1,2], and Xuesong Jin[1,2]

[1] School of Computer and Information Engineering, Harbin University of Commerce, Harbin 150028, China
1041451358@qq.com

[2] Heilongjiang Provincial Key Laboratory of Electronic Commerce and Information Processing, Harbin University of Commerce, Harbin 150028, China

Abstract. In image retrieval, the shape feature is one of the key features of image content description. At present, most of the widely used Fourier descriptors in shape descriptors are invariant in translation, rotation and scale expansion. But Fourier descriptors are susceptible to the location of the starting point. In this paper, an improved image retrieval method based on Fourier descriptors is proposed. First, the image is preprocessed and the edge of the image is extracted. Secondly, the starting point of the contour is determined by the minimum inertia axis. Then Fourier transform is used to get eigenvectors. Finally, the correlation coefficient is used to calculate the similarity. Experiments show that the Fourier Descriptor Image Retrieval Method based on the minimum inertia axis is more efficient than other methods in Swedish Leaf database.

Keywords: Image retrieval · Shape feature · Fourier descriptor · Minimum inertia axis

1 Introduction

Now, with the growing Internet technology, tens of thousands of product images are pouring into people's sight every day. Along with the influence of e-commerce on people's life and shopping habits, simple text information retrieval can no longer meet people's requirements for product retrieval. Content Based Image Retrieval [1, 2] mainly uses visual features such as color, shape, texture, spatial relationship, etc., and relies on image processing technology, recognition technology, artificial intelligence and computer vision technology to realize image retrieval [3]. In the image of the product, the shape is often associated with the target, which is in line with the visual habits of people to recognize the object, and has certain semantics. Therefore, the shape is widely used as a discriminating element in the field of content-based image retrieval. In many applications, shape captures most of the perceptual information of an object on an image, while colors and textures can often be omitted without affecting retrieval performance. But the shape may be affected by factors such as deformation, scaling,

M. Jia et al. (Eds.): WiSATS 2019, LNICST 281, pp. 241–249, 2019.
https://doi.org/10.1007/978-3-030-19156-6_23

orientation changes, noise and partial hiding. Therefore, accurate description of the shape is still a challenging technical issue.

For image retrieval systems based on shape features, the description of the shape of the image is very important. Shape features can be divided into two main categories: contour-based features and region-based features. The contour-based description method only uses the boundary information and loses the internal content of the shape, so the versatility is not high. The region-based description method utilizes the internal pixel information of the target shape, which can be applied to general occasions. However, all the region description methods currently extract the spatial features of the shape, so it is sensitive to subtle changes in noise and shape, and is resistant to interference. The ability is relatively poor.

In many existing shape feature descriptors, the Fourier descriptor has several desirable features, such as low computational complexity, sharpness and coarse to fine description, which makes it a popular descriptor. A new method for extracting Fourier descriptors that preserve the phase of Fourier coefficients is proposed by Sokic [4]. Introduce specific points, called pseudo-mirror points, and use them as shape orientation references. It helps extract the phase-preserving Fourier descriptor and is constant under translation, scaling, rotation and starting point changes. Performance and computational complexity measurements indicate that the proposed method is superior to other phase-based Fourier descriptors. El-ghazal et al. [5] proposed a new curvature-based Fourier descriptor (CBFD) shape retrieval. The proposed descriptor has an unconventional view of the curvature scale spatial representation of the shape profile because it is considered a two-dimensional binary image (hence the curvature scale image or CSI). The invariant descriptor is derived from the two-dimensional Fourier transform of the curvature scale image. This approach allows the descriptor to capture the detailed dynamics of the shape curvature and improve the efficiency of the shape matching process.

2 Image Shape Feature Extraction Based on Minimum Inertia Axis

2.1 Fourier Descriptor

First, the product image is binarized, and the binarized product image $p(x, y)$ is characterized by only two pixels of black and white. Black is the target pixel, denoted as $p(x, y) = 1$, white is the background pixel, denoted as $p(x, y) = 0$. Second extract the coordinates of the shape boundary from the image. In order to apply the shape description method, the equal length sampling is performed by the difference method, and the contour of the shape is resampled with a fixed number of points.

For subsequent analysis, it will be assumed that the shape profile is given by N boundary points $A(k) = (x_k, y_k)$, $k = 1, 2, \cdots, N-1$. If set $x(k) = x_k$, $y(k) = y_k$, and to represent them in the plural form, then get the coordinate sequence of the boundary [6]:

$$s(k) = x(k) + jy(k)(k = 1, 2, \cdots, N-1) \tag{1}$$

for which the Discrete Fourier Transform may be computed as in the following equation [6]:

$$S(k) = \sum_{k=1}^{K-1} s(k)^{-j2\pi uk/K}(k = 1, 2, \cdots, K-1) \tag{2}$$

The Fourier coefficient $S(k)$ is used to derive the Fourier descriptor. In the case of translation, rotation, scaling and starting point changes, the coefficient $S(k)$ must be constant. It can be easily seen from the formula that the invariance under rotation and starting point variation is achieved only by the magnitude of the Fourier coefficient, while the invariance under translation is achieved by ignoring the DC component (coefficient $S(0)$).

Since the Fourier descriptor is related to the scale, direction, and position of the starting point of the image shape, in order to identify shapes with rotation, translation, and scale invariance, the Fourier descriptor needs to be normalized. According to the Fourier transform property, the position of the starting point of the object shape boundary is shifted by α length, the object is magnified by β times, the rotation angle φ and the translation displacement (x_0, y_0), and the new shape Fourier transform coefficient $S'(k)$ [7]:

$$\begin{aligned} S'(k) &= f[(x' + y')\beta e^{j\varphi} + (x_0 + iy_0)] \\ &= \beta e^{j\varphi} f(x' + y')\beta e^{j\varphi} + f(x_0 + iy_0) = \beta e^{j\varphi} e^{-j\frac{2\pi}{K}k\alpha} S(k) + f(x_0 + iy_0) \end{aligned} \tag{3}$$

$$\Rightarrow \begin{cases} S'(0) = \beta e^{-j\varphi} S(0) + f(x_0 + iy_0), k = 0 \\ S'(k) = \beta e^{-j\varphi} e^{-j\frac{2\pi}{K}k\alpha} S(k), k = 1, 2, \cdots N-1 \end{cases} \tag{4}$$

$$\frac{\|S'(k)\|}{\|S'(1)\|} = \frac{\beta \left\| e^{-j\varphi} e^{-j\frac{2\pi}{K}k\alpha} S(k) \right\|}{\beta \left\| e^{-j\varphi} e^{-j\frac{2\pi}{K}\alpha} S(1) \right\|} = \frac{\|S(k)\|}{\|S(1)\|} \tag{5}$$

Where: $k = 1, 2, \cdots, N-1$, $\|\cdot\|$ indicates modulo. From the derivation formulas of Eqs. (3) and (4), it can be obtained that when the image shape is rotated φ and the starting position is transformed by α, the Fourier transform changes its phase $e^{j\varphi}e^{-j\frac{2\pi}{K}k\alpha}$; The object changes its amplitude β when it is scaled; when the object is translated, it only changes its $S(0)$ component $f(x_0 + iy_0)$. According to the ratio of the modulus of Eq. (5), the traditional normalized Fourier descriptor $Z(k)$ [8] is:

$$z(k) = \frac{\|S(k)\|}{\|S(1)\|}, k = 1, 2, \cdots, N-1 \tag{6}$$

The traditional normalized Fourier descriptor $z(k)$ eliminates the change of mode and phase through the ratio of the moduli, so that the Fourier descriptor has the rotation, translation and scale invariance of the shape. However, $z(k)$ is only identified using the modulus of the Fourier transform coefficient $S(k)$ as a feature, resulting in loss of image phase information. In general, phase information is very important for accurately identifying the shape of an object. All methods that are normalized by touch will result in an accuracy that is too low in image retrieval. In order to use the information contained in the phase of the Fourier coefficients, their invariance must be obtained at the starting point and direction change. If the starting point of the shape contour is determined, it can be easily implemented.

In the following sections, a novel method for determining the starting position of a shape will be introduced, which achieves the desired phase invariance.

2.2 Fourier Descriptor Based on Minimum Inertia Axis

Intra-class similarity and class similarity are actually improved by reducing the number of possible starting points. If compare one shape to all possible angles of another shape, even if they have no semantic relevance in those directions, it produces the best possible match between the shapes.

This paper presents a method for finding points with specific geometric and shape discriminating meanings. Set the starting point to the farthest point of the minimum inertia axis of the center of gravity and the intersection of the contours, and then fine tune around the intersection. Make sure the starting point of the contour C_1. The center of gravity formula is as follows [9]:

$$x_c = \frac{\sum p_i x_i}{\sum p_i}, y_c = \frac{\sum p_i y_i}{\sum p_i} \tag{7}$$

Where (x_i, y_i) is the coordinates of the pixel and p_i is the pixel value of the point.

In rigid body kinematics, it is pointed out that the axisymmetric rigid body with uniform mass distribution has the smallest moment of inertia when rotating around its axis of symmetry. The axisymmetric object presents two-dimensional shape information in the digital image. In the gray image, the target is composed of a pixel point set $\mathrm{p} = \{((\mathrm{x_i}, \mathrm{y_i})|\mathrm{i} \in [(\mathrm{x_i}, \mathrm{y_i})]\}$, where N is the target The number of pixels included, each of which can be considered equivalent to each of the quality micro-elements in the rigid body M. Then, the moment of inertia of the rigid body M for a straight line can be obtained by integrating the moment of inertia of each mass micro-element. Then the minimum inertia axis formula is as follows [10]:

$$I = \sum_{i=1}^{N} d_i^2 \tag{8}$$

Where $d_i = \frac{|y-(x-x_c)\cdot\tan\theta - y_c|}{\sqrt{1+\tan\theta^2}}$; (x_c, y_c) is the barycentric coordinates of the image; θ is the equal division of all pixel points of the image contour N parts, then the degree of gravity of the angle between the center of gravity and each boundary point and the main axis. After determining the minimum inertia axis, this paper determines the starting point as the farthest point between the minimum inertia axis and the contour intersection.

In the new normalization of the Fourier descriptor, the main direction φ of the normalized shape is the angle θ between the minimum inertia axis and the main coordinate axis. Since the main direction of the normalized shape is the horizontal direction, the main direction of the new shape is that the angle between the minimum inertia axis and the main direction is θ, and according to the derivation of Eq. (9), the boundary can be estimated by the main direction θ of the shape. The phase of the starting translational arc length α affects $e^{-j\frac{2\pi}{K}\alpha}$, there by eliminating the phase effect of the boundary starting point. Define a new normalized Fourier descriptor $z'(k)$, as shown in Eq. (10):

$$\frac{S'(1)}{\|S'(1)\|} = \frac{\beta e^{j\varphi} e^{-j\frac{2\pi}{K}k\alpha} S(1)}{\beta \| e^{j\varphi} e^{-j\frac{2\pi}{K}\alpha} S(1) \|} = e^{j\varphi} e^{-j\frac{2\pi}{K}\alpha} \tag{9}$$

$$z'(k) = \frac{s'(k) \cdot e^{j\theta}}{\|S(2)\|}, k = 1, 2, \cdots, N-1 \tag{10}$$

Since the details of the image correspond to the high-frequency part and the contour corresponds to the low-frequency part of the image, the high-frequency part of the outline is removed. Since the first point of the Fourier descriptor contains its high-frequency information, it is normalized. Use $\|S(2)\|$ when it is used.

2.3 Similarity Measure Algorithm and Evaluation Criteria

Similarity Measure Algorithm. In the content-based image retrieval, it is necessary to calculate the similarity matching between the image to be retrieved and the image in the database. Therefore, it is undoubtedly very important to define an appropriate visual feature similarity measurement method for image retrieval. Influence. The extracted visual features can be expressed in the form of vectors. In fact, the commonly used similarity measure methods are vector space models, that is, visual features are regarded as points in vector space, by calculating between two points. The proximity is a measure of the similarity between image features. This paper uses the Euclidean distance method.

The Euclidean Distance represents the distance between two points in the Euclidean space. The Euclidean distance between the two vectors f_{Q_i} and $f_{DB_{ji}}$ is calculated as follows [7]:

$$\delta(f_{Q_i}, f_{DB_{ji}}) = \sqrt{\sum_{i=1}^{Lg} (f_{DB_{ji}} - f_{Q_i})^2} \tag{11}$$

Which $f_{DB_{ji}}$ represents the i feature of the j image in database |DB|, Lg represents the number of images in the database.

Evaluation Criteria. In the field of image retrieval, the average retrieval precision and the average retrieval rate are generally used to evaluate the performance of the algorithm. For the image I_q to be retrieved, the precision and recall are defined as follows [11]:

$$\Pr ecision : P(I_q) = \frac{Number\ of\ related\ images\ retrieved}{Total\ number\ of\ images\ retrieved} \tag{12}$$

$$\Pr ecision : P(I_q) = \frac{Number\ of\ related\ images\ retrieved}{The\ total\ number\ of\ related\ images\ in\ the\ database} \tag{13}$$

For the image I_q to be retrieved, the average precision calculation formula (6) is shown in Eq. (14) [12]:

$$P(I_q, n) = \frac{1}{n}\sum_{i=1}^{|DB|} \left|Q(\varphi(I_i), \varphi(I_q))\right| \tag{14}$$

Where n represents the number of related pictures retrieved, |DB| represents the size of the database, and $\varphi(x)$ represents the type of x.

For the image to be retrieved I_q, the average recall calculation formula (6) is shown in Eq. (15) [12]:

$$P(I_q, n) = \frac{1}{N}\sum_{i=1}^{|DB|} \left|Q(\varphi(I_i), \varphi(I_q))\right| \tag{15}$$

Where N represents the total amount of images associated with the image I_q to be retrieved.

It can be seen from the above formulas (14) and (15) that each image in the image database is used as the image to be retrieved, and the calculated precision is averaged to obtain an average precision. Similarly, the image is obtained. Each image in the database is used as the image to be retrieved, and the calculated recall rate is averaged to obtain the average recall rate. The paper uses the average retrieval precision and the average retrieval rate as the evaluation criteria for retrieval performance.

3 Experimental Results and Analysis

3.1 Experimental Environment and Data

(1) Experimental environment: Matlab R2016b, Windows 10 operating system.
(2) Experimental data (Fig. 1):

Data preprocessing: Since the product images are all color images, the image is first converted into a binary image and the binary image is subjected to threshold processing; secondly, the coordinates of the edge points of the image contour are extracted, and the difference between the coordinate points is obtained with equal spacing. Contour coordinate point; then find the image centroid under the obtained coordinate

Fig. 1. An image of each plant in the Swedish Leaf database. Source: Swedish Leaf database as an experimental sample.

point to determine the minimum inertia axis of the image, and find the intersection of the minimum inertia axis and the image contour to determine the starting point of the Fourier transform next, and determine the image coordinate point after the starting point The Fourier transform is performed to obtain the feature vector. Finally, the image retrieval is realized by calculating the distance between the feature vector of the image to be retrieved and the feature vector of the image in the image database.

3.2 Image Shape Feature Extraction

As can be seen from the process of image feature extraction in Fig. 2, (a) is the original image of the leaves in the Swedish Leaf database, the size is 256 × 154, (b) is the

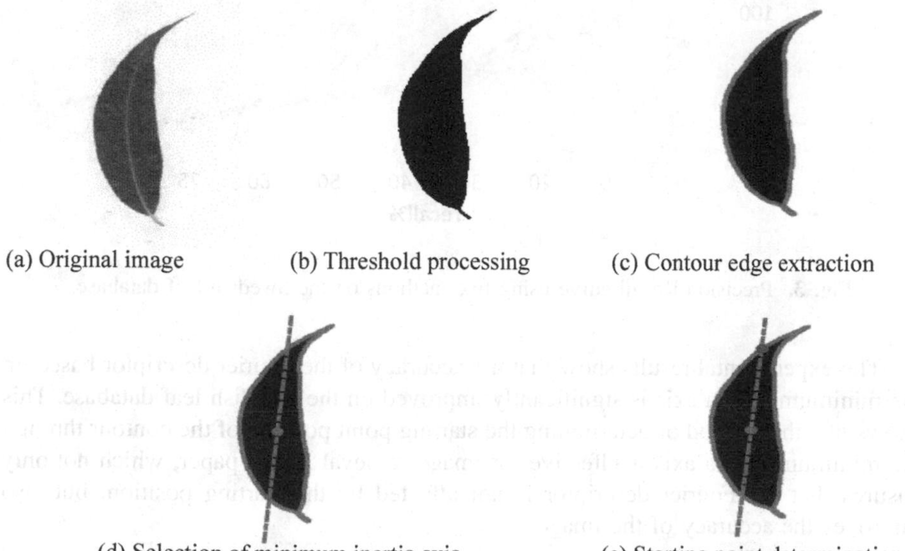

(a) Original image (b) Threshold processing (c) Contour edge extraction

(d) Selection of minimum inertia axis (e) Starting point determination

Fig. 2. Image feature extraction.

image threshold processing, using the automatic threshold processing method for the leaves The image is subjected to threshold processing; (c) is based on the contour edge extraction method. In the image retrieval based on Fourier descriptor, the required Fourier points are equidistant, so the equidistant interpolation method can guarantee The accuracy of the Fourier descriptor in the image retrieval process; (d) is the minimum inertia axis of the selected image; and (e) is the determination of the starting point of the image.

3.3 Feature Matching Results and Analysis

In the retrieval experiment, the number of boundary sample points for each shape contour is 256. A total of 50 low frequency Fourier coefficients are used to determine the similarity between the two shapes. Each shape in the database is treated as a query object. For each query, record the accuracy of the recall at each level. The FMAL accuracy retrieved is obtained by averaging all query results at each recall level. In theory, as the recall rate increases, so does the accuracy.

We compare the improved method with the retrieval of several widely used or recently introduced feature functions on two databases. These feature functions include CD, CC and FPD. 50 Fourier coefficients are reserved for each function to calculate the similarity between the two shapes.

Figure 3 shows the average accurate recall graph test on the Swedish leaf database, where each curve represents a method and the improved method is represented by MIAFD.

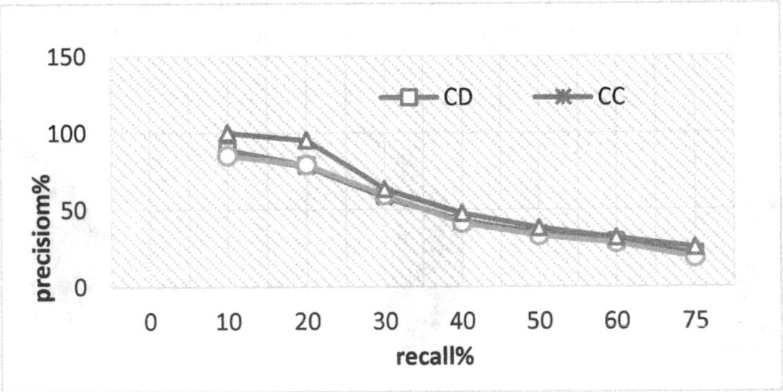

Fig. 3. Precision-Recall curve using five methods on the Swedish leaf database.

The experimental results show that the accuracy of the Fourier descriptor based on the minimum inertia axis is significantly improved on the Swedish leaf database. This shows that the method of determining the starting point position of the contour through the minimum inertia axis is effective for image retrieval in this paper, which not only ensures that the Fourier descriptor is not affected by the starting position, but also improves the accuracy of the image.

4 Conclusion

The shape description of the Fourier description is performed by determining the position of the starting point. Determining the starting point position by the minimum inertia axis is valuable for determining shape feature based retrieval. Where the starting point and rotation invariance are required, the minimum inertia axis determining starting point can be used to improve the shape description method. Combined with scale normalization and Fourier coefficient-based retention principles, they can be used for contour normalization to apply other more complex shape description techniques. Experiments performed on commonly used Swedish leaf databases have shown that this method is effective compared to other Fourier descriptors.

Acknowledgement. This work is supported by the Harbin Science and Technology Bureau outstanding subject leader fund project (2017RAXXJ055), and Nature Science Foundation of Heilongjiang Province (F2018020), and the Basic Scientific Research Operating Expense Project of Provincial Institutions of Higher Education in Heilongjiang (17XN003).

References

1. Datta, R., Joshi, D., Li, J., et al.: Image retrieval: Ideas, influences, and trends of the new age. ACM Comput. Surv. **40**(2), 1–60 (2008)
2. Madugunki, M., Bormane, D.S., Bhadoria, S., et al.: Comparison of different CBIR techniques. In: International Conference on Electronics Computer Technology, pp. 372–375 (2011)
3. Zhao, C., Ren, Y.: Research on shape-based image retrieval. Mod. Electron. Technol. **13**, 159–162 (2008)
4. Sokic, E., Konjicija, S.: Phase preserving Fourier descriptor for shape-based image retrieval. Signal Process. Image Commun. **40**(C), 82–96 (2016)
5. Bartolini, I., Ciaccia, P., Patella, M.: WARP: accurate retrieval of shapes using phase of fourier descriptors and time warping distance. IEEE Trans. Pattern Anal. Mach. Intell. **27**(1), 142–147 (2005)
6. Jain, A.K.: Fundamentals of Digital Image Processing, pp. 370–371. Prentice-Hall Press, Upper Saddle River (1989)
7. Wang, T., Liu, W., Sun, J., Zhang, H.: Using fourier descriptors to recognize object's shape. Comput. Res. Dev. **39**(12), 1714–1719 (2002)
8. Zhang, Y.: Image Processing and Analysis, 2nd edn. Tsinghua University Press, Beijing (1999)
9. Liang, N., Guo, L., Yu, Y.: A symmetry axis detected method based on the minimal value of moment of inertia. Microprocessor **6**, 62–64 (2009)
10. Shanmugavadivu, P., Sumathy, P., Vadivel, A.: FOSIR: fuzzy-object-shape for image retrieval applications. Neurocomputing **7**, 719–735 (2016)
11. Hong, T., Sun, H., Jin, X., et al.: Study on image retrieval algorithm based on local right-angle mean patterns. J. Harbin Univ. Commer. **7**(2), 172–174 (2017)

Analysis of the Classical Spectrum Sensing Algorithm Based on Transmitter

Xiaolin Jiang(✉), Susu Qu, and Zhengyu Tang

Heilongjiang University of Science and Technology, Harbin 150027, China
jlynner@163.com

Abstract. Spectrum sensing technology is implemented in cognitive radio spectrum, the basis of switching, spectrum management and spectrum sharing is the precondition of effective, reliable, wireless communication, the spectrum sensing algorithm based on sending and have energy detection, matched filtering test and cyclic stationary test three classical algorithms, detailed description of the classical algorithm, and through the simulation to compare the performance of three algorithms, put forward the suitable application scenario, provide some reference for researchers of the algorithm.

Keywords: Double threshold · Energy detection · Performance analysis

1 Introduction

Spectrum sensing technology is the basis for realizing spectrum switching, spectrum management and spectrum sharing in cognitive radio communication, and the prerequisite for effective and reliable wireless communication. Therefore, it is of great significance to carry out research on this aspect for the application and development of cognitive radio technology. The main task of the spectrum sensing process is to detect the spectrum hole through monitoring the use of spectrum resources, so as to provide the basis for cognitive users in the cognitive wireless network to be waiting for access to the idle frequency band, timely and accurate spectrum sensing information, and effectively avoid interference to the authorized users. On the premise of not affecting the communication of authorized users, cognitive users also realize the communication of information through the frequency band, so as to realize the sharing of spectrum resources. The perceived quality of the visible spectrum determines whether the spectrum resources can be utilized efficiently and directly determines the overall performance of the wireless communication network. Usually, in the study of spectrum perception, the key research issues include the design of the perception algorithm, which can realize the fast and efficient detection of spectrum information through algorithm research and improvement. The multi-user cooperative spectrum sensing strategy is studied so as to effectively solve the hidden terminal problem, make efficient use of multi-user data information, and realize spectrum detection more reliably. A series of issues such as how to make tradeoffs between perceptual time selection and spectral transmission efficiency are studied.

M. Jia et al. (Eds.): WiSATS 2019, LNICST 281, pp. 250–258, 2019.
https://doi.org/10.1007/978-3-030-19156-6_24

2 Classic Algorithms

According to the essence of spectrum perception, the spectrum perception problem can be transformed into the signal processing problem, so as to build the detection model. Spectrum perception completes the process of cognitive users to judge whether there is an authorized user signal in the frequency band that they are interested in from the received signals. At present, it is representative of Energy Detector (ED), matching Filter Detector (MFD), cycle-stationary Feature Detector (CFD), and so on [1].

In the cognitive radio network, the perception algorithm based on transmitter is mainly centered on the transmitter. The cognitive users in the network detect the authorized user signal information, and decide whether the frequency band is available or not according to the existence or not. The detection model is as follows:

$$y(t) = \begin{cases} n(t), & H_0 \\ hx(t) + n(t), & H_1 \end{cases} \tag{1}$$

Among them,

$y(t)$—Cognitive users receive signal information;
$x(t)$—Primary User information;
$n(t)$—Additive white gaussian noise;
h—Channel amplitude gain;
H_0—Only under noise conditions;
H_1—There are Primary User conditions.

2.1 Energy Detection

Energy detection is a relatively simple signal detection method, and its detection principle is shown in Fig. 1. The essence of energy detection is to realize the purpose of spectrum detection by measuring the energy of a signal on the frequency band and setting specific energy threshold value. If the frequency band is reached or exceeded, it is considered that the frequency band has been occupied. In the energy detection, the input signal is filtered through the front filter, and then after the transformation through A/D, the modulus and square of the input signal can be obtained. Alternatively, the time domain information can be converted to the frequency domain, that is, the received signal is filtered by the front filter, followed by the n-point FFT transformation, and then the modulus square of the frequency domain signal is obtained to obtain its energy value. Energy detection is the energy accumulation in a certain frequency band, that is, through the sum of N samples, the detection statistics are obtained. Then judgment is made through the judgment unit. If it is lower than the specific threshold value, the signal does not exist but only noise. If the detection statistic is higher than the set judgment threshold, the judgment signal exists [2].

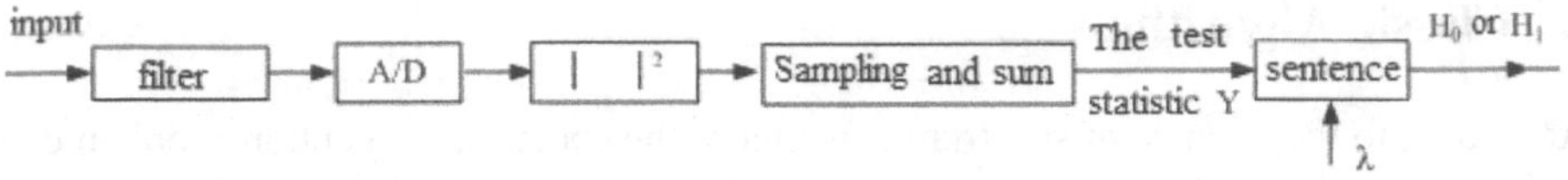

Fig. 1. Energy detection principle

In the above energy detection method, the judgment statistic Y can be expressed as

$$Y = \begin{cases} \chi^2_{2TW}, & H_0 \\ \chi^2_{2TW}(2\gamma), & H_1 \end{cases} \tag{2}$$

$\chi^2_{2TW}(2\gamma)$—The judgment statistics is subject to 2γ non-central chi-square distribution of 2TW;
χ^2_{2TW}—The central chi-square distribution of the statistic Y obeying degree of freedom is 2TW;
TW—Time and bandwidth product;
γ—SNR.

The method of energy detection is simple and easy to implement, and the theoretical technology has been very mature. At present, it is widely studied and discussed in signal detection, and various improved algorithms of energy detection have been derived. However, in the case of low signal-to-noise ratio (SNR), the authorized user's signal is very weak, which is usually submerged in noise. In addition to the impact of noise variance uncertainty, the performance of the energy detection algorithm is very poor [3]; Moreover, according to the basic model of energy perception, energy detection can only distinguish the existence of authorized users, and information such as the form of transmitting signals and the type of authorized users cannot be obtained.

2.2 Matched Filter

When the cognitive user knows the prior information of the authorized user signal, the input signal and the transmitting signal are multiplied by the multiplier, and the sampling judgment is used to obtain the test statistics, and then the judgment is compared with the specific threshold. In essence, the matched filter detection method is a coherent detection algorithm, which is the optimal linear filter with the maximum output signal-to-noise ratio and the maximum signal-to-noise ratio of the received signal [4]. Matching filtering detection is a common method in signal detection [5], and its block diagram is shown in Fig. 2.

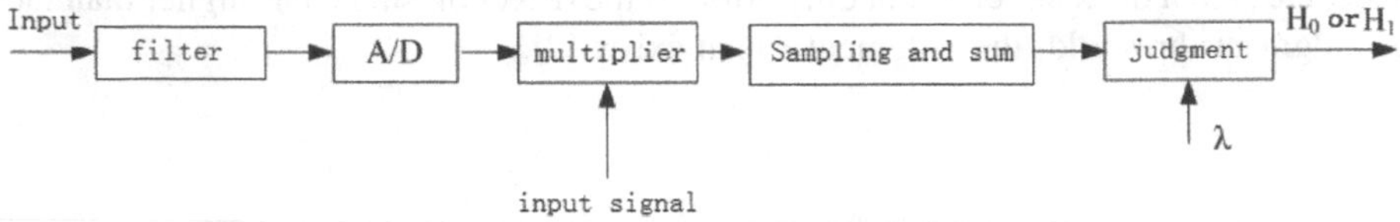

Fig. 2. The principle of matched filtering detection

If the input signal of the matched filter is

$$r(t) = s(t) + n(t) \tag{3}$$

Among them, $s(t)$ is PU, $n(t)$ is additive white Gaussian noise. Let's say that $s(t)$ and $n(t)$ are independent. After the input signal is prefiltered, A/D transformation is performed, and then the statistic Y is detected by multiplying the original transmitting signal and the received signal sampling:

$$Y = \sum_{n=0}^{N-1} r(n)s(n) \tag{4}$$

$r(n)$—$r(t)$ The received signal sequence obtained after sampling N points;
$s(n)$—$s(t)$ The sequence of transmitting signals obtained after sampling N points;
N—Sampling spot number.

Test statistics achieve the judgment by comparing with the set threshold value λ. When the threshold value λ is greater than, the judgment is "1", indicating the existence of the authorized user; otherwise, the judgment is "0", indicating that the authorized user does not exist.

The matching filtering detection algorithm adopts the coherent detection technology, which can achieve the advantages of relatively less time required for higher processing gain, and it can be known through theoretical derivation that the algorithm can maximize the output SNR [6]. But needs to know that originated in the process of implementation of correlation detection signal of a priori information, a priori information is accurate or not directly decides the matched filtering performance of detection algorithm, and the matched filtering detection algorithm implementation process is very high to the requirement of phase synchronization, synchronization technology must be used when using even equalization to meet the requirements, the process complexity is high, not easy to achieve.

2.3 Cycle-Stationary Feature Detection

In radio communications, the transmission of a signal is usually modulated. If the signal of the authorized user is modulated, the corresponding information will be pulse sequence, carrier, repetitive extension and cyclic prefix. This characteristic makes the modulated signal inherently periodic [43]. The so-called cyclic stability characteristic refers to the authorized user signal after modulation. Its mean value and autocorrelation function are both periodic. We can apply this characteristic by analyzing the spectral correlation function. The most important characteristic of the spectral correlation function is that the energy of the modulated signal can be separated from the energy of the noise signal. It is because the modulated signal correspondingly has inherent periodicity and spectral correlation, while the noise signal, because it is a broadband and static signal, has no intrinsic correlation. In this case, its periodic moment or periodic cumulative quantity or periodic cycle spectral value is zero. According to this characteristic, it can decide whether the authorized user information exists [7].

The cyclic stationary signal feature detection can overcome the shortcoming of energy detection and is little affected by the signal signal-to-noise ratio. The mutual interference between signals can also be eliminated through the circular stationary signal processing [8]. If the mean value $A_x(t) = E[x(t)]$ of a random process is a periodic function, we call it a first order cyclic stationary process. The mean value of a cyclic stationary process can be expressed as:

$$A_x(t) = \sum_{n=-\infty}^{\infty} A_x^{\alpha} e^{j2\pi\alpha t} \tag{5}$$

Among them, $\alpha = m/T_0$, T_0 is the period of the mean, A_x is the Fourier series coefficients and its calculation formula:

$$A_x(t) = \frac{1}{T_0} \int_{-T_0/2}^{T_0/2} A_x(t) e^{j2\pi\alpha t} dt \tag{6}$$

If $x(t)$ is a non-stationary complex exponential signal whose mean is zero, and its mean Fourier series expansion does not satisfy Eq. (5). If the correlation function $R_x(t, \tau)$ is a periodic signal, then x(t) is a second-order stationary process [9]. The correlation function of the random process is shown in formula (7).

$$R_x(t, \tau) = E\{x(t)x * (t - \tau)\} \tag{7}$$

Let me write it in terms of the average of time:

$$R_x(t, \tau) = \lim_{N \to \infty} \frac{1}{2N + 1} \sum_{n=-N}^{N} x(t + nT_0)x * (t + nT_0 - \tau)\} \tag{8}$$

Where N is the number of data. The periodic correlation functions $R_x(t, \tau)$ are continued to be carried out for Fourier series expansion, as shown in formula (9).

$$R_x(t, \tau) = \sum_{n=-N}^{N} R_x^{\alpha}(\tau) e^{j2\pi\alpha t} \tag{9}$$

Among $\alpha = m/T_0$, T_0 is the relevant cycle. The Fourier coefficients of the Fourier series is

$$R_x^{\alpha}(\tau) = \frac{1}{T_0} \int_{-T_0/2}^{T_0/2} R_x(t, \tau) e^{-j2\pi\alpha t} dt \tag{10}$$

So:

$$R_x^\alpha(\tau) = \lim_{T_0\to\infty} \frac{1}{T_0}\int_{-T_0/2}^{T_0/2} x(t)x*(t-\tau)e^{-j2\pi\alpha t}dt = <x(t+\frac{\tau}{2})x*(t-\frac{\tau}{2})e^{-j2\pi\alpha t}>_t \quad (11)$$

The Fourier coefficient in the corresponding Fourier series expansion represents the cyclic autocorrelation intensity of the loop frequency α, which is a function of phi, or the cyclic autocorrelation function for short. The autocorrelation function of the signal achieves coherent accumulation at different cyclic frequencies, and achieves or is nearly identical in phase, thus causing the cyclic spectrum of the input signal to appear spectral peak at some cyclic frequencies [9]. Fourier transform is applied to the cyclic autocorrelation function, so

$$S_x^\alpha(f) = \int_{-\infty}^{\infty} R_x^\alpha(\tau)e^{-j2\pi f\tau}d\tau \quad (12)$$

$S_x^\alpha(f)$ is the cyclic spectral density function. According to the above analysis, for stationary noise, it can be completely suppressed through cyclic spectrum, and for all kinds of non-stationary noise, as long as the periodic frequency of the signal and the periodic frequency of noise are different, it can be separated in the circular spectrum plane.

Rewrite Eq. (11) as follows:

$$R_x^\alpha(\tau) = <x(t+\frac{\tau}{2})e^{-j2\pi\alpha(t+\tau/2)}x*(t-\frac{\tau}{2})e^{-j2\pi\alpha(t-\tau/2)}>_t \quad (13)$$

$$\begin{cases} u(t) = x(t)e^{-j2\pi\alpha t} \\ v(t) = x(t)e^{j2\pi\alpha t} \end{cases} \quad (14)$$

The Fourier transform of the above formula is given

$$\begin{cases} U(f) = X(f+\alpha/2) \\ V(f) = X(f-\alpha/2) \end{cases} \quad (15)$$

Then, $R_x^\alpha(\tau) = R_{uv}(\tau) = <u(t+\frac{\tau}{2})v*(t-\frac{\tau}{2})>_t$, $u(t)$ is related to $v*(t)$. From a frequency domain perspective, the Fourier transform of $R_x^\alpha(\tau)$ can be expressed as the correlation of the spectrum of the signal up and down by the translation of the common component of $\alpha/2$ [12]. Therefore, the cyclic power spectral density function is also called spectral correlation function. However, the general noise signal does not have this cyclic stationary characteristic, so it is easy to distinguish the interference from the signal by using this difference, and extract the cyclic stationary signal information. The detection of cyclic stationary feature is based on this principle.

The spectrum sensing method based on cyclic spectral correlation detection USES the periodicity of the signal's autocorrelation function to detect the idle spectrum. Although it has the advantage of being able to distinguish between authorized user signals and interference signals, and is less affected by the uncertainty of noise variance, in some complex conditions, it can not distinguish between signals and noises through the periodicity of second-order statistics of cycle spectrum. In this context, high-order cycle statistics have been extensively studied. This is due to the strict cyclic stationarity of higher-order cyclic statistics, complete separation of stationary and circular stationary signals, effective suppression of any noise, and better receiver operating characteristic curve (ROC) [51]. Therefore, the theory of asymptotic optimization is used to construct the hypothesis testing model and test statistics of higher-order cyclic statistics [13], and the use of the higher-order cyclic statistical characteristics of authorized user signals to carry out spectrum perception is a hot research topic in recent years.

3 The Simulation Analysis

Energy detection, matched filtering detection and cyclic stationary feature detection are three classic non-cooperative sensing technologies based on receiver detection. Below is the additive gaussian white noise environment, $SNR = -15$ dB, the algorithm performances are simulated. Figure 3 shows the ROC performance simulation curves of these three classic perception technologies.

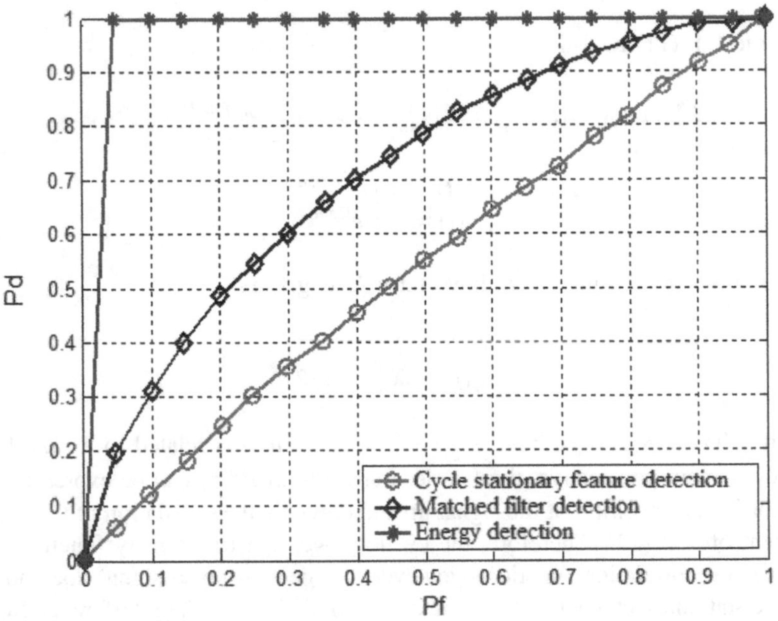

Fig. 3. SNR = 15 dB three classic ROC performance comparison of test method

It can be found from the figure that, for performance, the matched filter detection is obviously better than the energy detection and cyclic stationary detection methods, but in the process of implementation, because the matched filter detection requires to know a large amount of prior information of authorized users, which greatly limits its practical application in the cognitive radio system. In the simulation, an ideal energy detection model with assumed noise power is adopted. In this case, the energy detection performance is superior to the ordinary cyclic stationary detection.

4 Conclusion

The energy detection method is a nonuniform detection which simplifies the matching filter. The most remarkable feature of it is simple structure, easy to implement, good practicability, and energy detection does not need prior information of detection signal, so it has better universality. However, in the case of low signal-to-noise ratio (SNR), the detection time needs to be increased to improve the detection performance. In other words, the number of samples should be increased, but the complexity is also increased. Furthermore, the threshold value of energy detection is easily subject to noise fluctuation and cannot be determined accurately. For example, it will be difficult to set the threshold under the weak channel, and the detection performance is greatly affected by noise variance uncertainty. Moreover, the energy detector is not suitable for detection under broadband signal conditions, and more sophisticated signal processing methods should be developed for these signals. The ideal way to detect any signal is to match the filter, as its output SNR is maximized. However, for the matched filter to work effectively requires correct demodulation of the authorized user signal, which means that cognitive radio requires prior information of the authorized user signal at the physical and MAC levels. As described in the detection method, the signal is assumed to be known and a matching filter is constructed from the signal. But the inflexible part is that demodulation requires timing and carrier synchronization or even channel balancing to be consistent with the authorized user. If the prior information obtained is not accurate enough, the accuracy of the result of the matched filter detection will be greatly affected. The main advantage of a matched filter is that it takes very little time to achieve a high processing gain. However, one of its biggest drawbacks is the prior information needed to authorize users. Most of the modulating signals have the characteristics of stable circulation, so the cyclic power spectrum characteristic detection has the identifiability, and can extract the signal from the noise background. Considering that energy detection is susceptible to noise variance uncertainty, compared with energy detection, the detection performance of cyclic stationary feature is superior to energy detection in the case of low signal-to-noise ratio. This shows the anti-noise property of cycle stationary feature detection. But at the same time, the computational complexity is higher and the detection time is longer.

Acknowledgement. This work was supported by the Heilongjiang Province Natural Science Foundations of China (F2015019, F2015017 and E2016061), the Heilongjiang Province Postdoctoral Science Foundations (LBH-Z16054).

References

1. Seshukumar, K., Saravanan, R., Suraj, M.S.: Spectrum sensing review in cognitive radio. In: The International Conference on Emerging Trends in VLSI, Embedded System, Nano Electronics and Telecommunication System (ICEVENT), pp. 1–4 (2013)
2. Masonta, M.T., Mzyece, M., Ntlatlapa, N.: Spectrum decision in cognitive radio networks: a survey. IEEE Commun. Surv. Tutor. **15**(3), 1088–1107 (2012)
3. Tandra, R., Sahai, A.: Fundamental limits on detection in low SNR. In: Proceedings of the Wireless Comm Symposium on Signal Processing, pp. 464–469 (2005)
4. Xinzhi, Z., Rong, C., Feifei, G.: Matched filter based spectrum sensing and power level detection for cognitive radio network. In: IEEE Global Conference on Signal and Information Processing (GlobalSIP), pp. 1267–1270 (2014)
5. Cabric, D., Mishra, S.M., Brodersen, R.W.: Implementation issues in spectrum sensing for cognitive radios. In: Proceedings of Asilomar Conference on Signals, Systems and Computers (ACSSC 2004), pp. 772–776 (2004)
6. Ruolin, Z., Xue, L., Yang, T.C.: Real-time cyclostationary analysis for cognitive radio via software defined radio. In: IEEE Global Communications Conference (GLOBECOM), pp. 1495–1500 (2012)
7. Optimizing wideband cyclostationary spectrum sensing under receiver impairments. IEEE Trans. Sig. Process. **61**(15), 3931–3943 (2013)
8. Mishra, S.M., Sahai, A., Brodersen, R.W.: Cooperative sensing among cognitive radios. In: Proceedings of IEEE International Conference on Communications (ICC 2006), pp. 1658–1663 (2006)
9. Fan, R., Jiang, H.: Optimal multi-channel cooperative sensing in cognitive radio networks. IEEE Trans. Wirel. Commun. **9**(3), 1128–1138 (2010)
10. Zhi, T., Tafesse, Y., Sadler, B.M.: Cyclic feature detection with sub-Nyquist sampling for wideband spectrum sensing. IEEE J. Sel. Top. Sig. Process. **6**(1), 58–69 (2011)
11. Gardner, W.: Measurement of spectral correlation. IEEE Trans. Acoust. Speech Sig. Process. **34**(5), 1111–1123 (1986)
12. Jiang, X.L., Gu, X.M.: Double threshold collaborative spectrum sensing algorithm based on energy detection. J. Hei LongJiang Univ. Sci. Technol. 553–556 (2016)
13. Gezici, S., Celebi, H., Poor, H.V., Arslan, H.: Fundamental limits on time delay estimation in dispersed spectrum cognitive radio systems. IEEE Trans. Wirel. Commun. **8**(1), 78–83 (2009)

A New Type Double-Threshold Signal Detection Algorithm for Satellite Communication Systems Based on Stochastic Resonance Technology

Xiaolin Jiang[1,2](✉) and Ming Diao[1]

[1] Harbin Engineering University, Harbin 150000, China
jlynner@163.com
[2] Heilongjiang University of Science and Technology, Harbin 150000, China

Abstract. In order to further improve the accurate detection signal, reduce interference between signals, this paper designs a new type of signal detection algorithm for satellite communication systems, using stochastic resonance technology improve the signal-to-noise ratio of the input signal, the signal by using energy detection, double threshold, accurate judgment. The first step in the conventional energy of double threshold detection, the second step into the energy detection method based on stochastic resonance detection process. The experimental results show that this algorithm under the condition of low SNR signals effectively detect, promoted the whole satellite communication system performance.

Keywords: Satellite communication network · Stochastic resonance · Algorithm

1 Introduction

The increasing demand for wireless spectral resources in communication systems has led to an increasingly tight spectral resource, which is a bottleneck that restricts the development of wireless communications. The rapid growth of current data communication services increasingly requires satellite communication networks to have higher throughput and spectral efficiency. The current 4G satellite wireless communication network networking mode achieves full frequency multiplexing [1]. In the case of full frequency multiplexing, severe mutual interference often occurs between all the base stations transmitting the same frequency in the same frequency. The upcoming 5G satellite communication network will also adopt the same-frequency full-duplex technology, that is, in the same spectrum, the transmitting and receiving sides of the satellite communication simultaneously transmit and receive signals, and the full-duplex technology can break through the spectral resource usage restrictions of frequency division multiplexing and time division multiplexing, making the use of spectral resources more flexible. However, full-duplex technology requires extremely high interference cancellation capability, which poses a great challenge to interference cancellation technology. Effective detection of signals is the most important part of

M. Jia et al. (Eds.): WiSATS 2019, LNICST 281, pp. 259–272, 2019.
https://doi.org/10.1007/978-3-030-19156-6_25

reducing mutual interference [2, 3]. However, in satellite communication networks, information transmission is also highly susceptible to interference such as channel decay effects, how to perform effective signal detection under low SNR conditions is directly related to the performance of the entire satellite communication network system. People began to seek a new signal detection algorithm combining multiple technologies to reduce the negative impact on signal detection reliability when the SNR caused by channel decay is low [4]. Through investigation, it is found that the stochastic resonance theory provides a good technical improvement for better signal detection under low SNR. Stochastic resonance theory states that when a stochastic resonance occurs in a noisy system, part of the noise energy is converted into the energy of the useful signal, which greatly increases the SNR of the system [5]. Based on stochastic resonance technology, this paper uses a double threshold two step algorithm to achieve signal detection, which greatly improves the overall performance of the satellite communication network.

2 Bistable Stochastic Resonance Model

The classical deterministic equation with bistable properties can be expressed as:

$$S(x) = ax - bx^3 \tag{1}$$

a and b are adjustable parameters, both greater than zero. According to this deterministic equation, the corresponding potential function of the system can be obtained as:

$$U(x) = -ax^2/2 + bx^4/4 \tag{2}$$

The waveform of this function is shown in Fig. 1. From the picture, $U(x)$ has a maximum value at $x = 0$, has two minimum values at $x = \pm\sqrt{a/b}$. Corresponding to one barrier point and two potential well points of the system, at this time, potential well depth $U_0 = a^2/4b$. We also call this the height of base (6).

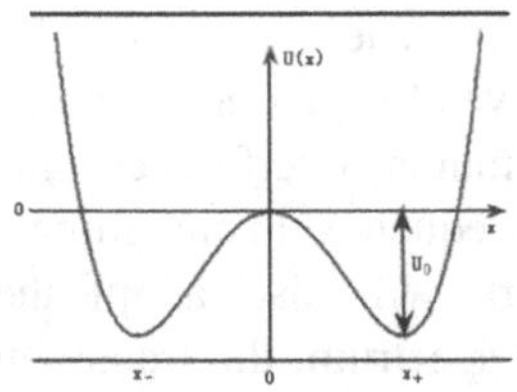

Fig. 1. Bistable system potential function characteristic curve

According to the stochastic resonance theory, if the values of a and b change, the depth and width of the well will change, but they will remain symmetrical. Given an initial state, the system will evolve differently, but will always stabilize at a certain point in $x = \pm\sqrt{a/b}$ or $x = 0$. When $a = b = 1$, the system potential function $U(x)$ and the state of the system evolve. At this time, the position of the bottom of the two symmetric wells is $x = \pm 1$, the position of the barrier is $x = 0$, and the height of the barrier is $U_0 = 1/4$.

Following, we analyze this nonlinear system, If assuming the motion of particles, if the initial value of the system is $x = 0$, the particles will stop at the unstable state of $x = 0$, until any slight interference, the particles will tend to a stable state of x_+ or x_-. If the particle is in the initial state $x < 0$, the particle will tend to the stable state of x_-. If the particle is in the initial state $x > 0$, the particle will tend to the stable state of x_+. When $t \to \infty$, the particle will stop approximating to the stable fixed point. It can be seen that the nonlinear system described by Eq. (1) has two stable states, and in the absence of the force outside the system, the system will eventually infinitely approach any one of the two stable fixed points, so Eq. (2) describes a bistable system.

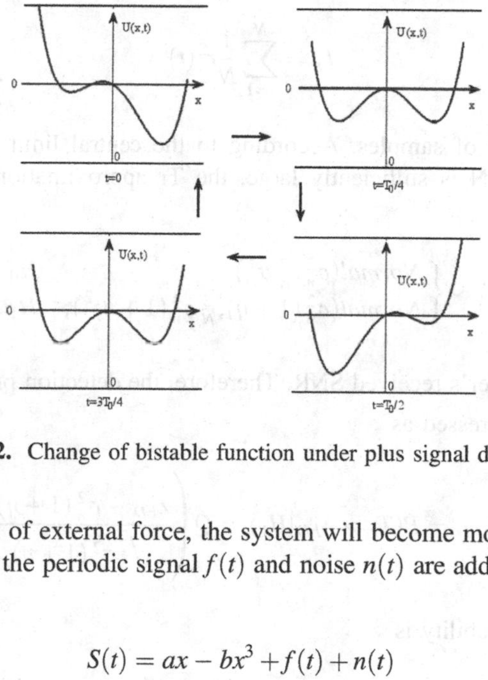

Fig. 2. Change of bistable function under plus signal driven

Under the action of external force, the system will become more complicated, but more meaningful. If the periodic signal $f(t)$ and noise $n(t)$ are added, the formula will change as

$$S(t) = ax - bx^3 + f(t) + n(t) \tag{3}$$

Physically: the particles moving in the potential well $U(x)$, the Langevin equation followed by $f(t)$ and $n(t)$. When there is an external periodic force $s(t) = A\cos\Omega t$, the potential function is modulated. In a period $T = 2\pi/\Omega$, it is apparent that the presence of a periodic external force causes the potential well to periodically tilt, as shown in Fig. 2, this tilt provides a condition for the systematic output state to cross the barrier and transition between the two potential wells, when the conditions are appropriate (7), the transition frequency is exactly equal to the periodic frequency of the signal, then the SR phenomenon occurs.

3 Algorithm Design and Analysis

Due to the random decay effects in a satellite communication environment, the energy of the user receiving other user signals at different times and at different locations is different. When the satellite communication environment between the user and other users is better, the conventional energy detection can also achieve better detection results, and the gain effect of the stochastic resonance system on the signal with better signal to noise is not obvious, so this time it is not necessary to use stochastic resonance processing. Therefore, we use a two-step signal detection improvement mechanism based on stochastic resonance.

3.1 System Model

Hypothesis test model for energy detection, whose energy detection statistic is calculated as (8)

$$T_r = \sum_{t=1}^{N} \frac{1}{N} r^2(t) \tag{4}$$

N is the number of samples. According to the central limit theorem, when the number of samples N is sufficiently large, the Tr approximation follows a normal distribution.

$$T_r \sim \begin{cases} Normal(\sigma_w^2, \frac{2}{N}\sigma_w^4), & H_0 \\ Normal(\sigma_w^2(1+\eta), \frac{2}{N}\sigma_w^4(1+\eta)^2), & H_1 \end{cases} \tag{5}$$

$\eta = \frac{h^2\sigma_s^2}{\sigma_w^2}$ is the user's received SNR. Therefore, the detection probability of energy detection can be expressed as

$$P_{D\_ED} = P(T_r > \lambda_{ED}|H_1) = Q\left(\frac{\lambda_{ED} - \sigma_w^2(1+\eta)}{\sqrt{\frac{2}{N}}\sigma_w^2(1+\eta)}\right) \tag{6}$$

False alarm probability is

$$P_{F\_ED} = P(T_r > \lambda_{ED}|H_0) = Q\left(\frac{(\lambda_{ED} - \sigma_w^2)}{\sqrt{\frac{2}{N}}\sigma_w^2}\right) \tag{7}$$

λ_{ED} is the decision threshold of energy detection. Under the Newman-Pearson criterion, when the target constant false alarm probability of a wireless communication network is given, the threshold can be obtained by the following formula.

$$\lambda_{ED} = \sqrt{\frac{2}{N}} Q^{-1}\left(\overline{P_{F\_ED}} + 1\right)\sigma_w^2 \tag{8}$$

3.2 Perceptual Mechanism Design

A new type double-threshold signal detection algorithm based on stochastic Resonance technology includes two stages of a first threshold detection and a second threshold detection. It is assumed that the channel is an AGWN fading channel, the first threshold detection phase adopts the conventional double threshold energy detection, and the second step deep detection uses the energy detection method based on stochastic resonance. The schematic is shown in Fig. 3.

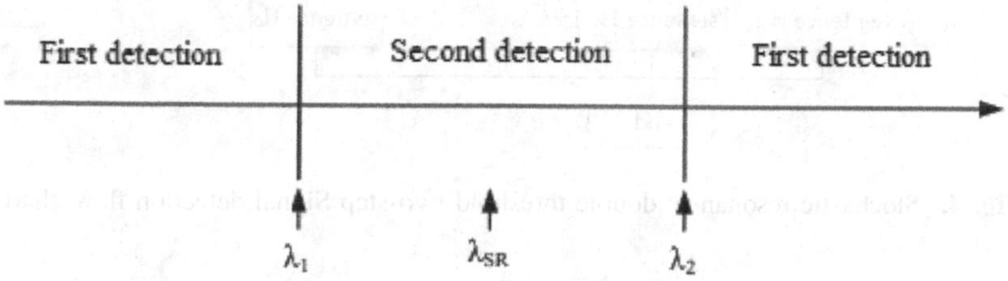

Fig. 3. Stochastic resonance, double threshold two-step sensing schematic

In the first step, the statistic is compared ($\lambda_1 < \lambda_2$) with the two thresholds λ_1 and λ_2 to determine its reliability and whether the second step of in-depth testing is required. If the statistic of the first threshold detection is outside the interval (λ_1, λ_2), it is considered to be reliable, and the second step of in-depth detection is not required at this time. If the statistic is greater than or equal to the upper limit λ_2, the user directly determines that H_1 is established. If it is less than the lower limit λ_1, the user directly determines that H0 is true. However, when the first threshold detection statistic falls within the interval (λ_1, λ_2), the statistic is considered to be unreliable and further in-depth detection is required. Since the unreliable statistic is usually caused by weak signal under H1 condition or strong noise under H_0 condition, in the two-step signal detection, when other user signals exist, the stochastic resonance system will only process weak signals. In the second step of the in-depth detection phase, the statistics formed by the output of the stochastic resonance system will be compared to the corresponding thresholds to arrive at a decision message as to whether or not the final other user signals are present. If the statistic is greater than or equal to the threshold, it is considered that the other user is using the sensing frequency band, and the user cannot access; if the threshold is less than the threshold, the sensing frequency band is considered to be idle. The flow chart is shown in Fig. 4.

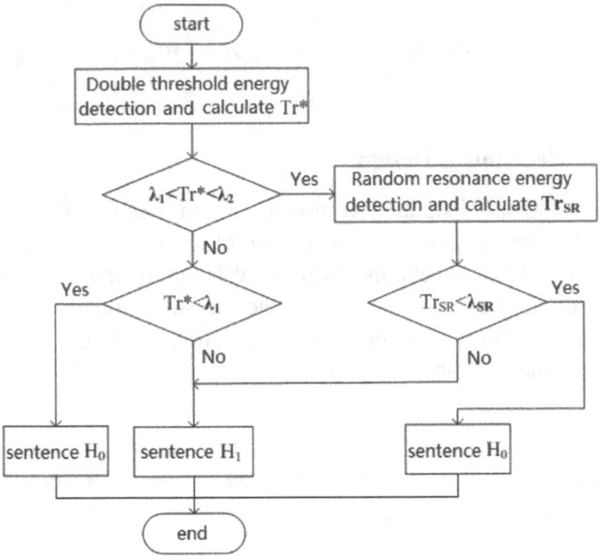

Fig. 4. Stochastic resonance, double threshold two-step Signal detection flow chart

3.3 Performance Analysis

(1) Parameter selection

The selection of thresholds plays a crucial role in the overall signal detection process. The thresholds of the first-stage sensing phase are assumed to be λ_1 and λ_2, respectively. In order to meet the requirements of the satellite communication network and fully utilize the idle frequency band, the improved perceptual algorithm based on stochastic resonance energy detection also needs to maintain a constant false alarm probability. In the following (9), Tr^* is used to represent the statistics of the first-stage sensing phase in the double-threshold signal detection algorithm based on stochastic resonance to distinguish the statistic Tr in the conventional single-level perceptual mechanism, which we discuss separately below.

Firstly, the decision threshold based on the stochastic resonance double threshold two step energy detection algorithm is discussed. Since the probability of constant false alarm is maintained, the threshold can be calculated by the Newman-Pearson criterion. However, in order to minimize the computational complexity, the lower threshold is defined as $\lambda_1 = \inf(\mathrm{Tr}^* : Tr_{SR} \geq \lambda_{SR})$, that is, the statistic after the stochastic resonance processing is greater than or equal to the minimum value of the first-order sensing phase statistic of the threshold λ_{SR}. When the statistic Tr is smaller than λ_1, it is not necessary to introduce a stochastic resonance process because the stochastic resonance process does not improve the performance of signal detection at this time. Under the Newman-Pearson criterion, the improved signal detection algorithm based on stochastic resonance energy detection should have the same constant false alarm probability as the conventional single-stage energy detector. The false alarm probability of a conventional single-stage energy detector can be calculated as

$$P_f = P(Tr \geq \lambda_{ED}|H_0) \tag{9}$$

λ_{ED} is the decision threshold of the conventional single-stage energy detection method. The stochastic resonance double threshold signal detection algorithm false alarm probability can be expressed as

$$\begin{aligned} P_f^* &= P(Tr^* \geq \lambda_2|H_0) \\ &\quad + P(Tr_{SR} \geq \lambda_{SR}|\lambda_1 \leq Tr^* < \lambda_2, H_0) \times P(\lambda_1 \leq Tr^* < \lambda_2|H_0) \end{aligned} \tag{10}$$

λ_{SR} is the decision threshold of the second-step perceptual stochastic resonance energy detection method.

Therefore, according to the Newman-Pearson criterion $P_f = P_f^*$

$$\begin{aligned} P(Tr \geq \lambda_{ED}|H_0) &= P(Tr^* \geq \lambda_2|H_0) \\ &\quad + P(Tr_{SR} \geq \lambda_{SR}|\lambda_1 \leq Tr^* < \lambda_2, H_0) \cdot P(\lambda_1 \leq Tr^* < \lambda_2|H_0) \end{aligned} \tag{11}$$

Depending on the characteristics of the stochastic resonance system, it can enhance other user signals input by the system when the conditions for generating stochastic resonance are met. Therefore, when other user signals are present, the user can obtain an enhanced received signal by stochastic resonance processing. However, when other user signals are not present, the stochastic resonance system will not function. Therefore, when $\lambda_2 \leq \lambda_{ED}$, under the H_0 condition, if the statistics of the first-stage sensing stage is less than λ_2, the statistics of the second-step sensing stage will not exceed λ_{SR}, because the Newman-Pearson criterion needs to maintain the same constant virtual alarm probability. This means that when $\lambda_2 \leq \lambda_{ED}$, there is

$$P(Tr_{SR} \geq \lambda_{SR}|\lambda_1 \leq Tr^* < \lambda_2, H_0) = 0 \tag{12}$$

Thus, the Eqs. (4–9) can be simplified to

$$P(Tr \geq \lambda_{ED}|H_0) = P(Tr^* \geq \lambda_2|H_0) \tag{13}$$

In the actual perception process, the statistic Tr and Tr* expressions are the same, so if and only if $\lambda_2 = \lambda_{ED}$, the above equation holds.

When $\lambda_2 > \lambda_{ED}$, P_f^* can be further expressed as

$$\begin{aligned} P_f^* &= P(Tr^* \geq \lambda_{ED}|H_0) - P(\lambda_{ED} \leq Tr^* < \lambda_2, H_0) \\ &\quad + P(Tr_{SR} \geq \lambda_{SR}|\lambda_1 \leq Tr^* < \lambda_{ED}, H_0) \cdot P(\lambda_1 \leq Tr^* < \lambda_{ED}|H_0) \\ &\quad + P(Tr_{SR} \geq \lambda_{SR}|\lambda_{ED} \leq Tr^* < \lambda_2, H_0) \cdot P(\lambda_{ED} \leq Tr^* < \lambda_2|H_0) \end{aligned} \tag{14}$$

Similarly, due to the Newman-Pearson criterion $P_f = P_f^*$, $P(Tr_{SR} \geq \lambda_{SR} | \lambda_1 \leq Tr^* < \lambda_{ED}, H_0) = 0$, the statistics Tr and Tr* expressions are the same (10), so

$$P(\lambda_{ED} \leq Tr^* < \lambda_2, H_0) = P(Tr_{SR} \geq \lambda_{SR} | \lambda_{ED} \leq Tr^* < \lambda_2, H_0) \times P(\lambda_{ED} \leq Tr^* < \lambda_2 | H_0) \quad (15)$$

According to the stochastic resonance linear response theory and the Newman-Pearson criterion, we can get $P(Tr_{SR} \geq \lambda_{SR} | \lambda_{ED} \leq Tr^* < \lambda_2, H_0) = 1$. So the above formula is always established. That is, when $\lambda_2 \geq \lambda_{ED}$, $P_f = P_f^*$ is always established. Since the upper threshold λ_2 is larger, the probability of performing the second step of perception is greater. Therefore, in order to minimize the computational complexity and ensure that the stochastic resonance system processes the weak signal, we select the upper threshold as $\lambda_2 = \lambda_{ED}$.

(2) Detection probability

According to the thresholds λ_1 and λ_2 determined in the previous section, the detection probability P_d^* of the two-step energy detection signal detection algorithm based on the stochastic resonance double threshold can be calculated as

$$P_d^* = P(Tr^* \geq \lambda_2 | H_1) + P(Tr_{SR} \geq \lambda_{SR} | \lambda_1 \leq Tr^* < \lambda_2, H_1) \cdot P(\lambda_1 \leq Tr^* < \lambda_2 | H_1) \quad (16)$$

In order to compare with the performance of stochastic resonance energy detection, we will explore the user detection probability using stochastic resonance energy detection, which can be expressed as

$$P_d = P(Tr_{SR} \geq \lambda_{SR} | H_1) \quad (17)$$

Using the full probability formula, we can get

$$\begin{aligned} P_d = {} & P(Tr_{SR} \geq \lambda_{SR} | Tr < \lambda_1, H_1) P(Tr < \lambda_1 | H_1) \\ & + P(Tr_{SR} \geq \lambda_{SR} | \lambda_1 \leq Tr < \lambda_2, H_1) P(\lambda_1 \leq Tr < \lambda_2 | H_1) \\ & + P(Tr_{SR} \geq \lambda_{SR} | Tr > \lambda_2, H_1) \cdot P(Tr > \lambda_2 | H_1) \end{aligned} \quad (18)$$

Because $\lambda_1 = \inf(\mathrm{Tr}^* : Tr_{SR} \geq \lambda_{SR})$, $P(Tr_{SR} \geq \lambda_{SR} | Tr < \lambda_1, H_1) = 0$. According to the rules selected above, in the presence of other users, if the stochastic resonance system works normally, when $Tr \geq \lambda_2$, there is naturally $Tr_{SR} \geq \lambda_{SR}$, so

$$P_d = P(Tr_{SR} \geq \lambda_{SR} | \lambda_1 \leq Tr < \lambda_2, H_1) P(\lambda_1 \leq Tr < \lambda_2 | H_1) + P(Tr > \lambda_2 | H_1) \quad (19)$$

Comparing (16) and (19), since the stochastic resonance double threshold two step detection algorithm and the stochastic resonance energy detection statistic are the same, both methods have the same detection probability.

The reference paper [11] and [12] proposed and discussed the compromise optimization of satellite communication network sensing and throughput. The perceptual time in a frame of user is obtained by maximizing the throughput of the satellite communication network, so

$$\max_{ts} R(\tau_s) = \frac{T_f - \tau_s}{T_f}\left[C_0 \mathrm{P}(\mathrm{H}_0)(1 - \mathrm{P}_f(\tau_s)) + C_1 \mathrm{P}(\mathrm{H}_1)(1 - \mathrm{P}_d(\tau_s)\right] \\ \text{s.t.} \quad P_d(\tau_s) > \overline{P_d} \tag{20}$$

Among, τ_s is sensing time, Tf is MAC frame length, C_0 represents the throughput of authorized users is not occupy the channel, C1 represents the throughput of authorized users is occupy the channel, $P_d(\tau_s)$ is the detection probability, $P_f(\tau_s)$ is the false alarm probability, $\overline{P_d}$ is the target detection probability required by the PU.

In fact, since the occupancy rate of the PU to the target frequency band is no more than 0.3, the maximum satellite communication network throughput R can be equivalent to the maximization function $R_0 = C_0 P(H_0)(1 - \tau/T)(1 - P_f(\tau))$. Among the new Algorithm, $\lambda_1 \leq Tr^* < \lambda_2$, so P can be written as:

$$\mathrm{P}_1 = P(\lambda_1 \leq Tr^* < \lambda_2/H_0) + P(\lambda_1 \leq Tr^* < \lambda_2/H_1) \tag{21}$$

In this paper, the average sensing time required: $\tau_{T-SR} = \tau_1 + P\tau_2$, so τ_1 and τ_2 can be obtained by optimizing the throughput in the algorithm. The Throughput optimization problem of the double-threshold signal detection algorithm based on stochastic resonance technology can be described as:

$$\max_{\tau_1,\tau_2} \mathrm{C_0P(H_0)}(1 - \frac{(\tau_1 + P_1\tau_2)}{T})(1 - \mathrm{P}_{F\_SR}) \\ \text{s.t. } \tau_1 + \tau_2 \leq T \tag{22}$$

To simplify the analysis, it is assumed that additive channel noise $n(t)$ fully meets the requirements for noise when stochastic resonance system synergizes. In other words, the input noise power is 0, so P_{F_SR} can be written as:

$$P_{F\_SR} = Q(1 + \frac{1}{\eta})Q^{-1}(\bar{P}_{D\_SR}) + \frac{1}{\eta}\sqrt{f_s(\tau_1 + \tau_2)/2} \tag{23}$$

Among, $\bar{P}_{D\_SR}$ is the target detection probability given to ensure the communication quality of PU, the formula (22) Can be further expressed as:

$$\max_{\tau_1,\tau_2} \mathrm{C_0P(H_0)}(1 - \frac{(\tau_1 + P_1\tau_2)}{T})(1 - Q(1 + \frac{1}{\eta})Q^{-1}(\bar{P}_{D\_SR}) + \frac{1}{\eta}\sqrt{f_s(\tau_1 + \tau_2)/2}) \\ \text{s.t. } \tau_1 + \tau_2 \leq T \tag{24}$$

When the perceived duration τ_1 or τ_2 is fixed, the optimization objective function is simplified into a convex optimization problem. For the one-dimensional convex optimization problem, the conventional efficient method can be used to solve the optimization problem.

4 Simulation Results and Analysis

The above theoretical derivation and analysis are verified by simulation. In order to improve the detection performance, a typical bistable system is used in the simulation. Its potential function is $V(x) = -\frac{1}{2}x^2 + \frac{1}{4}x^4$, other user signals use BPSK signals with a frequency of 10 kHz. The signal received by the user is a signal that superimposes additive white Gaussian noise after the other user signals and other BPSK interference signals pass through the flat slow fading channel.

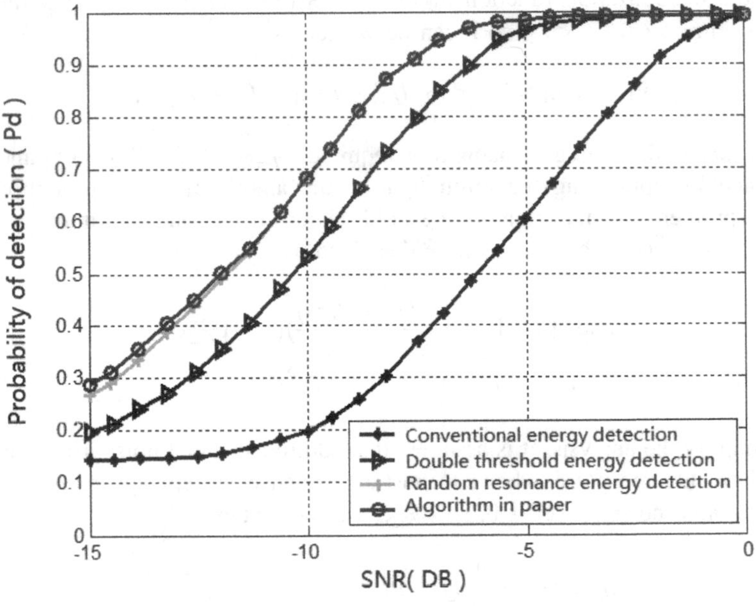

Fig. 5. Signal-to-noise ratio and the detection probability curve

Figure 5 shows the signal detection algorithm for conventional energy detection, double threshold energy detection, stochastic resonance energy detection and stochastic resonance double-threshold two-step energy detection under different conditions of sample number N = 1000 and false alarm probability of 0.05. Comparison of simulation probability under noise ratio conditions; Fig. 6 shows a comparison of receiver operating characteristics at a signal-to-noise ratio of −10 dB. It can be seen from the figure that compared with the conventional energy detection, based on the stochastic resonance energy detection algorithm, the detection probability is significantly improved under low noise conditions, the signal detection algorithm based on stochastic resonance energy detection and stochastic resonance double threshold two step energy detection is superior to conventional energy detection and dual-threshold energy detection algorithms. From the simulation diagram, we also found that the stochastic resonance energy detection and the double-threshold energy signal detection algorithms based on stochastic resonance have the same detection performance regardless of the conditions, which also verifies the correctness of the theoretical derivation.

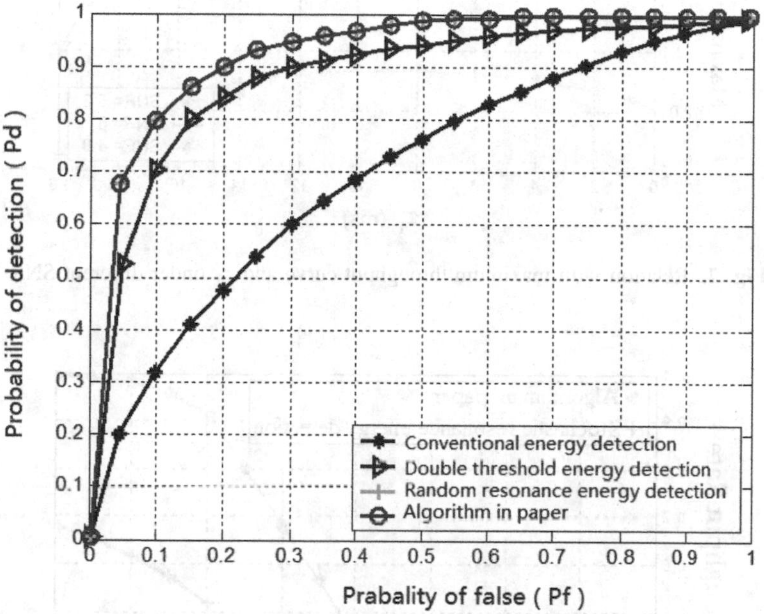

Fig. 6. Detection performance curve comparison chart

Now let's verify the throughput optimization problem. Take the MAC frame length as 60 ms. The sampling frequency of BPSK signal is 10 kHz. Assuming that P $(H_0) = P(H_1) = 0.5$, $\bar{P}_d = 0.9$. The maximum reachable throughput under different τ_1 and all possible τ_2 is shown in Fig. 7.

It can be seen that under different SNR, the curve of its maximum achievable throughput is convex. So, under all possible conditions, it can always find one that enables the maximum through put to be reached. When the SNR is at −5 dB, it reaches the maximum value $\tau_1 = 8$ ms, which is 2.2790. When the SNR is −5.2 dB, it reaches the maximum value $\tau_1 = 10$ ms, which is 2.0839.

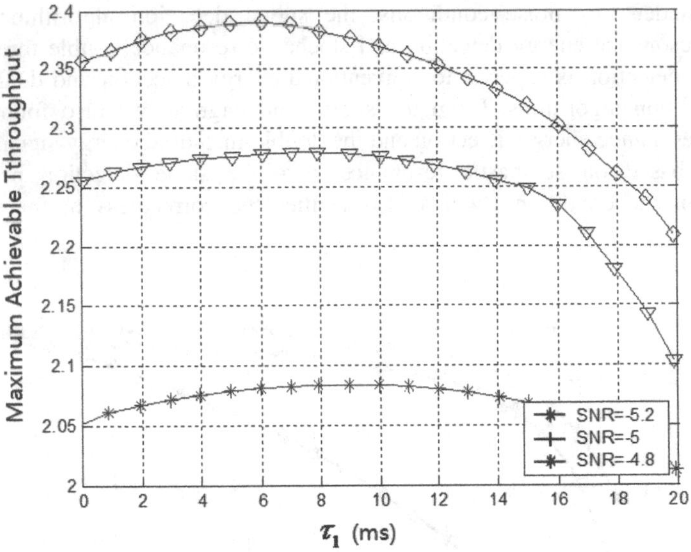

Fig. 7. Relation with maximum throughput curve and τ_1 under different SNR

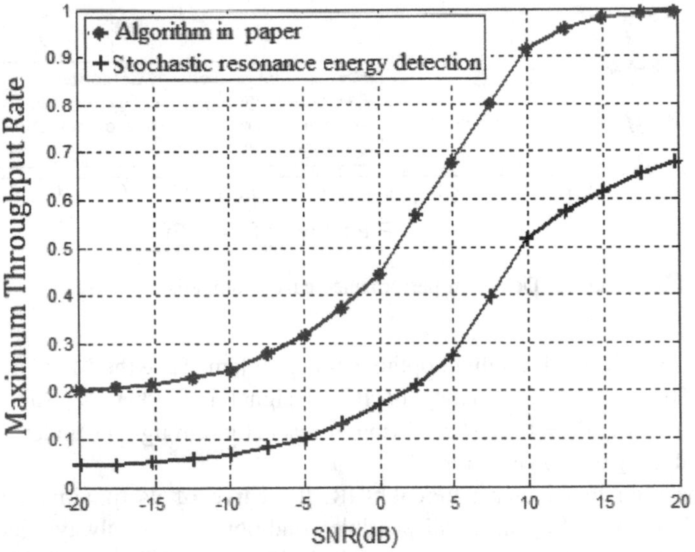

Fig. 8. The contrast of the Maximum throughput rate under different SNR

Furthermore, the maximum throughput rate and optimal average perceived time of the two algorithms are simulated under different signal-to-noise ratios. In the simulation condition, the SNR under H_0 condition is set to 20 dB, under H_1 condition is −10 dB, the MAC frame length is 50 ms, and P(H0) = 0.7, the detection probability is set to 0.9.

Figure 8 shows the comparison of maximum reachable satellite communication network throughput rate under different signal-to-noise ratios between the double-threshold signal detection algorithm based on stochastic resonance and the energy detection algorithm based on stochastic resonance. It can be seen from the simulation figure that compared with the energy detection method based on stochastic resonance, double-threshold signal detection algorithm based on stochastic resonance can achieve a large network throughput with less perception time.

5 Conclusion

In this paper, the satellite communication is performed under the condition of low SNR. According to the characteristics of the stochastic resonance system with enhanced other user signals received by the user, a double threshold signal detection algorithm based on stochastic resonance is proposed. And two decision thresholds are derived to determine the double threshold perception algorithm. When the access user needs to perform random resonance processing on the normal user signal received by the user, the effective detection of the small signal with low SNR condition is realized. The simulation results show that the detection performance is effectively improved. This method has higher signal detection efficiency, better universal applicability and throughput, so the double-threshold signal detection algorithm based on stochastic resonance improves the satellite communication network performance effectively.

Acknowledgement. This work is supported by Heilongjiang Natural Science Fund Project (F2015019, F2015017) (2017RAXXJ055), and Heilongjiang Provincial Postdoctoral Fund Project (LBH-Z16054).

References

1. He, D., He, C., Jiang, L.: Spectrum sensing approach based on optimal stochastic resonance technique under color noise background in cognitive radio networks. In: 2010 IEEE International Conference on Communications Workshops (ICC), pp. 1–4 (2010)
2. Lin, Y., He, C., Jiang, L.: A cyclostationary-based spectrum sensing method using stochastic resonance in cognitive radio. In: IEEE International Conference on Communications Workshops (ICC), pp. 1–5 (2010)
3. Chen, H., Varshney, P.K.: Theory of the stochastic resonance effect in signal detection—part II: variable detectors. IEEE Trans. Sig. Process. **56**(10), 5031–5041 (2008)
4. He, D., Lin, Y.P., He, C.: A novel spectrum sensing technique in cognitive radio based on stochastic resonance. IEEE Trans. Veh. Technol. **59**(4), 1680–1688 (2010)
5. Jia, M., Gu, X., Guo, Q., Xiang, W., Zhang, N.: Broadband hybrid satellite-terrestrial communication systems based on cognitive radio toward 5G. IEEE Wirel. Commun. **23**(6), 96–106 (2016)
6. Jia, M., Liu, X., Gu, X., Guo, Q.: Joint cooperative spectrum sensing and channel selection optimization for satellite communication systems based on cognitive radio. Int. J. Satell. Commun. Netw. **35**(2), 139–150 (2017)

7. Jiang, X.L., Gu, X.M.: Double threshold collaborative spectrum sensing algorithm based on energy detection. J. Hei LongJiang Univ. Sci. Technol. 553–556 (2016)
8. Chen, H., Varshney, P.K., Kay, S.M.: Theory of the stochastic resonance effect in signal detection: part I—fixed detectors. IEEE Trans. Sig. Process. **55**(7), 3172–3184 (2007)
9. Kawaguchi, M., Mino, H., Momose, K., Durand, D.M.: Stochastic resonance with a mixture of sub-and supra-threshold stimuli in a population of neuron models. In: IEEE International Conference on Engineering in Medicine and Biology Society (EMBC), pp. 7328–7331 (2011)
10. Wu, J.: A cooperative double-threshold energy detection algorithm in cognitive radio systems. In: IEEE International Conference on Wireless Communications Networking and Mobile Computing (2009)
11. Liang, Y.C., Zeng, Y.: Sensing-throughput tradeoff for cognitive radio networks. IEEE Trans. Wirel. Commun. **7**(4), 1326–1337 (2008)
12. Peh, E.C.Y., Liang, Y.C., Guan, Y.L.: Optimization of cooperative sensing in cognitive radio networks: a sensing-throughput tradeoff view. IEEE Trans. Veh. Technol. **58**(9), 5294–5299 (2009)

International Workshop on Advances in Communications and Computing for Internet-of-Things

Resource Allocation Schemes Based on Improved Beetle Antennae Search Algorithm for Collaborative Communication of the Unmanned Aerial Vehicle Network

Xujie Li[1,2(✉)], Lingjie Zhou[1], Ying Sun[1], Siyuan Zhou[1], and Mu Lu[3]

[1] College of Computer and Information, Hohai University, Nanjing 210098, China
lixujie@hhu.edu.cn
[2] Suqian Research Institute of Hohai University, Suqian 223800, China
[3] Jiangsu Suyuan Jierui Science & Technology Co., Ltd., Suqian 223800, China

Abstract. In this paper, the resource allocation problem for collaborative communication of unmanned aerial vehicle network is formulated and analyzed. In our scenario, the unmanned aerial vehicles (UAVs) are uniformly distributed in the network. We consider that multiple UAVs can share one channel resource. First, a system model is established and the resource allocation problem is formulated. Then a resource allocation scheme based on the improved beetle antennae search algorithm is proposed, which finds the optimum solution efficiently. Finally, the simulation results show that the performance of the proposed the improved beetle antennae search algorithm is better than that of random algorithm. This scheme provides an efficient optimization for resource allocation of collaborative communication of UAVs.

Keywords: Unmanned aerial vehicle (UAV) · Resource allocation · Beetle antennae search algorithm

1 Introduction

Unmanned aerial vehicle (UVA) is an aircraft operated by radio remote control equipment and automatic program control device. With the spread of the UAV project, UAVs have been introduced into application in recent years [1]. Therefore, the scarcity of the radio spectrum prompts us to consider improving the spectrum resources. Direct communication between UAVs can overcome the problem and improve the spectral efficiency.

In UAV communication system, when UAV pairs share the same spectrum resource with other UAV pairs, they will interfere with each other. So resource allocation is the important part of improving the spectrum resources which attracts many researchers all around the world. In [2], the authors analyze the deployment of an UAV as a base station to provide the wireless communications. The coverage and rate are mainly analyzed in two scenarios: a static UAV and a mobile UAV. Simulation results show that the optimal values for the UAV altitude can lead to maximum sum-rate and

M. Jia et al. (Eds.): WiSATS 2019, LNICST 281, pp. 275–282, 2019.
https://doi.org/10.1007/978-3-030-19156-6_26

coverage probability. The small world network theory is introduced into wireless sensor networks to improve the network performance. The authors introduce this theory into real-time of UAV and use the ant colony algorithm to realize real-time update and data transmission [3]. In [4], an adaptive vertical array antenna technique into wireless broadband modem for UAV communication is proposed to overcome the problem of the altitude limitation. The authors propose the frame structure and a resource allocation algorithm to satisfy the high network throughput. The result shows that this algorithm can allocate the resource effectively [5]. This paper focus on the use of UAVs in the scenario of the disaster and the frequency resource is considered that shared by the adjacent UAVs. The radio resource management system is proposed to improve the communication of the data [6]. In [7], the cooperative game theory is proposed to solve the problem for the resource allocation of UAVs group performing a task. In [8], the authors mainly discuss the power control, capacity optimization and suppression of interference in D2D communication system. In [9], a combining call admission control and power control scheme is proposed under guaranteeing QoS of user equipment (UE).

The main contributions of our work are as follows:

1. We propose a resource allocation scheme based on the improved beetle antennae search algorithm for collaborative communication of unmanned aerial vehicle network.
2. We select the system capacity as a factor for evaluating system performance.

The rest of this paper is organized as follows. In Sect. 2, we describe the system model of unmanned aerial vehicles (UAVs) network. In Sect. 3, a resource allocation scheme based on beetle antennae search algorithm is proposed and discussed. In Sect. 4, the capacity of the UVAs as the performance of the communication system is simulated and analyzed. Finally, the conclusion is drawn out in Sect. 5.

2 System Model and Problem Formulation

2.1 Channel Allocation Mode

There are two types of UAVs in collaborative communication network: transmitting unmanned aerial vehicles (TUAVs) and receiving unmanned aerial vehicles (RUAVs). In this scenario, we consider TUAVs and RUAVs come in pairs. We assume that all UAVs in the network are uniformly distributed inside a cube with the side length A. We analyze the transmission in the communication network as show in Fig. 1. When the UAVs share the same spectrum resources, they get the same frequency interference. The solid black line represents the communication link between the UAV pair. The remaining dotted line represents the interference of the RUAV from the other TUAVs at the same frequency.

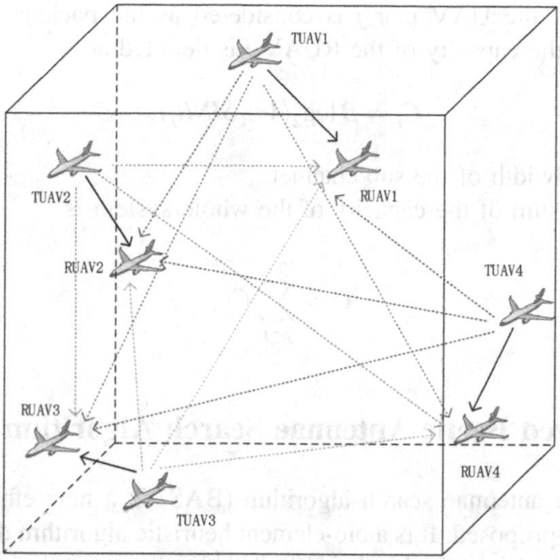

Fig. 1. The system model of the UAV

2.2 Problem Formulation

In the system model, M channel resources are allocated to N UAV pairs. We choose the maximum capacity to evaluate the performance. To guaranty the Quality of Service (QoS) of the system, the signal to interference plus noise ratio should be larger than SINR threshold β. When the UAVs communicate with each other, the interference of the RUAV j is:

$$I_j = \sum_{\substack{k \in \Re_m \\ k \neq j}} \frac{P_T}{d_{k,j}^{\alpha}} \tag{1}$$

Here, P_T is the transmitting power of the TUAV, $d_{k,j}$ denotes the distance between kth TUAV and jth RUAV, $\Re_m$ denotes the mth sub-channel, α is the path loss factor.

Therefore, during the communication period for the RUAV j, the SINR can be written as

$$SINR_j = \frac{P_T / d_j^{\alpha}}{I_j + N_0} \tag{2}$$

Here, d_j denotes the distance between TUAV j and RUAV j, N_0 is the noise power.

For UAV pairs, the UAV piar j is considered as the package m. According to Shannon theorem, the capacity of the RUAV j is denoted as

$$C_j = B\log_2(1 + SINR_j) \tag{3}$$

Here, B is the bandwidth of the sub-channel.

Obviously, the sum of the capacity of the whole system is

$$C = \sum_{j=1}^{N} C_j \tag{4}$$

3 The Improved Beetle Antennae Search Algorithm

In 2017, the beetle antennae search algorithm (BAS) is a new efficient search optimization algorithm proposed. It is a bio-element heuristic algorithm developed inspired by the foraging behavior of the beetles [10]. This intelligent optimization algorithm is different from those swarm intelligence algorithms. There is only one individual search for the better solution in the each iteration. Therefore, the computational complexity of the algorithm is greatly reduced.

3.1 Description of the Beetle Antennae Search Algorithm

The beetles forage for food depending on the strength of the food smell. They have two antennae which are used to judge the direction of the food. If the left antenna receives a stronger smell than the right one, the beetle will fly to the left; otherwise it will fly to the right. Each foraging process corresponds to the each iteration of finding the optimal solution.

The initial solution of the beetle antennae search algorithm is the initial position of the beetle, which is randomly generated. x^t denotes the position of the beetle at t time instance. *dir* denotes the direction vector of the right antennae pointing to the left antennae and it is random in each step. The beetle can search in the k-dimension space, so that x^t and *dir* are k-dimension vector. *dir* is defined as follows:

$$\begin{aligned} dir &= rands(k, 1) \\ dir &= dir/norm(dir) \end{aligned} \tag{5}$$

Here, the rands (.) denotes the random function, and the norm (.) denotes the normalization function.

Step represents the search step and changes with the iteration times. The initial step is larger for search for global optimal solution. *eta* is the attenuation coefficient of the search step. d_0 represents the distance between the two antennae. c is a constant and the ratio of *step* to d_0. n denotes the iteration times. The initial values of these parameters are as follows: $step = 10$, $eta = 0.95$, $c = 5$, $n = 100$.

After the initialization, the value of objective function of the left antennae and right antennae can be generated according to the Eq. (6).

$$\begin{aligned} f_l &= f(x + dir * d_0) \\ f_r &= f(x - dir * d_0) \end{aligned} \tag{6}$$

The objective function values are judged by the function sign (.). The expression of the x^t is as followed:

$$x^t = x^{t-1} - \text{step}^t dir * sign(f(x_l - x_r)) \tag{7}$$

By comparing f(x^t) and f(x^{t-1}), keep the maximum value of the function is preserved.

The solution of the algorithm will eventually evolve to a convergence with enough the iteration times. We will obtain the solution and optimal objective function value.

3.2 The Improved Beetle Antennae Search Algorithm

The beetle algorithm is originally used to solve the optimal problem of continuous function, but the practical application problem in this paper is combinatorial optimization. We refer the mutation operation of genetic algorithm to carry out mutation operation on the position of the beetle. Therefore, we can improve the diversity of solutions and avoid falling into the local optimum too early in the iteration process. The detailed steps of the improved beetle antennae search algorithm are as follows:

1. **Initialization**
   x^t is randomly generated as the initial solution. Each value of vector x^t represents which channel the UAV pair is in. For example, x^t = (3, 2, 5, 1, 3, 4, 1, 5, 2…) denotes the UAV_1 and UAV_5 share the third sub-channel, UAV_2 and UAV_9 share the second sub-channel, UAV_3 and UAV_8 share the fifth sub-channel and so on. The value of the vector x^t is an integer limited between 1 and 5.
2. **Search for the new solution**
   The spatial dimension of the optimal solution searched by the algorithm is k. When k is larger than 2, the direction of the left or right doesn't make much sense anymore. We consider the left and the right is a random direction in k-dimension space. We refer the mutation operation of genetic algorithm, randomly selecting a value in the k-dimension vector and mutating it. The mutation operation is to randomly select a part of the position to mutate to produce a better position. The purpose of doing so is to maintain the diversity of the position.
3. **Stopping criteria**
   With the increasing of the iteration times, the solution of the improved algorithm will evolve to a convergence. Finally, we achieve the best solution and global optimal objective function value (Table 1).

Table 1. Improved beetle antennae search algorithm specific steps

Improved beetle antennae search algorithm specific steps:
1. Parameter settings.
2. First, randomly generate the solution corresponding to the left and right antennae, and then calculate the objective function values.
3. Compare the values of objective function and select the larger value $f(x^t)$ to compare with the value of $f(x^{t-1})$. Keep the maximum value of the function is preserved
4. Judge whether the iteration is over. If not, return to step 2.

4 Simulations and Discussions

In our simulation, we assume that TUAVs follow a uniform distribution in the cube. The side length of the model is A. The RUAVs follow a uniform distribution centered on the corresponding TUAVs in the sphere of the radius L. Simulation parameters are summarized in Table 2.

Table 2. Simulation parameters.

Parameter	Value	Parameter	Value
Model length A	200 m	The number of UAV pairs	20
L	30 m	The bandwidth of the sub-channel B	0.2 MHz
Path loss factor α	4	The transmission power of UAV	0.01 W
SINR threshold β	4.6 dB	N_0	−90 dBm

Figure 2 shows the capacity of UAV communications with the change of the iteration times by using different algorithms. We make this simulation by Monte Carlo method. We analyze the system capacity performance of the beetle antennae search algorithm and random algorithm. The blue line represents the minimum value during the iterative process. It can be seen that beetle antennae search algorithm has the ability of searching the global optimal solution and is not easy to run into the local optimization solution. Compared with the random algorithm, the beetle antennae search algorithm has better performance and the fast convergence speed.

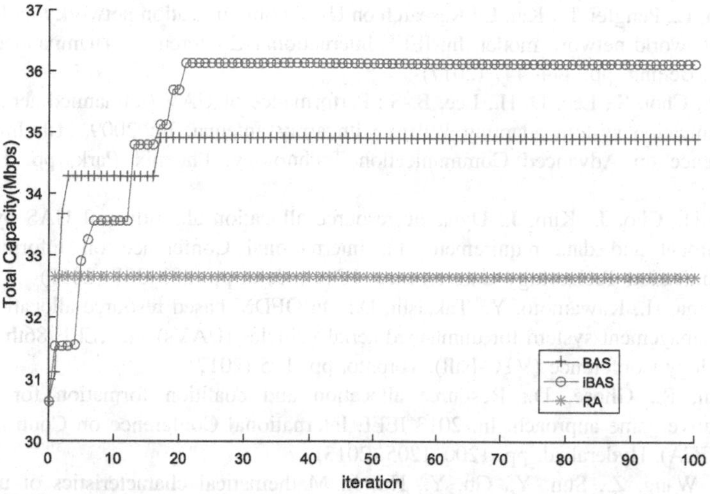

Fig. 2. The capacity of UAV communications

5 Conclusions

In this paper, the resource allocation problem for collaborative communication of unmanned aerial vehicle group is formulated and analyzed. In our scenario, UAVs are uniformly distributed in the network. We establish a system model and formulate the resource allocation problem. To improve the performance of the system communication, a resource allocation scheme based on beetle antennae search algorithm is proposed. Beetle antennae search algorithm finds the optimum solution efficiently. Finally, the simulation results show that the performance of the proposed beetle antennae search algorithm is better than that of random algorithm. This result can be applied for the resource allocation UAVs collaborative communication.

Acknowledgements. This work was supported in part by the Fundamental Research Funds for the Central Universities (No. 2017B14214, 2018B53114), Six Talent Peaks project in Jiangsu (No. DZXX-008), National Natural Science Foundation of China (No. 61301110) and Research & Development Plan of Suqian City (No. H201719).

References

1. Jiang, H., Zhang, Z., Wu, L., Dang, J.: Three-dimensional geometry-based UAV-MIMO channel modeling for A2G communication environments. IEEE Commun. Lett. **22**(7), 1438–1441 (2018)
2. Mozaffari, M., Saad, W., Bennis, M., Debbah, M.: Unmanned aerial vehicle with underlaid device-to-device communications: performance and tradeoffs. IEEE Trans. Wirel. Commun. **15**(6), 3949–3963 (2016)

3. Jingnan, L., Pengfei, L., Kai, L.: Research on UAV communication network topology based on small world network model. In: IEEE International Conference on Unmanned Systems (ICUS), Beijing, pp. 444–447 (2017)
4. Park, P., Choi, S., Lee, D.-H., Lee, B.-S.: Performance of UAV (unmanned aerial vehicle) communication system adapting WiBro with array antenna. In: 2009 11th International Conference on Advanced Communication Technology, Phoenix Park, pp. 1233–1237 (2009)
5. Cheon, H., Cho, J., Kim, J.: Dynamic resource allocation algorithm of UAS by network environment and data requirement. In: International Conference on Information and Communication Technology Convergence (ICTC), Jeju, pp. 383–387 (2017)
6. Nishiyama, H., Kawamoto, Y., Takaishi, D.: On OFDM-based resource allocation in LTE radio management system for unmanned aerial vehicles (UAVs). In: IEEE 86th Vehicular Technology Conference (VTC-Fall), Toronto, pp. 1–5 (2017)
7. Bardhan, R., Ghose, D.: Resource allocation and coalition formation for UAVs: a cooperative game approach. In: 2013 IEEE International Conference on Control Applications (CCA), Hyderabad, pp. 1200–1205 (2013)
8. Li, X., Wang, Z., Sun, Y., Gu, Y., Hu, J.: Mathematical characteristics of uplink and downlink interference regions in D2D communications underlaying cellular networks. Wirel. Pers. Commun. **93**(4), 917–932 (2017)
9. Li, X., Zhang, W., Zhang, H., Li, W.: A combining call admission control and power control scheme for D2D communications underlaying cellular networks. China Commun. **13**(10), 137–145 (2016)
10. Zhu, Z., Zhang, Z., Man, W., Tong, X., Qiu, J., Li, F.: A new beetle antennae search algorithm for multi-objective energy management in microgrid. In: 2018 13th IEEE Conference on Industrial Electronics and Applications (ICIEA), Wuhan, pp. 1599–1603 (2018)

A Novel Resource Optimization Algorithm for Dynamic Networks Combined with NFV and SDN

Qian Zhang[1], Xiaohua Qiu[2], and Xiaorong Zhu[1(✉)]

[1] Nanjing University of Posts and Telecommunications, Nanjing 210003, China
xrzhu@njupt.edu.cn

[2] Nanjing Institute of Technology, Nanjing 210003, China

Abstract. Various services of Internet of Things (IoT) require flexible network deployment to guarantee different quality of services (QoS). Aiming at the problem of service function chain deployment, in this paper, we propose the combination of NFV and SDN to optimize resources. Considering forwarding cost and traffic load balance, a joint optimization model of virtual network function (VNF) placement and service function chain routing is given and is proved to be NP-Hard. In order to solve this model, we propose two heuristic algorithms. One is the service function chain deployment algorithm of First Routing Then Placing (FRTP) and the other is the Placing Followed by Routing (PFBR) based on node priority. Simulation results show that the former can reduce forwarding times and bandwidth consumption than the latter. And PFBR algorithm outperforms in balancing network traffic load and improving the acceptance ratio of the chain requests compared with other algorithms.

Keywords: IoT · VNF · Service function chain deployment · Node priority · Load balance

1 Introduction

With the development of the Internet of Things, the demands of various services are increasingly diversified [1]. For example, the ideal latency for Internet of Vehicles is almost zero; it is necessary to control the lowest packet loss and ultra-low latency in industrial manufacturing; the mobile video surveillance networks need higher bandwidth.

To satisfy those distinct QoS requirements simultaneously, Software Defined Networking (SDN) could offer smart routing and scheduling solutions. Network Function Virtualization (NFV) uses virtualization to eliminate dependencies on

Foundation Items: National Natural Science Foundation of China (61871237), National Science and Technology Major Project (2017ZX03001008), Postgraduate Research & Practice Innovation Program of Jiangsu Province (KYCX17_0767), Natural Science Foundation of the Higher Education Institutions of Jiangsu Province (16KJA510005) and YKJ201422.

M. Jia et al. (Eds.): WiSATS 2019, LNICST 281, pp. 283–296, 2019.
https://doi.org/10.1007/978-3-030-19156-6_27

dedicated hardware and consolidates different types of network devices onto industry-standard and high-capacity servers, switches or storage [2], which reduces costs of network equipment meanwhile enhancing the sharing capacity of network resources and quality of service. And virtualization in the form of network slicing could be used to isolate IoT use-cases with conflicting requirements.

Although the combination of SDN and NFV is expected to meet the diversified demands of services of the Internet of Things, NFV abstracts and finely decomposes network services, making its components more complex. The service function chain (Service Function Chain, SFC) deployment is the key challenge. Due to its large size of services and high dynamic network load, the complex service-driven dynamic network construction mechanism of Internet of Things is a challenge for both the current and future network. The existing dedicated network faces severe defects such as stiff network architecture, unreasonable function plane partitioning and difficulty in network upgrades and maintenance, which makes it hard to cope with the ever-changing requirements of the Internet of Things.

For the resource allocation of NFV, the authors of [3] propose a comprehensive cost model to meet the needs of users and achieve the lowest cost. Moens et al. consider the scenario where physical network functions and virtual network functions coexist [4], then decide what kind of the functions to be placed to make full use of the physical and virtual resources. Reference [5] uses graph theory to solve the problem of resource allocation in NFV, where network functions and servers (with multiple virtual machines) are regarded as two disjoint subsets in a bipartite graph. The resource utilization and the bandwidth utilization are weighed with the coefficients so as to achieve load balancing in the network [6]. Nam et al. [7] introduce the NFV to the radio access network. It is possible to allocate nearby base stations to obtain a lower latency experience. NFV is extended to the radio access section [8], and the main drawback is that each function can only be deployed once, and be placed on different nodes, which, to some extent, introduces link latency. Reference [9] locates the scene in the enterprise network, and it is committed to reducing the total cost of deploying virtual network functions. In order to implement service chain deployment, [10] considers sharing virtual network functions among service chains (SCs) and avoiding bandwidth consumption by deploying adjacent VNFs in one node. Reference [11] aims at minimizing NFV nodes as an optimization target for the VNFs sharing of multiple SFCs.

Although an increasing number of the researches on NFV resource allocation and SDN routing strategies, there are still many areas need to be improved. For example, in most researches, VNFs required by service function chains merely occupy a single kind of resource, and almost do not consider the case where multi-dimensional resources such as computation and storage are needed at the same time. In addition, some papers focus on one aspect of NFV resource allocation or SDN routing strategies, resulting in local optimal solution. How to coordinate the relationship between them deserves further study.

In this context, this paper studies the resource allocation method of NFV and SDN in dynamic service network. According to the dynamic changes of network status and service characteristics, a joint optimization model is proposed to determine the resource allocation and routing strategies of service-driven optimal transmission performance. In order to facilitate the optimization model, we propose two heuristic algorithms according to the order of VNFs placement and service flow routing. One is the service function chain deployment algorithm of First Routing Then Placing (FRTP) and the other is the Placing Followed by Routing (PFBR) based on node priority. The former is more focused on reducing forwarding times and bandwidth consumption than the latter. And PFBR algorithm outperforms in balancing network traffic load and improving the acceptance ratio of the chain requests compared with other algorithms.

The rest of this paper is organized as follows. Section 2 describes the problem of deployment of service function chain. In Sect. 3, a joint optimization model of virtual network function placement and service function chain routing is given. We present our solutions in Sect. 4. In Sect. 5, we validate the algorithms and discuss the results. Section 6 concludes the paper.

2 System Description

In this paper we assume that the service function chain deployment involves two aspects. In one aspect, we place a series of virtual network functions on the NFV enabled nodes to meet user-customized network services. And the other is that, the paths are selected according to the demands of service function chain until a complete end-to-end service path is formed.

In order to perform the resource allocation of the service function chains, we model the physical network as a undirected graph denoted by $G = (V, E)$, where $V = \{v_n | n = 1, 2, \ldots, N\}$ represents the set of nodes and E is the set of the links. Resource capacity of each node is C_n^t and is associated with its type $t \in T$ (e.g., computing, storage and so on). To be noted that if $C_n^t > 0, t \in T$, the node v_n can host different VNFs unless its capacity is less than the demand of VNFs. Otherwise, the node v_n only be able to forward packets. Each link $e \in E$ is associated with a bandwidth capacity B_e.

There are many kinds of VNFs, f_x represents the x_th kind in the VNF set $F = \{f_x | x = 1, 2, \ldots, X\}$. The resource demands of f_x is $C_x^t, t \in T$. Service function chain is composed by a series of VNFs and need to be traversed in particular order. Suppose there are a total of K service function chains in a period of time, the set of which can be expressed as $S = \{S^k | k = 1, 2, \ldots, K\}$. For S^k, it contains source node, destination node and a series of VNFs and can be expressed as $N^k = \{s^k, f_1^k, f_2^k, \ldots, f_M^k | f_m^k \in F, d^k\}$, where $m = 0$ and $m = M + 1$ represents the source and destination node respectively. Then, the set of neighbor nodes of f_m^k are represented as $\eta^k(m)$, which indicates the adjacent virtual functions of f_m^k.

And $E^k = \{(s^k, f_1^k), (f_1^k, f_2^k), \ldots, (f_{M-1}^k, f_M^k), (f_M^k, d^k)\}$ describes the logical link set. Suppose that the QoS of S^k can be represented by r^k, the demand of bandwidth. In addition, $q_{mx}^k \in \{0, 1\}$ is introduced in our model. It implies whether the kind of f_m^k in S^k is f_x and hence its resource requirement is indicated as $\sum_{x \in X} q_{mx}^k \cdot C_x^t, t \in T, T = \{\text{computing, storage,} \ldots\}$.

As shown in Fig. 1, the service function chain requires five VNFs. On the one hand, five virtual network functions are assigned at physical node 1, 2, 3, 4, 3. On the other hand, the computed path by the controller is (s,1)→(1,2)→(2,3)→(3,5)→(5,4)→(4,3)→(3,t). Both of the two aspects represent resource allocation and link mapping in one service function chain.

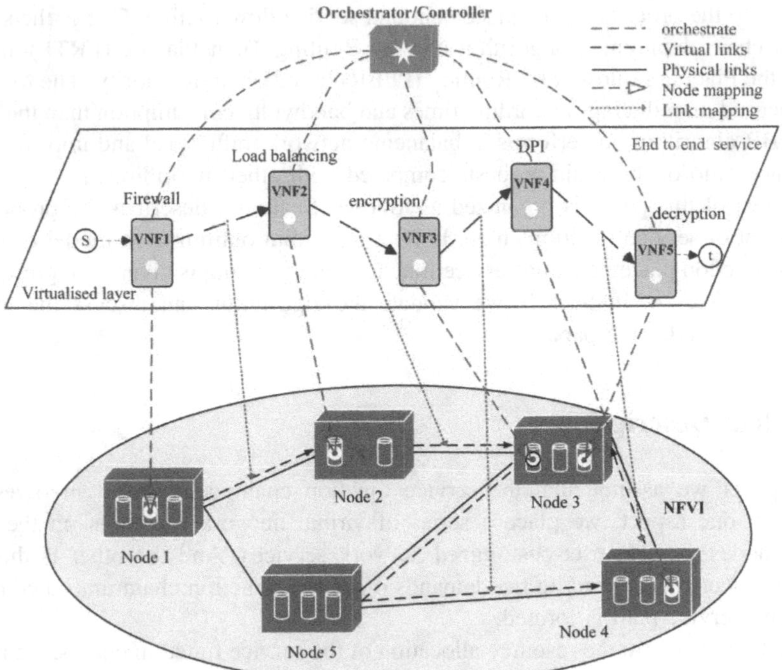

Fig. 1. Resource allocation and link mapping in one service function chain

As a consequence, we define several sets of variables to indicate above process. The first is $a_m^k(n)$, and it equals 1 if f_m^k in S^k is placed on node v_n, and 0 otherwise. The next is $l_{m_1m_2}^{k,p}(n_1, n_2)$, and it equals 1 when the logical link $(m_1, m_2) \in E^k$ of S^k is routed by the path p from node n_1 to n_2, where $p \in P(n_1, n_2)$ and $P(n_1, n_2)$ is the link set between node n_1 and n_2. The last is $\varphi^k \in \{0, 1\}$, it equals 1 if the S^k is accepted, and 0 otherwise. Furthermore, if $\varphi^k = 0$, then $\sum_{n \in N} a_m^k(n) = 0$ and $\sum_{p \in P(n_1,n_2)} l_{m_1m_2}^{k,p}(n_1, n_2) = 0$.

3 Service Function Chain Deployment

The service function chain is regard as a form of service. From the user's point of view, the key is real-time response. But from long-term of network operation, it is essential to improve resource utilization. Accordingly, the optimization goal of this paper consists of two aspects. One is to minimize the total forwarding costs of service function chains as (1). It is related to forwarding times and bandwidth requirements. And the other is to balance the traffic load as much as possible. We use the degree of load balancing to measure the maximum link utilization in the network and they are represented as (2) and (3) respectively. The lower degree of load balancing is, the more balanceable the traffic loads are.

It should be noted that if the request is not deployed, the total forwarding cost and the link utilization are lower. However, which cannot satisfy their needs. Penalty functions are introduced when SFCs are rejected, and they are expressed as (4) and (5). Therefore, the overall objective is formulated as (6), where coefficients and indicate the weight of the two different aspects.

$$C_{forward} = \sum_{S^k \in S} \sum_{(m_1,m_2)\in E^k} \sum_{n_1,n_2 \in N} \sum_{p \in P(n_1,n_2)} l^{k,p}_{m_1 m_2}(n_1,n_2) \cdot r^k \cdot |p| \quad (1)$$

$$d_{load} = \max_{e \in E} R_e / B_e \times 100\% \quad (2)$$

$$R_e = \sum_{S^k \in S} \sum_{(m_1,m_2)\in E^k} \sum_{n_1,n_2 \in N} \sum_{p \in P(n_1,n_2)} l^{k,p}_{m_1 m_2}(n_1,n_2) \cdot r^k \quad (3)$$

$$C_{penalty} = \sum_{S^k \in S} (1-\varphi^k) r^k \cdot \max_{p \in P(s^k,d^k)} |p| \quad (4)$$

$$d_{penalty} = \left(\sum_{S^k \in S} (1-\varphi^k) r^k \right) \Big/ \min_{e \in E} B_e \quad (5)$$

$$\min \alpha \cdot (C_{forward} + C_{penalty}) + \beta \cdot (d_{load} + d_{penalty}) \quad (6)$$

$$\sum_{n \in N} a^k_m(n) \le 1, \quad \forall m \in N^k, S^k \in S \quad (7)$$

$$\sum_{f^k_n \in s^k} \sum_{n \in N} a^k_m(n) = \varphi^k \cdot \left(|N^k| - 2\right), \quad \forall S^k \in S \quad (8)$$

$$\sum_{S^k \in s} \sum_{f^k_m \in S^k} \sum_{x \in X} a^k_m(n) \cdot q^k_{mx} \cdot C^t_x \le C^t_n, \forall t \in T, \forall n \in N \quad (9)$$

$$\sum_{n_1,n_2 \in N} \sum_{p \in P(n_1,n_2)} l^{k,p}_{m_1 m_2}(n_1,n_2) = a^k_{m_1}(n_1) \times a^k_{m_2}(n_2)$$
$$\forall (m_1,m_2) \in E^k, \forall S^k \in S \quad (10)$$

$$l^{k,p_1}_{m_1 m_2}(n_1,n_2) + l^{k,p_2}_{m_1 m_2}(n_2,n_1) \le 1$$
$$\forall n_1,n_2 \in N, \forall S^k \in S, \forall (m_1,m_2) \in E^k \quad (11)$$
$$\forall p_1 \in P(n_1,n_2), p_2 \in P(n_2,n_1)$$

$$\sum_{S^k \in S} \sum_{(m_1,m_2)\in E^k} \sum_{n_1,n_2 \in N} \sum_{p \in P(n_1,n_2)} l^{k,p}_{m_1 m_2}(n_1,n_2) \cdot r^k \le B_e \quad (12)$$
$$\forall e \in P(n_1,n_2)$$

$$\sum_{n_2 \in N} l^{k,p_1}_{m_1 m_2}(n_1,n_2) - \sum_{n_2 \in N} l^{k,p_2}_{m_1 m_2}(n_2,n_1) = a^k_{m_1}(n_1) - a^k_{m_2}(n_1)$$
$$\forall (m_1,m_2) \in E^k, \forall S^k \in S \quad (13)$$
$$\forall p_1 \in P(n_1,n_2), \forall p_2 \in P(n_2,n_1).$$

$$r^k \le \min(B_e - R_e),\ e \in P(n_1, n_2),\ l^{k,e}_{m_1 m_2}(n_1, n_2) = 1$$
$$\forall n_1, n_2 \in N, \forall S^k \in S \tag{14}$$

Constraint (7) indicates that any VNFs other than the source and destination of the SFCs, at most selects one physical node to be placed; the constraint (8) indicates whether S^k is accepted, if it is, the required VNFs must be allocated one physical node to host them. Constraints (9) indicate that the resources required by the VNFs cannot exceed the resources available on the nodes. $a^k_{m_1}(n_1) \times a^k_{m_2}(n_2)$ of constraints (10) represents the adjacent VNFs $f^k_{m_1}$ and $f^k_{m_2}$ in S^k are placed on n_1 and n_2 respectively, and one path between them should be routed. Constraint (11) represents each logical link in one SFC cannot be mapped to a bi-directional link; the constraint (12) indicates that the aggregation bandwidth on the physical link cannot exceed the link bandwidth; Constraints (13) ensures that the logical links of S^k map to a continuous path of the physical topology, and constraints (14) guarantee quality of service.

The resource optimization problem of combination of NFV and SDN studied in this paper is a NP-hard problem [10]. If all the nodes are guaranteed to have the same available resources, the node can be regarded as a fixed-capacity packet and the requested VNFs are objects in different sizes. It is converted to a normal problem called binary-knapsack. Suppose that B_e is infinite, which means that the routing is not important, the problem becomes a pure VNF placement, which has been proved to be NP-hard. Therefore, the resource optimization problem of combination of NFV and SDN studied in this paper is proved to be an NP-hard problem.

4 Heuristic Algorithms

In order to solve above NP-hard problem in reasonable time, we propose two heuristic algorithms according to the order of VNFs placement and traffic flow routing. First Routing Then Placing (FRTP) algorithm is to choose paths for SFCs firstly, and then place the required VNFs orderly along the chosen paths. Another Placing Followed by Routing (PFBR) algorithm is just the opposite. Firstly, the VNFs required by SFCs are assigned to some nodes whose priorities are relatively high. Then, the source node, the intermediate node and the destination node are connected together into a complete path. During the placement phase of PFBR algorithm, the priority of nodes is given as (15).

$$w(v_n) = \left(1 - \frac{hop_n}{\max_{j \in N}(hop_j)}\right) \cdot \left(\frac{rec_n}{\max_{j \in N}(rec_j)}\right) \tag{15}$$

The priority of a node is determined by the available resources of the node and the number of hops introduced by the node, where, indicates the number of forwarding hops introduced by the node, represents the total amount of available resources of the node, indicates the maximum number of forwarding hops and implies the maximum amount of available resources.

Algorithm 1. First Routing Then Placing algorithm

1: **function** FRTP (S, F, $G=(V,E)$)

2: *order SFC*←order SFCs by r^k in decreasing order

3: *cost*=0; *Accept*=0; p_k, *paths*={0}; $\pi_k, \pi = 0$;

4: $\forall S^k \in S$:

5: **if** $r^k > \lambda$ **then**

6: $p \leftarrow$ Shortest_path(G, s^k, t^k)

7: **if** $D_k^t \le \sum_{v_n \in p} C_n^t, \forall t \in T$ && $r_k \le \min_{e \in p}(B_e - R_e)$ **then**

8: $\forall f_m^k \in N^k$, $v_n \in p$:

9: place f_m^k to v_n;

10: $\pi_k \leftarrow \pi_k \cup v_n$; $p_k \leftarrow p_k \cup p$;

11: cost=cost+$r^k \cdot |p_k|$; Accept++;

12: update C_n^t, B_e;

13: **else**

14: Remove p_k in G; continue;

15: **end if**

16: **else** $p \leftarrow$ K_Shortest_path(G, s^k, t^k);

17: repeat 9-20;

18: **end if**

19: Add π_k to π; p_k to *paths*;

20: **end function**

Both of the FRTP and PFBR algorithm proposed in this paper decide different paths for requests with different bandwidth requirements. Once the request arrives, we judge whether the demand of bandwidth exceeds the threshold λ. If it exceeds, the request is regarded as a high bandwidth service request, we try to guide traffic to the shortest path so as to reduce forward times and bandwidth consumption. Otherwise, we try to search a path which has more available link resources, which can balance the network traffic load. Algorithms 1 and 2 give the pseudocode of the heuristic solutions respectively. Both of them take as input a set of SFC requests S, and a set of VNFs annotated with the network topology graph. In initial step, we order SFCs by r^k in decreasing order.

Besides, the outputs include π, a set of nodes which host the required VNFs, routing paths and etc.

Algorithm 2. Placing Followed by Routing algorithm

1: function PFBR (S, F, $G=(V,E)$)

2: *order* SFC←order SFCs by r^k in decreasing order

3: cost=0; Accept=0; $p_m^k, p_k, paths=\{0\}; \pi_k, \pi = 0$;

4: $\forall S^k \in S$:

5: calculate $w(v_i) = (1 - \frac{hop_i}{\max_{j \in N}(hop_j)}) \cdot (\frac{rec_i}{\max_{j \in N}(rec_j)})$;

6: *order* v_n ← order v_i by $w(v_i)$ in decreasing order

7: $\forall f_m^k \in S^k$, $v_n \leftarrow order\ v_i$:

8: **if** $D_k^t \leq C_n^t, \forall t \in T$ **then**

9: place f_m^k to v_n;

10: $\pi_k \leftarrow \pi_k$ U v_n;

11: **if** $r^k > \lambda$ **then**

12: $\forall (s^k, \pi_k), (\pi_k, t^k)$:

13: $p_1^k \leftarrow$ Shortest_path(G, s^k, π_k);

14: **if** $r_k \leq \min_{e \in p_1^k}(B_e - R_e)$ **then**

15: Add Add p_1^k *to* p_k;

16: cost=cost+ $r^k \cdot |p_k|$;Accept++;

17: update C_n^t, B_e;

18: **else** Remove p_k in G; continue;

19: **end if**

20: **else**

21: $p_1^k \leftarrow K_$Shortest_path(G, s^k, π_k);

22: repeat 17-19;

23: **end if**

24: **else**

25: Remove v_n in G; continue;

26: **end if**

27: Add π_k to π; p_k to *paths*

28: **end function**

5 Experiment Result

In order to evaluate the algorithms proposed in this paper, we verify the feasibility of the proposed model and the effectiveness of the proposed algorithm. In terms of total forwarding costs and degree of load balancing coupled with the acceptance ratio of requests, the proposed heuristic algorithms are compared with Routing before Placement (RBP) algorithm proposed in [12]. During the routing phase, RBP algorithm is always searching shortest path for each demand unless resource constraints are violated. Then, VNFs are placed on the path greedily. If no such path satisfies all resource constraints, the demand is rejected.

5.1 Experimental Environment and Settings

In simulation experiment, we use Matlab2015a for program simulation and run them on the Windows 10 with Intel Core i7-6900, 3.40 GHz CPU and 8 GB RAM.

Our experiment adopts random network topology with 20 to 100 nodes. Each node has three resource types. The total amount of resources follows a uniform distribution with an average of 100 and a variance of 30, and the average link capability is about 200. There are 10 types of VNFs in the VNFs set. And 3 to 6 kinds of which are required of a SFC. Each type of resource is required by one VNF is 0.4 to 1 unit. The bandwidth demand r^k of each SFC varies from 1 to 5 units, and λ is the average of overall bandwidth requirements. In our experiment, the number of SFCs is increased from 200 to 1000.

5.2 Performance Analysis

Figurc 2 demonstrates that total forwarding cost increases with the number of SFCs. When the nodes in the network is fixed as 50, the total forwarding cost of FRTP algorithm is lower than that of PFBR based on node priority, and the results of them are higher than RBP algorithm. However, only consider the cost of forwarding is not comprehensive, because it is related with the forward times and bandwidth demands of SFCs. Figure 3 shows the degree of load balancing as the number of SFCs increases. In the aspect of load balancing, FRTP algorithm is inferior to that of PFBR algorithm based on node priority, and it shows stronger advantages than the RBP algorithm without load balancing.

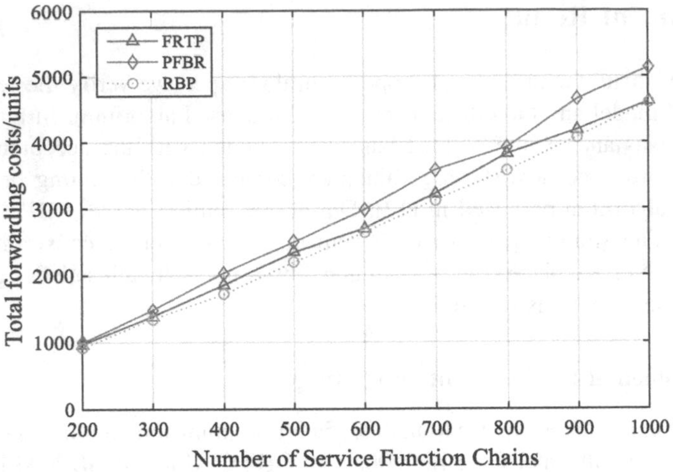

Fig. 2. Total bandwidth occupation of the number of SFCs

When the network size gradually increases, the total forwarding costs do not vary greatly. This is due to the fact that the average distances generated by random networks are about the same. RBP algorithm holds a slight advantage in forwarding cost, while FRTP and PFBR algorithm show little difference. Figure 4 shows the degree of load balancing when the network size gradually increases. Generally, PFBR algorithm outperforms than FRTP algorithm in load balancing, and RBP algorithm is inferior to the algorithms proposed in this paper. The average running time of the algorithms increases with the increasing of the number of SFCs and nodes. As shown in Figs. 5 and 6, the average running time of FRTP algorithm is lower than that of PFBR algorithm, because the latter takes more time to calculate the node priority. RBP algorithm takes least time in the traffic routing phase without load balancing.

Furthermore, a set of experiments are carried out with 20 nodes to verify the requests acceptance ratio. Figure 7 shows the acceptance ratio of various algorithms under different number of SFCs. Obviously, PFBR algorithm can balance the traffic load better than other algorithms, and can make greater use of resources. As a result, the acceptance ratio of requests is obviously improved compared with other algorithms.

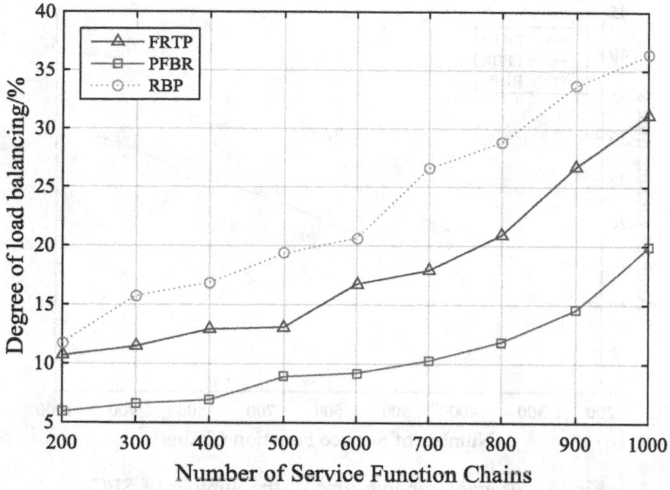

Fig. 3. Degree of load balancing versus the number of SFCs

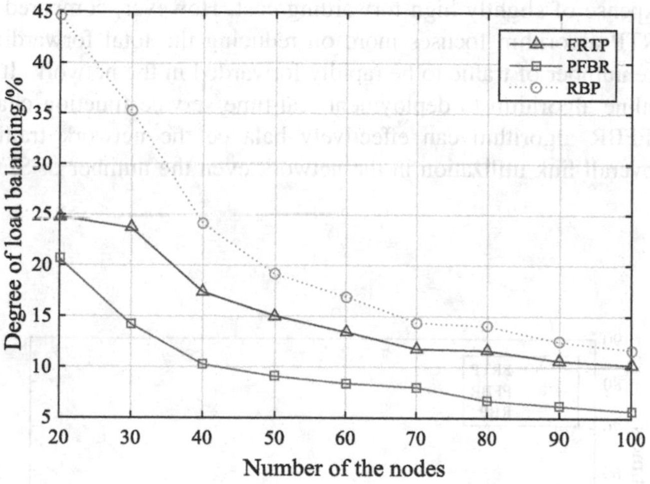

Fig. 4. Degree of load balancing versus nodes in the network

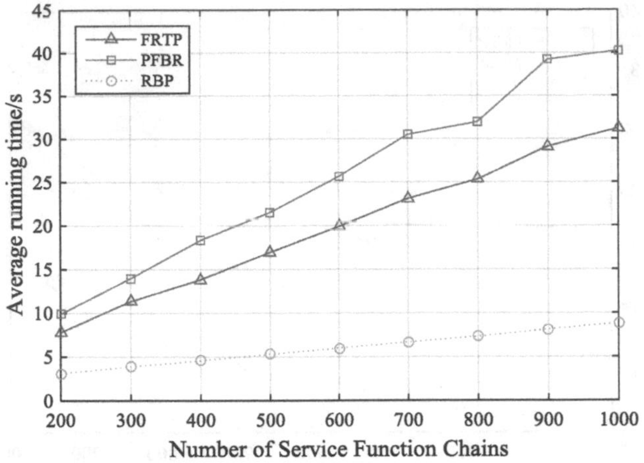

Fig. 5. Average running time of the number of SFCs

To sum up, compared with RBP algorithm, the two algorithms proposed in this paper can more remarkably balance the traffic load and improve the requests acceptance ratio at the expense of slightly high forwarding cost. However, compared with PFBR algorithm, FRTP algorithm focuses more on reducing the total forwarding cost and enables a large number of traffic to be rapidly forwarded in the network. It can also be used as an online algorithm to deployment real-time service function chains. On the other hand, PFBR algorithm can effectively balance the network traffic load and improve the overall link utilization in the network even the number of SFCs or nodes are large.

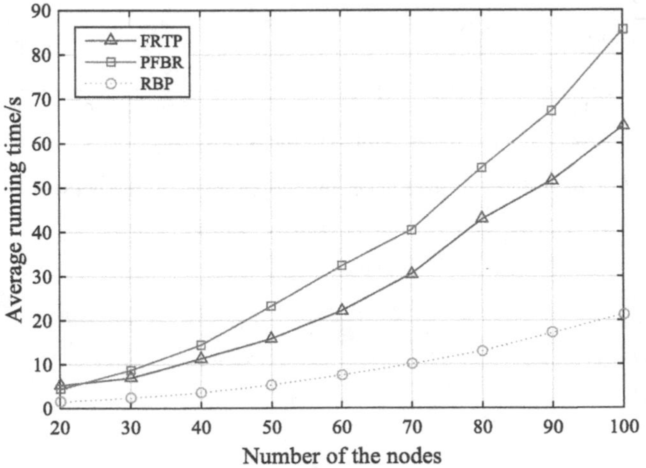

Fig. 6. Average running time versus the number of nodes in the network

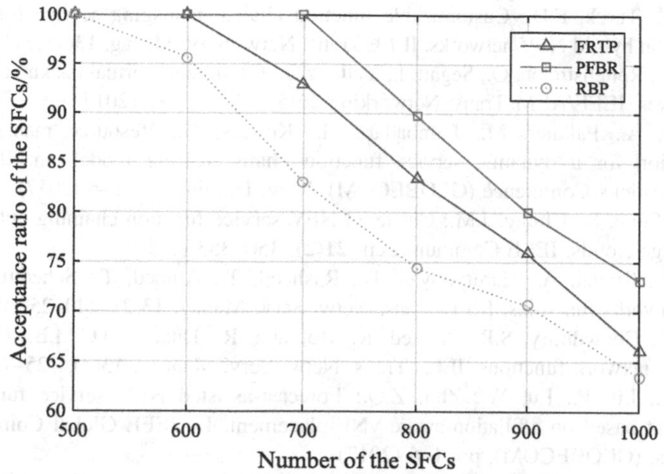

Fig. 7. Acceptance ratio under different intensity of SFCs

6 Conclusion

In this paper, we propose a joint optimization model of service function chain placement and routing algorithm. Then two heuristic algorithms are proposed according to the order of VNFs placement and traffic flow routing. The simulation results show that FRTP can make a large number of data packets be rapidly forwarded, which can reduce service function chaining time and improve user experience to a certain extent. Although PFBR algorithm is slightly inferior in reducing the total forwarding cost, the advantage in load balancing is prominent, which improves the request acceptance ratio of requests. The beneficial combination of the two algorithms enables more flexible deployment of the service function chains. However, given the traffic load balancing in the network, the time overhead of proposed two algorithms increases rapidly when the scale of network and the number of service function chains get larger. Therefore, in the future work, we expect to study more optimized methods such machine learning to balance the load and improve the ratio of acceptance of requests while reducing the time overhead as much as possible.

References

1. Bizanis, N., Kuipers, F.A.: SDN and virtualization solutions for the Internet of Things: a survey. IEEE Access **4**, 5591–5606 (2016)
2. Mechtri, M., Ghribi, C., Soualah, O., Zeghlache, D.: NFV orchestration framework addressing SFC challenges. IEEE Commun. Mag. **55**(6), 16–23 (2017)
3. Wang, L., Lu, Z.M., Wen, X.M., Knopp, R., Gupta, R.: Joint optimization of service function chaining and resource allocation in network function virtualization. IEEE Access **4**, 8084–8094 (2016)

4. Moens, H., Turck, F.D.: Customizable function chains: managing service function chain variability in hybrid NFV networks. IEEE Trans. Netw. Serv. Manag. **13**(4), 711–724 (2016)
5. Kanizo, Y., Rottenstreich, O., Segall, I., Yallouz, J.: Optimizing virtual backup allocation for middleboxes. IEEE/ACM Trans. Networking **25**(5), 2759–2772 (2017)
6. Leivadeas, A., Falkner, M., Lambadaris, I., Kesidis, G.: Resource management and orchestration for a dynamic service function chain steering model. In: IEEE Global Communications Conference (GLOBECOM), Kiev, Ukraine, pp. 1–6 (2017)
7. Nam, Y., Song, S., Chung, J.M.: Clustered NFV service function chaining optimization in mobile edge clouds. IEEE Commun. Lett. **21**(2), 350–353 (2017)
8. Riggio, R., Bradai, A., Harutyunyan, D., Rasheed, T., Ahmed, T.: Scheduling wireless virtual networks functions. IEEE Trans. Netw. Serv. Manag. **13**(2), 240–252 (2016)
9. Bari, M.F., Chowdhury, S.R., Ahmed, R., Boutaba, R., Duarte, O.C.M.B.: Orchestrating virtualized network functions. IEEE Trans. Netw. Serv. Manage. **13**(4), 725–739 (2016)
10. Sun, Q.Y., Lu, P., Lu, W., Zhu, Z.Q.: Forecast-assisted NFV service function chain deployment based on affiliation-aware vNF placement. In: IEEE Global Communications Conference (GLOBECOM), pp. 1–6 (2017)
11. Savi, M., Tornatore, M., Verticale, G.: Impact of processing costs on service function chain placement in network functions virtualization. In: IEEE Conference on Network Function Virtualization and Software Defined Network, pp. 191–197 (2015)
12. Nguyen, T.M., Fdida, S., Pham, T.M.: A comprehensive resource management and placement for network function virtualization. In: 2017 IEEE Conference on Network Softwarization (NetSoft), Bologna, Italy, pp. 1–9 (2017)

Vehicle Localization Using Joint DOA/TOA Estimation Based on TLS-ESPRIT Algorithm

Shanjie Zhang[1(✉)], Yi Shi[1], Rui Zhang[2], Feng Yan[2], Yi Wu[3], Weiwei Xia[2], and Lianfeng Shen[2]

[1] Collaborative Innovation Center of Advanced Microstructures, Nanjing University, Nanjing 210093, People's Republic of China
mf1623045@smail.nju.edu.cn, yshi@nju.edu.cn

[2] National Mobile Communications Research Laboratory, Southeast University, Nanjing 210096, People's Republic of China
{zhangrui09, feng.yan, wwxia, lfshen}@seu.edu.cn

[3] Key Laboratory of OptoElectronic Science and Technology for Medicine of Ministry of Education, Fujian Provincial Key Laboratory of Photonics Technology, Fujian Normal University, Fuzhou 350007, People's Republic of China
wuyi@fjnu.edu.cn

Abstract. In this paper, a high-resolution vehicle positioning estimation algorithm based on existing Vehicle to Infrastructure (V2I) communications is proposed to achieve joint estimation of vehicle target's direction of arrival (DOA) and time of arrival (TOA). We adopt the Estimating Signal Parameters via Rotational Invariance Techniques (ESPRIT) algorithm based on total least squares (TLS) to estimate the DOA and TOA, and the vehicle location can be obtained from the estimated parameters. The TLS-ESPRIT algorithm not only has a relatively small amount of computation to meet the real-time requirements of vehicle localization, but also has the advantage of strong anti-noise. We also introduce unscented Kalman filter (UKF) to further improve the localization accuracy of the TLS-ESPRIT algorithm and to reduce the influence of noise interference. The simulation results show that compared with the traditional 2D-ESPRIT parameter estimation methods without UKF and the Global Positioning System (GPS), this method has better performance of positioning parameter estimation.

Keywords: Vehicle location · TLS-ESPRIT · Direction of arrival (DOA) · Arrival time (TOA) · Kalman filter

1 Introduction

With the rapid development of intelligent transportation system (ITS), many emerging application techniques appear in the Internet of Vehicles, such as traffic flow control, road safety, automatic driving, and Vehicle queuing Network [1]. The realization of these applications can not be separated from the accurate and reliable perception of the vehicle position information. Currently, different positioning methods can be used for the precise positioning of the traveling vehicle. One of the most widely used

M. Jia et al. (Eds.): WiSATS 2019, LNICST 281, pp. 297–309, 2019.
https://doi.org/10.1007/978-3-030-19156-6_28

positioning methods is the Global Navigation Satellite System (GNSS) represented by Global Positioning System (GPS). Its positioning error is generally about 10 m, and the best positioning accuracy that the GPS positioning method can achieve after optimization is between 3 m to 7 m, such as differential GPS [2]. However, the positioning accuracy of GPS is affected by the use environment. For example, in an occluded urban environment or a high-speed driving scene, due to the presence of unstable factors such as signal multipath and target driving speed, the positioning error will be greatly increased to 15 m [3, 4]. Therefore, in ITS, the accuracy of satellite positioning does not satisfy the need for more precise positioning within one meter in applications such as collaborative driving or collision avoidance [5]. However, it is also possible to use roadside unit (RSU) positioning based on Dedicated Short-Range Communication (DSRC) to meet the requirements of ITS positioning accuracy. Therefore, vehicle positioning parameter estimation algorithm for obtaining a wireless positioning signal by communicating with the RSU has the significance of research.

The RSU serves as pre-deployed road facilities and provides positioning parameters such as Received Signal Strength (RSS), Time of Arrival (TOA) and Direction of Arrival (DOA) through communication between the vehicle and roadside infrastructure (V2I). For wireless access in vehicular environment (WAVE), dedicated short range communications (DSRC) technology is one of the earliest developed and most mature communication technology. It supports wireless access based on the IEEE 802.11p protocol to provide high-speed, low-latency inter-vehicle and vehicle-to-infrastructure communication services [6], and spreads orthogonal frequency division multiplexing (OFDM) signal in its radio channel [7]. Therefore, the estimation of the positioning parameters contained in signals such as DOA and TOA is an important research content in vehicle positioning. Joint DOA/TOA parameter estimation has many advantages, not only can improve the positioning accuracy through multiple roadside unit coverage, but also can greatly reduce the number of deployment of roadside nodes compared to a single positioning parameter estimation. Theoretically, only one roadside node can be used to locate the target vehicle [8]. In a super-resolution channel parameter estimation method based on a Uniform Linear Array (ULA), the ESPRIT algorithm has many performance advantages over the Multiple Signal Classification (MUSIC) algorithm. For example, the DOA estimation accuracy and computational complexity are significantly better than the MUSIC algorithm [9], and no two-dimensional spatial peak search is needed. In addition, the two-dimensional matrix pencil (2D-MP) proposed in [10] is a direct data-domain method that does not require calculation of signal covariance matrix, but the disadvantage of this method is that three or more RSUs are needed to provide Sufficient range reference signal.

The novelty of this paper is to propose a low-complexity ESPRIT algorithm based on Total least squares (TLS). Joint parameter estimation of DOA and TOA is achieved by analyzing multipath channel frequency response (CFR) of OFDM signals. In addition, unscented Kalman filter (UKF) is also used to reduce the channel noise interference to improve the joint parameter estimation accuracy. At low signal-to-noise ratio (SNR), the proposed TLS-ESPRIT algorithm overcomes the disadvantages of poor positioning accuracy of multi-signal classification and its real-time performance is much better than the MUSIC algorithm. The precise position information of vehicle is finally obtained by recombining the velocity components through joint observations of

DOA and TOA. This article is organized in the following order: Sect. 2 provides a vehicle positioning system model. The proposed calculation principles of the TLS-ESPRIT localization algorithm and the UKF filtering algorithm are described in Sect. 3. Section 4 discusses the performance of the algorithm and simulation results. Finally, the Sect. 5 is the summary of this article and the discussion of the follow-up tasks.

2 Positioning System Model

It is assumed that the roadside node units have been pre-deployed in the vehicle positioning system beside the bidirectional lanes, and that the communication distances of these roadside unit sets can cover the entire road, and the position information of these roadside units is known to the vehicle. In this system, both the roadside unit and the vehicle are equipped with DSRC terminal equipment, so the V2I communication between the roadside unit and the vehicle is accomplished through the 802.11P protocol. A multi-antenna array is also installed at the driving vehicle to detect the frequency response of the multi-path channel of the received OFDM signal. In addition, the vehicle can also obtain the current speed vector data through the navigation or speed sensor device carried by itself. The location scenario of driving vehicles in an urban environment is shown in Fig. 1.

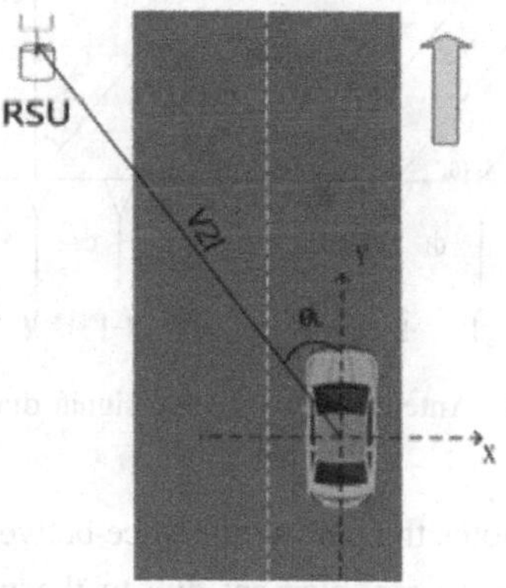

Fig. 1. RSU-based vehicle location scenario

In addition, the on-board unit is also equipped with an M antenna receiving array. We assume that the antenna array spacing is a fixed value and is generally half of the signal wavelength. The transmitted signal $S_T(t)$ is received by the antenna array via L propagation paths, only one of which is along the line of sight (LOS) and others are considered as non-line-of-sight propagation. According to [11], the time domain signal received by the mth antenna element in a uniform linear array (ULA) can be expressed as:

$$S_{m,k}(t) = \sum_{l=1}^{L} e^{\frac{-j2\pi d(m-1)\sin\theta_l}{\lambda_k}} \beta_l S_T(t - \tau_l) + N_{m,k}(t) \quad (1)$$

In (1), the interval of ULA is $d_1 = d_2 = d_3 = \cdots = d_{M-1} = d$. λ_k is the kth subcarrier wavelength of the OFDM signal, β_l is the complex attenuation coefficient of different paths, and $S_T(t - \tau_l)$ is the signal transmitted by the roadside unit. θ_l, τ_l corresponds to DOA and TOA for different propagation paths, respectively. $N_{m,k}$ is the zero mean additive white Gaussian noise (AWGN) of different subcarriers on different antennas. In [12], the complex time domain received signals of different antennas can also be expressed as:

$$S_{m,k} = \sum_{l=1}^{L} \beta_l e^{-j2\pi\left\{ d(m-1)\frac{\sin\theta_l}{\lambda_k} + [f_D + (k-1)f_S]\tau_l \right\}} + N_{m,k} \quad (2)$$

Where f_D is the Doppler frequency shift, f_S is the subcarrier frequency interval, and k is the number of subcarriers of the OFDM signal, in the range of [1 ,⋯, K]. The antenna index value m is in the range [1 ,⋯, M], the propagation path of the OFDM signal is shown in Fig. 2.

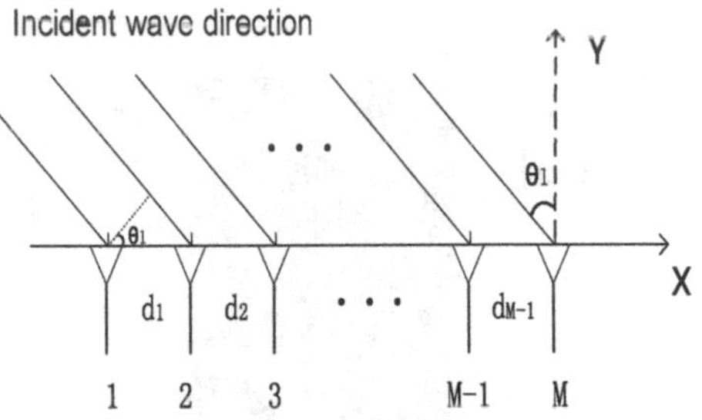

Fig. 2. Antenna array receive signal diagram

In (2), $d(m-1)\frac{\sin\theta_l}{\lambda_k}$ denotes the phase difference between the mth antenna element in the ULA and the reference array element due to the propagation path difference. According to [13], we rewrite $S_{m,k}$ into a vector form:

$$S = H\beta_l + n \quad (3)$$

In (3), H denotes the transmission channel matrix, β_l is the path-dependent complex attenuation coefficient vector, and $[]^T$ denotes the transposition of the vector.

$$S(n) = [s_1(n), s_2(n), s_3(n), \cdots, s_M(n)]^T$$

$$n(n) = [n_1(n), n_2(n), n_3(n), \cdots, n_M(n)]^T$$

$$H = \begin{bmatrix} h_{1,1}(\theta_1, \tau_1) & h_{1,2}(\theta_2, \tau_2) & \cdots & h_{1,L}(\theta_L, \tau_L) \\ h_{2,1}(\theta_1, \tau_1) & h_{2,2}(\theta_2, \tau_2) & \cdots & h_{2,L}(\theta_L, \tau_L) \\ \vdots & \vdots & \ddots & \vdots \\ h_{M,1}(\theta_1, \tau_1) & h_{M,2}(\theta_2, \tau_2) & \cdots & h_{M,L}(\theta_L, \tau_L) \end{bmatrix}$$

$$h_{M,L}(\theta_L, \tau_L) = e^{-j2\pi\left\{ d(M-1)\frac{\sin\theta_L}{\lambda_k} + [f_D + (k-1)fs]\tau_L \right\}}$$

$$\beta_l = [\beta_1, \beta_2, \beta_3, \cdots, \beta_L]^{\mathrm{T}}$$

Then the total least squares algorithm (TLS-ESPRIT) is used to jointly estimate the DOA and TOA of the received signal, and then use UKF to further optimize the estimation result.

3 Parameter Estimation Algorithm

3.1 Total Least Squares Based ESPRIT Algorithm (TLS-ESPRIT)

In the parameter estimation of the received signal, it is assumed that the number of antennas M of the ULA at the receiving end is greater than the multipath number L of signal propagation, and the former [1: $M-1$] array antennas and the last [2: M] arrays in Fig. 2 are taken respectively. The elements form two sub-antenna arrays. By default, the first sub-array receives the signal vector S_1(n), and the second sub-array receives the signal vector S_2(n). Available from (3):

$$S_1 = [s_1(n), s_2(n), s_3(n), \cdots, s_{M-1}(n)]^{\mathrm{T}} = H_1.\beta_l + n_1 \tag{4}$$

$$S_2 = [s_2(n), s_3(n), s_4(n), \cdots, s_M(n)]^{\mathrm{T}} = H_2.\beta_l + n_2 \tag{5}$$

In (4) and (5), the matrice H_1, H_2 are

$$H_1 = \begin{bmatrix} h_{1,1}(\theta_1, \tau_1) & h_{1,2}(\theta_2, \tau_2) & \cdots & h_{1,L}(\theta_L, \tau_L) \\ h_{2,1}(\theta_1, \tau_1) & h_{2,2}(\theta_2, \tau_2) & \cdots & h_{2,L}(\theta_L, \tau_L) \\ \vdots & \vdots & \ddots & \vdots \\ h_{M-1,1}(\theta_1, \tau_1) & h_{M-1,2}(\theta_2, \tau_2) & \cdots & h_{M-1,L}(\theta_L, \tau_L) \end{bmatrix}$$

$$H_2 = \begin{bmatrix} h_{2,1}(\theta_1, \tau_1) & h_{2,2}(\theta_2, \tau_2) & \cdots & h_{2,L}(\theta_L, \tau_L) \\ h_{2,1}(\theta_1, \tau_1) & h_{2,2}(\theta_2, \tau_2) & \cdots & h_{2,L}(\theta_L, \tau_L) \\ \vdots & \vdots & \ddots & \vdots \\ h_{M,1}(\theta_1, \tau_1) & h_{M,2}(\theta_2, \tau_2) & \cdots & h_{M,L}(\theta_L, \tau_L) \end{bmatrix}$$

Thus, (5) can be written as:

$$S_2 = H_1 \Phi \beta_l + n_2 \tag{6}$$

$$\Phi = diag\{e^{-2\pi j \alpha_1}, e^{-2\pi j \alpha_2}, \cdots, e^{-2\pi j \alpha_L}\} \tag{7}$$

$$\alpha_l = d \times \sin\theta_l / \lambda_k + f_s \times \tau_l, l = 1, \cdots, L \tag{8}$$

The DOA and TOA of the incident multipath signal are included in the diagonal matrix Φ. If the corresponding rotation-invariant relationship between the subarrays can be obtained, the vehicle positioning information can be extracted. Combine S_1 and S_2 into a new matrix S_3.

$$S_3 = \begin{bmatrix} S_1 \\ S_2 \end{bmatrix} = \begin{bmatrix} H_1 \\ H_1 \bullet \Phi \end{bmatrix} \beta_l + \begin{bmatrix} n_1 \\ n_2 \end{bmatrix} = \widehat{H}\, \beta_l + \widehat{n} \tag{9}$$

Solving the Autocorrelation Matrix of S_3 in (9).

$$R_{S_3} = E[S_3\, S_3^{\mathrm{T}}] = \widehat{H}\, R_{\beta_l}\, \widehat{H}^{\mathrm{H}} + \delta^2 N \tag{10}$$

In the above formula, $(.)^{\mathrm{H}}$ represents the Hermitian transpose, $R_{\beta_l} = E[\beta_l\, \beta_l^{\mathrm{H}}]$ and δ^2 is the variance of Gaussian white noise. $N = \begin{bmatrix} E_{M-1} & J \\ J^H & E_{M-1} \end{bmatrix}$, E_{M-1} is an $M-1$ order identity matrix, and J is a $M-1$ order square matrix with all subdiagonals of 1.

Solving the generalized eigenvalues of R_{S3} results in $\lambda_1 \geq \lambda_2 \geq \cdots \geq \lambda_L \geq \lambda_{L+1} = \cdots = \lambda_{2M-2} = \delta^2$. Let the eigenvectors of the first L corresponding large generalized eigenvalues make up the signal subspace $I = [I_1, I_2, \cdots, I_L]$, because the columns of the matrix I and the columns of the direction matrix can be expanded into the same subspace:

$$\mathrm{span}\{I\} = \mathrm{span}\{\hat{H}\} \tag{11}$$

so there is a unique $L \times L$ order non-singular matrix A such that

$$I = \widehat{H} \times A \tag{12}$$

decompose the signal subspace I into two $M-1 \times L$ matrices I_1, I_2, where $I_1 = H_1 A, I_2 = H_1 \Phi A$, and construct the $M-1 \times 2L$ matrix $I_{12} = [I_1, I_2]$, from which $(I_{12})^{\mathrm{H}} \times I_{12}$ is obtained:

$$\begin{bmatrix} I_1^{\mathrm{H}} \\ I_2^{\mathrm{H}} \end{bmatrix} [I_1 \quad I_2] = \begin{bmatrix} A^{\mathrm{H}} \\ A^{\mathrm{H}} \Phi^{\mathrm{H}} \end{bmatrix} H_1^{\mathrm{H}} H_1 [A \quad \Phi A] \tag{13}$$

Solve the eigenvalues of the (13) and their corresponding eigenvectors, and sort the eigenvalues from largest to smallest $\Lambda_1 \geq \Lambda_2 \geq \ldots \geq \Lambda_L \geq \Lambda_{L+1} = \ldots = \Lambda_{2L} = 0$, corresponding the feature vectors are u_1, u_2,..., u_L,..., u_{2L}. So (13) can also be expressed as

$$(I_{12})^H \times I_{12} = U\Lambda U^H \tag{14}$$

In (14), Λ is a diagonal matrix consisting of eigenvectors. U is a $2L \times 2L$ square matrix and is divided into blocks as follows.

$$U = \begin{bmatrix} U_{11} & U_{12} \\ U_{21} & U_{22} \end{bmatrix} \tag{15}$$

available by (15)

$$A^{-1}\Phi A = -U_{12}\,U_{22}^{-1} \tag{16}$$

The eigenvalue decomposition on the right side of the equal sign of (16) results in L eigenvalues g_1, g_2, ···, g_L. The DOA and TOA of the target vehicle are given by the following formula:

$$\widehat{\tau}_l = \frac{-\arg(g_l)}{2\pi f_S} \tag{17}$$

$$\widehat{\theta}_l = \arcsin\left[\frac{-\arg(g_l)\lambda}{2\pi d}\right] \tag{18}$$

In (18), λ is the carrier wavelength of the received signal, so the position information of the vehicle can be accurately measured by (17), (18). The proposed 2D-ELSITE algorithm achieves automatic pairing by joint diagonalization of DOA and TOA parameters, which can effectively overcome the problem of degraded estimation performance of the 1D-ESPRIT algorithm caused by changes in the carrier frequency offset caused by the mobility of the target vehicle [16].

3.2 Unscented Kalman Filter (UKF)

The essence of Kalman filtering is to reconstruct the state vector of the positioning system from the measured values. According to the measurement value of the vehicle positioning system, the noise interference is filtered out from the noise-polluted system, and the estimated performance degradation under low SNR environment can be overcome. Unscented Kalman filter (UKF) is a method that approximates nonlinear distribution using sigma points and is based on UT (Unscented Transform) transformation. Compared with the extended Kalman filter (EKF), UKF does not approximate the nonlinear function and there is no defect caused by omitting Taylor's expansion of higher-order terms, which increases the estimation accuracy and robustness of strongly nonlinear systems [15]. The UKF proposed in this paper can not only reduce the channel noise and the influence of estimation error, but also predict the DOA and TOA of the next moment of the vehicle through the velocity component. The UKF filtered system equation is given by:

$$\begin{cases} X(k) = FX(k-1) + Gw(k-1) \\ Z(k) = h[X(k)] + u(k) \end{cases} \tag{19}$$

In (19), $X(k)$ is N rows state column vector, $Z(k)$ is M rows observation column vector, $w(k)$, $u(k)$ are zero mean Gaussian state noise and Gaussian observation noise, F is an $N \times N$ state transition matrix, G is the noise input matrix of the system, and h is a nonlinear transformation function, i.e., $E^{N\times 1} \Rightarrow E^{M\times 1}$. If the state vector of the sigma sample point at time k is $X_S(k|k)$, the one-step state estimation and observation estimation formula of the sample point at $k-1$ time is:

$$\begin{cases} X_S(k|k-1) = F\bullet\ X_S(k-1) \\ Z_S(k|k-1) = h[X_S(k-1)] \end{cases} \tag{20}$$

A one-step prediction of the system state estimation and state covariance estimation of UKF is:

$$\begin{cases} X(k|k-1) = \sum_{S=0}^{2n} W_S X_S(k|k-1) \\ A(k|k-1) = \sum_{S=0}^{2n} W_S X'\bullet X'^T \end{cases} \tag{21}$$

In (21), $X' = X(k|k-1) - X_S(k|k-1)$, the one-step prediction of the observational estimation and observation covariance estimation is:

$$\begin{cases} Z(k|k-1) = \sum_{S=0}^{2n} W_S Z_S(k|k-1) \\ B(k|k-1) = \sum_{S=0}^{2n} W_S Z' \times Z'^T \end{cases} \tag{22}$$

In (22), $Z' = Z(k|k-1) - Z_S(k|k-1)$, the full state vector of UKF and the state covariance can be expressed as:

$$\begin{cases} K(k) = \frac{A(k|k-1)}{B(k|k-1)} \\ X(k) = X(k|k-1) + K(k)[Z(k) - Z(k|k-1)] \\ A(k) = A(k|k-1) - K(k)B(k|k-1)K^T(k) \end{cases} \tag{23}$$

In (23), $K(k)$ denotes the Kalman gain. In (21) and (22), W_S denotes the weights of different *sigma* points. The DOA and TOA components in the initial state vector X(0) can be obtained by (17) and (18), we also let the UKF state vector be:

$$X(k) = [\theta(k), \tau(k), V_X(k), V_Y(k)]^T \tag{24}$$

$\theta(k), \tau(k)$ respectively represent the DOA and TOA of the LOS path at time k, and V_X and V_Y are the traveling speeds in the X and Y directions in Fig. 1, respectively.

4 Simulation Results

This paper proposes that TLS-based positioning estimation algorithm needs a 2M-2 × 2M-2 order, once 2L × 2L order and L × L order eigenvalue decomposition. In practical applications, the computational complexity is also related to the number of samples N in digital signal processing. It can be approximated as O(N3) [14]. In this simulation, the proposed algorithm with and without UKF filters were simulated in the vehicle location scenario, and GPS was added for comparison. The vehicle positioning accuracy based on DOA and TOA estimation was studied, and the effectiveness of parameter estimation using UKF was illustrated. The vehicle's positioning scenario is that the vehicle travels along a road with a length of about 1 km and a width of 10 m at a constant speed and Simulation parameters for vehicle position estimation are shown in Table 1.

Table 1. Simulation parameters

Parameter	Numeric value
Multipath number	4
Number of receiving antennas	12
Antenna spacing	Half the wavelength
Center frequency	5.9 GHz
Bandwidth	10 MHz
Number of subcarriers	24
Speed of vehicle	30 m/s
Road length and width	1000 m/10 m
Input SNR	50 db

Vehicle tracking is achieved at the vehicle using a vehicle-mounted ULA array to receive broadcast packets and extract the DOA/TOA of LOS through the 2D-ESPRIT algorithm.

In the simulation, we continuously track the vehicle for more than 30 s. We record the position information generated by the DOA/TOA parameter estimation method with and without the UKF filter and the GPS positioning method in the Y direction and the X direction, respectively. The evaluation criterion of the positioning simulation is the positioning accuracy error, that is, the absolute value of the difference between the estimated position and the actual position of the Y-X axis coordinate. The simulation results of the Y-X axis are shown in Figs. 3 and 4 below:

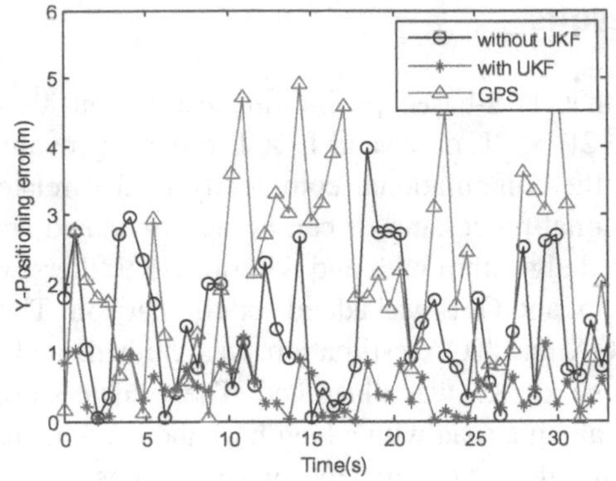

Fig. 3. Positioning accuracy of the DOA/TOA estimation method on the Y-axis

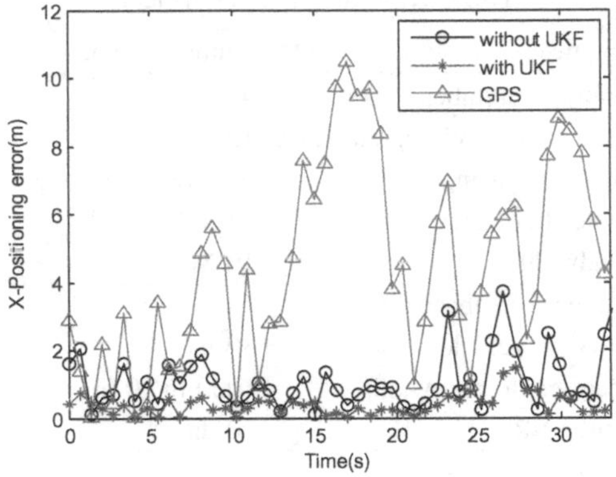

Fig. 4. Positioning accuracy of the DOA/TOA estimation method on the X-axis

In Figs. 3 and 4 above, the positioning error between the conventional 2D-ESPRIT estimation algorithm without UKF, the GPS positioning and the proposed positioning estimation algorithm in the Y and X directions are respectively shown to change over time. As shown in Fig. 3, in the Y direction (traveling direction), the positioning error of the conventional 2D-ESPRIT algorithm without UKF varies significantly within a range of 3 m with time. In addition, the GPS positioning is affected by measurement noise in various aspects and the positioning error is even up to about 5 m. While the accuracy of the proposed positioning algorithm with UKF doesn't fluctuate with time, and the positioning accuracy can remain stable during the tracking period, about 1 m. Figure 4 shows that in the X direction, the positioning accuracy of the algorithm presented in this paper can remain stable over time, and its error reaches a decimeter level around 0.5 m. The accuracy of the conventional estimation algorithm without UKF in the early stage is slightly inferior to the algorithm proposed in this paper. However, since the vehicle is far away from the RSU, accuracy loss is caused in the later period. The accuracy loss of GPS is more obvious with time and it can no longer meet the application requirements. Therefore, the positioning estimation algorithm with UKF proposed in this paper has much better performance than the traditional two-dimensional subspace estimation algorithm and the GPS positioning in the resolution and stability of location accuracy.

In addition to the above criteria, this paper also uses two-dimensional Euclidean distance to represent the estimated error of position coordinates, i.e., from which the probability distribution of the error can be obtained. The cumulative distribution function (CDF) of the estimated error generated by the UKF filtering positioning algorithm is as shown in Fig. 5.

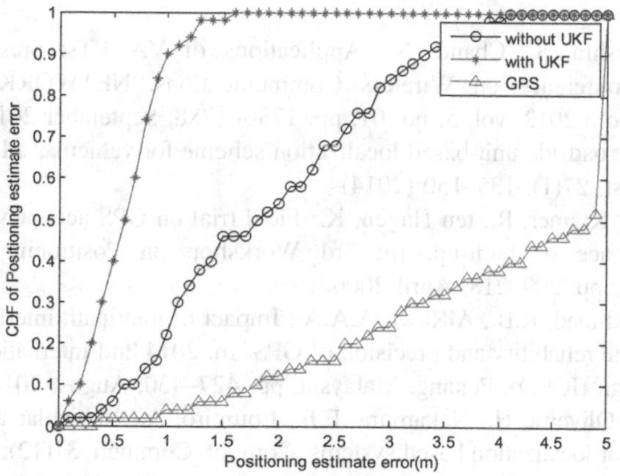

Fig. 5. Cumulative distribution function (CDF) generated by different localization algorithms

The above figure shows that the proposed ESPRIT estimation algorithm with UKF has absolute advantages over traditional algorithms and GPS in terms of reliability. For example, the proposed positioning algorithm can make the error value of the 98% vehicle positioning sample less than 1.5 m. However, if the vehicle positioning using the traditional 2D-ESPRIT estimation algorithm and making the estimation error within 1.5 m, the percentage can only reach 46%, and the percentage of GPS positioning to achieve the same positioning error standard is even lower, only 6%.

5 Conclusion

We propose a vehicle location algorithm based on DOA/TOA joint estimation in this paper. The ESPRIT algorithm utilizes the rotation invariance of the ULA received signal and performs super-resolution estimation of the spatial spectrum through the principle of total least squares (TLS). Different from the traditional two-dimensional spatial spectrum estimation algorithm, the proposed algorithm also introduces the Unscented Kalman Filter (UKF) to overcome the noise interference in the V2I communication environment, which greatly improves the accuracy and reliability of DOA and TOA estimation. Therefore, it is possible to obtain fairly accurate vehicle positioning information to meet the demand for high-precision positioning by the Intelligent connected vehicle. In addition, our follow-up work will also in-depth study of the number of ULA elements, RSU coverage dimensions and real-time constraints and other conditions on the vehicle positioning accuracy, in order to achieve the vehicle positioning accuracy optimization.

Acknowledgment. This work is supported in part by the National Natural Science Foundation of China (No. 61571128, 61471164, 61601122 and 61741102).

References

1. Kumar, V., Mishra, S., Chand, N.: Applications of VANETs: present & future. In: International Conference on Wireless Communications, NETWORKING and Mobile Computing-Wicom 2012, vol. 5, no. 01, pp. 1780–1788, September 2013
2. Chia-Ho, O.: A roadside unit-based localization scheme for vehicular ad hoc networks. Int. J. Commun. Syst. **27**(1), 135–150 (2014)
3. Modsching, M., Kramer, R., ten Hagen, K.: Field trial on GPS accuracy in a medium size city: the influence of built-up. In: 3rd Workshop on Positioning, Navigation and Communication, pp. 209–218, April 2006
4. Younis, H.K., Ahmad, R.B., AlRawi, A.A.A.: Impact of multipath interference and change of velocity on the reliability and precision of GPS. In: 2014 2nd International conference on Electronic Design (ICED), Penang, Malaysia, pp. 427–430, August 2014
5. Boukerche, A., Oliveira, H., Nakamura, E.F., Loureiro, A.: Vehicular ad hoc networks: a new challenge for localization based systems. Comput. Commun. **31**(12), 2838–2849 (2008)
6. Zeadally, S., Hunt, R., Chen, Y.S., Irwin, A., Hassan, A.: Vehicular ad hoc networks (VANETs): status, results, and challenges. Telecommun. Syst. **50**(4), 217–241 (2012)
7. Elazab, M., Noureldin, A., Hassanein, H.S.: Integrated cooperative localization for connected vehicles in urban canyons. In: Proceedings of IEEE GlobeCom, San Diego, CA, USA, pp. 1–6, December 2015
8. Sarkar, T., Ji, Z., Kim, K., Medouri, A., Salazar-Palma, M.: A survey of various propagation models for mobile communication. IEEE Ant. Prop. Mag. **45**(3), 51–82 (2003)
9. Vikas, B., Vakula, D.: Performance comparision of MUSIC and ESPRIT algorithms in presence of coherent signals for DoA estimation. In: International Conference on Electronics, Communication and Aerospace Technology, pp. 403–405, April 2017
10. Gaber, A., Omar, A.: A study of wireless indoor positioning based on joint TDOA and DOA estimation using 2-D matrix pencil algorithms and IEEE 802.11ac. IEEE Trans. Wirel. Commun. **14**(5), 2440–2454 (2015)
11. Hongmei, Z., Zhenguo, G., Fu, H.: High resolution random linear sonar array based MUSIC method for underwater DOA estimation. In: Proceedings of 32nd Chinese Control Conference, Xi'an, China, pp. 4592–4595, July 2013
12. Chen, L., Qi, W.: Joint 2-D DOA and TOA estimation for multipath OFDM signals based on three antennas. IEEE Commun. Lett. **22**(2), 324–327 (2018)
13. Zhang, X., Gao, X., Xu, D.: Multi-invariance ESPRIT-based blind DOA estimation for MC-CDMA with an antenna array. IEEE Trans. Veh. Technol. **58**(8), 4686–4690 (2009)

14. Kim, S., Oh, D., Lee, J.: Joint DFT-ESPRIT estimation for TOA and DOA in vehicle FMCW radars. IEEE Antennas Wirel. Propag. Lett. **14**, 1710–1713 (2015)
15. Yao, H., Tianqi, Z., Qingsha, G., et al.: A method improving the accuracy of UKF. Comput. Simul. **27**(3), 348–352 (2010)
16. Oh, D., Kim, S., Yoon, S.-H., Chong, J.-W.: Two-dimensional ESPRIT-Like shift-invariant TOA estimation algorithm using multi-band chirp signals robust to carrier frequency offset. IEEE Trans. Wirel. Commun. **12**(7), 3130–3139 (2013)

Social Trusted D2D Seed Node Cluster Generation Strategy

Weifeng Lu[1(✉)], Xiaoqiang Ren[1], Jia Xu[1], Siguang Chen[2], Lijun Yang[2], and Jian Xu[3]

[1] School of Computer Science, Nanjing University of Posts and Telecommunications, Nanjing 210003, China
luwf@njupt.edu.cn
[2] College of IoT, Nanjing University of Posts and Telecommunications, Nanjing 210003, China
[3] School of Computer Science and Engineering, Nanjing University of Science and Technology, Nanjing 210094, China

Abstract. In this paper, we propose a Device-to-Device (D2D) seed node cluster generation strategy based on coalitional game in social trusted D2D communication system. First, in the premise that the D2D seed node not harm the interests of other nodes and the cooperative power cost considered, a simple distributed algorithm is adopted to form independent and disjoint coalitions to maximize the throughput of the seed node cluster. Then the social trusted framework is introduced to make the segmentation of coalitions effectively meet the requirements of social security. The simulation results show that compared with the node cluster of the traditional cellular network and non-coalitional game, the system throughput of which is maintained at a higher level with social security ensured as well.

Keywords: D2D communication · Coalitional game · Social trusted · Throughput · Node cluster

1 Introduction

With the explosive growth of mobile data traffic, the load of base stations and spectrum resources are nearly saturated. The advantages of D2D communication in data offloading and distribution are making it the mainstream and center of the next generation mobile network, although D2D initially exists as a technical support option for public security services. In the process of D2D providing a variety of in-cell applications and services, it is obviously unfeasible that the simple direct connection on the basis of existing research considering only physical factors without any social awareness toward trust. Therefore, the method combining D2D communication with social awareness emerges and becomes a hot topic in D2D research.

M. Jia et al. (Eds.): WiSATS 2019, LNICST 281, pp. 310–322, 2019.
https://doi.org/10.1007/978-3-030-19156-6_29

In this paper, we focus on promoting the whole throughput and safety coefficient of the social trusted D2D seed node cluster. The major contents of this paper are summarized as follows:

1. Applying the concept of coalitional game into the architecture of system model, proposing a new social aware D2D communication model.
2. Dividing the social relationships into five categories which corresponding five different kinds of social trust coefficient. Social trust classification will help selecting the seed node to join the cluster and enhancing the security of it.
3. Considering the system throughput and social trust coefficient of the seed nodes, the concept of safety throughput is proposed.

The remainder of this paper is organized as follows. In Sect. 2, the related work is briefly described. Section 3 introduces the proposed multi-nodes cooperation model and social relationship model under the framework of coalitional game. In Sect. 4, we present seed node cluster generation algorithm. Section 5 gives performance analysis of proposed algorithm and Sect. 6 draws conclusion of this paper.

2 Related Work

2.1 Social Awareness in D2D Communication

A D2D relay nodes set allocation strategy is presented in [1] based on D2D communication interruption probability and social parameters, which reduces the outage probability, optimizes the system throughput and solves the optimal power allocation for D2D users (DUEs) equipment and D2D relay equipment problems as well. On this basis, a D2D relay communication interference coordination algorithm introducing social relations is proposed in [2], in which relay node selection using the key characteristics of social relations can significantly improve the security and the connection success rate of D2D communication and reduce the cost of the relay detection. In [3], it is pointed that user distribution density and communication distance are important factors affecting the social perception of D2D communication. D2D node data distribution has the social attribute too [4]. By analyzing the interest difference within social users, the author proposes a logic structure detection method based on user interest difference. Accordingly, [5] considers the small scale cluster with DUEs sharing similar interests to optimize cell resource allocation. [6] designs a D2D node set prediction mechanism based on the social interest, in which data sharing is based on DUE cluster sharing similar interest. Considering the mobility of DUES and different interests, the author proposes a distributed mobile embedded social aware caching scheme to cache the shared content in the partitioned form. [7] ensures the size of the DUE set but ignores the influence of social relationships. Due to the mobility and inclination of social networks, DUE always inevitably has social relationship with a specific D2D node and exchanges a large amount of information.

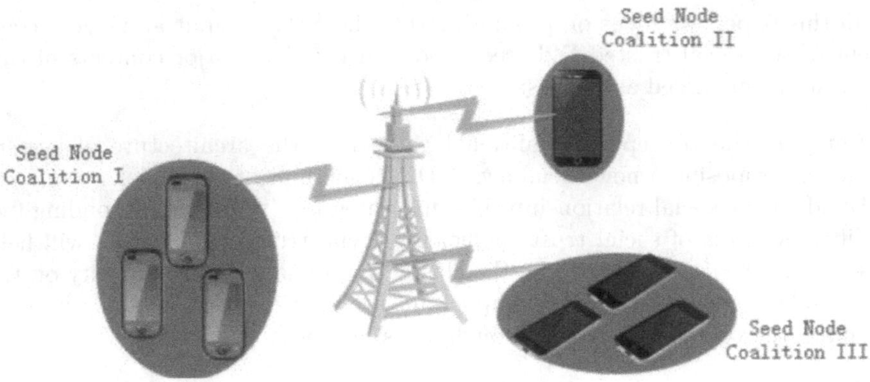

Fig. 1. System model

2.2 Security Challenges in Social-Aware D2D Communication

[8] and [9] use historical social relationships of DUES to group users and explore the probability of the user joining a node cluster. In the field of mobile communications, the combination of social network parameters for directional data transmission can significantly increase the efficiency of wireless communications and user intimacy. Introducing social networks into D2D communication has great potential in solving D2D communication technology problems, improving the effectiveness of the system and designing a new communication system [10–14].

3 Social Trusted Multiple Seed Nodes Cooperation Model

The emergence of D2D communication has subverted the traditional mobile network architecture. D2D communication simplifies the network topology between users and base stations and increases the topology among D2D users. A part of the user nodes share work of data offloading and distribution from the base station. The other users obtain the base station resources by establishing D2D connections with these nodes, which are the so-called seed nodes in this paper.

3.1 Throughput Payoff of the Coalition

We consider a single cell D2D communication model as shown in Fig. 1 with D2D seed nodes and a base station (BS). Each seed node is regarded as the transmitter while BS is regarded as a receiver. All seed nodes in the cell are defined as $N = \{1, ..., T\}$, where $S \subseteq N$ is a coalition containing N users. In TDMA transmission network, it is assumed that time is divided into equally slots. In this way, in non-cooperative scenario, a seed node takes up one time slot, which means T numbers of seed nodes need T time slots to transmit data.

This can be defined as node-level information transmission. While in cooperative scenario, seed nodes compose different disjoint coalitions, each of which can be regarded as a virtual MIMO device. All the seed nodes of a coalition take up a time slot to carry out a transmission. T times of node-level information transmission are carried out. Due to the mobility and the time-variability of the trust coefficient of the seed nodes, the current coalition segmentation is no longer optimal any more, so the next distributed autonomous coalition segmentation is needed. It is assumed that the transmission service arrival of each seed node obeys the same independent Poisson distribution. According to ergodicity, each coalition can be dispatched and the probability of being dispatched is roughly the same as the ratio of the number of users in the coalition and the number of the total users in the system.

Based on the above assumption, the virtual system formed by a coalition S with size $|S| \times T$ can be modeled as:

$$r_S = G_S + H_S z_S \tag{1}$$

where $z_S = [z_1, ..., z_{|S|}]^T$ is the transmit signal vector of each symbol period in coalition S. Each element in z_S represents the signal sent by each seed node in the coalition S. The signal vector received by the BS receiver in each symbol period is expressed as $r_S = [r_1, ..., r_{|S|}]^T$, in which each element is a signal received by BS. $G_S = [G_1, ..., G_{|S|}]^T$ is the independent and identically distributed additive complex Gauss white noise vector of BS receiver.

According to information theory, for Gauss channel, the best distribution of the transmitting signal is also the Gauss signal. It is reasonable to make the element of z_S independent and identically distributed Gauss variable with zero mean value. The covariance matrix of the transmitting signal z_S is:

$$Q_S = E\left[z_S \cdot {z_S}^{\dagger}\right] \tag{2}$$

where ${z_S}^{\dagger}$ is the conjugate transposed matrix of z_S. For a cooperative coalition S, we consider the path loss model between the seed node and the base station in n slots. The fast fading channel matrix ${H_S}^n$ of $T \times |S|$ is adopted where each element represents the channel fading coefficient from the seed node to BS receiver int n slots:

$${h_i}^n = e^{j{\phi_i}^n} \sqrt{\kappa / {d_i}^{n\alpha}} \tag{3}$$

where α is a path fading index and κ is a path fading constant. ${\phi_i}^n$ and ${d_n}^i$ are the signal phase and distance from the seed node i to the base station receiver in n numbers of time slots respectively.

Since we consider a TDMA system, it can be defined that a fixed transmitting power limitation for each time slot, i.e., regardless of the number of seed nodes in a coalition, the total transmit power is limited to:

$$P_S = tr(Q_S) = tr(E[z_S \cdot {z_S}^{\dagger}]) \tag{4}$$

where $tr(\cdot)$ represents the trace of a matrix which can be obtained by summing the diagonal elements of the matrix. The average power limit is applied to all the seed nodes transmitting end of the active coalition set at the time slot. In the non-cooperative scenario, the power limitation above is the same as the power limitation of the active seed nodes in each slot. In fact, due to ergodicity, for each time slot, the long-time power limitation is the same as what of each time slot for each seed node. In this system, only one coalition is allowed to transmit in a time slot, which meas transmitting data will not be interfered by other coalition. Thus, the capacity of the virtual coalition set in one time slot with power limitation is:

$$\begin{aligned} &C_S = \max_{Q_S} I(z_S; r_S) = \max \log\left(\det\left(I_T + H_S \cdot Q_S \cdot {H_S}^{\dagger}\right)\right) \\ &s.t.\ tr[Q_S] \leq P_S. \end{aligned} \tag{5}$$

Finally, according to the water-filling power allocation of each seed node in the coalition, the transmission speed of the seed node j of the coalition S in n time slots can be defined as:

$$C_j = \log\left(1 + \frac{{P_j}^n {\lambda_j}^n}{\sigma^2}\right) \tag{6}$$

In order to form the aforementioned coalition and benefit from the tradeoff between throughput and security, the social trust coefficient of each seed node is evaluated next.

3.2 User Social Relationship Model

In the analysis of social networks, this paper considers the social relationships between DUEs and the social relationships between D2D devices. The social relationships are divided into the following two categories and five types with trust coefficient set for each of them.

User Social Relationship. First, this paper defines a human social relationship (HSR) to indicate the willingness of each D2D node to exchange data with other nodes. This parameter is determined by the degree of familiarity and trust and the frequency of data exchange between D2D node users and the frequency of data exchange. Another type of user social relationship is the market value relationship (MPR). This parameter is determined by the expected benefits that can be obtained by two nodes performing D2D communication. In other words, the establishment of D2D communication guided by this factor is due to the high common interest between the two nodes.

Device Social Relationship. In this type of social relationship, there are not many users actively intervening existing. Instead, D2D device owners and D2D device manufacturers set up rules for trust evaluation. For example, there are co-location device relationship (C-LDR) and co-work device relationship (C-WDR). The former indicates that the two devices that will establish D2D communication have once shared a specific location information (e.g., the family relationship of human society), the latter means that two D2D devices once exchanged resources (e.g., the cooperation between human society) in a D2D communication. Finally, we define an ownership device relationship (ODR) for two D2D devices that belong to the same user. The various relationships and their trust coefficient are shown in Table 1.

Table 1. Social relationship

Social relationship	Relation type	Relation description	Trust coefficient
HSR	User social relationship	Familiarity between D2D nodes	[0, 1]
MRP	User social relationship	Expected benefits that can be obtained by two nodes performing D2D communication	0.2
C-LDR	Device social relationship	Devices sharing a specific location information	0.8
C-WDR	Device social relationship	Devices sharing public experience	0.6
ODR	Device social relationship	Devices that belong to the same user	1

According to the above-mentioned social relationship model, We can describe the social relationship of D2D seed nodes as:

$$r_j = r_i = p_{i,j} \cdot s_{i,j} \tag{7}$$

Where $s_{i,j} \in [0,1]$ represents the social relationship between a D2D communication pair. $p_{i,j}$ is a bisection function. If user i and user j are close to each other, $p_{i,j}$ takes 1; otherwise, it takes 0.

$s_{i,j}$ in the above parameters is decided by the social relationship between users and the social relationship between devices in the previous statement:

$$s_{i,j} = \alpha \cdot H_{i,j} + (1 - \alpha) \cdot D_{i,j} \tag{8}$$

Where $H_{i,j}$ is determined by the social relationships between users in Table 1. Apparently, the HSR and MPR in previous belong to $H_{i,j}$. While C-LDR, C-WDR and ODR belong to $D_{i,j}$ categories. When a D2D communication pair has multiple relationships of the same type (e.g, there is a user social relationship and a market value relationship at the same time), we select an item with the highest coefficient of trust as $H_{i,j}$. It is because closer social relationships will provide securer D2D connections and improve the performance of D2D connections in this way. In addition, we also set a weighting parameter α to dynamically adjust the proportion of user social relationship and device social relationship between the D2D communication pairs according to a specific application scenario. The extreme case where *alpha* is equal to 1 or 0 indicates that there is only user social relationship or only device social relationship between the D2D communication pairs. A more thorough analysis of all possible communication scenarios is beyond the scope of this article. Therefore, if there is no explicit designation, the default value of *alpha* is 0.5. i.e., we consider the importance of user social relationship and device social relationship to be the same.

Considering the actual throughput and social trust coefficient of seed nodes, we can get the safety throughput of each seed node in one time slot:

$$T_j = C_j \cdot r_{i,j} \tag{9}$$

where C_j defined in (6) represents the transmission speed and r_j defined in (7) represents the social trust coefficient of seed node j respectively.

4 Social Trusted Seed Node Cluster Generation Algorithm Based on Coalitional Game

The generation problem of D2D seed node cluster is modeled as a utility non-transferable coalitional game. The proposed game model can characterize the trade-off between improving system throughput and ensuring node security. By analyzing the formation process and the structure of the coalition, all the seed nodes in the cluster are guaranteed to have higher transmission speed and social trust coefficient.

Specifically, utility non-transferable coalitional game can be defined as $(\mathcal{N}, \mathcal{V}, \mathcal{S})$, in which $\mathcal{N}$ is the set of all game participants with all seed node included. $\mathcal{S} = \{S_1, ...S_k, ...S_K\}$is called a coalition structure and its constituent element $S_k (1 < k < K)$ s a coalition that satisfies $\forall k' \neq k$, $S'_k \bigcap S_k = \varnothing$ and $\bigcup_{k=1}^{K} S_k = \mathcal{N}$. ν is the eigenfunction of coalitional game, which is obtained based on the safety throughput of seed nodes. Since it is a utility non-transferable coalitional game, $\nu(S_k)$ is the set of all $|S_k|$-dimensional utility vectors that S_k can guarantee, which gives each coalition $S_k \subseteq \mathcal{N}$ a subset $\nu(S_k) \subseteq \mathbb{R}^{|S_k|}$:

$$\nu(S_k) = \{\phi(S_k) | \phi(S_k) = (\phi_i(S_k))_{i \in S_k}\} \tag{10}$$

where $\phi(S_k)$ is a vector and the elements in $\phi(S_k)$ represent the safety throughput of participant i in coalition S_k:

$$\phi(S_k) = T_i, i \in S_k, S_k \in \mathcal{S} \tag{11}$$

where T_i is defined in (9). Then we can define the utility function of each coalition $\mathcal{S} \subseteq \mathcal{N}$:

$$\nu_S^n = |\mathcal{S}| T_S^n \tag{12}$$

The aim of this paper is to increase the security throughput as much as possible. As water-filling power considered as the cost of coalition, there will be coalitions with strong desire to deviate from the major coalition and break it into independent and disjoint minor ones. Thus, the major coalition is not always the best coalition structure. With the basic concept of coalitional game described in the previous sections, we can design a self-organizing coalitional game algorithm in D2D communication networks, which is based on the simple principle of merger and separation and allows an improved segmentation $\prod_N$ as follows:

Principle of Merger. For any coalition set $\{S_1, ..., S_j\}$, as long as the condition $\{U^l_{j-1}\} \triangleright \{S_1, ..., S_l\}$ is satisfied, the coalition set is merged, i.e. $\{S_1, ..., S_l\} \rightarrow \{U^l_{j=1} S_j\}$, where each S_i represents a coalition.

Principle of Separation. For any coalition $U^l_{j=1} S_j$, as long as the condition $\{S_1, ..., S_l\} \triangleright \{U^l_{j=1} S_j\}$ is satisfied, the coalition set is separated, i.e. $\{U^l_{j-1}\} \rightarrow \{S_1, ..., S_l\}$, where each S_i represents a coalition.

In short, if merger (or separating) produces a $\triangleright$based priority set, multiple coalitions will merge or separate. The article [14] shows that any iteration of merger or separation will terminate. So it is feasible to design a coalitional game algorithm by merger and separating. In the seed node cooperation coalitional game, it is very attractive to use Pareto criterion as a comparison relation of the merger-separation principle. Under the effect of the Pareto criterion, at least one seed node can increase its personal payoff with this merger only if it does not reduce the payoff of other seed nodes. The coalition will merge. Similarly, at least one seed node in the coalition can directly increase its personal payoff by this separation only when it does not harm the payoff of other seed nodes. Therefore, a merger or separation decision depends on the fact that all seed nodes must benefit from this merger or separation. As a result, any merger (separation) form can be reached when it allows at least one seed nodes to increase payoff and all related users guarantee their payoff meanwhile. The algorithm we propose is summarized as follows:

Algorithm 1. Social trusted seed node cluster generation algorithm

---

Initialization: $\prod_N \leftarrow \{1, 2, .., N\}, C_i \leftarrow 0, H^0_i, \alpha \leftarrow 0.5, n \leftarrow 1 \forall i$
repeat
1) Each seed node selects a potential coalition partner meeting the requirements $r_j > 0$
2) Calculate node transmission speed by formula (6)
3) Calculate the social trust coefficient of each seed node by formula (7)
4) Each node joins a coalition that guarantees maximum security throughput by formula (9) and (11)

until Convergence to a stable and optimal coalition segmentation

---

Theorem 1. *Iterative operations based on Merger-Separation (M-S) criterion will be terminated.*

Proof. Proposition 1 guarantees that social trusted seed node cluster generation algorithm can converge. In addition, the complexity of algorithm is closely related to the number of M-S operations. There are a total number of $N-1$ attempts in the merger operation. Considering the worst scenario, i.e., to traverse all the coalitions in the coalition structure and achieve separation operations, the number of operations required is Baer number. Stability is one of the most important concepts for a coalition game because that of the segmentation means that no combination of the participants can improve the payoff by separating. The stability of the coalition structure obtained by the proposed game model is analyzed below.

Theorem 2. *The coalition structure S obtained by social trusted seed node cluster generation algorithm is stable.*

Proof. It is pointed out in [14] that the coalition structure is stable only if it is the result of the iteration of the M-S criterion. The social trusted seed node cluster generation algorithm is based on the M-S iteration process, so it can directly use the above theorem to verify the correctness. Conversely, if the proposed algorithm cannot be terminated, the final coalition structure cannot be formed. Proposition proved.

5 Simulations

5.1 Simulation Scenario and Parameters

In this section we verify the effectiveness of the proposed algorithm. Considering a single-cell scenario with simplified interference. The cell radius is 500 m, the maximum D2D communication distance is 50 m, the base station transmit power is 46 dBm, the seed node transmit power is 23 dBm and the number of users is [10, 100]. The remaining parameters are shown in Table 2.

Table 2. Core simulation parameters

Parameters	Value
Maximum D2D range	30 m
Cell radius	100 m
Base station transmit power	46 dBm
User transmit power	23 dBm
D2D link establishment time	1 s
Node movement model	Levy flight
Amount of users	[10, 100]
$H_{i,j}$	[0, 1]
$D_{i,j}$	[0.6, 0.8, 1]

5.2 Simulation Results and Analysis

In the communication scenario, the communication entities (seed nodes and non-seed nodes) are subject to the free movement of Levi's flight. The discovery of the D2D device and the establishment of the D2D connection are completed by the base station using the appropriate network protocol. Data transmission between the D2D nodes Out-of-band is completed out-of-band (e.g. Wi-Fi and LTE parallel). In order to verify the efficiency of the strategy, the following scenarios are used as a comparison:

Cellular Solution. Connect using only traditional cellular links.

Simple D2D Connection. Two D2D devices covered by cellular are connected in the shortest distance with base station acting as a security assessment.

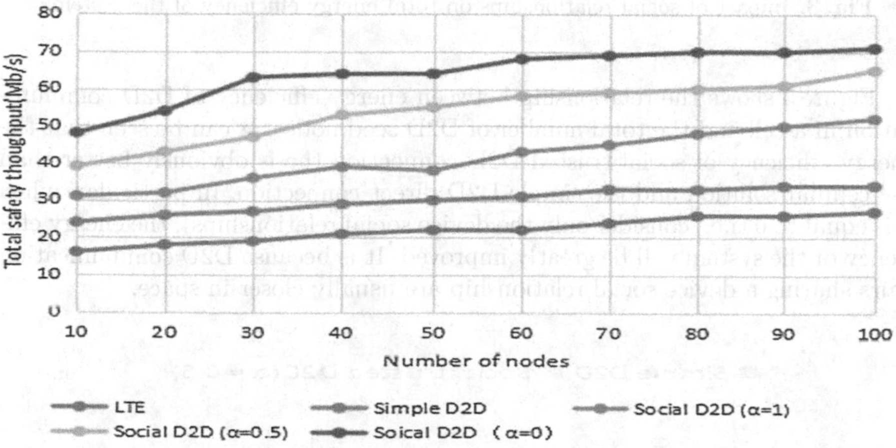

Fig. 2. Impact of social relationships on system throughput

Social Trusted D2D Connection. A D2D node cluster is established based on the method in previous of this paper. The cellular coverage of the seed node is guaranteed while the cellular coverage of other non-seed nodes is not. The security assessment is self-assessed by the D2D linker. In order to evaluate the impact of social relationships between users and social relationships of devices, α will be taken as 0, 0.5, 1 for comparison.

Figure 2 shows the relationship between the total safety throughput and the total number of D2D seed nodes in the cell. As is shown, the total safety throughput of social trusted D2D connections is always better than the cellular solution and the simple D2D direct connection within the range of the number of users. Specifically, when α is equal to 0 (i.e. consider social relationships of devices). The result shows that the social trust coefficient between devices higher, the safety throughput of the system will greatly improve.

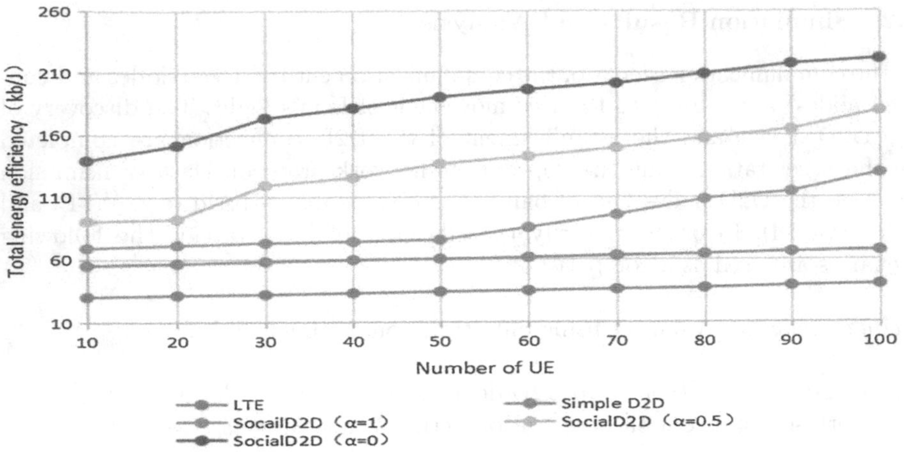

Fig. 3. Impact of social relationships on total energy efficiency of the system

Figure 3 shows the relationship between energy efficiency of D2D communication in a cell and the total number of D2D seed nodes. It can be seen that the energy efficiency of social trusted D2D connection the is obviously better than the cellular solution and the simple D2D direct connection. In particular, when α is equal to 0 (i.e., consider only the device social relationships), the energy efficiency of the system will be greatly improved. It is because D2D communication pairs sharing a device social relationship are usually closer in space.

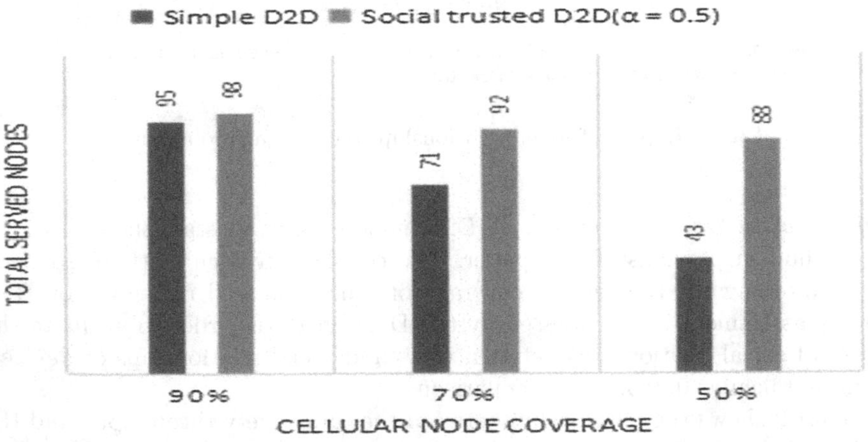

Fig. 4. Impact of social relationships on number of served nodes in the system

Further, in the right subplot of Fig. 4 we report on the proportion of users served with a simple D2D link or a social trusted D2D cluster. As we learn from this plot, when the available cellular coverage area is particularly small, in the case of the simple D2D solution the number of users that establish a D2D connection is low. This is due to the fact that under-coverage users reside in proximity to the BS and thus receive higher channel quality compared to that on the D2D link. As a consequence, a higher number of users may be served through the infrastructure links with the BS. On the contrary, the percentage of users served via D2D connections is three times higher for the proposed social trusted D2D solution. The explanation of this result lies in our solution being able to also provide connectivity to those users who are outside the cellular coverage (i.e., within D2D clusters). Note that this important outcome is achieved due to the operation of our social-based secure cluster formation scheme.

6 Conclusions

In this paper, we combine social relationships with D2D communication and adopt the method of coalitional game to propose a D2D seed node cluster generation algorithm toward social trust. This paper introduces two models, multiple seed node cooperation model and user relationship model. Based on this, this paper proposes the concept of security throughput, which maximizes throughput of seed node clusters on the premise of security. Simulation results proves the effect of our solution.

Acknowledgements. Foundation Items: The National Natural Science Foundation of China for Youth (61201160, 61602263); The Natural Science Foundation of Jiangsu Province (BK20131377, BK20151507, BK20160916); The Natural science fund for colleges and universities in Jiangsu Province under Grants (16KJB510034); The six talent peaks project in Jiangsu Province (XYDXXJS-044); A Project Funded by the Priority Academic Program Development of Jiangsu Higher Education Institutions (yx002001); The Jiangsu Overseas Research and Training Program for University Prominent Young and Middle-aged Teachers and Presidents; Sponsored by NUPTSF (Grant Nos. NY212012, NY214065, NY216020); National Natural Science Foundation of China under grant number (61872186).

References

1. Asadi, A., Mancuso, V., Gupta, R.: DORE: an experimental framework to enable outband D2D relay in cellular networks. IEEE/ACM Trans. Netw. **PP**(99), 1–14 (2017)
2. Zhang, Z., Zhang, P., Liu, D., et al.: SRSM-based adaptive relay selection for D2D communications. IEEE Internet of Things J. **PP**(99), 1 (2017)
3. Yi, W., Liu, Y., Nallanathan, A.: Modeling and analysis of D2D millimeter-wave networks with poisson cluster processes. IEEE Trans. Commun. **PP**(99), 1 (2017)
4. Wang, Z., Shahmansouri, H., Wong, V.: How to Download More Data from Neighbors? A Metric for D2D Data Offloading Opportunity. IEEE Educational Activities Department (2017)

5. Feng, Z., Gulliver, T.A.: Effective small social community aware D2D resource allocation underlaying cellular networks. IEEE Wirel. Commun. Lett. **PP**(99), 1 (2017)
6. Li, J., Liu, M., Lu, J., et al.: On social-aware content caching for D2D-enabled cellular networks with matching theory. IEEE Internet of Things J. **PP**(99), 1 (2017)
7. Doppler, K., Rinne, M., Wijting, C., et al.: Device-to-device communication as an underlay to LTE-advanced networks. Mod. Sci. Technol. Telecommun. **47**(12), 42–49 (2009)
8. Li, Y., Wu, T., Hui, P., et al.: Social-aware D2D communications: qualitative insights and quantitative analysis. IEEE Commun. Mag. **52**(6), 150–158 (2014)
9. Zhang, B., Li, Y., Jin, D., et al.: Social-aware peer discovery for D2D communications underlaying cellular networks. IEEE Trans. Wirel. Commun. **14**(5), 2426–2439 (2015)
10. Chen, X., Proulx, B., Gong, X., et al.: Exploiting social ties for cooperative D2D communications: a mobile social networking case. IEEE/ACM Trans. Netw. **23**(5), 1471–1484 (2015)
11. Chen, S., Wang, K., Zhao, C., Zhang, H., Sun, Y.: Accelerated distributed optimization design for reconstruction of big sensory data. IEEE Internet of Things J. **4**(5), 1716–1725 (2017)
12. Chen, S., Zhao, C., Wu, M., Sun, Z., Zhang, H., Leung, V.C.M.: Compressive network coding for wireless sensor networks: spatio-temporal coding and optimization design. Comput. Netw. **108**, 1339–1351 (2016)
13. Chen, S., Zhou, J., Zheng, X., Ruan, X.: Energy-efficient data collection scheme for environmental quality management in buildings. IEEE Access **6**, 57324–57333 (2018)
14. Apt, K.R., Witzel, A.: A generic approach to coalition formation. Int. Game Theory Rev. **11**(3), 347–367 (2009)

A Puncturing Algorithm for Mixing 2-Kernel and 3-Kernel Polar Codes

Xiaojun Zhang(✉), Chen Chen, Jianming Cui, Geng Chen, and Hengzhong Li

Shandong University of Science and Technology,
Qingdao, Shandong, People's Republic of China
zhangxiaojun@sdust.edu.cn

Abstract. In this paper, a puncturing algorithm for mixing 2-kernel and 3-kernel polar codes is presented. The puncturing sequence is generated based on the capacity of channels and the upper bound of minimum block error probability for successive cancellation (SC) decoding. We use the capacity-zero puncturing model, the decoding algorithm of mother codes can still be adopted. An improved greedy algorithm of computing the maximization of the minimum distance is proposed to select the information set. The maximum number of punctured bits is limited to $[1, 2^{n-2})$ when the length of subcodes $M \in (2^{n-2} * 3, 2^n)$. Simulation results show that the block error rate based on the mixing kernels is better than that based on 2-kernel.

Keywords: Polar codes · Multi-kernel · Length-compatible · Puncturing

1 Introduction

The original polar codes, proposed by Arikan [1], are capacity-achieving linear block codes. It is recursively constructed by the binary kernel matrix $\begin{bmatrix} 1 & 0 \\ 1 & 1 \end{bmatrix}$. However, the code length is limit to be $N = 2^n$. [2] has proved that $l \times l$ kernel is granted for the polarization effect, where $l > 2$. It code length is $N = l^n$ [3]. To achieved more flexible code length, [4] presents construction methods based on multi-kernel, $N = l_1^n \times l_2^m$. This method is still restricted to achieve arbitrary code length.

In general, puncturing [5] and shorten [9] is a technique to implement higher code rate and wide range of code lengths. [6] proposed a puncturing pattern. Since the punctured channels don't transmit the information, they are treated as zero-capacity channels (completely noisy channels). We call this category as the capacity-zero (C0) puncturing model. The pattern punctures bits from the frozen set, which limits the performance of puncturing. [7] proposed a low-complexity puncturing algorithm, which selects the first m bits of the output as puncturing bits. It gets a better performance of the block error rate (BLER) than LET and WCDMA by using the successive cancellation list (SCL) decoder. However, all

M. Jia et al. (Eds.): WiSATS 2019, LNICST 281, pp. 323–332, 2019.
https://doi.org/10.1007/978-3-030-19156-6_30

the above puncturing schemes are based on the mother codes $N = 2^n$, and the performance is worse when too many bits are punctured.

This paper proposes a puncturing algorithm based on polar construction mixing kernels of sizes 2 and 3, when the length of subcodes $M \in (2^{n-1}, 2^{n-2}*3)$. We can puncture the bits from mother code $N = 2^{n-2} * 3$ and combine the original puncturing algorithms when $M \in (2^{n-2} * 3, 2^n)$, the maximum number of punctured bits is limited to $[1, 2^{n-2})$. It is proved that the puncturing code is still applicable to the original SCL decoder. For short code lengths, the minimum distance has a large impact on performance, the polarization effect is not crucial. Theoretically, the punctured table can be acquired by optimization of distance spectrum or minimum Hamming distance. It is discovered that the maximal minimum-distance spectrum can be acquired by using recursion [8]. We propose the puncturing algorithm to select the punctured bits and use the improved greedy algorithm to select the information bits.

The rest of this paper is organized as follows. In Sect. 2, a brief review is given to the mixing 2-kernel and 3-kernel polar code. The proposed puncturing method is presented in Sect. 3. Numerical results are provided in Sect. 4. Finally, Sect. 5 concludes the paper.

2 Preliminaries

Since the code length is $N = n_1 \times \cdots \times n_s$, the generator matrix is defined as $G_N \triangleq T_{n_1} \otimes \cdots \otimes T_{n_s}$, where $\otimes$ denote Kronecker product, n_i denote the dimension of kernel and $T_2 = \begin{bmatrix} 1 & 0 \\ 1 & 1 \end{bmatrix}$, $T_3 = \begin{bmatrix} 1 & 1 & 1 \\ 1 & 0 & 1 \\ 0 & 1 & 1 \end{bmatrix}$, the dimensions of kernels 2×2, 3×3 respectively. If we select the first bit as the information bit, then the largest minimum distance is 3. For the size of the information set is 2, the last two bits are selected and the minimum distance is 2. If we select all the bits as information bits, the minimum distance is 1. The minimum-distance spectrum is $S_{T_3} = (3, 2, 1)$. For example, because of the recursive operation of generator matrix, it is cleared that $N_6 = T_2 \otimes T_3 = \begin{bmatrix} T_3 & 0 \\ T_3 & T_3 \end{bmatrix}$. The minimum-distance spectrum $S_{T_6} = sort(T_3, T_3 + T_3)$, where $sort(x)$ denotes the sorting of vector x in the decreasing ordering. The information set A and the frozen set A^c are acquired by the greedy algorithm, which is based on maximize minimum-distance spectrum. The binary output vector $X = \{x_1, x_2, \cdots, x_N\}$ can be acquired form the binary output vector $U = \{u_1, u_2, \cdots, u_N\}$ with G_N, $X = UG_N$. As in the binary case, the indices of X are required to be reshuffled. For each stage $i > 1$, the permutation matrix P_{i} can be calculated as

$$P_i = (Q_i | Q_i + N_{i+1} | Q_i + 2N_{i+1} \cdots | Q_i + (N/N_{i+1}) N_{i+1}) \qquad (1)$$

Where Q_i is the canonical permutation, it is introduced in [4]. Assume that the $n_j \times n_j$ is the dimension of the j-th kernel of the Kronecker product, $N_{\mathrm{i}} = \prod_{j=1}^{i-1} n_j$, the last stage $P_s = Q_s$. Then the output indices are acquired in the first stage by P_1. Then we can get the X permutation in the final, in Sect. 3 we will show an example in detail.

The reliability of output is calculated with Bhattacharyya parameter over BEC channels. The subchannels' capacity of T_3 is

$$\begin{cases} I(W_3^1)=I(W_1)I(W_2)I(W_3) \\ I(W_3^2)=I(W_1)+I(W_2)I(W_3)-I(W_1)I(W_2)I(W_3) \\ I(W_3^3)=I(W_1)+I(W_2)-I(W_1)I(W_2) \end{cases} \quad (2)$$

Multi-kernel polar code can calculate the error probability of subchannel by using Gaussian approximation (GA). In the case of binary additive white Gaussian noise channel (B-AWGNC), it assumes that all-zero bits are transmitted, and the probability density function (PDF) of likelihood ratios (LLRs) is $a_N^i \sim N(m_N^i, 2m_N^i)$, where $m_1^1 = 2/\sigma^2$. The recursive formulas of LLRs are calculated by

$$m_{3N}^{3i-1} = \varphi^{-1}(1-(1-m_N^i)^3) \quad (3)$$

$$m_{3N}^{3i-2} = \varphi^{-1}(1-(1-m_N^i)^2) + m_N^i \quad (4)$$

$$m_{3N}^{3i} = 2m_N^i \quad (5)$$

Where

$$\varphi(x) = \begin{cases} 1-\frac{1}{\sqrt{4\pi x}}\int_{-\infty}^{\infty}\tanh\frac{u}{2}\cdot exp(-\frac{(u-x)^2}{4x})du & x \geq 10 \\ 0 & x=0 \end{cases} \quad (6)$$

$\varphi(x)$ can be calculated by

$$\varphi(x) = \begin{cases} \sqrt{\frac{\pi}{x}}(1-\frac{10}{7x})exp(-\frac{x}{4}) & x \geq 10 \\ exp(-0.4527x^{-0.86}+0.00218) & 0<x<10 \end{cases} \quad (7)$$

Assume all-zero vectors are transmitted, the estimate of u is determined to 1 when the LLR is less than 0. The probability over $(-\infty, 0)$ is the error probability of SC decoding

$$p_e(i) = \int_{-\infty}^{0} \frac{1}{2\sqrt{\pi m_N^{(i)}}} \cdot exp(\frac{-(x-m_N^{(i)})^2}{4m_N^{(i)}})dx \quad (8)$$

3 Puncturing Algorithm for Mixing 2-Kernel and 3-Kernel Polar Codes

In this section, the paper analyzes the impact of each punctured bit on the other bits and the feasibility of puncturing algorithm for mixing 2-kernel and 3-kernel polar code. We propose the method of puncturing input bits for mixing of kernel polar codes, and apply the quasi-uniform puncturing (QUP) algorithm to the proposed mixing 2-kernel and 3-kernel construction method. After puncturing, the minimum-distance spectrum is used to select the information set A and the frozen set A^c.

Theorem 1. *Regardless of the puncturing from the input bits or the output bits, it can receive the same number of channel with zero-capacity at the other side by using T_3 kernel.*

Proof. For T_3, the input bits of LLRs with SC decoder are calculated by

$$L(u_1) = 2tanh^{-1}(tanh\frac{L(y_1)}{2}tanh\frac{L(y_2)}{2}tanh\frac{L(y_3)}{2}) \tag{9}$$

$$L(u_2) = 2tanh^{-1}(tanh\frac{L(y_2)}{2}tanh\frac{L(y_3)}{2})+(-1)^{u_1}L(y_1) \tag{10}$$

$$L(u_3) = (-1)^{u_1}L(y_2) + (-1)^{u_1 \oplus u_3}L(y_3) \tag{11}$$

If one bit is punctured, one of the output sequence y_1^3 does not have any message. We will puncture one bit and make one of $\{L(y_1); L(y_2); L(y_3)\}$ be 0. No matter what the situation is, that will lead to $L(u_1) = 0$. The capacity of subchannels can also be calculated by (2). When puncturing one bit from input bits, the result of $I(W_3^1) = 0$ remains no matter which one is chosen in $\{W_1, W_2, W_3\}$. For other stages, due to T_2, it can acquire the same number of channel with zero-capacity at both sides. In every stage, it can get the same number of channels with zero-capacity at the both side. And the one which is puncturing the first bit in T_3 as the optimal puncturing pattern. It can be noticed that the input bit u_1 corresponds exactly to the output bit y_1. When the subcodes $M \in (2^{n-1}, 2^{n-2} * 3)$, it just needs to puncture 2^{n-2} bits at most.

Theorem 2. *Suppose that the length of subcodes $M \in (2^{n-1}, 2^{n-2} * 3)$, the number of puncturing codes m. Puncturing the bits $\{y_1, \cdots, y_m\}$ from the output bits, the corresponding input bits must be the bits with zero-capacity.*

Proof. Assume that the error probability of the sub-channel is $p_e(i)$. The overall block error probability upper bound of polar code is obtained by

$$\text{BLER} \leq \sum_{i \in A} p_e(i) \tag{12}$$

Based on the minimum estimate of $\sum p_e(i)$, we can get the structure and the best performance. Therefore, when a bit in T_3 is punctured, we can select the optimal puncturing pattern which minimizes BLER. The punctured bits can be regarded as $L(y_i) \sim N(0, 0)$, where $E(x)$ denotes the mean of LLRs

$$E(u_1) = \varphi^{-1}(1 - (1 - E(y_1))(1 - E(y_2))(1 - E(y_3))) \tag{13}$$

$$E(u_2) = \varphi^{-1}(1 - (1 - E(y_2))(1 - E(y_3))) + E(y_1) \tag{14}$$

$$E(u_3) = E(y_1) + E(y_2) \tag{15}$$

Table 1 enlists the error probability of subchannels for T_3 after puncturing one bit. In case of puncturing the first bit or third bit of T_3, the minimum block error probability upper bound can be obtained.

Considering of the Theorem 1, we determine that the first bit in the T_3 is the unique puncturing position. The output sequence after polarization can be acquired using (1) when one bit is punctured. An example is given in Fig. 1.

Table 1. The error probability of subchannels for T_3 after puncturing one bit

Punctured bit	u_1	u_2	u_3	*Total*
u_1		0.2605	0.0786	0.3391
u_2	0.2606		0.1587	0.4193
u_3	0.2606	0.0786		0.3391

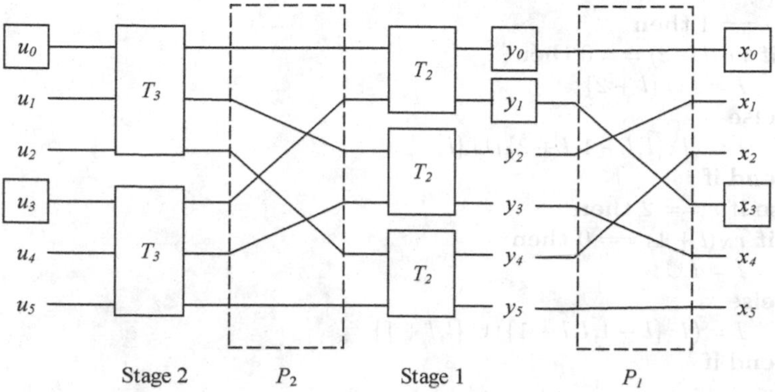

Fig. 1. Tanner graph of mixing 2-kernel and 3-kernel polar code with $N = 6$

Since stage 2 is the last stage, $P_2 = Q_2$, $Q_2 = \begin{pmatrix} 1\,2\,3\,4\,5\,6 \\ 1\,3\,5\,2\,4\,6 \end{pmatrix}$, we can get P_1 by all the other P_i, $P_1 = (P_2)^{-1} = \begin{pmatrix} 1\,2\,3\,4\,5\,6 \\ 1\,4\,2\,5\,3\,6 \end{pmatrix}$. The output order can be calculated with P_1. The polar code for $N = 6, M = 4, m = 2$, the puncturing vector $\mathbf{P} = (p_1, p_2, p_3, p_4, p_5, p_6)$, where $p_i \in \{0, 1\}$ denotes the corresponding output bits. $\mathbf{P}$ is set to all ones initially, the output x_i is punctured when $p_i = 0$. The algorithm is described as:

Step1: Set the first m bits as zeros of $\mathbf{P}$.
Step2: Update permutation by P_1 and obtain the puncturing set of input bits, B.

We find that the bits, which is the first bit of each T_3, are already in the first third of the output sequence. So any bits in the first third of output bits can be punctured. If the punctured bits from output sequence have zero-capacity, the corresponding input bits must be the bits with zero-capacity calculating by (2).

After puncturing the bit of T_3, the generator matrix is $\begin{bmatrix} 0\,1 \\ 1\,1 \end{bmatrix}$, the minimum-distance spectrum is $S'_{T_3} = (2, 1, 0)$, the corresponding position of input bits are $\{u_2; u_2, u_3; \phi\}$. If we delete columns corresponding to the punctured positions from, $G_N = T_2^{\otimes n} \otimes T_3$ and the vector $r'_N = (2, 1)^{\otimes n} \otimes S'_{T_3}$, where r'_N is an unsorted version of the minimum-distance spectrum. We set $I = \{\}$, at each step we will select one row add to I.

Algorithm 1. Information set to minimum distance

```
Initialize the set I = {}
Load N-vector r_N
Load B
for i = 1, ..., K do
    l = argmax(r_N)
    q = (l mod 3)
    r_N(l) = 0;
    if q == 1 then
        if r_N(l + 2) == 0 then
            I = I ∪ {l + 2}
        else
            I = (I\{l, l + 1, l + 2}) ∪ {l}
        end if
    else if q == 2 then
        if r_N(l + 1) == 0 then
            I = I ∪ l
        else
            I = (I\{l − 1, l, l + 1}) ∪ {l, l + 1}
        end if
    else
        I = (I\{l − 2, l − 1, l}) ∪ {l − 2, l − 1, l}
    end if
end for
```

For instance, $M = 5$ and $K = 3$. When $M \in (2^2, 2^1 * 3)$, we will use the puncturing algorithm for mixing 2-kernel and 3-kernel polar code. When the code lengths is $N = 2^1 * 3^1 = 6$, the puncturing vector is initialized as $\mathbf{P} = (1,1,1,1,1,1)$. After the first step and reshuffling permutations, $\mathbf{P} = (0,1,1,1,1,1)$, the punctured position is u_1. The generator matrix G_6 is depicted as

$$G_6 = \begin{bmatrix} 0\,0\,0\,0\,0\,0 \\ 0\,0\,1\,0\,0\,0 \\ 0\,1\,1\,0\,0\,0 \\ 0\,1\,1\,1\,1\,1 \\ 0\,0\,1\,1\,0\,1 \\ 0\,1\,1\,0\,1\,1 \end{bmatrix} \tag{16}$$

The sequence of the minimum-distance spectrum is $S_{T_6} = (5,3,2,2,1,0)$. The information set I is initially empty.

Step1: $l = \{4\}$, $q = 1, r_N(6) \neq 0$, $I = 4$.
Step2: $l = 5$, $q = 2, r_N(6) \neq 0$, $I = \{5,6\}$.
Step3: $l = 1$, $q = 1, r_N(3) = 0$, $I = \{3,5,6\}$.

4 Numerical Results

When $M \in (2^{n-1}, 2^n)$, the method of this paper combines with the QUP algorithm based on the original polar code, which can effectively reduce the number of punctured bits, and improve the decoding performance. For instance, when $M \in [128, 192]$, the number of punctured bits based on proposed algorithm are represented in Fig. 2(a). And Fig. 2(b) shows the number of punctured bits based on the original polar codes. It shows that the proposed algorithm less 64 bits than that based on the original polar codes.

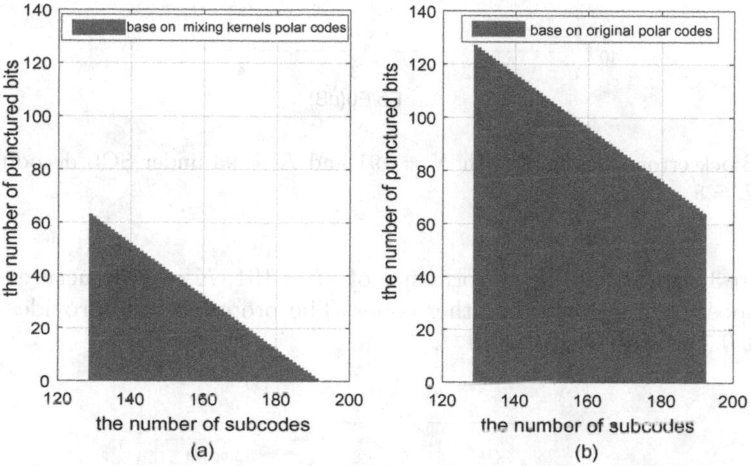

Fig. 2. The number of punctured bits needed for different subcodes

When $M \in (2^{n-1}, 2^{n-2} * 3)$, the proposed method effectively reduces the punctured bits based on the mother codes being equal to 1/4 of the original codes. When $M \in (2^n * 3, 2^{n+2})$, it can still puncture the bits based on original polar code. Because of the above improvements, the research can limit the maximal number of punctured bits to 2^{n-1}. Moreover, compared with the original polar code puncturing algorithm based on the 2-kernel polar code, the decoding based on the mother decoder, and complexity of the multi-kernel polar code decoder is lower than that of the original polar code. Therefore, the proposed algorithm has lower complexity compared to the decoder and encoder of the state-of-the-art punctured polar code.

In Figs. 3 and 4, the paper compares BLER performance of the proposed puncturing algorithm over AWGN channel against the punctured and shortened polar code based on the original polar code. We adopt the SCL decoding with $L = 8$. When $M = 191$ and dimension $K = 96$, the mother code based on multi-kernel of length $N = 192$, and others use mother code based on the original polar code of length $N = 256$.

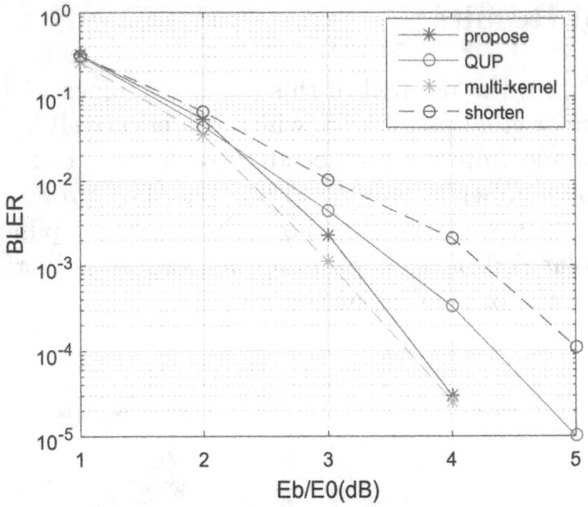

Fig. 3. Block error rates for length $N = 191$ and $K = 96$ under SCL decoding with list size $L = 8$

Figure 3 shows that the performance of $M = 191$, $K = 96$ punctured codes. The proposed outperform the other codes. The proposed code provides a gain of about 0.55 dB at BLER of 10^{-4}.

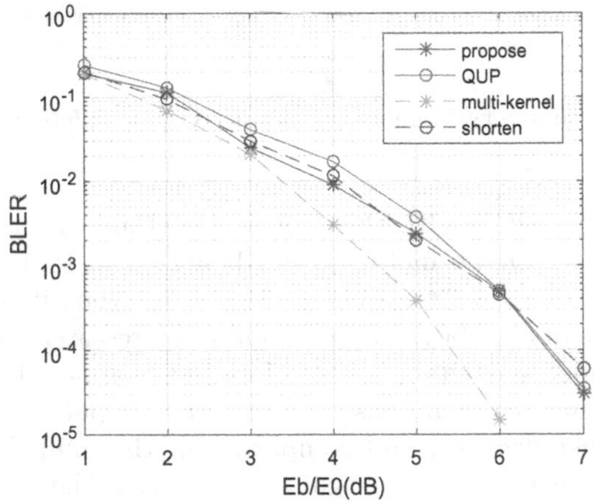

Fig. 4. Block error rates for length $N = 40$ and $K = 20$ under SCL decoding with list size $L = 8$

Figure 4 depicts that the performance of a code of length $M = 40$ and dimension $K = 20$. The BLER of the proposed is close to that of the shorten polar code. This shows that the proposed algorithm should be further optimized in adopting larger-scale and varied kernel not only use T_3 to construct the multi-kernel. The proposed puncturing algorithm based on multi-kernel significantly outperforms QUP puncturing algorithm which is based on original 2-kernel polar code. It is expected that this heuristic algorithm can apply puncturing algorithm to multi-kernel polar code, when larger puncturing ratio in practical applications is required.

5 Conclusions

In this paper, we present a puncturing algorithm for mixing 2-kernel and 3-kernel polar code. When $M \in (2^{n-1}, 2^{n-2} * 3)$, the proposed algorithm for mixing codes can puncture less 2^{n-2} bits than the others. We further improve the greedy algorithm, which is suitable for puncturing algorithm, to find the information set. Simulation results show that the proposed algorithm can have similar or even better performance than that based on 2-kernel polar code.

Acknowledgment. This work was supported in part by the NSFC (61701284, 61472229, 61471224), Project funded by China Postdoctoral Science Foundation (2016M592216) and Qingdao postdoctoral research project (2016125), Sci. & Tech. Development Fund of Shandong Province of China (2016ZDJS02A11), and SDUST Research Fund (2015TDJH102). 2017 Humanities and Social Sciences Research Program of University in Shandong (J17ZZ27).

References

1. Arikan, E.: Channel polarization: a method for constructing capacity-achieving codes for symmetric binary-input memoryless channels. IEEE Press **55**(7), 3051–3073 (2009)
2. Korada, S.-B., Sasoglu, E., Urbanke, R.: Polar codes: characterization of exponent, bounds, and constructions. IEEE Trans. Inf. Theory **56**(12), 3253–6264 (2010)
3. Wang, X., Zhang, Z., Zhang, L.: On the SC decoder for any polar code of length $N = l^n$. In: Wireless Communications and Networking Conference, pp. 485–489. IEEE, Istanbul (2014)
4. Gabry, F., Bioglio, V., Land, I., Belfiore, J.C.: Multi-kernel construction of polar codes. In: 2017 IEEE International Conference on Communications Workshops (ICC Workshops), pp. 761–765. IEEE, Paris (2017)
5. Eslami, A., Pishro-Nik, H.: A practical approach to polar codes. In: IEEE International Symposium on Information Theory Proceedings, pp. 16–20. IEEE, St. Petersburg (2011)
6. Zhang, L., Zhang, Z., Wang, X., Yu, Q.: On the puncturing patterns for punctured polar codes. In: IEEE International Symposium on Information Theory, pp. 121–125. IEEE, Honolulu (2014)
7. Niu, K., Chen, K., Lin, J.-R.: Beyond turbo codes: rate-compatible punctured polar codes. In: 2013 IEEE International Conference on Communications (ICC), pp. 3423–3427. IEEE, Budapest (2013)

8. Bioglio, V., Gabry, F., Land, I., Belfiore, J.-C.: Minimum-distance based construction of multi-kernel polar codes. In: 2017 IEEE Global Communications Conference, GLOBECOM 2017, pp. 1–6 (2016). IEEE Global Communications Conference 18(12), 2081–2084
9. Wang, R., Liu, R.: A novel puncturing scheme for polar codes. IEEE Commun. Lett. **18**(12), 2081–2084 (2016)

A Quick Adaptive Migration Algorithm for Virtual Network Function

Yizhong Wang[1], Xiaorong Zhu[1(✉)], and Xiaohua Qiu[2]

[1] Nanjing University of Posts and Telecommunications, Nanjing 210003, China
xrzhu@njupt.edu.cn
[2] Nanjing Institute of Technology, Nanjing 210003, China

Abstract. The combination of software defined network (SDN) and network function virtualization (NFV) solves some problems in traditional networks, such as service deployment and configuration and management of network resources. However, it also introduces new problems such as network load imbalance. Virtual network function (VNF) migration is an effective way to solve these problems. In this paper, we propose a quick adaptive migration algorithm for VNF, which combines pre-calculation and real-time calculation to reduce the cost of migration. When the node triggers the light-overload-threshold, we perform a pre-calculation of migration for the node and set the result-set. When the node is overloaded, we perform the migration if the result-set is unexpired, otherwise we perform the real-time migration solution. Simulation results show that this algorithm can effectively reduce the number of migration, improve the stability of the system and reduce the overall network migration overhead of the system.

Keywords: Virtual network function · Migration algorithm · Multi-objective decision-making

1 Introduction

With the development of network and the large-scale application of Internet of things (IoT) technology, massive terminal access network. Traditional network architecture is confronted with many problems, such as bloated protocols, difficult business deployment and inflexible resource scheduling [1], so it is urgent to propose new technology to change this situation. Network function virtualization (NFV) and software defined network (SDN) came into being. NFV [2] technology can run the virtual network function on the general hardware, SDN can control the traffic forwarding path, and make the network programmable.

Currently, there have been cases with NFV and SDN technology in the network [3]. In SDN-NFV networks, programmable switches forward targeted traffic to the

---

Foundation Items: National Natural Science Foundation of China (61871237), National Science and Technology Major Project (2017ZX03001008), Natural Science Foundation of the Higher Education Institutions of Jiangsu Province (16KJA510005) and YKJ201422.

M. Jia et al. (Eds.): WiSATS 2019, LNICST 281, pp. 333–347, 2019.
https://doi.org/10.1007/978-3-030-19156-6_31

appropriate network functional unit for processing, so dynamic deployment of network functions may result in unbalanced load between network control domains.

To address the issue of load imbalance in such NFV and SDN deployments, researchers introduce virtual network function (VNF) migration. VNF migration means removing VNF from the original physical machine and redeploying at a better location. VNF migration and virtual machine migration have similarities in some respects. Both of them occupy various types of network resources of the nodes, and the destination nodes of migration need to meet their performance requirements. However, the biggest difference between VNF migration and virtual machine migration [4] lies in that the VNF instances have a specific type and belong to one or several service function chains, and the service function chains usually have end-to-end performance requirements.

The researchers proposed different VNF migration strategies and migration methods from different perspectives. VNF has a variety of migration strategies, such as the horizontal scaling technology in the literature [5], the resources occupied by the VNF are allocated when being instantiated. When the demand changes, VNF instance should be directly removed without being changed. The vertical scaling technique is adopted in the literature [6–8], and the resources allocated to VNF are distributed dynamically with the change of business requirements. In this paper, the vertical scaling technology is used. When a VNF allocates a certain amount of resources during instantiation, when the requirements change, the resources occupied by the VNF change correspondingly until the VNF is triggered to migrate.

In the literature [9], a traffic cycle model and a system cost function are proposed, and the problem of VNF migration is transformed into a periodic migration problem of mapping strategy. The scenario proposed in this solution is a data center with a low traffic period, which cannot effectively migrate the traffic non-periodic scene. A distributed elastic control algorithm based on switch migration is proposed in [10]. This migration scheme can achieve load balancing among nodes, but the end-to-end delay constraint of the SFC is not considered in the migration process.

In view of the deficiencies of the above methods, this paper proposes a fast adaptive migration algorithm for network functions based on multidimensional environment perception, and adds the coordination of migration pre-calculation and real-time computation to reduce the real-time computation cost of network migration. The structure of the article is as follows: The second part gives the model of VNF migration problem in NFV network. The third part gives the optimization problem of reducing the network migration cost and reducing the number of VNF migration, and proposes a method of migration pre-calculation and real-time calculation. In the fourth part, we present a heuristic algorithm to solve the problem, which is used to solve the selection problem of the VNFs to be migrated and the migration destination nodes. The simulation results and analysis will be given in the fifth part, and the last part will give the conclusion.

2 System Model

This chapter will present the problem of VNF migration in NFV network. A network model is designed to describe the dynamic change of demand in NFV network, the occupation of various resources by VNF, and the conditions of triggering VNF migration.

2.1 Problem Statement

In SDN and NFV networks, there are many nodes, and each node has computing, bandwidth and storage resources. According to service requirements, we place the corresponding service function chain in the network. Each SFC consists of a series of ordered virtual network functions. According to the end-to-end delay performance requirement of the SFC, the VNF is placed on an appropriate node and occupies various resources of the node.

With the change of service requirements, due to the use of vertical scaling technology, the resources occupied by the corresponding VNFs also change. The scenario studied in this paper is to achieve fast network load balancing by reasonably selecting VNFs to be migrated and migrated destination nodes.

In the migration process, the performance requirements of the VNF to be migrated and the end-to-end performance needs of the service function chain to be migrated need to be considered. By reasonably selecting the destination node, the overall system migration cost and the migration times are reduced.

2.2 Network Model

We use one directed graph, $G = (V^{Node}, E)$, to represent the physical network, where V^{Node} is the set of the nodes, and E is the set of its edges. The characteristics of server nodes and links are described as follows:

- N_w^{core}: processing capacity of the node w in term of the number of cores that it has;
- N_w^{mem}: memory capacity of the node w in term of the number of gigabytes that it has;
- C_{ij}: bandwidth of the physical link between node i and node j;

V^{VNF}represents the set of virtual network function (VNF), The characteristics of VNF are described as follows:

- n_y^{core}: processing capacity of the VNF y;
- n_y^{mem}: memory capacity of the VNF y;
- c_y: bandwidth capacity of the VNF y;
- a_{ij}: binary variable assuming the value 1 if the VNF v_i is embedded in node n_j, otherwise its value is 0;

The usage of a certain resource of a node is defined as the ratio of the used resource in the current node to the total resource. The condition for triggering the migration calculation is that any resource usage is greater than its preset threshold $T_k, T_k \in (0, 1), k = 1, 2, 3$, and each type of resource has its own threshold.

The set of service function chains (SFC) is $F = \{f_1, f_2, \ldots, f_n\}$, the maximum time delay constraint for SFC f_n is τ_n, therefore, when the VNF belongs to SFC f_n (only consider that each VNF instance belongs to a SFC), the sum of the additional delay τ_+

and the original delay τ_0 should be less than τ_n, i.e. $\tau_+ + \tau_0 < \tau_n$. We define a boolean variable b_{ik} to denote whether virtual network function v_i migrates or not, i.e., $b_{ik} = 1$ if the virtual network function v_i is moved to network node n_k, otherwise $b_{ik} = 0$.

The destination node should not overburden after the VNF moves in. It can be expressed by

$$\sum_{l \in V^{VNF}} n_l^{core} \cdot a_{lk} + n_i^{core} \cdot b_{ik} < T_1 \cdot N_{w_k}^{core} \tag{1}$$

$$\sum_{l \in V^{VNF}} n_l^{mem} \cdot a_{lk} + n_i^{mem} \cdot b_{ik} < T_2 \cdot N_{w_k}^{mem} \tag{2}$$

$$\sum_{l \in V^{VNF}} c_l \cdot a_{lk} + c_i \cdot b_{ik} < T_3 \cdot \sum_{k \neq j, l \in V^{VNF}} C_{jk} \tag{3}$$

The cost of migration $F(cost, times)$ is defined as a function of migration overhead $f(cost)$ and the number of migrations $f(times)$.

$$F(cost, times) = \lambda \cdot f(cost) + \mu \cdot f(times) \tag{4}$$

where λ and μ are weight coefficients.

Migration overhead $f(cost)$ is the sum of VNF migration calculation time and implementation migration time. The number of migrations $f(times)$ is the number of VNF migrations that occur during system operation. Implementation migration time [5] defines the out-of-service time due to the VNF implementing the migration. The downtime of VNF v_i is defined as the time for VNF v_i to migrate from node n_j to node n_k.

3 The Optimization Problem

In this chapter, we propose a multi-objective optimization problem to reduce the VNF migration overhead and the number of VNF migrations in the NFV network and improve the system stability. In order to reduce the real-time computing overhead of VNF migration in the system, a method of collaborative migration pre-calculation and real-time calculation is proposed to reduce the system migration cost.

3.1 System Modeling

This paper proposes a migration algorithm that migrates virtual network functions from overload node to idle node. Through the perception of computing resources, storage resources and communication resources, we can solve the problem of the migration of virtual network function (VNFMP) and realize Network Load balancing.

$$
\begin{aligned}
\min \quad & \{\lambda \cdot f(cost) + \mu \cdot f(times)\} \\
subject\ to: & \sum a_{ij} = 1 \quad a_{ij} \in \{0,1\} \\
& \frac{\sum\limits_{i \in V^{VNF}} n_i^{core} \cdot a_{ij}}{N_{w_j}^{core}} < T_1, \quad \forall w \in V^{Node} \\
& \frac{\sum\limits_{i \in V^{VNF}} n_i^{mem} \cdot a_{ij}}{N_{w_j}^{mem}} < T_2, \quad \forall w \in V^{Node} \\
& \frac{\sum\limits_{i \in V^{VNF}} c_i \cdot a_{ij}}{\sum\limits_{k \neq j, k \in V^{Node}} C_{jk}} < T_3, \quad \forall w \in V^{Node} \\
& \sum_{l \in V^{VNF}} n_l^{core} \cdot a_{lk} + n_i^{core} \cdot b_{ik} < T_1 \cdot N_{w_k}^{core} \\
& \sum_{l \in V^{VNF}} n_l^{mem} \cdot a_{lk} + n_i^{mem} \cdot b_{ik} < T_2 \cdot N_{w_k}^{mem} \\
& \sum_{l \in V^{VNF}} c_l \cdot a_{lk} + c_i \cdot b_{ik} < T_3 \cdot \sum_{k \neq j, l \in V^{VNF}} C_{jk} \\
& a_{ij} \cdot b_{ik} \cdot \Delta\tau_{jk+} + \tau_0 < \tau_{max}, v_i \in f_n
\end{aligned}
\tag{5}
$$

where T_1, T_2, T_3 respectively represent the thresholds of occupancy rate of computing, storage and communication resources in network nodes. $\tau_{\max}$ represents the maximum tolerable delay of the service function chain to which VNF v_i belongs.

The objective function represents that the cost of migration is defined as a function of migration overhead and the number of migrations. The first constraint ensures that each virtual network feature must be deployed on only one network node. The second to the fourth constraints ensure that the occupancy of computing, storage and communication resources of each network node does not exceed its preset threshold. The fifth to the seventh constraints ensure that the destination network node is not overloaded after the virtual network function is moved in. The last constraint ensures that the sum of the original delay and the additional delay caused by the virtual function migration is smaller than the upper limit of the delay of the service function chain to which it belongs.

3.2 Cooperation of Migration Pre-calculation and Real-Time Calculation

The main migration overhead for VNF migration is the time overhead for solving VNF migration scenarios and the time overhead for implementing VNF migration. When the number of nodes increases, the time and cost for the migration plan calculation increases sharply. In order to reduce the time overhead of solving the migration scheme, this paper presents a migration algorithm that combines migration pre-calculation and real-time calculation. We set the appropriate light overload threshold and overload threshold for the system to reduce the VNF real-time computing overhead. In order to ensure the validity of the results of the migration estimate, we add the time stamp to the result of the migration calculation, set a reasonable timeout time, and then carry out the migration calculation again after the result set migration scheme timeout expires.

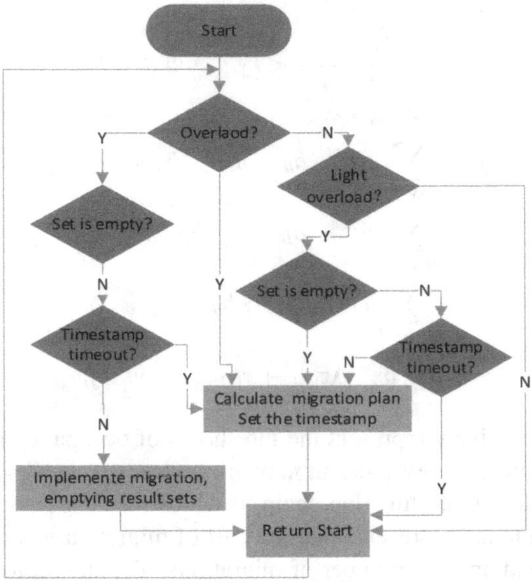

Fig. 1. Cooperation of migration pre-calculation and real-time calculation

As shown in Fig. 1, the implementation procedure of the migration algorithm for migration precomputation and real-time computation collaboration is as follows: Monitoring node resource usage, when the node is overloaded, we check the node's migration scheme result set. If the result set is not empty and the timestamp does not expire, we immediately implement the migration, and empty the node calculation result set, and continue to determine the status of the node. If the node is overloaded, the result set of the node migration scheme is empty, or the timestamp expires, the migration is performed in real time. When the node triggers the light overload threshold but does not trigger the overload threshold, we check the result set of the node migration scheme. If it is null or the timeout expires, we need calculate the node migration scheme again to ensure the validity of the migration scheme.

The pre-calculation and real-time calculation in the system adopt the same migration algorithm. The parameters received by the algorithm include the state of the node, the occupation of each resource by the VNF deployed on the node, and the related state information of other nodes in the system.

4 Heuristic Algorithm for Solving the Problem

The VNFMP problem is an NP-hard problem that can be proven through multiple commodity flows. This section divides VNFMP into two parts: the choice of the VNF to be migrated and the choice of the migrating destination. And two heuristic algorithms are proposed to solve these two problems respectively.

4.1 VNF Selection Algorithm for Migration

Based on experience, the earliest to reach the upper limit of resource types often become the bottleneck to improve performance. Therefore, we need to consider the situation of node overload caused by insufficient resources. We introduce a resource-aware RAIL [11] algorithm to make the decision to migrate the VNF.

When an overload occurs on a node and VNF migration is required, we need to select the VNF to be migrated according to the overload resource type, so as to reduce the resource occupation rate of the overloaded node to a reasonable extent as soon as possible. We define a ternary variable (α, β, γ) to represent the overloaded state of three resources of the node. When computing resources overload, α assignment is 1, otherwise 0, as same as storage resources and communication resources.

We define the migration index θ_i, based on the multi-dimensional environment of perception using RIAL dynamic weight settings. According to the usage of the corresponding resource, the weight of the overloaded resource is greater than 1, the weight of the lightly loaded resource is less than 1, and the greater the migration index of the virtual function used by the overloaded resource is.

$$\theta_i = \sum_K \left\{ \alpha_k \cdot \frac{1}{1 - x_k} + (1 - \alpha_k) \cdot (1 - x_k) \right\} \cdot \chi_{ik} \quad K = (Core, Mem, Com) \tag{6}$$

where α_k indicates whether resource type k is overloaded, x_k represents the occupancy of the resource type k of the node, χ_{ik} indicates the occupancy rate of VNF v_i to node K-type resources.

We sort all the VNF on the overload node according to the migration index, and select the VNF with the highest migration index into the VNF migration sequence.

Algorithm 1: VNF Selection Algorithm For Migration

Set VNF f which to be migrated is empty

VNF set on the node w_j is F_j

Set temporary variable temp=0;

for each VNF f_i in F_j

  calculate θ_i of f_i according to RAIL

  if θ_i >temp

    temp= θ_i

    $f = f_i$

  end if

end for

4.2 Migration Destination Node Selection Algorithm

The selection of migration destination nodes needs to first consider the constraints of VNF migration, including the resource requirements of the VNF to be migrated and the end-to-end performance constraint of the service chain of the function where it is located. In the case of satisfying the constraints, it is necessary to select a node with more types of residual resources and less delay, as a destination node. The choice of the optimal node needs to make the multi-objective decision-making, so the TOPSIS algorithm is used to select the destination node.

The first step is to select the nodes that satisfy the delay constraint according to the end-to-end performance requirement of the service function chain to which the VNF belongs.

$$a_{ij} \cdot b_{ik} \cdot \Delta\tau_{jk+} + \tau_0 < \tau_{\max}, v_i \in f_n \tag{7}$$

In the second step, we select the nodes that meet the performance requirements of the VNF; and the nodes will not overload after the VNF moves in.

In the third step, we use TOPSIS algorithm [12] to calculate the node's immigration index. We need to calculate the positive and negative ideal solutions, and calculate the distance between the positive and negative ideal solutions and get the immigration index of the nodes.

$$T_{i+} = \min\{T_{ki} | k \in N_3\}, i \in \{1,2,3\} \tag{8}$$

$$\tau_{+} = \min\{\tau_k | k \in N_3\} \tag{9}$$

$$T_{i-} = \max\{T_{ki} | k \in N_3\}, i \in \{1,2,3\} \tag{10}$$

$$\tau_{-} = \max\{\tau_k | k \in N_3\} \tag{11}$$

We find the ideal and negative ideal solutions, and then compute the euclidean distance θ_{ok+} between the node and the positive ideal solution and the euclidean distance θ_{ok+} between the node and the negative ideal solution.

$$\theta_{ok+} = \sqrt{\sum_{i=1}^{3} [\gamma_i (T_{ki} - T_{i+})]^2 + [\gamma_4 (\tau_k - \tau_+)]^2} \tag{12}$$

$$\theta_{ok-} = \sqrt{\sum_{i=1}^{3} [\gamma_i (T_{ki} - T_{i-})]^2 + [\gamma_4 (\tau_k - \tau_-)]^2} \tag{13}$$

where γ_i represents the weight of each indicator, which is a predefined value. So that we can get the immigration index θ_{ok}. The larger the immigration index is, the closer the node is to the ideal solution. We choose to move in the node with the largest index as the destination node.

$$\theta_{ok} = \frac{\theta_{ok-}}{\theta_{ok-} + \theta_{ok+}} \tag{14}$$

Algorithm 2 Migration Destination Node Selection Algorithm

initial
  Destination node v =null
  VNF f_0 to be migrated
  Set of not overloaded nodes N_1
  Set of nodes N_2 =null, N_3 =null
  Set temporary variables temp=0
  Initialize bestNode,worstNode
end initial
for each v_i in N_1
  if $\Delta\tau_i < \tau_0$
    add v_i into N_2
  end if
end for
for each v_i in N_2
  if v_i satisfied the resource requirement of f_0
    add v_i into N_3
  end if
end for
calculate bestNode, worstNode in N_3 according to TOPSIS
for each v_k in N_3
  calculate θ_{ok} of v_k according to TOPSIS
  if θ_{ok} >temp
    temp= θ_{ok} , $v = v_k$
  end if
end for

5 Simulation and Performance Analysis

In this section, we evaluate the performance of the proposed heuristic at different node sizes through simulation experiments and compare it with other algorithms.

5.1 Simulation Settings

The initial size of the network is set to 100 nodes and randomly generates 500 links, which is equivalent to a medium-sized ISP network [13]. Each node is assigned a storage resource, a calculation resource, and a communication resource, each of which has 10 normalized units and a link delay of 1 to 10 random units. The traffic in the network is random, so the corresponding virtual network function is changing dynamically. We assume that each network service function chain consists of 2 to 5 virtual network functions, with 1 to 5 virtual network functions placed on each node. In order to improve the stability of the system, some idle nodes are placed in the network, that is, nodes that do not have the function of virtual network.

5.2 Performance Analysis

All the simulation algorithms are showed in Table 1. The first is RAIL & TOPSIS collaborative resource awareness (RT) algorithm, which can sense multi-domain resources through RAIL algorithm and make multi-objective decision through TOPSIS to find the best migration scheme. However, this algorithm will increase the computational complexity and increase the time spent in migration calculation. The second one is a fixed weight algorithm, which uses a fixed weight to find the VNF to be migrated. The third algorithm is a simple instant migration algorithm. When selecting a migration destination node, the algorithm finds any node which satisfies the performance and delay constraints as the migration destination node. The fourth algorithm is Pre-Calculation RAIL & TOPSIS (PRT) algorithm, which adds pre-calculation and real-time calculation synergy to the RAIL & TOPSIS algorithm to reduce the solution time and reduce the migration overhead.

Table 1. Comparison of algorithm differences

Algorithm	Similarity	Differences
RT algorithm	——	——
Fixed weight algorithm	Using TOPSIS to find dest-node	Using a fixed weight to find the VNF to be migrated
Simple instant algorithm	Using RAIL to find which VNF to be migrated	Choosing any node that satisfies constraints can be the dest-node
PRT algorithm	Using RAIL and TOPSIS algorithm	Adding cooperation of pre-calculation and real-time calculation

Figure 2 shows the total system migration costs under different migration algorithms. It can be seen from the figure that as the node size increases, the total system migration cost also increases. The total migration cost of RT algorithm is higher than other algorithms due to its high computational complexity. With the increase of node size, the migration overhead increases sharply. When the node size exceeds 400, the total migration of Simple Instant Migration algorithm begins to increase dramatically, becoming the algorithm with the highest total cost of migration.

Figure 3 shows the comparison of the number of transitions per unit time under different migration algorithms. It can be seen from the figure that the number of system migration times per unit time increases with the number of nodes. The number of RT algorithm migration is obviously less than the other two algorithms. Compared with RT

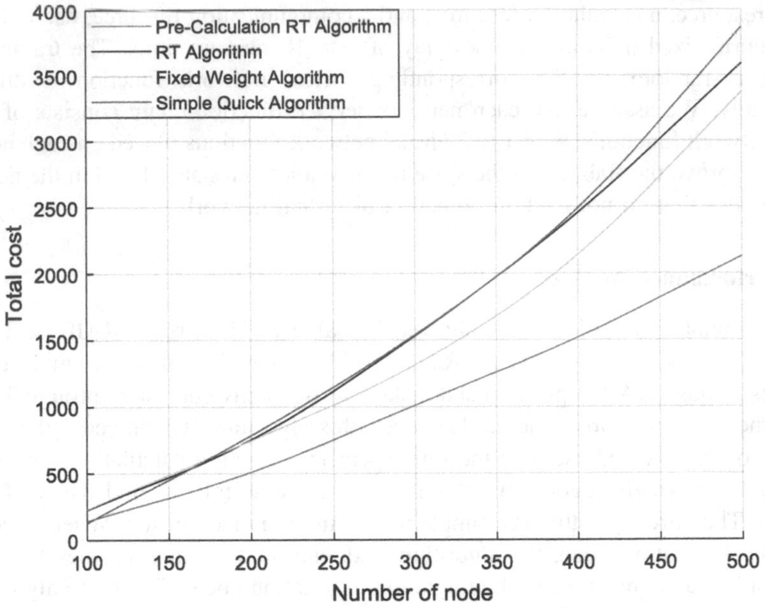

Fig. 2. Comparison of total migration costs

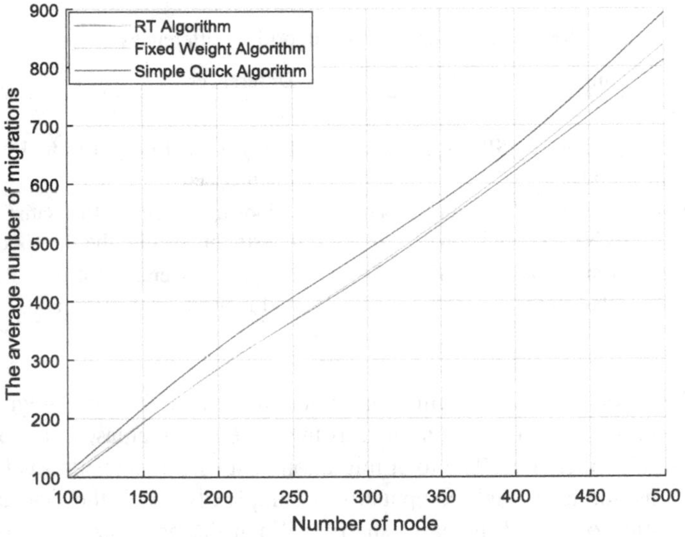

Fig. 3. Comparison of average migration times

algorithm and fixed weight algorithm, it can be concluded that resource awareness through RAIL algorithm can effectively reduce the number of migration. Compared with RT algorithm and simple real-time algorithm, it can be concluded that multi-objective decision making through TOPSIS can effectively reduce the number of migration.

Figure 4 shows the average resource utilization of the destination node when selecting the destination node for the RT algorithm and the simple real-time algorithm. It can be found that the TOPSIS algorithm can achieve load balancing in the network more effectively and make the resource utilization of each node in the network more balanced. Figure 5 shows the single migration cost of VNF under different algorithms. It can be seen from the figure that the cost of single migration is obviously higher than other algorithms due to the large migration cost and fewer migration times of RT algorithm.

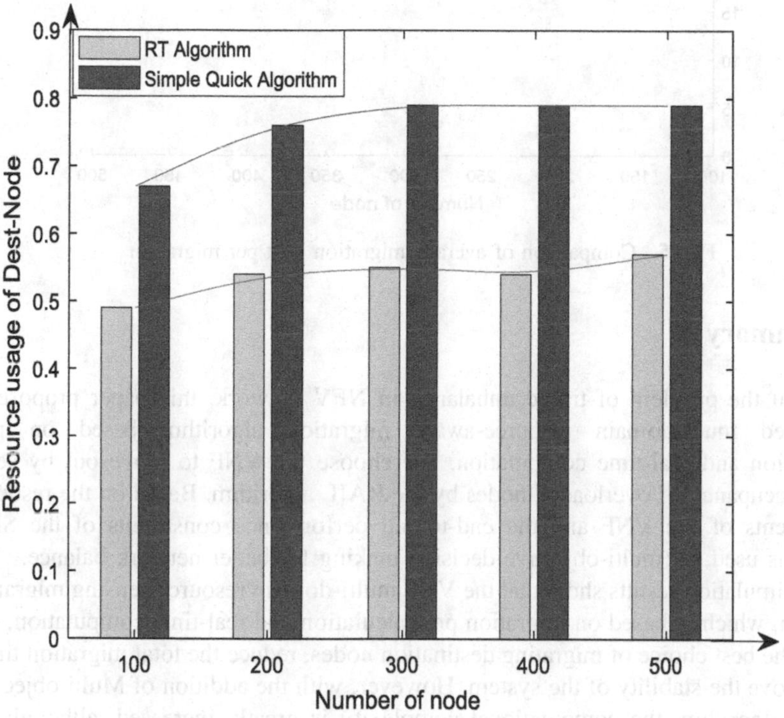

Fig. 4. Resource utilization ratio of destination node

In summary, RT algorithm can effectively reduce the number of migration, and achieve a more balanced network, but it also bring sa higher computational complexity what increases the migration calculation time, resulting in a higher single migration costs. In order to keep the advantages of RT algorithm and reduce the computation time of migration, a PRT algorithm is proposed, which is a combination of pre-calculation and real-time calculation. After adding pre-calculation, it can effectively reduce the migration calculation time, so as to reduce the migration cost. At the same time, the migration cost is almost the same as RT algorithm, which makes the cost of single migration significantly lower than other algorithms.

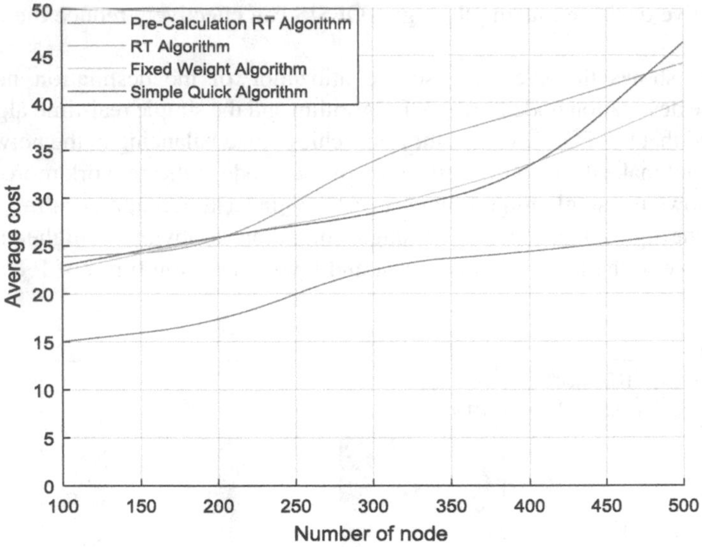

Fig. 5. Comparison of average migration cost per migration

6 Summary

Aiming at the problem of traffic unbalance in NFV network, this paper proposes a VNF-based multi-domain resource-aware migration algorithm based on pre-computation and real-time computation. We choose the VNF to move out by sensing the occupancy of overloaded nodes by the RAIL algorithm. Based on the resource requirements of the VNF and the end-to-end performance constraints of the SFC, TOPSIS is used for multi-objective decision making for better network balance.

The simulation results show that the VNF multi-domain resource sensing migration algorithm, which is based on migration pre calculation and real-time computation, can achieve the best choice of migrating destination nodes, reduce the total migration times and improve the stability of the system. However, with the addition of Multi-objective decision algorithm, the computational complexity is greatly increased, although the migration estimation mechanism can reduce the overall migration calculation cost, but the cost of the single real-time migration computation still cannot be reduced, which needs further research.

References

1. Xiong, G., Hu, Y.X., Tian, L., et al.: A virtual service placement approach based on improved quantum genetic algorithm. Front. Inf. Technol. Electron. Eng. **17**(7), 661–671 (2016)
2. Wen, T., Yu, H., Sun, G., et al.: Network function consolidation in service function chaining orchestration. In: 2016 IEEE International Conference on Communications (ICC), pp. 1–6. IEEE (2016)

3. Faraci, G., Schembra, G.: An analytical model to design and manage a green SDN/NFV CPE node. IEEE Trans. Netw. Serv. Manag. **12**(3), 435–450 (2015)
4. Moens, H., De Turck, F.: VNF-P: a model for efficient placement of virtualized network functions. In: 2014 10th International Conference on Network and Service Management (CNSM), pp. 418–423. IEEE (2014)
5. Ghaznavi, M., Khan, A., Shahriar, N., et al.: Elastic virtual network function placement. In: 2015 IEEE 4th International Conference on Cloud Networking (CloudNet), pp. 255–260. IEEE (2015)
6. Gember-Jacobson, A., Viswanathan, R., Prakash, C., et al.: OpenNF: enabling innovation in network function control. In: ACM Conference on SIGCOMM, pp. 163–174. ACM (2015)
7. Rajagopalan, S., Dan, W., Jamjoom, H., et al.: Split/merge: system support for elastic execution in virtual middleboxes. In: USENIX Conference on Networked Systems Design and Implementation, pp. 227–240 (2013)
8. Sherry, J., Chang, L., Popa, R.A., et al.: BlindBox: deep packet inspection over encrypted traffic. In: ACM Conference on Special Interest Group on Data Communication, pp. 213–226. ACM (2015)
9. Eramo, V., Ammar, M., Lavacca, F.G.: Migration energy aware reconfigurations of virtual network function instances in NFV architectures. IEEE Access **5**, 4927–4938 (2017)
10. Cheng, G.: Based on the meta-capabilities of the network functional combination of key technologies. PLA Information Engineering University (2015)
11. Chen, L., Shen, H., Sapra, K.: RIAL: resource intensity aware load balancing in clouds. In: Proceedings of IEEE, INFOCOM, 2014, pp. 1294–1302. IEEE (2014)
12. Wang, Z.H., Zhan, W., Qiu, W.H.: Application of an optimized entropy-TOPSIS multicriteria decision making model to facilities management. Int. J. Plant Eng. Manag. **11**, 129–136 (2006)
13. Xia, J., Cai, Z., Xu, M.: Optimized virtual network functions migration for NFV. In: 2016 IEEE 22nd International Conference on Parallel and Distributed Systems (ICPADS), pp. 340–346. IEEE (2016)

Blockchain-Based SDN Security Guaranteeing Algorithm and Analysis Model

Zhedan Shao, Xiaorong Zhu(✉), Alexander M. M. Chikuvanyanga, and Hongbo Zhu

Nanjing University of Posts and Telecommunications, Nanjing 210003, China
xrzhu@njupt.edu.cn

Abstract. Although Software Defined Networking (SDN) has a lot of advantages, it also leads to some security issues such as DDoS/DoS attacks, unauthorized access, and single point of failure. To improve the security and efficiency of the SDN control plane, we propose a novel consensus algorithm–Simplified Practical Byzantine Fault Tolerance (SPBFT) to transfer messages between controllers and then establish an analysis model to analyze the security and performance of SPBFT based on game theory. In this paper, we apply blockchain technology in SDN to build a readable, addable, and unmodifiable distributed database which maintains a list of updated system activities and time stamps in each controller. The simplified three-step consensus algorithm SPBFT makes the message transfer and verification carry out efficiently in parallel. In addition, we use recovery mechanism and credibility assessment on the primary controller to increase the invulnerability of system. Simulation results show that compared with the PBFT algorithm, the proposed algorithm can significantly improve system performances in terms of security and efficiency.

Keywords: SDN · Security · Blockchain · Consensus algorithm

1 Introduction

Software Defined Networking (SDN) is a new technology that separates control planes from the data plane to support network virtualization. Compared with traditional networks, SDN has many advantages such as the separation of control and data planes, programmability, dynamic flow control, and centralized control management. However, it poses some threats in security such as DDoS/DoS attacks, illegal access, and single point of failure which can limit the large-scale deployment and application of SDN in many scenarios. The SDN control plane serves as the center of centralized control. For the attacker, attacking control plane is the most effective method to destroy the network. Therefore, the key measure lies in the effective security protection mechanism for the control level.

Foundation Items: National Natural Science Foundation of China (61871237), National Science and Technology Major Project (2017ZX03001008), and Natural Science Foundation of the Higher Education Institutions of Jiangsu Province (16KJA510005).

M. Jia et al. (Eds.): WiSATS 2019, LNICST 281, pp. 348–362, 2019.
https://doi.org/10.1007/978-3-030-19156-6_32

Blockchain refers to the technology of collectively maintaining a reliable database through decentralization and de-trust. It is actually a series of data blocks generated by using cryptography correlation. Each data block contains information for valid confirmation of multiple transactions. This storage method makes it difficult to tamper with information once it has been recorded.

The characteristics of the blockchain, such as de-trust, openness, and non-destructive information, coincide with the requirements of the distributed SDN architecture. Moreover, smart contracts of blockchain can be better configured under the programmability of SDN.

Regarding to the current situation of SDN security, the advantages and disadvantages of the SDN is analyzed from the perspective of security and possible attack behaviors is illustrated from three levels, including DDoS and illegal intrusion attacks for the control plane in [1]. These two points should be contained in the consideration of the security mechanism design in this paper. The authors of [2] summarize and analyze the security problems caused by the programmable data plane and point out possible loopholes in the future data plane. Security architecture platforms are proposed based on SDN [3, 4], however the more granular security scheme is not mentioned. Some authors are considering the methods to deal with specific DoS attacks in SDN which are useful for SDN security but lack of integrity [5–7]. Researches on the security of the control plane for the core of the SDN architecture is still relatively one-sided, and many are based on the scenario of a single controller or a specific attack method.

With respect to the application of blockchains in security, the authors of [8] establish a blockchain-based electronic medical record system that applies blockchains to data structures and source layers. The system monitors the data request actions from all requesters through smart contracts to prevent the medical data of patients from being stolen, making medical records traceable and checkable. The authors of [9] build a user-centric content distribution system with blockchain to implement a decentralized proxy mechanism which enables Content Providers (CPs) and Technology Enablers (TEs) to compete and negotiate with each other to instantiate the best content distribution session, but specific negotiation mechanism is not proposed. The authors of [10] establish a smart grid water network architecture that uses the blockchain as a link to store data to ensure the verification of information and the correctness of data. The use of basic cryptographic primitives makes the system more secure and user-friendly. It can input user data to complete multi-party security protocols and prevent privacy leakage and data abuse. [11] proposes a two-step protocol that securely shares health data to each node in the network in a pervasive social network (PSN). For access control and node verification, the author authorizes a security component as an access control provider and believes that blockchain technology can further enhance the security of this system. The authors of [12] argue that blockchains need to adapt to their own characteristics according to different systems. It is proposed that the direction in the future is to overcome blockchain restrictions such as most of the blockchains can only complete 7 transactions per second.

The literatures show that blockchain has been succeeded in security aspect [8–12]. The blockchain creates a good structural foundation for the architecture protection with its decentralized, smart and convenient use, information confidentiality, integrity and traceability. However, at present, there are still few literatures on the use of blockchain in SDN. [13] proposes a new type of blockchain-based distributed cloud architecture, including device layer, fog layer, and cloud layer, so that controller fog nodes at the edge of the network can meet the required design principles. However, the internal structure of controller proposed above still adopts the traditional SDN controller structure without adding the blockchain feature and putting forward a specific security mechanism.

Therefore, we propose an SDN security mechanism based on blockchain with distributed SDN architecture. The controllers are intelligently distributed in different geographical locations to alleviate "single-point failure" so to avoid serious widespread network crashes. We use blockchain technology to build a blockchain database together on SDN controllers. The block records the real-time system activities and the time stamps, thus making the entities activities traceable. A simplified consensus algorithm named Simplified Practical Byzantine Fault Tolerance (SPBFT) is proposed to verify the messages transmitted between blocks which contains the communication time restriction, the recovery mechanism and the credibility assessment. In addition, we establish an analysis model to evaluate the security and performance of consensus algorithms and make simulation on the proposed consensus algorithms.

2 Blockchain-Based SDN Security System Model and Guaranteeing Mechanism

This paper proposes a security SDN system model and guaranteeing mechanism based on blockchain. The system model adds block to each controller to store security verification information in the control plane and deals with different security issue with different contracts. Communication guaranteeing algorithm between controllers SPBFT and emergency strategy are proposed based on consensus algorithm and smart contract respectively, according to two kinds of attack, the illegal invasion and DDoS attacks.

2.1 Blockchain-Based SDN Security System Model

To guarantee the security of the SDN system model, we mainly take the following four aspects into consideration: system reliability, scalability, confidentiality of information, and non-repudiation. The system model is shown in Fig. 1.

We adopt a horizontal distributed controller architecture to divide the network into different independent areas. Each area is controlled by a separate controller. Different controllers construct the entire network view through a consensus algorithm to prevent single point of failure and improve the system reliability.

The network between controllers is equivalent to a P2P network. Each controller exists equally. In this case, System can add new controllers with some verification of other legal controllers. From the perspective of global security and load balancing, it is necessary to dynamically update the global topology and link state information, such as the switch port status, link utilization, and host CPU usage, to form a global network view. Real-time updated data is recorded in blockchains, and global views can be created in each controller.

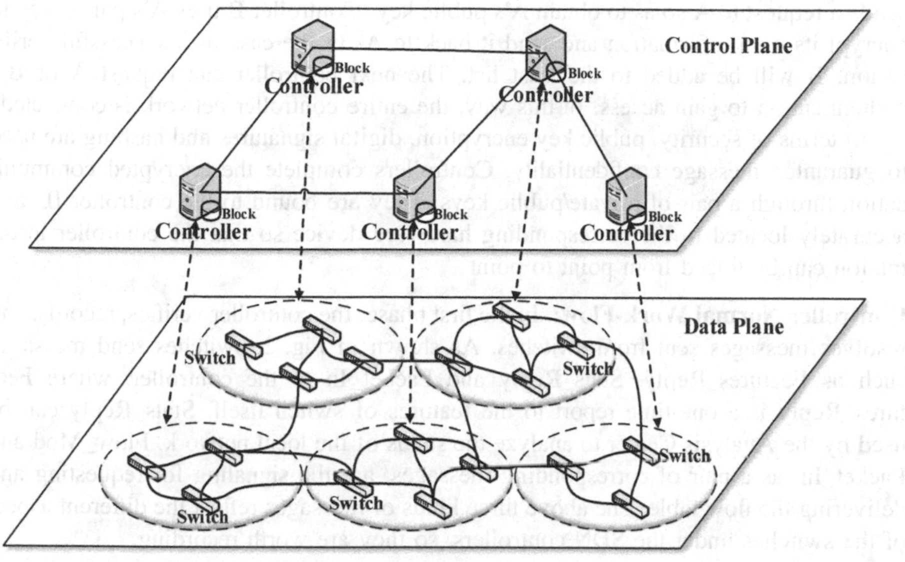

Fig. 1. Blockchain-based SDN security system model.

For a controller, the function can be divided into two phases, prevention phase and processing phase. In the prevention phase, the security mechanism of the SDN control plane mainly includes two aspects: preventing the access of unauthorized controllers and preventing attackers from falsifying shared database information. The main approach is to authenticate by exchanging data between SDN controllers. The controller has its own verification information and stores the verification information of other controllers. Through the encrypted data transmission, information verification and obtaining consensus to anti-falsification forgery. Uniform data distributed storage between controllers makes it difficult to tamper with the information of a single controller. During the processing phase, the controller detects abnormal traffic and determines whether there is an attack. Through the detection of the analysis center, the mitigation of smart contracts can automatically react to attacks.

2.2 Blockchain-Based SDN Control Plane Work-Flow

Controller Join Process: Based on the centralized control of SDN, the control plane needs to ensure the security of the controller node and the confidentiality of the information transmission. The generation of the controller does not depend on the "mining" model in the public chain, but up to the administrator. Therefore, adding the new controllers can be verified by the administrator which is the first protection of the control plane.

At the very beginning, the administrator randomly determines an initial controller A to receive connection requests from other controllers. The initial controller A has a private key and a public key. The controller B who wants to join the controller layer sends a request to A so as to obtain A's public key. Controller B uses A's public key to encrypt its own information and send it back to A. In the case of a successful verification, B will be added to the trust list. The next controller can request A or B's authentication to gain access. In this way, the entire controller network is connected.

In terms of security, public key encryption, digital signatures and hashing are used to guarantee message confidentiality. Controllers complete the encrypted communication through a pair of private/public keys. They are bound to the controller ID and accurately located to the corresponding hardware device so that the controller information can be traced from point to point.

Controller Normal Work-Flow: In the first phase, the controller verifies, records, and resolves messages sent from switches. As shown in Fig. 2, switches send messages such as Features_Reply, Stats_Reply and Packet_In to the controller, where Features_Reply is a one-time report to the features of switch itself. Stats_Reply can be used by the Analysis Center to analyze the status of the local network. Flow_Mod and Packet_In, as a pair of corresponding messages, are the signaling for requesting and delivering the flow table. The above three kinds of messages reflect the different aspect of the switches under the SDN controllers, so they are worth recording.

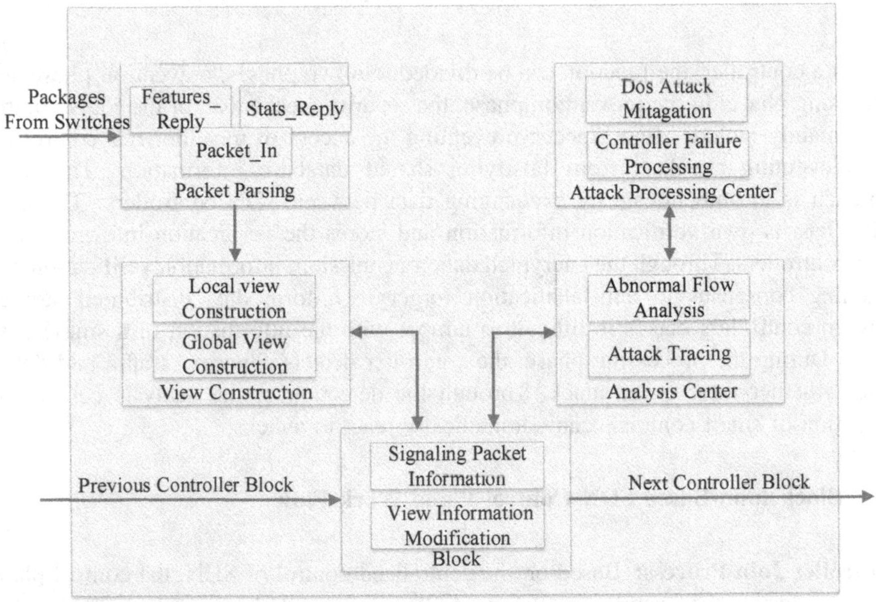

Fig. 2. Blockchain-based SDN controller internal structure.

In the second phase, the topology state of the route and the state set of the switch are extracted to construct a topology map of the network flow which dynamically display the local traffic. At the same time, the above four kinds of information are stored in the local block, so as to trace back to the source when problem occurs.

In the third phase, each data is uploaded to the block to form a global view. This process can be divided into periodicity and triggered modes. When the network runs smoothly, each controller independently manages its own domain. In this case, the global network topology is periodically updated. However, when a controller issues an alert message, the global view is immediately updated so that each controller can grasp the overall situation and provide feedback on the alert controller.

Requests for uploading global views need to be verified by other controllers. Thus, each operation for the management of the global view of the controller and the modification of the global view will be recorded in the block. For controllers with successful recording, the percentage of trust value is a larger percentage of each account.

In the fourth phase, the information and state data of each controller and switch recorded in the block will be analyzed to determine the type of attack and use intelligent contracts to automatically make response strategies.

2.3 Consensus Algorithm Based Security Guaranteeing Algorithm Among SDN Controllers

This paper proposes a Simplified Practical Byzantine Fault Tolerance consensus algorithm based on Practical Byzantine Fault Tolerance (PBFT) algorithm.

The SPBFT algorithm proposed in this paper has made up for the shortcomings of PBFT that low consensus efficiency, poor self-healing, and invulnerability. It simplifies the PBFT consensus process and makes the message transfer and verification carry out in parallel. It also grades requests to ensure that urgent requests can be handled quickly and efficiently. A credibility assessment that the controller with the highest degree of trust value is used as the primary controller to prevent invasion has been added. The malicious controller can be found with the guide of primary controller and measures will be taken to restore its availability. The changes above make SPBFT more suitable for the application of SDN.

The workflow of the SPBFT algorithm is as follows:

(a) A certain controller (named A) that wants to broadcast a request to other controllers.
(b) The other controllers verify the source of the request.
(c) If the others verify that controller A is valid, the execution of the request continues, and a reply is sent to controller A. Otherwise the system stops executing the request and enters the defense state. The controller with highest degree of trust value becomes primary and dominates the normal controller against the effects of the bad controller. After the defense phase the trust value is cleared to restart the next view.
(d) Controller A waits for f + 1 replies from different controllers (replies with the same result) and the reply is the result of the request operation.
(e) Operation results are recorded in the controller's block to calculate the trust value and weight of all controllers.

SPBFT uses a three-phase protocol to broadcast requests to other controllers, Prepare, Commit, Reply, as shown in Fig. 3. The red lines express the processes of

SPBFT and the black lines express that of PBFT. PBFT was originally applied to a distributed system mainly consisting of state machines. It needs to perform the same serialization processing on distributed nodes, which are not exhaustive in SDN. In PBFT, a five-phase protocol, there are two consensuses in Prepare and Commit phase to guarantee the same decision and operation in each node. However, In SPBFT, we need only one consensus to ensure the identity and decision at one time. Because there are many types of requests in SDN. Request processing with different priorities can be queued, so there is no need to sort the requests in a fixed manner in the SDN. The requests can be automatically executed according to request priority and the same-level request first-in-first-out principle.

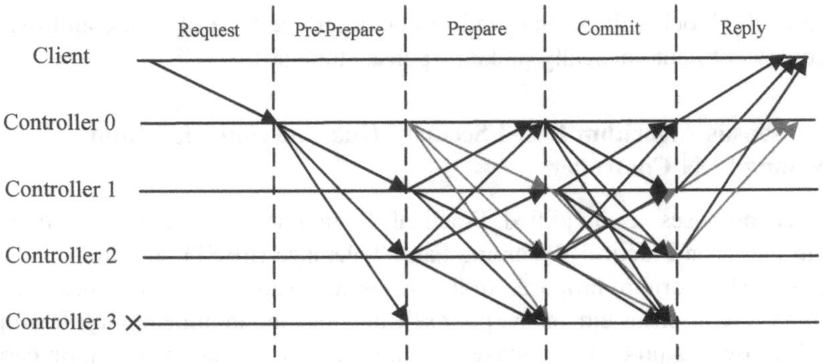

Fig. 3. SPBFT and PBFT normal working phases (Color figure online)

In SPBFT, the Prepare phase is mainly to confirm the validity of the request and the controller. In the subsequent Commit phase, the controllers reach an agreement and execute the request. In the Reply phase is mainly to inform the request controller of the completion of the request.

In the Prepare phase, we provide authentication mainly in the form of encryption and Q&A.

Controller A broadcasts a prepare message to other controllers, this information $<(prepare, v, n, h, a, d)_{en}, m>$ contains the view v, request number n, controller A's own information h, request content m, the question answer a, and the content summary d. Wherein, v represents the view where the controller is located. n is the sequence number down ordered by the requesting controller A according to its own stored request. h is the information used by the controller to prove itself, and a represents that the answer to the problem set by the primary controller. d is a summary of the content m. The subscript en indicates the encryption process. The prepare message is sent to each controller and this information is inserted into the block.

When the controller i receives the prepare message from controller A, it determines whether the information matches. If it matches, the controller receives the prepare message and enters the following commit phase. Messages $<(commit, v, n, d, i)_{en}>$ are broadcast to other controllers other than A, and prepare and commit messages are appended to the log.

When a controller has previously received a prepare message that is in the same view and number is also n, but the digest is different, the controller will reject the message and report the situation to the primary controller and record the exception in the blockchain.

In the Commit phase, the controller executes the request with the principle of the minority when the malicious controller is limited.

The controller collects the commit messages to determine whether the controller is prepared by checking the view, serial number *n*, and request summary. When there are *f* commits from different controllers that is prepared, it means that $<(commit, v, n, d, i)_{en}>$ is true, then the status of the request on this controller is considered to be executable. As a result, the operation is performed according to the request.

Once each controller receives different result of the request, it reports to the primary controller to check. If the controller has not received a certain controller information within a few request periods, it may be that the link between the two controllers is interrupted or there is a bad controller. At this point, the situation message is also sent to the primary controller for verification.

Thus, we also enhance system security by limiting communication time, adding recovery mechanisms, and assessing trustworthiness.

Limited Communication Time: In order to guarantee the security of information transmission and tamper-proof, it is necessary to ensure that the transmission time of each message is within a certain range. Therefore, we set a maximum delay Δ. If the transmission delay of the message is less than Δ, the message is considered to be valid. Otherwise if the transmission delay of the message is greater than Δ, the message may be intercepted and tampered or the communication failure occurred. In this case, the transmission has failed and the message will be ignored. The maximum delay Δ can be expressed by the maximum arrival delay counted on previous view.

Recovery Mechanism: After each synchronization, if the primary controller receives more than 1/3 of the replica controllers reporting a controller out of response time, the primary controller broadcasts a message to other replica controllers to contact with the controller. If the replica controller finds the controller working normally, it receives a short message $<(OK, v, n)_{en}>$ to confirm the status of the controller. If not, the reply message is sent to the primary controller and the unconnected controller is suspected to have been compromised. To avoid further damage, the primary controller generates a new request (isolation command) that requires the switch under the problematic controller to be assigned to other replica controllers. When $f + 1$ replica controllers agree to this request, the identity certificate is used to inform the switch to execute the instructions so that the problematic controller is effectively isolated. The Attack Processing Center performs subsequent checks and repairs on the problematic controller.

Credibility Assessment: We uses the service as a measure of the credibility of the evaluation criteria.

In our SDN network, services are used as the "transactions" stored in the blockchain. We define the credibility in SDN from two aspects, utility and time. For the unity, it can be considered from two parts, control plain and data plain. In control plain, each service should be verified before being stored. The number of valid services also means the number of controller that being verified successfully. In data plain, the more switches the controller manage, the more important the controller is. For the time aspect, the normal working hours and rounds to a certain extent reflect invulnerability of controllers. Therefore, we define *Trust* as the trust value of each controller calculated by following parameters. S, W, M, R represent the proportion of valid services, the number of managed switches, the duration and the rounds of normal work, respectively.

$$Trust = \alpha S + \beta W + \chi M + \delta R (0 < \alpha < 1, 0 < \beta < 1, 0 < \chi < 1, 0 < \delta < 1) \quad (1)$$

$$\alpha + \beta + \chi + \delta = 1 \quad (2)$$

In the above formula, α, β, χ, δ express the weight parameters for the above four indicators.

Adding an assessment standard to the blockchain to determine the master-slave relationship of the controller participating in the contract. In this way, the system can solve the security risks as soon as possible.

2.4 Smart Contract Based DDoS/DoS Attack Protection Mechanism

This paper uses the Analysis Center and Attack Processing Center in the SDN security system model to collaboratively complete the implementation of protection contracts for DDoS/DoS attacks.

The threat of the control plane is mainly caused by DDoS/DoS attacks from the data plane. Attackers send large amounts of meaningless packets to SDN switches, so that the switch needs to request the flow table frequently from the controller. There is another way that the attacker hijacks or forges a switch to allow malicious traffic to flow to the other controller. Excessive flow table requests and controller resource usage can be considered that there may be DDoS/DoS attacks.

Attack Detection and Mitigation: For DDoS/DoS attacks, smart contracts periodically check the status of the controller with traversing the states, transactions, and trigger conditions contained in each contract one by one. Then the conditional transaction is pushed to the queue to be verified and wait for consensus. Transactions that do not satisfy the trigger condition will continue to be stored on the blockchain. Once the Analysis Center detects abnormal traffic, it triggers the generation of a DDoS/DoS Alert Contract and broadcasts it. First step is to verify the security of each controller and ensure its validity. The verified controller will enter the consensus set. After most of the verification nodes reach a consensus, they select the most reliable primary controller according to the trust mechanism of the consensus algorithm. The primary controller generates the DDoS/DoS Mitigation Contract and distributes it to other controllers to alleviate the alarm controller's DDoS/DoS attack. For the sake of fairness, the primary controller cannot be re-elected in two consecutive views.

Follow-Up Protection: The smart contract implements a confidence system based on a consensus algorithm as a guarantee to ensure the correct execution of the incident resolution. After the alarm is eliminated, the alarming controller needs to perform a series of verification operations to eliminate the security risks at the control level. At the same time, each controller sends status information to the block to analyze the current status of the alarming controller, the mitigation effect, the impact on other controllers and the origin of this attack. Each attack interval event will also be recorded in the block for systematic analysis.

3 Security and Performance Analysis Model on SPBFT Algorithm

In this paper, we use game theory to analyze the SPBFT algorithm.

Definition: The game is defined as $\Gamma = \{I, S, U\}$. where $I = \{a, d\}$ is the participant, a denotes the attacker and d denotes the defender, i.e. the controller. $S = \{t_a, t_d\}$ defines the strategy set of attacker and controller. $U = \{u_a, u_d\}$ is the utility function of attacker and the controller.

Assuming that there are n controllers and the attacker attacks r controllers at the same time with the attack speed t_a which means the duration that attacker breaks through the firewall of the controller itself and tampers with the controller information. $N(t_a)$ means number of the requests that have been sent in the period t_a. The total time is T. The verification is initiated in the process of request processing, so request initiation interval equals verification interval. We assume that the request initiation time interval t_d obeys the exponential distribution with the parameter λ. The number of controllers recovered in each attack period is Y.

In the next attack time ta, the controller will send a request with a probability of

$$P(N(t_a) = 1) = \lambda t_a e^{-\lambda t_a} \tag{3}$$

In the next attack time ta, more than one request will be sent with a probability of

$$P(N(t_a) \geq 1) = 1 - P(N(t_a) = 0) = 1 - e^{-\lambda t_a} \tag{4}$$

In a certain attack time ta, the probability of a successful attack for attackers is

$$X = 1 - P(N(t_a) \geq 1) = e^{-\lambda t_a} \tag{5}$$

Therefore, during this time, there are $X \times r$ controllers that will be intruded.

During attack period i, we assume there are $M(i)$ controllers that will be intruded and $M(i)$ can be expressed by

$$M(i) = \sum_{k \in [1,i]} (X \times r) - \sum_{k \in [1,i-1]} Y \tag{6}$$

Therefore, the probability of a successful attack to a certain controller can be obtained by

$$PT = \frac{M(i)}{n} \tag{7}$$

For a certain attacker, we define the cost includes intrusion cost C_{a1} that is the cost of intruding controllers and the penalty cost C_{a2} that is the cost of the attack being detected. If the attack succeeds, it will get the successful intrusion gain B_a.

For a certain defender, we define the cost C_d that is the cost of the controller failing to resist intrusion. If the controller operates normally, it will get the daily gain B_{d1}. In the case that controller successfully discovered the attack, it will get the profit B_{d2}.

Therefore, the attacker's utility function can be expressed as

$$u_a = B_a \times PT - C_{a1} - C_{a2} \times (1 - PT) \tag{8}$$

And the defender's utility function is

$$u_d = B_{d1} \times (1 - PT) + B_{d2} \times \frac{Y}{r} - C_d \times PT \tag{9}$$

Table 1 shows the comparison of different consensus algorithms. Compared with PBFT, the proposed SPBFT has advantages over error node tolerance. It contributes to that even if at most one-third of nodes is invaded, only if the primary node has not been invaded, thc system may still keep in normal state. In addition, we also see that SPBFT has good trading performances. PBFT cannot meet the demand for high message volume of SDN network. However, SPBFT can simplify the process of verification and consensus and reduce the number of signaling.

Table 1. Consensus parameter comparison.

Consensus algorithm	PBFT	SPBFT
Number of nodes	3f + 1	3f + 1
Error node tolerance	At most 1/3 error nodes, but also depends on the primary controller	At most 1/3 error nodes
Consensus efficiency	General	High
Invulnerability	General	High

In the aspect of invulnerability, SPBFT uses the trusted data in the blockchain for analysis to find the invaded controller and has the mechanism to handle with the suspected controller, while PBFT does not. In that case, SPBFT can obviously slow down the overall speed of the system being compromised. When attacked, the system can respond quickly and stop it in time. Each block records various activities of the system and records time stamps, making each entity's implement self-inspection and self-recovery under the certain attacks. After mitigation of attacks, activity analysis and source track of the entities that generate the activity are carried out.

Furthermore, in terms of architecture, distributed decentralized security architecture can avoid large-scale network anomalies which are brought by "single point of failure". Also, other normal controllers assist problem controllers to get out of trouble. Under this architecture, we use identity and traffic as the focus of outlier monitoring to ensure the normal operation of the controller. The programmability of SDN makes this architecture easy to extend.

In the aspect of confidentiality and integrity of information, each controller manages its own private key and distributes the public key using blockchain technology. Blocks store encrypted segments of controller information without any third party access and control so that privacy protection can easily be achieved. The blockchain consists of a readable, addable, and non-removable distributed database, maintaining the block's record list. With the containing of time stamp and links to the previous block, the blockchain provides a security guarantee that, once recorded, the data cannot be modified.

4 Simulation Results and Analysis

In this paper, PBFT is used as the baseline of the algorithm to compare with SPBFT proposed in this paper with Matlab2015b. The request arriving intervals and the controller processing request intervals are both assumed to be with exponential distributions. We use the shortest path algorithm to transmit the signaling. Simulation parameters are shown in Table 2.

Table 2. Simulation parameters.

Parameters	Distribution	Mean	Var
Request arriving interval (ms)	Exponential	1.1	1.23
Controller processing interval (ms)	Exponential	1.1	1.23
Link delay (ms)	Uniform	1	0.34
Number of periods	N/A	60	N/A

We compare consensus time of normal controller with the probability of 1 and 2/3. Figure 4 shows the simulation results. The abscissa is the number of controllers and the ordinate is the mean consensus time. From the simulation results, the consensus time of the two algorithms is not much different when the number of nodes is less than 10. The consensus time of the SPBFT algorithm saves about 1/3 of the PBFT when the number of nodes is higher than 10.

Figure 5 shows the comparison of signaling overhead between two algorithms. The abscissa is the number of controllers and the ordinate is the average signaling overhead. Signaling overhead increases as the number of controller nodes increases. The signaling overhead of the SPBFT algorithm is approximately 50% lower than that of the PBFT algorithm.

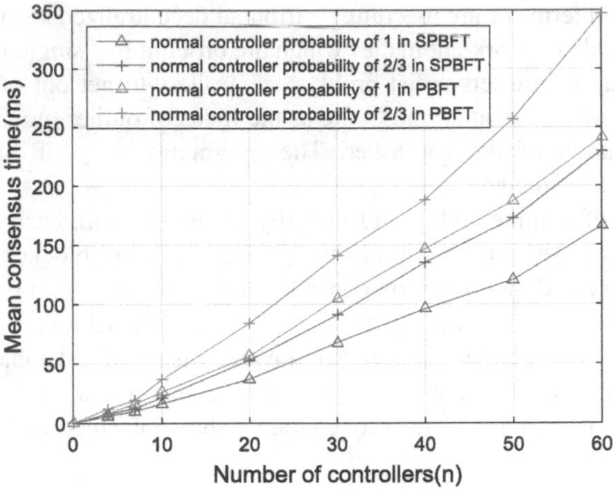

Fig. 4. Mean consensus time comparison.

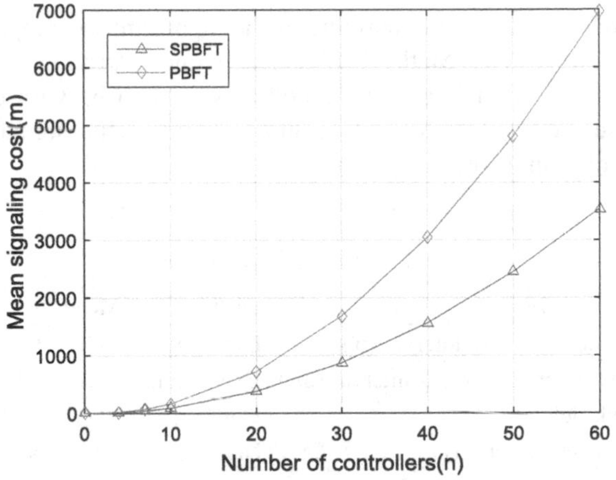

Fig. 5. Mean signaling overhead comparison.

This paper analyzes the complexity of the algorithm using the running time of the two algorithms in the program. A total of 20 runs were performed and averaged to obtain the algorithm complexity simulation results shown in Fig. 6. The abscissa is the number of controllers and the ordinate is the complexity. As shown, the complexity of the algorithm increases with the number of controllers. The complexity of the SPBFT algorithm is lower than that of the PBFT algorithm. Also, as the number of nodes increases, the complexity of the SPBFT algorithm rises more slowly than that of the PBFT algorithm.

In Fig. 7, we compare the invulnerability with and without using SPBFT algorithm under the same attack strength based on the analysis model proposed in this paper. The abscissa is the proportion of controllers being attacked, and the ordinate is the number

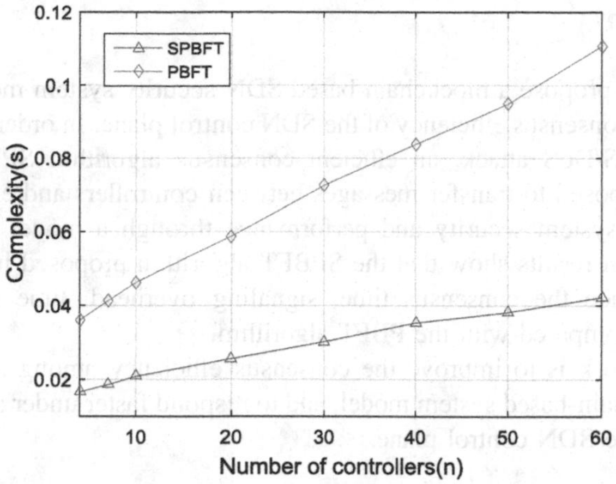

Fig. 6. Time complexity comparison

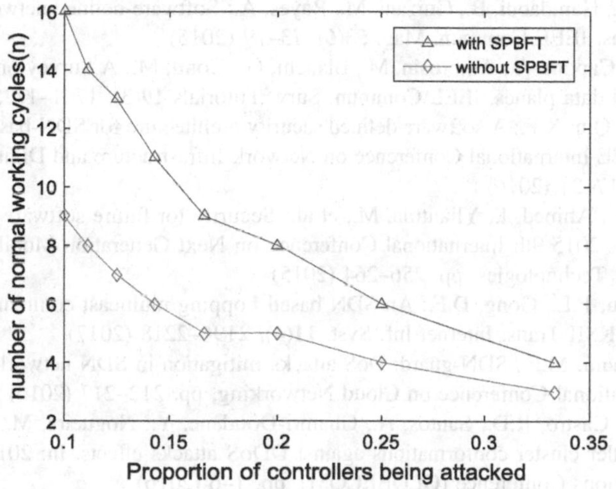

Fig. 7. Invulnerability comparison

of normal working cycles. As the proportion of attackers attacking the controller increases, the normal working cycle of the controller is shortened. The recovery strategy in this algorithm makes the control plane run normally for a longer time under the same intensity of attack.

Compared with the PBFT algorithm, the SPBFT algorithm reduces the one-time broadcast consensus, so the mean consensus time, signaling overhead, and time complexity are reduced, which is more in line with the SDN requirements of fast response. In addition, SPBFT uses the primary controller as the subject of the recovery measures implementation. Thus, under the same intensity of attack, the system can persist for longer with SPBFT algorithm.

5 Conclusion

In this paper, we propose a blockchain-based SDN security system model to improve the security and consensus efficiency of the SDN control plane. In order to avoid illegal access and DDoS/DoS attack, an efficient consensus algorithm SPBFT and smart contracts are proposed to transfer messages between controllers and execute requests. We analyze the system security and performance through a model based on game theory. Simulation results show that the SPBFT algorithm proposed in this paper can significantly reduce the consensus time, signaling overhead, time complexity and invulnerability, compared with the PBFT algorithm.

Our future work is to improve the consensus efficiency among SDN controllers under the blockchain-based system model, and to respond faster under attacks to ensure the security of the SDN control plane.

References

1. Dabbagh, M., Hamdaoui, B., Guizani, M., Rayes, A.: Software-defined networking security: pros and cons. IEEE Commun. Mag. **53**(6), 73–79 (2015)
2. Dargahi, T., Caponi, A., Ambrosin, M., Bianchi, G., Conti, M.: A Survey on the security of stateful SDN data planes. IEEE Commun. Surv. Tutorials **19**(3), 1701–1725 (2017)
3. Liang, X.D., Qiu, X.F.: A software defined security architecture for SDN-based 5G network. In: 2016 IEEE International Conference on Network Infrastructure and Digital Content (IC-NIDC), pp. 17–21 (2016)
4. Liyanage, M., Ahmed, I., Ylianttila, M., et al.: Security for future software defined mobile networks. In: 2015 9th International Conference on Next Generation Mobile Applications, Services and Technologies, pp. 256–264 (2015)
5. Zhao, Z., Liu, F.L., Gong, D.F.: An SDN based hopping multicast communication against DoS attack. KSII Trans. Internet Inf. Syst. **11**(4), 2196–2218 (2017)
6. Dridi, L., Zhani, M.F.: SDN-guard: DoS attacks mitigation in SDN networks. In: 2016 5th IEEE International Conference on Cloud Networking, pp. 212–217 (2016)
7. Macedo, R., Castro, R.D., Santos, A., Ghamri-Doudane, Y., Nogueira, M.: Self-organized SDN controller cluster conformations against DDoS attacks effects. In: 2016 IEEE Global Communications Conference (GLOBECOM), pp. 1–6 (2016)
8. Xia, Q., Sifah, E.B., Asamoah, K.O.: MeDShare: trust-less medical data sharing among cloud service providers via blockchain. IEEE Access **5**, 14757–14767 (2017)
9. Herbaut, N., Negru, N.: A model for collaborative blockchain-based video delivery relying on advanced network services chains. IEEE Commun. Mag. **55**(9), 70–76 (2017)
10. Rottondi, C., Verticale, G.: A privacy-friendly gaming framework in smart electricity and water grids. IEEE Access **5**, 14221–14233 (2017)
11. Zhang, J., Xue, N., Huang, X.: A secure system for pervasive social network-based healthcare. IEEE Access **4**(1), 9239–9250 (2016)
12. Anjum, M., Sporny, A.: Sill: blockchain standards for compliance and trust. IEEE Cloud Comput. **4**(4), 84–89 (2017)
13. Sharma, P.K., Chen, M.Y., Park, J.H.: A software defined fog node based distributed blockchain cloud architecture for IoT. IEEE Access **6**, 115–124 (2017)

An ESPRIT Parameter Estimation Algorithm Based on Non-circular Signal for MIMO Radar

Jurong Hu[1(✉)], Ying Tian[1], Evans Baidoo[1], Xiaoyong Ni[2], and Lei Zha[1]

[1] College of Computer and Information, Hohai University, Nanjing, China
hujurong@sina.com, 1354563810@qq.com,
ebaidoo2@hhu.edu.cn, 1045634657@qq.com

[2] College of Computer and Information, University of Electronic Science and Technology of China, Chengdu, China
852808792@qq.com

Abstract. In this paper, a method of parameter estimation based on Non-Circular Signal via two-dimensional ESPRIT algorithm for MIMO radar is proposed. The algorithm considers the characteristic of the maximum non-circularity signal, and utilizes not only the covariance matrix but also the pseudo-covariance matrix to obtain the data matrix of the non-circular signal. This algorithm expands the received signal data matrix by data recombination, which increases the number of effective array elements of MIMO radar and improves the utilization of echo information. Then the parameter estimates are obtained by using the two-dimensional ESPRIT algorithm. Compared with the ESPRIT algorithm developed in other references, this algorithm has higher accuracy of parameter estimation in the case of lower signal-to-noise ratio or fewer array elements. Meanwhile, the algorithm can improve the accuracy of parameter estimation when the targets are close together. Simulation results indicate that the proposed algorithm improves the performance significantly.

Keywords: Parameter estimation · Two dimensional ESPRIT algorithm · Non-circular signal · MIMO radar

1 Introduction

Multiple-input–multiple-output (MIMO) radar is a new type of system radar, which utilizes multiple antennas to simultaneously transmit orthogonal waveforms and uses multiple antennas to receive the reflected signals. It has been shown that MIMO radars have many potential advantages over conventional phased-array radars [1]. According to the antennas configuration, MIMO radars can be divided into two types. One is called distributed MIMO radar, and the second one is the collocated MIMO radar, which is studied in this paper. In recent years, different methods have been developed for estimating DOD and DOA of multiple targets in collocated MIMO radar. Capon algorithms [2] have been used for angle estimation in bistatic MIMO radar, while multiple signal classification algorithms [3] can also work well for angle estimation.

M. Jia et al. (Eds.): WiSATS 2019, LNICST 281, pp. 363–369, 2019.
https://doi.org/10.1007/978-3-030-19156-6_33

However, the above mentioned algorithms require the spectrum searches, which lead to high computational complexity. In [4], a rotational invariance techniques (ESPRIT) algorithm is proposed for angle estimation, and the reduced-dimensional transformation is employed to reduce the complexity. Aiming at the problem that the traditional ESPRIT algorithm has poor performance under the background of Gaussian white noise, [5] improves the traditional ESPRIT algorithm. It divides the planar array into multiple subspace arrays, and applies the ESPRIT algorithm to each antenna which improves the parameter estimation accuracy and resolution. However, the ESPRIT algorithm in [5] is still not perfect in parameter estimation when the distances of several far-field targets are close. In [6], the non-circular signal used in the radar system has potential advantages for improving the performance of all aspects of the radar. Therefore, this paper further studies the MIMO radar angle estimation algorithm based on non-circular signals.

The main objective of this paper is to propose a parameter estimation method based on Non-circular (NC) signal via two-dimensional (2-D) ESPRIT algorithm (NC-2D-ESPRIT). The studied algorithm considers the characteristics of the maximum non-circularity signal, and converts the real signal into maximum non-circularity signals by phase shifting [7], which uses the covariance matrix and the pseudo covariance matrix [8, 9] of the maximum non-circular signal to obtain the data matrix of the non-circular signal. Then, this algorithm expands the received signal data matrix by data recombination [10], which achieves the purpose of increasing the number of effective array elements of MIMO radar. Compared to the ESPRIT [5], the proposed algorithm has slightly better parameter estimation performance and improves the accuracy of parameter estimation when the distance of multiple targets is relatively close.

The remainder of this paper is structured as follows. Section 2 develops the system model on NC signal, and Sect. 3 proposes the parameter estimation theory of NC-2D-ESPRIT. Section 4 analyzes the simulation results, while the conclusion is presented in Sect. 5.

2 System Model

Consider a MIMO radar system with Uniform linear array of transmitters and receivers which utilizes M transmitters to transmit orthogonal signals and N receivers to receive the reflected signals. Define $d_t = \mathrm{N}d_r$, d_r is the distance from the transmitter to transmitter, d_r is the distance from the receiver to receiver. Thus, the M + N array elements of the transmitting and receiving arrays are equivalent to M $\times$ N-dimensional virtual transceiver array.

The signal received by the virtual transceiver array after filtering can be expressed as

$$\mathrm{Y} = \begin{bmatrix} Y_1 \\ Y_2 \\ \vdots \\ Y_N \end{bmatrix} = \begin{bmatrix} A_x D_1(A_y) \\ A_x D_2(A_y) \\ \vdots \\ A_x D_N(A_y) \end{bmatrix} \mathrm{S} + \begin{bmatrix} W_1 \\ W_2 \\ \vdots \\ W_N \end{bmatrix} \tag{1}$$

Where $A_x = [a_x(\theta_1, \varphi_1), a_x(\theta_2, \varphi_2), \ldots, a_x(\theta_K, \varphi_K)]$ is the direction matrix of M array elements along the x-axis in which $a_x(\theta_k, \varphi_k)$ represents the signal from the signal source corresponding to the array response of the virtual transceiver array in the x-axis direction. $A_y = [a_y(\theta_1, \varphi_1), a_y(\theta_2, \varphi_2), \ldots, a_y(\theta_K, \varphi_K)]$ is the direction matrix of N array elements along the y-axis in which $a_y(\theta_k, \varphi_k)$ represents the signal from the signal source corresponding to the array response of the virtual transceiver array in the y-axis direction, and $\mathbf{W} = [W_1, W_2, \ldots, W_N]$ is the received noise matrix. S is a data matrix for noncircular signals [9] as follow:

$$S = \Psi S_0 = [S(1), S(2), \ldots, S(P)] \tag{2}$$

Where $\Psi = \{e^{j\Psi_1}, e^{j\Psi_2}, \ldots e^{j\Psi_k}\}$, and the different values on its diagonal lines represent the non-circular phase of non-circular sources, $S_0 = [s_{01}, s_{02}, \ldots, s_{0k}]^T$, S_0 is a real valued matrix, and s_{0k} represents the zero initial phase real signal of the maximum non-circular signal obtained by phase shifting.

3 Principle of Direction of Arrival Estimation Algorithm Based on NC-2D-ESPRIT

The data matrix Y received by the virtual transceiver array established in this paper is extended [14] as follows:

$$Y' = \begin{bmatrix} Y \\ JY^* \end{bmatrix} = \Lambda S_0 + W' \in C^{2MN \times P} \tag{3}$$

Where J is an MN × MN-dimensional exchange matrix with all the anti-corner elements being 1, the rest of the positions take the value 0, and $Y^* \in C^{MN \times P}$ represents the conjugate matrix of matrix Y, A is the joint direction vector matrix after extending the transceiver array, $W' = \begin{bmatrix} W \\ JW^* \end{bmatrix}$ is the restructured noise matrix.

Define two sub-matrices from A to satisfy:

$$A_2 = A_1 D_2(A_y) = A_1 \psi_1 \tag{4}$$

Where, A_1 respectively denote the first N-1 rows of matrix A and A_2 denote the last N-1 rows of matrix A. Then, the covariance matrix of data in (3) will be $R_{zz} = E[Y' Y'^H]$ [8] can be decomposed. Taking the larger k eigenvalues obtained by the decomposition to form the signal subspace as $\mathbf{E}_s$, whose K columns are the eigenvectors associated with the K largest eigenvalues of R_z. For DOD estimation, the matrix $\mathbf{E}_s$ is dividing into E_{x1} and E_{y1}, which are obtained as follows:

$$\begin{bmatrix} E_{x1} \\ E_{y1} \end{bmatrix} = \begin{bmatrix} A_1 T_4 \\ A_1 D_2(A_y) T_4 \end{bmatrix} \tag{5}$$

Where T_4 is a full rank non-singular matrix, from the rotational invariance property of the antenna array, (5) satisfies $E_{y1} = E_{x1}T_4^{-1}\Psi_y T_4 = H_y T_4$, therefore, its least-squares solution can be expressed as:

$$\widehat{\mathrm{H}}_y = E_{x1}^{+}E_{y1} \tag{6}$$

Decompose the eigenvalue of $\widehat{\mathrm{H}}_y$ to get $\widehat{\mathrm{T}}_4 = \Gamma T_4$, $\widehat{\Psi}_y = \Gamma\Psi_y\Gamma^{-1}$ and $\widehat{r}_{yk} = \cos\widehat{\theta}_k sin\widehat{\Psi}_k$. Where Γ is a permutation matrix, $\widehat{r}_{yk}$ indicates that the eigenvalue position of $\widehat{\mathrm{H}}_y$ is K.

Similarly, for DOA estimation, by reconstructing the signal subspace we can get as follows:

$$E_s' = E_s\widehat{T}_4^{-1} = \mathrm{A}T_4\widehat{T}_4^{-1} = \mathrm{A}\Gamma^{-1} \tag{7}$$

Define two signal sub-matrices E_{x2} and E_{y2} from E_s' and two sub-matrices A_3 *and* A_4 from A to satisfy:

$$E_{x2} = A_3\Gamma^{-1} \tag{8}$$

$$E_{y2} = A_4\Gamma^{-1} = E_{x2}\Gamma\Psi_x\Gamma^{-1} = E_{x2}H_x \tag{9}$$

Then the estimated value that can be solved by the least squares method as follows:

$$\widehat{\mathrm{H}}_x = E_{x2}^{+}E_{y2} \tag{10}$$

Decompose the eigenvalue of $\widehat{\mathrm{H}}_x$ to get $\widehat{\Psi}_x = \Gamma\Psi_x\Gamma^{-1}$, $\widehat{r}_{Xk} = \cos\widehat{\theta}_k sin\widehat{\Psi}_k$. Where $\widehat{r}_{Xk}$ indicates that the eigenvalue position of $\widehat{\mathrm{H}}_x$ is K. In practice, the estimation of the elevation angle and azimuth of the MIMO radar based on NC-2D-ESPRIT can be obtained by the combination of Eqs. (11) and (12) as follows.

$$\widehat{\theta}_k = cos^{-1}\sqrt{(\widehat{r}_{Xk}^2 + \widehat{r}_{yk}^2)} \tag{11}$$

$$\widehat{\Psi}_k = tan^{-1}\sqrt{\frac{\widehat{r}_{yk}}{\widehat{r}_{Xk}}} \tag{12}$$

4 Simulations

This section discusses the capability of the proposed algorithm in fields of target angle resolution, array number and signal-to-noise ratio (SNR). Assume that there are K = 3 independent targets with the angles being $(25^{\circ}, -20^{\circ})$, $(45^{\circ}, 10^{\circ})$, $(35^{\circ}, -10^{\circ})$, $\mathrm{M} = 6$, $\mathrm{N} = 6$, $LC = 200$, and the number of snapshots is P = 100 times.

Table 1 shows, compared with the ESPRIT [8], the estimated performance is significantly improved regardless of the azimuth or the pitch angle differs by 0.5°. It indicates that the algorithm can achieve a difference of 0.5° between the target angles under multiple targets. Therefore, the algorithm improves the radar resolution.

Table 1. The comparison of the difference of 0.5° between the target angles

SNR	Angle condition			
	Azimuth difference between 0.5°		Elevation difference between 0.5°	
	ESPRIT [8] RMSE/°	NC-ESPRIT RMSE/°	ESPRIT [8] RMSE/°	NC-ESPRIT RMSE/°
0 dB	1.3400	0.3973	0.9712	0.3840
5 dB	0.5741	0.1705	0.4860	0.1682
10 dB	0.2351	0.0919	0.1589	0.0905
15 dB	0.1240	0.0507	0.0854	0.0487
20 dB	0.0740	0.0286	0.0583	0.0251
25 dB	0.0400	0.0154	0.0334	0.0146
30 dB	0.0287	0.0086	0.0232	0.0078

Figure 1 shows the effect of SNR when estimating the target angle using the ESPRIT [8] and the NC-2D-ESPRIT algorithm. Increase the SNR from 0 dB to 30 dB at 2 dB, while other simulation conditions remain unchanged. We take the average of the RMSE of the three targets for comparison. It can be discovered that the angle estimation performance curve of the proposed algorithm is obviously better than that of the ESPRIT algorithm [8]. Furthermore, we can get that the RMSE of the proposed algorithm is lower. And the performance estimation of the proposed algorithm is obviously better than the ESPRIT algorithm [8], especially in low SNR.

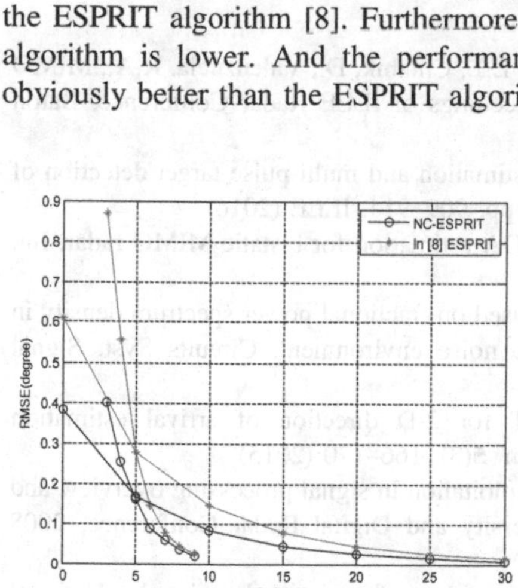

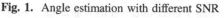

Fig. 1. Angle estimation with different SNR

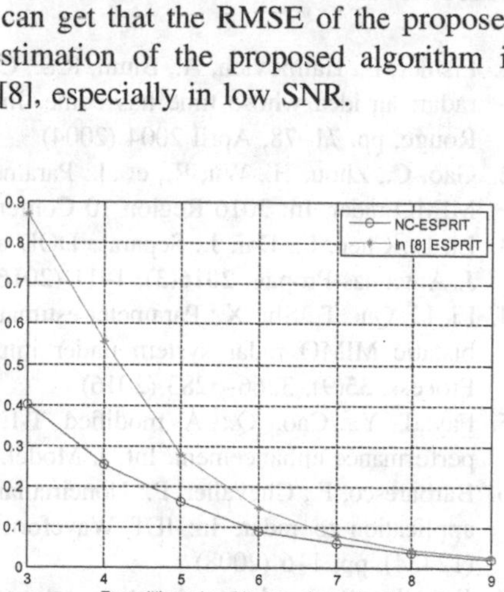

Fig. 2. Angle estimation comparison with different array elements

Figure 2 presents the effect of signal-to-array elements by using the two algorithms when change the number of transmitting and receiving elements from 3 to 9 at an interval with SNR = 10 dB.

It is shown that, the accuracy on parameter estimation of the proposed algorithm is significantly higher than the ESPRIT [8] under the same elements. When the number of elements is fewer, the RMSE of the proposed algorithm still remains small, indicating that parameters can still be accurately estimated. With the increasing number of array elements, both algorithms can estimated exactly. However, setting a large number of array elements will lead to an increase in the amount of calculation and energy, so in practice, we need to consider the actual situation and the integrated environment.

5 Conclusion

In this paper, a parameter estimation algorithm based on Non-Circular Signal via two-dimensional ESPRIT algorithm for MIMO radar has been discussed. This algorithm introduces the maximum non-circularity signal, and combines the ESPRIT algorithm to estimate MIMO radar parameters. Simulations show that the algorithm improves the accuracy of angle estimation regardless of the number of different elements or different SNR, especially in low SNR and fewer elements. Furthermore, the algorithm can achieve accurate estimation when the angle difference between multiple targets is 0.5°. In summary, the proposed algorithm provides a more convenient solution for MIMO radar parameter estimation.

References

1. Fishler, E., Haimovich, A., Blum, R.S., Cimini, L.J., Chizhik, D., Valenzuela, R.A.: MIMO radar: an idea whose time has come. In: Proceedings of IEEE Radar Conference, Baton Rouge, pp. 71–78, April 2004 (2004)
2. Gao, C., Zhou, H., Wu, R., et al.: Parameter estimation and multi-pulse target detection of MIMO radar. In: 2016 Region 10 Conference, pp. 909–914. IEEE (2016)
3. Li, L., Chen, F., Dai, J.: Separate DOD and DOA estimation for bistatic MIMO radar. Int. J. Antennas Propag. **2016**(3), 1–11 (2016)
4. Li, L., Qiu, T., Shi, X.: Parameter estimation based on fractional power spectrum density in bistatic MIMO radar system under impulsive noise environment. Circuits Syst. Signal Process. **35**(9), 3266–3283 (2016)
5. Fayad, Y., Cao, Q.: A modified T-ESPRIT for 2-D direction of arrival estimation performance enhancement. Int. J. Model. Optim. **5**(3), 166–170 (2015)
6. Barbaresco, F., Chevalier, P.: Noncircularity exploitation in signal processing overview and application to radar. In: IET Waveform Diversity and Digital Radar Conference, 2008 (12434), pp. 1–6 (2008)
7. Jian, L.: Research on direction estimation algorithm of non-circular signals. National University of Defense Technology (2007)
8. Chargé, P., Wang, Y.D., Saillard, J.: A non-circular sources direction finding method using polynomial rooting. Signal Process. **81**(8), 1765–1770 (2001)

9. Zoubir, A., Chargé, P., Wang, Y.: Non circular sources localization with ESPRIT. In: Proceedings of the European Conference on Wireless Technology (2003)
10. Haardt, M., Römer, F.: Enhancements of unitary ESPRIT for non-circular sources. In: International Conference on Acoustics, Speech and Signal Processing, II, pp. 101–104. IEEE (2004)

An Improved Target Location Algorithm of MIMO Radar Based on Fuzzy C Clustering

Jurong Hu, Lei Zhan(✉), Evans Baidoo, Xujie Li, and Ying Tian

College of Computer and Information, Hohai University, Nanjing, China
hujurong@sina.com, 1045634657@qq.com,
{ebaidoo2,lixujie}@hhu.edu.cn, 1354563810@qq.com

Abstract. This paper deals with multi-target localization in statistical MIMO radar. An improved target locating algorithm is proposed which combines Kalman filtering with fuzzy C clustering. The Kalman filter is utilized to acquire the information of target location and fuzzy C clustering is used for data fusion as there are multiple receivers in radar. For target locating in MIMO radar, we first utilize the maximum likelihood estimation algorithm to estimate the parameters of targets. To eliminate the influence of noise on the parameter estimation, we take advantage of the gliding property of Kalman filter to process the result of parameter estimation. All these processing data from different receivers is fused by fuzzy C cluster to obtain the parameters estimation of all targets. We give scenarios including MIMO radar and targets to analyze the performance of this target location algorithm. With considering the effects of noise, the position of receivers and transmitters and the moving of targets, the analysis is carried out by evaluating the location accuracy of the algorithm. The simulation result shows that the proposed method can locate multiply targets effectively and improves the location accuracy.

Keywords: Statistical MIMO radar · Multi-target localization · Kalman filtering · Fuzzy C clustering

1 Introduction

MIMO (Multiple-input multiple-output) radar is a new kind of system radar. It is superior to traditional radar in target detection and parameter estimation. Target positioning is one of the core issues in the fields of radar, sonar and UAV interaction and it is performed by processing the echo. Typical methods include the Maximum Likelihood method and the Best Linear Unbiased Estimation method.

A series of solutions are proposed for the MIMO radar which take the distance equation on target localization into consideration. Wang et al. achieved target localization by hyperbolas without considering the effect of transmit and receive antennas [2]. Yang et al. proposed a hyperbolic localization algorithm based on the measurement of the arrival time of the transmitting/receiving antenna. This algorithm solves the local convergence problem in the traditional algorithm and analyzes the influence of transmitting/receiving antenna pairs on the positioning accuracy. But it requires an

M. Jia et al. (Eds.): WiSATS 2019, LNICST 281, pp. 370–376, 2019.
https://doi.org/10.1007/978-3-030-19156-6_34

initial estimate close to the target position [3]. These algorithms require transmit and receive antenna to meet time synchronization strictly.

For the research of processing echo information in statistical MIMO radar, the proposed method achieves target positioning directly. Two approximate ML algorithms are proposed with the influence of noise [4]. Taking phase error correction into consideration, the author solved the problem of multi-target localization under the circumstances of phase mismatch [5]. The method achieves positioning of multiple targets by estimating alternately the reserve reflection coefficient and phase difference. A method that paired target distances with Doppler frequency estimates in different observation channels to estimate the target position is proposed [6]. The research on the accuracy of the target position estimation needs to be further developed.

In order to enhance the performance multiple targets location, an improved localization algorithm based on fuzzy C clustering and Kalman filtering is proposed. Fuzzy C clustering can form new clusters from data that have similarity to existing categories and process position parameter estimation on information fusion. Kalman filtering estimates the state of a dynamic system from a series of incomplete and noise measurement. The algorithm achieves multi-target positioning and solves the situation where two adjacent targets appear in the air.

2 Radar System Model

The signal model focuses on multiple targets $\left(\mathrm{x_q}, \mathrm{y_q}, \mathrm{z_q}\right)(\mathrm{q} = 1, 2, \ldots, \mathrm{N})$ in the far field of transmitting and receiving antenna. Figure 1 illustrates the model. We express the received signals which originate from the transmitter and are reflected by the target:

$$r_n^{(q)}(t) = \sqrt{E/M \sum\nolimits_{m=1}^{M} \zeta \rho_{mn}(X_q) s_m(t - \tau_{mn}(X_q)) + w_n(t)} \quad (1)$$

Where, ζ represents coincident reflectivity, $\mathrm{w_n}(\mathrm{t})$ is Gaussian white noise, and f_c is carrier frequency.

The distance between the transmitting antenna and the target and the distance between the receiving antenna and the target can be written as follows:

$$d(T_m, X_q) = \sqrt{(x_{tm} - x_q)^2 + (y_{tm} - y_q)^2 + (z_{tm} - z_q)^2}$$

$$d(R_n, X_q) = \sqrt{(x_{rn} - x_q)^2 + (y_{rn} - y_q)^2 + (z_{rn} - z_q)^2} \quad (2)$$

Where, $\tau_{\mathrm{tm}}(\mathrm{x_q})$ represents propagation delay of the signal from transmitting antenna to target, $\tau_{\mathrm{rn}}(\mathrm{X_q})$ is the delay of signal from target to receive antenna, as follows:

$$\tau_{mn}(X_q) = \tau_{tm}(X_q) + \tau_{rn}(X_q) = d(R_n, X_q)/C + d(T_m, X_q)/C$$

$$\rho_{mn}(X_q) = exp(-j2\pi f_c \tau_{mn}(X_q)) \tag{3}$$

3 Target Location Method

In the proposed method, it estimates the position of target using maximum likelihood. Where, $X_q = [x_q, y_q, z_q]^T$ represents the position of target and we can puts the unknown parameters into the vector $\theta = [x, y, z, \zeta_{q1}, \zeta_{q2}]^T$. The Joint Probability Density Function of observation is determined by the vector, as follows:

$$p(r;\theta) = exp\left\{ -\frac{1}{\sigma^2} \sum\nolimits_{n=1}^{N} \int_T |r_n(t) - \zeta_q E/M \sum\nolimits_{m=1}^{M} \rho_{mn}(X_q) s_m(t - \tau_{mn}(X_q))\}|^2 dt \right\}$$

$$\widehat{\theta}_{ML} = \arg\{max[lgp(r;\theta)]\} = arg\{max\{max[lgp(r;X_q,\zeta_{q1},\zeta_{q2})]\}\} \tag{4}$$

Where, $(.)^*$ represents conjugate, maximum likelihood estimation is expressed as:

$$\widehat{X}_{qML} = arg\left\{ max\left[\sum\nolimits_{m=1}^{M} \sum\nolimits_{n=1}^{N} \rho^*_{mn}(X_q) \int r_n(t) s^*_m(t - \tau_{mn}(X_q))dt \right] \right\} \tag{5}$$

Where, the coordinate $X_c = (\widehat{x}_c, \widehat{y}_c, \widehat{z}_c)$ of the target position parameter is obtained.

The target position estimation parameters obtained are placed in the set $C_k^{Q \times G}$. The number of targets is used as the number of clusters c, and the state prediction value of target is a center of the class, and the other collections under the same condition.

The state equation to find the classification center at the time of k is:

$$X_q(k) = A_q X_q(k-1) + B_q u_q(k-1) + w_q(k) \tag{6}$$

The measurement equation of the moment by the formula is written as:

$$z_q(k) = H_q X_q(k) + v_q(k) \tag{7}$$

Where, $X_q(k)$ represents the state of target q at the moment of k, A_q is the state transition matrix, $w_q(k)$ represents the system noise vector, H_q is the observation matrix, I_q represents the identity matrix, $u_q(k), v_q(k)$ represent the process and measurement noise respectively. The covariance $Q_q(k)$ and $R_q(k)$ are Gaussian white noise. Where, $K_q(k)$ is the Kalman gain matrix, and $\widehat{X}_q(k+1)$ is the best filter value.

The state prediction equation of target is obtained by Kalman filtering as follows:

$$\widehat{X}_q(k+1) = \widehat{X}_q(\overline{k}) + K_q(k)\left(z_q(k) - H_q \widehat{X}_q(\overline{k})\right)$$

$$v_q(k) = X_q(k) - H_q \widehat{X}_q(\overline{k})$$

$$P_q(k) = \left(I_q - K_q(k)H_q\right)P_q\left(\overline{k}\right)$$

$$S_q(k+1) = H_q P_q\left(\overline{k}\right)H_q^T + R_q(k) \tag{8}$$

Where, $v_q(k)$ is innovation and $P_q(k)$ represents filter covariance, $S_q(k+1)$ is innovation of covariance matrix. The state prediction of target is the classification center.

The Mahalanobis distance formula calculate the distance between all target position parameter estimations and the classification center. The formula is given by:

$$d_q^2 = v_q(k)' S_q(k) v_q(k) \tag{9}$$

If the distance between the position parameter and target state predicted value is less than or equal to a threshold, then it is the effective measured value. Otherwise, it was rounded off. Effective position parameter estimation $Y_l(l = 1, 2, \ldots, L)$ is judged by the threshold. We can put it into the other set and divide the data into class $C(C = Q)$. Where, $P = \{P_1, \ldots, P_c, \ldots, P_C\}$ is defined as cluster center. The data belongs to a class and has a membership degree of u_{cl} we find that the objective function is:

$$J(W, P) = \sum\nolimits_{l=1}^{L} \sum\nolimits_{c=1}^{C} (u_{cl})^{m2} \|Y_l - P_c\|^2 \tag{10}$$

Where, m2 is the fuzzy weighted index. When $J(W, P)$ taking the minimum, using the Lagrange multipliers method can be written in the following form as:

$$u_{cl} = \left[\sum\nolimits_{c2=1}^{C} \left(\|Y_l - P_c\|^2 / \|Y_l - P_{c2}\|^2\right)^{\frac{2}{m2-1}}\right]^{-1} \tag{11}$$

Iteration stops until the threshold reached, and the range is $1.5 \le m2 \le 2.5$. We put target location parameters into a collection as $Q = \{Z_1, Z_2, \ldots, Z_Q\}$, they are averaged:

$$z_q^n = 1/N1 \sum\nolimits_{n1=1}^{N1} z_{qn1}^n (n = 1, 2, \ldots, N) \tag{12}$$

Where, z_{qn1}^n represents the estimation of all position parameters of the receiving antenna for target, and N1 is the number of position parameter estimation.

Data fusion processes for $Z_1, Z_2, \ldots, Z_Q$. Assume that the observation error is Gaussian white noise. The position parameters estimated of linear fusion are expressed by:

$$Z_{qf} = f_1 Z_q^1 + f_2 Z_q^2 + \ldots + f_R Z_q^R \left(f_j = \frac{1/\sigma_n^2}{\sum_{n=1}^{N} 1/\sigma_n^2} \right) \tag{13}$$

Kalman filtering filtered it for the target by means of Z_{qf}, and the state value based on the fusion measurement is obtained. Where the state is estimated as:

$$Z_{qf}(k) = AZ_{qf}(k-1) + Bu_{qf}(k-1) + w_{qf}(k) = H_{qf}Z_{qf}(k) + v_{qf}(k) \tag{14}$$

Where, A_{qf} is the state transition matrix of the system, $w_{qf}(k)$ represents the system noise vector, and H_{qf} is the observation matrix, $u_{qf}(k)$ is the process noise, and $v_{qf}(k)$ is the measurement noise, $Q_{qf}(k)$ and $R_{qf}(k)$ are the Gaussian white noise.

Where, $P_{qf}(k)$ is Filter covariance, $K_{qf}(k)$ represents Kalman gain, $P_{qf}(\overline{k})$ is the prediction error covariance, $\widehat{Z}_{qf}(k+1)$ is Optimal Filter, the vectors are expressed as:

$$P_{qf}(k) = \left(I_{qf} - K_{qf}(k)H_{qf}\right)P_{qf}(\overline{k})$$

$$K_{qf}(k) = P_{qf}(\overline{k})H_{qf}^T\left[H_{qf}P_{qf}(\overline{k})H_{qf}^T + \sigma_f^2 I_{qf}\right]^{-1}$$

$$v_{qf}(k) = Z_{qf}(k) - H_{qf}\widehat{Z}_{qf}(\overline{k})$$

$$P_{qf}(\overline{k}) = A_{qf}P_{qf}(k-1)A_{qf}^T + Q_{qf}(k)$$

$$\widehat{Z}_{qf}(k+1) = \widehat{Z}_{qf}(k) + K_{qf}(k)\left[\left(z_{qf}(k) - H_{qf}\widehat{Z}_{qf}(k)\right)\right] \tag{15}$$

4 Simulation and Analysis

This section presents simulations to verify the accuracy and resolution performance of the proposed approach. It is assumed that there are three pairs of transmit/receive antennas that they are both time and space aligned. The sampling period is 1 s. There are 5 targets with different initial positions, speeds, and accelerations. The process noise and measurement noise are Gaussian white noise, the signal-to-noise ratio is 10 dB, and the fuzzy weight is two.

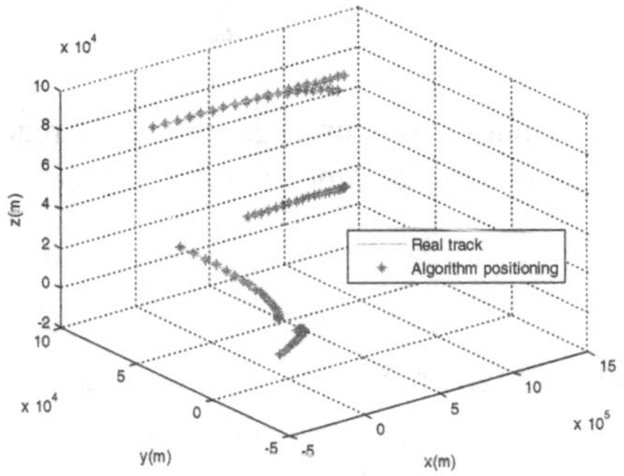

Fig. 1. Estimate target plots of improved algorithm

The target real motion trajectory and algorithm estimation points after Monte Carlo experiments are shown in Fig. 1. The trace is the target estimate of the improved algorithm. The position estimation point of the algorithm has a high coincidence degree with the target motion curve, so the positioning of maneuvering target can be achieved. It can be seen that there is no disorder in the algorithm which solves the problem of positioning of adjacent target.

Assuming that the signal-to-noise ratio of the simulation environment is 10 dB, in the 0–50 s time period, the root mean square error of the estimated position of the algorithm is obtained. After Monte Carlo experiments, Fig. 2 is an RMSE plot of the proposed algorithm for estimating multiple target locations at different times. As the motion time of target increased in the airspace, the root mean square error of target parameter estimation is increased, and the positioning effect is gradually deteriorated.

Setting the signal-to-noise ratio range to 0–24 dB when the time t = 1 s, t = 2 s, t = 3 s and t = 4 s in motion, the root mean square error of target 1, target 2, target 3 and target 4 at different time is obtained by simulation. In Fig. 3, with the signal-to-noise ratio increasing, the positioning performance is improved continuously. When the signal-to-noise ratio range to 0–10 dB, it has a great influence on the positioning performance of the algorithm. The algorithm is less affected relatively by it when the signal-to-noise ratio is 0 dB. When the signal-to-noise ratio is constant, the positioning performance decreased with the extension of the target motion time.

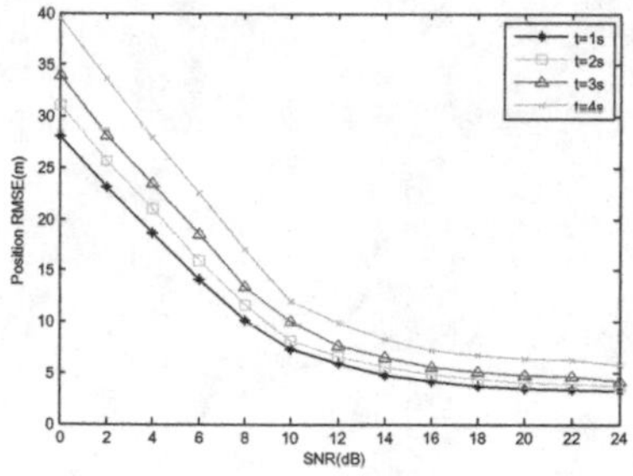

Fig. 2. The root mean square error

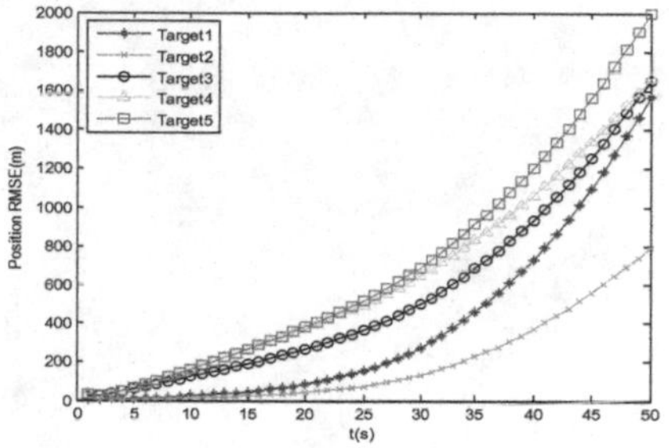

Fig. 3. Position effect under different SNR

5 Conclusion

In this paper, we have proposed an improved multi-target locating method in MIMO radar. Firstly, the maximum likelihood estimation algorithm is used to process the echo to obtain the target position parameter estimation. Then the iterative method is used to solve the ML equation to obtain the position parameter estimation. The localization algorithm based on fuzzy C cluster and Kalman filtering obtains the target parameter estimation. The algorithm is simulated by MATLAB software. The effects of SNR, receiving/transmitting antenna and target motion time on estimation accuracy are analyzed. The simulation results show that the proposed algorithm can locate multi-target and improved effectively the resolution ratio of positioning adjacent targets in the airspace.

References

1. Li, J., Stoica, P.: MIMO Radar Signal Processing. Wiley-IEEE Press, Hoboken (2009)
2. Wang, H., Guo, H.: Hyperbolic localization method for MIMO radar. In: Radar Symposium, pp. 880–885. IEEE (2011)
3. Yang, H., Chun, J., Chae, D.: Hyperbolic localization in MIMO radar systems. IEEE Antennas Wirel. Propag. Lett. **14**, 618–621 (2015)

4. Xia, W., He, Z.: On the maximum likelihood method for target localization using MIMO radars. Sci. China Inf. Sci. **53**(10), 2127–2137 (2010)
5. Sun, B., Chen, H., Zou, H.: Sparsity-aware multi-target localization for distributed MIMO radar against phase synchronisation mismatch. IET Commun. **10**, 2269–2275 (2016)
6. Chen, J., Chen, X., Zhu, Y.: Multi-target localization and velocity estimation method for statistical MIMO radar. Telecommun. Technol. (2013)
7. Haimovich, A.M., Blum, R.S., Cimini, L.J.: MIMO radar with widely separated antennas. IEEE Sig. Process. Mag. **25**(1), 116–129 (2007)
8. Li, Q., Li, R., Ji, K., et al.: Kalman filter and its application. In: International Conference on Intelligent Networks and Intelligent Systems, pp. 74–77. IEEE (2015)
9. Waltz, E., Llinas, J.: Multisensor Data Fusion, pp. 25–42. Artech House, Boston (2008)
10. Julier, S.J., Uhlmann, J.K., Durrant-Whyte, H.F.: A new approach for filtering nonlinear systems. In: Proceedings of the American Control Conference, vol. 3, pp. 1628–1632. IEEE (2002)

A Resource Allocation Scheme Based on Predatory Search Algorithm for Ultra-dense D2D Communications

Xujie Li[1(✉)], Ying Sun[1], Lingjie Zhou[1], Yanli Xu[2], and Siyuan Zhou[1]

[1] College of Computer and Information, Hohai University, Nanjing 210098, China
lixujie@hhu.edu.cn

[2] College of Information Engineering, Shanghai Maritime University, Shanghai 201306, China

Abstract. In this paper, resource allocation problem for ultra-dense D2D communications is studied. In ultra-dense scenarios, the number of D2D user equipments (DUEs) is far bigger than the number of cellular user equipments (CUEs). The dense user equipments (UEs) increase the complexity of resource allocation problem. Firstly, the system model of ultra-dense D2D communications is described. Then the resource allocation problem of ultra-dense D2D communications is formulated. Next a fast resource allocation algorithm based on predatory search algorithm is proposed and analyzed. Finally, the analysis and simulation results validate that the performance of proposed scheme is very efficient and has a low algorithmic complexity. This scheme can be applied into the ultra-dense D2D communication networks.

Keywords: Device to device · Resource allocation · Predatory search algorithm

1 Introduction

Now, satellite communications and terrestrial communications playing more and more significant role in the future information transmission [1–3]. To meet the demand of bandwidth efficiency improvement and more data services requirement, device-to-device (D2D) communication is presented. D2D communication system allows the terminals in proximity to directly communicate each other via the base station (BS). It will effectively improve spectrum efficiency and reduce terminal transmission power. It has become a key technique for 5G network and Internet of Things (IoT) [4–6]. Meanwhile, the concept of ultra-dense networks emerges to accommodate more user equipments (UEs).

In ultra-dense D2D communications, the resource allocation problem gets more challenging due to the randomness of the positions of the massive UEs. Meanwhile, the positions of the UEs will change frequently because of their movements. This makes the resource allocation problem more difficult to solve. In this case, it is very hard to obtain a better resource allocation scheme while guaranteeing the QoS of all UEs using

M. Jia et al. (Eds.): WiSATS 2019, LNICST 281, pp. 377–386, 2019.
https://doi.org/10.1007/978-3-030-19156-6_35

the traditional techniques. So we need to find a fast and efficient algorithm to solve the problem. Compared with other feasible algorithms, the predatory search algorithm has stronger global searching ability and faster convergence speed. Base on the idea of the predatory search algorithm, a resource allocation scheme based on predatory search algorithm for ultra-dense D2D communications is proposed in this paper.

It is generally known that resource allocation is an important problem in D2D communication. So there are many researchers who focus on this field according to the different application scenarios [6–12]. But in the work above, the conventional optimization methods are used to solve the resource allocation issues. Meanwhile, some researchers implement intelligent optimization methods to allocate the resource. To optimally get the number of frequency channels required in the system, Lee et al. proposed Genetic Algorithm (GA) with frequency hopping technique [13]. A GA scheme combining resource allocation and user matching algorithm is presented to minimize the intra-cell interference and maximize the throughput in this system [14].

In general speaking, the above algorithms are not suitable for the ultra-dense D2D communications where the number of DUE pairs is far bigger than that of CUE. In ultra-dense D2D communications, multiple DUE pairs share one sub-channel with one CUE. Due to the randomness of the positions of the massive UEs, it is very hard to obtain a fast and efficient resource allocation scheme while guaranteeing the QoS of all UEs. So we need to find an efficient algorithm to solve the problem. Compared with other intelligent algorithms, the predatory search algorithm has stronger global searching ability and faster convergence speed. The conventional predatory search algorithm was first presented by Linhares in 1998 [15]. This algorithm is a spatial search strategy simulating predation behavior of animals and it is used in solving combinatorial optimization problems. For the predators in the search process, the most well-known search strategy is as follows. When there is no prey and traces of prey, predators search for prey at a rapid speed in a certain direction in the whole predator space; once found prey or prey signs, they immediately change their movement, slow down, tour continually, search for a concentrated area in the vicinity of the discovery of prey or signs of prey, and keep on approaching the prey. After searching for a period of time without finding a prey, the predator will give up this concentrated area and continue to find the prey in the whole predator space. This is the famous Area-Restricted search strategy, and it is described in different species such as birds, lizards, many predators and other acts. This predation behavior appears to be adaptive and efficient for different environments and prey distribution. For example, if the search space is aggregated or randomly distributed, the Area-Restricted search can maximize the probability of successful search by performing a continuous search near the prey. As shown in Fig. 1, the search strategy for this predation of an animal can be summarized as the following two searches.

Search 1 (regular search): Conduct a full search throughout the search space until you find a prey or prey sign and go to search 2 for region search.
Search 2 (region search): We do concentrated search in the vicinity of the discovery of prey or signs of prey, and search for a lot of times and do not find prey, then give up local search, go to search 1 for regular search.

Inspired by this, the resource allocation scheme based on predatory search algorithm for ultra-dense D2D communications is proposed in this paper. The main contributions of our work are as follows:

1. We propose a fast and efficient resource allocation scheme based on predatory search algorithm for ultra-dense D2D communications.
2. We evaluate the system performance of ultra-dense D2D communications.

This paper is organized as follows. In Sect. 2, we establish and explain our system model in detail. In Sect. 3, problem formulation is presented. Then we propose a fast resource allocation scheme based on predatory search algorithm for ultra-dense D2D communications and evaluate the system performance of ultra-dense D2D communications in Sect. 4. Simulation results are presented in Sect. 5, and the conclusion is drawn out in Sect. 6.

2 System Model

In frequency division duplex cellular network, one sub-channel is only allocated to one CUE. We assume a single cellular network with K sub-channels, where N CUEs and M DUE pairs coexist, as shown in Fig. 1. We denote the transmitter and receiver of one DUE pair as DTUE and DRUE, respectively. In our cellular network, CUEs and DTUEs are evenly distributed in the cell with the radius of R. Meanwhile, DRUEs are evenly located in the circles with the radius of L, and the centers of the circle are the DTUEs. One sub-channel is only occupied by one CUE, but it can be shared by multiple DUE pairs. To make full use of the advantages of D2D technology, we solve the intricate resource allocation problem in the case that M is much larger than N. Meanwhile, uplink resources are easy to reuse for D2D communications compared with downlink resources. Therefore, we mainly consider the case of uplink resources sharing.

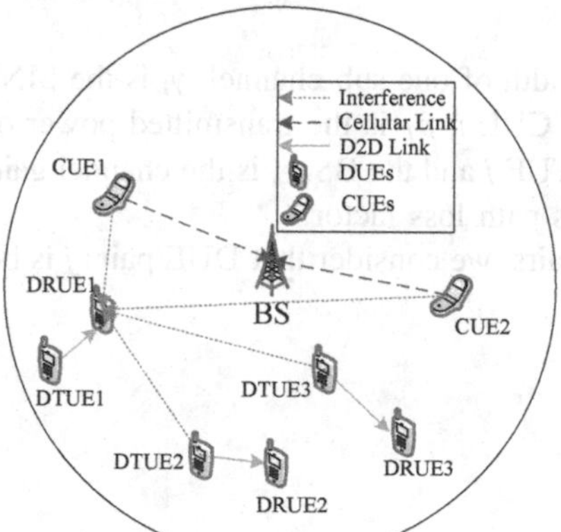

Fig. 1. System model of D2D communications.

3 Problem Formulation

As mentioned above, we assume that K sub-channels are provided by the communication network, where N CUEs and M DUE pairs coexist. Let $S = (K, N, M)$. The sets of CUEs and DUE pairs are denoted as $\mathbb{C} = (1, 2, \cdots, N)$ and $\mathbb{D} = (1, 2, \cdots, M)$. Meanwhile, one CUE only occupies one sub-channel, but multiple DUE pairs can share one sub-channel. Then we have $N \leq K$. Now, we can consider one sub-channel as one package. So there are K packages. What we need to do is to allocate all DUE pairs to K packages. The ith package is denoted as $\Re_i$, $i = (1, 2, \cdots, K)$. The Fig. 2 shows an example of $S = (4, 3, 10)$. The goal that D2D technology is introduced into cellular networks is to improve bandwidth efficiency and network throughput. So throughput is selected as the optimizing criterion in this paper.

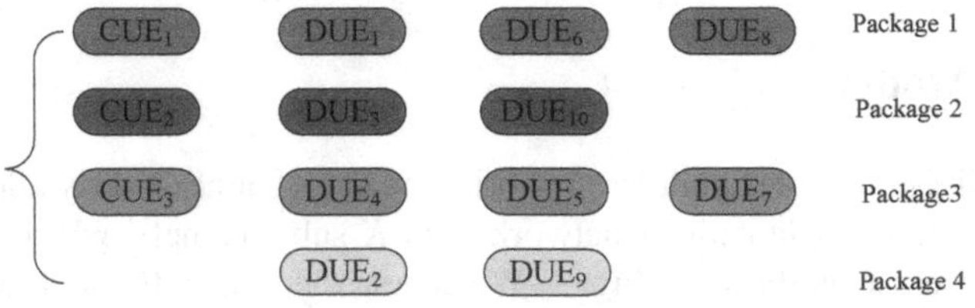

Fig. 2. An example of channel resource allocation.

The objective function is the performance indicator which needs to be optimized. In general, the network capacity is selected as the optimization objective. Obviously, the total capacity consists of two parts: CUEs and DUE pairs. For CUE i, the capacity is written as

$$Cc_i = B\log_2(1+\gamma_i) = B\log_2\left(1+\frac{p_i z_i}{\sum\limits_{\{D_j \in \Re_m | C_i \in \Re_m\}} p_T s_j^{\alpha} + N_0}\right) \tag{1}$$

Here, B is the bandwidth of one sub-channel. γ_i is the SINR value of CUE i, p_i is the transmitted power of CUE i, p_T is the transmitted power of the DTUE k, s_j is the channel gain between DTUE j and the BS, z_i is the channel gain between BS and CUE i, N_0 is noise power, α is path loss factor.

Similarly, for DUE pairs, we consider that DUE pairs j is belong to package m, i.e. $j \in \Re_m$. Then, we have

$$Cd_j = B\log_2(1+\beta_j)$$
$$= B\log_2\left(1+\frac{p_T x_j}{\sum\limits_{\{C_i\in\Re_m|D_j\in\Re_m\}} p_i h_{i,j} + \sum\limits_{\substack{\{D_k\in\Re_m|D_j\in\Re_m\}\\ k\neq j}} p_T g_{k,j} + N_0}\right) \quad (2)$$

Here, β_j is the SINR value of DRUE j, x_j is the channel gain between DRUE j and DTUE j, $h_{i,j}$ is the channel gain between CUE m and DRUE j, $g_{k,j}$ represents the channel gain between DRUE j and DTUE k.

Therefore, the total capacity can be calculated as

$$C = \sum_{i=1}^{N} Cc_i + \sum_{j=1}^{M} Cd_j \quad (3)$$

Here, γ_i is maintained constant because power control scheme is applied into the CUEs. So the capacities of CUEs are considered as constant and denoted as C_c. Then the capacity is written as

$$C = \sum_{j=1}^{N} Cc_i + \sum_{j=1}^{M} Cd_j = N * C_c + B\sum_{j=1}^{M}\log_2(1+\beta_j) \quad (4)$$

Next, we can get the optimization objective as:

$$\mathbb{Q}_1 : \max N * C_c + B\sum_{j=1}^{M}\log_2(1+\beta_j) \quad (5a)$$

$$\text{subject to} : \gamma_i = \Gamma \ \ \forall i \in (1\cdots N) \quad (5b)$$

$$\beta_j \geq \Gamma \ \ \forall j \in (1\cdots M) \quad (5c)$$

$$0 < p_i \leq p_{\max} \quad \forall i \in (1\cdots N) \quad (5d)$$

4 Resource Allocation Scheme Based on Predatory Search Algorithm

In this section, a fast resource allocation scheme based on predatory search algorithm for ultra-dense D2D communications is proposed. In D2D communications, CUEs have a higher priority over DUE pairs. So we must guarantee the QoS of CUEs firstly. Then DUE pairs will try best to access network with sharing resources whist their QoSs are guaranteed. For our scenario, some definitions and parameters are described as follows.

1. Coding

For CUEs, CUE i is allocated to ith sub-channel by default. We define an allocation scheme as $S = (s_1, \cdots, s_i, \cdots, s_M)$. The dimension of S corresponds to the number of DUE pairs, every bit represents one DUE pair. The value of s_i means that *i*th DUE pair use the index of package.

2. The selection of initial point

Generally speaking, we can select the initial point randomly.

3. Definition of neighbourhood

The neighbourhood is related to the scope of search and result precision. So it is crucial to the algorithm. In many research papers, the neighborhood node can be obtained by the reversion or bit mutation. However, the objective functions of neighborhood nodes fluctuate greatly. So it is not suitable to our scenario. As mentioned before, an allocation scheme corresponds to a code in base S. Let us take $S = (4, 3, 10)$ for example. We consider that a point A is (1, 4, 3, 2, 3, 4, 2, 1, 3, 1), then the neighborhood of point A is defined as the set including the points which only have a different bit compared with point A and the value of the different bit is smaller or bigger than A by one. For example, the neighborhood of point A includes (1, 4, 3, 2, 3, 4, 2, 1, 3, 2), (1, 4, 3, 2, 3, 4, 2, 1, 3, 4), (1, 4, 3, 2, 3, 4, 2, 1, 2, 1), (1, 4, 3, 2, 3, 4, 2, 1, 4, 1), and so on.

4. Description of parameters
   (1) *NumLevel*: the maximum limit level is *NumLevel* + 1.
   (2) *Cthreshold*: the pointer threshold for increasing the limit level.
   (3) *Lthreshold*: When *Level* increases to *Lthreshold*, it indicates that the algorithm has performed multiple valid searches in the restricted area without finding an improved solution. Then the algorithm abandons the region-limited search mode.
   (4) *LhighThreshold*: It indicates a high fitness value for the search mode. It means that the algorithm will stop if the algorithm still does not find a new improved solution while completing the search of *Lthereshold* limit levels in the normal search mode.

Here the maximum limit level number *NumLevel* + 1 is equal to 6, the pointer threshold for increasing the limit level *Cthreshold* is equal to 1, the limit level of the area limit search mode *Lthereshold* is equal to 1, the high fitness value for the search mode *LhighThreshold* is equal to 4.

Based on the above basis, a predatory search algorithm is proposed as follows:

(1) Initialize system parameters: the number of all sub-channels, SINR threshold, the transmitting power of the D2D, the numbers of CUE and DUE pairs, the positions of UEs, *NumLevel*, *Cthreshold*, *Lthreshold* and *LhighThreshold*.

(2) The resource allocation scheme is encoded as $S = (s_1, \cdots, s_i, \cdots, s_M)$. s_i is the number of sub-channels which is allocated to DUE *j*, and its value ranges from 1 to *N*.
(3) Randomly select an initial point a, a $\in \Omega$, where Ω is the set of all possible values. Let the optimal solution $b = a$, the counter $k = 0$, the limit level of search $l = 0$. Then initialize the limit set *res*[*NumLevel*].
(4) If $l <$ *NumLevel*, we take 5% points of neighborhood of *a* to construct $N'(s)$, and obtain the point *Mresult* which is corresponded by its maximum function value (the function value in the algorithm is the channel capacity), then turn to step 5; Otherwise, the resources are allocated according to the scheme corresponding to the optimal solution *b*.
(5) If the function value corresponding to *Mresult* falls between res[*l*] and the function values corresponding to *b*, that is, $Z(Mresult) \in (res[l], Z(b))$, let $a = Mresult$, then go to step 7; otherwise turn to step 6.
(6) If $Z(a) > Z(b)$, let $b = a$, $m = 0$, $k = 0$, recalculate the limit set and turn to step 4; Otherwise, go to next step.
(7) Let $k = k + 1$. If $k > Cthreshold$, let $l = l + 1$ and $k = 0$, then go to next step; Otherwise, turn to step 4.
(8) If $l = Cthreshold$, let $l = LhighThreshold$, and go to step 4; Otherwise, go directly to step 4.

5 Simulation and Discussion

In our simulations, we assume that three CUEs and ten DTUEs are distributed in the cell. Simulation parameters are described in Table 1.

Table 1. Parameter settings in our simulation

Parameter	Value and unit	Parameter	Value and unit
Cell radius (*R*)	600 m	*L*	20 m
Path loss factor (α)	4	The number of DUE pairs (*M*)	10
The number of CUEs (*N*)	3	The maximum transmitted power of CUE	2 W
SINR threshold (β)	4.6 dB	The transmitted power of DTUE P_T	0.001 W
N_0	−105 dBm	*Cthreshold*	1
NumLevel	5	*LhighThreshold*	4
Lthereshold	1		

The channel capacity of the D2D communication using the predator search algorithm and other algorithms is compared in Fig. 3. It can be seen from the figure that although the method of resource allocation based on random algorithm is simple, the result is very poor. The exhaustive algorithm can find out the optimal resource allocation method, but the exhaustive method is to traverse all feasible allocation schemes, so the computation is large and time consuming. And the predator-based search algorithm is computationally small and not time-consuming, and it can converge quickly to the optimal result of the exhaustive algorithm.

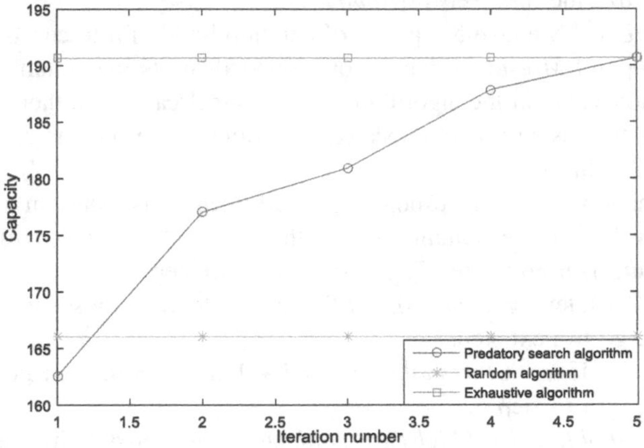

Fig. 3. The capacity of D2D communications.

At the same time, Fig. 4 demonstrates the average transmission power of CUEs based on these three algorithms. The exhaustive algorithm needs maximal transmission power compared with the proposed predatory search algorithm and random algorithm. The reason is that the exhaustive algorithm can get best resource allocation result which gets the maximum system capacity and lead to consume much energy.

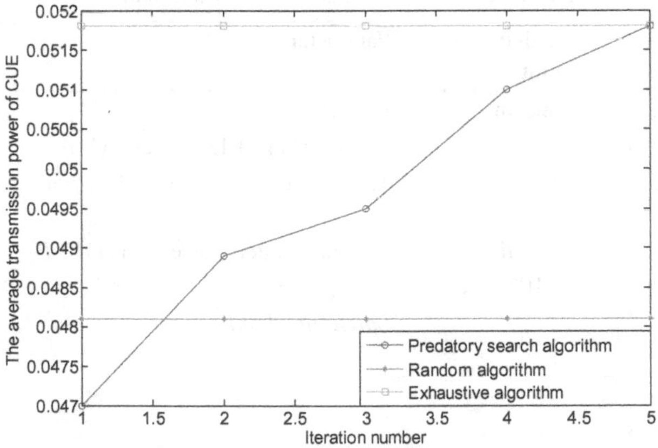

Fig. 4. The average transmission power of CUEs.

6 Conclusions

In this paper, the ultra-dense D2D communication system model where M DUE pairs and N CUEs coexist is described. Then resource allocation problem for ultra-dense D2D communications is formulated and analyzed. Next, a fast and efficient resource allocation scheme based on predatory search algorithm for ultra-dense D2D communications is presented. Finally, the analysis and simulation results validate that the performance of proposed scheme. This scheme can be applied into the ultra-dense D2D communication networks.

Acknowledgments. This work was supported in part by the Fundamental Research Funds for the Central Universities (No. 2017B14214, 2018B53114), Six Talent Peaks project in Jiangsu (DZXX-008) and National Natural Science Foundation of China (No. 61701168, 61601283, 61301110).

References

1. Jia, M., Gu, X., Guo, Q., Xiang, W., Zhang, N.: Broadband hybrid satellite-terrestrial communication systems based on cognitive radio toward 5G. IEEE Wirel. Commun. **23**(6), 96–106 (2013)
2. Jin, M., Liu, X., Gu, X., Guo, Q.: Joint cooperative spectrum sensing and channel selection optimization for satellite communication systems based on cognitive radio. Int. J. Satell. Commun. Network. **35**(2), 139–150 (2017)
3. Jia, M., Liu, X., Yin, Z., Guo, Q., Gu, X.: Joint cooperative spectrum sensing and spectrum opportunity for satellite cluster communication networks. Ad Hoc Netw. **58**(C), 231–238 (2016)
4. Li, X., Wang, Z., Sun, Y., Gu, Y., Hu, J.: Mathematical characteristics of uplink and downlink interference regions in D2D communications underlaying cellular networks. Wirel. Pers. Commun. **93**(4), 917–932 (2017)
5. Jia, M., Yin, Z., Guo, Q., Liu, G., Gu, X.: Downlink design for spectrum efficient IoT network. IEEE Internet Things J. **5**(5), 3397–3404 (2018)
6. Jia, M., Yin, Z., Li, D., Guo, Q., Gu, X.: Toward improved offloading efficiency of data transmission in the IoT-cloud by leveraging secure truncating OFDM. IEEE Internet Things J. **1**(99), 1–8 (2018)
7. Cicalò, S., Tralli, V.: QoS-aware admission control and resource allocation for D2D communications underlaying cellular networks. IEEE Trans. Wirel. Commun. **17**(8), 5256–5269 (2018)
8. Zhang, B., Mao, X., Yu, J.L., Han, Z.: Resource allocation for 5G heterogeneous cloud radio access networks with D2D communication: a matching and coalition approach. IEEE Trans. Veh. Technol. **67**(7), 5883–5894 (2018)
9. Feng, L., et al.: Resource allocation for 5G D2D multicast content sharing in social-aware cellular networks. IEEE Commun. Mag. **56**(3), 112–118 (2018)
10. Li, X., Shankaran, R., Orgun, M., Fang, G., Xu, Y.: Resource allocation for underlay D2D communication with proportional fairness. IEEE Trans. Veh. Technol. **67**(7), 6244–6258 (2018)

11. Ahmed, M., Shi, H., Chen, X., Li, Y., Waqas, M., Jin, P.: Socially aware secrecy-ensured resource allocation in D2D underlay communication: an overlapping coalitional game scheme. IEEE Trans. Wirel. Commun. **17**(6), 4118–4133 (2018)
12. Wang, H., Wang, J., Ding, G., Wang, L., Tsiftsis, T., Sharma, P.: Resource allocation for energy harvesting-powered D2D communication underlaying UAV-assisted networks. IEEE Trans. Green Commun. Network. **2**(1), 14–24 (2018)
13. Lee, Y.H., et al.: Using genetic algorithm with frequency hopping in device to device communication (D2DC) interference mitigation. In: 2012 International Symposium on Intelligent Signal Processing and Communications Systems, pp. 201–206 (2012)
14. Yang, C., Xu, X., Han, J., ur Rehman, W., Tao, X.: GA based optimal resource allocation and user matching in device to device underlaying network. In: Wireless Communications and Networking Conference Workshops (WCNCW), pp. 242–247 (2014)
15. Linhares, A.: Preying on optima: a predatory search strategy for combinatorial problems. In: 1998 IEEE International Conference on Systems, Man, and Cybernetics, pp. 2974–2978 (1998)

A Low-Complexity Channel Estimation Method Based on Subspace for Large-Scale MIMO Systems

Cheng Zhou[1], Zhengquan Li[1,2(✉)], Song Xing[3], Qiong Wu[1,2,5], Yang Liu[1,4], Baolong Li[1], and Xiaoqing Zhao[1]

[1] Jiangsu Provincial Engineering Laboratory of Pattern Recognition and Computational Intelligence, Jiangnan University, Wuxi 214122, China
{6171918020,6171918007}@stu.jiangnan.edu.cn, {lzq722, qiongwu,lblong}@jiangnan.edu.cn, ly71354@163.com

[2] National Mobile Communication Research Laboratory, Southeast University, Nanjing 210096, China

[3] Department of Information Systems, California State University, Los Angeles, USA
sxing@calstatela.edu

[4] The National Key Laboratory of Millimeter Wave, Southeast University, Nanjing 210096, China

[5] Department of Electronic Engineering, Tsinghua University, Beijing 100084, China

Abstract. In large-scale multiple-input multiple-output (LS-MIMO) systems, singular value decomposition (SVD) or eigenvalue decomposition (EVD) are common channel estimation schemes. However, the computational complexity of two estimators limits the application in LS-MIMO systems. Motivated by this, in order to reduce the complexity, a novel method that combines fast single compensation approximated power iteration (FSCAPI) algorithm with iterative least square with projection (ILSP), FSCAPI-ILSP, is proposed in this paper, In the proposed method, the received signals subspace is estimated by the FSCAPI algorithm firstly, then the initial channel estimation is obtained by the pilot signals. Finally, we combine it with the ILSP algorithm to improve the accuracy of the channel estimation. Compared with the conventional methods, the proposed scheme degrades the computational complexity significantly. Simulated results indicate the provided method is better than its counterparts and improves the channel estimation accuracy effectively.

Keywords: Channel estimation · Semi-blind · Large scale MIMO · Subspace tracking

1 Introduction

Due to high demand for speed and spectrum utilization in the next-generation communication systems, the concept of large scale multiple-input multiple-out (LS-MIMO) system which is also called massive MIMO has been deemed as an important approach

M. Jia et al. (Eds.): WiSATS 2019, LNICST 281, pp. 387–397, 2019.
https://doi.org/10.1007/978-3-030-19156-6_36

for future communication system networks [1–3]. In such systems, at the base station (BS), there is large number of antennas equipped, which is able to serve tens of users in the same frequency band simultaneously [4–7]. Therefore, it achieves higher spectral efficiency [8] and significantly improves the capacity and reliability of wireless systems. LS-MIMO technology can significantly degrade the transmit power, and enhance the power efficiency. For the LS-MIMO system, the channel vectors are superiority of LS-MIMO is reflected with the antennas increase, channel vectors are approximately orthogonal under rich scattering environments. In addition, as the number of antennas at the BS increases, the influences caused by noise and the fast fading tend to be negligible [9].

To obtain higher performance and reduce pilot overhead [10], the orthogonal pilot symbols are restricted due to the finite coherence time. Thus, adjacent cells typically use non-orthogonal or reuse the same orthogonal pilot sequences for channel estimation, which causes pilot contamination [11] However, the imperfect channel state information (CSI) will degrade the accuracy of channel estimation. Numerous papers have been given that accurate CSI determines the quality of LS-MIMO systems. Therefore, it is vitally important for such systems to obtain high-accuracy channel estimation [12–15]. However, in LS-MIMO systems, the channels need to be estimated may be excessive. Consequently, effective channel estimation methods for reducing the complexity are urgently required.

Many methods have been proposed for resolving the problem in channel estimation. Specifically, in [16, 17] compressive sensing method was introduced to estimate the channel to degrade the complexity. In [18], the authors proposed a method based on EVD, which assumed that channel vectors are perfectly orthogonal, thus each channel vector can be uniquely characterized by an eigenvector having at most a multiplicative scalar ambiguity, which will be resolved with a few pilot sequences. But the channel vectors are only approximately orthogonal in practice. In [19], the authors proposed the SVD-based scheme, and the analysis showed that the inter-cell interference (ICI) can be completely eliminated with an infinite antennas and data symbols, but there is still a residual ICI. Therefore, semi-blind channel estimation (SBCE) is able to substantially degrading ICI impact in practical LS-MIMO systems require further investigation. Unfortunately, the disadvantage of the EVD and SVD is that the computational complexity is too high, which is $O(M^3)$, M represents the quantity of the antennas. So as M increase, it is not practical to use the two methods for LS-MIMO systems.

In this paper, we concentrate on mitigating the computational complexity and further improving the estimation accuracy, a low-complexity subspace adaptive SBCE method is introduced for LS-MIMO, which is comprised two parts designed to degrade the complexity and improve the performance of channel estimation, respectively. Primary contributions of each part are summarized as below:

(1) In [20], to carry out pilot decontamination, the received signal is projected into the subspace. It was indicated that pilot contamination is able to degrade effectively by means of subspace projection when the data sequences length and the BS antennas are enough large. Moreover, the number of dimensions of the received signals is degraded by the subspace projection processing. However, to obtain the signal subspace, the SVD procedure is required on a high-dimensional matrix,

which is consisted of all the received symbols. Therefore, we should find a better computationally effective method to determine the dominant subspace. our proposed scheme estimates the received signals subspace by using the FSCAPI algorithm [21], which has quickly convergence and better signal subspace tracking performance, compared to that of [18, 19], it can achieve lower computational complexity and accelerate the estimation of signal subspace. In [21], to obtain the signal subspace faster, the FSCAPI algorithm is proposed, which is referred as paper [19]. Compared to latter, the former has better performance in computational complexity and tracking.

(2) Having obtained the signal subspace, an initial estimation can be got with short uplink pilot symbols, however, there will be a deviation which caused by finite sample data rather than real data. Therefore, to degrade the estimation error, we combine it with the ILSP signal detection algorithm [22] to improve the performance. The procedures of the ILSP algorithm are summarized as below. Firstly, it takes use of the obtained initial channel estimate which has discussed above to carry out data detection, and then, the detected data are used to re-estimate the channel. Considering single-cell systems performance is the upper bound of the multi-cell systems [17] in LS-MIMO systems with multi-user. So, in this paper, we mainly research the single-cell system.

The remainder of the paper is consisted as follows: Sect. 2 presents the system model. Section 3 describes the proposed subspace-based low-complexity SBCE method and extends complexity analysis. In Sect. 4, we establish and discuss the simulation results. Finally, the conclusion is derived in Sect. 5.

Notation: In this paper, vectors (matrices) are represented as lower-case (upper-case) boldface letters. Superscripts $(\cdot)^*$, $(\cdot)^{\mathrm{T}}$, $(\cdot)^{\mathrm{H}}$, and $(\cdot)^+$ are the conjugate, transpose, Hermitian, and the Moore-Penrose inversion operators, respectively. $\mathbf{I}_M$ is the size $M \times M$ identity matrix, $[\cdot]_i$ denotes matrix *i*-th column, the *(i, j)*-th element of a matrix is representing by $[\cdot]_{i,j}$, the Euclidean norm of a vector is $\|\cdot\|$, the operator $\mathbf{E}\{\cdot\}$ is the expectation.

2 System Model

Given a typical single-cell LS-MIMO system with multi-user shares the same frequency band, considering a frequency-flat fading uplink transmission in a communication system works at mechanism called time-division duplex (TDD). Thus downlink (DL) channels are able to obtain by transposing the uplink (UL) channels because of the reciprocity. At the BS, there are M antennas, and K users each equipped single antenna are served simultaneously, usually $K \ll M$ is assumed. Then the uplink received signal vector $\mathbf{r} \in \mathrm{C}^{M\times 1}$ is

$$\mathbf{r} = \sqrt{p_u}\mathbf{G}\mathbf{s} + \mathbf{w}, \tag{1}$$

the uplink channel matrix represents by $\mathbf{G} \in \mathrm{C}^{M\times K}$, between user k and antenna m, the channel coefficient is represented by $g_{m,k} = [\mathbf{G}]_{m,k}$ The elements of $\mathbf{G}$ are considered to be independent and identically distributed (i.i.d.), and circularly-symmetric Gaussian random variables with zero mean and unit variance ($CN(0, 1)$), $\mathbf{s} \in C^{K\times 1}$ is transmitted symbols (p_u is the signal-to-noise ratio(SNR)), the additive white Gaussian noise (AWGN) is $\mathbf{w} \in C^{M\times 1}$ and satisfies $CN(0, \mathbf{I})$ distribution at the BS.

3 Subspace-Based Low-Complexity Channel Estimation

In this part, based on FSCAPI-ILSP, we present a subspace-based low-complexity SBCE scheme for multiuser LS-MIMO systems. Specifically, the proposed algorithm is mainly composed of two steps. In the first step, the received vectors subspace can be obtained by using FSCAPI algorithm to degrade the computational complexity, and then the initial channel estimation matrix is able to be obtained. In the second stage, to further obtain better performance, ILSP algorithm is combined. The details of the proposed scheme are presented in the following.

3.1 Problem Formulation and Resolve

The SBCE fully exploits both the pilots and the data symbols, thus it outperforms the totally blind channel estimator. According to large numbers theorem, as antennas at the BS are very big, for example as $M \to \infty$, the channel vectors will become asymptotically orthogonal between the BS and users, i.e. $(1/M)\mathbf{G}^{\mathrm{H}}\mathbf{G} \to \mathbf{I}_k$. This is a vitally feature in LS-MIMO systems. It is helpful to analyze subspace-based low-complexity SBCE. In particular, the subspace-based SBCE exploits the received signals characteristic, which is able to achieve better tradeoff between performance and complexity. The received signal $\mathbf{r}$ covariance matrix is computed as

$$\mathbf{cov}_r = \mathrm{E}\{\mathbf{r}\mathbf{r}^{\mathrm{H}}\} \tag{2}$$

However, in practical, the sample covariance matrix is usually substituted by Eq. (3). Therefore, the estimation of the covariance matrix $\hat{\mathbf{C}}_r$ in (3) will be approximated as

$$\hat{\mathbf{C}}_r = \frac{1}{N}\sum_{t=1}^{N}[\mathbf{r}(t)][\mathbf{r}(t)]^{\mathrm{H}} \tag{3}$$

As N tends to infinity, the matrix $\hat{\mathbf{C}}_r$ will gradually converge to the real. Since $\hat{\mathbf{C}}_r$ is a Hermitian matrix, and its SVD is given by $\hat{\mathbf{C}}_r = \mathbf{R}\boldsymbol{\Sigma}\mathbf{R}^{\mathrm{H}}$, where the column vectors of $\mathbf{R} \in C^{M\times M}$ are the singular vectors of $\hat{\mathbf{C}}_r$, $\boldsymbol{\Sigma} \in C^{M\times M}$ represents a diagonal matrix, which elements are consisted of the M singular values. More specifically, $\mathbf{R}$ can be divided into $\mathbf{R} = [\mathbf{R}_s, \mathbf{R}_n]$, where $\mathbf{R}_s \in C^{M\times K}$ represents the signal subspace, the noise subspace is represented by $\mathbf{R}_n \in C^{M\times(M-K)}$. In [19], we can know that $\mathbf{R}_s$ is the largest K singular value that correspond to the singular vectors of $\hat{\mathbf{C}}_r$, which can be used to estimate $\mathbf{G}$, the corresponding channel estimation [24] is

$$\tilde{\mathbf{G}} = \mathbf{R}_s \mathbf{E}_j, \tag{4}$$

where $\mathbf{E}_j$ is considered as the ambiguity matrix. Thus as long as $\mathbf{E}_j$ is known, the channel matrix $\mathbf{G}$ can be estimated from $\mathbf{R}_s$. Therefore, the short uplink pilots are invoked for resolving the ambiguity matrix $\mathbf{E}_j$. At the BS, the received pilot symbols $\mathbf{Y}^{\mathrm{p}} \in \mathbb{C}^{M \times N_{\mathrm{p}}}$ can be expressed as

$$\mathbf{Y}^{\mathrm{p}} = \sqrt{p_{\mathrm{t}}}\mathbf{G}\mathbf{\Phi} + \mathbf{N}, \tag{5}$$

where pilot matrix $\mathbf{\Phi} \in \mathbb{C}^{K \times N_{\mathrm{p}}}$ satisfies $\mathbf{\Phi}\mathbf{\Phi}^{\mathrm{H}} = \mathbf{I}_k$, and N_{p} is the pilots sequences length, which are transmitted by users. p_{t} is the transmit power, noise matrix $\mathbf{N} \in \mathbb{C}^{M \times N_{\mathrm{p}}}$ follows i.i.d. $\mathcal{CN}(0, 1)$. According to (5), $\mathbf{G}$ can be estimated by invoking $\mathbf{Y}^{\mathrm{p}}$ as

$$\hat{\mathbf{G}}^{\mathrm{p}} = \frac{1}{\sqrt{p_{\mathrm{t}}}}\mathbf{Y}^{\mathrm{p}}\mathbf{\Phi}^{\mathrm{H}}. \tag{6}$$

For resolving the ambiguity matrix $\mathbf{E}_j$ in the signal subspace $\mathbf{R}_s$, based on the estimation channel with the aid of pilot, we can address the ambiguity matrix as

$$\mathbf{E}_j = (\mathbf{R}_s)^{\mathrm{H}}\hat{\mathbf{G}}^{\mathrm{p}}. \tag{7}$$

Thus, from Eqs. (4) and (7), the corresponding channel estimation is

$$\tilde{\mathbf{G}} = \mathbf{R}_s\mathbf{E}_j = \mathbf{R}_s(\mathbf{R}_s)^{\mathrm{H}}\hat{\mathbf{G}}^{\mathrm{p}}. \tag{8}$$

From what has discussed above, it can be seen that a key factor is to get the signal subspace estimation from the received signal in the SBCE methods. The commonly used channel estimation methods based on EVD or SVD are not easy to carry out for real-time application in practical systems due to high computational complexity.

3.2 The Proposed Method and Performance Analysis

For the purpose of obtaining the estimation of the signal subspace faster and reduce the deviation caused by using finite sample data rather than real data, we propose a method that combines the ILSP signal detection algorithm with the FSCAPI algorithm to reduce computational complexity and improve channel estimation accuracy. In this part, the complexity of the FSCAPI-ILSP is analyzed. Additionally, the proposed method is compared to other SBCEs. In [21, 23], the authors obtain the signal subspace estimation of the received signal by using FSCAPI algorithm, which will adopt in this paper.

As discussed above, because the covariance matrix is made of the finite sample data rather than real data, there must be a deviation. Thus, joint FSCAPI-based method and ILSP method is introduced. Defining $K \times N$ dimensional matrix $\mathbf{S}_l$ is the data signals sent by K users to the BS, and channel $\mathbf{G}_l$ is $M \times K$-dimensional matrix, $\mathbf{W}_l$ is the noise matrix, so the received signal $\mathbf{Y}_l$ is expressed as

$$\mathbf{Y}_l = \sqrt{p_u}\mathbf{G}_l\mathbf{S}_l + \mathbf{W}_l \tag{9}$$

where $\mathbf{Y}_l$ = [**r**(1), **r**(2), …, **r**(*N*)], $\mathbf{S}_l$= [**s**(1), **s**(2), …, **s**(*N*)], $\mathbf{W}_l$= [**w**(1), **w**(2), …, **w**(*N*)]. The operation procedures of ILSP method is introduced as below. First of all, assuming the channel $\mathbf{G}_l$ is estimated from the initial procedure by using FSCAPI, and next the data are detected by using least-squares method, and the result can be written as

$$\tilde{\mathbf{S}}_l = \arg\min_{S_l \in \chi} \left\| \frac{1}{\sqrt{p_u}} \tilde{\mathbf{G}}_l^{+} \mathbf{Y}_l - \mathbf{S}_l \right\|_F^2 \tag{10}$$

The values of the transmitted signal is represented by the set χ, next, the detected signals $\tilde{\mathbf{S}}_l$ are considered as the real transmitted signals and used to re-estimated the channel via least-squares, so the estimation of the channel matrix is

$$\tilde{\mathbf{G}}_l = \frac{1}{\sqrt{p_u}} \mathbf{Y}_l \tilde{\mathbf{S}}_l^{+} \tag{11}$$

From Eqs. (10) and (11), our problem can be solved by using the ILSP algorithm [22]. And making use of the initial estimation channel by FSCAPI scheme, the joint FSCAPI and ILSP algorithm is proposed. The primary procedures of the proposed algorithm are summarized in **Algorithm 1**.

3.3 Analysis of Computational Complexity

Both EVD and SVD algorithms are requiring NM^2 complex multiplication when calculating the auto-correlation matrix of received signal samples. If the dimension of the matrix is $M \times M$, calculating the accurate EVD and SVD, the complex multiplications is needed $(4/3)M^3$ and $11M^3$ separately, and the SBCE algorithm in [18] needs $8MK^2N_p + (4N_p + 1)MK + O(K^3)$ complex multiplications to calculate the ambiguity matrix. MK complex multiplications are also required when calculate final estimation of **G**. In [19], to get pilot-based channel estimation, the SBCE algorithm based on SVD demands $MKN_p + MK$ complex multiplications, and it also requires $2MK^2$ complex multiplications to get the estimation of **G**. The computational complexity in [11] is primarily depended on SVD, LS algorithm and the iteration times. In Table 1, it is shown the different complexity about various estimation schemes.

Algorithm 1 The FSCAPI-ILSP Based Channel estimation algorithm

Step 1) Calculate the estimation channel based on pilot using (6).
Step 2) Calculate received signals subspace.
For $t = 1,2,\ldots,N$
Given: $\mathbf{r}(t)$.
Using the FSCAPI Algorithm in [24] to obtain the $\Lambda(t)$
End for
Step 3) Let $\mathbf{R}_s = \Lambda(t)$, resolve the ambiguity matrix $\mathbf{E}_j$ using (7)
Step 4) Obtain the initial channel estimation matrix using (8)
Step 5) Initialize, choose number of iterations K_{step}, assume $k = 0$,
For: k+=1

$$\tilde{S}_{l,k} = \arg\min_{S_l \in \chi} \left\| \frac{1}{\sqrt{\mathrm{p_u}}} \tilde{\mathbf{G}}_{l,k}^{+} \mathbf{Y}_l - S_l \right\|_F^2$$

$$\tilde{\mathbf{G}}_{l,k} = \frac{1}{\sqrt{\mathrm{p_u}}} \mathbf{Y}_l \tilde{S}_{l,k}^{+}$$

Repeat until $\mathrm{k} = K_{\text{step}}$

Table 1. Computational complexity compared in different algorithms

Algorithm	Complexity
SVD-ILSP [11]	$K_{\text{step}}(MK(N_p + 1)) + 11M^3 + NM^2 + 2MK^2 + MKN_p + MK$
EVD-BASED [18]	$(4/3)M^3 + NM^2 + 8MK^2N_p + (4N_p + 2)MK + O(K^3)$
SVD-BASED [19]	$11M^3 + NM^2 + 2MK^2 + MKN_p + MK$
FSCAPI-BASED [23]	$2M^2K + MK(N_p + 1) + 3(MK + K^2) + 2M + 6K$
PROPOSED	$K_{\text{step}}(MK(N_p + 1)) + 2M^2K + MK(N_p + 1) +$ $3(MK + K^2) + 2M + 6K$

In Table 1, the complexity is compared in different Algorithms with the proposed scheme by taking the length of pilot N_p into account. Due to the BS antennas M are much more than the users K in LS-MIMO systems usually, thus the proposed scheme enjoys lower complexity than others methods

4 Numerical Results

The Monte Carlo simulation is conducted to analyze the proposed scheme performance in large-scale multi-user MIMO system, only single-cell system is considered. The normalized mean square error (NMSE) is regarded as the performance metric is formulated as

$$NMSE = \frac{tr\{(\tilde{\mathbf{G}} - \mathbf{G})^H (\tilde{\mathbf{G}} - \mathbf{G})\}}{MK}. \tag{12}$$

A comparative analysis of channel estimation performance is performed under various signal-to-noise ratios (SNR) and different antenna numbers, respectively. Assuming the terminals are $K = 10$ in each cell, and $\mu = 0.995$ is the value of forgetting factor, pilot symbols are set to $N_p = K$ of each user. BPSK modulation is used for the transmission of data symbols.

Figure 1 shows the NMSE performance versus the received SNR under various channel estimation schemes, where the BS antennas are assumed to be $M = 100$, and the samples are assumed to be $N = 100$. As we can see, the performance of the EVD estimator almost unchanged with the SNR is increasing, that is because the ambiguity matrix is approximates assumed to be a diagonal matrix, but in real conditional, this assumption is invalid. As the simulation results shown, we can conclude that the proposed scheme performance is nearly same with the SVD-ILSP estimator, and they also show a tendency to decrease linearly, and also outperform than others estimators.

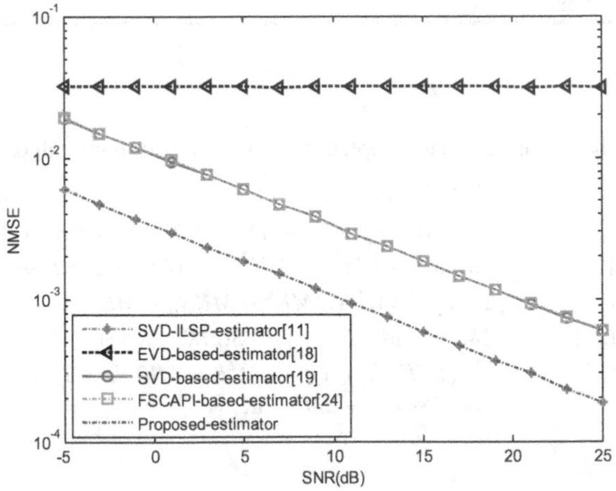

Fig. 1. The performance of NMSE for different schemes versus SNRs with $M = 100$, $N = 100$ are compared.

Figure 2 depicts different channel estimators performance with SNR = 20 dB versus different BS antennas. It shows that the performance of the NMSE in all methods are degrading with the antennas increasing, and it further proves the proposed scheme is better than SVD, EVD and FSCAPI schemes versus different antennas. But on the other hand, we can observe that with BS antennas are increasing, the NMSE reduction is not so obviously, the main reason of this phenomenon is caused by the large-scale fading coefficient of the users.

Figure 3 compares the computational complexity of different algorithms versus number of receive antennas with the samples set $N = 100$, the pilot symbols are setting

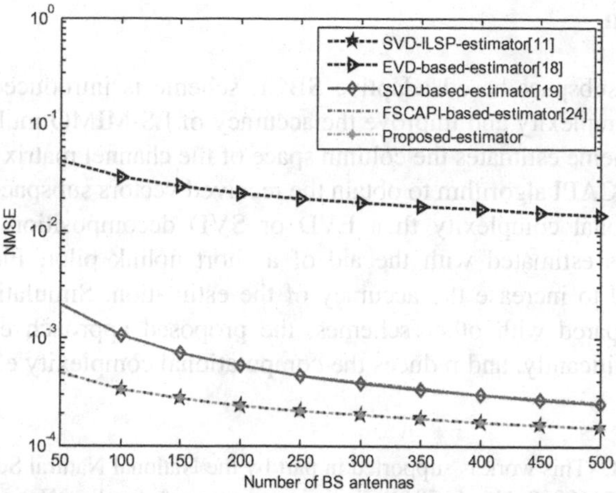

Fig. 2. NMSE comparison with different methods versus antennas with the fixed SNR = 20 dB.

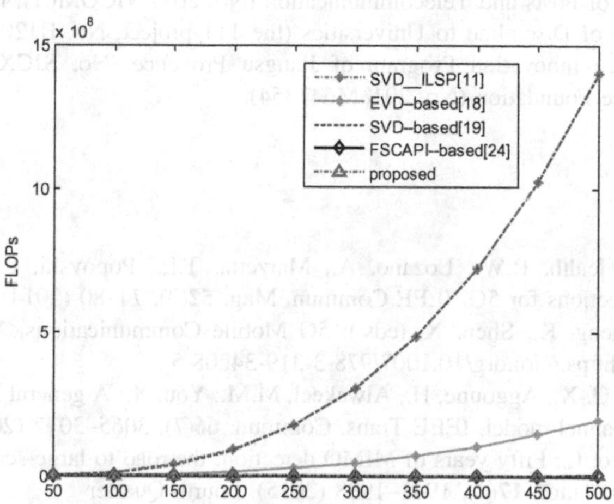

Fig. 3. Comparison of FLOPs in different algorithms versus receive antennas M, with $N_P = K$=10, N = 100, K_{step} = 5

to $N_p = K$=10 of each user, the number of iterations K_{step} = 5. It is observed that the proposed scheme is much lower complexity than SVD-based and SVD-ILSP, especially when M is increasing, the computational complexities of the latter two schemes are too high while the proposed scheme is slightly increased. Therefore, our proposed scheme is less computational complexity as compared with other schemes.

5 Conclusion

In this paper, a subspace-based adaptive SBCE scheme is introduced to reduce the computational complexity and improve the accuracy of LS-MIMO multi-user systems. The proposed scheme estimates the column space of the channel matrix firstly, which is relying on the FSCAPI algorithm to obtain the received vectors subspace and it requires lower computational complexity than EVD or SVD decomposition. And then, the channel matrix is estimated with the aid of a short uplink pilot. Finally, the ILSP algorithm is used to increase the accuracy of the estimation. Simulation results have shown that compared with other schemes, the proposed approach exhibits a better performance significantly, and reduces the computational complexity effectively in LS-MIMO system.

Acknowledgement. This work is supported in part by the National Natural Science Foundation of China (No. 61571108 & No. 61701197), the open research fund of National Mobile Communications Research Laboratory of millimeter wave, Southeast University (No. 2018D15), the open research fund of the National Key Laboratory of millimeter wave, Southeast University (No. K201918), and the Open Foundation of Key Laboratory of Wireless Communication, Nanjing University of Posts and Telecommunication (No. 2017WICOM01), the Programme of Introducing Talents of Discipline to Universities (the 111 project, No. B12018), Postgraduate Research & Practice Innovation Program of Jiangsu Provence (No. SJCX18_0646), China Postdoctoral Science Foundation (No. 2018M641354).

References

1. Boccardi, F., Health, R.W., Lozano, A., Marzetta, T.L., Popovski, P.: Five disruptive technology directions for 5G. IEEE Commun. Mag. **52**(2), 74–80 (2014)
2. Xiang, W., Zheng, K., Shen, X. (eds.): 5G Mobile Communications, 1st edn. Springer, Cham (2017). https://doi.org/10.1007/978-3-319-34208-5
3. Wu, S., Wang, C.-X., Aggoune, H., Alwakeel, M.M., You, X.: A general 3D non-stationary 5G wireless channel model. IEEE Trans. Commun. **66**(7), 3065–3077 (2018)
4. Yang, S., Hanzo, L.: Fifty years of MIMO detection: the road to large-scale MIMOs. IEEE Commun. Surv. Tutor. **17**(4), 1941–1988 (2015). Fourth Quarter
5. Ngo, H.Q., Larsson, E.G., Marzetta, T.L.: Energy and spectral efficiency of very large multiuser MIMO systems. IEEE Trans. Commun. **61**(4), 1436–1449 (2013)
6. Cheng, M., Yang, S., Fang, X.: Adaptive antenna-activation based beamforming for large-scale MIMO communication systems of high speed railway. China Commun. **13**(9), 12–23 (2016)
7. Zhou, C., Gu, Y., He, S., Shi, Z.: A robust and efficient algorithm for coprime array adaptive beamforming. IEEE Trans. Veh. Technol. **67**(2), 1099–1112 (2018)
8. Larsson, E.G., Edfors, O., Tufvesson, F., Marzetta, T.L.: Massive MIMO for next generation wireless systems. IEEE Commun. Mag. **52**(2), 186–195 (2014)
9. Rusek, F., et al.: Scaling up MIMO: opportunities and challenges with very large arrays. IEEE Sig. Process. Mag. **30**(1), 40–60 (2013)
10. Qi, C., Huang, Y., Jin, S., Wu. L.: Sparse channel estimation based on compressed sensing for massive MIMO system. In: Proceedings of IEEE International Conference on Communications (ICC 2015), London, June 2015, pp. 4558–4563 (2015)

11. Wang, Q.Z., Qiu, C.C.: Subspace-based semi-blind channel estimation for massive MIMO systems. Comput. Eng. Appl. **54**(8), 91–95 (2018)
12. Gao, Z., Dai, L., Lu, Z., Yuen, C., Wang, Z.: Super-resolution sparse MIMO-OFDM channel estimation based on spatial and temporal correlations. IEEE Commun. Lett. **18**(7), 1266–1269 (2014)
13. Gao, Z., Dai, L., Yuen, C., Wang, Z.: Asymptotic orthogonality analysis of time-domain sparse massive MIMO channels. IEEE Commun. Lett. **19**(10), 1826–1829 (2015)
14. Wan, L., Han, G., Jiang, J., Rodrigues, J.J.P.C., Feng, N., Zhu, T.: DOA estimation for coherently distributed sources considering circular and noncircular signals in massive MIMO systems. IEEE Syst. J. **11**(1), 41–49 (2016)
15. Zhou, C., et al.: Direction-of-arrival estimation for coprime array via virtual array interpolation. IEEE Trans. Sig. Process. **66**(22), 5956–5971 (2018)
16. Nguyen, S.L.H., Ghrayeb, A.: Compressive sensing-based channel estimation for massive multiuser MIMO systems. In: Proceedings of IEEE Wireless Communications and Networking Conferences (WCNC), Shanghai, China, April 2013, pp. 2890–2895 (2013)
17. Ngo, H.Q., Larsson, E.G., Marzetta, T.L.: The multi-cell multiuser MIMO uplink with very large antenna arrays and a finite-dimensional channel. IEEE Trans. Commun. **61**(6), 2350–2361 (2013)
18. Ngo, H.Q., Larsson, E.G.: EVD-based channel estimation in multi-cell multiuser MIMO systems with very large antenna arrays. In: IEEE International Conference on Acoustics, Speech and Signal Processing (ICASSP), Kyoto, Japan, pp. 3249–3252 (2012)
19. Badeau, R., David, B., Richard, G.: Fast approximated power iteration subspace tracking. IEEE Trans. Sig. Process. **53**(8), 2931–2941 (2005)
20. Müller, R.R., Cottatellucci, L., Vehkaperä, M.: Blind pilot decontamination. IEEE J. Sel. Top. Sig. Process. **8**(5), 773–786 (2014)
21. Wei, Z., Lu, H.: Fast single compensation approximated power iteration subspace tracking algorithm. J. North Univ. China (Nat. Sci. Ed.) **33**(4), 381–386 (2012)
22. Talwar, S., Viberg, M., Paulraj, A.: Blind separation of synchronous co-channel digital signals using an antenna array. I. Algorithms. IEEE Trans. Sig. Process. **44**(5), 1184–1197 (1996)
23. Xu, F, Xiao, Y, Wang, D.: Adaptive semi-blind channel estimation for massive MIMO systems. In: 2014 12th International Conference on Signal Processing (ICSP), pp. 1698–1702. IEEE (2014)
24. Hu, A., Lv, T., Lu, Y.: Subspace-based semi-blind channel estimation for large-scale multi-cell multiuser MIMO systems. In: IEEE 77th Vehicular Technology Conference (VTC Spring), Dresden, pp. 1–5, June 2013

An Improved Gauss-Seidel Algorithm for Signal Detection in Massive MIMO Systems

Xiaoqing Zhao[1], Zhengquan Li[1,2(✉)], Qiong Wu[1,2,3], Yang Liu[1,4], Baolong Li[1], Ziyan Jia[5], and Cheng Zhou[1]

[1] Jiangsu Provincial Engineering Laboratory of Pattern Recognition and Computational Intelligence, Jiangnan University, Wuxi 214122, China
{6171918007,6171918020}@stu.jiangnan.edu.cn, {lzq722, qiongwu,lblong}@jiangnan.edu.cn, ly71354@163.com

[2] National Mobile Communication Research Laboratory, Southeast University, Nanjing 210096, China

[3] Department of Electronic Engineering, Tsinghua University, Beijing 100084, China

[4] The National Key Laboratory of Millimeter Wave, Southeast University, Nanjing 210096, China

[5] School of Electrical and Information Engineering, Jiangsu University of Technology, Changzhou, China
jiaziyan@jsut.edu.cn

Abstract. Massive multiple input multiple output (MIMO) is a promising technology that has been proposed to meet the requirement of the fifth generation wireless communications systems. For uplink massive MIMO systems, the typical linear detection such as minimum mean square error (MMSE) shows near-optimal performance. However, due to the direct matrix inverse, the computational complexity of the MMSE detection algorithm is too high, especially when there are a large number of users. Thus, in this paper, we propose an improved Gauss-Seidel algorithm by utilizing delayed over relaxation (DOR) scheme, which is named as delayed over relaxation Gauss-Seidel (DRGS) algorithm. The basic idea of the DOR scheme is to combine the predicted iterative step $(n + 1)$ with the iteration of step $(n - 1)$. The scheme can provide a significant improvement of the convergence speed for iterative algorithm. The theoretical analysis of DRGS algorithm shows that the proposed algorithm can reduce the computational complexity from $O(K^3)$ to $O(K^2)$, where K is the number of users. Simulation results verify that the DRGS algorithm can achieve almost the same BER performance as that of MMSE detection with a small number of iterations.

Keywords: Massive MIMO system · Delayed over relaxation Gauss-Seidel algorithm · MMSE detection · BER

M. Jia et al. (Eds.): WiSATS 2019, LNICST 281, pp. 398–407, 2019.
https://doi.org/10.1007/978-3-030-19156-6_37

1 Introduction

Massive multiple-input multiple-output (MIMO) is widely considered as one of the most emerging technologies for future wireless communications [1–5]. Differing from the traditional MIMO (4×4, 8×8), massive MIMO systems are equipped with hundreds of antennas at the base station (BS) to serve user equipment (UE) simultaneously [6, 7]. It has been proved that massive MIMO can better meet the requirement of fast date rate, high spectral efficiency and wide coverage than conventional MIMO systems through theoretical analysis. Unfortunately, the augment of antennas increases the dimensions of matrix, which results in a significant increase in the computational complexity of signal processing [8].

The optimal detection algorithm, such as maximum likelihood (ML) detection algorithm, is highly impractical because of vast calculations [9]. To achieve near-optimal performance, several linear signal detection algorithms, such as zero-forcing (ZF) and minimum mean square error (MMSE), have been proposed [10]. Unfortunately, the algorithms mentioned above have high computational complexity due to a full matrix inversion operation, notably when the number of users is large.

Therefore, it is necessary to simplify matrix inversion calculation for massive MIMO systems. Recently, many effective researches about low complexity approximate matrix inversion have been conducted [11–16]. One typical category is to replace calculating matrix inversion directly with polynomial expansion (PE) [11, 12]. But, it is not practical for massive MIMO systems for a marginal reduction in complexity. The other category is based on iterative algorithms, such as Richardson algorithm [13], Jacobi algorithm [14] and Gauss-Seidel algorithm [15]. The Richardson algorithm [13] was proposed to avoid the high complexity caused by direct matrix inversion. Nevertheless, its convergence requires a large number of iterations which would lead to prohibitive complexity for massive MIMO systems. Therefore, in order to reduce the number of iterations, the approach based on Jacobi algorithm [14] was presented. Numerous studies have showed that the convergence rate of the conventional Jacobi algorithm is lower in comparison with the conventional Gauss-Seidel (GS) algorithm [15]. Based on the conventional GS algorithm, GS algorithm with initialization is proposed in [16], which can accelerate the convergence rate and reduce the number of iterations. But existing GS-based detectors still exhibit slow convergence rates.

In order to further improve the conventional GS detection algorithm for massive MIMO systems. The GS algorithm utilizes the delayed over-relaxation [17] approach to quicken the convergence rate, which brings about a reduction in iterations and computational complexity. According to simulation results, it is proved that the proposed algorithm can solve the matrix inversion problem in an iterative procedure with low complexity.

The remainder of this paper is organized as follows: we introduce the uplink system model in Sect. 2. Section 3 describes the proposed algorithm based on GSI algorithm and provides the analysis of computational complexity. Section 4 presents and discusses the simulation results. Finally, the conclusion is drawn in Sect. 5.

Notation: In this paper, lower-case boldface letters represent the column vectors (e.g., **h**), and the upper-case boldface letters refer to the matrices (e.g., **H**). **H**(*i*, *j*) represents the (i, j) element of matrix $\mathbf{H}$. For the matrix $\mathbf{H}$, $\mathbf{H}^T$, $\mathbf{H}^H$, and $\mathbf{H}^{-1}$ indicate the transpose, the Hermitian transpose, and the inverse of $\mathbf{H}$, respectively. In addition, $\mathbf{I}_K$ denotes the $K \times K$ identify matrix.

2 System Model

We consider an uplink massive MIMO system employing N antennas at the BS to serve K single-antenna users simultaneously. Not that in such system, N is larger than K.

Let vector $\mathbf{s_c}= (s_{c,1}, s_{c,2}, \ldots, s_{c,K})^T$ represent the complex-valued transmitted signal vector from K users. The transmitted symbol $s_{c,i}$ is modulated and mapped to one point of A which denote a complex M-QAM scheme. The matrix $\mathbf{H}_c \in \mathbb{C}^{N\times K}$ denotes the flat Rayleigh fading channel matrix, and the entries of $\mathbf{H}_c$ are independently and identically distributed (i.i.d.) with zero mean and unit variance [18, 19]. The vector $\mathbf{n_c}= (n_{c,1}, n_{c,2}, \ldots, n_{c,K})^T$ denotes the additive white Gaussian noise with mean is zero and corresponding variance is σ_n^2. Then, the complex received signal vector $\mathbf{y_c}= (y_{c,1}, y_{c,2}, \ldots, y_{c,K})^T$ can be expressed as:

$$\mathbf{y}_c = \mathbf{H}_c\mathbf{s}_c + \mathbf{n}_c \tag{1}$$

For ease of presentation and computation, the complex-valued system model can be translated to real-valued system model as

$$\underbrace{\begin{bmatrix} \mathrm{Re}\{\mathbf{y}_c\} \\ \mathrm{Im}\{\mathbf{y}_c\} \end{bmatrix}}_{\mathbf{y}} = \underbrace{\begin{bmatrix} \mathrm{Re}\{\mathbf{H}_c\} & -\mathrm{Im}\{\mathbf{H}_c\} \\ \mathrm{Im}\{\mathbf{H}_c\} & \mathrm{Re}\{\mathbf{H}_c\} \end{bmatrix}}_{\mathbf{H}} \underbrace{\begin{bmatrix} \mathrm{Re}\{\mathbf{s}_c\} \\ \mathrm{Im}\{\mathbf{s}_c\} \end{bmatrix}}_{\mathbf{s}} + \underbrace{\begin{bmatrix} \mathrm{Re}\{\mathbf{n}_c\} \\ \mathrm{Im}\{\mathbf{n}_c\} \end{bmatrix}}_{\mathbf{n}} \tag{2}$$

where Re{.} and Im{.} denote the real and imaginary parts, respectively. Note that $\mathbf{y} \in \mathbb{R}^{2K\times 1}$, $\mathbf{s} \in \mathbb{R}^{2K\times 1}$, $\mathbf{n} \in \mathbb{R}^{2K\times 1}$, accordingly $\mathbf{H} \in \mathbb{R}^{2K\times 2K}$.

2.1 MMSE Detector

The task of signal detector is to obtain the estimated value of $\mathbf{s}$ from the channel matrix $\mathbf{H}$ and the received vector $\mathbf{y}$. It is well known that the MMSE detector is proved to have near-optimal performance for massive MIMO systems. Thus, utilizing the MMSE detector, the resulting estimated symbol vector $\hat{\mathbf{s}}$ can be given by

$$\hat{\mathbf{s}} = \left(\mathbf{H}^H\mathbf{H} + \sigma_n^2\mathbf{I}_{2K}\right)^{-1}\mathbf{H}^H\mathbf{y} = \mathbf{A}^{-1}\mathbf{b} \tag{2}$$

where $\mathbf{A} = \mathbf{H}^H\mathbf{H} + \sigma_n^2\mathbf{I}_{2K}$ is the MMSE weighting matrix, and $\mathbf{b} = \mathbf{H}^H\mathbf{y}$ is the output of the matched filter, respectively. Note that $\mathbf{A}$ is symmetric positive definite and diagonally dominant [20]. The computational complexity of direct matrix inversion is $O(K^3)$, which is too high for massive MIMO systems, especially when the number of user is large. Therefore, we can convert the MMSE algorithm into solving the following linear equation as

$$\mathbf{As} = \mathbf{b} \tag{3}$$

which can be solved in an iterative way.

2.2 Conventional Gauss-Seidel Algorithm

In order to avoid the direct matrix inversion, GS algorithm was proposed in [15]. Consider the decomposition of $\mathbf{A}$ as $\mathbf{A} = \mathbf{D} - \mathbf{L} - \mathbf{U}$, where $\mathbf{D}$ is composed of diagonal elements of $\mathbf{A}$, $\mathbf{L}$ and $\mathbf{U}$ represent the strictly lower triangular matrix and the upper triangular matrix of $\mathbf{A}$, severally. Then we can utilize GS iterative algorithm to solve (3) which can be written as:

$$\hat{\mathbf{s}}_{n+1} = (\mathbf{D} - \mathbf{L})^{-1}(\mathbf{U}\hat{\mathbf{s}}_n + \mathbf{b}) \tag{5}$$

where $\hat{\mathbf{s}}_n$ is the estimated transmitted vector at the n iteration.

3 Low-Complexity Signal Detection Algorithm

In this section, we propose an improved signal detection algorithm based on GS algorithm for massive MIMO systems. Through the theoretical analysis of convergence, the proposed DRGS algorithm can achieve good convergence rate. Then we analyze the complexity of the proposed DRGS algorithm.

3.1 DRGS Algorithm

The delayed over relaxation (DOR) method [17] is introduced briefly. The form of iterative solution method for linear equation can be cast in the following general form:

$$\mathbf{s}_{n+1} = \mathbf{G}\mathbf{s}_n + \mathbf{f} \tag{5}$$

As we all know, if the spectral radius of the matrix $\mathbf{G}$, hereinafter $\rho(\mathbf{G})$, is smaller than unity, the GS algorithm is convergent. And the smaller $\rho(\mathbf{G})$, the faster the convergence of the algorithm [21]. Therefore, the DOR method was utilized to achieve better performance of convergence. The main idea of the DOR method is combing the iteration of the predicted step $(n+1)$ with the iteration of step $(n-1)$. As described above, the modified relaxation step of system (5) can be expressed as:

$$\begin{cases} \mathbf{s}^*_{n+1} = \mathbf{G}\mathbf{s}_n + \mathbf{f} \\ \mathbf{s}_{n+1} = w\mathbf{s}^*_{n+1} + (1-w)\mathbf{s}_{n-1} \end{cases} \tag{6}$$

where w represents the relaxation parameter. The DOR method leads to a significant improvement of the convergence rate of iterative algorithm.

Next, we employ the DOR method to GS algorithm, which is named as DRGS algorithms. As mentioned before, the form of Gauss-Seidel algorithm can be denoted as

$$\hat{\mathbf{s}}^{(n+1)} = (\mathbf{D}-\mathbf{L})^{-1}\mathbf{U}\hat{\mathbf{s}}^{(n)} + (\mathbf{D}-\mathbf{L})^{-1}\mathbf{b} \tag{7}$$

The principle of DRGS algorithm is to modify the iterative step by DOR method. By substituting (7) into (6), the form of joint DOR method and GS algorithm can be described as follow:

$$\begin{cases} \hat{\mathbf{s}}^{*}_{n+1} = (\mathbf{D}-\mathbf{L})^{-1}\mathbf{U}\hat{\mathbf{s}}_{n} + (\mathbf{D}-\mathbf{L})^{-1}\mathbf{b} \\ \hat{\mathbf{s}}_{n+1} = w\hat{\mathbf{s}}^{*}_{n+1} + (1-w)\hat{\mathbf{s}}_{n-1} \end{cases} \tag{8}$$

Furthermore, as well known, the initial value of **s** plays an important role in the convergence rate and the detection accuracy of the iterative algorithm when the number of iterations is limited. Thus, we take diagonal matrix **D** and lower triangular matrix **L** into consideration to approximate $\mathbf{A}^{-1}$ and represent the initial solution as $\mathbf{s}_0 = (\mathbf{D}-\mathbf{L})^{-1}\mathbf{b}$.

3.2 Convergence Proof

The convergence of the proposed DRGS is analyzed on a theoretical basis in this section. As [17] shows, the convergence rate of DRGS method is closely related to $\rho(\mathbf{G})$. Therefore, the spectral radius of G is considered firstly. We define the $\mathbf{G} = (\mathbf{D}-\mathbf{L})^{-1}\mathbf{U}$, where $\mathbf{U} = \mathbf{L}^{T}$.

Theorem 1: Let $\mathbf{G} \in \mathbb{C}^{2K\times 2K}$ has eigenvalues $\lambda_i, i = 1:2K$. Then the spectral radius ρ(G) is [21, 22]: $\rho(\mathbf{G}) = \max_{1\le i\le 2K}|\lambda_i|$.

At first, we set **r** as an arbitrary $2K \times 1$ non-zero real-valued vector. On the basic of the definition of eigenvalue, we have:

$$\begin{aligned} \mathbf{Gr} &= (\mathbf{D}-\mathbf{L})^{-1}\mathbf{L}^{T}\mathbf{r} = \lambda_i\mathbf{r} \\ \mathbf{L}^{T}\mathbf{r} &= \lambda_i(\mathbf{D}-\mathbf{L})\mathbf{r} \end{aligned} \tag{9}$$

Multiple by $\mathbf{r}^{T}$ on both sides of (9), we can get

$$\mathbf{r}^{T}\mathbf{L}^{T}\mathbf{r} = \lambda_i\mathbf{r}^{T}(\mathbf{D}-\mathbf{L})\mathbf{r} \tag{10}$$

Then we transpose both sides of (11) simultaneously, where $\mathbf{D} = \mathbf{D}^{T}$. Another equation can be obtained as

$$\mathbf{r}^{T}\mathbf{L}\mathbf{r} = \lambda_i\mathbf{r}^{T}(\mathbf{D}-\mathbf{L}^{T})\mathbf{r} \tag{11}$$

Add (11) and (10) will lead to

$$\mathbf{r}^{T}(\mathbf{L}^{T}+\mathbf{L})\mathbf{r} = \lambda_i\mathbf{r}^{T}(\mathbf{D}-\mathbf{L}-\mathbf{L}^{T})\mathbf{r} \tag{12}$$

As shown earlier, we can depose **A** as $\mathbf{A} = \mathbf{D} - \mathbf{L} - \mathbf{L}^{T}$. Combine (12) and the decomposition form of **A**, we have

$$(1 - \lambda_i)\mathbf{r}^T\mathbf{Dr} = (1 + \lambda_i)\mathbf{r}^T\mathbf{Ar} \tag{13}$$

Since the MMSE filtering matrix $\mathbf{A}$ is positive definite matrix, thus, the diagonal matrix $\mathbf{D}$ of $\mathbf{A}$ is positive definite. Then we can infer that $\mathbf{r}^T\mathbf{Ar} > 0$ and $\mathbf{r}^T\mathbf{Dr} > 0$. Further, we can get $(1 - \lambda_i)(1 + \lambda_i) > 0$, which indicates $|\lambda_i| < 1$. Combing the conclusion and Theorem 1, we can get $\rho(\mathbf{G}) < 1$.

As [17] shows, assume the iterative matrix of the DRGS algorithm is $\mathbf{M}$ and $w \in (1, 2)$, when the spectral radius $\rho(\mathbf{G}) > \sqrt{w - 1}$, the spectral radius of $\mathbf{M}$ can be written as

$$0 < \rho(\mathbf{M}) < \rho(\mathbf{G}) < 1 \tag{14}$$

Hence, we can get the proposed DRGS algorithm is convergent.

3.3 Computational Complexity Analysis

For massive MIMO systems, computational complexity is one of the important factors in measuring the performance of detector. The complexity is defined as the required real multiplications in solving $\mathbf{A}^{-1}$. Focus on the iterative form of DRGS algorithm, we calculate the complexity in each step. Firstly, the complexity of $\hat{\mathbf{x}}^*_{n+1}$, which is the same as the conventional GS algorithm, is equal to $4K^2$. Then, to achieve $\hat{\mathbf{x}}_{n+1}$, we require to calculate two scalar multiplication with $2K \times 1$ vector with the complexity is $4K$.

In Table 1, we compare the complexity of the proposed algorithm DRGS with the Jacobi algorithm and GS algorithm. As is shown in this table, the proposed algorithm has almost the same computational complexity as the conventional Jacobi algorithm and GS algorithm. Thus, the complexity of DRGS almost no increase in complexity and is much lower than the traditional MMSE signal detection.

Table 1. Computational complexity comparison of different algorithms

Algorithm	Complexity (iteration times T)
MMSE	$(5/3)K^3 + (3/2)K^2 + (8/3)K$
Jacobi [14]	$4K^2 + 10K + (4K^2 - 2K)T$
GS [16]	$8K^2 + 4K + 4K^2T$
DRGS	$4K^2 + 4K + (4K^2 + 4K)T$

4 Simulation Results

In this section, we utilize Monte-Carlo simulation to evaluate the proposed algorithm. In order to verify the performance of the DRGS algorithm, we provide bit error rate (BER) simulation result compared with the conventional GS algorithm. The BER performance of the typical MMSE is used as the benchmark for comparison. We consider the Rayleigh fading channel model as channel model. And the channel matrix

$\mathbf{H}_c$ follow the complex-valued Gaussian distribution with zero mean and unity variance. And the simulation environment is assumed to be the uplink massive MIMO system with 128 × 32 and 256 × 64, respectively. The 64QAM modulation scheme is utilized in the simulations.

Figure 1 illustrates the BER performance of the proposed DRGS algorithm against the relaxation parameter *w*. For comparison, we set the signal-to-noise (SNR) as 14 dB and the number of iterations is $T = 3$. The minimum BER is almost 10^{-6} for $N \times K = 128 \times 32$ and $N \times K = 256 \times 64$, when selecting the optimal relaxation parameter. Fortunately, we can find the optimal *w* is 1.1 for both above-mentioned systems. Moreover, according to extensive simulation results, it is found that the optimal relaxation parameter w is invariable when the result of (*N*/*K*) is fixed. Thus, the optimal *w* is easily to be ascertained when the result of (*N*/*K*) have been known.

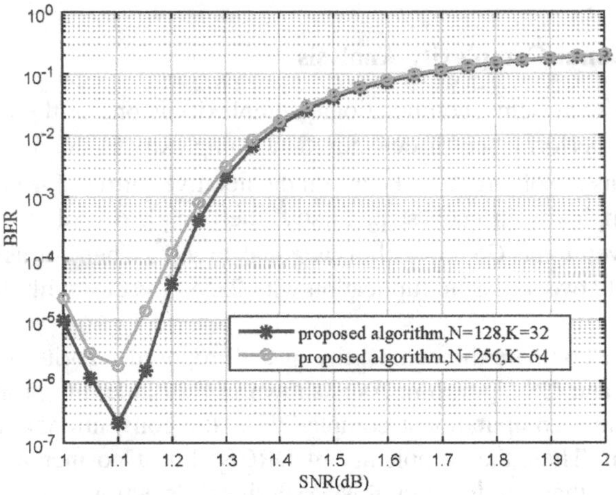

Fig. 1. BER performance of the proposed DRGS detection algorithm against the relaxation parameter *w*.

Figure 2 shows the comparison between the proposed DRGS algorithm with the Jacobi detection algorithm [14] and GS detection [16] algorithm, and the BER performance of the typical MMSE signal detection is utilized as the benchmark. The relaxation parameter *w* is considered to be set as $w = 1.1$. It is observed that the BER of both algorithms are closer to that of MMSE algorithm when the number of iterations increases. In addition, the proposed DRGS algorithm performs better in BER than the conventional algorithms with the same number of iterations. As we can observe in Fig. 2, in order to achieve the BER of 10^{-5}, the SNR required by the proposed algorithm is 12 dB, and the SNR required by the Jacobi algorithm and GS algorithm is more than 16 dB, when $T = 3$. Therefore, the convergence rate of our proposed DRGS algorithm is faster as compared with the conventional algorithm.

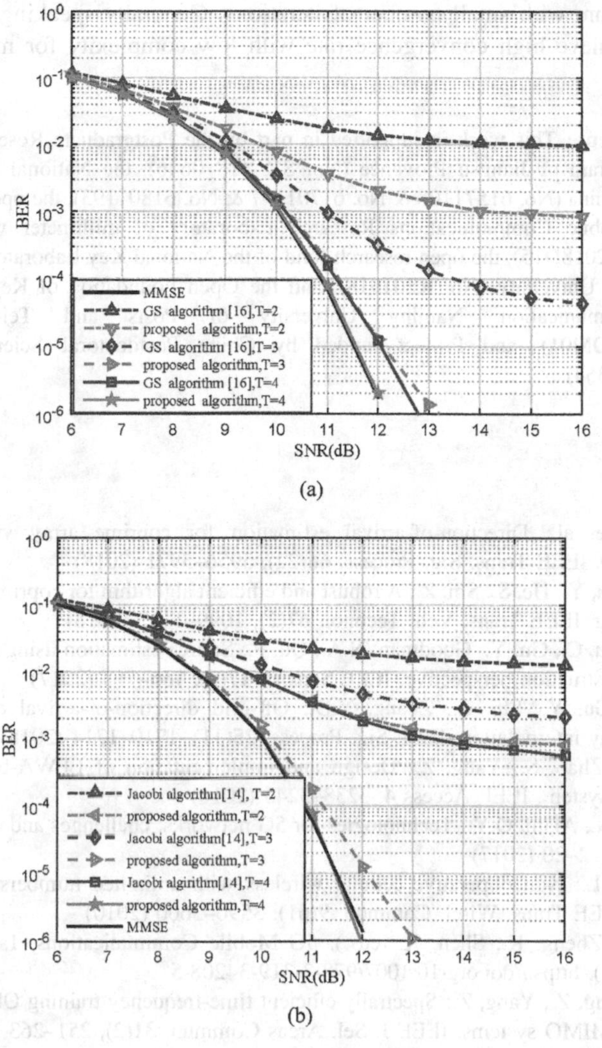

Fig. 2. BER performance comparison between the proposed algorithm and the conventional iterative algorithm with 64QAM modulation.

5 Conclusion

In this paper, we propose an improved GS algorithm that called DRGS algorithm in signal detection for massive MIMO systems. The DRGS algorithm is proved to realize MMSE solution and avoid direct matrix inversion and reduce the complexity from $O(K^3)$ to $O(K^2)$. In addition, through theoretical analysis and simulation results, it is proved that the DRGS algorithm can reach the approximate performance of typical

MMSE algorithm with small number of iterations. Generally speaking, the proposed DRGS can achieve high convergence rate with low complexity for massive MIMO systems.

Acknowledgement. This work is supported in part by the Postgraduate Research & Practice Innovation Program of Jiangsu Provence (No. SJCX18_0646), the National Natural Science Foundation of China (No. 61571108 & No. 61701197 & No. 61801193), the open research fund of National Mobile Communications Research Laboratory of millimeter wave, Southeast University (No. 2018D15), the open research fund of the National Key Laboratory of millimeter wave, Southeast University (No. K201918), and the Open Foundation of Key Laboratory of Wireless Communication, Nanjing University of Posts and Telecommunication (No. 2017WICOM01), and Project funded by China Postdoctoral Science Foundation (No. 2018M641354).

References

1. Zhou, C., et al.: Direction-of-arrival estimation for coprime array via virtual array interpolation. IEEE Trans. Sig. Process. **66**(22), 5956–5971 (2018)
2. Zhou, C., Gu, Y., He, S., Shi, Z.: A robust and efficient algorithm for coprime array adaptive beamforming. IEEE Trans. Veh. Technol. **67**(2), 1099–1112 (2018)
3. Shi, Z., Zhou, C., Gu, Y., Goodman, N.A., Qu, F.: Source estimation using coprime array: a sparse reconstruction perspective. IEEE Sens. J. **17**(3), 755–765 (2017)
4. Zhou, C., Gu, Y., Shi, Z., Zhang, Y.D.: Off-grid direction-of-arrival estimation using coprime array interpolation. IEEE Sig. Process. **25**(11), 1710–1714 (2018)
5. Zheng, K., Zhao, S., Yang, Z.: Design and implementation of LPWA-based air quality monitoring system. IEEE Access **4**, 3238–3245 (2016)
6. Al-Falahy, N., Alani, O.Y.: Technologies for 5G networks: challenges and opportunities. IT Prof. **19**(1), 12–20 (2017)
7. Marzetta, T.L.: Noncooperative cellular wireless with unlimited numbers of base station antennas. IEEE Trans. Wirel. Commun. **9**(61), 3590–3600 (2010)
8. Xiang, W., Zheng, K., Shen, X. (eds.): 5G Mobile Communications, 1st edn. Springer, Cham (2017). https://doi.org/10.1007/978-3-319-34208-5
9. Dai, L., Wang, Z., Yang, Z.: Spectrally efficient time-frequency training OFDM for mobile large-scale MIMO systems. IEEE J. Sel. Areas Commun. **31**(2), 251–263 (2013)
10. Chockalingam, A., Rajan, B.S.: Large MIMO Systems, 1st edn. Cambridge University Press, New York (2014)
11. Shariati, N., Bjornson, E., Bengtssson, M., Debbah, M.: Low-complexity polynomial channel estimation in large-scale MIMO with arbitrary statistics. IEEE J. Sel. Top. Sig. Process. **8**(5), 815–830 (2014)
12. Wu, M., Yin, B., Wang, G., Dick, C., Cavallaro, J.R., Studer, C.: Large-scale MIMO detection for 3GPP LTE: algorithms and FPGA implementations. IEEE J. Sel. Top. Sig. Process. **8**(5), 916–929 (2014)
13. Gao, X., Dai, L., Yuen, C., Zhang, Y.: Low-complexity MMSE signal detection based on Richardson method for large-scale MIMO systems. In: 80th Vehicular Technology Conference, Vancouver, BC, pp. 1–5 (2014)
14. Qin, X., Yan, Z., He, G.: A near-optimal detection scheme based on joint steepest descent and Jacobi method for uplink massive MIMO systems. IEEE Commun. Lett. **20**(3), 276–279 (2016)

15. Wu, Z., Zhang, C., Xue, Y., Xu, S., You, X.: Efficient architecture for soft-output massive MIMO detection with Gauss-Seidel method. In: 2016 IEEE International Symposium on Circuits and Systems (ISCAS), Montreal, QC, pp. 1886–1889 (2016)
16. Zhang, C., Wu, Z., Xue, Y., Studer, C., Zhang, Z., You, X.: Efficient soft-output Gauss-Seidel data detector for massive MIMO systems. IEEE Trans. Circ. Syst. I Reg. Pap. 1–12 (2018)
17. Antuono, M., Colicchio, G.: Delayed over-relaxation for iterative methods. J. Comput. Phys. **321**, 892–907 (2016)
18. Wang, G., Xiang, W., Yuan, J.: Outage performance for compute-and-forward in generalized multi-way relay channels. IEEE Commun. Lett. **16**(12), 2099–2102 (2012)
19. Xiao, L., et al.: Efficient compressive sensing detectors for generalized spatial modulation systems. IEEE Trans. Veh. Technol. **66**(2), 1284–1298 (2017)
20. Sun, Y., Li, Z., Zhang, C., Zhang, R., Yan, F., Shen, L.: Low complexity signal detector based on SSOR iteration for large-scale MIMO systems. In: 2017 9th International Conference on Wireless Communications and Signal Processing (WCSP), Nanjing, pp. 1–6 (2017)
21. Björck, Å.: Numerical Methods in Matrix Computations. TAM, vol. 59. Springer, Cham (2015). https://doi.org/10.1007/978-3-319-05089-8
22. Gao, X., Dai, L., Hu, Y., Wang, Z., Wang, Z.: Matrix inversion-less signal detection using SOR method for uplink large-scale MIMO systems. In: 2014 IEEE Global Communications Conference, Austin, TX, pp. 3291–3295 (2014)

Research on the Integrated Working Mode Based on Positive and Negative Frequency Modulation in Radar Communication Integration

Quanrui Zhao and Aijun Liu(✉)

Harbin Institute of Technology, Weihai 264209, China
mylaj@hitwh.edu.cn

Abstract. Nowadays, the fast development of the digital circuits results in a more and more high digital level of radar system. Especially, the development of the solid-state active module, the high-speed multi-digital A/D convertor, the direct digital synthesizer (DDS), and universal use of the high-speed digital signal processor provide an outstanding basis of the radar communication integration. Minimum Shift Keying Linear Frequency Modulation (MSK-LFM) is a novel multifunctional radar waveform. For all above, this paper proposes an integrated working mode based on positive and negative frequency modulation in radar communication integration. In the mode, the radar main station transmits positive linear modulation frequency signals, however, the communication affiliated station transmits negative linear modulation frequency signals. Their orthogonality causes less interference. Through the derivation, the method for the orthogonality improvement is obtained. The effectiveness of this working mode is proved by the simulations.

Keywords: Radar communication integration · MSK-LFM · LFM

1 Introduction

Recently, radar communication integration has been a focus point at home and abroad. In the references [1], Chen proposed using linear frequency modulation: LFM signal as the carrier of minimum shift keying (MSK) [2] signal to form a new MSK-LFM signal with both radar detection function and communication function, and theoretically analyzed the signal. It was proved that MSK-LFM is no worse than LFM on the performance of range and velocity acquisition [3, 4, 5]. For integrated waveform, there are difficulties such as large interference in practical applications [6, 7, 8], so the working mode with the same frequency and the same time based on positive and negative frequency modulation is proposed in order to study the system of integrated signal, and its principle of working mode and orthogonality are studied. Through simulation, it is concluded that the orthogonality of radar signal processing is related to modulation data and the time-bandwidth product.

M. Jia et al. (Eds.): WiSATS 2019, LNICST 281, pp. 408–414, 2019.
https://doi.org/10.1007/978-3-030-19156-6_38

2 Same-Time and Same-Frequency Working Mode

Same-time and Same-frequency working mode means that the radar waveform and the communication waveform are sent at the same wavelength and at the same time. Its schematic diagram is shown in Fig. 1.

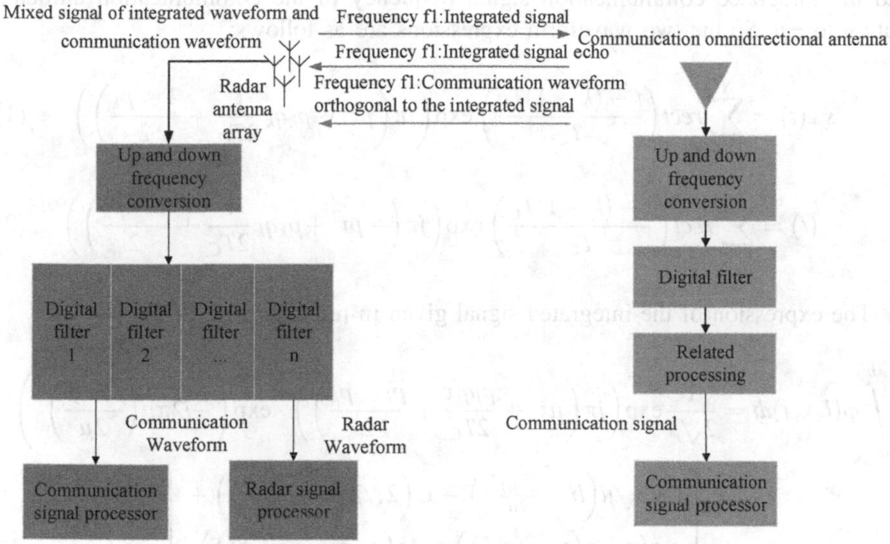

Fig. 1. Same-time and Same-frequency working mode

(1) the MSK-LFM signal waveform with a frequency of f1 sent by the radar main station is used to complete the detection and communication functions simultaneously.
(2) Communication from the station to the radar main station sends a signal of integrated waveform orthogonal to the radar waveform and with a frequency of f1, which is used to complete communication from the station to the radar main station.
(3) When the communication receives the integrated signal from the radar main station from the station, the communication signal is obtained after down-conversion, digital filtering and correlation processing demodulation, then the communication function is completed.
(4) Waveform of communication from communications affiliated stations and radar echo could reach the radar main station at the same time, but the two signals are orthogonal, so they will not produce interference. The two orthogonal signal, after completing down frequency conversion, digital filtering, correlation processing and matching processing, radar echo complete detection function in the radar signal processor, communication signals complete the communication function in communication processor.

3 Orthogonal Analysis of Radar Performance

Integration of radar echo signals and communication signals may arrive at the main radar station at the same time, only when two waveform quadrature to each other it will not produce interference, so this section will analyze the orthogonality of the radar signal processing. Set the integrated signal frequency of the radar main station to $+\mu$, and the integrated communication signal frequency of the communication affiliated station to $-\mu$. So the two waveform expressions are as follows:

$$s_{+}(t) = \sum_{k=1}^{N} rect\left(\frac{t-(k-1)T_C}{T_C}\right)\exp\left(j\pi\left(\mu t^2 + p_k q_k \frac{t}{2T_C} + \frac{1-p_k}{2}\right)\right) \tag{1}$$

$$s_{-}(t) = \sum_{k=1}^{N} rect\left(\frac{t-(k-1)T_C}{T_C}\right)\exp\left(j\pi\left(-\mu t^2 + p_k q_k \frac{t}{2T_C} + \frac{1-p_k}{2}\right)\right) \tag{2}$$

The expression of the integrated signal given in references [4, 9, 10] is:

$$\int_a^b \varphi(l,k,t)dt = \frac{1}{2\sqrt{\mu}}\exp\left(j\pi\left(\mu\tau^2 + \frac{p_l q_l \tau}{2T_C} + \frac{p_l - p_k}{2}\right)\right)\cdot\exp\left(-j2\pi\mu\left(\frac{f_0+f}{2\mu}\right)^2\right) \cdot \begin{bmatrix} C\left(2\sqrt{\mu}\left(b+\frac{f_0+f}{2\mu}\right)\right) - C\left(2\sqrt{\mu}\left(a+\frac{f_0+f}{2\mu}\right)\right) + \\ jS\left(2\sqrt{\mu}\left(b+\frac{f_0+f}{2\mu}\right)\right) - jS\left(2\sqrt{\mu}\left(a+\frac{f_0+f}{2\mu}\right)\right) \end{bmatrix} \tag{3}$$

We can obtain the correlation coefficient between the integrated waveforms of positive and negative frequencies. The correlation coefficient of integrated waveforms of positive and negative frequency modulation is simulated to analyze how to improve the cross-property. Simulation parameters are set as follows:

In Fig. 2: radar bandwidth is 30 MHz, radar pulse width is 10 μs and modulation data number is 10.

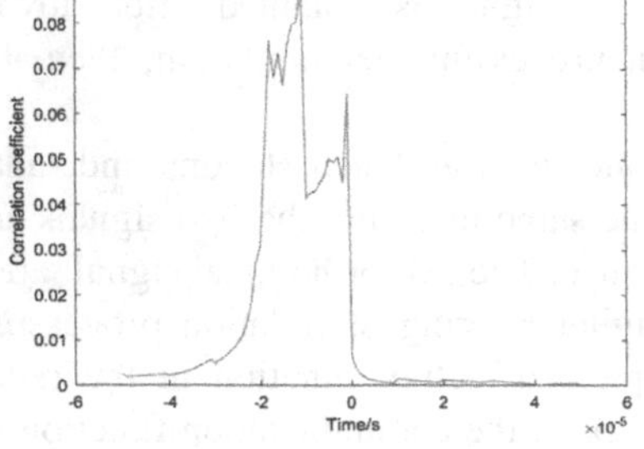

Fig. 2. Simulation of parameter one

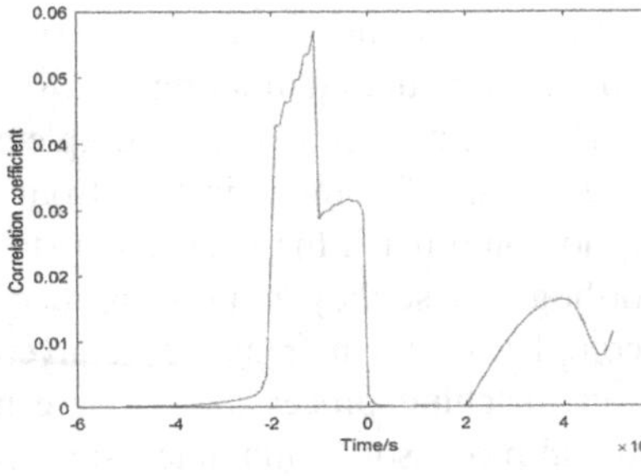

Fig. 3. Simulation of parameter two

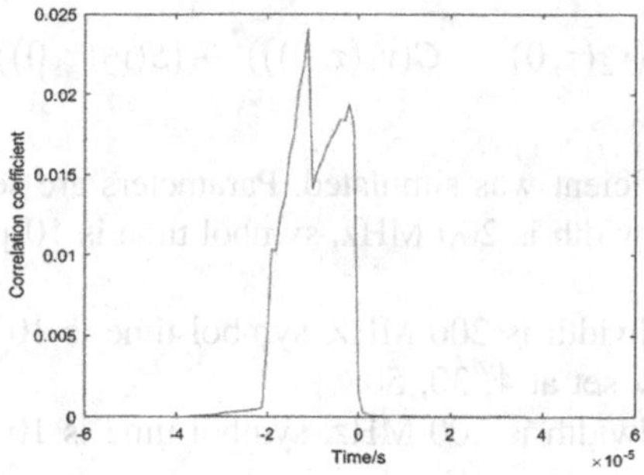

Fig. 4. Simulation of parameter three

In Fig. 3: radar bandwidth is 30 MHz, radar pulse width is 10 μs and modulation data number is 100.

In Fig. 4: radar bandwidth is 500 MHz, radar pulse width is 10 μs and modulation data number is 10.

It can be seen that the orthogonality of integrated waveforms with positive and negative frequencies is affected by the number of modulated data and time-bandwidth product. According to the simulation results, the orthogonality of the integrated waveform with positive and negative frequency modulation will be improved with the increase of time-bandwidth product. But as the number of modulation data increases, the integration of the signal spectrum is increased, so the best way to improve the positive rate of integration waveform orthogonality method is to increase the time-bandwidth product.

4 Orthogonal Analysis of Communication Signal

The upper limit and lower limit of integral can be obtained:

$$\begin{cases} v_1(\tau,f) = 2\sqrt{\mu}\Big((k-1)T_C + \tau + \frac{1}{2\mu}\cdot\Big(\frac{p_k q_k}{4T_C} - \mu\tau + f\Big)\Big) \\ v_2(\tau,f) = 2\sqrt{\mu}\Big(kT_C + \frac{1}{2\mu}\cdot\Big(\frac{p_k q_k}{4T_C} - \mu\tau + f\Big)\Big) \end{cases} \tag{4}$$

When $-T_C \leq \tau \leq 0$, the lower and upper limits are:

$$\begin{cases} v_1(\tau,f) = 2\sqrt{\mu}\Big((k-1)T_C + \frac{1}{2\mu}\cdot\Big(\frac{p_k q_k}{4T_C} - \mu\tau + f\Big)\Big) \\ v_2(\tau,f) = 2\sqrt{\mu}\Big(kT_C + \tau + \frac{1}{2\mu}\cdot\Big(\frac{p_k q_k}{4T_C} - \mu\tau + f\Big)\Big) \end{cases} \tag{5}$$

By substituting equation, the interrelationship number expression can be obtained:

$$\rho(\tau) = \frac{1}{2\sqrt{\mu T_C}}\sqrt{(C(v_2(\tau,0)) - C(v_1(\tau,0)))^2 + (S(v_2(\tau,0)) - S(v_1(\tau,0)))^2} \quad (6)$$

The correlation coefficient was simulated. Parameters are set as follows:

In Fig. 5: radar bandwidth is 200 MHz, symbol time is 10 μs and modulation data is 500.

In Fig. 6: radar bandwidth is 200 MHz, symbol time is 10 μs, modulation data is 500 and k is respectively set at 4, 30, 50.

In Fig. 7: radar bandwidth is 200 MHz, symbol time is 10 μs, modulation data is 500, $k = 1 \sim 200$.

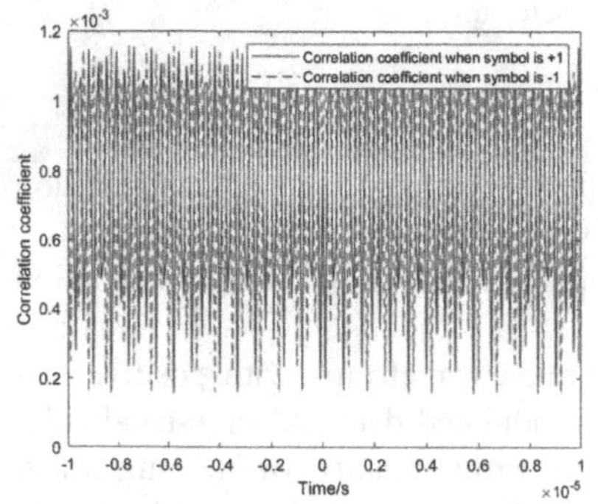

Fig. 5. The correlation coefficient different position of symbol

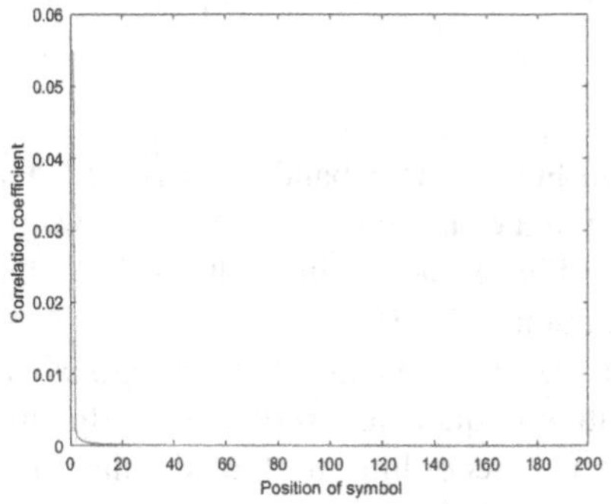

Fig. 6. The correlation coefficient under between symbol is +1 and −1

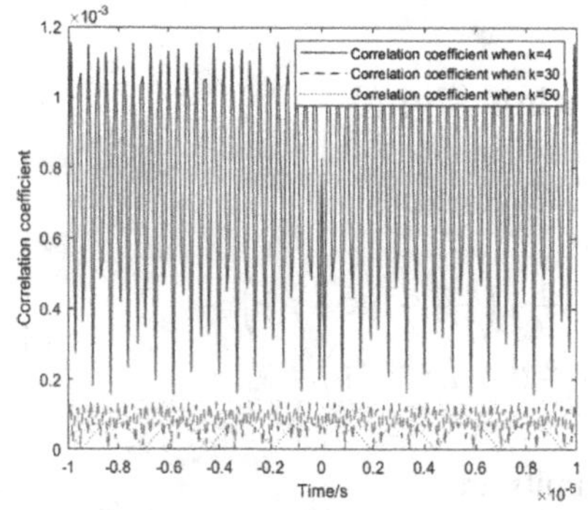

Fig. 7. The correlation coefficient under different k values

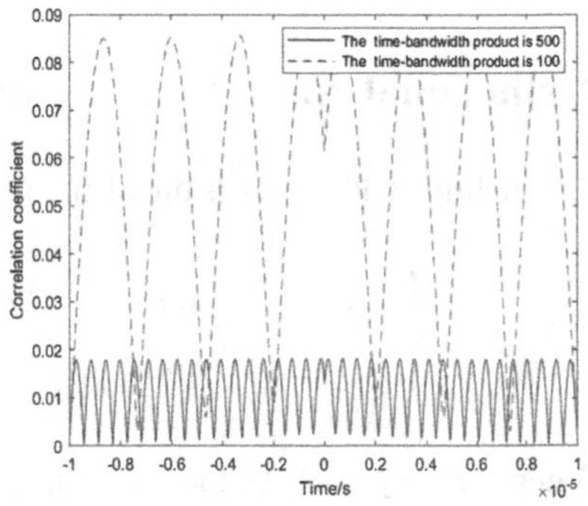

Fig. 8. The correlation coefficient of the different product of time and bandwidth

In Fig. 8: radar bandwidth is 50 MHz and 10 MHz, symbol time is 10 μs and modulation data is 200.

By analyzing the simulation results, it can be seen from Fig. 5 that the correlation coefficient when the symbol is +1 and −1 is basically the same. In other words, the symbol is +1, or −1, which has no effect on orthogonality. As can be seen from Figs. 6 and 7, with the increase of k value, the correlation coefficient between the reference signals of radar echo and communication matched filtering decreases, and the orthogonality performance improves. Moreover, the correlation coefficient changes greatly for different k values, which means that the later symbol is affected by the radar echo, resulting in a smaller probability of error. Figure 8 shows that as the time-bandwidth product of the symbol increases, the correlation coefficient decreases and the orthogonality becomes better.

5 Conclusion

In the working mode of integrated signal in the same frequency synchronous, radar main station transmits the positive linear modulation frequency integrated signals, and the communication affiliated station uses the negative modulation frequency integrated signals. The less interference results from their orthogonality. Through simulation, it is concluded that the orthogonality of radar signal processing is related to modulation data and the time-bandwidth product. However, the larger the modulation number is, the more serious the spectrum expansion is. Therefore, the method of increasing the time-bandwidth product can be adopted to improve the orthogonality of the two signals. Finally, the correlation coefficient is analyzed, which is independent of the code element polarity, and will decrease with the increase of the time-bandwidth product. And the further the position is, the better the orthogonal performance is.

Acknowledgement. This work was supported in part by the National Key R&D Program of China under Grant 2017YFC1405202, in part by the National Natural Science Foundation of China under Grant 61571159 and Grant 61571157, and in part by the Public Science and Technology Research Funds Projects of Ocean under Grant 201505002.

References

1. Chen, X., Wang, X., Xu, S., Zhang, J.: A novel radar waveform compatible with communication. In: International Conference on Computational Problem-Solving, pp. 177–181. IEEE (2011)
2. Pasupathy, S.: Minimum shift keying: a specially efficient modulation. IEEE Commun. Mag. **17**(7), 14–22 (1979)
3. Levanon, N., Mozeson, E.: Radar Signals. Wiley, New York (2004). Chap. 4
4. Zhipeng, L.: Radar communication integrated waveform research, p. 93. Beijing Institute of Technology, Beijing (2015)
5. Papoulis, A.: Signal Analysis. McGraw-Hill, New York (1977)
6. Roberton, M.: Integrated radar and communication based on chirped spread-spectrum techniques. In: IEEE MTT-S International Microwave Symposium Digest, Philadelphia, pp. 611–614 (2003)

7. Yankun, S.: Research on airborne application of radar communication integrated waveform, p. 34. University of Electronic Science and Technology, Chengdu (2013)
8. Xiaoming, T.: Overview of integrated development of radar communication. In: Proceedings of the 16th Information Theory Academic Annual Meeting of Chinese Institute of Electronics. Information Society of China Electronics Society (2009)
9. Bello, P.A.: Characterization of randomly time-variant linear channels. IEEE Trans. Commun. Syst. **11**, 360–393 (1963)
10. Xue, Z.: Modulation and demodulation of MSK signals. Beijing University of Posts and Telecommunications, Beijing (2013)

Late Main Track

Landsat-8 Image Restoration Based on Kernel Density Regression

Yuchen Li[1], Jiang Qian[2,3](✉), Yong Wang[2,4,5], Xiaobo Yang[3], and Bin Duo[6]

[1] Yingcai Honors College, UESTC, Chengdu 611731, Sichuan, China
[2] School of Environment and Resources, UESTC, Chengdu 611731, Sichuan, China
jqian@uestc.edu.cn
[3] School of Information and Communication Engineering, UESTC, Chengdu 611731, Sichuan, China
[4] Department of Geography, Planning, and Environment, East Carolina University, Greenville, NC 27858, USA
[5] Institute of Remote Sensing Big Data, Big Data Research Center of UESTC, Chengdu 611731, Sichuan, China
[6] College of Information Science and Technology, Chengdu University of Technology, Chengdu, China

Abstract. A multi-temporal kernel density regression (KDR) method is proposed in this paper for reflectance restoration. Kernel density regression perform optimization to search the best regression coefficients. The proposed method is applied on the Landsat-8 dataset, and shows a better estimation of the true pixel value from the contaminated images.

Keywords: Reflectance restoration · Multi-temporal · Kernel density regression

1 Introduction

Clouds are the biggest occlusion in the optical remote sensing images. Since electromagnetic waves can be strongly attenuated and interfered when reflected in the cloud layer, the quality of the optical remote sensing image is greatly reduced due to the reflection of the cloud, and the accuracy of the optical application results is greatly reduced. Therefore, it is crucial to retrieve the landscape reflectance from cloud corrupted images.

Fmask algorithm [1] is a kind of object-based method, which uses the precise measurement of Near Infrared (NIR) Band and the Brightness Temperature

This work was supported by the National Natural Science Foundation of China under Grant 61401077 and the China Postdoctoral Science Foundation under Grant 2015M580784.

M. Jia et al. (Eds.): WiSATS 2019, LNICST 281, pp. 417–423, 2019.
https://doi.org/10.1007/978-3-030-19156-6_39

(BT) for cloud and cloud shadow detection of Landsat-8 data. The algorithm needs a lot of information, e.g. the satellite sensor‘s view angle, the illuminating angle, brightness, spectral variability and temperature probability, etc. By this method, a relatively accurate cloud shape detection can be obtained. However, because of the difficulty of getting the prior information motioned above, the practicality of Fmask is greatly reduced when the images of the land is the only information we have.

The number of works focused on reflectance restoration in optical remote sensing images with time series is quite small. When there is no cloud in the sky, the reflection of the underlying landscape is usually small due to the continuity of the natural landscape. When the cloud appears, the pixel value will change greatly. Most multi-temporal methods detect clouds by analyzing pixel quality changes in time-series images.

Another algorithm adopted the method based on adaptive threshold is multi-temporal cloud detection (MTCD) [3]. The reflectance variations in both red and blue bands is recorded. The result is that although the algorithm shares an effective competence, the high requirement of a clear reference image with little or no cloud covered weaken its practicality. Besides, one of our conference paper [5] applies mean shift algorithm to extract the pixels' model through multi-temporal images and a cloud-free image is created. The cloud is then detected by thresholding the difference pixel value between the target image and reference image.

Creating a different reference image at each moment is a more efficient and reasonable approach from a more realistic perspective. In this article, we exploit KDR to restore pixel values in multi-temporal images which is contaminated by clouds. We determine the pattern of changes for each pixel based on the time series, while providing a recovered image for each moment. By KDR process, we can get the best regression coefficients and the clear restored images of underlying landscape for the whole time series. Through the kernel density estimation, the probability density of the residual value is calculated and we choose the coefficient corresponding to the maximum probability density as the regression coefficient. Then we can use the regression function to estimate the true pixel value.

2 Methodology

Suppose that:

$$y_i = f(x_i) + \varepsilon_i, i = 1, 2..., n \tag{1}$$

where $f(\cdot)$ is the regression function, y_i is the measurement which gives reflectance of one pixel at sampling instant x_i, n is the number of the samples. Because the cloud layer has a big impact on the detected pixel quality, the measurement y_i could deviate far away from the true reflectance of the pixel in some times.

Since in the natural world, the ground landscape usually changes continuously, so the pixels' reflectance always changes slowly in image series. Therefore, the function $f(\cdot)$ can be assumed to be of an 3-order local smoothness, i.e., the model can be approximated as:

$$y_i = \beta_0 + \beta_i x_i + \beta_2 x_i^2 + \beta_3 x_i^3 \tag{2}$$

Let $X_i = [y_i, x_i, x_i^2, x_i^3]^T$, $\beta = [-1, \beta_1, \beta_2, \beta_3]^T$, we have

$$\beta^T X_i + \beta_0 = 0, i = 1, 2..., n \tag{3}$$

Thus the problem of solving coefficients of the polynomial becomes the problem of searching the parameter β and β_0 which fit all of the data $\{X_i, i = 1, 2, ..., n\}$ best, and it equals pursuit a unit normal vector $\alpha = \beta / norm(\beta)$, norm$(\cdot)$ is a normalization function, and $\alpha_0 = \beta_0 / norm(\beta)$. In the solving process, we firstly set a normalized vector α, and then perform orthogonal projection of each X_i on it, we will obtain n projected values. If the true vector α is selected for projection, the projected values will concentrate at $-\beta_0$. We introduce the metric of kernel density estimation to make quantitative analysis of concentration. We use the kernel function $K(\cdot)$ to find the probability density function of its distribution $p_\alpha(\cdot)$:

$$p_\alpha(u) = \frac{1}{N h_\alpha} \sum_{i=1}^{n} K\left(\frac{u - \alpha X_i}{h_\alpha}\right) \tag{4}$$

where $p_\alpha(u)$ is the density estimate at point u, N is the total number of the points of the sample set, h_α is the bandwidth of kernel function with certain α.

Here we use the Epanechnikov function [6] as the kernel function $K(\cdot)$:

$$K(x) = \begin{cases} \frac{3}{4}(1 - x^2), & x^2 < 1 \\ 0, & else \end{cases} \tag{5}$$

The probability density function $p_\alpha(\cdot)$ can reflect if we find the true parameter α, $p_\alpha(\cdot)$ will have the maximum peak if the true vector α is found, and the mode is $-\alpha_0$.

Then the optimization of the parameter, i.e., $\hat{\alpha}$, can be calculated as:

$$\hat{\alpha} = arg \max_\alpha p_\alpha(u) \tag{6}$$

By solving this optimization problem, we can get the regression coefficients $\hat{\alpha}$ and the true value of the pixel value y_i can be estimated by the regression as:

$$\hat{y}_i = -\frac{\alpha_0}{\alpha_1} - \frac{\alpha_2}{\alpha_1} x_i - \frac{\alpha_3}{\alpha_1} x_i^2 - \frac{\alpha_4}{\alpha_1} x_i^3 \tag{7}$$

which corresponds to the clear pixel at time i.

The gray information algorithm is used in this paper to deal with the multi-temporal optical remote sensing images for reflectance restoration. The method is divided into two parts. The first step is preprocessing (i.e. calibration, region of interest selection) and the second is reflectance restoration. The data preprocessing is that co-registering all the images in Landsat-8 OLI dataset before the process of value restoration of pixels, which allows a cloud-contaminated image to be fully acquired in a fixed area in one year. In order to reduce the computational complexity of processing the whole images of the dataset, we use some sub-images that cropped out from the registered images for the purpose of results demonstration. After the preprocessing above, the restoration result of kernel density estimation algorithm is shown on the set of sub-images in Sect. 2.

Here we denote $D = \{S_1, S_2, ..., S_{25}\}$ with $S_i \in R^{M \times N}$ the sub-image dataset of a certain area at 25 time instants. The reflectance of that underlying landscape is assumed as changes slowly and gradually within a short time period. However, if the land is contaminated by cloud or other optical contaminant, the pixel's reflectance will have a sudden change.

Here we select the pixel at (m, n) as an example to illustrate the effect of the algorithm. The Landset-8 satellite scans the same place every 16 days and after 25 times of scanning, pixel located at (m, n) can obtain 25 reflectance measurements, which can be denoted by notation above as $D_{m,n} = \{S_1(m, n), S_2(m, n), ..., S_{25}(m, n)\}$. Equation (7) provided the robust regression estimate of $D_{m,n}$ and the cloud can be detected if the pixel value is far away from the model. In Fig. 1, it gives the regressed reflectance result of given $D_{m,n}$, and the robust regression result is denoted by the red line and the cloud corrupted measurements are denoted by the blue star line. It can be noted that the outliers with pixel values 66, 45 at time instants 13, 14 correspond to thick cloud and those with pixel values 36 at time instants 17 correspond to extremely thin cloud. Through kernel density estimation we can find the best fit coefficients. Kernel density function of the projection $\alpha^T X_i + \alpha_0$ of the pixel located at (m, n) have one largest main peak which close to zero. Figure 2 gives the result of kernel density function with respect to the pixel at (150,150). The maximum value of the probability density function is at the zero point of the coordinate axis, and the highest peak of the kernel density estimation is also at zero point, so it can be explained that the regression equation is very close to the original pixel value.

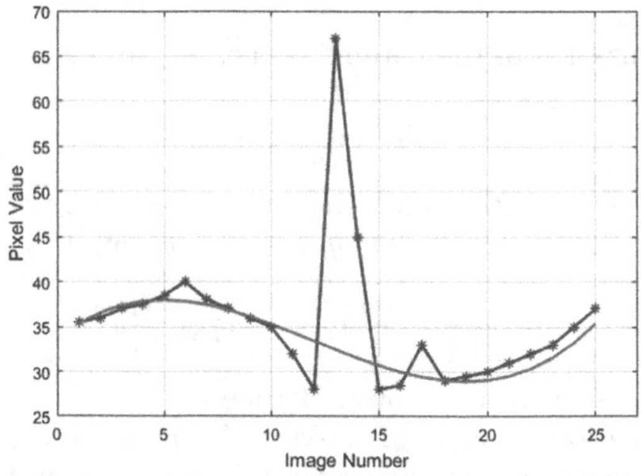

Fig. 1. Cloud corrupted pixel value against the time series and the kernel density estimation based regression. (Color figure online)

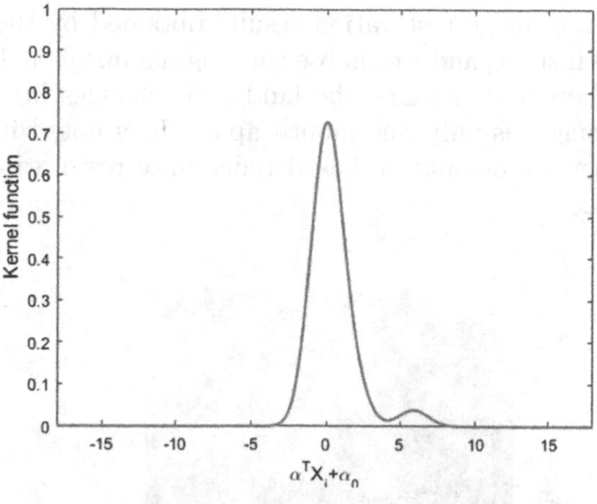

Fig. 2. The estimated probability density function after KDR.

3 Preliminary Results

For validating the effectiveness of the algorithm, our algorithm is tested with the time series data of Landsat-8 OLI images of 011/036 (path/row) acquired from 15 March, 2013 to 2 July, 2014, which can be downloaded at http://earthexplorer.us.gs.gov. The images centered at 34°55′10″N and 74°7′15″W were near Norfolk, Virginia, USA. A set of sub-image with configuration of 501 (columns) × 501 (rows) were extracted from each image in dataset. The illustration of the images we used in this time series can be found in Fig. 3, where the images are sorted line by line in order of time growth.

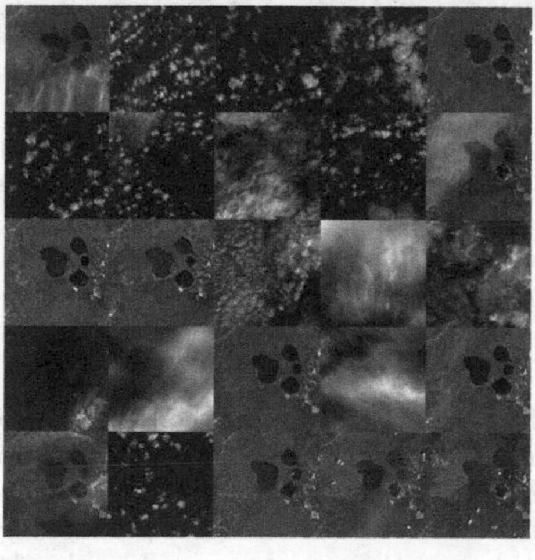

Fig. 3. Raw RGB images sorted by time. (Color figure online)

Figure 4 gives the image restoration results obtained by the proposed algorithm at 14th time instant, and we choose the original image at 12th time instant as ground truth, herein we assume the landscape changes little since the shot time of the two images is only one month apart. It is noted in Fig. 4 that the proposed kernel density estimation based reflectance restoration algorithm has a good performance.

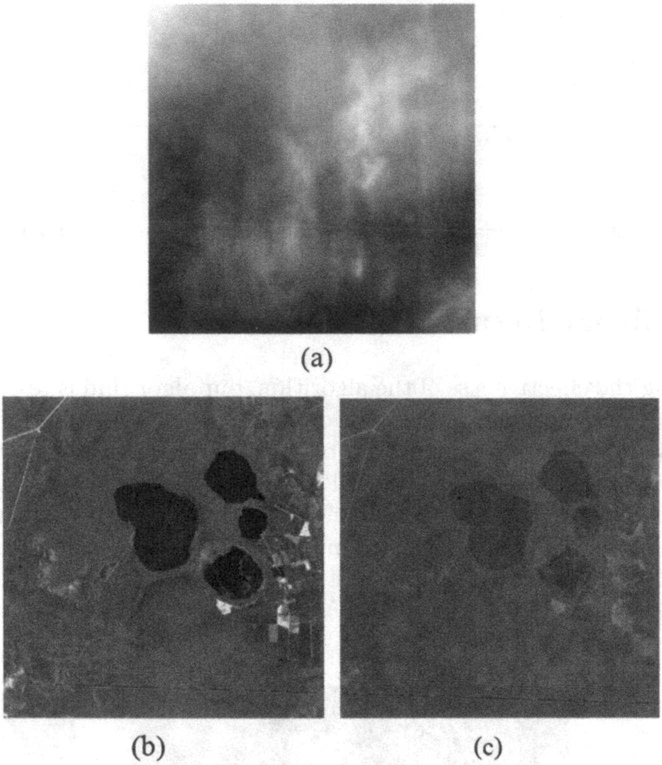

Fig. 4. Image restoration result at 14th time instant. (a) Original cloud contaminated image; (b) The original image in the 12th time instant; (c) The result of the proposed method.

4 Conclusion

A multi-temporal reflectance restoration method is proposed in this article by kernel density estimation regression model. With this method, we can obtain a cloud free image at any time instant. It can work automatically without reference image. For each time instant, a restored image is produced by fitting robustly of the pixels of the multi-temporal images corrupted by the cloud. Those restored images show the inherent gradual change of the landscape with time instants.

The limitation of the method is that the effect of extremely thin cloud components cannot be avoid and the degree of reduction of images in urban areas is relatively low because the difference between the reflectance and the pixel value corrupted by cloud is too small to discriminate.

References

1. Zhu, Z., Woodcock, C.E.: Object-based cloud and cloud shadow detection in Landsat imagery. Remote Sens. Environ. **118**, 83–94 (2012)
2. Li, M., Liew, S., Kwoh, L.: Automated production of cloud-free and cloud shadow–free image mosaics from cloudy satellite imagery. In: Proceedings of the ISPRS Congress, Istanbul, 12–13 July 2004 (2004)
3. Hagolle, O., Huc, M., Pascual, D.V., Dedieu, G.: A multi-temporal method for cloud detection, applied to FORMOSAT-2, VENuS, LANDSAT and SENTINEL-2 images. Remote Sens. Environ. **114**(8), 1747–1755 (2010)
4. Han, Y., Kim, B., Kim, Y., Lee, W.: Automatic cloud detection for high spatial resolution multi-temporal images. Remote Sens. Lett. **5**(7), 601–608 (2014)
5. Qian, J., Luo, Y., Wang, Y.: Cloud detection of optical remote sensing image time series using mean shift algorithm. In: IEEE International Geoscience and Remote Sensing Symposium (IGARSS), pp. 560–562 (2016)
6. Epanechnikov, V.A.: Non-parametric estimation of a multivariate probability density. Theory Probab. Appl. **14**, 153–158 (1969)

Design and Verification of a Novel Switching Architecture for Onboard Processing

Chenhua Sun, Bo Yin, and Zhibin Dou(✉)

The 54th Research Institute of China Electronics Technology Group Corporation, Shijiazhuang 050000, Hebei, China
dzbjet@126.com

Abstract. To overcome the problems caused by conventional ground routing protocols applied in the satellite communication network, a novel switching architecture is proposed. The proposed architecture employs layer-2 switching for same port and IP routing for different ports. Furthermore, the onboard IP switching process is well designed. OPNET is applied to build a satellite network simulation environment based on onboard IP switching. Simulation results demonstrate that the switching architecture meets the requirements of onboard IP data packet switching for both inter-beam, between beams and between satellites.

Keywords: Space based backbone network · Switching architecture · Satellite communication

1 Application Scenarios

With the improvement of the processing ability of satellite platform and payload, communication satellites can realize not only bent pipe, but also data regeneration and even routing and switching technology. The development of satellite communication system based on IP packet switch extends the ground network to outer space. IP packet switch onboard can provide internet communication service for anybody at anywhere. Furthermore, satellite communication can stay connected if the ground-control system is breakdown or encounters failures, which improves the viability of satellite communication systems. The network structure of satellite communication system based on IP packet switch is shown in Fig. 1.

M. Jia et al. (Eds.): WiSATS 2019, LNICST 281, pp. 424–431, 2019.
https://doi.org/10.1007/978-3-030-19156-6_40

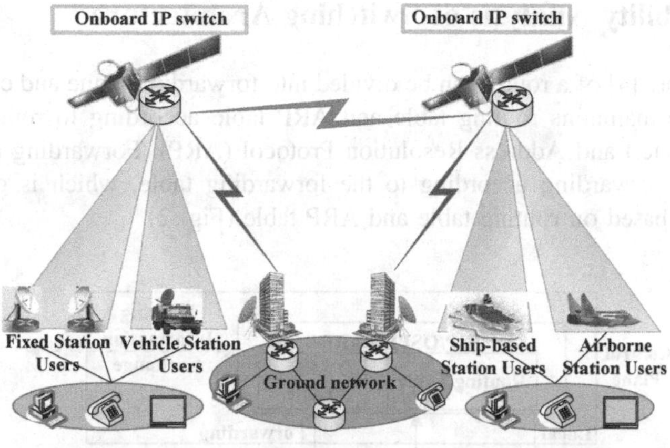

Fig. 1. Network structure of satellite communication system based on IP packet switch

2 Related Work

Typical satellite communication systems which are capable of onboard switching include SpaceWay system, IRIS system and TAST system. Among them, TSAT system [1] attempts to use onboard MPLS switching. However, due to the restrictions of funds and technologies, TSAT project ended in 2009.

- **SpaceWay System**

SpaceWay system [2] employs onboard fixed length packet switching method to implement IP packet routing and switching. Ingress flows and egress flows are of standard IP packets for both satellite terminals and ground equipment. In the satellite terminal, each IP packet is divided into one or more fixed length SpaceWay packets. The MAC layer addresses of the destination node and the downlink beam which the destination node located in are inserted in the SpaceWay packet header. Then, the SpaceWay satellite analyzes the packet header and extracts the two addresses to implement onboard switching. The transformation from IP addresses to SpaceWay addresses is achieved through a collaboration of satellite terminal and satellite network control center.

- **IRIS System**

IRIS system [3] attempts to develop space router based on radiation-resistant PowerPC CPU. With the help of this router, a series of IP-based applications, e.g. web and VoIP, can build the communication link directly without via the ground relay station, which decreases the Space-Ground communication delay (the delay for GEO satellite is about 250 ms). IRIS system installs a Cisco 18400 spaceborne IP router, which can be configured flexibly onboard according to ground control commands, to process routing and switching of IP packets. Satellite employs IP data packet to transmit data, which allows direct access to the network and achieves a faster communication.

3 Adaptability Analysis of Switching Architecture

The architecture [4] of a router can be divided into forwarding plane and control plane. Control plane maintains routing table and ARP table according to routing protocol (RIP, OSPF, etc.) and Address Resolution Protocol (ARP). Forwarding plane implements packet forwarding according to the forwarding table, which is generated by control plane based on routing table and ARP table (Fig. 2).

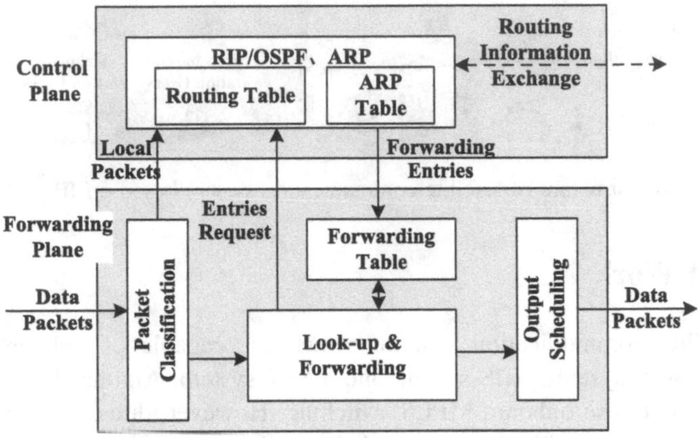

Fig. 2. Architecture of a router on ground

In the following of this section, the adaptability of switching architecture in satellite communication systems based on spaceborne IP switching is analyzed in the aspect of processing and switching for different kinds of data packets (IP unicast data packets, IP multicast data packets, ARP data packets).

3.1 IP Unicast Data Packet

After receiving an IP unicast data packet, the forwarding plane decides whether the packet should be received locally according to the MAC address. Data packet with the router's MAC address is accepted. Otherwise, the data packet is discarded directly and will not be forwarded by the same port. Then, the data packet is classified according to its IP address. Data packet with local IP address is sent to control plane and data packet with non-local IP address is forwarded based on the matching results of forwarding table.

As a result, if the switching architecture of the ground router is adopted on the satellite directly, IP unicast data packets from two satellite terminals under the same beam cannot be transmitted correctly. Because the IP unicast data packet from the source terminal is discarded directly by the satellite router due to the MAC address of the packet is different from the MAC address of the satellite router.

3.2 IP Multicast Data Packet

IP multicast data packets can be divided into data packets and management packets. The switching architecture of data packet is the same as the IP unicast data packet, i.e. a router looks up multicast IP address in multicast routing table and forwards the packet. For management packets (applied in RIP [5], OSPF [6], etc.), a router decides whether the packet should be received locally according to the multicast IP address and will not forward the packet by the same port.

As a result, if the switch architecture of the ground router is adopted on the satellite directly, multiple ground routers under the same beam and the satellite router form a point-to-multipoint network. The routing information from one ground router will not be forwarded to other ground routers under the same beam, and ground routers cannot obtain the routing information of next hop. Figure 3 shows that ground router with RIP protocol can only obtain routing information from different beams if the switch architecture of the ground router is adopted on the satellite directly.

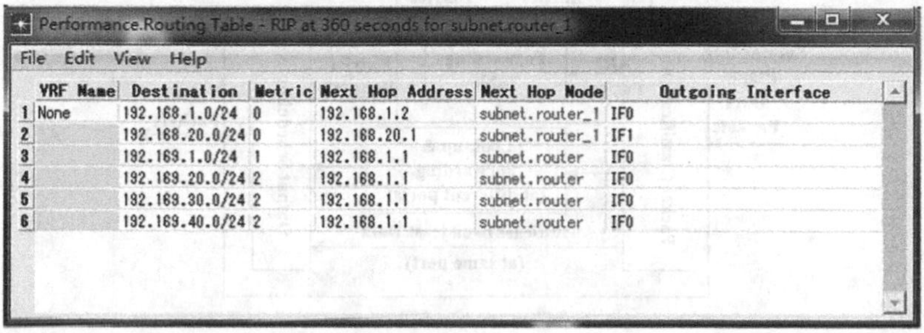
Performance.Routing Table - RIP at 360 seconds for subnet.router_1
File Edit View Help

	VRF Name	Destination	Metric	Next Hop Address	Next Hop Node	Outgoing Interface
1	None	192.168.1.0/24	0	192.168.1.2	subnet.router_1	IF0
2		192.168.20.0/24	0	192.168.20.1	subnet.router_1	IF1
3		192.169.1.0/24	1	192.168.1.1	subnet.router	IF0
4		192.169.20.0/24	2	192.168.1.1	subnet.router	IF0
5		192.169.30.0/24	2	192.168.1.1	subnet.router	IF0
6		192.169.40.0/24	2	192.168.1.1	subnet.router	IF0

Fig. 3. RIP routing information on ground router

3.3 ARP Data Packet

After receiving an ARP data packet, the forwarding plane classifies the packet according to its MAC address. Data packet with local address or broadcast address is sent to the control plane. Otherwise, the data packet is discarded directly and will not be forward by the same port.

As a result, if the switch architecture of the ground router is adopted on the satellite directly, the ARP data packets from two satellite terminals under the same beam cannot be processed properly. Because the MAC address of ARP data packet from the source terminal is broadcast address and the packet is sent to control plane rather than being forwarded to the destination terminal.

It can be seen from the above analysis that, if the switch architecture of the ground router is adopted on the satellite directly, forwarding of certain IP data packets or ARP data packets will be affected, which causes the routing protocol failing to converge. Therefore, it is necessary to provide adaptive design for the environment of onboard IP switch.

4 Switching Architecture Design for Onboard Processing

Considering layer-2 switching and IP routing in ground network, and taking into account the communication requirements among satellite terminals under the same beam and the limitation of the storage capacity of spaceborne IP switch payload, this paper proposes a novel switching architecture. In this architecture, layer-2 switching happens at the same port, and IP routing happens between different ports. Combined with the optimization design such as proactive forwarding entries distribution in routing table and ARP table self-learning, the proposed architecture meets the requirements of onboard IP data packet switching (Fig. 4).

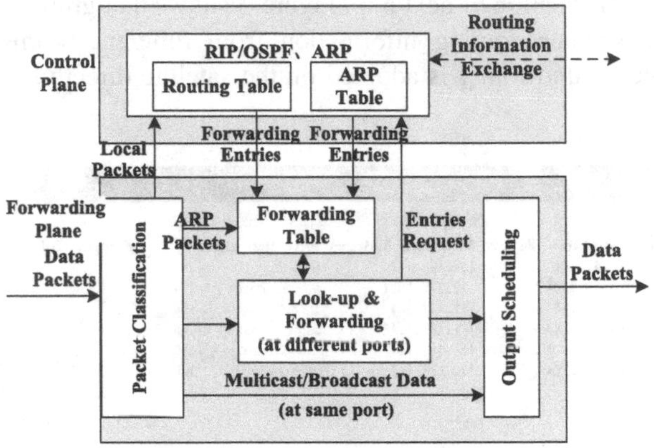

Fig. 4. Onboard IP switching architecture

- **Layer-2 Switching at the Same Port**

The following section illustrates the IP data switching process at the same port by taking satellite terminal 1 to visit satellite terminal 2 which is at the same port as an example. When satellite terminal 1 receives IP data packet, the layer-2 address of next hop (satellite terminal 2) is obtained by looking up the routing table according to the destination IP address. Satellite terminal 1 adds its layer-2 address and satellite terminal 2's layer-2 address as the header of IP data packet and encapsulated it into a satellite transmission frame before sending it to the onboard IP router.

After receiving the satellite transmission frame, the onboard IP router extracts the layer-2 address of data packet and determines this address is different from its own layer-2 address. Then, the frame is sent directly to the downlink interface for transmission and the onboard layer-2 switching process at the same port is accomplished.

Satellite terminal 2 receives the satellite transmission frame and determines the layer-2 address of the data packet is the same as its own layer-2 address. Then, the frame is accepted and the IP data packet is recovered. After that satellite terminal 2 sends the IP data packet to its corresponding user.

- **IP Routing and Switching among Different Ports**

The following section illustrates the IP data switching process at different ports by taking satellite terminal 1 to visit satellite terminal 2 which is at different ports as an example. When satellite terminal 1 receives an IP data packet, the layer-2 address of next hop (satellite terminal 2) is obtained by looking up the routing table according to the destination IP address. Satellite terminal 1 add its layer-2 address and the onboard IP router's layer-2 address as the header of IP data packet and encapsulates it into a satellite transmission frame before sending it to the onboard IP router.

After receiving the satellite transmission frame, the onboard IP router extracts the layer-2 address of data packet and determines this address is the same as its own layer-2 address. Then, the IP data packet is recovered and the corresponding IP address is extracted. The desired port is obtained by looking up the forwarding table according to the IP address. Then the IP data packet is encapsulated into a satellite transmission frame and is sent to the downlink interface for transmission. With this, the onboard layer-2 switching process at different ports is accomplished.

Satellite terminal 2 receives the satellite transmission frame and determines the layer-2 address of the data packet is the same as its own layer-2 address. Then, the frame is accepted and the IP data packet is recovered. After that satellite terminal 2 sends the IP data packet to its corresponding user.

5 Simulation and Verification

In order to test the ability of the above onboard IP switching architecture, OPNET is applied to build satellite network simulation environment. There is 1 onboard IP router and 6 earth stations (employing ground router and data terminal simulator), as shown in Fig. 5. Port 1 of onboard IP router connects earth stations 1, 2, 3 and port 2 of onboard IP router connects earth stations 4, 5, 6. The router uses RIP protocol to configure the communication service parameters under the same beam and different beams, so as to verify the routing convergence and data transmission performance with the proposed switching architecture.

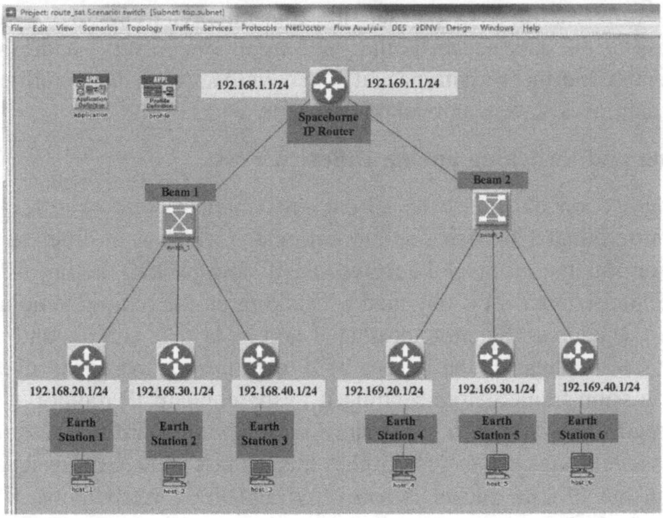

Fig. 5. Satellite network simulation environment with onboard IP switching architecture

Figure 6 shows the routing convergence results of ground router with RIP routing protocol. It can be seen that, by employing the proposed switching architecture, ground router can obtain the routing information under the same beam or different beams.

Performance.Routing Table - RIP at 360 seconds for subnet.router_1

	VRF Name	Destination	Metric	Next Hop Address	Next Hop Node	Outgoing Interface
1	None	192.168.1.0/24	0	192.168.1.2	subnet.router_1	IF0
2		192.168.20.0/24	0	192.168.20.1	subnet.router_1	IF1
3		192.168.30.0/24	1	192.168.1.3	subnet.router_2	IF0
4		192.168.40.0/24	1	192.168.1.4	subnet.router_3	IF0
5		192.169.1.0/24	1	192.168.1.1	subnet.router	IF0
6		192.169.20.0/24	2	192.168.1.1	subnet.router	IF0
7		192.169.30.0/24	2	192.168.1.1	subnet.router	IF0
8		192.169.40.0/24	2	192.168.1.1	subnet.router	IF0

Fig. 6. RIP routing information on ground router

The transmitting performance of earth terminals with the proposed switching architecture is given in Fig. 7. Simulation results show that data from earth station terminals can transmit data under the same beam or different beams.

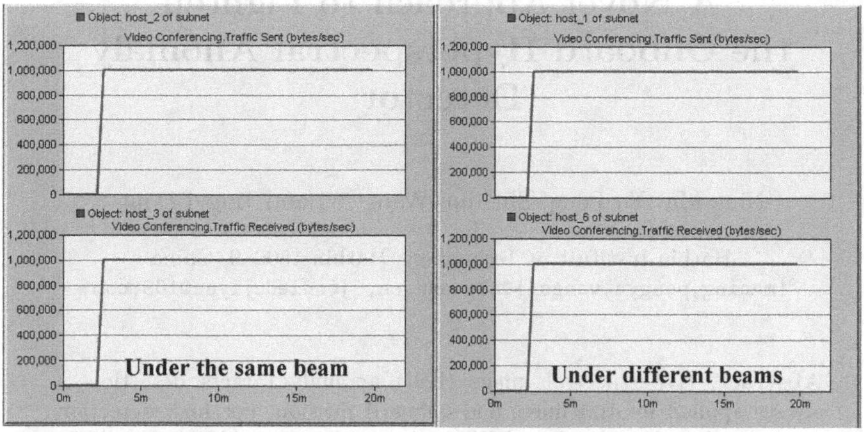

Fig. 7. Transmitting performance of earth terminals

6 Conclusion

A novel switching architecture suitable for satellite communication network application based on onboard IP switching is proposed. The traditional ground routing protocols will not converge and IP data packets will not be properly processed when applied in the onboard IP routers as downlink beam is broadcast in nature. The proposed architecture employs a hybrid switching strategy: layer-2 switching within same port and IP routing for different ports, combined with the optimization design such as proactive forwarding entries distribution in routing table and ARP table self-learning, to overcome the existing problems and enable routing convergence and data transmission. Simulation results show that the proposed architecture meets the requirements of onboard IP data packet switching.

References

1. Everett, M., Haines, J., Touch, J., et al.: TSAT network architecture. In: Military Communications Conference, MILCOM 2008. IEEE (2008)
2. Whitefield, D., Gopal, R., Arnold, S.: Spaceway now and in the future: on-board IP packet switching satellite communication network. In: Military Communications Conference, MILCOM 2006. IEEE (2006)
3. Florio, M., Fisher, S.J., Mittal, S., Yaghmour, S.: Internet routing in space: prospects and challenges of the IRIS JCTD. In: Military Communications Conference, MILCOM 2007. IEEE (2007)
4. Aweya, J.: IP router architectures: an overview. Int. J. Commun. Syst. **14**(5), 447–475 (2001)
5. Malkin, G.: RIP Version 2. IETF RFC 2453 (Standards Track) (1998)
6. Moy, J.: OSPF Version 2. IETF RFC 2328 (Standards Track) (1998)

A Novel Approach to Lighten the Onboard Hyperspectral Anomaly Detector

Ning Ma, Yu Peng, Shaojun Wang(✉), and Jingyi Dong

Harbin Institute of Technology, Harbin 150080, China
{maning,pengyu,wangsj}@hit.edu.cn, jennied_jiyue@163.com

Abstract. Hyperspectral image (HSI) anomaly targets detection is always applied for timeliness and onboard mission. For high detection accuracy, deep learning based HSI anomaly detectors (ADs) are widely employed in recent researches. However, their huge network scale for high-level representation ability leads to great computation burden for the onboard computation system. To decrease the computation complexity of the detector, a lightweight network is expected for the HSI AD. In this paper, by creating a multiobjective optimization with nondominated sorting genetic algorithm II (NSGA-II), an automatic evolution based deep learning network HSI AD (Auto-EDL-AD) is proposed to explore a lightweight network. The experimental results on an HSI dataset show that the proposed Auto-EDL-AD can generate an optimal network for the HSI anomaly detection which reaches up to 170% speedup without any detection accuracy loss.

Keywords: Hyperspectral image · Deep learning · Real-time processing · Multiobjective optimization

1 Introduction

As an important remote sensing technology, hyperspectral image (HSI) can reflect the material of the ground objects with spectral information from the hundreds of narrow contiguous bands and the spatial information. It is widely used in precision agriculture, environmental protection, military mission and city plan by classification, anomaly target detection (AD) and targets recognization. In those applications, anomaly detection is widely required to found the interest targets along with the image capture.

In general, an anomaly target is defined as an object or pixel which is different from its surrounding background. The anomaly targets present in a lower probability than the background, such as a fire point in a forest. To provide an early alarm for disaster monitor, the traditional processing procedure which contains image collection, data compression, downlink transmission, data decompression,

M. Jia et al. (Eds.): WiSATS 2019, LNICST 281, pp. 432–445, 2019.
https://doi.org/10.1007/978-3-030-19156-6_41

and targets detection is too long to fit the response requirement. A simple procedure that executed the detection onboard besides with the remote image collecting become a promising approach. However, the restriction on weight, power, size and the hash space environment seriously limit the onboard computing performance. Furthermore, the sharply increased spectral number and the spatial precision brings more burdens for the detector. Therefore, it is significant to lessen an onboard HSI AD for a real-world detection mission.

With the effort from the researchers all over the world, a various of HSI ADs have been proposed, such as the Reed-Xiaoli detector (RXD) [13], low probability detection [1] and random-selection-based anomaly detector (RSAD) [5], which is based on the whole HSI scene, namely global based detector. While to reduce the processing delay for a quick response, locally based detectors are studied which employ a small window slid on the HSI to detect the targets after the data collection, such as local based RXD (LRXD). For local based detector, the output delay is approximately equal to the time of capturing a certain number lines of pixels (depend on the height of the local window). To reduce such delay for real-time applications, a series of various RXD, such as progressive band processing of anomaly detection (PBP-AD) [2], real-time causal RXD (RT-CK-RXD) [3]. are proposed. By using a half window to replace the local window, the processing delay can be decreased to several milliseconds. However, those detectors have been based an assumption that the HSI background follows the Gaussian distribution while this assumption cannot be always right for real-world HSI and leads to false alarm.

To get a higher detection accuracy, the sparse representation theory based detectors are proposed, such as collaborative representation based anomaly detector (CRD) [8], sparse representation-based detector (SRD) [9]. In CRD, a dictionary is first set up by the pixels in a local window to represent the under test pixels which is in the central of the local window. A normal pixel can be represented with a sparse vector in a small residual, but an anomaly pixel cannot be. So, the anomaly pixel can be identified.

With the development of machine learning, especially the high-level representation ability of the deep learning, more deep learning based HSI ADs are proposed for high detection accuracy, such as stacked denoising autoencoder (SDAE) anomaly detection [16], Deep Belief Network (DBN) HSI AD [11], Weight based SAE HSI AD [12] and Transferred Deep Learning based HSI AD [10]. According to the fact that the anomaly targets are in low appearance probability, in the training stage, the anomaly pixels contribute less to optimize the parameters of the network than the background pixels. Therefore, during the detection, the residual of the anomaly pixel is greater than the residual of the background pixel. With the deep network structure and the abundant non-linear function of the neurons, the features can be learned well and a better detection accuracy can be reached. However, the large scale of the network leads to a huge computation which sets an enormous challenge for real-time onboard detection in a satellite.

To balance the conflicts between the detection accuracy and the computation amount, a minimum scale network which performs high detection accuracy is expected for the onboard HSI AD. In this paper, a multiobjective optimization is proposed to find the probable solution for the above problem with the nondominated sorting genetic algorithm II. For deep learning based online HSI AD, an automatic deep learning network constructing method (Auto-EDL-AD) is proposed to generate the hyperparameters and model structure by a nondominated sorting genetic algorithm II. With the proposed method, a small scale of deep learning model is built to accelerate the detection without accuracy loss for onboard HSI AD.

The remainder of the paper is arranged as follow. A common deep learning based HSI AD is introduced briefly in Sect. 2. In Sect. 3, the details of the proposed approach are stated. A real HSI data set is employed to validate the proposed approach in Sect. 4.

2 Deep Learning Based Online HSI AD

Recently, deep learning based methods have performed as a promising technology for hyperspectral image anomaly detection. A widely studied network for HSI AD is the multiplayer stacked auto-encoder which learns the high-level features of the HSI by its abundant non-linear functions. After the model training, the features of an HSI pixel can be extracted and represented by the middle layer (code layer) of the network. Due to the anomaly pixel performs less contribution to build the network, the residual of the anomaly pixel is higher than that of the background pixel. Such residual can be employed to mitigate the local contamination. By calculating the distance between the under test pixels and its surrounding pixels, the anomaly score can be figured out to determine the anomaly pixels. In general, a deep learning based HSI AD can be described as in Fig. 1.

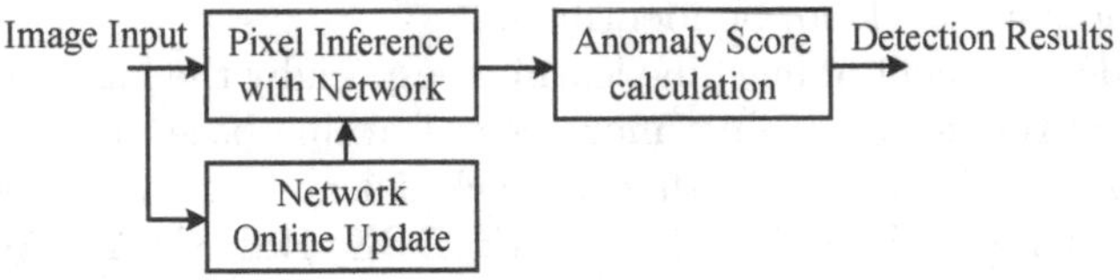

Fig. 1. The structure of a common deep learning based HSI AD

An autoencoder network is stacked by several layers as in Fig. 2 in a symmetrical structure. The layers are connected together by the connection weights. Through mapping the output as equal as possible with the input data during the training, the network can be learned the features of HSI in an unsupervised way.

As shown in Fig. 2, the layers are constructed by different number of neurons which deal the inputs with a non-linear activation function. In general, the sigmoid function, Rectified Linear Unit (ReLu) function or Leaky Relu function

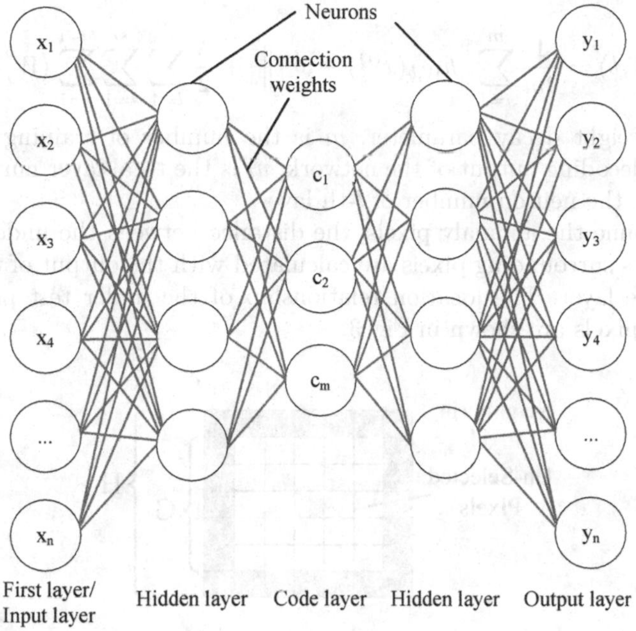

Fig. 2. The structure of a SAE network

are selected as the activation function. For onboard HSI AD mission, considering the computer resources limitation, the Leaky ReLu function is selected which is described as in formula 1. Its derivative is described as in formula 2.

$$f(z) = \begin{cases} z \quad when\ z > 0; \\ \alpha \cdot z \quad when\ z \leq 0; \end{cases} \tag{1}$$

$$f'(z) = \begin{cases} 1 \quad when\ z > 0; \\ \alpha \quad when\ z \leq 0; \end{cases} \tag{2}$$

where z is the input of each neuron. α is the leaky value.

For HSI AD application, the neurons number of the first layer and the output layer are equal to the spectral band number of the HSI. The output of neurons in the $(l+1)$-th layer is represented as $a^{(l+1)}$ or $h_{W,b}(x)$ in formulas 3a and 3b.

$$z^{(l+1)} = W^{(l)} a^{(l)} + b^{(l)} \tag{3a}$$

$$h_{W,b}(x) = a^{(l+1)} = f(z^{(l+1)}) \tag{3b}$$

where $W^{(l)}$ and $b^{(l)}$ denote the connection weight and the bias of the l-th layer respectively. Both of them are updated during the training.

To get the parameters W and b, a model training is executed by minimizing the loss function as formula 4 with gradient descent [7].

$$J(W,b) = \frac{1}{2m}\sum_{i=1}^{m}\left\|h_{W,b}(x^{(i)}) - y^{(i)}\right\|^2 + \frac{\lambda}{2}\sum_{l=1}^{n_{l-1}}\sum_{i=1}^{s_l}\sum_{j=1}^{s_{l+1}}(W_{ji}^{l})^2 \tag{4}$$

where λ is weight decay parameter, m is the number of training samples, y denotes the decoding output of the network, n_l is the total layer numbers of the network, s_l is the neuron number of l-th layer.

To determine the anomaly pixels, the distance between the under test pixel (PUT) and its surrounding pixels are calculated with the output of the neurons in the middle layer. The location relationship of the under test pixel and its surrounding pixels are shown in Fig. 3.

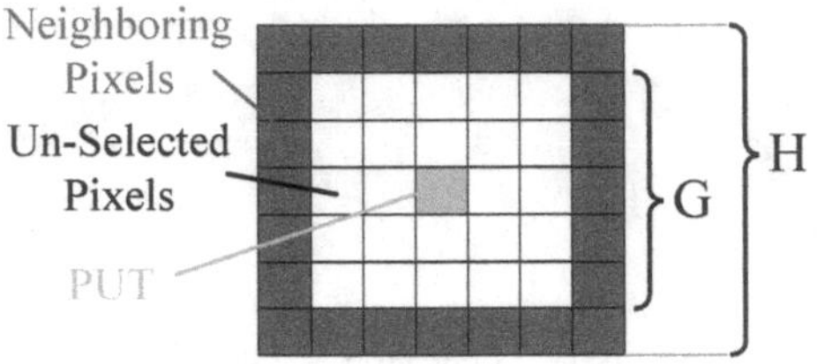

Fig. 3. The location relationship between PUT and surrounding pixels.

To reduce the anomaly pixels selected as background pixels in surrounding pixels, the Un-Selected pixels in Fig. 3 are employed. If some anomaly pixels located in outside as background pixels, it is called local anomaly contamination. The contamination may lead to a false alarm. To mitigate such contamination, the reconstruction errors from the network are employed as weights to adjust the contribution of each neighboring pixels in the anomaly score calculation as in formula 5. A PUT with a greater anomaly score means that it is more likely to be an anomaly targets.

$$\delta_d = 1/K\sum_{j=1}^{K}1/t_j(\sum_{i=1}^{D}|x_{ji} - y_i|^2)^{1/2}, \tag{5}$$

where K is the total number of local neighboring pixels, t is the weight of local pixel which is reciprocal of its reconstruction error and is described as formula 6.

$$t = \sum_{i=1}^{B}|x_i - \hat{x}_i|^2, \tag{6}$$

where B is spectral bands number of the input HSI. $\hat{x}$ is the output of the network.

For the onboard mission, the low delay response and high processing throughput contradict the limitation of onboard computing resources. To reduce such gap, a light-weight network which can keep the detection accuracy with fewer neurons in each layer should be designed by exploring the network design space.

3 The Proposed Light-Weight Network Exploring Approach

To build up a light-weight network for the onboard HSI AD mission, a deep learning network structure exploring approach is proposed. The computation amount and the detection accuracy are employed as two objects for optimization. Both of them are related to the factors including neurons number, local window size, leaky value α of the network in formula 1. However, the computation amount and the detection accuracy conflict with each other with a latent relation. It is a constrained multiobjective optimization problem. In fact, this is a multi-objective programming (MOP) problem which is an NP-hard problem. In this paper, a genetic algorithm based optimization approach named nondominated sorting genetic algorithm II (NSGA-II) [14] is employed to build up an automatic evolution deep learning based HSI AD (Auto-EDL-AD). The basic flow of the NSGA-II is shown in Fig. 4.

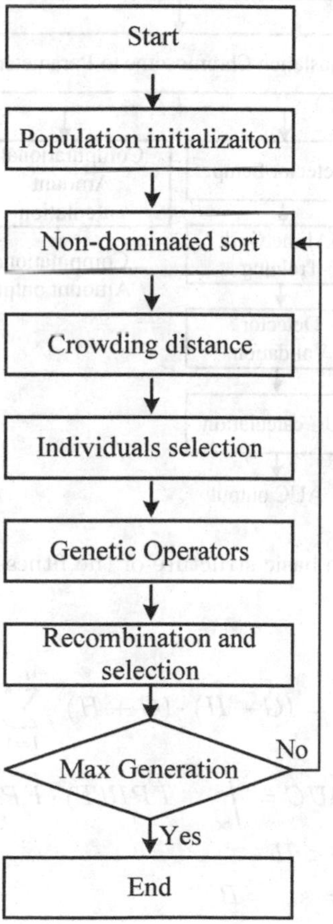

Fig. 4. The basic flow of the NSGA-II.

As shown in Fig. 4, the population is initialized within a specified range. The chromosome vector is generated which not only contains the basic genes but also contains the results of the fitness function and the crowding distance information.

The goal of the optimization is to maximize the detection accuracy and minimize the computation amount, the optimization model can be described as formula 7. Both of the objects are calculated depending on basic genes in the fitness function which is as shown in Fig. 5. Based on the effects for both of the objects, the neurons number, local window size, leaky value α of the network are employed as basic genes for the NSGA-II. The range of the basic genes are listed in Table 1. The objects are calculated as the formula 8 and the formula 11.

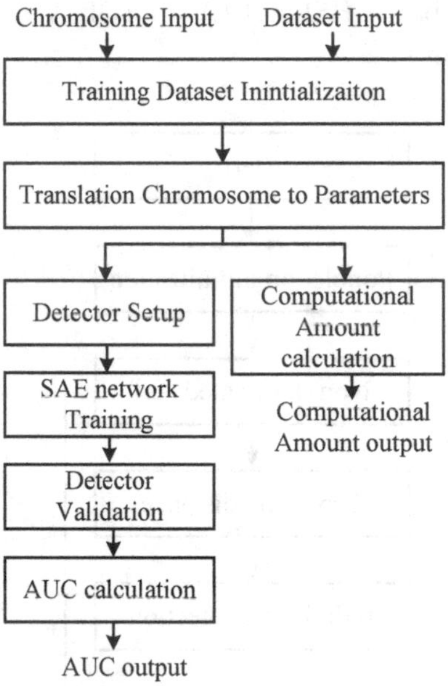

Fig. 5. The basic structure of the fitness function.

$$\begin{cases} min\ C = (G - H) \cdot (G + H) \cdot \sum_{l=1}^{n_{l-1}} s_l \cdot s_{l+1} \\ max\ AUC = \int_{\infty}^{-\infty} TPR(T) \cdot FPR(T) dT \\ s.t.\ \ G < H \\ \quad s_1 = s_{n_l} = B \\ \quad s_l > s_{l+1}, l < n_l/2 \\ \quad s_l < s_{l+1}, l > n_l/2 \end{cases} \tag{7}$$

where B is spectral bands number of the input HSI. H and G are the local window height and the guard window height of the local window. s_l is the neurons number of a layer. C is the computation amount as in formula 8. AUC is the area under the curve which is defined in formula 11.

The first object is to minimize the computation amount C which is approximatively quantized in terms of the number of multiply operations by the number of the neurons and the window size as formula 8.

$$C = (G - H) \cdot (G + H) \cdot \sum_{l=1}^{n_l - 1} s_l \cdot s_{l+1} \tag{8}$$

where H and G are the local window height and the guard window height of the local window respectively as shown in Fig. 3. From the previous researches [12], the n_l is set as 5. Due to the symmetrical structure of the autoencoder network, the neurons number of the first and the last layer are equal to the spectral band number B. Therefore, only the neuron number of the second (n_2) and the middle layer (n_m) are employed as the basic genes. The range of the n_2 and the n_m are specified as the Table 1.

Table 1. The range of the basic genes list.

Gene name	Leaky value α	n_2	n_m	H	G
Data type	Real	Integer	Integer	Integer	Integer
Maximum value	1	100	80	30	29
Minimum value	0.0001	20	1	8	6

The second object is to maximize the area under the curve (AUC) value which is used to indicate the detection accuracy. AUC is a common criterion to evaluate a detector in terms of accuracy. The curve is the receiver operating characteristic curve (ROC) which is created by drawing the true positive rate (TPR) against the false positive (FPR) when changing the threshold value for the anomaly score. TPR and FPR are defined as formulas 9 and 10 respectively. The anomaly score is the result of the detector which has been introduced in formula 5.

$$TPR = \frac{TP}{TP + FN} \tag{9}$$

where TP represents the true positive, which is the number of the correctly identified anomaly pixels. FN represents the false negative, which is the number of the incorrectly identified background pixels.

$$FPR = \frac{FP}{FP + TN} \tag{10}$$

where FP represents the false positive, which is the number of the incorrectly identified anomaly pixels. TN represents the true negative, which is the number of the correctly identified background pixels.

A greater AUC value means a high detection accuracy performance of a detector. The AUC value varies between 0 and 1. AUC is given by formula 11.

$$AUC = \int_{\infty}^{-\infty} TPR(T) \cdot FPR(T) dT \tag{11}$$

where T is the threshold value.

As shown in Fig. 4, after population initialization, a non-dominated sort and the crowding distance computing are executed for the chromosomes to gain its rank and the crowding distance to decide the position in the front. During the evolution process, the individuals with better fitness results are selected as a parent in the individual selection stage of the Fig. 4. To get the offspring chromosome, the crossover and mutation operator is performed in the genetic operator stage, the fitness results are calculated in this stage as well. The best solution depends on the rank and the crowding distance are selected for offspring generation. More details about NSGA-II can be found in Ref. [14].

After exploration, Pareto optimal solutions can be generated which contains a series of basic genes. Then, a balanced decision between computation amount and the detection accuracy can be made based on those solutions.

4 Experiments and Results

To evaluate the proposed Auto-EDL-AD, a real HSI dataset is employed in the experiment. The dataset is captured over the Sandiego airport by the Airborne Visible Infrared Imaging Spectrometer (AVIRIS). The wavelength is from 0.4 µm–2.4 µm. The color image of the dataset is shown in Fig. 6. A part of the image with the size of 100 × 100 as shown in Fig. 7(a) is employed for the experiment. 166 spectral bands are selected from the 224 bands after removing the water absorption and low signal-to-noise ration bands with the central frequency of 0.37 µm–0.38 µm, 0.90 µm–0.97 µm, 1.11 µm–1.16 µm, 1.33 µm–1.50 µm and 1.78 µm–1.98 µm [4,6,15]. 38 planes are regarded as the anomaly objects for the HSI AD. The ground truth which indicates the location of the anomalies is shown in Fig. 7(b).

The classic HSI anomaly detector Reed-Xiaoli detector(RXD) which always used as the baseline algorithm for the HSI anomaly detection research, a state-of-the-art HSI AD, collaborative representation HSI anomaly detector (CRD) [8] and an SAE based AD (SAE-AD) [12] are implemented for comparison. The ROC and the AUC are employed as the criteria to evaluate the accuracy which has been introduced in Sect. 3. The throughputs of the above detectors are given as well to illustrate the computational efficiency. All the detectors are run by Matlab 2017a on a Dell T7910 workstation which contains 2 Intel Xeon CPU with the type of E5-2630 at 2.4 GHz and 32 Gigabyte Double-Data-Rate Three Synchronous Dynamic Random Access Memory (DDR3 SDRAM).

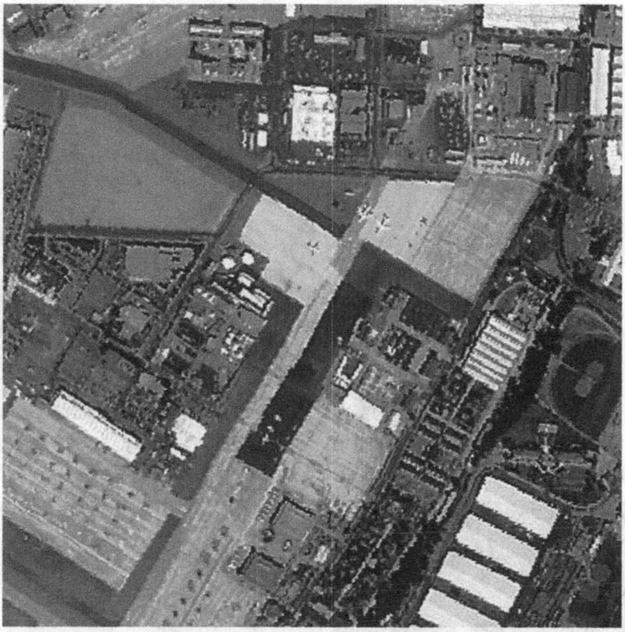

Fig. 6. The color image of the Sandiego airport HSI dataset.

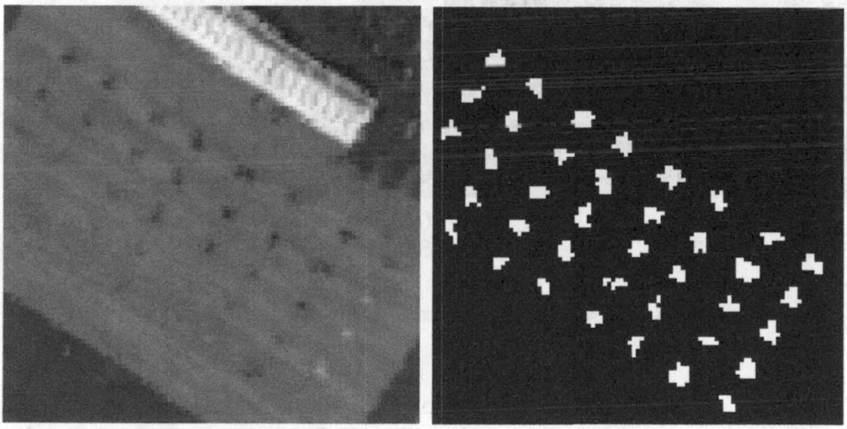

(a) The colour image and the anomaly targets of the Sandiego data set.

(b) The ground truth image of the Sandiego data set.

Fig. 7. The colour image and the ground truth image of Sandiego data set

The detection results from the proposed Auto-EDL-AD, RXD, CRD and SAE-AD are given in term of anomaly score in Fig. 8.

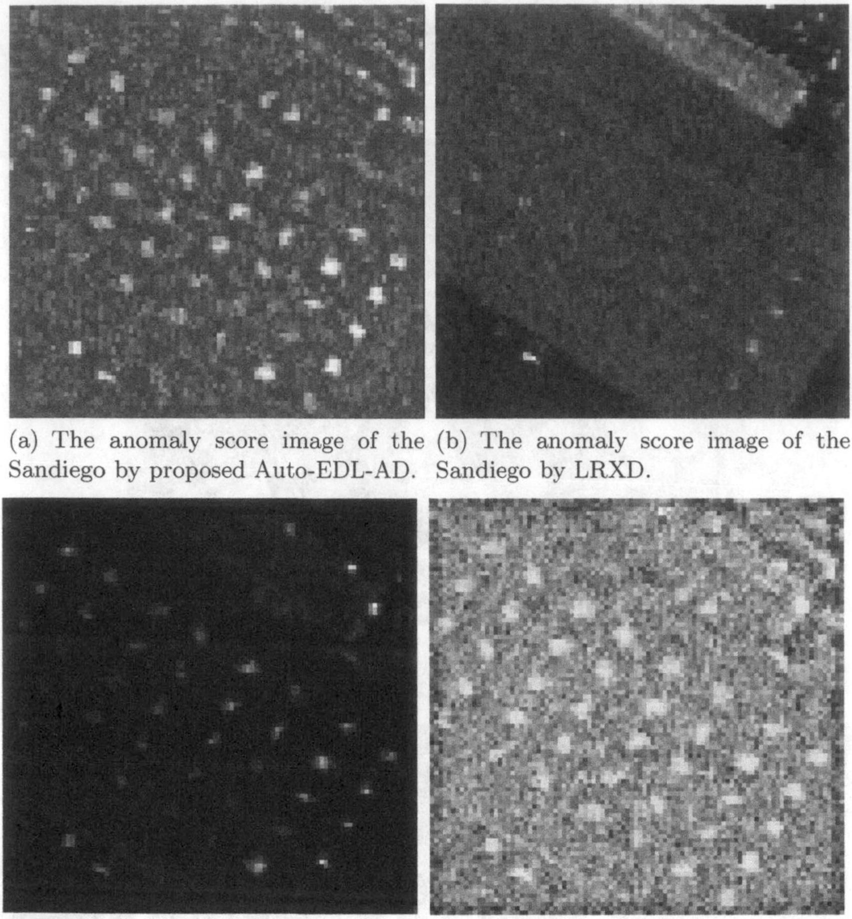

(a) The anomaly score image of the Sandiego by proposed Auto-EDL-AD. (b) The anomaly score image of the Sandiego by LRXD.

(c) The anomaly score image of the Sandiego by CRD. (d) The anomaly score image of the Sandiego by SAE-AD.

Fig. 8. The detection results for the Sandiego dataset.

The ROC curve of those detectors for the Auto-EDL-AD, RXD, CRD, and SAE-AD are given in Fig. 9. The AUC value and the processing time are listed in Table 2.

The anomaly score is converted to gray image in Fig. 8. The whiter pixel has a higher probability to be an anomaly pixel than the background pixel. From the Fig. 8(a), the proposed Auto-EDL-AD can indicate most of the anomaly objects clearly. From detection results by LRXD in Fig. 8(b), the anomaly targets show almost the same brightness with the background for the Sandiego dataset. In the results by CRD as shown in Fig. 8(c), the background are suppressed at a low level, while some of the anomaly pixels are suppressed to be the same level with background pixel. Figure 8(d) shows that the result difference between

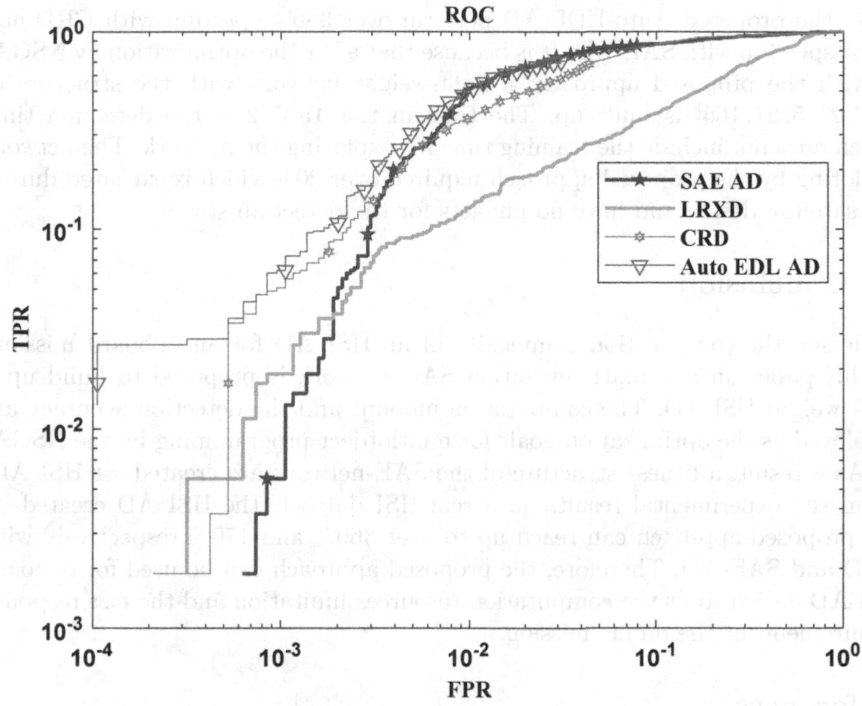

Fig. 9. The ROC curve for sandiego dataset.

anomaly pixels and the background pixels is not very great and more false alarm is generated.

From the definition of the ROC, a detector whose curve is located higher than others performs better. In Fig. 9, the ROCs are drawn for proposed Auto-EDL-AD, SAE-AD, LRXD and the CRD. The proposed Auto-EDL-AD outperforms other detectors in low FPR (FPR ≤ 0.01). When FPR ≤ 0.01, The ROC curve of the proposed Auto-EDL-AD overlap the ROC curve of CRD.

Table 2. The AUC value and the time consumption.

Detector name	Auto-EDL-AD	LRXD	CRD	SAE-AD
AUC value	0.922	0.776	0.917	0.914
Detection time (s)	9.41	80.01	34.38	16.23

From the Table 2, the AUC value of the proposed Auto-EDL-AD is almost the same with the state-of-the-art CRD and the SAE-AD. Due to comparison detectors are run with the same platform, less computation time means low computational complexity for a detector. From the Table 2, in term of the process time, the proposed Auto-EDL-AD perform over 360% speedup with CRD and 172% speedup with SAE-AD. It is because that after the optimization by NSGA-II with the proposed approach, a light-weight network with the structure of [166, 21, 5, 21, 166] is built up. The time in the Table 2 is the detection time which does not include the training time for exploring the network. The network exploring by the proposed approach required over 20 h which is executed during the satellite design and have no impacts for the detection stage.

5 Conclusion

To lessen the computation complexity of an HSI AD for an onboard mission, in this paper an automatic evolution SAE network is proposed to build up a light-weight HSI AD. The computation amount and the detection accuracy are employed as the optimization goals for multiobject programming by the NSGA-II. As a result, a fitness structure of the SAE-network are created for HSI AD. From the experimental results on a real HSI dataset, the HSI AD created by the proposed approach can reach up to over 360% and 170% respectively with CRD and SAE-AD. Therefore, the proposed approach can be used for onboard HSI AD design to fit the computation resources limitation and the fast response requirement for the online mission.

References

1. Chang, C.I., Chiang, S.S.: Anomaly detection and classification for hyperspectral imagery. IEEE Trans. Geosci. Remote Sens. **40**(6), 1314–1325 (2002). https://doi.org/10.1109/tgrs.2002.800280
2. Chang, C.-I., Li, Y., Hobbs, M.C., Schultz, R.C., Liu, W.-M.: Progressive band processing of anomaly detection in hyperspectral imagery. IEEE J. Sel. Top. Appl. Earth Obs. Remote Sens. **8**(7), 3558–3571 (2015). https://doi.org/10.1109/jstars.2015.2415782
3. Chen, S.-Y., Wang, Y., Wu, C.-C., Liu, C., Chang, C.-I.: Real-time causal processing of anomaly detection for hyperspectral imagery. IEEE Trans. Aerosp. Electron. Syst. **50**(2), 1510–1533 (2014). https://doi.org/10.1109/taes.2014.130065
4. Curran, P.J., Dungan, J.L.: Estimation of signal-to-noise: a new procedure applied to AVIRIS data. IEEE Trans. Geosci. Remote Sens. **27**(5), 620–628 (1989). https://doi.org/10.1109/tgrs.1989.35945
5. Du, B., Zhang, L.: Random-selection-based anomaly detector for hyperspectral imagery. IEEE Trans. Geosci. Remote Sens. **49**(5), 1578–1589 (2011). https://doi.org/10.1109/TGRS.2010.2081677
6. Gao, B.C., Heidebrecht, K.B., Goetz, A.F.H.: Derivation of scaled surface reflectances from AVIRIS data. Remote Sensi. Environ. **44**(2–3), 165–178 (1993). https://doi.org/10.1016/0034-4257(93)90014-o
7. Hinton, G., Osindero, S., Teh, Y.: A fast learning algorithm for deep belief nets. Neural Comput. **7**(18), 1527–1554 (2006). https://doi.org/10.1162/neco.2006.18.7.1527
8. Li, W., Du, Q.: Collaborative representation for hyperspectral anomaly detection. IEEE Trans. Geosci. Remote Sens. **53**(3), 1463–1474 (2015A). https://doi.org/10.1109/tgrs.2014.2343955

9. Li, J., Zhang, H., Zhang, L., Ma, L.: Hyperspectral anomaly detection by the use of background joint sparse representation. IEEE J. Sel. Top. Appl. Earth Obs. Remote Sens. **8**(6), 2523–2533 (2015). https://doi.org/10.1109/jstars.2015.2437073
10. Li, W., Wu, G., Du, Q.: Transferred deep learning for anomaly detection in hyperspectral imagery. IEEE Geosci. Remote Sens. Lett. **5**(14), 597–601 (2017). https://doi.org/10.1109/LGRS.2017.2657818
11. Ma, N., Wang, S., Yu, J., Peng, Y.: A DBN based anomaly targets detector for HSI. In: Asundi, A.K., Zhao, H., Osten, W. (eds.) AOPC 2017: 3D Measurement Technology for Intelligent Manufacturing, vol. 10458, pp. 1–6 (2017). https://doi.org/10.1117/12.2285766
12. Ma, N., Peng, Y., Wang, S., Gao, W.: A weight SAE based hyperspectral image anomaly targets detection. In: Proceedings of the International Conference on Electronic Measurement & Instruments (ICEMI), Yangzhou, China, October 2017, pp. 511–515. IEEE (2017). https://doi.org/10.1109/ICEMI.2017.8265874
13. Reed, I.S., Yu, X.L.: Adaptive multiple-band CFAR detection of an optical pattern with unknown spectral distribution. IEEE Trans. Acoust. Speech Sig. Process. **38**(10), 1760–1770 (1990). https://doi.org/10.1109/29.60107
14. Ramesh, S., Kannan, S., Baskar, S.: Application of a fast and elitist multi-objective genetic algorithm to reactive power dispatch. Serb. J. Electr. Eng. **6**(6), 119–133 (2009). https://doi.org/10.1109/4235.996017
15. Rodger, A., Lynch, J.M.: Determining atmospheric column water vapour in the 0.4–2.5 μm spectral region. In: Proceedings of the AVIRIS Workshop Pasadena, California, USA, 27 February–02 March 2001. Jet Propulsion Laboratory (JPL) publication (2001)
16. Zhao, C., Li, X., Zhu, H.: Hyperspectral anomaly detection based on stacked denoising autoencoders. J. Appl. Remote Sens. **11**, 1–19 (2017). https://doi.org/10.1117/1.jrs.11.042605

Detection Probability Analysis of Spectrum Sensing over Satellite Fading Channel

Xiaogu Huang[1,2], Xiaojin Ding[3,4], Haoyu Li[1,2], Yunfeng Wang[1,2], and Gengxin Zhang[1,2](✉)

[1] Key Laboratory of Broadband Wireless Communication and Sensor Network Technology, Nanjing University of Posts and Telecommunications, Nanjing 210003, China
zgx@njupt.edu.cn

[2] "Telecommunication and Network" National Engineering Research Center, Nanjing University of Posts and Telecommunications, Nanjing 210003, China

[3] Jiangsu Engineering Research Center of Communication and Network Technology, Nanjing University of Posts and Telecommunications, Nanjing 210003, China

[4] National Mobile Communications Research Laboratory, Southeast University, Nanjing 210096, China

Abstract. In this paper, we investigate spectrum sensing relying on multiple satellites, which can achieve global seamless spectrum sensing, due to the feature of wide coverage. We conceive a pair of satellite based spectrum sensing schemes, namely hard combination oriented energy detection based spectrum sensing (HC-EDSS) and semisoft-combination double-threshold oriented energy detection based spectrum sensing (SD-EDSS). In the HC-EDSS scheme, secondary users send their decision results to fusion center in order to get the final decision. By contrast, secondary users not only send their decision results, but also send some individual information to fusion center in the SD-EDSS scheme. We also derive the closed-form of the probability of detection over satellite fading channel. In our performance evaluations, the conceived HC-EDSS and SD-EDSS schemes outperform the conventional single user oriented energy detection based spectrum sensing (SU-EDSS) in terms of its probability of detection. Moreover, the SD-EDSS scheme achieves the best probability of detection among them, demonstrating the advantage of increasing the accuracy of spectrum sensing.

Keywords: Spectrum sensing · Satellite communication · Energy detection

1 Introduction

Satellite communications [1] is an outgrowth of modern technology to meet the demand of greater capacity and higher communication quality. It is suited to network which has wide coverage because it can overcome the problem of long distances and desolate terrains (desert, ocean, forest, etc.) [2]. For the remote and sparsely populated locations, satellites can actually provide communication access, which may be the cheapest solution in these cases [3]. However, As continuously increasing demand for

M. Jia et al. (Eds.): WiSATS 2019, LNICST 281, pp. 446–454, 2019.
https://doi.org/10.1007/978-3-030-19156-6_42

broadcast, multimedia and interactive services, the usable satellite spectrum is becoming scarce [4, 5]. Although the spectrum resources is so scarce, many of the licensed spectrum resources are still underutilized, which causes the waste of spectrum resources [6]. It is extremely urgent to improve the spectrum utilization in satellite communications.

In order to raise the spectrum utilization, many wireless communication theories and related technologies have been proposed, such as multi-antenna technology, adaptive technology, etc. Although these technologies have improved the spectrum efficiency to a certain extent, they are far from satisfying the growing demand for spectrum resources. Cognitive radio [7] technology can effectively solve the problem of low spectrum efficiency caused by fixed allocation strategy in satellite communication system. Spectrum sensing is part of cognitive radio, which consists of multi-node cooperative spectrum sensing and single-node spectrum sensing [8]. The aim of spectrum sensing is mainly to detect whether the primary user (PU) occupies a channel to prevent interference with the PU's communication [9]. There are many detection methods in spectrum sensing. Energy detection [10], which is simple and has the characteristics of not requiring priori information about the transmitted signal, is the most widely used spectrum sensing technology.

Although signal often transmits over fading channel in real life, most of existed works are based on non-fading channel [11]. In [12], the author analyses the performance of spectrum sensing system in Rician fading channel and Nakagami channel. In [13], a semisoft combination scheme based on local double-threshold decision has been proposed to improve the probability of detection. In [14], a novel spectrum sensing system is proposed to perform wideband spectrum sensing over fading channel. In [15], author proposed a simple land mobile satellite channel model for the convenience of calculation.

In this paper, the satellite channel is regarded as the Shadowed-Rician fading channel. Theoretical probability of detection under this channel is derived and compared with the simulated value. In addition, cooperative spectrum sensing is introduced in order to improve the probability of detection under Shadowed-Rician fading channel. The satellite performs as secondary user (SU) and sends the decision result to the information fusion center (FC). FC fuses all received information for global decision. In this paper, the SD-EDSS method is applied, which is also compared with some classic cooperative strategy.

The rest of this paper is organized as follows. In Sect. 2, energy detection has been reviewed. In Sect. 3, The system model for Shadowed-Rician fading channel is presented. The simulation results are shown in Sect. 4. Finally, The conclusions are given in Sect. 5.

2 System Model

As we can see in Fig. 1, there are N satellite as SUs in the system model. SUs detect the signal from PU and then send their decision results to FC. FC fuses all the local decision results and makes decision about whether the signal exists.

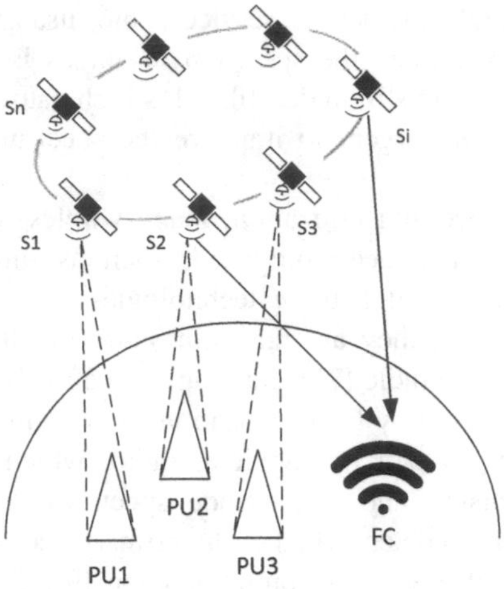

Fig. 1. System model

The aim of spectrum sensing is to determine whether a licensed band is used by the PU or not. The problem can be formulated as [12].

$$x(t) = \begin{cases} n(t) & H_0 \\ hs(t) + n(t) & H_1 \end{cases}, \tag{1}$$

where *n(t)* is the additional white Gaussian noise (AWGN), *s(t)* represents the signal from PU, *h* is the channel gain. Both H_1 and H_0 are the two states of signal, presence or absence.

In local detection, energy detection is used. The essence of energy detection is the accumulation of received signal power on spectrum band, and the accumulated energy is compared with the predefined threshold. The principle of energy detection is shown in Fig. 2.

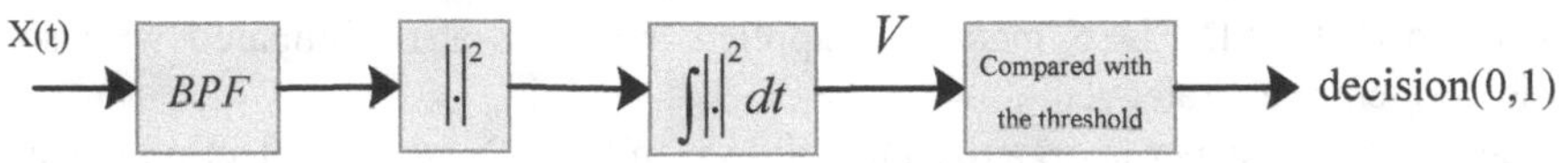

Fig. 2. The principle of energy detection

The energy received by SU can be expressed as $Y = \sum_{i=1}^{2u} x^2(i)$ and Y obeys the chi-square distribution as

$$Y \sim \begin{cases} x_{2u}^2 & H_0 \\ x_{2u}^2(2\gamma) & H_1 \end{cases}, \tag{2}$$

where γ is signal-to-noise (SNR). The probability distribution function (PDF) of Y is given by

$$f_Y(y) = \begin{cases} \frac{1}{2^u\Gamma(u)} y^{u-1} e^{-\frac{y}{2}} & H_0 \\ \frac{1}{2}\left(\frac{y}{2\gamma}\right)^{\frac{u-1}{2}} e^{-\frac{2\gamma+y}{2}} I_{u-1}(\sqrt{2\gamma y}) & H_1 \end{cases}, \quad (3)$$

where $\Gamma(u)$ is the gamma function, $I_{u-1}(x)$ represents the modified Bessel function of order *u* − *1*.

3 Performance Analysis of the Probability of Detection

3.1 Analysis of the Probability of Detection over AWGN Channel

In this subsection, we analyze the probability of detection of single user oriented energy detection based spectrum sensing (SU-EDSS) over AWGN channel for comparison purpose. If energy detection is applied in a non-fading environment, the probability of detection (P_d) and probability of false alarm (P_f) for energy detection can be obtained as follows [16]

$$\begin{aligned} P_d &= \Pr(Y > \lambda \mid H_1) = Q_u(\sqrt{2\gamma}, \sqrt{\lambda}) \\ P_f &= \Pr(Y > \lambda \mid H_0) = \frac{\Gamma(u, \frac{\lambda}{2})}{\Gamma(u)}, \end{aligned} \quad (4)$$

where λ is detection threshold, $Q_u(a, b)$ represents the Marcum-Q function, and $\Gamma(u, \frac{\lambda}{2})$ refers to incomplete gamma function.

3.2 Analysis of the Probability of Detection over Satellite Fading Channel

SU-EDSS: As aforementioned, The content above is based on the AWGN channel. When the signal transmits through satellite channel, instantaneous channel gain h in the model is varying due to the fading/shadowing of the channel. P_d for fading channel can be obtained by averaging over fading statistics [17],

$$\overline{P_d} = \int_{\gamma} P_d f(\gamma) d\gamma = \int_{\gamma} Q_u(\sqrt{2\gamma}, \sqrt{\lambda}) f(\gamma) d\gamma, \quad (5)$$

where $f(\gamma)$ is the probability distribution function (PDF) of SNR under fading/shadowing. However, the P_f under the fading channel is still the same as that under the AWGN channel due to P_f is independent of signal-to-noise ratio (SNR).

In this paper, satellite channel can be seen as Shadowed-Rician fading channel, thus, based on [15], the PDF of $|h|^2$ can be given by

$$f_{|h|^2}(x) = \alpha_0 e^{-\beta_0 x} {}_1F_1(m_0; 1; \delta_0 x), \quad x \geq 0 \tag{6}$$

where $\alpha_0 = \frac{1}{2b_0}\left(\frac{2b_0 m}{2b_0 m+\Omega}\right)^m$, $\beta_0 = \frac{1}{2b_0}$, $\delta_0 = \frac{\Omega}{2b_0(2b_0 m+\Omega)}$, the parameter Ω represents the average power of the LOS component, $2b_0$ is the average power of the scatter component, and m is the Nakagami parameter ranging from 0 to ∞. For $m = 0$, the envelope of h obeys the Rayleigh distribution, which is associated to urban region with complete obstruction of the LOS. While for $m = \infty$, it follows the Rician distribution, which is associated to open region with no obstruction of the LOS.

According to Eq. 5, given γ is the SNR and $\gamma_s = |h|^2\gamma$, the PDF of γ_s can be shown as

$$f_{\gamma_s}(x) = \frac{1}{\gamma} \times f_{|h|^2}\left(\frac{x}{\gamma}\right) = \frac{\alpha_0}{\gamma} e^{-\frac{\beta_0}{\gamma}x} {}_1F_1(m_0; 1; \frac{\delta_0 x}{\gamma}), \quad x \geq 0 \tag{7}$$

where ${}_1F_1(m_0; 1; \delta_0 x)$ is the general hypergeometric function.

The closed-form formula for P_d under Shadowed-Rician fading channel may be obtained (after some manipulation) by substituting $f_{\gamma_s}(x)$ into Eq. 5.

$$\begin{aligned} P_d = C_1 \sum_{n=0}^{\infty} C_2 \Big\{ & \Gamma(n+1)(2b_0\gamma)^{n+1} \\ & - e^{-\frac{\lambda}{2}} \sum_{j=u}^{\infty} \left[\frac{\lambda^j \Gamma(n+1) 2^{n+1-j} (b_0\gamma)^{n+1-j}}{(2b_0\gamma+1)^{n+1}\Gamma(j+1)} \times {}_1F_1\left(n+1; j+1; \frac{2\lambda b_0\gamma}{4b_0\gamma+2}\right) \right] \Big\}, \end{aligned} \tag{8}$$

where $C_1 = \frac{1}{2\gamma b_0}\left(\frac{2b_0 m}{2b_0 m+\Omega}\right)^m$, $C_2 = \frac{(m)_n \Omega^n}{(1)_n n!(2\gamma b_0)^n (2b_0 m+\Omega)^n}$, and $(m)_n = \frac{\Gamma(m+n)}{\Gamma(m)}$ is an incremental factorial whose length is n.

HC-EDSS: To improve P_d, cooperative spectrum sensing is introduced. 'K-out-of-N' rule [18] is used in this paper, which adds all the decision results from SUs and compares the obtained value with a predefined threshold K. Assuming there are N spectrum detection nodes detecting the states of the channel, the decision result is as follow.

$$\begin{cases} H_1: & \sum_{i=1}^{N} D_i \geq K \\ H_0: & \sum_{i=1}^{N} D_i < K \end{cases}. \tag{9}$$

The cooperative detection performance metrics (Q_d and Q_f) for '*K-out-of-N*' rule are derived as follows

$$Q_d = \sum_{i=k}^{N} \binom{N}{i} \prod_{j=1}^{i} P_{d,j} \prod_{v=1}^{N-i} (1 - P_{d,v})$$
$$Q_f = \sum_{i=k}^{N} \binom{N}{i} \prod_{j=1}^{i} P_{f,j} \prod_{v=1}^{N-i} (1 - P_{f,v}). \tag{10}$$

SD-EDSS: With the aid of double threshold [19], the result of local energy detection transmitted to FC can be shown as

$$\begin{cases} send\,0, & if\, Y \leq \lambda_1 \\ send\, \frac{Y-\lambda_1}{\lambda_2-\lambda_1}, & if\, \lambda_1 < Y < \lambda_2\,, \\ send\,1, & if\, Y \geq \lambda_2 \end{cases} \tag{11}$$

where Y is the energy received by each SU.

In FC, weighting factor of each SU is given according to the reliability of its local decision results. In this way, SU not only reports the local decision result through the report channel, but also reports its theoretical P_d at its received SNR. The weighting factor can be shown as the ratio between the P_d and the average P_d, The expression is $W_i = \frac{P_{d,i}}{\overline{P_d}}$, where $\overline{P_d} = \frac{1}{N}\sum_{i=1}^{N} P_{d,i}$. FC uses the calculated weighting factors to weight-add all the local decision results as global result, which will then be compared to predefined threshold.

4 Simulation Results

In this section, performance evaluations are demonstrated through simulations. The QPSK signal is assumed to be the PU signal, and the satellites are assumed to be the SUs. SUs can accomplish the detection of the wireless spectrum resource to determine the occupancy of the PUs. A cognitive radio network which has one PU and four SUs is considered. The comparison between the theoretical and simulated values under the Shadowed-Rician fading channel are analyzed. In our numerical results, the fading channel parameters are seen as the average shadowing $(b, m, \Omega) = (0.126, 10.1, 0.835)$. The threshold at the central node $K = \frac{N}{2} = 2$.

Figure 3 shows the comparison of the theoretical P_d and simulated P_d under the Shadowed-Rician fading channel. It can be concluded from this picture that the expression derived in this paper is basically consistent with the simulation values, which can prove the correctness of the formula derivation. Furthermore, the performance of the spectrum detection is improved with the increase in SNR.

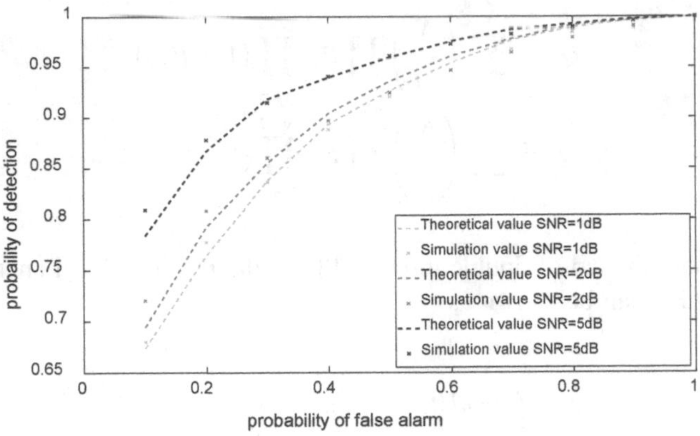

Fig. 3. P_d vs. P_f plot of comparison between the theoretical P_d and simulated P_d

Figure 4 demonstrates P_d of SU-EDSS, HC-EDSS and SD-EDSS, while P_f is predefined as 0.1. It is seen that SD-EDSS has better performance than other two methods, which illustrate using SD-EDSS could significantly improve the performance of P_d under the Shadowed-Rician fading channels as more information is available to FC in SD-EDSS.

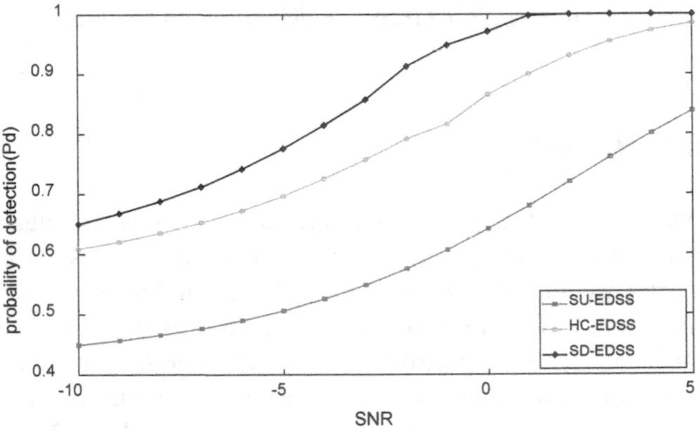

Fig. 4. P_d vs. P_f plot of comparison among the SU-EDSS, HC-EDSS and SD-EDSS

5 Conclusion

In this paper, we conceived spectrum sensing schemes for a cognitive radio network consisting of multiple satellites. We explored satellite based cooperative spectrum sensing, called HC-EDSS and SD-EDSS, respectively. We also derived the performance of spectrum sensing over satellite fading channel. It was shown that the probability of detection of the SD-EDSS is better than that of SU-EDSS and HC-EDSS schemes, demonstrating that cooperative spectrum sensing can dramatically improve the probability of detection.

Acknowledgement. The work presented in this paper is partially supported by the National Science Foundation of China (No. 91738201), the National Key Research and Development Program of China under grant 2016YFE0200200, the open research fund of National Mobile Communications Research Laboratory, Southeast University (No. 2018D16), the Natural Science Research of Higher Education Institutions of Jiangsu Province (No. 18KJB510030), and the Open Research Fund of Jiangsu Engineering Research Center of Communication and Network Technology, NJUPT.

References

1. Sodnik, Z., Furch, B., Lutz, H.: Optical intersatellite communication. IEEE J. Sel. Top. Quantum Electron. **16**(5), 1051–1057 (2010)
2. Qu, Z., Zhang, G., Xie, J.: LEO satellite constellation for Internet of Things. IEEE Access **85**, 18391–18401 (2017)
3. Lagunas, E., Sharma, S.K., Maleki, S., et al.: Resource allocation for cognitive satellite communications with incumbent terrestrial networks. IEEE Trans. Cogn. Commun. Netw. **1** (3), 305–317 (2017)
4. Murroni, M., Popescu, V., Fadda, M., et al.: Robust multi-rate modulation for cognitive radio communications over land mobile satellite channel at Ku-band. Int. J. Satell. Commun. Netw. **35**, 503–515 (2016)
5. Su, J., Yang, S., Xu, H., et al.: A stackelberg differential game based bandwidth allocation in satellite communication network. China Commun. **15**(8), 205–214 (2018)
6. Tsiropoulos, G.I., Dobre, O.A., Ahmed, M.H., et al.: Radio resource allocation techniques for efficient spectrum access in cognitive radio networks. IEEE Commun. Surv. Tutorials **18** (1), 824–847 (2016)
7. Mitola, J.I., Maguire, G.Q.J.: Cognitive radio: making software radios more personal. IEEE Pers. Commun. **6**(4), 13–18 (1999)
8. Wang, X., Jia, M., Guo, Q., et al.: Reputation-based cooperative spectrum sensing algorithm for mobile cognitive radio networks. China Commun. **14**(1), 124–134 (2017)
9. Yucek, T., Arslan, H.: A survey of spectrum sensing algorithms for cognitive radio applications. IEEE Commun. Surv. Tutorials **11**(1), 116–130 (2009)
10. Salt, J.E., Nguyen, H.H.: Performance prediction for energy detection of unknown signals. IEEE Trans. Veh. Technol. **57**(6), 3900–3904 (2008)
11. Raymo, F.M.: Digital processing and communication with molecular switches. Adv. Mater. **14**(6), 401–414 (2010)
12. Digham, F.F., Alouini, M.S., Simon, M.K.: On the energy detection of unknown signals over fading channels. IEEE Trans. Commun. **55**(1), 21–24 (2007)
13. Zhang, X., Li, Y., Zhang, Z.: Cooperation spectrum sensing algorithm based on improved majority rule. J. Comput. Inf. Syst. **8**(18), 7457–7464 (2012)
14. Sun, H., Nallanathan, A., Cui, S., et al.: Cooperative wideband spectrum sensing over fading channels. IEEE Trans. Veh. Technol. **65**(3), 1382–1394 (2016)
15. Abdi, A., Lau, W.C., Alouini, M.S., et al.: A new simple model for land mobile satellite channels: first- and second-order statistics. IEEE Trans. Wirel. Commun. **2**(3), 519–528 (2003)

16. Digham, F.F., Alouini, M.S., Simon, M.K.: On the energy detection of unknown signals over fading channels. In: IEEE International Conference on Communications, vol. **5**, pp. 3575–3579 (2003)
17. Peh, E.C.Y., Liang, Y.C., Guan, Y.L.: Optimization of cooperative sensing in cognitive radio networks: a sensing-throughput tradeoff view. IEEE Trans. Veh. Technol. **58**(9), 5294–5299 (2009)
18. Huang, X., Han, T., Ansari, N.: On green-energy-powered cognitive radio networks. IEEE Commun. Surv. Tutorials **17**(2), 827–842 (2018)
19. Verma, P., Singh, B.: Throughput maximization by alternative use of single and double thresholds based energy detection method. Optik-Int. J. Light Electron Opt. **127**(4), 1635–1638 (2016)

Link Assignment and Information Transmission Route Planning for BDS Inter-satellite Link Network

Hongbo Zhao[1(✉)], Shurui Zhou[1], Yue Jia[2], Bo Pang[3], and Wenquan Feng[1]

[1] School of Electronic and Information Engineering, Beihang University, Xueyuan Road No. 37, Haidian District, Beijing 100191, China
bhzhb@buaa.edu.cn

[2] School of Aeronautics and Astronautics, Sichuan University, 1st Ring Road, Jinjiang District, Chengdu 610065, China

[3] China Academy of Space Technology, Youyi Road No. 102, Haidian District, Beijing 100094, China

Abstract. Satellites of the third generation BeiDou Navigation Satellite System (BDS) will be equipped with Ka-band antennas and communicate through point-to-point Inter-Satellite Links (ISLs). Link assignment and routing algorithms of other Global Navigation Satellite Systems (GNSSs) are not suitable for BDS ISL due to its unique communication system. This article mainly focuses on inter-satellite link assignment and routing problem in BDS ISL network which is a new challenge and has no mature algorithm proposed specially for it before. Firstly, time slot matrix assigning algorithm is put forward to solve link assignment problem based on characteristic of BDS ISL. Performance of this algorithm is simulated and ISL network topology designed by this algorithm is proved to be good in aspects of average number of links, average position dilution of precision (PDOP) and other important indicators. Secondly, on the basis of determined network topology, this paper provides a heuristic route planning strategy for information transmission in BDS ISL network. Path Combinational Optimization algorithm based on Simulated Annealing (PCO-SA) is proposed and elaborated in this paper. By combining PCO-SA and adjusted Contact Graph Routing (CGR) algorithm, a common solution for routing problem of navigation related data can be achieved. Simulation results compared with other route planning methods show that PCO-SA can not only significantly increase success ratio of route planning, but also optimize average time delay and hop of planned path.

Keywords: BDS · Inter-satellite link · Link assignment · Route planning · Simulated annealing

M. Jia et al. (Eds.): WiSATS 2019, LNICST 281, pp. 455–478, 2019.
https://doi.org/10.1007/978-3-030-19156-6_43

1 Introduction

BeiDou Navigation Satellite System is a global satellite navigation system independently constructed by China. It aims to provide high accurate positioning, navigation and timing services. In accordance with the construction plan, satellite constellation of the third generation BDS will be composed with three Geostationary Earth Orbit (GEO) satellites, three Inclined Geosynchronous Satellite Orbit (IGSO) satellites and 24 Medium Earth Orbit (MEO) satellites [1] (In the rest of this article, BDS refers to the third generation BDS if not specifically declared). It is impossible for domestic monitoring stations in China to track and communicate with all satellites all day long. Therefore, inter satellite links (i.e., wireless links for communication and ranging between satellites) can be used to improve the service performance of the navigation satellite system [2].

ISLs were first implemented in the GPS Block IIR satellites [3]. GPS ISLs work in the ultrahigh frequency band. Every satellite transmits a ranging signal in its own scheduled slot, and all its visible navigation satellites can receive the signal. With the technique development, the wide beam ISL system will be gradually upgraded to narrow beam with time division to reach better pointing flexibility and higher communication efficiency [4, 5]. The GPS will upgrade its ISL to the Ka or V band in the next stage to enhance the ISL performance [6]. Exploratory studies carried for other GNSSs such as GLONASS and Galileo also demonstrate the narrow beam ISL system [7, 8]. In a word, other GNSSs are planning on developing narrow-beam ISL systems, but there is no mature implementation until now.

As for BDS, Ka-band phased-array antennas will be equipped on satellites of the third generation BDS to achieve precise orbit determination and autonomous navigation [9]. Satellites communicate with each other for inter-satellite ranging and data transmission via Ka-band point beam inter-satellite links. In this communication system, one satellite can only communicate with one other satellite through bidirectional ISL simultaneously. To achieve higher ranging accuracy, satellites are demanded to connect with other satellites within short time period. In addition, satellites create telemetry data constantly in its life cycle and receive commands from ground facilities intermittently. Data are downlinked and uplinked between space segment and ground segment. These demands bring two problems. The first one is link assignment problem, that is, how to arrange the ISL antennas to build link with other satellites ensuring both ranging observations' quantity and information transmission quality. The second one is how to plan routes for all information to be transmitted based on the ISL network determined in the first problem.

Link assignment for communication between satellites has been discussed in many literatures [10–14]. Efficient algorithms for broadband low earth orbit (LEO) satellite systems were put forward to avoid dynamics and enhance communication performance of inter satellite links. But these algorithms are not suitable for link assignment in BDS for the reason that point-to-point communication is used in BDS ISL which is completely different with the mature broadcast communication in GPS or other fully researched broadband communication. In addition, ranging channel and data channel are synchronous in BDS ISL. So when planning ISL network topology, ranging needs and data transmission needs should both be taken into consideration. Focusing on narrow beam link between navigation satellites, Yang et al. proposes a timeslot scheduling method to achieve more observation and faster transmission of telemetry data [15]. But BDS is consist of space segment and ground segment, so BDS ISL network is a generalized network including satellite nodes and ground station nodes, which is different from Yang's work. Besides, there are several types of information to be transmitted instead of only telemetry data.

When it comes to routing problem, BDS ISL network can be considered as a special kind of delay-tolerant network. Routing algorithms in delay tolerant network are usually reactive without full knowledge of information in advance [16, 17]. But in BDS ISL network, transmission tasks of various navigation information within a time period are usually known a prior. This is the first difference with other routing problems. In addition, routing plan in BDS ISL network has low failure tolerance due to limited connectivity. For these reasons, route planning can be transformed into combinational optimization problem, which is quite different from fully-researched reactive routing protocol. The path set can be programmed in advance by ground station facilities who have sufficient computing capability. Then satellites just connect with each other according to the plan, and communication tasks just go as expected.

In conclusion, the topology design and routing plan problem for BDS ISL network have quite unique characteristics and are lack of targeted research. Based on the characteristics of BDS ISL, this paper provides solution to solve the whole problem. Firstly, link assigning algorithm is put forward. The ISL link assignment problem is converted into solving time slot assignment matrix. The solution can not only satisfy the ranging needs, but also provide a good topology structure for data transmission. Then, the paper proposes the path combination optimization algorithm based on simulated annealing (PCO-SA). By combining PCO-SA and adjusted contact graph routing algorithm for path searching, route planning problem for variable navigation messages can be solved effectively.

The structure of this paper is as follows: Sect. 2 introduces the principle and processing method of link assignment for MEO ISL network of BDS. Link assigning algorithm with large average inter-satellite link number, small ranging PDOP, and high connectivity between ground and space segment is proposed. Section 3 provides a route planning scheme for BeiDou navigation data transmission based on the determined link topology. In Sect. 3, contact graph routing is adjusted and applied in path searching. And PCO-SA is proposed. In Sect. 4, the link assigning method and PCO-SA are simulated respectively. Performances of algorithms are demonstrated. Section 5 summarizes the work of this paper and looks forward to the future work in BDS ISL.

2 Inter-satellite Link Assignment in BDS

2.1 Link Assigning Principles in BDS ISL Network

Under the new challenge, ISL network including the whole constellation is too complicated with three various types of satellites. So it has to be noted that in this paper, we are concerned about and will focus on MEO satellites since they are main satellites to carry out navigation mission. In addition, ISL network in this article refers to generalized ISL network composed of satellite nodes and ground station nodes.

Due to the constraints of satellite platform and the signal system, inter-satellite link antennas equipped in each satellite are very limited. The "Point to Point" communication between satellites is realized by these limited Ka-band phased array antennas. The goal of the ISL communication is inter-satellite ranging and data transmission, and signal of these two tasks are modulated on the same carriers. So, the two tasks share the same ISL network topology simultaneously. Since inter-satellite ranging is the primary task, network topology should firstly meet its requirements and try to increase ranging accuracy. Meantime, satellites receive commands and transmit telemetry track and control (TT&C) data, navigation data and other data via links between satellites and the ground stations. It also brings requirements to ISL network topology.

In this paper, we assume that the one MEO satellite is equipped with only one Ka-band antenna. Considering the commands of inter-satellite ranging and data transmission in BDS ISL, we conclude the principles of link assignment and network topology design as follows:

- Satellites should establish links with as many other satellites as possible within link assigning time period. The links number and geometry configuration of linked satellites should ensure high ranging accuracy.
- To satisfy the communication tasks between the space segment and the ground segment, ground stations are supposed to establish satellite-ground links with their visible satellites as long as they can.

Refer to the finite state automaton framework proposed in [14], we take T as the minimum link assignment period. In every time period T, the visibility and the relative position among all nodes in the ISL network are assumed to be fixed.

T is equally divided into K segments and each segment is called time slot. The topological structure doesn't change with each slot. Switching of links and changes of topological structure occur at the instant when the slot starts and ends. Under this link processing mechanism, for each minimum assignment period T with S nodes in the network, the inter-satellite connection relationship can be represented by an S*K matrix, i.e., time slot assignment matrix.

2.2 Link Assigning Method for BDS ISL Network

In this section, according to the principles mentioned above, the method for inter-satellite link assignment problem is proposed. Time slot link assignment matrix generated by this method can provide good topology for both inter-satellite ranging and data transmission. The flow chart is shown in Fig. 1 below.

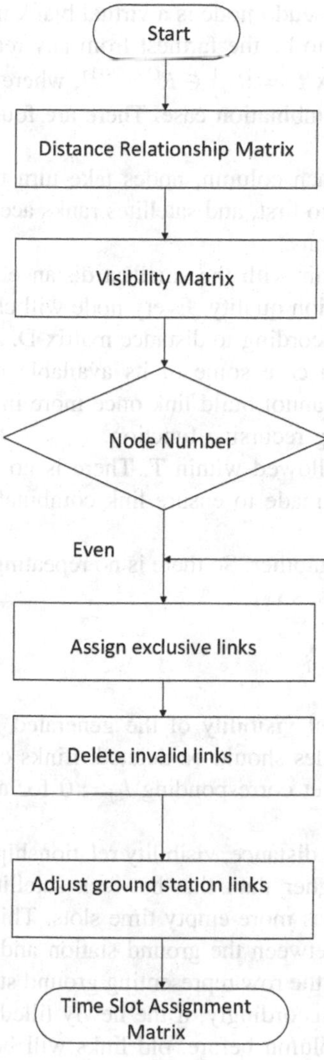

Fig. 1. Flow chart of the time slot matrix assignment algorithm

1. Firstly, we create the distance matrix, $D = [d_{i,j}] \in R^{N\times(N-1)}$, to represent the distance sequence between pairs of nodes. N denotes the total number of nodes in the ISL network. $D(i,:)$ is sorted from near to far by distance from other nodes to node i;
2. Then, we create the visibility matrix V. $V = [v_{i,j}] \in R^{N\times N}$ denotes the visible relationship among all pairs of nodes within T. $v_{i,j} = 0$ means that node i and node j are invisible within T. Conversely, $v_{i,j} = 1$ means this pair of nodes has the opportunity to contact with each other;
3. Preprocess when nodes number is odd: when the number of network nodes is odd, a pseudo node will be added and the total number O equals to N + 1. If N is even,

preprocessing is omitted, and O = N. The pseudo node is a virtual blank node with no position information. But we enforce it to be the farthest from any real node;

4. Assign exclusive links: we create the matrix $L = \left[l_{i,j}\right] \in R^{O\times(O-1)}$, where $l_{i,j}$ is the linking node with node i in the j-th link combination case. There are four rules in generating matrix L:
   a. Matrix L is generated by column. In each column, nodes take turn to choose their connecting node. Ground stations go first, and satellites ranks according to their average distance with ground stations.
   b. When choosing linking nodes, nodes pair with the smallest distance takes the first priority for the sake of communication quality. Every node will choose the nearest node in its available nodes set according to distance matrix D. Available nodes set is updated for every node in case some of its available nodes are chosen and linked by other nodes and cannot build link once more in this slot. This step can be implemented by calling recursive function.
   c. For any node, repeating links are not allowed within T. There is no repeating element in each row of L. This rule is made to ensure link combinations represented by each column are exclusive.
   d. ISLs are bidirectional from one node to another. So there is no repeating element in each column of L. Nodes are in pairs, so

$$l_{l_{i,j},j} = i \tag{1}$$

5. Delete unpractical links: Considering actual visibility of the generated links, the unpractical links composed of invisible nodes should be deleted. Links containing pseudo nodes should be deleted too. We set corresponding $l_{i,j} = 0$ for all invalid links.
6. Adjust links from ground station: Due to far distance, visibility relationship between ground station and satellites is much tougher than that between satellites. After deleting unpractical links, ground station has more empty time slots. This violates the target to guarantee data transmission between the ground station and satellites segment. So in this step, empty elements in the row representing ground station will be filled with visible satellites circularly. Accordingly, if the newly filled satellites have connected with other nodes in the column before, old links will be deleted. After this, K columns with the least 0 element will be chosen as the final time slot assignment matrix.

After steps mentioned above, time slot assignment matrix $L = \left[l_{i,j}\right] \in R^{N\times K}$ represents ISL network topology within T, where N is the total number of nodes including satellites and ground station, K is the number of slots in T. $l_{i,j}$ denotes linking node of node i in time slot j, if $l_{i,j} = 0$, this node has no link in time slot j.

3 Route Planning for BDS ISL Network

Based on network topology determined by link assigning algorithm put forward in Sect. 2, this section is focused on information route planning problem in BDS ISL network. Firstly, we adjust and apply contact graph routing (CGR) for path searching in this unique network. Secondly and most importantly, path combinational optimal algorithm based on simulated annealing is proposed. By combining path searching and path combinational optimization algorithm, a common route planning method for navigation related message transmission in BDS ISL network is provided.

To be consistent with link assignment period, T = 1 min is set as time duration of path combinational optimization period. Without doubt, the network is still the generalized inter-satellite link network composed of ground station nodes and 24 MEO satellites nodes of BDS-3.

3.1 Path Searching Algorithm

3.1.1 Characteristics of Navigation Related Message

Considering real scenarios of navigation satellite system, we choose 4 typical categories of information including telemetry data, autonomous navigation data, operation control data, and telecommand data. Basic attributes for all kinds of message are as follows: data size, priority, source node, destination node, hop limit, message generation time, and message survival time.

- Hop limit: Maximum hop for message transmission. If exceeded, completeness and correctness of transmitted message may not be ensured.
- Generation time: The moment when the message is generated. A message can only enter the network after it has been generated.
- Message Survival Time: The time duration from message generation time to message expiration time. If transmission can't be completed in message survival time, message expires.

3.1.2 Path Searching Algorithm for Single Message

To arrange information transmission by path combinational optimization, feasible paths for single message should be searched firstly. Contact graph routing (CGR) is a path searching algorithm brought forward by Burleigh [18]. This algorithm is often applied in interplanetary networks or satellites networks around the earth [19]. It is especially fit for delay-tolerant networks whose links are discontinuous and have long time delay [20]. Therefore, CGR can be applied in searching feasible paths for navigation related messages here.

Basic principle of CGR is to start from the destination node and constantly move to "transmit node" who has valid link with "current node". By recursively calling contact review procedure (CRP), the algorithm can find all feasible paths for the message considering its data size and network capacity.

It has to be noted that, so far, no CGR algorithm has been introduced in literature focusing on BDS ISL specifically. To meet unique messages attributes and constrictions in this problem, CGR is adjusted for BDS ISL here. We consider the link assignment as a contact plan for the network. The specific algorithm flow pseudo code and variable declaration of adjusted CGR are as follows (Table 1 and Fig. 2):

Table 1. CGR variables definitions

Variables	Definitions
$S_{exclude}$	Nodes that have been chosen and should not be included in the same path again
h_{limit}	Number of remaining hops of the path
h_{max}	Max hop of the message
t_{ddl}	The latest time for the message to be transmitted in current path
t_{in}	Message's generation time
$t_{survival}$	Message's longest living time before it expires
D	Current node
N_{src}	Source node of the message
N_{dest}	Destination node of the message
t_{slot}	Duration of one slot
XMT_D	Nodes that have chance to send messages to D according to contact plan
$t_{tranmit}$	Duration time needed to transmit the message
ECC	Data size of the message
$m_{linkrate}$	Data rate of the link whose transmitting node is *m*
m_{start}	Start time of the link whose transmitting node is *m*
m_{stop}	Stop time of the link whose transmitting node is *m*
P_D	Collection of all paths that start from source node and end at node D
P_{Dm}	Collection of all paths whose start node is the source node and last two nodes are m and D

Initialization

$S_{exclude} \leftarrow \emptyset,\ h_{limit} \leftarrow h_{max},\ t_{ddl} \leftarrow t_{in} + t_{survival},\ D \leftarrow N_{dest},\ P_D \leftarrow \emptyset$

CGR_CRP(CG,D)

```
S_exclude ← ∅ ∪ D
if h_limit < 1 then
   return;
end if
i_max ← t_ddl/t_slot
for i ← i_max to 1 do
   m ← XMT_D_i
   t_tranmit ← 2 * ECC/m_linkrate
   t_ddl ← t_ddl − t_tranmit
   if m_start > t_ddl or ECC > m_linkrate then continue
   else
      if m = N_src then
         t_ddl ← min(t_ddl, m_stop − t_tranmit)
         if t_in ≥ t_ddl then continue
         else
            P_Dm ← {N_src, D}
         end if
      else
         if m ∈ S_exclude then continue
         else
            t_ddl ← min (t_ddl, m_stop − t_tranmit)
            get P_m by executing CGR_CRP (CG,m)
            generate P_Dm by adding D to the end of all paths in P_m
         end if
      end if
   P_D ← P_D ∪ P_Dm
end for
```

Fig. 2. Pseudo code of the adjusted CGR algorithm

3.1.3 Path Screening

After CGR, a great number of feasible paths may be searched out. In this situation, several paths with better performance are chosen and other "bad" paths will not join the follow-up combinational optimization process. Path screening can avoid the efficiency reduction caused by too many meaningless paths.

In this article, time delay and hop number are two indicators that determine paths performance. Considering the difference between their dimension units and physical meaning, we use the formula

$$P = delay/C + hop \tag{2}$$

to describe the comprehensive performance of planned paths, where *delay* denotes time delay of the path, *hop* denotes how many hops the path go through and C is a constant. The formula means, in our performance calculation rule, adding C seconds time delay has the same negative effect with adding one hop.

In a word, when too many paths are feasible than wanted, path screening can be executed by calculating the P value of all paths and choosing several needed paths with the minimum P.

3.2 Path Combinational Optimal Algorithm Based on Simulated Annealing

Feasible path set of all messages to be transmitted can be known by path searching. But due to limited network capacity, congestion occurs if all messages are transmitted according to their own optimal path. In other words, when some link is included in many messages' best path, summation data size of these messages will exceed the link capacity. To avoid path plan failure caused by such path conflict, optimization should be done in advance to make sure the planned path set for all messages are executable. The core principle is to arrange paths for as many messages as possible. Besides, performance of the planned path is also supposed to be optimized.

In this section, a heuristic framework based on simulated annealing is used for combinatorial optimization. The simulated annealing method has small computational complexity and high versatility [21]. When the number of iterations is large enough, it can converge with the probability of 1. The core idea of simulated annealing is to accept worse performed new solution with certain probability which decreases along the iteration process. Therefore, this method can probabilistically jump out of the local optimal solution and finally approach the global optimal solution. Flow chart of PCO-SA proposed in this paper is shown in the Fig. 3 below.

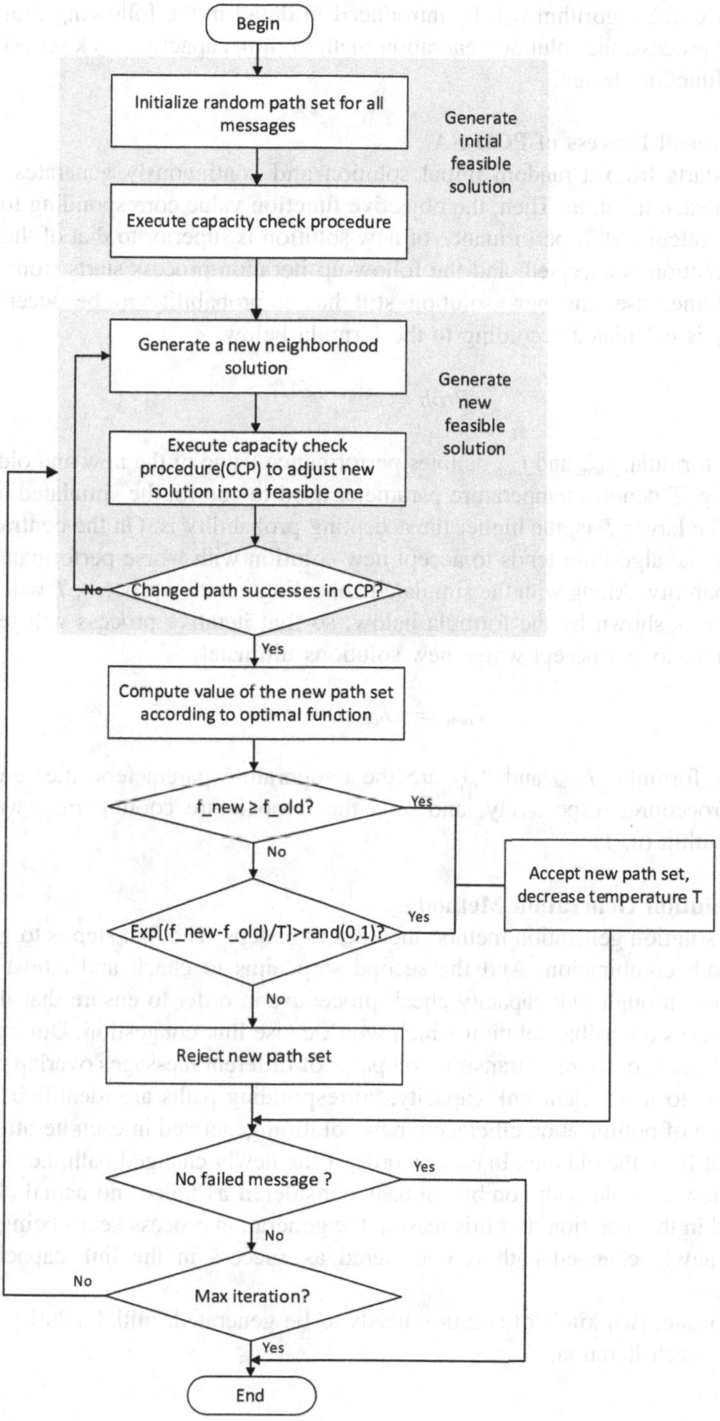

Fig. 3. The flow chart of PCO-SA

The PCO-SA algorithm will be introduced in detail in the following four aspects: the overall process, the solution generation method, link capacity check procedure, and objective function design.

3.2.1 Overall Process of PCO-SA

PCO-SA starts from a random initial solution and continuously generates one new solution in each iteration. Then, the objective function value corresponding to the new solution is calculated. If performance of new solution is superior to that of the old one, the new solution is accepted, and the follow-up iteration process starts from this new solution. Otherwise, the new solution still has a probability to be accepted. The probability is calculated according to the formula below.

$$Prob = e^{(f_{new} - f_{old})/T} \tag{3}$$

In this formula, f_{new} and f_{old} denotes performance value of the new and old path set respectively. T denotes temperature parameter used to control the simulated annealing process. The larger T is, the higher the accepting probability is. On the contrary, when T is small, the algorithm tends to accept new solution with worse performance with a small probability. Along with the simulated annealing iterative process, T will continue to decrease as shown by the formula below, so that iterative process will tend to be stable and no longer accept worse new solutions ultimately.

$$T_{new} = \alpha T_{old}, 0 < \alpha < 1 \tag{4}$$

In this formula, T_{new} and T_{old} are the temperature parameters after and before cooling procedure, respectively, and α is the temperature cooling rate, which is a constant within (0, 1).

3.2.2 Solution Generation Method

The basic solution generation method includes two steps. The first step is to generate a random path combination. And the second step aims to check and adjust the path combination through link capacity check procedure in order to ensure that the generated path set is a feasible solution which won't cause link congestion. During the link capacity check procedure, if transmission paths of different messages overlap and cause conflict due to insufficient link capacity, corresponding paths are identified as failed. For the sake of optimization efficiency, new solution generated in each iteration should be different from the old one. In other words, if the newly changed path, i.e., difference between new and old path combination, is considered as failed, no actual changes is introduced in this iteration. For this reason, the generation process keeps being repeated until the newly changed path is considered as success in the link capacity check procedure.

In step one, two kinds of solution needs to be generated: initial solution and new solution in each iteration.

For M messages to be transmitted, we represent the whole feasible path set obtained by CGR with $R_i = \{r_{ij}\}(1 \leq j \leq p_i, 1 \leq i \leq M)$, where R_i is the path set of the i-th message, it has p_i paths in total, r_{ij} denotes the j-th path in feasible path set of the i-th message. Each path is actually a sequence of nodes with time information. So each path combination for all messages can be represented by

$$Pathcomb = [x_1, x_2, \ldots, x_M] \tag{5}$$

where x_i is the number x_i path in path set for the i-th message. If x_i is 0, it means the path chosen for the i-th message fails to pass link capacity check procedure.

Simulated annealing can start from any starting point, so this paper generates a random initial solution. That is, for each message i, an integer number $x_i(1 \leq x_i \leq p_i)$ is randomly selected to generate an initial path combination of M pieces of message.

In the follow-up new solution generation process in each iteration, message m is randomly selected, and the original chosen path number x_m is replaced with another random integer which is in the range of (1, p_m) and different from the original x_m. The obtained $Pathcomb_{new}$ is a neighborhood solution of $Pathcomb_{old}$.

After the first step mentioned above, link capacity check must be performed as follow-up step to adjust the generated solution to a feasible one.

3.2.3 Link Capacity Check Procedure

The core idea of the link capacity check is to check whether the total data to be transmitted will exceed the link capacity in the network according to path combination. If true, it decides some messages whose paths are engaged in conflict are successful and the remaining messages are failed.

The process of link capacity check procedure is as follows.

- First, generate the order for messages to go through the link capacity check. There are three principles for generating.
  - The checking order is generated according to priority. Messages that have higher priority ranks higher in the checking order.
  - For messages of the same priority, the checking order is randomly arranged.
  - Checking order corresponding to the message whose path has been replaced this time should be moved to the first place among messages with the same priority.

  These principles can ensure that overall the high-priority messages are more advantageous in the sequential checking. And the checking order generated in each iteration is different from each other, which can bring randomness to the exploration process. Besides, newly replaced path has a greater chance of being successfully arranged and jumping out of the solution generation loop thanks to a higher checking order.
- Then, perform link capacity check procedure according to the checking order. If the path chosen for certain message can be added without leading to insufficient link capacity, it is determined as successful. Message data size is added to corresponding occupied capacity of link included in the path. If the data to be transmitted

overflows after adding this message, path arrangement of this message fails. Link capacity of all links in the network is still the same as when the message was not added. This step is repeated until all messages have been checked.

There is a special case that may happen in BDS ISL network route planning worth mentioning. When a message is generated in current route planning period, but its effective lifetime ends at next period, some feasible paths of this message path will include links belongs to next period. Messages spanning across periods result in the problem that some links of current period are occupied by information generated in previous period, and some information occupies the link capacity of the next period. To solve this problem, "Folding Principle" is put forward and applied. If the path of certain message occupies links of the second period, when calculating the occupied capacity of network links, links in the second period are folded into the first period. Since the link topology of the second period is consistent with the first period, message size is subtracted from current link capacity of corresponding links in the first period. For BDS, generally, the visibility between nodes does not change substantially in 2 consecutive minutes. Based on this assumption that topology of the next period is the same as the previous one, interaction between periods is replaced by optimization within current period, this is called the "Folding Principle".

3.2.4 Objective Function

For the route planning issue of information in the satellite navigation system, we mainly focus on three indicators: success ratio, time delay, and hop number. Among them, Success ratio is the primary indicator used to evaluate the effect of route planning since key objective of route planning problem is to arrange as many messages as possible. Time delay and hop number reflect the performance of the successfully planned path. The smaller the delay is, the faster message reaches the destination node. The smaller hop number is, the better performance is. That is because too many transit node may cause unnecessary errors in the process of information unpacking and grouping.

Accordingly, when designing the objective function, we pay the most attention to improving the success ratio. Performance indicators of the successfully planned path are also take into consideration. For information that is successfully planed, we define its value function as:

$$S_m = (pri_m \times pri_m)/(hop_m + delay_m/C) \tag{6}$$

where pri_m is the priority of the message, hop_m and $delay_m$ denotes time delay and hop number of this path, C is the same constant as that in (2) which represents the proportional relationship between time delay and hop number on final performance.

For messages fails to be arranged, penalty function is as follows.

$$P_m = -(pri_m \times pri_m) \tag{7}$$

It means, when the information arrangement fails, the negative penalty for the total value is only related to its priority. The higher the priority is, the greater the penalty is.

For any path combination of M messages to be transmitted, the corresponding combined value function is

$$f_M = \sum\nolimits_{m \in SuccessMessage} S_m + \sum\nolimits_{m \in FailMessage} P_m \tag{8}$$

High-priority messages have a greater impact on the result, so the result is iterated toward the trend that high-priority messages are beneficial. And for the same message, penalty function calculates bigger than value function. Failure causes more significant influence to the whole value. Therefore, success ratio increases as the iteration process.

4 Computational Results

In this section, we simulate and analyze the performance of the two algorithms put forward respectively in Sects. 2 and 3, namely link assigning algorithm and PCO-SA. Algorithms are simulated based on real satellites constellation of the third generation BDS. Note that no ground station placement plan for the third generation BDS has been published so far. In this paper, only one ground station is included in generalized ISL network for the reason that one station is the most basic scene considering practical construction progress. Basic scene can be expanded to multiple ground stations with link assigning algorithm and PCO-SA running the same steps. Here we choose Beijing (39°55′N 116°23′E), the capital of China, as location of the only ground station. Distance between space segment and ground segment is far beyond distance between potential ground stations in China so ground station in Beijing can be typical representative.

The proposed methods were implemented using MATLAB. And the Ka-band ISL antennas have a pitch angle limit of 60°. The visibility and positions were calculated using STK software.

The basic simulation conditions are as follows (Table 2):

Table 2. Simulation condition

Simulation condition	Parameter
Simulation start time	20180101 00:00:00
Network Nodes	24 MEO satellites + 1 Ground station
T	1 min
K	20

Parameters used to simulate navigation related messages are as follows (Table 3):

Table 3. Parameters of messages to be transmitted

Message type	Priority	Generation rule	Data size	Hop limit	Message survival time
Telemetry information	4	One telemetry message from each satellite to ground station in each time slot	8192 bit	4	60 s
Auto-navigation information	3	One auto-navigation message from each satellite to its connecting satellites in each time slot	2048 bit	1	60 s
Telecommand data	2	Message from ground station to corresponding telecommand satellite within a uniform time distribution in every 60 s	102400 bit	4	60 s
Operating control information	1	Message from ground station to corresponding operating control satellite within a uniform time distribution in every 60 s	102400 bit	4	60 s

4.1 Performance of Link Assigning Algorithm

We generate the link assignment matrix for every minute according to the algorithm in Sect. 2.2. Then we calculate the average number of links, average PDOP and average hop between ground station and satellites. The results are shown as follows (Table 4):

Table 4. Performance of link assignment method

Performance index	Best	Worst	Average
Average number of distinct links for satellites	18.2917	17	17.6697
Average PDOP	1.0555	1.2570	1.1480
Average hop from ground station to satellites	1.5417	1.7500	1.6259
Average number of distinct links for ground station	11	6	8.9792

According to the simulation results, satellites build links with 17.6697 nodes on average, and the difference between the best and worst results is not big. The robust performance can satisfy the needs for satellite nodes to ranging with as many other satellites as possible. The average PDOP equals to 1.148. This is much smaller than 3, which is considered to represent a ranging geometric configuration good enough. High precision ranging can be guaranteed. Ground station builds links with 9 satellites on average, and the average communication hop is 1.6259. Space segment and ground segment are highly connected.

In conclusion, the proposed method can generate ISL network which not only satisfies the design principles mentioned in Sect. 2, but also provides promising network topology structure for the follow-up route planning. It is a quite practical method to apply in link assignment for BDS ISL network.

4.2 Performance of PCO-SA

4.2.1 Parameter Configuration of Objective Function

From Eq. (2), the objective function and, more specifically, the choice of the C determine the final optimization result including the hop number and the time delay. In order to determine appropriate value of C, we set the following simulation conditions: space segment is consisted of 24 MEO satellites of BDS, the ground station has 6 visible satellites, data rate of links between satellites is 102.4 Kbps, data rate of links between ground station and satellites is 204.8 Kbps. We calculate the average time delay and hop number under different C values. The results are shown as follow (Fig. 4):

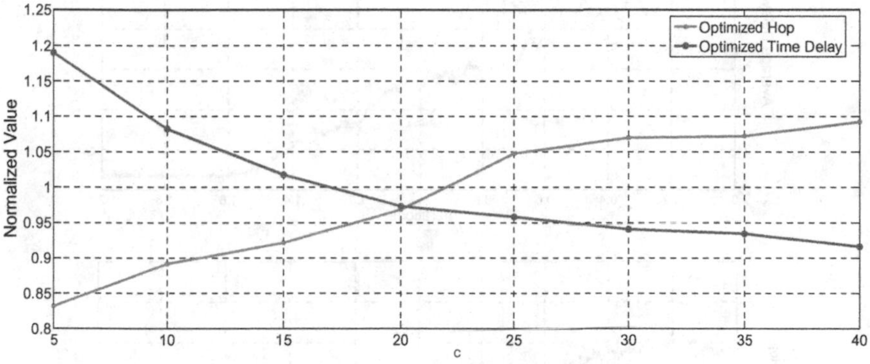

Fig. 4. The choice of the C value

It is obvious from the figure that when value of C equals to 20, the optimization result of hop number and time delay are in equilibrium. So, we choose C = 20 as the parameter in objective function.

4.2.2 Parameter Configuration of Simulated Annealing

After multiple simulations, we discover that 20000 is the most proper maximum iteration number for our problem to acquire results good enough without too long computational time. In the "cooling" process, we set $T_0 = 273$ as the initial temperature. Temperature decreasing parameter α is set to 0.9995.

4.2.3 Simulation on Telemetry Message Route Planning Using PCO-SA

Based on the generated ISL network topology and parameters set above, experiments on PCO-SA are performed. Firstly, gradual convergence trends of three indicators in the optimization process are shown. Secondly, we compare the performance of proposed PCO-SA with other path plan methods under different data rate. Thirdly, we compare the performance of PCO-SA with other methods with different number of ground station's visible satellites.

Only one type of navigation related information can be selected in the simulation for the sake of single variable principle. Since telemetry information is generated continuously by satellites and needs to be transmitted to the ground in a short period of time, it's quite challenging to arrange the massive data. Also, telemetry information is of high transmission priority which exists in all navigation scenes. For these reasons, telemetry data of BDS is selected here.

The visible satellites number of ground station is set to 6. Data rate of links between satellites is 102.4 Kbps, data rate of links between ground station and satellites is 204.8 Kbps (Fig. 5).

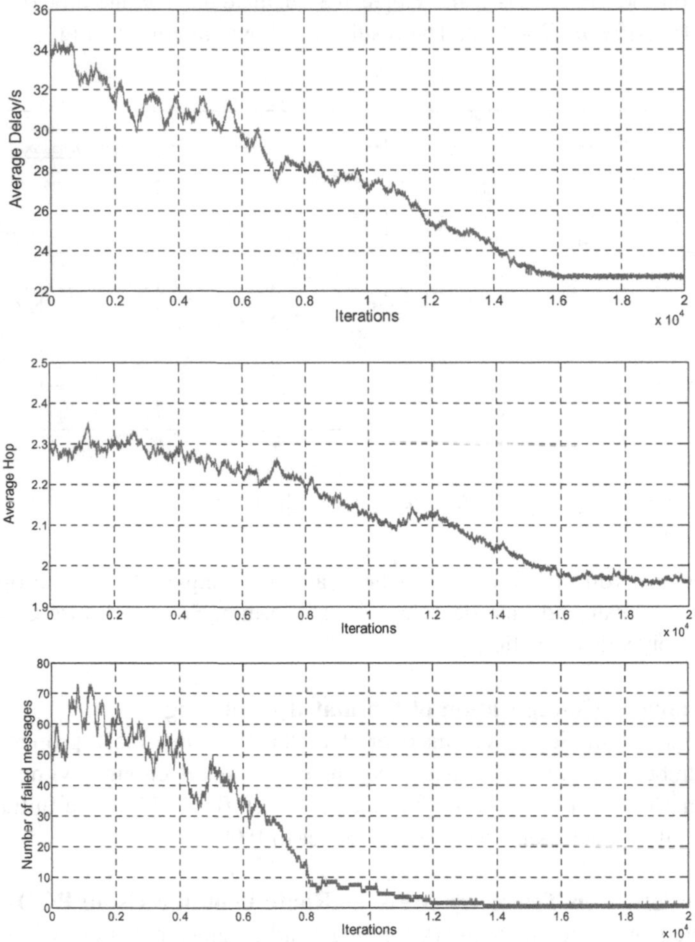

Fig. 5. Trends of indicators in the optimization process

According to the figure, the failed-to-plan paths number gradually decreases to 0 as the iteration goes. Average time delay and hop number of planed paths decrease and finally stabilize.

Then, we compared the performance of PCO-SA and other methods under different link data rates. As far as we know, no mature route planning method for BDS ISL has been proposed before. So three principles are used to generate path plan. MinDelay principle denotes to a scheme where all messages choose the minimum delay path for themselves. Similarly, all messages choose their minimum hop path in MinHop principle. Random principle denotes to random path combination. After generation process of these three principles, capacity check procedure mentioned in Sect. 3.2.3 is executed to adjust the solutions to feasible ones.

In this simulation, the visible satellites number of ground station is 6. Data rate of links between ground station and satellites is 204.8 Kbps. Data rates of links between satellites are 51.2 Kbps, 102.4 Kbps and 204.8 kbps respectively. All results are average values from 50 times of experiments. Results are shown in Fig. 6.

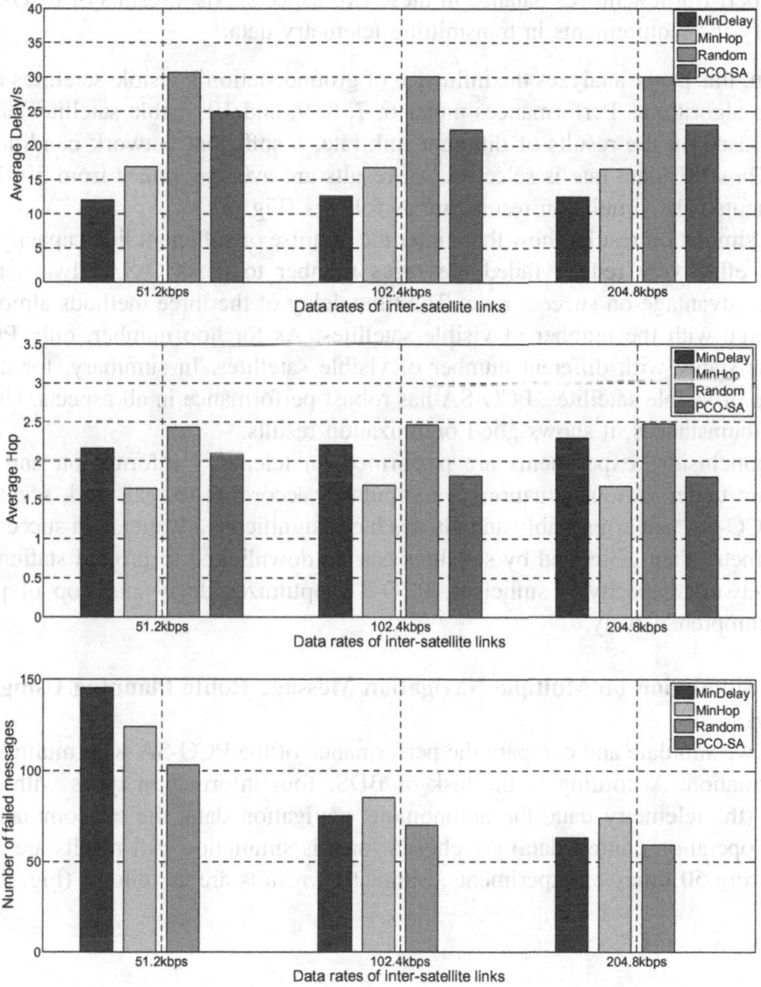

Fig. 6. Performance of algorithms with different ISL data rates

According to the simulation results, we can conclude that:

- Under different inter-satellite link rates, all messages' paths are successfully planned using PCO-SA with. PCO-SA has absolute advantage in success ratio among other principles.
- Compared with random principle, PCO-SA has little optimization on time delay and hop number under ISL link data rate of 50.2 Kpbs. Due to limited link capacity, performance on these two aspects is sacrificed to improve the success ratio. When network capacity is sufficient with data rate of 102.4 Kpbs or 204.8 Kpbs, PCO-SA can significantly improve the performance of successfully planned path.
- Compared with MinDelay principle, PCO-SA doesn't have advantages in time delay. Compared with MinHop principle, PCO-SA has no advantages in hop number. But it achieves balance in these two aspects. Also, results of PCO-SA can satisfy the requirements in transmitting telemetry data.

Then, this paper analyzes the influence of ground station's visible satellites number on these algorithms. Performances under 6, 7, 8, 9, and 10 visible satellites are compared. Based on the results of different link rate, a sufficient network condition with 102.4 Kbps ISL data rate is selected. All results are average values from 50 times of experiments. The simulation results are as follows (Fig. 7):

The simulation results show that under the premise of sufficient link capacity, PCO-SA can effectively reduce failed messages number to 0. PCO-SA always has the absolute advantage on success ratio. The time delay of the three methods almost does not change with the number of visible satellites. As for hop number, only PCO-SA performs stably with different number of visible satellites. In summary, for different numbers of visible satellites, PCO-SA has robust performance in all aspects. Under all these circumstances, it shows good optimization results.

In conclusion, experiments are performed on telemetry information and results show that under various situations we simulated according to real work scenarios in BDS, PCO-SA performs stably and always has a significant advantage in success ratio. All telemetry data generated by satellites can be downlinked to ground station. Also, when network capacity is sufficient, PCO-SA optimizes delay and hop of planned routes comprehensively.

4.2.4 Simulation on Multiple Navigation Message Route Planning Using PCO-SA

Finally, we simulate and compare the performance of the PCO-SA with multiple kinds of information. According to the task of BDS, four information types with various priority (the telemetry data, the autonomous navigation data, the telecommand data, and the operation control data) are chosen for this simulation. All results are average values from 50 times of experiments. Simulation results are as follows (Fig. 8):

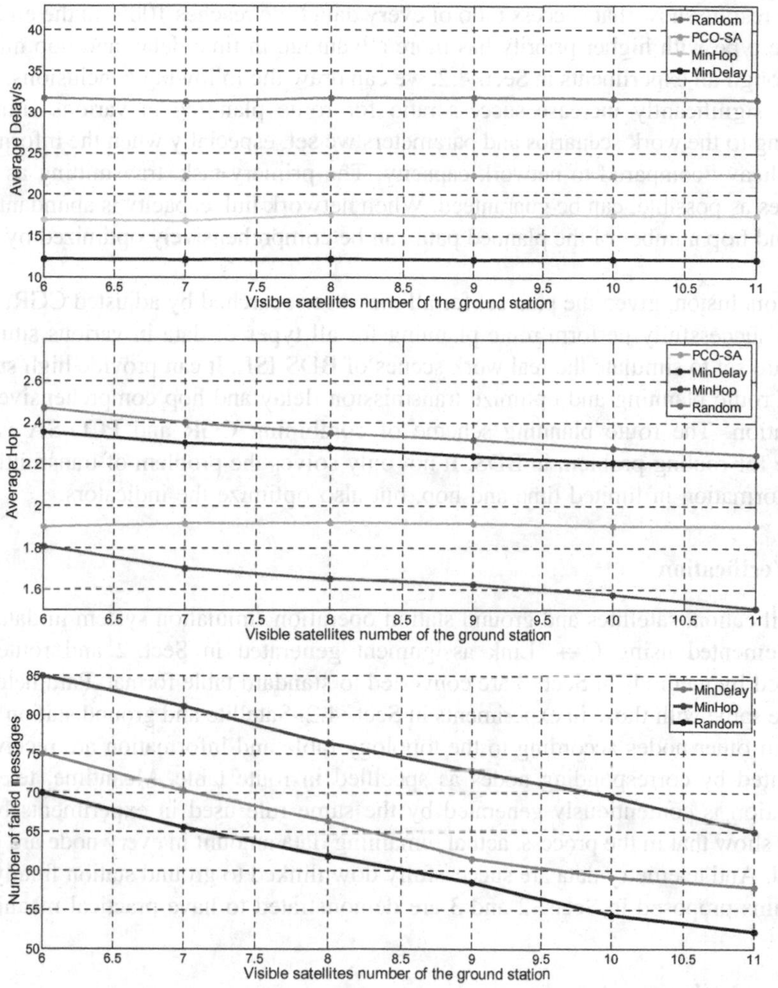

Fig. 7. Performance of algorithms with different number of ground station's visible satellites

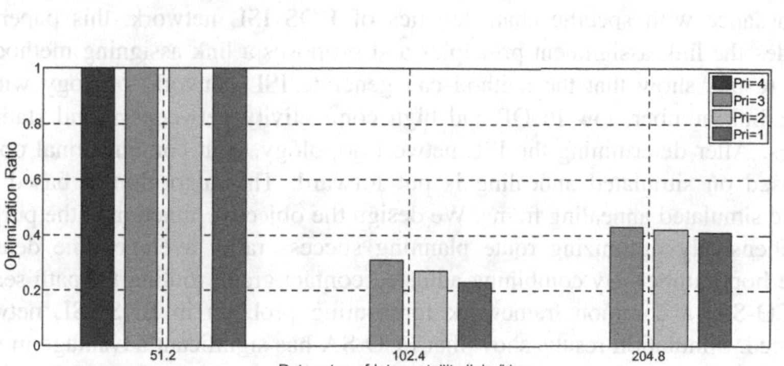

Fig. 8. Performance of different information using PCO-SA

The results show that success ratio of every data type reaches 100% in the end. And message type with higher priority has more advantage in time delay and hop number.

Through all experiments in Sect. 4.2, we can draw the following conclusions: PCO-SA can significantly increase success ratio for route planning in various situations according to the work scenarios and parameters we set, especially when the information load is heavy compared to network capacity. The primary task, transmitting as many messages as possible, can be guaranteed. When network link capacity is abundant, time delay and hop number of the planned path can be comprehensively optimized by PCO-SA.

In conclusion, given the path set for all messages searched by adjusted CGR, PCO-SA can successfully perform route planning for all types of data in various situations which are set to simulate the real work scenes of BDS ISL. It can provide high success ratio of route planning and optimize transmission delay and hop comprehensively for information. The route planning scheme of combining CGR and PCO-SA is very suitable for routing problem in BDS. It not only solves the problem of transmitting all task information in limited time and hop, but also optimize the indicators.

4.3 Verification

For verification, satellites and ground station operation simulation system in data level is implemented using C++. Link assignment generated in Sect. 2 and route plan generated by methods in Sect. 3 are converted to standard table format. Parameters are set to be same with those in experiments in Sect. 4.2. Satellite and ground station nodes link with other nodes according to the topology table and information are received or transmitted by corresponding nodes as specified in route table. Meantime, telemetry information is contentiously generated by the same rule used in experiments before. Results show that in the process, actual remaining data amount in every node are just as planned. And telemetry data are successfully downlinked to ground station finally. The algorithms proposed in Sects. 2 and 3 are demonstrated to have practical meanings.

5 Conclusion

In accordance with specific characteristics of BDS ISL network, this paper firstly concludes the link assignment principles and proposes a link assigning method. Simulation results show that the method can generate ISL network topology with high average link number, low PDOP and high connectivity between ground station and satellites. After determining the ISL network topology, path combinational optimization based on simulated annealing is put forward. This algorithm is based on the heuristic simulated annealing frame. We design the objective function at the purpose of comprehensively optimizing route planning success ratio, average time delay, and average hop number. By combining adjusted contact graph routing for path searching and PCO-SA, a common framework for routing problem in BDS ISL network is introduced. Simulation results show that PCO-SA has significant advantage in success ratio of route planning compared with other three principles. Time delay and hop number can also be optimized through PCO-SA. In addition, PCO-SA has great stability under various situations including different link data rate and different visibility condition of ground station. At last, we compare the performance among different information using PCO-SA. In addition of guaranteed high success ratio, messages with high priority can take more advantages in time delay and hop number.

In conclusion, link assignment method and route planning scheme of combining CGR and PCO-SA put forward in this paper are demonstrated to perform advantageously in solving the topological design and routing problem in BDS ISL network.

Algorithms introduced in this paper are specifically targeted at inter-satellite link network composed of MEO satellites and ground station in BDS. Under the trend of air and space integration, future work on more complicated network including GEO, IGSO or even communication satellites still remains to be accomplished.

References

1. BeiDou Navigation Satellite System Signal In Space Interface Control Document Open Service Signal B1C (Version 1.0). http://en.beidou.gov.cn/SYSTEMS/Officialdocument/. Accessed 15 Oct 2018
2. Abusali, P.A.M., Tapley, B.D., Schutz, B.E.: Autonomous navigation of global positioning system satellites using cross-link measurements. J. Guidance Control Dyn. **21**(2), 321–327 (2015)
3. Fisher, S.C., Ghassemi, K.: GPS IIF-the next generation. In: Proceedings of the IEEE, Seal Beach, CA, pp. 24–47 (1999)
4. Vasavada, Y., Gopal, R., Ravishankar, C.: Architectures for next generation high throughput satellite systems. Int. J. Satellite Commun. Network. **34**(4), 523–546 (2016)
5. Wu, Y.L., Yang, J., Chen, J.Y.: Route analysis of satellite constellation based on directional crosslink with narrow-beam antenna. In: Wang, Y., Li, T. (eds.) Practical Applications of Intelligent Systems. AINSC, vol. 124, pp. 639–650. Springer, Berlin (2011). https://doi.org/10.1007/978-3-642-25658-5_76
6. Maine, K., Anderson, P., Bayuk, F.: Communication architecture for GPS III. In: IEEE Aerospace Conference Proceedings (2004)
7. Fernández, F.A.: Inter-satellite ranging and inter-satellite communication links for enhancing GNSS satellite broadcast navigation data. Adv. Space Res. **47**(5), 786–801 (2011)
8. Wang, D.X., Jie, X., Feng, X., Rui, G., Xie, J.S., Chen, J.P.: Development and prospect of GNSS autonomous navigation based on inter-satellite link. J. Astronautics **37**, 1279–1285 (2016)
9. Yang, Y., Yangyin, X., Jinlong, L., Yang, C.: Progress and performance evaluation of BeiDou global navigation satellite system: data analysis based on BDS-3 demonstration system. Sci. China Earth Sci. **61**(5), 614–624 (2018)
10. Harathi, K., Krishna, P., Newman-Wolfe, R.E., Chow, Y.C.: A fast link assignment algorithm for satellite communication networks. In: Twelfth International Phoenix Conference on Computers and Communications, pp. 401–408. IEEE (1993)
11. Noakes, M.D., Cain, J.B., Nieto, J.W., Althouse, E.L.: An adaptive link assignment algorithm for dynamically changing topologies. IEEE Trans. Commun. **41**(5), 694–706 (1993)
12. Markus, W., Jochen, F., Frédéric, W., Gérard, M.: Topological design, routing and capacity dimensioning for ISL networks in broadband LEO satellite systems. Int. J. Satellite Commun. **19**(2001), 499–528 (2001)

13. Liu, Z., Guo, W., Deng, C., Hu, W.: Perfect match model based link assignment for optical satellite network. In: IEEE International Conference on Communications, pp. 4149–4153. IEEE (2014)
14. Chang, H.S., Kim, B.W., Chang, G.L., Min, S.L.: FSA-based link assignment and routing in low-earth orbit satellite networks. IEEE Trans. Veh. Technol. **47**(3), 1037–1048 (1997)
15. Yang, D., Yang, J., Xu, P.: Timeslot scheduling of inter-satellite links based on a system of a narrow beam with time division. GPS Sol. **21**, 1–13 (2016)
16. Sushant, J., Kevin, F., Rabin, P.: Routing in a delay tolerant network. In: Proceedings of the 2004 Conference on Applications, Technologies, Architectures, and Protocols for Computer Communications, pp. 145–158. ACM (2004)
17. Jones, E.P.C., Li, L., Schmidtke, J.K., Ward, P.A.S.: Practical routing in delay-tolerant networks. IEEE Trans. Mob. Comput. **6**(8), 943–959 (2007)
18. Burleigh, S.: Contact Graph Routing. http://tools.ietf.org/html/draft-burleigh-dtnrg-cgr-01. Accessed 15 Oct 2018
19. Birrane, E., Burleigh, S., Kasch, N.: Analysis of the contact graph routing algorithm: bounding interplanetary paths. Acta Astronaut. **75**(2), 108–119 (2012)
20. Araniti, G., Bezirgiannidis, N., Birrane, E., Bisio, I., Burleigh, S., Caini, C.: Contact graph routing in DTN space networks: overview, enhancements and performance. IEEE Commun. Mag. **53**(3), 38–46 (2015)
21. Bertsimas, D., Tsitsiklis, J.: Simulated annealing. Stat. Sci. **8**(1), 10–15 (1993)

Resource Allocation Based on Auction Game of Satellite Avionics System

Rui Wang, Xiao-dong Han(✉), Yang Li, Chao Wang, and Xi Zhou

Institute of Telecommunication Satellite, China Academy of Space Technology, Beijing 100094, China
willingdong@163.com

Abstract. Along with the development of spacecraft technology, the demands for intelligence and autonomy of future satellites are promoting. However, the operational capability of processor and transmittability of bus are mainly the factors against the promotion in existing satellite avionics system. Moreover, the efficient allocation method for computing and storage resource based distributed architecture is also the valid measures to improve the efficiency of satellite avionics system. In this paper, we focus on the resource limitation of processing units, and mention the resource allocation based auction game of satellite avionics system, advance the use ratio of free resource and optimize the power consumption.

Keywords: Auction game · Satellite avionics system · Resource allocation

1 Introduction

The avionics system is popularly known as the generic terms of spacecraft electronic system, which have the characteristics as based on computer networks, advanced micro-electronic designing and manufacturing technique, and using systematic, integrated and optimized designing in electronic equipment of different subsystem and their function, to improve the performance and reliability. Since 21st century, the avionics system is defined as the complicated electronic system base on progressive large scale integrated circuit, hybrid integrated circuit, and realized in using satellite information network architecture. The avionics system is applied in designing of GEO (Geostationary Earth Orbit) communications satellites of our contrary, and its bearer function is mainly satellite data management [1].

The existing avionics system of GEO satellite communications satellite and subsequent platforms is mainly constitute by SMU (Satellite Management Unit) and ISU (Integrated Service Unit), and connected to the other subsystems and equipment by data bus. It bears the operating system and application software, and in charges of the

Foundation Items: The Foundation of Preview of Equipment (No. 30501050403, 30501050405), National Natural Science Foundation of China (No. 61471360), The major projects of national science and technology (No. 2017ZX01013101-003).

M. Jia et al. (Eds.): WiSATS 2019, LNICST 281, pp. 479–487, 2019.
https://doi.org/10.1007/978-3-030-19156-6_44

telemetry data collection and tele-command distribution, autonomously thermal control and energy management, FDIR (Failure Detection, Isolation and Recovery) and so on. The SMU and ISU have independent processer, software and storage, could realize the function like software updating and recovery, important data preservation [2, 3].

Along with the development of spacecraft technique, the progressing and carrying capacity improving, application of large-scale reconfigurable satellite platform, the performance enhancement of operating system and application software, the mature of autonomously system optimization and failure detection, means the remarkable promotion of satellite autonomy and intelligence. In the future space-based networks, the avionics system could process basic works and preservation of satellite system even whole space-based networks like data collection, storage and distribution, management of distributed computing resource, contingency plan of failure conduction and recovery by prestored handling mechanism as the satellite programming and management center. The operation of these prestored mechanisms makes independently management of resource and basic function preservation possible.

However, the operational capability of processor and transmittability of data bus are the principal factors which affect the further development of autonomy and intelligence. The insufficient of progressing capacity makes operating complicate resource management and distribution algorithm occupy high range of computing resource, and reduces the operating efficiency of avionics system. The lacks of transmittability of data bus restricts the data exchanging rate among the center progressing unit and distributed processing unit, makes most of distributed progressing unrealizable.

Against upper problems, in following design of communications satellite avionics system, it contains the solution of operational capacity of processor and transmittability of data bus. At the same time, it also needs corresponding resource allocation method, which mainly contains efficient resource allocation method designing for calculation and storage resource in distributed system, to avoid the influence of efficient promotion of avionics system with the improvement of hardware condition.

In this paper, we design a method of resource allocation in satellite avionics system. And the rest of the paper is organized as follows. After introducing the system model and auction game algorithm in distributed satellite processing unit in Sect. 2, the process of resource allocation is discussed in Sect. 3. In Sect. 4, we give the numerical results and analysis. Finally, conclusions are drawn in Sect. 5.

2 System Model

At this stage, the main architecture of satellite avionics system is in Fig. 1. In this figure, the satellite management unit, platform integrated unit and payload integrated unit are equipment of avionics, and connected to the other equipment by data bus (1553B) to exchange telemetry data and tele-commands. Except satellite management unit, the other equipment also has the function of important data storage and recovery. But restricted by the storage space, they could not save too much data. And the 1553B data bus only support 1 Mbps bandwidth, it cannot satisfy the demand to storage and distributed processing. In future communication satellite platform designing, the high-speed bus system is applicative, like SpaceWire. Different from the bus topology of

1553B bus, SpaceWire bus is in architecture of star topology include router [4–6]. As the initiator and participant of resource allocation, the integrated service units have the same configuration performance. And the method in this paper could be implemented not only in distributed system but also in system have central management unit.

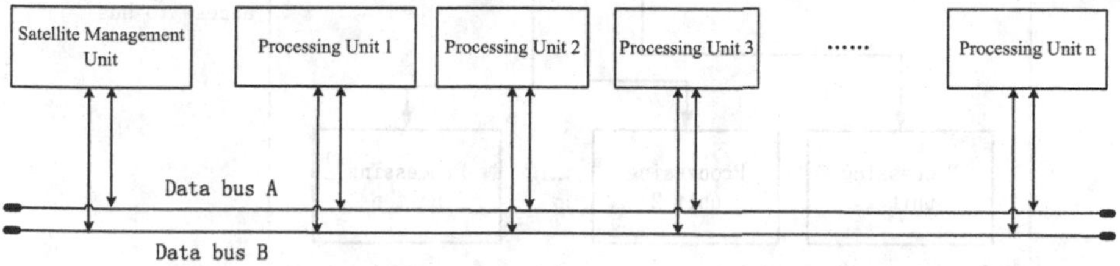

Fig. 1. Architecture of satellite avionics system-bus topology

The algorithm of resource allocation in this paper is the distributed algorithm base on first price sealed-bid (FPSB) auction game. The reason to use the game method to design algorithm is as follows:

(1) The development direction in future avionic system is modularity and intelligence. Therefore, the satellite process units have the independent module qualified computing resource, and format distributed network construction. The central resource management algorithm has poor adaptability to this construction.
(2) Restricted to the limited energy and computing resource, repeated game and iterative algorithm method are inapplicable to the environment of avionic system, waste computing resource, generate more communication overhead, and occupy the bandwidth of communication links [7–10].

The algorithm in this paper could be described as follows: first, cooperative computing means the processing units offer their own computing resource to help the other processing units. The network architecture is in Fig. 2.

Define the parameters: R_s is the computing resource of the initiator in cooperation, and R_{r_i} is the computing resource of the i_{th} participant r_i. W_i is the bandwidth in communications. p_{r_i} is the power in cooperation of participant. Q_{r_i} is the total power of participant. η is the cooperative efficiency. α_i is a function of $p_s \cdot k_i$ is a power price parameter of participant r_i, always larger than 1 and known to r_i itself. The efficiency of participant is expressed as

$$\eta = \frac{R_s}{R_{ri} W_i P_{ri}} \tag{1}$$

The initiator occupies more resource, the participant spend less. And the cooperative efficiency is inversely proportional to consumed power and occupied throughput of bus. From the relationship before, the price generated by participant could be described as

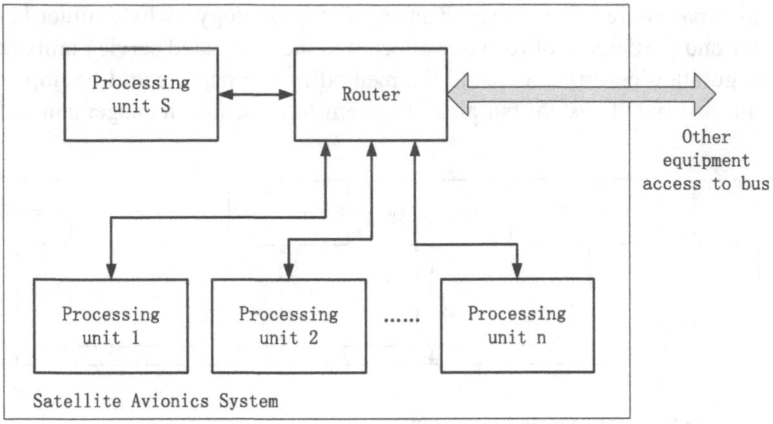

Fig. 2. Architecture of satellite avionics system-star topology

$$\alpha_i(R_s) = k_i R_{ri}(R_s) = \frac{k_i R_s}{\eta(mW_i + tP_{ri})} \tag{2}$$

It has the following properties: while $k_i = 1$, r_i gains no profit from helping the initiator but only cover the cost caused due to the consumed power for cooperation. While $k_i > 1$, r_i makc the profit of $(k_i - 1)R_{ri}$. Therefore, r_i has a minimum value of k_i given as

$$k_i^{\min} = 1 + a\exp(-b(Q_{ri} - P_{ri})) \tag{3}$$

Where $a > 0$, $b > 0$, this function denotes that the minimum value of price is increasing with the improving of power of participant in cooperative computing, and reduces the success rate of this participant in auction. While the participant success in auction, its profit is $(k_i^{\min} - 1)R_{r_i}$. The occupied resource of cooperation computing of initiator could be expressed as

$$C_i = R_s + \alpha_i \tag{4}$$

Combined to function (2), we can get

$$C_i = R_s + k_i R_{ri} = R_s\left(1 + \frac{k_i}{\eta(mW_i + tP_{ri})}\right) \tag{5}$$

From function (5), we can find that C_i is linear function of R_s, so C_i is continuous of R_s in given data field, and have the minimum value in this field. According to Kakutani fixed point theorem, it exists at least one Nash equilibrium point. The participants based on FPSB auction game algorithm could choose the auction strategy with best profit. Follow this strategy; the system will in a steady state after the participant adjust their strategy self-adaptively.

3 Process of Auction Game Algorithm

In satellite, the processing unit S which initiates the auction game (resource allocation initiator) implement the demand of resource allocation based on its margin of computing resource (or the margin of storage resource, which means the idleness of CPU/storage space, and so on. They have the same variation trend. The increasing of margin reduces the demand of cooperation. We only use computing resource for instance). The initiator computes the resource R_s in cooperation, and allocates it by broadcasting on bus to the other n processing units which are the potential participant of the auction game (resource allocation participant).

The potential participant r_i receives the broadcasting message and gets the information of initiator includes R_s, and calculates W_i, R_{r_i} and p_{r_i}. Based on the result, mentions the price α_i and join the auction by feedback message on bus to the initiator.

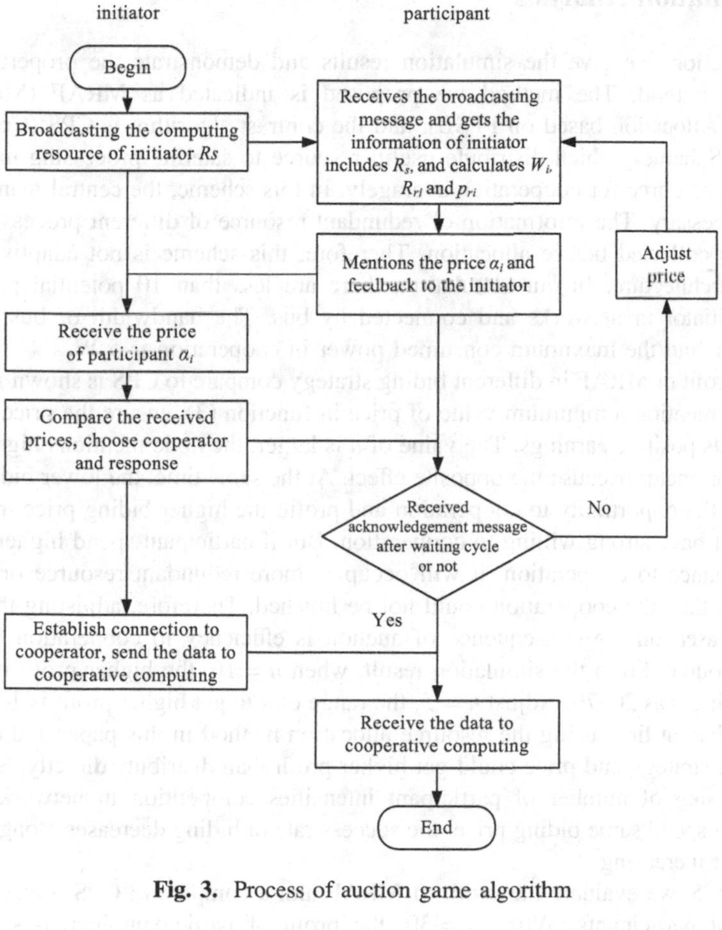

Fig. 3. Process of auction game algorithm

The initiator gets the price from participant in given waiting cycle, then confirms the participant which given the lower price as the bid winner, and establishes the link to it. And send the cooperative data as the proportion of occupying resource, finish distribution.

The winner participant will receive the acknowledgement message and establish link, receive cooperative data from initiator, finish distribution.

The loser participant will not receive the acknowledgement after given waiting cycle, and then consider bidding failure in auction. It will change its auction strategy and improve price when the resource condition permitted, present in the next auction.

The process of auction game algorithm could be expressed in Fig. 3.

Following the program of initiator and participant, the resource allocation could be established. And the course could be finished by satellite processing units autonomously without overall planning and management of central management unit.

4 Simulation Analysis

In this section, we give the simulation results and demonstrate the property of our proposed method. The method we proposed is indicated as MRAF (Method of Resource Allocation based on FPSB), and the contrast algorithm is CPS (Centralized Planning Scheme), which distribute useful resource to satellite processing units have redundant resource for cooperation averagely. In this scheme, the central management unit is necessary. The information of redundant resource of different processing units should be collected before allocation. Therefore, this scheme is not adaptive to distributed architecture. In our simulation, there are less than 10 potential participant except initiator in networks and connected by bus. The bandwidth of bus is set as 100 Mbps, and the maximum consumed power in cooperation is 5 W.

The profit of MRAF in different biding strategy compare to CPS is shown in Fig. 4. The node mention a minimum value of price in function (3), ensure the price satisfied criteria gets positive earnings. The value of a is larger, the node mentions higher price, and the parameter because the opposite effect. At the same time, the lower biding price decreases the opportunity to cooperation and profit; the higher biding price means the participant have strong willing to cooperation. But if participant spend higher price to get the chance to cooperation, it will occupies more redundant resource or exceeds limitation, then the cooperation could not be finished. Therefore, adjusting the biding strategy based on the consequence of auction is efficiency to cooperation based on useful resource. From the simulation result, when $n = 10$, the higher profit is acquire while setting a as 20–70. Adjust $n = 5$, the range of a to get higher profit is 10–40. We can find that, at first, using the resource allocation method in this paper and adjusting the biding strategy and price could get higher profit than distribute directly. Secondly, the increasing of number of participant intensifies competition in networks. If the participant spend same biding price, the success rate of biding decreases along with the participant increasing.

In Fig. 5, we evaluate the profit of MRAF aim a compare to CPS under different number of participants. When $a = 30$, the profit of participant increases with the increasing of number of participants, and get extreme point at $n = 6$ then decreases, but always higher than the profit of CPS. When $a = 60$, the growth is slow and average profit is higher. We can find that MRAF could get higher profit and the positive strategy get lower profit than passive strategy while the network contains fewer nodes. It means the increasing number of nodes intensifies competition in networks.

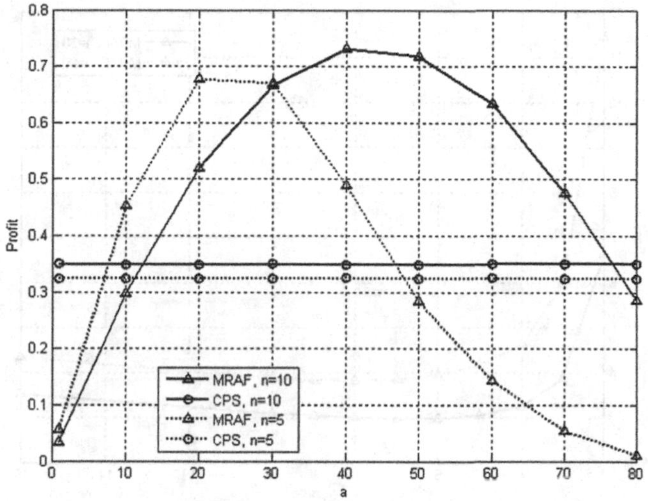

Fig. 4. The profit of MRAF in different biding strategy compare to CPS

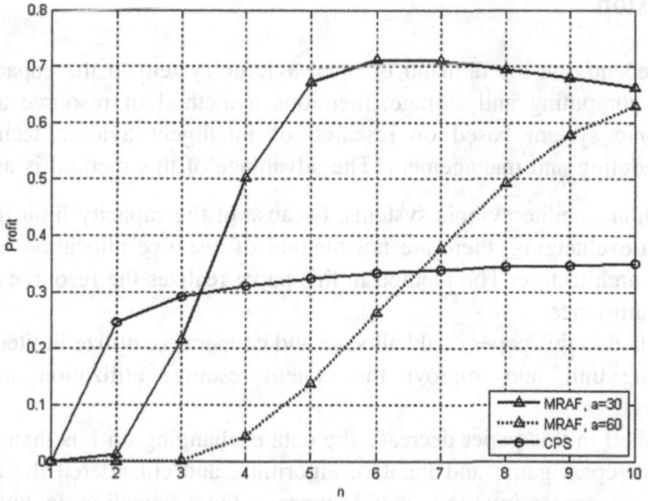

Fig. 5. The profit of MRAF aim *a* compare to CPS under different number of participants

Figure 6 shows the trend of average biding price of MRAF with different strategy along with the number of participant in network. We can find that fewer participants make them spend higher biding price. But too high price could not acquire profit, which is expressed in Fig. 5. When $a = 60$, $n = 2$, the high biding price makes resource to cooperation exceeds the limitation; with the increasing of number of participants, the average price is decreasing and profit increasing.

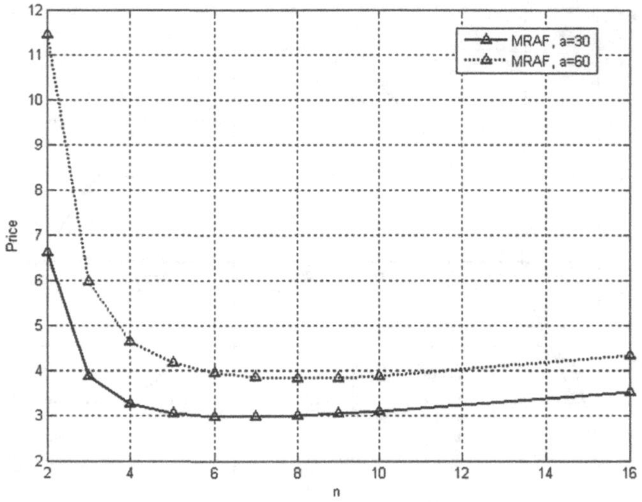

Fig. 6. The biding price of MRAF in different strategy under different number of participants

5 Conclusion

This paper depends on the demand of open avionic system to the capacity of communications, computing and storage, mentions a method of resource allocation of satellite avionic system based on research of intelligent avionic technology and resource scheduling and management. The advantage of this method is as follows:

(1) In common satellite avionic systems, because of the capacity limit in computing and data exchanging, there are not method of resource allocation in distributed network architecture. The method in this paper realizes the resource allocation in this circumstance.
(2) The method in this paper could allocate and cooperative utilize limited resource of processing unit, and improve the system resource utilization and operating efficiency.
(3) The method in this paper decrease the data exchanging on bus than the methods based on repeat game and iterative algorithm, and considered the limitation of resource in processing unit, could improve the occupation in bandwidth and power consuming.

The designing of process of resource allocation algorithm and simulation result prove the effectiveness of this method, and realize coordinating and allocation autonomously in distributed architecture of satellite avionic system, acquire higher profit than centralized planning scheme.

References

1. Wang, J.: Development state and thought of the satellite synthesized electronic system. Spacecraft Eng. **5**(5), 68–73 (2007)
2. Li, X., Shi, S., Li, G.: Integrated electronics system of micro-satellite. Spacecraft Eng. **17**(1), 30–35 (2008)
3. Zhang, F., Chu, W., Fan, X., et al.: Research on architecture of integrated modular avionics. Electron. Opt. Control **16**(9), 47–51 (2009)
4. Feng, X., Lan, H.: New generation aerospace bus technology. Aeronaut. Manuf. Technol. **2012**(3), 98–99 (2012)
5. Zhao, J., He, B.: Onboard data system based on SpaceWire bus. J. Spacecraft TT&C Technol. **2009**(2), 98–99 (2013)
6. ECSS-E-ST-50-12C, SpaceWire-Links, nodes, routers and networks. ESA, Noordwijk (2008)
7. Tsiropoulou, E.E., Vamvakas, P., Papavassiliou, S.: Energy efficient uplink joint resource allocation non-cooperative game with pricing. In: IEEE Wireless Communications and Networking Conference, pp. 2352–2356 (2012)
8. Zappone, A., Jorswieck, E.: Non-cooperative resource allocation in relay-assisted MIMO MAC systems with partial CSI: a game-theoretic approach. In: 2011 IEEE International Conference on Communications (ICC), vol. 57, no. 4, pp. 1–5 (2011)
9. Ma, Y., Chen, H., Lin, Z., et al.: Distributed and optimal resource allocation for power beacon-assisted wireless-powered communications. IEEE Trans. Commun. **63**(10), 3569–3583 (2015)
10. Zhang, X., Ji, H., Li, Y., et al.: Energy efficient transmission in relay based cooperative networks using auction game. In: 2013 IEEE Wireless Communications and Networking Conference (WCNC), pp. 2123–2127 (2013)

Outage Probability Analysis for Hybrid Satellite and Terrestrial Network with Different Combining Schemes

Guoqiang Cheng[1,2](✉), Zhi Lin[1], Min Lin[2,3], Qingquan Huang[1], and Jian Ouyang[3]

[1] College of Communications Engineering, Army Engineering University of PLA, Nanjing 210007, China
chenggq1994@163.com

[2] Nanjing Institute of Telecommunication Technology, Nanjing 210007, China

[3] Key Lab of Broadband Wireless Communication and Sensor Network Technology, Ministry of Education, Nanjing University of Posts and Telecommunications, Nanjing 210003, China

Abstract. In this paper, we investigate the outage probability (OP) of a hybrid satellite and terrestrial cooperative network (HSTCN) with the terrestrial relay having multiple antennas. Here, it is assumed that the satellite channel undergoes the shadowed-Rician fading, while terrestrial channel follows correlated Rayleigh fading. By supposing that statistic channel state information (CSI) of relay-destination link is available at the relay, we first obtain the end-to-end output signal-to-noise ratio (SNR) expression of the HSTCN. Then, the closed-form expressions of the outage probability for the considered system are derived, where two combining schemes, namely, selection combing (SC) and maximal-ratio combining (MRC) protocols are utilized at the destination to combine signals form the satellite and relay. Finally, numerical results are given to validity of the OP analysis, and reveal the performance difference of the two combining schemes.

Keywords: Satellite communication · Correlated Rayleigh · Multi-antennas

1 Introduction

Satellite communication is known as its wide coverage and convenience for remote communication [1]. In order to extend the coverage of satellite and achieve high data transmission, especially when the line of sight link (LOS) is blocked by obstacles, the hybrid satellite-terrestrial cooperative networks were proposed [2].

Supported in part by the Key International Cooperation Research Project under Grant 61720106003, in part by National Natural Science Foundation of China under Grant 61801234 and 61271255.

M. Jia et al. (Eds.): WiSATS 2019, LNICST 281, pp. 488–496, 2019.
https://doi.org/10.1007/978-3-030-19156-6_45

Since the potential value of HSTCNs, many researchers studied this issue. The authors in [3] addressed a problem of amplify-and-forward (AF) based HSTCN in which the MRC was applied at the destination, and the average symbol error rate (ASE) of this system was given. In [4], the authors studied the secrecy performance of a HSTCN in the presence of multiple eavesdroppers, furthermore, they also assumed that the perfect CSI was available at the relay and they considered different cooperative protocols at the relay, namely decode-and-forward (DF) and AF. The authors in [5] considered a HSTCN with AF based relay, in which the satellite node and destination node were equipped with multi-antenna while the relay node was equipped with single antenna, the outage probability of this system was evaluated. The authors in [6] analyzed the ergodic capacity of a best relay selection HSTCN, in which statistic CSI of relay-destination links was available at the relays. Furthermore, they considered two different cases that DF and AF were applied at the relay, respectively.

Although many researchers such as [3–6] have studied the performance form many angles, they haven't considered the situation that the relay-destination link follows correlated Rayleigh fading and the CSI of this link is statistical such as [7], especially when there are different combining protocols applied at the destination. To fill this gap, we consider a HSTCN with a multi-antenna DF relay where the satellite links undergo the shadowed-Rician fading and the terrestrial link undergoes the correlated Rayleigh fading. Moreover, in order to fully analyze the performance of this system, we assume that the destination applies SC and MRC protocols, respectively. Then, we analyze the outage probability of these two schemes and obtain the closed-form expressions, as far as the authors known, this is the first time that such expressions are obtained. Finally, the numerable results are provided to confirm the correctness of these expressions and show the different performance of the two combining protocols.

2 System Model

We consider a HSTCN in which the satellite source (S) communicates with a terrestrial destination (D) with the aid of a terrestrial relay (R), similar as [8]. We assume that the S-R and S-D links follow the shadowed-Rician fading and the R-D link undergoes the correlated Rayleigh fading. The satellite and the terrestrial user nodes are both installed a signal antenna, while the terrestrial relay node is equipped with N antennas.

The process of the communication in this HSTCN can be divided into two time slots. During the first time slot, S sends its signal $x_s(t)$ to R and D with the average power $\mathrm{E}\left[|x_s(t)|^2\right] = 1$, the received signal at R and D are expressed as [9]

$$y_{d1}(t) = \sqrt{P_s} h_{sd}(t) x_s(t) + n_{d1}(t), \tag{1}$$

$$y_r(t) = \sqrt{P_s} \mathbf{w}_{sr}^H \mathbf{h}_{sr} x_s(t) + n_r(t), \tag{2}$$

wherc P_s denotes the transmit power of S, h_{sd} and $\mathbf{h}_{sr} = [h_1, h_2, \cdots, h_N]^T$ the channel coefficient of S-D link and S-R link, respectively, $\mathbf{w}_{sr} \in \mathbf{C}^{N \times 1}$ the receive beamforming (BF) weight vector at R, $n_{d1(t)}$ and $n_r(t)$ represent the zero mean additive white Gaussian noise (AWGN) with variances σ_0^2 and σ_1^2 at D and R, respectively. Then, the signal-to-noise ratios (SNRs) at D and R during the first time phase are, respectively, given by

$$\gamma_{d1} = \frac{P_s}{\sigma_0^2} |h_{sd}|^2, \tag{3}$$

$$\gamma_r = \frac{P_s}{\sigma_1^2} \mathbf{h}_{sr}^H \mathbf{w}_{sr} \mathbf{w}_{sr}^H \mathbf{h}_{sr}. \tag{4}$$

During the second time phase, R processes the received signal $y_r(t)$ and employs the DF strategy and sends the re-encoded signal $x_r(t)$ with $\mathrm{E}\left[|x_r(t)|^2\right] = 1$ to D with weight vector $\mathbf{w}_{rd} \in \mathbf{C}^{N \times 1}$. Thus, the received signal at D from the relay can be modeled as

$$y_{d2}(t) = \sqrt{P_r} \mathbf{h}_{rd}^H \mathbf{w}_{rd} x_r(t) + n_{d2}(t), \tag{5}$$

with $n_{d2}(t)$ is the zero mean additive white Gaussian noise (AWGN) with $E\left[n_{d2}(t)^2\right] = \sigma_2^2$. When applying the DF protocol applied at R, the SNR of S-R-D link is given by [10,11]

$$\gamma_{df} = \min\{\gamma_r, \gamma_{d2}\}, \tag{6}$$

where

$$\gamma_{d2} = \frac{P_r}{\sigma_2^2} \mathbf{w}_{rd}^H \mathbf{h}_{rd} \mathbf{h}_{rd}^H \mathbf{w}_{rd}. \tag{7}$$

Since D receives signals both from S and R, we consider D applies two different combining protocols to combine the signal, namely, MRC and SC.

(1) By applying SC at D, the output SNR is given by

$$\gamma_{SC} = \max\{\gamma_{df}, \gamma_{d1}\} = max\{min\{\gamma_r, \gamma_{d2}\}, \gamma_{d1}\}, \tag{8}$$

(2) By applying MRC at D, the output SNR is given by

$$\gamma_{MRC} = \gamma_{df} + \gamma_{d1} = min\{\gamma_r, \gamma_{d2}\} + \gamma_{d1}. \tag{9}$$

3 Problem Formulation and Preliminary Results

We consider a optimization problem to maximize the end-to-end SNRs, namely, γ_{SC} and γ_{MRC} with the constrained of transmit BF weight vectors of this system.

$$\max_{\mathbf{w}_{sr}, \mathbf{w}_{rd}} \gamma_i \quad s.t. \|\mathbf{w}_{sr}\| = 1, \|\mathbf{w}_{rd}\| = 1, \tag{10}$$

where $(i = SC, MRC)$. Since γ_{d1} is not affected by $\mathbf{w}_{sr}, \mathbf{w}_{rd}$, and according to (8) and (9), the optimization problem (10) can be reformulated as the following two optimization problem, namely

$$\max_{\mathbf{w}_{sr}} \gamma_r = \frac{P_s}{\sigma_1^2} \mathbf{w}_{sr}^H \mathbf{h}_{sr} \mathbf{h}_{sr}^H \mathbf{w}_{sr} \quad s.t. \|\mathbf{w}_{sr}\| = 1, \tag{11}$$

$$\max_{\mathbf{w}_{rd}} \gamma_{d2} = \frac{P_r}{\sigma_{d2}^2} \mathbf{w}_{rd}^H \mathbf{h}_{rd} \mathbf{h}_{rd}^H \mathbf{w}_{rd} \quad s.t. \|\mathbf{w}_{rd}\| = 1. \tag{12}$$

Then, we focus on the design of receive and transmit BF at R.

3.1 Satellite Downlink Channels

For the optimization problem (11), obviously, the solution is MRC [12], so we have $\mathbf{w}_{sr} = \mathbf{h}_{sr}/\|\mathbf{h}_{sr}\|$. Such that, the maximal value of γ_r is given by

$$\gamma_r = \overline{\gamma}_r |\mathbf{h}_{sr}|^2, \tag{13}$$

where $\overline{\gamma}_r = \frac{P_s}{\sigma_1^2}$ presents the average SNR at S, and $|\mathbf{h}_{sr}|^2 = \sum_{i=1}^N |h_i|^2$.

In this paper, we assume the satellite links undergo Shadowed-Rician fading, thus the probability density functions (PDFs) of $|h_i|^2$ $(i = 1, 2 \cdots N)$ can be expressed as [12,13]

$$f_{|h_i|^2}(x) = \alpha_i \exp(-\beta_i x) {}_1F_1(m_i; 1; c_i x), \tag{14}$$

where $\alpha_i = (2b_i m_i/(2b_i m_i + \Omega_i))^{m_i}/2b_i$, $\beta_i = 1/2b_i$, $c_i = (\Omega_i/(2b_i m_i + \Omega_i))/2b_i$, $(i = 1, \cdots N)$, Ω_i is the average power of the LOS component, $2b_i$ is the average power of the multi-path component and m_i the Nakagami-m parameter. We assume that S-R link is *ii.d* fading channels, such that, we denote $\Omega_1 = \cdots = \Omega_N = \Omega b_1 = \cdots = b_N = b, m_1 = \cdots = m_N = m$, hence the subscript $i = 1, \cdots N$ can be dropped, meanwhile, we retain our focus in the case of Nakagami-m parameter taking integer values, *i.e.* $m \in \mathrm{N}$. With the help of [12], ${}_1F_1(m; 1; cx)$ becomes

$${}_1F_1(m; 1; cx) = \exp(cx) \times \sum_{k=0}^{m-1} \frac{(-1)^k (1-m)_k (cx)^k}{(k!)^2}, \tag{15}$$

with $(x)_n = x(x+1) \cdots (x+n-1)$. Then, by applying (15) to (14), the PDF of $|h_i|^2$ can be denoted as

$$f_{|h_i|^2}(x) = \sum_{k=0}^{m-1} \underbrace{\frac{(-1)^k (1-m)_k c^k}{(k!)^2}}_{\xi(k)} \times \alpha x^k \exp(-(\beta - c)x). \tag{16}$$

After some mathematical calculation, the PDF of $|\mathbf{h}_{sr}|^2$ is given by [12]

$$f_{|\mathbf{h}_{sr}|^2}(x) = \sum_{k_1=0}^{m-1} \cdots \sum_{k_N=0}^{m-1} \Xi(N) x^{\Lambda-1} \exp(-(\beta - c)x), \tag{17}$$

where $\Lambda \triangleq \sum_{i=1}^{N} k_N + N$ and

$$\Xi(N) = \prod_{i=1}^{N} \xi(k_i)\alpha^N \prod_{j=1}^{N-1} B(\sum_{l=1}^{j} k_l + j, k_{j+1} + 1), \tag{18}$$

with $B(\cdot,\cdot)$ denoting the beta function [14]. Thus the PDF of γ_r can be obtained as

$$f_{\gamma_r}(x) = \sum_{k_1=0}^{m-1} \cdots \sum_{k_N=0}^{m-1} \frac{\Xi(N)x^{\Lambda-1}}{\overline{\gamma}_s{}^{\Lambda}} \exp\left(-\frac{\beta-c}{\overline{\gamma}_s}x\right). \tag{19}$$

Meanwhile, S-D link also undergoes the shadowed-Rician fading with the parameters (m_0, b_0, Ω_0), such that, the PDF of γ_{d1} can be expressed as

$$f_{\gamma_{d1}}(x) = \sum_{k=0}^{m_0-1} \frac{\xi(k)}{\overline{\gamma}_s^{k+1}} \alpha_0 x^k \exp\left(\frac{-(\beta_0-c_0)}{\overline{\gamma}_s}x\right). \tag{20}$$

3.2 Terrestrial Downlink Channel

We assume the R-D link follows correlated Rayleigh fading, such as the related work [15], thus $\mathbf{h}_{rd}(N \times 1)$ can be modeled as [15,16]

$$\mathbf{h}_{rd}(t) = \frac{1}{\sqrt{L}} \sum_{l=1}^{L} \rho_l(t)\,\mathbf{a}(\theta_l), \tag{21}$$

where $\theta_l \in \left[\overline{\theta}_l - \Delta\theta_l/2, \overline{\theta}_l + \Delta\theta_l/2\right]$ is the angle-of-departure (AOD) of the l-th path signal with $\overline{\theta}_l$ being the mean cluster AOD and $\Delta\theta_l$ the angular spread, respectively, $\rho_l\ (0, \sigma^2)$ denote the fading coefficient of the path signal, respectively. Without loss of generality, $\rho_l(t)$ in (21) is modeled as a complex Gaussian random variable with zero mean and unit variance. If uniform linear array (ULA) is employed at the transmitter, the downlink array steering vector $\mathbf{a}(\theta_l)$ is given by

$$\mathbf{a}(\theta_l) = \left[1, exp\left(j\kappa d_a \cos\theta_l\right), \ldots, exp\left(j\left(N-1\right)\kappa d_a \cos\theta_l\right)\right]^T, \tag{22}$$

with $\kappa = \frac{2\pi}{\lambda_{rd}}$ being the wavenumber, λ_{rd} the carrier wavelength and d_a the inter-element spacing. Then, we put our attention on the optimization problem (12) to maximize the received SNR at D for R-D link. Specifically, the statistical CSI of R-D link is available at R as our assumption. In this case, R only know the matrix of $\mathbf{h}_{rd}$, that is, $R = E\left[\mathbf{h}_{rd}\mathbf{h}_{rd}^H\right]$. Such that, the optimization problem (12) can be denoted as

$$\begin{aligned} \max_{\mathbf{w}_{rd}} \gamma_{d2} &= \bar{\gamma}_r \mathbf{w}_{rd}^H \underbrace{E\left[\mathbf{h}_{rd}\mathbf{h}_{rd}^H\right]}_{R} \mathbf{w}_{rd}, \\ s.t. \quad & \|\mathbf{w}_{rd}\| = 1. \end{aligned} \tag{23}$$

Then, with the help of singular value decomposition (SVD) to R [17], we have that

$$\mathbf{R} = \mathbf{V}\mathbf{\Phi}\mathbf{V}^H, \quad \mathbf{\Phi} = \operatorname{diag}\left(\lambda_1, \ldots, \lambda_N\right), \quad \mathbf{V} = \left[\mathbf{v}_1, \ldots, \mathbf{v}_N\right], \tag{24}$$

where $\mathbf{V}$ is the unitary matrix with $\mathbf{v}_j\,(j=1,\ldots,N)$ being the corresponding eigenvectors, $\mathbf{\Phi}$ the eigenvalue matrix with eigenvalues $\lambda_j\,(j=1,\ldots,N)$ which are arranged in decreasing order. With the aid of Generalized Rayleigh entropy formula, we have that

$$\mathbf{w}_{rd}^{H}\mathbf{R}\mathbf{w}_{rd} \le \lambda_{\max}(\mathbf{R}) = \lambda_1, \tag{25}$$

with the equality sign holding when $\mathbf{w}_{rd}$ equals to the eigenvector corresponding to λ_1. Such that, the solution of optimization (12) is $\mathbf{w}_{rd}=\mathbf{v}_1$. Meanwhile, by using the Kronecker model, $\mathbf{h}_{rd}$ can be denoted as

$$\mathbf{h}_{rd} = \mathbf{R}^{\frac{1}{2}}\widetilde{\mathbf{h}}_{rd}, \tag{26}$$

where $\widetilde{\mathbf{h}}_{rd} = \left[\widetilde{h}_{rd,1},\ldots,\widetilde{h}_{rd,N}\right]^T$ with $\widetilde{h}_{rd,i} \sim CN(0,1)$ being i.i.d random variables. Such that, γ_{d2} can be rewritten as

$$\begin{aligned}\gamma_{d2} &= \bar{\gamma}_r\left|\mathbf{w}_{rd}^{H}\mathbf{h}_{rd}\right|^2 = \bar{\gamma}_r\left|\mathbf{v}_1^{H}\mathbf{R}^{\frac{1}{2}}\widetilde{\mathbf{h}}_{rd}\right|^2\\ &= \bar{\gamma}_r\widetilde{\mathbf{h}}_{rd}^{H}\mathbf{R}^{H}\mathbf{v}_1\mathbf{v}_1^{H}\mathbf{R}^{\frac{1}{2}}\widetilde{\mathbf{h}}_{rd}\\ &= \bar{\gamma}_r\lambda_1\left|\widetilde{h}_{rd,1}\right|^2.\end{aligned} \tag{27}$$

Then, after some mathematical calculation, the PDF of γ_{d2} is given by

$$f_{\gamma_{d2}}(x) = \frac{1}{\lambda_1\bar{\gamma}_r}e^{-\frac{x}{\lambda_1\bar{\gamma}_r}}. \tag{28}$$

4 Outage Probability

Outage probability is defined as the probability that the SNR falls below a certain threshold γ_{th}, thus the OPs of this system when SC and MRC are applied at D, namely, P_{SC}^{out} and P_{MRC}^{out} are given by

$$\begin{aligned}P_{SC}^{out} &\triangleq \Pr\{\gamma_{SC} < \gamma_{th}\} = \Pr\{\max\{\gamma_{df},\gamma_{d1}\} < \gamma_{th}\}\\ &= F_{\gamma_{df}}(\gamma_{th}) \times F_{\gamma_{d1}}(\gamma_{th})\\ P_{MRC}^{out} &\triangleq \Pr\{\gamma_{MRC} < \gamma_{th}\} = \Pr\{(\gamma_{df}+\gamma_{d1}) < \gamma_{th}\}\\ &= \int_0^x F_{\gamma_{df}}(x-\tau) \times f_{\gamma_{d1}}(\tau)d\tau,\end{aligned} \tag{29}$$

with $F_{\gamma_{df}}(\gamma_{th}) = 1-(1-F_{\gamma_r}(\gamma_{th}))\times(1-F_{\gamma_{d2}}(\gamma_{th}))$, $F_{\gamma_i}(x)$, $(i \triangleq r, d1, d2)$ being the cumulative distribution function (CDF) of γ_i. with the help of [14], the CDF of γ_{d1} can be written as

$$F_{\gamma_{d1}} = \sum_{k=0}^{m_0-1}\frac{k!\xi(k)\alpha_0}{(\beta_0-c_0)^{k+1}}\left(1-\sum_{l=0}^{k}\frac{(\beta_0-c_0)^l{\gamma_{th}}^l}{l!\bar{\gamma}_s^l}\times\exp(\frac{-(\beta_0-c_0)\gamma_{th}}{\bar{\gamma}_s})\right). \tag{30}$$

Such that, the CDF of γ_{df} can be obtained as

$$F_{\gamma_{df}} = \left[1-\sum_{k_1=0}^{m-1}\cdots\sum_{k_N=0}^{m-1}\sum_{r=0}^{\Lambda-1}\frac{(\Lambda-1)!\Xi(N){\gamma_{th}}^r}{r!\bar{\gamma}_s^r(\beta-c)^{\Lambda-r}}\exp\left(-\left(\frac{\beta-c}{\bar{\gamma}_s}+\frac{1}{\lambda_1\bar{\gamma}_r}\right)\gamma_{th}\right)\right], \tag{31}$$

(1) In the case of SC applied at D, with the help of Eqs. (29) - (31), P_{SC}^{out} can be written as (32)

$$\begin{aligned} P_{SC}^{out} &= F_{\gamma_{df}}(\gamma_{th}) \times F_{\gamma_{d1}}(\gamma_{th}) \\ &= \sum_{k=0}^{m_0-1} \frac{k!\xi(k)\alpha}{(\beta_0-c_0)^{k+1}} \left(1 - \sum_{l=0}^{k} \frac{(\beta_0-c_0)^l {\gamma_{th}}^l}{l!\bar{\gamma}_s^t} \exp(\frac{-(\beta_0-c_0)\gamma_{th}}{\bar{\gamma}_s})\right) \\ &\times \left[1 - \sum_{k_1=0}^{m-1} \cdots \sum_{k_N=0}^{m-1} \sum_{r=0}^{\Lambda-1} \frac{(\Lambda-1)!\Xi(N){\gamma_{th}}^r}{r!\bar{\gamma}_s^r(\beta-c)^{\Lambda-r}} \exp\left(-\left(\frac{\beta-c}{\bar{\gamma}_s} + \frac{1}{\lambda_1\bar{\gamma}_r}\right)\gamma_{th}\right)\right]. \end{aligned} \tag{32}$$

(2) In the case of MRC applied at D, the OP is given by (32)

$$\begin{aligned} P_{MRC}^{out} = & \sum_{k=0}^{m_0-1} \frac{k!\xi(k)\alpha_0}{(\beta_0-c_0)^{k+1}} \left(1 - \sum_{l=0}^{k} \frac{(\beta_0-c_0)^l {\gamma_{th}}^l}{l!\bar{\gamma}_s^t} \exp\left(\frac{-(\beta_0-c_0)\gamma_{th}}{\bar{\gamma}_s}\right)\right) \\ & - \sum_{k=0}^{m_0-1} \sum_{k_1=0}^{m-1} \cdots \sum_{k_N=0}^{m-1} \sum_{r=0}^{\Lambda-1} \frac{(\Lambda-1)!\Xi(N)\alpha_0\xi(k){\gamma_{th}}^{(k+r+1)}}{r!\bar{\gamma}_s^{(r+k+1)}(\beta-c)^{\Lambda-r}} \exp\left(-\left(\frac{\beta-c}{\bar{\gamma}_s} + \frac{1}{\lambda_1\bar{\gamma}_r}\right)\gamma_{th}\right) \\ & \times B(r+1, k+1)_1F_1\left(k+1, r+k+2, \left(\frac{1}{\lambda_1\bar{\gamma}_r} + \frac{(\beta-c)-(\beta_0-c_0)}{\bar{\gamma}_s}\right)\gamma_{th}\right) \end{aligned} \tag{33}$$

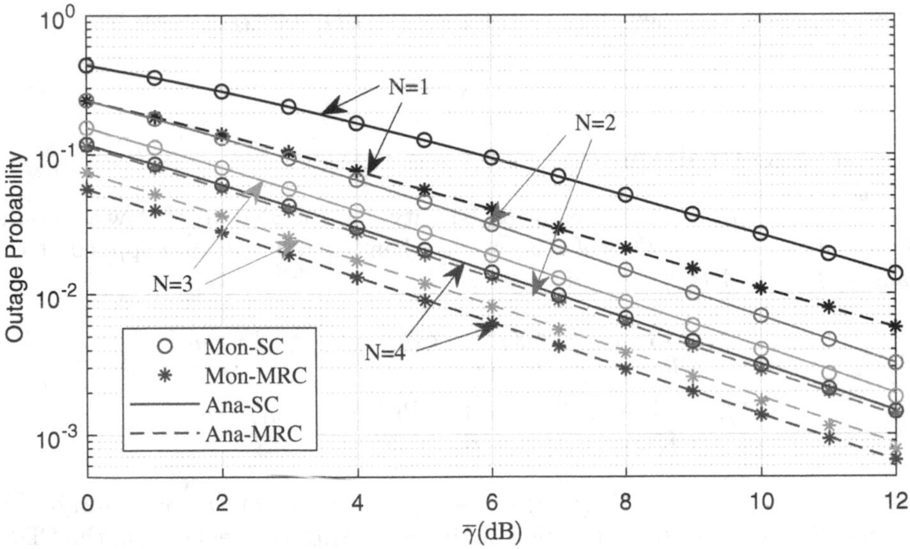

Fig. 1. Outage probability of the system

5 Simulation Results

In this section, we provide the simulation results to testify the validity of expressions of OP in the last section, the results also shows the influence of the antennas' number and different combining protocol to the OP of this system. The simulation results are obtained with 10^7 channel realizations, and we assume that $\overline{\gamma} = \overline{\gamma}_r = 2\overline{\gamma}_s$, $\gamma_{th} = 0\,\text{dB}$ for both the satellite and terrestrial links.

Figure 1 shows the OP of the system in the case that different protocols applied at D and different antennas' number equipped at R. We assume that $b = 0.251$, $m = 5$, $\Omega = 0.278$ and $\theta = 5°$, $L = 10$. It can be clearly observed that the OP curves are corresponding ti the analysis curves, while the performance gets better with the increase of antennas' number at relay no matter in any scheme. And we find that the performance of the system when MRC applied at D is better than the case that SC applied at D, which means MRC is more efficient than SC for combining.

6 Conclusion

In this paper, we analyze the performance of a HSTCN with a DF based terrestrial relay which is equipped with multi-antennas. We consider MRC and SC combing schemes at D for this system to detail the analysis, the expressions of OP are obtained. According to the numerical results, we find that the performance of this system gets better with these reasons: the increase of antennas' number at terrestrial relay and the enhancing of combining protocol at the destination.

References

1. Lin, M., Lin, Z., et al.: Joint beamforming for secure communication in cognitive satellite terrestrial networks. IEEE J. Sel. Areas Commun. **36**(5), 1017–1029 (2018)
2. Paolo, C., Giovanni, G., Sastri, K.: A survey on mobile satellite systems. Int. J. Satellite Commun. Netw. **28**(1), 29–57 (2010)
3. Bhatnagar, M.R., Arti, M.K.: Performance analysis of AF based hybrid satellite-terrestrial cooperative network over generalized fading channels. IEEE Commun. Lett. **17**(10), 1912–1915 (2013)
4. Huang, Q., Lin, M., An, K., Ouyang, J., Zhu, W.: Secrecy performance of hybrid satellite-terrestrial relay networks in the presence of multiple eavesdroppers. IET Commun. **12**(1), 26–34 (2018)
5. An, K., Lin, M., Liang, T., et al.: Performance analysis of multi-antenna hybrid satellite-terrestrial relay networks in the presence of interference. IEEE Trans. Commun. **63**(11), 4390–4404 (2015)
6. Zhao, Y., Chen, H., Xie, L., Wang, K.: Exact and asymptotic ergodic capacity analysis of the hybrid satellite-terrestrial cooperative system over generalised fading channels. IET Commun. **12**(11), 1342–1350 (2018)
7. Lin, Z., Lin, M., et al.: Robust secure beamforming for 5G cellular networks coexisting with satellite networks. IEEE J. Sel. Areas Commun. **36**(4), 932–945 (2018)
8. Arti, M.K., Bhatnagar, M.R.: Beamforming and combining in hybrid satellite-terrestrial cooperative systems. IEEE Commun. Lett. **18**(3), 483–486 (2014)
9. Sreng, S., Escrig, B., Boucheret, M.L.: Exact symbol error probability of hybrid/integrated satellite-terrestrial cooperative network. IEEE Trans. Wirel. Commun. **12**(3), 1310–1319 (2013)
10. Ju, M.C., Kim, I.M., Dong, I.K.: Joint relay selection and relay ordering for DF-based cooperative relay networks. IEEE Trans. Commun. **60**(4), 908–915 (2012)

11. An, K., Ouyang, J., Lin, M., et al.: Outage analysis of multi-antenna cognitive hybrid satellite-terrestrial relay networks with beamforming. IEEE Commun. Lett. **19**(7), 1157–1160 (2015)
12. Miridakis, N.I., Vergados, D.D., Michalas, A.: Dual-hop communication over a satellite relay and shadowed Rician channels. IEEE Trans. Veh. Technol. **64**(9), 4031–4040 (2015)
13. Abdi, A., Lau, W.C., Alouini, M.S., Kaveh, M.: A new simple model for land mobile satellite channels: first- and second-order statistics. IEEE Trans. Wirel. Commun. **2**(3), 519–528 (2003)
14. Gradshteyn, I.S., Ryzhik, I.M.: Table of Integrals, Series, and Products. Academic Press, San Diego (2010)
15. Lin, M., Yang, L., Zhu, W.P., et al.: An open-loop adaptive space-time transmit scheme for correlated fading channels. IEEE J. Sel. Topics Sig. Process. **12**(2), 147–158 (2008)
16. Dakdouki, A.S., Tabulo, M.: On the eigenvalue distribution of smart-antenna arrays in wireless communication systems. Antennas Propag. Mag. IEEE **46**(4), 158–167 (2004)
17. Lin, M., Ouyang, J., Zhu, W.P.: Joint beamforming and power control for device-to-device communications underlaying cellular networks. IEEE J. Sel. Areas Commun. **34**(1), 138–150 (2016)

UAV Tracking with Proposals Based on Optical Flow

Min Jia[1], Zheng Gao[1(✉)], Zhisong Hao[2], and Qing Guo[1]

[1] School of Electronics and Information Engineering, Harbin Institute of Technology, Harbin 150001, China
alexzgao@outlook.com

[2] The 54th Research Institute of China Electronics Technology Group Corporation, Shijiazhuang 050000, Hebei, China

Abstract. UAV tracking is aimed to infer the location of the object from the videos captured by an aerial viewpoint. The challenges mainly focus on fast motion, scale variation and aspect ratio variation. The region proposal in image detection can detect the object candidates in the image, which can be leveraged to find the optimal location of the object. In this paper, a tracking algorithm using Farneback optical flow is proposed to provide object proposals for correlation filter for robust tracking under aerial scenarios. The Farneback flow estimates the motion of the object between adjacent frames and an improved FAST detector is adopted to detect the keypoints that contain the local patterns of the object from the last frame. The object proposal is obtained by computing translations of the keypoints. The final proposal is determined by computing the bounding box that encloses the keypoints. A correlation filter from KCF is used to detect the object on the proposal. The quantitative evaluation results on OTB100 show the advantage of the proposed tracker to state-of-the-art trackers in accuracy, especially under fast motion.

Keywords: UAV tracking · Farneback · FAST · Correlation filter

1 Introduction

Generic object tracking has made significant progress these years. The tracking-by-detection framework focuses on applying image detection techniques to tracking systems and achieves great success. Since the feature detection has accomplished superior results in object representation, the tracking algorithm based on feature detector tends to perform better in accuracy than traditional trackers, which are developed by estimating the motions of the object between two adjacent frames [1]. The traditional feature detectors (e.g., HOG, LINEMOD) are proposed to represent the local features in the image and perform incredibly well on feature representation tasks, which contributes to the improvement of feature detection.

In order to construct feature detectors beyond manual design, some researchers begin to explore the study of learning neural networks from the training dataset to represent the objects. The application of neural network accounts for the success in image detection and classification in recent years [2]. Inspired by the work related to

M. Jia et al. (Eds.): WiSATS 2019, LNICST 281, pp. 497–505, 2019.
https://doi.org/10.1007/978-3-030-19156-6_46

neural network, the literatures that discuss deep tracking algorithms built upon deep learning have attracted more attention recently [3]. Held et al. [4] first propose GOTURN, a tracking method based on deep regression network that can run in real time. GOTURN uses the deep regression network to learn the connection between the object appearance and the object location by estimating the motions, which is completely different from the methods with convolutional neural network (CNN) for feature detection and classification. Since the classification network has excellent performance for the description of the object, Bertinetto et al. [5] adopts an offline trained CNN for feature detection by computing convolutional features.

However, there are only few literatures related to UAV tracking. Compared to generic object tracking, the main challenges are different. Mueller et al. [6] argue that for UAV tracking, the primary challenges include fast motion, scale variation and aspect ratio variation.

Zhu et al. [7] introduce the idea of region proposal in image detection to object tracking to deal with fast motion. A search strategy for object location beyond local search is proposed to detect the object candidates and the detection is performed on the proposals. They extract the edge map for the current frame first and then find the bounding boxes that enclose the contours based on Edge Boxes. The object candidates are in the closed boundaries. However, the object proposal strategy based on contours faces two major problems: (1) it is likely to produce an edge map with lots of false proposals that do not contain the object especially when the textures of the background are diverse; (2) the objects with similar aspect ratio to the object of interest will seriously interfere the detection on the proposal boxes, such as tracking for pedestrians on the street.

Generally, the object can be represented with some keypoints. The keypoint contains local structures of the object and is widely used in many fields like face recognition, pose estimation, gesture detection, etc. The local keypoint reflects the tree-structured structure of the object and connection of different parts. Therefore, we would like to track the trajectories of the keypoints along the adjacent frames and estimate the motions of the keypoints to infer the object proposals.

The main work in this paper is to combine optical flow and correlation filter in [8] for UAV tracking. The optical flow is used to compute motions of the keypoints and estimate the object proposals. The correlation filter is performed on the object candidates for accurate detection of the object.

The main contributions of our work are summarized as follows. First, we leverage the Farneback optical flow for object candidate estimation. The flow keeps tracks of the keypoints inside the object and provides information of potential location of the object, which is beyond the local search strategy broadly used in the current trackers. Second, a FAST detector with local threshold is proposed to detect the local strong keypoints inside the bounding box. The keypoints in the previous frame is employed to predict the locations in the current frame based on the flow. The rectangle that encloses the keypoints indicates the proposal of the object. Note that the proposed tracker is called OFT in this paper.

2 Correlation Filter

The correlation filter is meant to solve ridge regression problem with DFT operation for high speed. The correlation filter is used to perform convolution operation to compute the similarity to the object for the test sample. The training samples are generated by cyclic shifts of the base sample and construct a circulant matrix, which can be expressed with DFT matrix. Supposed that the set of samples is denoted by $\{\boldsymbol{x}_i\}$, and the regression labels are $\{y_i\}$. The optimal solution to the ridge regression problem is found by solving the following loss function:

$$\boldsymbol{w}^* = \arg\min_{\boldsymbol{w}} \|X\boldsymbol{w} - \boldsymbol{y}\|_2^2 + \lambda\|\boldsymbol{w}\|_2^2 \tag{1}$$

where X is the circulant matrix composed of the positive sample (i.e., base sample) and negative samples (i.e., shifted samples from the base sample) as the rows, $\boldsymbol{w}$ is the correlation filter, and λ is a regularization parameter that balances the residual error and generalization. The regression function $f(\boldsymbol{x}) = \boldsymbol{w}^T\boldsymbol{x}$ outputs the detection score for the test sample $\boldsymbol{x}$, which decides the label of the sample. The work in [8] proves that the solution to (1) is closed-form with $\boldsymbol{w} = (X^H X + \lambda I)^{-1} X^H \boldsymbol{y}$. However, the closed-form solution requires inversion operation, which is expensive in matrix operation and time consuming. Since the circulant matrix can be expressed as a function over its DFT transformation and DFT matrix, the matrix X can be diagonalized as follows:

$$X = F diag(\hat{\boldsymbol{x}}) F^H \tag{2}$$

where $\hat{\boldsymbol{x}}$ is the expression of $\boldsymbol{x}$ in Fourier domain, and F represents the DFT matrix with $\hat{\boldsymbol{x}} = \sqrt{n}F\boldsymbol{x}$. The closed-form solution can be solved efficiently with (2):

$$\hat{\boldsymbol{w}} = \frac{\hat{\boldsymbol{x}} \odot \hat{\boldsymbol{y}}}{\hat{\boldsymbol{x}}^* \odot \hat{\boldsymbol{x}} + \lambda} \tag{3}$$

where $\odot$ performs the product in an element-wise way. The optimal solution is computed efficiently in Fourier domain and the real solution is obtained via inverse DFT. To improve the classification performance in non-linear space, the kernel trick is used to obtain a non-linear function $f(\boldsymbol{z}) = \boldsymbol{w}^T\phi(\boldsymbol{z}) = \boldsymbol{\alpha}^T\phi(X)\phi(\boldsymbol{z}) = \sum_i \alpha_i \kappa(\boldsymbol{z}, \boldsymbol{x}_i)$, where $\boldsymbol{w} = \sum_i \alpha_i \phi(\boldsymbol{x}_i) = \phi(X)^T\boldsymbol{\alpha}$ is expressed in kernel space, $\phi(\boldsymbol{z})$ maps the original space of $\boldsymbol{z}$ to a high-dimensional space, $\kappa(\boldsymbol{z}, \boldsymbol{x}_i)$ performs the dot-product $\kappa(\boldsymbol{z}, \boldsymbol{x}_i) = \phi(\boldsymbol{z})^T\phi(\boldsymbol{x}_i)$. Thus the optimal solution can be performed over $\boldsymbol{\alpha}$ instead of $\boldsymbol{w}$:

$$\boldsymbol{\alpha}^* = \arg\min_{\boldsymbol{\alpha}} \|\phi(X)\phi(X)^T\boldsymbol{\alpha} - \boldsymbol{y}\|_2^2 + \lambda\|\phi(X)^T\boldsymbol{\alpha}\|_2^2 \tag{4}$$

The solution to (4) can be written as:

$$\hat{\alpha} = \frac{\hat{y}}{\widehat{k}^{xx} + \lambda} \tag{5}$$

where $k^{xx'}$ is composed of elements $k_i^{xx'} = \kappa(x', x_i)$, x_i is the i-th row of X, and $k^{xx'}$ is the DFT transformation of $k^{xx'}$. The regression function in Fourier domain can be expressed as:

$$\widehat{f}(z) = \widehat{k}^{xz} \odot \widehat{\alpha} \tag{6}$$

The regression function outputs a 2-dimensional response map and the maximum value in the map corresponds to the location of the object.

The correlation filter is evaluated on the neighboring region surrounding the tracked location from the last frame. However, the local sampling strategy cannot deal with fast motion. In this paper, the optical flow is adopted to compute the motions and infer the object proposals.

3 Proposals Based on Optical Flow

The basic idea of object proposal is to use Farneback optical flow to estimate the motions in the image and decide final proposal based on the keypoints of the object. The keypoints are detected by FAST detector with local threshold and the object proposal is estimated by computing the bounding box enclosing the keypoints.

3.1 Farneback Optical Flow

Farneback uses a quadratic polynomial to formulate the intensity of the pixel in the local region. The approximation over local coordinates $\boldsymbol{x}$ for the neighboring region of one pixel can be written as:

$$I(\boldsymbol{x}) = \boldsymbol{x}^T \boldsymbol{A} \boldsymbol{x} + \boldsymbol{b}^T \boldsymbol{x} + c \tag{7}$$

where $\boldsymbol{A} \in \mathbb{R}^{2\times2}$, $\boldsymbol{b} \in \mathbb{R}^2$ and c are coefficients of the quadratic polynomial, which can be computed with weighted least square algorithm. The polynomial is a function with respect to the horizontal and vertical coordinates $\boldsymbol{x} = (x, y)$. Since the local region surrounds the point of interest, the estimated coefficients vary when the point in the center changes.

When the point moves to the new position in the next frame by displacement $\boldsymbol{d}$, the approximation can be rewritten as:

$$\begin{aligned} I_2(\boldsymbol{x}) &= I_1(\boldsymbol{x} - \boldsymbol{d}) = (\boldsymbol{x} - \boldsymbol{d})^T \boldsymbol{A}_1 (\boldsymbol{x} - \boldsymbol{d}) + \boldsymbol{b}_1^T (\boldsymbol{x} - \boldsymbol{d}) + c_1 \\ &= \boldsymbol{x}^T \boldsymbol{A}_1 \boldsymbol{x} + (\boldsymbol{b}_1 - 2\boldsymbol{A}_1 \boldsymbol{d})^T \boldsymbol{x} + \boldsymbol{d}^T \boldsymbol{A}_1 \boldsymbol{d} - \boldsymbol{b}_1^T \boldsymbol{d} + c_1 \\ &= \boldsymbol{x}^T \boldsymbol{A}_2 \boldsymbol{x} + \boldsymbol{b}_2^T \boldsymbol{x} + c_2 \end{aligned} \tag{8}$$

where $A_2 = A_1$, $b_2 = b_1 - 2A_1 d$, $c_2 = d^T A_1 d - b_1^T d + c_1$. If A_1 is non-singular, the displacement d can be obtained by:

$$d = -\frac{1}{2} A_1^{-1} (b_2 - b_1) \tag{9}$$

In general case for A_1, the translation is solved by minimizing the following objective function:

$$d^* = \arg\min_{d} \|Ad - \Delta b\|_2^2 \tag{10}$$

where $\Delta b = b_2 - b_1$. However, the optimization on a single point is unreliable as the motion of the point can be affected by the noise. Therefore, the minimization is expanded to the neighboring region of the point:

$$d(x)^* = \arg\min_{d(x)} \sum_{\Delta x \in \Omega} w(\Delta x) \|A(x + \Delta x) d(x) - \Delta b(x + \Delta x)\|_2^2 \tag{11}$$

where Ω represents the neighboring region of the point x, $w(\Delta x)$ denotes a 2-dimensional weight function that controls the influence of the points in the local region on the objective function. The solution to (11) can be expressed as:

$$d(x) = \left(\sum w A^T A\right)^{-1} \sum w A^T \Delta b \tag{12}$$

3.2 FAST Detector with Local Threshold

The FAST detector is improved by adopting a local threshold strategy. The local threshold is aimed to detect the strong keypoints in the local region. FAST tries to find the pixels whose intensity is brighter or darker than the pixels surrounding it. The candidate pixel c is compared with local pixels that lie on the line of a circle with radius 3. The total number of the local pixels is 16. Suppose that the intensity of one pixel is $I(c)$ and the local pixel around it is $I(c \to p)$. If there are N contiguous pixels with greater or smaller intensities than $I(c)$ by a threshold T, the candidate pixel is decided as a keypoint.

FAST uses a global threshold for the detection of all points in the image. In this paper, we adopt a local threshold strategy to detect the points whose intensity is considerably different from the surrounding pixels. Assuming that the candidate pixel is close to the pixels in the eight-neighbor region. If the difference between the candidate pixel and the eight-neighbor pixels is high, the candidate pixel can be affected by the noise. Thus the difference in intensity in the neighboring region can be used to control the strength of the threshold. The pixel that is heavily affected by the noise corresponds to high threshold; otherwise, the pixel is detected with small threshold. The proposed local threshold is expressed as follows:

$$T = (k\sigma_{3\times3})^{\left(1-\frac{C\left(\max_i|e_i|/\sum_i|e_i|\right)-1}{C-1}\right)} = (k\sigma_{3\times3})^{\frac{C}{C-1}\left(1-\left(\max_i|e_i|/\sum_i|e_i|\right)\right)} \tag{13}$$

where $C = 8$ is the number of the pixels in the eight-neighbor region, I_i represents the pixels in the region. $e_i = I_c - I_i$ is computed to evaluate the difference between the candidate pixel I_c and its neighboring pixels I_i and $\sigma_{3\times3} = \sum_i |e_i|/C$ is the average difference. k is a constant to adjust the strength of the threshold. Moreover, the confidence term $1 - \left(C\left(\max_i|e_i| \Big/ \sum_i |e_i|\right) - 1\right) \Big/ (C-1)$ evaluates the distribution of the intensity difference in the neighboring region and varies from 0 to 1. If the differences are close to each other, the distribution item approaches 0; otherwise, it approaches 1. If the distribution is not uniform and some differences are larger than the others, which means the candidate pixel is considerably brighter or darker than its neighboring pixels, the confidence term decreases and the threshold reduces accordingly.

4 Performance Evaluation

The evaluation is performed on OTB100 to compare the performance between the proposed tracker and 2 state-of-the-art methods. The evaluated methods include high-speed tracking with kernelized correlation filters (KCF) [8], learning to track at 100 fps with deep regression networks (GOTURN) [4]. KCF trains a correlation filter on HOG feature space. The difference between the proposed method and KCF is that the object proposal strategy is adopted to handle fast motion. GOTURN learns to estimate the motions of the object along the frames and predict its location with a deep regression network.

4.1 Evaluation Criteria

The comparisons in terms of precision and success are performed to evaluate the performance of the trackers. The one-pass evaluation (OPE) in [6] is used as the evaluation metric. OPE means that the tracker runs on test video without restarting during process and the average precision or success rate is computed to evaluate the tracker.

The first metric is precision rate, which is defined as the Euclidean distance in pixels between the center of the tracked location and the ground truth bounding box.

The second one is success rate. The overlap score of the tracked location in one frame is defined as:

$$s = area(ROI_T \cap ROI_G)/area(ROI_T \cup ROI_G) \tag{14}$$

where ROI_T denotes the tracked bounding box and ROI_G represents the ground truth bounding box. $\cap$ and $\cup$ are the intersection and union operation of these two boxes respectively and $area(\bullet)$ means the area of the box in pixels. Given an overlap threshold τ, the percentage of the frames whose overlap score is larger than τ is defined as the success rate.

The precision plot shows the center location errors over the frames. The success plot shows the success rates at different overlap thresholds from 0 to 1.

4.2 Quantitative Comparisons

The overall OPE plots on all videos from OTB100 are given in Fig. 1. The proposed OFT is the top tracker in terms of both precision and success. The precision results at 20 pixels and success results at overlap threshold 0.5 are reported to evaluate the quantitative performance. The top two trackers are OFT and KCF. OFT achieves 0.7188 in precision and 0.6306 in success and thus outperforms KCF with precision 0.6918 and success 0.5219 by 2.7% and 10.87%, respectively. The comparisons in precision and success indicate that the proposed proposal strategy contributes to the improvement of the accuracy.

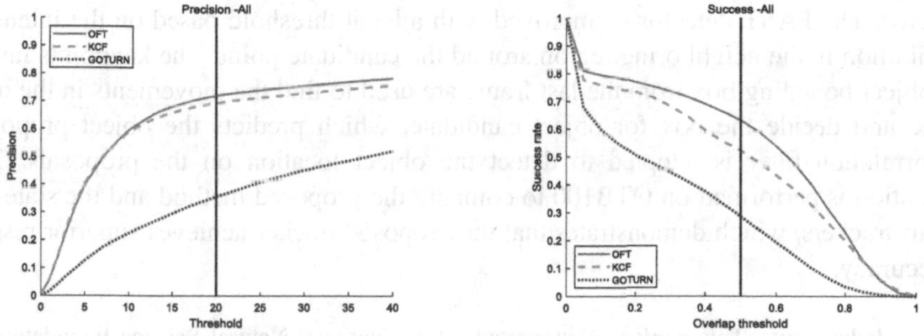

a) Precision b) Success

Fig. 1. Overall performance in OPE.

The evaluation results on fast motion challenge are shown in Fig. 2. Compared to the results of the overall performance, OFT accomplishes greater improvements for fast motion. The results for OFT are 0.6405 in precision and 0.6116 in success, compared to KCF with 0.5690 in precision and 0.5187 in success. The gap between OFT and KCF confirms that the object proposal can deal with fast motion effectively.

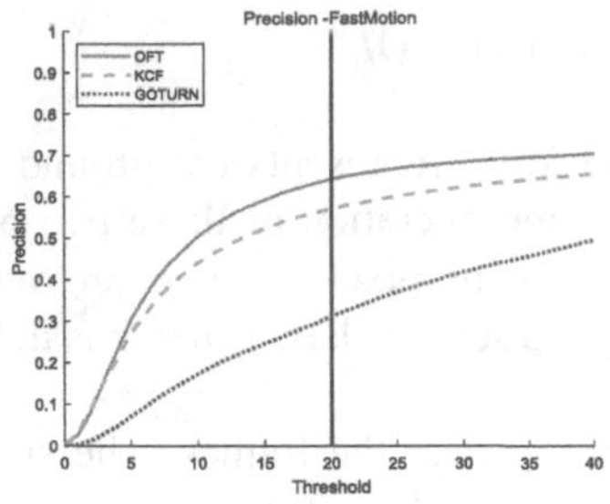

a) Precision

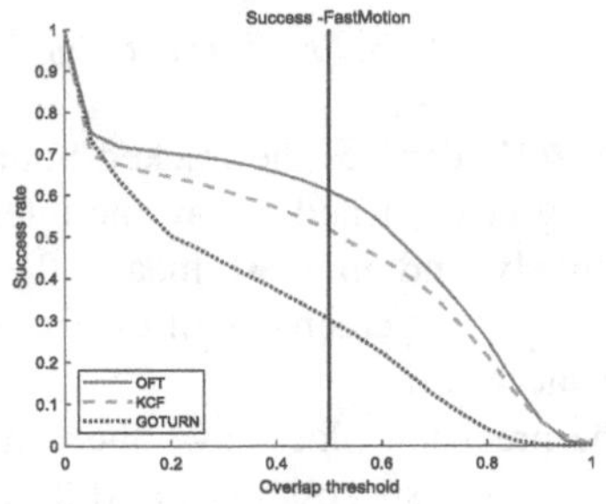

b) Success

Fig. 2. OPE under fast motion.

5 Conclusion

Although the generic tracking has made significant progress in recent years, the UAV tracking for videos captured from aerial viewpoints still faces challenges such as fast motion, scale variation and aspect ratio variation. Inspired by the idea of region proposal in image detection, an object proposal strategy is proposed to infer the object candidates based on Farneback flow. First, the Farneback flow is computed to find the connections between two adjacent frames by estimating the motions in the image. Then the keypoints that represent the local structures of the object are detected with a FAST detector. The FAST detector is improved with a local threshold based on the intensity distribution in the neighboring region around the candidate point. The keypoints inside the object bounding box from the last frame are used to find the movements in the next frame and decide the box for object candidate, which predicts the object proposal. A correlation filter is adopted to detect the object location on the proposals. The evaluation is performed on OTB100 to compare the proposed method and the state-of-the-art trackers, which demonstrates that the proposed tracker achieves superior results in accuracy.

Acknowledgement. This work was supported by the National Natural Science Foundation of China (No. 61671183, 61771163 and 91438205) and the Open Research Fund of State Key Laboratory of Space-Ground Integrated Information Technology (No. 2015_SGIIT_KFJJ_TX_02).

References

1. Li, P., Wang, D., Wang, L., Lu, H.: Deep visual tracking: Review and experimental comparison. Pattern Recognit. **76**, 323–338 (2018)
2. Cai, Z., Vasconcelos, N.: Cascade R-CNN: delving into high quality object detection. In: 2018 IEEE Conference Computer Vision Pattern Recognition, Salt Lake City, UT (2018)
3. Choi, J., Chang, H.J., Yun, S., Fischer, T., Demiris, Y., Choi, J.Y.: Attentional correlation filter network for adaptive visual tracking. In: 2017 IEEE Conference Computer Vision Pattern Recognition, Honolulu, HI, pp. 4828–4837 (2017)

4. Held, D., Thrun, S., Savarese, S.: Learning to track at 100 FPS with deep regression networks. In: Leibe, B., Matas, J., Sebe, N., Welling, M. (eds.) ECCV 2016. LNCS, vol. 9905, pp. 749–765. Springer, Cham (2016). https://doi.org/10.1007/978-3-319-46448-0_45
5. Bertinetto, L., Valmadre, J., Henriques, J.F., Vedaldi, A., Torr, P.H.S.: Fully-convolutional siamese networks for object tracking. In: Hua, G., Jégou, H. (eds.) ECCV 2016. LNCS, vol. 9914, pp. 850–865. Springer, Cham (2016). https://doi.org/10.1007/978-3-319-48881-3_56
6. Mueller, M., Smith, N., Ghanem, B.: A benchmark and simulator for UAV tracking. In: Leibe, B., Matas, J., Sebe, N., Welling, M. (eds.) ECCV 2016. LNCS, vol. 9905, pp. 445–461. Springer, Cham (2016). https://doi.org/10.1007/978-3-319-46448-0_27
7. Zhu, G., Porikli, F., Li, H.: Beyond local search: tracking objects everywhere with instance-specific proposals. In: 2016 IEEE Conference Computer Vision Pattern Recognition, Las Vegas, NV, pp. 943–951 (2016)
8. Henriques, J.F., Caseiro, R., Martins, P., Batista, J.: High-Speed Tracking with Kernelized Correlation Filters. IEEE Trans. Pattern Anal. Mach. Intell. **37**(3), 583–596 (2015)

A New Gateway Switching Strategy in Q/V Band High Throughput Satellite Communication Systems Feeder Links

Jiahao Yang, Wenkai Zhang, Mingchuan Yang(✉), and Yanyong Su

Communication Research Center, Harbin Institute of Technology, Harbin 150001, Heilongjiang, China
mcyang@hit.edu.cn

Abstract. A main obstacle to limit the capacity of next generation Terabit/s broadband satellite communication is the limited spectrum available in the Ka band. A feasible solution is to move the feeder link to the higher Q/V band, where spectrum is more available. However, the Q/V band is sensitive to rainfall attenuation. Compensating for the falling caused by rainfall, gateway diversity is considered to ensure the required feeder link availability. So far, many strategies for gateway diversity have been proposed, and each of them has its own advantages, so it is imperative to research gateway switching strategies. In this paper, a modified switch and stay combining strategy named TH-SSC is proposed for a Q/V band feeder link, which is suitable for three gateways to switch and we make an analysis and simulations about its performance. It can be seen that this modified TH-SSC strategy is pragmatic and has better performance in some aspects.

Keywords: Gateway diversity · Q/V band · Rain attenuation · Outage probability

1 Introduction

High-throughput satellite (HTS) systems are receiving increasing attention due to the tremendous demand for interactive services. At present, satellite communication systems would provide hundreds of Gigabit services and it is estimated that next generation satellites will require capacity of one Terabit/s (1000 Gbps) by 2020 [1]. A main obstacle for satellite to achieve Terabit/s is the limited spectrum of about 2 GHz available in the Ka band. An expected way is to move the feeder link to the higher Q/V band, where larger bandwidths, up to 5 GHz, are available [2], which not only promotes future system to achieve higher throughput, but also frees up the whole Ka-band spectrum for the user link. However, due to heavy rain attenuation, moving the feeder link to Q/V band imposes considerable strain on the link-budge. There are some strategies to compensate for fading, like Power control and adaptive modulation and coding (ACM) techniques, which are not sufficient to make up for high signal degradations up to 15–20 dB. Gateway diversity is considered as a powerful Fade Mitigation Technique (FMT) to ensure the required feeder link availability.

M. Jia et al. (Eds.): WiSATS 2019, LNICST 281, pp. 506–514, 2019.
https://doi.org/10.1007/978-3-030-19156-6_47

Gateway diversity is a familiar and mature technique with rich literature, Equal Gain Combining (EGC) and Maximum Ratio Combining (MRC) have been studied in [3] towards achieving transmit diversity. However, these two ways both require precise channel phase information and two gateways are active, which demands huge overhead and strict synchronization.

Since no phase information is required and have higher gateway utilization efficiency, Switch and Stay Combining (SSC) and Selection Combining (SC) strategies have been proposed in many literatures [3–5]. In order to get better performance, many scholars have improved on the basis of the above strategies. Based on SSC strategy, [6] proposed several improved strategies which establish a Markov model. In [7], a modified SSC (MSSC) scheme is proposed to reduce the number of gateway handover.

There are still many studies that promote switching strategies from two gateways to multiple gateways [8–10], which provides a better trade-off between outage and switching rate and have better gateway utilization, but we need compare signal information of active gateways and redundant gateways, which increases the complexity compared with SSC strategies.

Based on the SSC strategy, this paper proposes a three-gateway switching strategy named TH-SSC which is more pragmatic in reality. It has better performance in terms of outage probability and frequency of handovers while maintaining lower handover complexity. The utilization of gateway of original SSC strategy is 50%, but now we enhance it closed to 67%.

The remainder of this paper is organized as follows. Section 2 introduces the system model which is used in this paper. Section 3 studies the modified switching strategy and analysis the performance of it. Numerical results are presented in Sect. 4. Concluding remarks are provided in Sect. 5.

2 Research Scenario and System Model

Two active gateways, namely GW_1 and GW_2, separated by a distance of D_1, which distances from the backup gateway GW_3, D_2, D_3 and communicate with the GEO satellite through a feeder link operating in the Q/V band. The approach is depicted in the Fig. 1

Assume that the active GW transmits the signal s(t) having an average power E_1 and E_2. The decision on switching is taken at discrete time instants $t = NT$, where N is an integer and T is the interval between switching instants. The channel between GW_i and the satellite at $t = NT$ is denoted by $h_i[n] = |h_i[n]|e^{j\theta_i}$, where i = 1, 2, 3 and θ_i is the phase component of GW_i.

The channel amplitude, $|h_i[n]|$, can be estimated using a beacon signal received from the satellite. The clear sky signal-to-noise ratio (SNR) for the feeder uplink is then defined as SNR_{CS}, The actual SNR for the link between GW_i and the satellite at $t = NT$ can be obtained by $SNR_R = |h_i[n]|^2 E/N = |h_i[n]| SNR_{CS}$.

It is well known that the Lognormal distribution is an acceptable model for describing statistical data on rainfall rate, especially in areas with low rainfall rates [11]. Let the rain attenuation at GW_i be A_i, then we can obtain the following formulas (1),

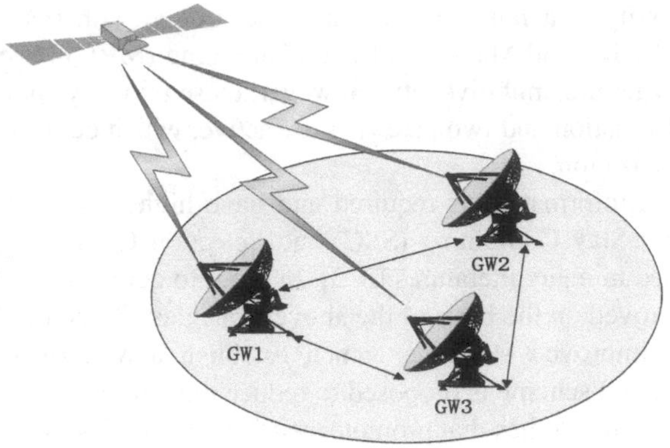

Fig. 1. The strategy of TH-SSC

where $< \ln A_i >$ and δ_i are the mean and standard deviation of $\ln A_i$. ρ is the spatial correlation coefficient for two GWs separated by a distance of D km, which can be obtained by formula $\rho_{ij} = 0.94\ \exp(-\frac{D}{30}) + 0.06\ \exp(-(\frac{D}{500})^2)$.

$$A_i = -10\log_{10}(|h_i[n]|^2) \quad \alpha_i = \frac{\ln A_i - < \ln A_i >}{\delta_i}$$
$$f_{A_iA_j}(A_i, A_j) = \frac{1}{2\pi A_i A_j \sigma_i \sigma_j \sqrt{1-\rho^2}} \exp(-\frac{1}{2(1-\rho^2)}[\alpha_i^2 - 2\rho_{ij}\alpha_i\alpha_j + \alpha_j^2]) \tag{1}$$

We can think if the distance exceeds 100 km, it is basically no longer relevant. Assuming that the uplink signal-to-noise ratio SNR_{CS} is fixed in clear sky, the satellite received signal power is directly related to the rainfall attenuation. According to strategy, gateway switching from active GW_i to redundant GW_j occurs if SNR_R is lower than threshold, which is rainfall attenuation $A_i > \beta_i$, β_i is the threshold of rainfall attenuation.

3 TH-SSC Based Gateway Switching Strategy

3.1 Switching State Analysis

We now study the outage performance of TH-SSC. Assuming the outage threshold of GW_i is β_i, which is the attenuation when outage occurs. The switching rules is as follows.

(1) When the active gateway is GW_1 and GW_2 at time $t = NT$,
If $A_1 > \beta_1$ switching between GW_1 and GW_3
Else if $A_1 < \beta_1$ and $A_2 > \beta_2$, switching between GW_2 and GW_3
(2) When the active gateway is GW_1 and GW_3 at time $t = NT$,
If $A_3 > \beta_3$ switching between GW_2 and GW_3
Else if $A_3 < \beta_3$ and $A_1 > \beta_1$, switching between GW_2 and GW_1

According to the switching rule, when the rain attenuation of the two active gateways is higher than the respective thresholds, there will be a gateway outage; when the rain attenuation of the three active gateways is higher than the respective thresholds, two gateways will be outage. Threshold vary depending on the link attenuation characteristics.

In general, we think that the distance between satellite gateways is several hundred kilometers. So we can approximate that the rainfall attenuation is not related to each other. Assuming the outage threshold of GW_i is β_i, which is equal with switching threshold.

We can use the Markov chain to solve parameters such as outage probability, switching rate, and average gain. First we need to define the nine states in the Markov chain, as shown in Table 1 below.

Table 1. 9 kinds of transmission status of switching

State at $t = N(T-1)$	Active GWs	Relationship	State at $t = NT$
State 1	GW1, GW2	$A_1 > \beta_1$	GW2, GW3
State 2	GW1, GW2	$A_1 < \beta_1, A_2 > \beta_2$	GW1, GW3
State 3	GW1, GW2	$A_1 < \beta_1, A_2 < \beta_2$	GW1, GW2
State 4	GW1, GW3	$A_3 > \beta_3$	GW1, GW2
State 5	GW1,GW3	$A_3 < \beta_3, A_1 > \beta_1$	GW2, GW3
State 6	GW1, GW3	$A_1 < \beta_1, A_3 < \beta_3$	GW1, GW3
State 7	GW2,GW3	$A_2 > \beta_2$	GW1, GW3
State 8	GW1, GW3	$A_2 < \beta_2, A_3 > \beta_3$	GW1, GW2
State 9	GW1, GW3	$A_2 < \beta_2, A_3 < \beta_3$	GW2, GW3

Define P_i as the probability of GW_i outage, we can obtain formula (2)

$$P_i = \Pr(A_i > \beta_i) = \int_{\beta_i}^{\infty} f_i(A_i)dA_i = \int_{\beta_i}^{\infty} \frac{1}{2\pi A_i \sigma_{\ln A_i}} \exp(-\frac{\alpha_i^2}{2})dA_i, i = 1,2,3 \quad (2)$$

We can conclude from Table 1 that the next possible state of State 1 is State 7, State 8, and State 9. Since the links are considered to be uncorrelated, it can be concluded that the probability of switching from state 1 to state 7 is P_2. So we can get the transition matrix M as formula (3).

$$M=\begin{vmatrix} 0 & 0 & 0 & 0 & 0 & 0 & P_2 & P_3(1-P_2) & (1-P_3)(1-P_2) \\ 0 & 0 & 0 & P_3 & P_1(1-P_3) & (1-P_3)(1-P_1) & 0 & 0 & 0 \\ P_1 & P_2(1-P_1) & (1-P_1)(1-P_2) & 0 & 0 & 0 & 0 & 0 & 0 \\ P_1 & P_2(1-P_1) & (1-P_1)(1-P_2) & 0 & 0 & 0 & 0 & 0 & 0 \\ 0 & 0 & 0 & 0 & 0 & 0 & P_2 & P_3(1-P_2) & (1-P_3)(1-P_2) \\ 0 & 0 & 0 & P_3 & P_1(1-P_3) & (1-P_3)(1-P_1) & 0 & 0 & 0 \\ 0 & 0 & 0 & P_3 & P_1(1-P_3) & (1-P_3)(1-P_1) & 0 & 0 & 0 \\ P_1 & P_2(1-P_1) & (1-P_1)(1-P_2) & 0 & 0 & 0 & 0 & 0 & 0 \\ 0 & 0 & 0 & 0 & 0 & 0 & P_2 & P_3(1-P_2) & (1-P_3)(1-P_2) \end{vmatrix} \tag{3}$$

Define π_i as the probability that state i appears, P_{i_j} as the probability that transform from state i to state j. We can obtain formula (4) as follows:

$$\begin{cases} \pi_j = \sum_{i=1}^{9} P_{i\_j} \times \pi_i \\ \sum_{i=1}^{9} \pi_i = 1 \end{cases} \tag{4}$$

Assuming $\vec{\pi} = [\pi_1, \pi_2, \cdots, \pi_9]$, then $\vec{\pi} = \vec{\pi}M$, we can get formula (5), where $\Delta = P_1 + P_2 + P_3$, $\lambda = P_1P_2P_3$

$$\begin{aligned} \vec{\pi} = (&\frac{P_1P_3}{\Delta}, \frac{P_2P_3 - \lambda}{\Delta}, \frac{P_3 - P_1P_3 - P_2P_3 + \lambda}{\Delta}, \frac{P_2P_3}{\Delta}, \frac{P_1P_2 - \lambda}{\Delta}, \frac{P_2 - P_1P_2 - P_2P_3 + \lambda}{\Delta}, \\ &\frac{P_1P_2}{\Delta}, \frac{P_1P_3 - \lambda}{\Delta}, \frac{P_1 - P_1P_2 - P_1P_3 + \lambda}{\Delta}) \end{aligned} \tag{5}$$

3.2 Outage Probability Analysis

Probability of an outage (SNR below the threshold at two gateways) is (6)

Where $P(i,j) = \Pr(A_i > \beta_i, A_j > \beta_j, \mathrm{A}_{another} < \beta_{another})$

$$\begin{aligned} P_{OUT1} &= P(1,2) + P(1,3) + P(2,3) \\ &= (\pi_1 + \pi_2 + \pi_3) \times \mathrm{P_1P_2} + (\pi_4 + \pi_5 + \pi_6) \times \mathrm{P_1P_3} + (\pi_7 + \pi_8 + \pi_9) \times \mathrm{P_2P_3} \end{aligned} \tag{6}$$

Probability of two outages (SNR below the threshold at all gateways) is (7)

$$\begin{aligned} P_{OUT2} = (\pi_1 + \pi_2 + \pi_3) \times \mathrm{P_1P_2P_3} + (\pi_4 + \pi_5 + \pi_6) \times \mathrm{P_1P_2P_3} + (\pi_7 + \pi_8 + \pi_9) \\ \times \mathrm{P_1P_2P_3} = \mathrm{P_1P_2P_3} \end{aligned} \tag{7}$$

So the frequency at which the outage occurs is as formula (8)

$$f_{OUT} = \frac{P_{OUT1} + 2P_{OUT2}}{3T} \tag{8}$$

3.3 Switching Frequency Analysis

When the system is in the state 1, 2, 4, 5, 7, and 8, the switching frequency of each active gateway in the average unit time is as formula (9)

$$f_{sw} = \frac{P_{SW}}{2T} = \frac{\pi_1 + \pi_2 + \pi_4 + \pi_5 + \pi_7 + \pi_8}{2T} \tag{9}$$

3.4 Average Gain Analysis

Transmit gain occurs when a switching event occurs. As shown above, consider transmit gain at 6 kinds of states. Assume that the probability density function of the attenuation on the GW_i link is $f_i(A)$, and transmit gain at state i is G_i, so the average gain G is as formula (10)

$$\begin{aligned} G &= \pi_1 G_1 + \pi_2 G_2 + \pi_4 G_4 + \pi_5 G_5 + \pi_7 G_7 + \pi_8 G_8 \\ &= (\frac{\pi_1}{P_1}) \int_{\beta_3}^{\infty} \int_{0}^{\infty} f_3(A_3) f_1(A_1)(A_1 - A_3) dA_3 A_1 + (\frac{\pi_2}{P_2}) \int_{\beta_2}^{\infty} \int_{0}^{\infty} f_3(A_3) f_2(A_2)(A_2 - A_3) dA_3 A_2 \\ &+ (\frac{\pi_3}{P_3}) \int_{\beta_3}^{\infty} \int_{0}^{\infty} f_2(A_2) f_3(A_3)(A_3 - A_2) dA_2 A_3 + (\frac{\pi_4}{P_1}) \int_{\beta_1}^{\infty} \int_{0}^{\infty} f_2(A_2) f_1(A_1)(A_1 - A_2) dA_2 A_1 \\ &+ (\frac{\pi_5}{P_2}) \int_{\beta_2}^{\infty} \int_{0}^{\infty} f_1(A_1) f_2(A_2)(A_2 - A_1) dA_1 A_2 + (\frac{\pi_6}{P_3}) \int_{\beta_3}^{\infty} \int_{0}^{\infty} f_1(A_1) f_3(A_3)(A_3 - A_1) dA_1 A_3 \end{aligned} \tag{10}$$

4 Numerical Result and Discussion

The mean and variance of rainfall fading are 5 dB and 25 dB respectively. For each strategy, each gateway has a simulation of 1,000,000 times between 20 km and 200 km. 200 km is represented by dots, and 20 km is represented by stars. The simulation results are as follows:

In Fig. 2, we compare the outage probability of the three strategies under different thresholds. We can be informed that TH-SSC strategy is worse than SSC strategy, but better than single gateway strategy in bad conditions. However, TH-SSC is close to SSC strategy in good conditions.

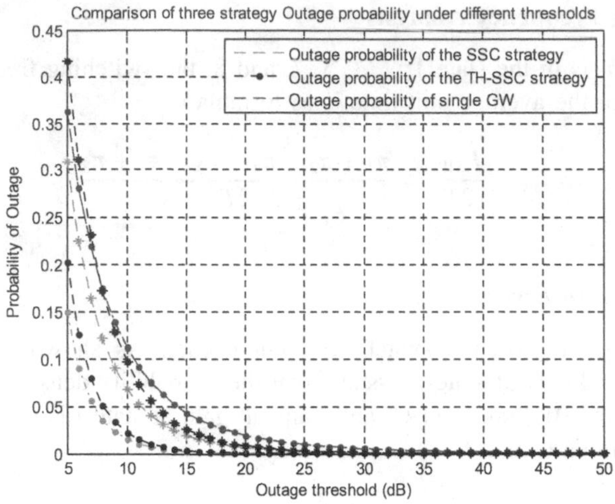

Fig. 2. Comparisons of three strategy's outage probability

In Fig. 3, we show the performance of outage probability under different thresholds, which illustrates that TH-SSC strategy is better than SSC strategy, especially in bad conditions.

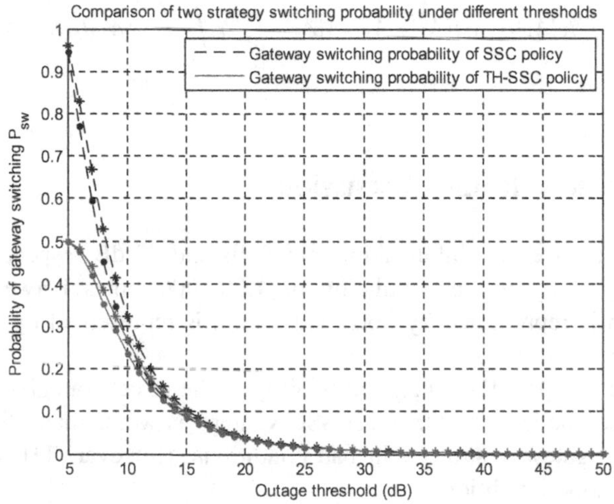

Fig. 3. Comparisons of two strategy's switching probability

In Fig. 4, we present the transmit gain of SSC and TH-SSC strategies under different thresholds. It is obvious that TH-SSC strategy is much better than SSC strategy.

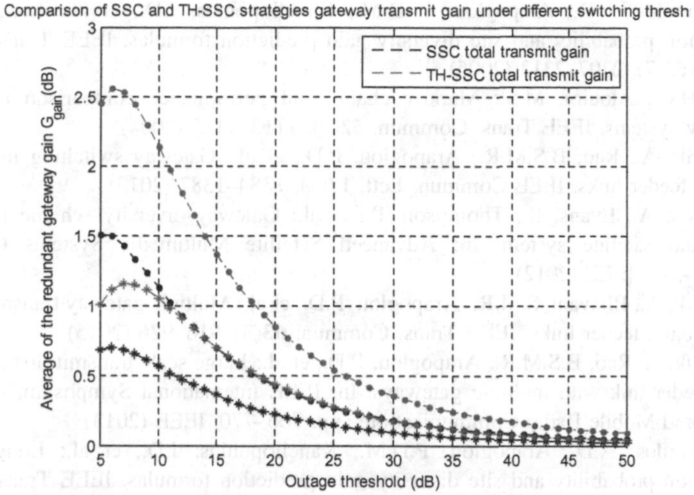

Fig. 4. Comparisons of two strategy's transitions gain

5 Conclusion

In this paper, a modified switch and stay scheme for Q/V band feeder link has been studied, which is a strategy include two active gateways and one redundant gateway and don't need sort by the received signal to noise ratio of different gateways. Through simulation, it can be seen that TH-SSC strategy is much better than SSC in transmit gain and switching probability, but in bad channel conditions, it is worse than SSC strategy in outage probability. It is further seen that advantages of TH-SSC is mainly in lower costs.

Acknowledgements. The paper is sponsored by National Natural Science Foundation of China (No. 91538104; No. 91438205).

References

1. Kyrgiazos, A., Evans, B., Thompson, P., et al.: Gateway diversity scheme for a future broadband satellite system. In: Advanced Satellite Multimedia Systems Conference, pp. 363–370. IEEE (2012)
2. Vidal, O., Verelst, G., Lacan, J., et al.: Next generation high throughput satellite system. In: IEEE First AESS European Conference on Satellite Telecommunications, pp. 1–7. IEEE (2012)
3. Arapoglou, P.D., Shankar, B., Panagopoulos, A., et al.: Gateway diversity strategies in Q/V band feeder links. In: Ka & Broadband Communications Conference (2013)
4. Kyrgiazos, A., Evans, B.G., Thompson, P.: On the gateway diversity for high throughput broadband satellite systems. IEEE Trans. Wireless Commun. **13**(10), 5411–5426 (2014)

5. Panagopoulos, A.D., Arapoglou, P.-D.M., Kanellopoulos, J.D., et al.: Long-term rain attenuation probability and site diversity gain prediction formulas. IEEE Trans. Antennas Propag. **53**(7), 2307–2313 (2005)
6. Yang, H.C., Alouini, M.S.: Markov chains and performance comparison of switched diversity systems. IEEE Trans. Commun. **52**(7), 1113–1125 (2004)
7. Gharanjik, A., Rao, B.S.M.R., Arapoglou, P.D., et al.: Gateway switching in Q/V band satellite feeder links. IEEE Commun. Lett. **17**(7), 1384–1387 (2013)
8. Kyrgiazos, A., Evans, B., Thompson, P., et al.: Gateway diversity scheme for a future broadband satellite system. In: Advanced Satellite Multimedia Systems Conference, pp. 363–370. IEEE (2012)
9. Gharanjik, A., Bhavani, S.M.R., Arapoglou, P.D., et al.: Multiple gateway transmit diversity in Q/V band feeder links. IEEE Trans. Commun. **63**(3), 916–926 (2015)
10. Gharanjik, A, Rao, B.S.M.R., Arapoglou, P.D., et al.: Large scale transmit diversity in Q/V band feeder link with multiple gateways. In: IEEE International Symposium on Personal Indoor and Mobile Radio Communications, pp. 766–770. IEEE (2013)
11. Panagopoulos, A.D., Arapoglou, P.D.M., Kanellopoulos, J.D., et al.: Long-term rain attenuation probability and site diversity gain prediction formulas. IEEE Trans. Antennas Propag. **53**(7), 2307–2313 (2005)

Channel States Information Based Energy Detection Algorithm in Dual Satellite Systems

Weizhong Zhang, Mingchuan Yang(✉), Wenqiu Wei, and Qing Guo

Communication Research Center, Harbin Institute of Technology,
Harbin 150001, Heilongjiang Province, China
mcyang@hit.edu.cn

Abstract. Satellite communication which is a crucial part in wireless communication field faces the spectrum scarcity problem. Therefore, exploring a suitable spectrum sharing mechanism has become a key issue in ensuring the full utilization of satellite users while improving the spectrum utilization of existing spectrum. Cognitive communication is an emerging solution to solving spectrum problems in wireless systems. An important part of cognitive radio is spectrum awareness, which is used for acquiring information about the spectral opportunities. One of the spectrum sensing methods is spectrum sensing, which utilizes spectrum holes in multiple fields to sense the presence or absence of primary users by using signal processing techniques. This paper studies some cognitive scenarios and systems for satellite communication, and then proposes a spectrum sensing algorithm based on the channel states information to solve the problem of large transmission loss in satellite cognitive scenarios.

Keywords: Satellite communication · Cognitive radio · Spectrum sensing · Channel states information

1 Introduction

Satellite communication (satcom) plays a key role in wireless communications because of its wide coverage and the ability to provide new services that are different from terrestrial networks. It extends the coverage of services on land-based fixed and mobile networks today. Like ground systems, satellite systems are facing spectrum scarcity due to increasing demand for communications services [1].

Cognitive communication is a new solution, which can solve the problem of spectrum scarcity in wireless systems. Although the solution started with software defining the concept of radio, it allows primary and cognitive users to coexist. The concept of Cognitive Radio (CR) was firstly proposed by Mitola in the late 1990's [2]. He defines CR as "a very intelligent radio with self and perception, including language and vision and cognitive ability of radio environment". The main task of CR is to sense the radio environment near CR, find the free spectrum resources, and allocate these spectrum resources reasonably, while not interfering with the primary user. An important part of CR is spectrum awareness [3], which is used for acquiring information about the spectral opportunities. Spectrum awareness methods include spectrum sensing, database, beacon transmission-based methods and so on. The information of

M. Jia et al. (Eds.): WiSATS 2019, LNICST 281, pp. 515–523, 2019.
https://doi.org/10.1007/978-3-030-19156-6_48

the surrounding spectrum can be obtained by spectrum sensing. Spectrum sensing uses digital signal processing technology to detect whether the surrounding spectrum is idle. According to the different digital signal processing technologies used, spectrum sensing technology can be divided into the following categories [4], such as energy detection, eigenvalue based spectrum sensing and so on. The application of energy detection algorithm in satellite communication is an important topic.

SatCom's research on CR technology is still in its infancy. In the terrestrial wireless system environment, CR has been tested and studied, but its application in satellite communications is facing great challenges. Therefore, the CoRaSat project studies and develops CR technology in SatCom system to make more effective use of spectrum. Considering the following two main categories, CoRaSat studies the importance of cognition in SatCom and possible coexistence scenarios: hybrid satellite-ground systems and dual satellite systems [5]. Because of large transmission loss in satellite communication systems, the signal received by secondary user has a very small power, this will lead to poor performance of energy detection [6]. Therefore, when applying CR to satellite communication, energy detection algorithm must be modified. This paper proposes a spectrum sensing algorithm based on the channel states information, which can solve the above problem well.

The rest of this paper is organized as follows. Section 2 describes some cognitive systems for satellite communication. Section 3 proposes a spectrum sensing algorithm based on channel states information in dual satellite systems. The simulation results and discussion are presented in Sect. 4. Then Finally the conclusions are offered in Sect. 5.

2 Cognitive Systems for Satellite Communication

In this part, we study the possible coexistence scenarios considering the following two main categories: Hybrid satellite-terrestrial systems and dual satellite systems. The hybrid systems can be beneficial to both terrestrial and satellite operators depending on which system is primary.

2.1 Hybrid Satellite-Terrestrial Systems

Cognitive hybrid systems include two main categories: (a) Primary satellite system with the secondary terrestrial system; (b) Secondary satellite system with the primary terrestrial system. Cognitive hybrid system (a) is shown in Fig. 1.

In this system, the satellite uplink is primary communication link, the terrestrial uplink is secondary communication link. The interference of the system mainly comes from the interference of the primary user's signal to the base station and the secondary user, and the interference of the satellite from the base station and the secondary user's signal. According to Ref. [7], The intelligent CR method can only be used for ground transmission and satellite up-link transmission. Because of the wide coverage of satellites, satellite downlink can't share dynamic spectrum. Because the earth station carries out highly directional transmission, satellite upstream links cause less interference to the ground system. However, the upstream link with low elevation has stronger interference than the upstream link with high elevation. Terrestrial communication systems share the same spectrum band as satellite uplink.

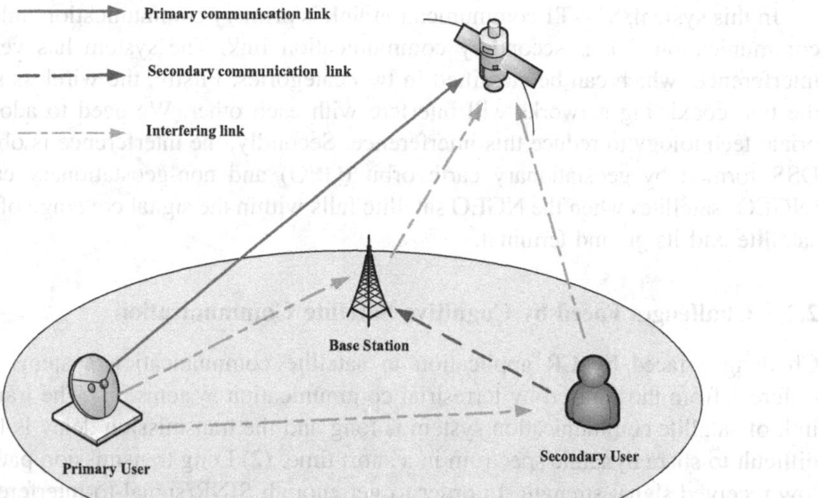

Fig. 1. Cognitive hybrid system

2.2 Dual Satellite Systems

In the dual satellite system (DSS), two satellites work in the same frequency band and share space and spectrum resources. DSS models a satellite scenario as follows (Fig. 2):

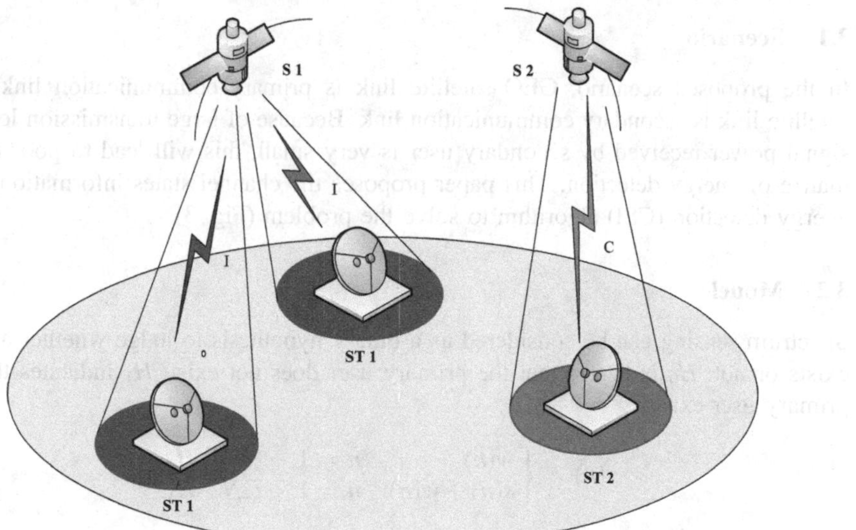

Fig. 2. Cognitive dual satellite system (C: cognitive, I: incumbent, S: satellite, ST: Secondary Transmitter)

In this system, S1-ST1 communication link is primary communication link, S2-ST2 communication link is secondary communication link. The system has very strong interference, which can be classified in two categories. Firstly, the wireless signals of the two coexisting networks will interfere with each other. We need to adopt appropriate technology to reduce this interference. Secondly, the interference is observed in DSS formed by geostationary earth orbit (GEO) and non-geostationary earth orbit (NGEO) satellites when the NGEO satellite falls within the signal coverage of the GEO satellite and its ground terminal.

2.3 Challenges Faced by Cognitive Satellite Communication

Challenges faced by CR application in satellite communication systems are quite different from those faced by terrestrial communication systems. (1) The transmission link of satellite communication system is long and the transmission delay is large. It is difficult to share dynamic spectrum in a short time. (2) Long transmission path leads to low received signal strength. In order to get enough SINR(signal-to-interference-plus-noise ratio), the receiver needs to install high gain antenna. This makes it very difficult to sense the spectrum of such signals [8]. (3) In satellite communication systems, the coverage of satellite beams is larger than that of ground cells. If there are multiple transmitters working in the same frequency band, such as cellular base stations, the sum of the interference generated by these devices will increase the interference level of the satellite, which will result in the inability to receive useful signals from the beam area.

3 Channel States Information Based Energy Detection Algorithm in Dual Satellite Systems

3.1 Scenario

In the proposed scenario, GEO satellite link is primary communication link, LEO satellite link is secondary communication link. Because of large transmission loss, the signal power received by secondary user is very small, this will lead to poor performance of energy detection. This paper proposes the channel states information based energy detection (CSI) algorithm to solve the problem (Fig. 3).

3.2 Model

Spectrum sensing can be considered as a binary hypothesis to judge whether a signal exists or not: H_0 indicates that the primary user does not exist; H_1 indicates that the primary user exists.

$$y(n) = \begin{cases} w(n) & n = 1, \cdots N \quad H_0 \\ s(n) + w(n) & n = 1, \cdots, N \quad H_1 \end{cases} \tag{1}$$

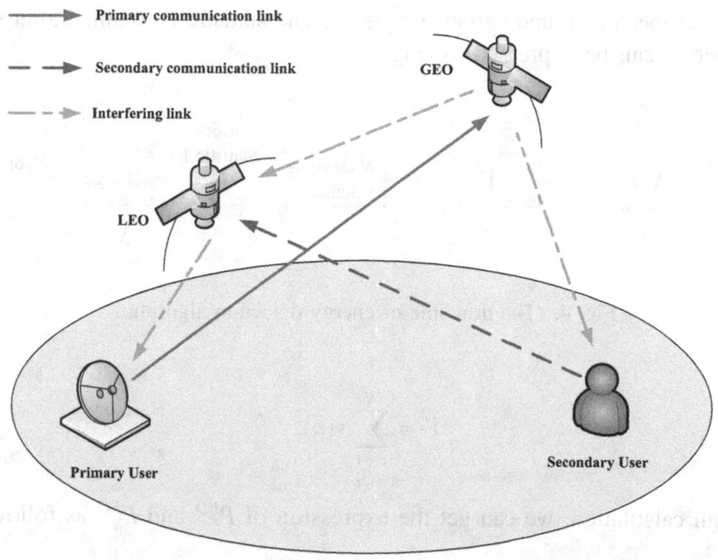

Fig. 3. GEO-LEO dual satellite system (LEO: low earth orbit, GEO: geostationary earth orbit)

Where $y(n)$ is received signal, $s(n)$ is useful signal, $w(n)$ is noise signal, N is the number of samples. Probability of Detection (P_d) and Probability of False-alarm (P_f) are two main indexes to measure spectrum sensing performance. Detection probability indicates that spectrum is occupied and the spectrum sensing result is H_1, that is, $P_d = P(H_1|H_1)$. False alarm probability indicates that spectrum is not occupied and the spectrum sensing result is H_1, that is, $P_f = P(H_1|H_0)$. Obviously, the larger the P_d, the smaller the interference from secondary users to primary users is, and the larger the P_f, the greater the probability that secondary users will miss the available spectrum resources. Therefore, the influence of spectrum sensing parameters on the performance of the algorithm can be measured by the receiver operating characteristic curve (ROC) corresponding to P_d and P_f.

3.3 Channel States Information Based Energy Detection Algorithm

The principle of the algorithm is to accumulate energy in a certain frequency band to get the energy detection statistic Y. If the value of Y is higher than the selected threshold lambda, the signal exists; otherwise, only noise signal exists. We assume that the interference noise is Gaussian white noise $w(t)$ and its amplitude obeys the normal distribution of mean zero and variance σ_w^2, and then assume that the amplitude of the primary user's signal $s(t)$ obeys the normal distribution of mean zero and variance σ_s^2, finally, we assume that the noise sampling values are independent and identically distributed, and are independent of the sampling values of the signals. We sampled $w(t)$ at N points and regarded the sampling result $w(1), \cdots, w(N)$ as a random variable. Obviously, these N random variables will obey the normal distribution of mean zero and variance σ_w^2. Similarly, because the amplitude of $w(t) + s(t)$ obeys the normal distribution of mean zero and variance $\sigma_w^2 + \sigma_s^2$, the N random variables of $w(1) + s(1), \cdots, w(N) + s(N)$ obtained by N-point sampling also obey the normal distribution of mean zero and variance $\sigma_w^2 + \sigma_s^2$. The statistic Y obtained after sampling and summation can be expressed as (Fig. 4):

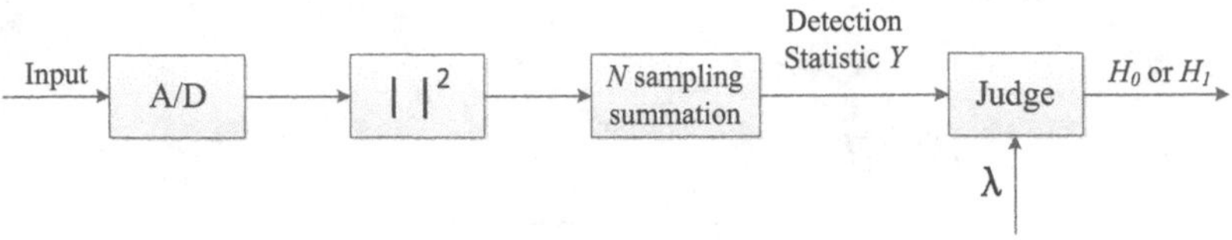

Fig. 4. The principle of energy detection algorithm

$$Y = \sum_{n=1}^{N} y(n)^2 \tag{2}$$

Through calculation, we can get the expression of P_f^{ED} and P_d^{ED} as follows:

$$P_f^{ED} = Q\left(\frac{\lambda - N\sigma_w^2}{\sqrt{2N\sigma_w^2}}\right) \tag{3}$$

$$P_d^{ED} = Q\left(\frac{\lambda - N(\sigma_w^2 + \sigma_s^2)}{\sqrt{2N}(\sigma_w^2 + \sigma_s^2)}\right) \tag{4}$$

Where $Q(x) = \int_x^{\infty} \frac{1}{\sqrt{2\pi}} \exp\left(-\frac{1}{2}t^2\right) dt$.

When applying spectrum sensing algorithm to this satellite cognitive system, energy detection algorithm must be modified. This paper proposes the CSI algorithm which maps the current channel state statistic $\widetilde{Y}$ by the channel statistics of the previous L detections. The previous L detections are $Y_i = \{Y_1, Y_2, \ldots Y_L\}$, in which Y_L represents the state closest to the current channel state (Fig. 5).

Fig. 5. Inference of the current channel state statistic

The current statistic $\widetilde{Y}$ can be described as follows:

$$\widetilde{Y} = \sum_{i=1}^{L} Y_i \tilde{f}(L - i + 1) = \sum_{i=1}^{L} \frac{Y_i e^{-\eta(L-i+1)}}{\sum_{j=1}^{L} e^{-\eta j}} \tag{5}$$

Where, $\tilde{f}(k) = \frac{e^{-\eta k}}{\sum_{j=1}^{L} e^{-\eta j}}$ is an attenuation function, $\eta = \log(1/(1-\theta))$ stands for the forgetting factor, the value of which depends on the transition probability (θ) of the primary user's channel state. In the following simulation, the value of θ is 0.5, which means that whether the primary user's channel is occupied or not is completely random.

Through calculation, we can get the expression of P_f and P_d as follows:

$$P_f = P_f^{ED} + \left(1 - P_f^{ED}\right) Q((\lambda - \tilde{\mu})/\tilde{\sigma}) P_f^{ED} \tag{6}$$

$$P_d = P_d^{ED} + (1 - P_d^{ED}) Q((\lambda - \tilde{\mu})/\tilde{\sigma}) P_d^{ED} \tag{7}$$

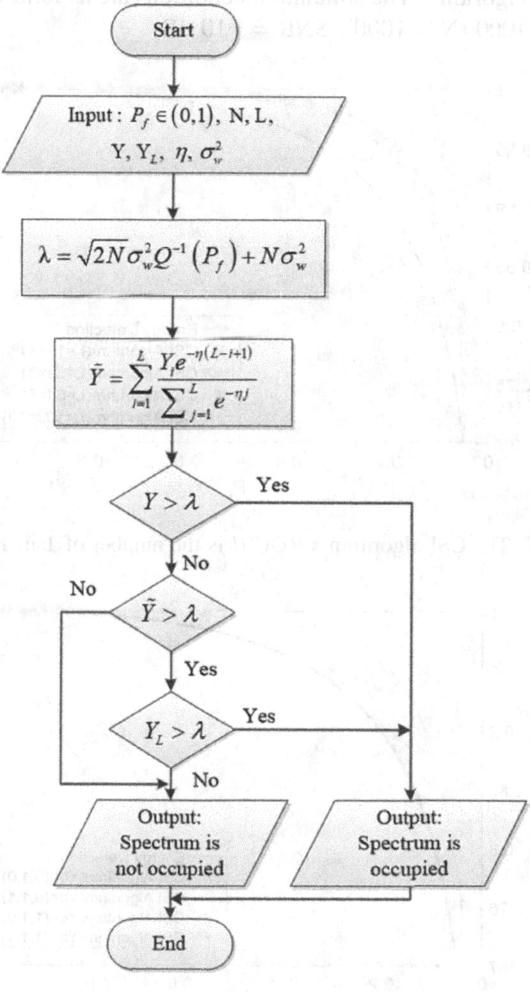

Fig. 6. The flowchart of CSI algorithm

Where,

$$\tilde{\mu} = \sum_{k=1}^{L} \tilde{f}(L+1-k)Y_c(k)N(\sigma_s^2 + \sigma_w^2) + \sum_{k=1}^{L} \tilde{f}(L+1-k)(1 - Y_c(k))N\sigma_w^2 \tag{8}$$

And $Y_c(k) = \{Y_c(1), Y_c(2), \ldots Y_c(L)\}$ is the state vector of the former L channels. The flowchart of CSI algorithm is as follows (Fig. 6):

4 Simulation Results and Discussion

Simulation analysis of receiver operating characteristic should be carried out to get the performance of the algorithm. The simulation conditions are as follows: The number of sampling points is 1000 (N = 1000), SNR = −10 dB.

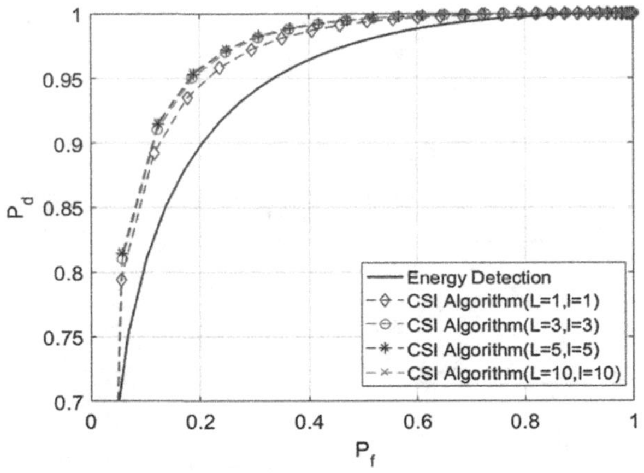

Fig. 7. The CSI algorithm's ROC (l is the number of 1 in $Y_c(k)$)

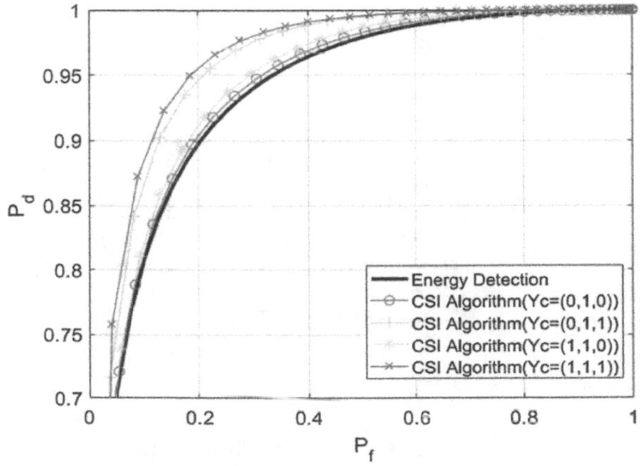

Fig. 8. The CSI algorithm's ROC

Figure 7 shows that the performance of the modified algorithm increases slightly with the increase of L. This is due to the fact that the current channel state statistic $\widetilde{Y}$ calculated by channel states can more accurately reflect the real average energy of the signal. However, when the number of L increases to a certain extent, the value of the signal power can be accurately estimated, which makes the increase of L can't bring about further improvement of the performance. Figure 8 shows that the performance of CSI algorithm is better than that of energy detection. And the performance will be better when the state closest to the current channel state is occupied.

5 Conclusions

Satellite communication which is a key part in wireless communication field faces the spectrum scarcity problem due to continuously increasing demand for broadcast, multimedia and interactive services. Applying cognitive radio to satellite communication can deal with the above problem well. After analyzing some cognitive scenarios and systems for satellite communication, we know that the energy detection algorithm should be modified in satellite cognitive communication systems. This paper proposes a spectrum sensing algorithm based on the channel states information. Simulation results show the performance of the proposed algorithm is better than that of the energy detection, and CSI algorithm solves the problem that the signals are weak at the reception point because of large transmission loss in satellite cognitive scenarios.

Acknowledgements. The paper is sponsored by National Natural Science Foundation of China (No. 91538104; No. 91438205).

References

1. Xiao, L.L., Liang, X.J., Li, X.: Development and application of satellite mobile communication system. Commun. Technol. **50**(6), 1093–1100 (2017)
2. Mitola, J., Maguire, G.: Cognitive radio: making software radios more personal. IEEE Pers. Commun. **6**(4), 13–18 (1999)
3. Zeng, Y., Liang, Y.C.: Eigenvalue-based spectrum sensing algorithms for cognitive radio. IEEE Trans. Commun. **57**(6), 1784–1793 (2009)
4. Axell, E., Leus, G., Larsson, E., Poor, H.: Spectrum sensing for cognitive radio: state-of-the-art and recent advances. IEEE Sig. Process. Mag. **29**(3), 101–116 (2012)
5. Chatzinotas, S., Ottersten, B., Gaudenzi, R.D.: Cooperative and Cognitive Satellite Systems. Academic Press, Cambridge (2015)
6. Wang, X.: The application of cognitive radio technology in satellite communication. Wirel. Interconnect. Technol. 3–4 (2017)
7. Kandeepan, S., Nardis, L.D., Benedetto, M.G.D., Guidotti, A., Corazza, G.E.: Cognitive satellite terrestrial radios. In: Global Telecommunications Conference (2011)
8. Höyhtyä, M.: Secondary terrestrial use of broadcasting satellite services below 3 GHz. Wireless Mob. Netw. **5**, 1–14 (2013)

Power Allocation Scheme for Decode-and-Forward Cooperative Communications in Rician Fading Channels

Wenqiu Wei, Weizhong Zhang, and Mingchuan Yang(✉)

Communication Research Center, Harbin Institute of Technology,
Harbin 150001, Heilongjiang Province, China
mcyang@hit.edu.cn

Abstract. Given to the performance of the resource utilization in the cooperative communication systems, the paper proposed a novel power allocation scheme in the Decode and Forward cooperative communication scenario. Based on the analysis of the system model and the fading channel model, the paper proposed an optimized power allocation scheme using optimization theory to minimize the outage probabilities of the communication system, for the accuracy and reliability of each link's transmission. Simulation results are presented to illustrate that optimized power allocation in terms of minimum outage probabilities offers better outage performance than common power allocation in cooperative diversity systems.

Keywords: Cooperative communication · Rician fading · Decode-and-Forward (DF) · Outage probability · Power allocation

1 Introduction

Cooperative communication technique in fading channel environments has been a hot research area for several years, because of its perfect performance in wireless communication environments [1, 2]. The principle of this technique is to make use of the broadcasting transmission characteristics of wireless signals in the channel, thus all nodes in the system can help their partners transmit information while sending their own information, thus forming a system that can obtain the same performance gain as MIMO (Multiple Input Multiple Output). Its basic idea is to share and transmit information by sharing partners' antennas and channels, so as to combat channel fading, improve communication reliability and reduce terminal burden.

Outage probability is another expression of link capacity. When the link capacity is lower than the data rate required by the user, outage events will occur, resulting in transmission errors. Outage probability is often used to measure the frequency of communication system outage events, so as to evaluate the performance of wireless systems.

Many papers have been published to deal with the resource allocation schemes to improve the performance of the cooperative communication systems under different cooperative communication schemes conditions (e.g., [3, 4]). In practice, Doppler

M. Jia et al. (Eds.): WiSATS 2019, LNICST 281, pp. 524–531, 2019.
https://doi.org/10.1007/978-3-030-19156-6_49

effect, shadow effect and multipath effect exist in satellite mobile communication. These effects affect the performance of communication system and even cause communication interruption. They are typical fading channels. Cooperative communication technology is an effective technology to mitigate fading channels and enhance communication quality, and the cooperative relay networks can be deployed in line-of-sight (LOS) environment [5]. Therefore, it is very necessary to study the property of the power allocation scheme in such fading environment. In this paper, we proposed an optimized power allocation algorithm in the three-node Decode and Forward (D-F) cooperative communication scenario.

2 Models and Formulas

2.1 System Model

In wireless networks, there are many system models of cooperative communication, and different definitions correspond to different system models. For example, the number of relay forwarding determines whether it is a two-hop or multi-hop model, and the number of relays determines whether it is a single-relay or multi-relay model. In order to facilitate the research, we simplify the model and only consider single source and single destination nodes. The three-node system model includes a source node denoted with S, a relay node denoted with R, and a destination node denoted with D. Each node has a single antenna. Figure 1 is the three-node system model.

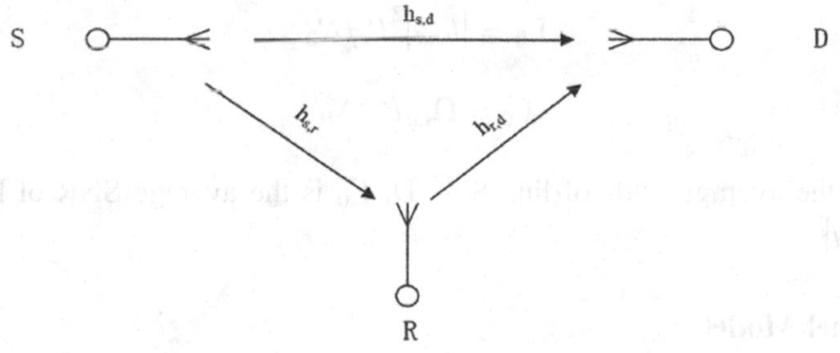

Fig. 1. Cooperative communication system model.

In the terrestrial wireless circumstances, the S and the R operate in the same frequency band and use the half duplex mode like reference [6]. There are two stages in the process of signal transmission: the first stage is that the R receives the signals sent by the S and the D receives the signals sent by the S too, and the expressions of the signals they receive are as follows

$$y_{s,d} = \sqrt{P_s} h_{s,d} x_s + n_{s,d} \tag{1}$$

$$y_{s,r} = \sqrt{P_s} h_{s,r} x_s + n_{s,r} \tag{2}$$

where P_s is the transmitted power of S, x_s is the transmitted signal. $h_{s,d}$ and $h_{s,r}$ are the corresponding link channel coefficients of link S $\rightarrow$ D and link S $\rightarrow$ R, $n_{s,d}$ and $n_{s,r}$ are Gauss white noise (AWGN) of direct link S $\rightarrow$ D and link S $\rightarrow$ R, which have zero-mean and variance N_0 [3].

In the next stage, the relay node receives the signal sent by the source node, and then performs the decoding operation. And only when the decoding is correct will the next step be carried out. At this point, the destination node receives a signal that is

$$y_{rd} = \sqrt{P_r} h_{r,d} x_s + n_{r,d} \tag{3}$$

where P_r is the relay transmitted power, $h_{r,d}$ is the channel coefficients of link R $\rightarrow$ D.

The instantaneous average signal-to-noise ratio (SNR) of source node-relay node and relay node-destination node are set as

$$\Gamma_1 = \left|h_{s,r}\right|^2 P_s/N_0, \Gamma_2 = \left|h_{r,d}\right|^2 P_r/N_0 \tag{4}$$

$$\bar{\Gamma}_1 = \Omega_{s,r} P_s/N_0, \bar{\Gamma}_2 = \Omega_{r,d}/P_r N_0 \tag{5}$$

where Γ_1 is the instantaneous SNR of link S $\rightarrow$ R and $\bar{\Gamma}_1$ is the average SNR of link S $\rightarrow$ R, while Γ_2 is the instantaneous SNR of link R $\rightarrow$ D and $\bar{\Gamma}_2$ is the average SNR of link R $\rightarrow$ D. $\Omega_{s,r} = E[h_{s,r}]$, $\Omega_{s,d} = E[h_{s,d}]$, in which $E[g]$ denotes expectation.

The instantaneous SNR of the link S $\rightarrow$ D is given in (6), and the average SNR of the link S $\rightarrow$ D is described as (7).

$$\Gamma_0 = \left|h_{s,d}\right|^2 P_s/N_0 \tag{6}$$

$$\bar{\Gamma}_0 = \Omega_{s,d} P_s/N_0 \tag{7}$$

where Γ_0 is the average SNR of link S $\rightarrow$ D, $\bar{\Gamma}_0$ is the average SNR of link S $\rightarrow$ D $\Omega_{r,d} = E[h_{r,d}]$.

2.2 Channel Model

In Rician fading channel, assuming that $h_{s,d}$, $h_{s,r}$ and $h_{r,d}$ are unrelated coefficients, non-central χ^2 is the basis of its power distribution, and the degree of freedom is two. Each resulting SNR (i.e., Γ_0, Γ_1 and Γ_2) has the same distribution. In a Rician fading channel, SNR's probability density function (PDF) is defined as

$$p(\gamma) = [(1+K)/\bar{\gamma}] \exp[-K - (1+K)x/\bar{\gamma}] \times I_0(2\sqrt{K(1+K)x/\bar{\gamma}}) \tag{8}$$

Where $\bar{\gamma}$ is an average SNR per symbol. K is the Rician K-factor defined as the ratio of the power in the LOS component to the power in the other (non-LOS) multipath components, is the zero-order modified Bessel function of the first kind.

According to reference [7], the instantaneous SNR's cumulative distribution function (CDF) is given in (9).

$$P(\gamma) = 1 - Q(\sqrt{2K}, \sqrt{2(1+K)\gamma/\bar{\gamma}}) \tag{9}$$

where $Q(\alpha, \beta)$ is the first-order Marcum Q function.

3 Optimized Power Allocation Scheme

In information theory, channel capacity rest with the received signal' SNR. Hence, for the system, the Γ_0, Γ_1 and Γ_2 is closely related to the outage probability. In the system model assumed in this paper, the destination node will receive two sets of signals, one from the relay link and the other from the direct link. Two sets of signals are combined based on the choice of merging mode. When the SNR threshold is fixed, for direct link, outage occurs when the instantaneous received SNR drops below the threshold, for relay link, outage occurs when the instantaneous received SNR of any single hop link is less than the threshold. When the SNR of two links is lower than the threshold SNR at the same time, the outage state of the whole system occurs [8]. Therefore, if the probability of making wrong decisions at the destination node can be reduced, then the transmission accuracy and reliability of each link can be guaranteed.

As shown in (4) and (6), it is important to allocate the source transmit power and the relay transmit power for minimizing outage probability.

As mentioned above, when the SNR of direct link and relay link is lower than the threshold SNR γ_{th} at the same time, the whole cooperative diversity system will be interrupted, and the probability of outage is

$$P_{out} = \Pr\{\Gamma_0, \min(\Gamma_1, \Gamma_2) < \gamma_{th}\} \tag{10}$$

where $\min(g)$ returns the minimum value.

In the direct link, the outage probability of the direct link is

$$P_{out1} = \Pr(\Gamma_0 < \gamma_{th}) \tag{11}$$

As was mentioned before, in the relay link, outage probability is a complementary event with more than two thresholds. Hence, the outage probability is given by

$$P_{out2} = 1 - \Pr\{\Gamma_1 > \gamma_{th}\}\Pr\{\Gamma_2 > \gamma_{th}\} \tag{12}$$

Combined with the (9), we have

$$\begin{aligned} P_{out} = P_{out1} \times P_{out2} = 1 - Q(\sqrt{2K_{sr}}, \sqrt{2(1+K_{sr})\gamma_{th}/\bar{\Gamma}_1}) \times Q(\sqrt{2K_{rd}}, \sqrt{2(1+K_{rd})\gamma_{th}/\bar{\Gamma}_2}) \\ \times [1 - Q(\sqrt{2K_{sd}}, \sqrt{2(1+K_{sd})\gamma_{th}/\bar{\Gamma}_0})] \end{aligned} \tag{13}$$

where $K_{s,d}$ is the Rician K-factor of the channel from the S to the D, $K_{s,r}$ from the S to the R, and $K_{r,d}$ from the R to the D.

The Marcum Q function is defined by [7]

$$Q(\alpha,\beta) = \exp(-(x^2+\alpha^2)/2)\sum_{k=0}^{\infty}(\alpha/\beta)^k I_k(\alpha\beta) \tag{14}$$

Its first-order formula is given as follows:

$$Q(\alpha,\beta) = \int_{\beta}^{\infty} x\exp(-(x^2+\alpha^2)/2)I_0(\alpha x)dx \tag{15}$$

As is shown in (15), we can't use the integral form without upper bound to express the outage probability function that with closed form directly. For simplicity of calculation, under the condition of upper bound is limited, the closed form approximation of outage probability CDF is obtained. Therefore, its closed-form is given in (16).

$$\begin{aligned} P_{out} = &\{1-\exp(-[(1+K_{sr})\gamma_{th}/\bar{\Gamma}_1+K_{sr}])\sum_{k=0}^{20}[K_{sr}\bar{\Gamma}_1/(1+K_{sr})\gamma_{th}]^{k/2}I_k(2[K_{sr}(1+K_{sr})\gamma_{th}/\bar{\Gamma}_1]^{k/2}) \\ &\times \exp(-[(1+K_{rd})\gamma_{th}/\bar{\Gamma}_2+K_{rd}])\sum_{k=0}^{20}[K_{rd}\bar{\Gamma}_2/(1+K_{rd})\gamma_{th}]^{k/2}I_k(2[K_{rd}(1+K_{sd})\gamma_{th}/\bar{\Gamma}_2]^{k/2})\} \\ &\times \{1-\exp(-[(1+K_{sd})\gamma_{th}/\bar{\Gamma}_0+K_{sd}])\sum_{k=0}^{20}[K_{sd}\bar{\Gamma}_0/(1+K_{sd})\gamma_{th}]^{k/2}I_k(2[K_{sd}(1+K_{sd})\gamma_{th}/\bar{\Gamma}_0]^{k/2})\} \end{aligned} \tag{16}$$

In this paper, we study the optimal power allocation problem with minimum outage probability under two constraints: the maximum power allowed to be consumed by a given packet in the whole propagation process from source to destination and the power provided by each relay node. The two constraints are total power constraints p_{tot} and maximum power $p_{\max}$ per hop. We should note that $p_{\max} < p_{tot} \le 2p_{\max}$.

Therefore, the problem is formulated is that under the condition of $p_1+p_2=p_{tot}$, $0 \le p_n \le p_{\max}\, n=1,2$, get the minimum value of P_{out}.

The problem formulated is an optimization problem. When drawing in linear proportion, the outage probability function is convex. Furthermore, they form a convex set because of all the constraints are linear [9], this is the cause of an optimization problem which has a unique optimal solution.

We use Lagrange multiplier maximization method, the modified objective function can be written as

$$P_{opt} = P_{out} + \eta(p_1+p_2-p_{tot}) + \mu_1(p_1-p_{\max}) + \mu_2(p_2-p_{\max}) + \delta_1 p_1 + \delta_2 p_2 \tag{17}$$

where η, μ_1, μ_2, δ_1 and δ_2 are constants.

4 Simulation Evaluation and Discussion

In this part, numerical results are used to show the optimal power allocation scheme. Assume the system channels are mutually independent identical Rician fading channels, and we have $K_{s,d} = K_{s,r} = K_{r,d} = K$. Set data rate R to 1 bits/Hz, so $\gamma_{th} = 2^{2R} - 1 = 3$. Set $p_{\max}/p_{tot}$ to 0.8. Define the ratio of the fading powers of the corresponding channels, $\Omega_{s,d} : \Omega_{s,r} : \Omega_{r,d}$. Considering whether the K factor and the fading power ratio are the same, we can divide them into two cases: one is that the K factor is the same but the fading power ratio is different, the other is opposite to the first case, and has different K factor and the same fading power ratio.

4.1 Optimal Power Allocation with Different Power Fading Ratios

Set $K = 3$. Figures 2 and 3 show the performance of the optimized power allocation scheme when the outage probability varies with the ratio. The outage performance is compared with the following two situations: 1. Uniform power distribution of the system. 2. Only direct links exist.

From Figs. 2, 3 it can be observed that, with high total power, outage probability of the optimal power allocation scheme and the uniform power allocation scheme tend to be identical under same fading power ratio condition. So the optimal power allocation is not necessary when the total power budget is large. It could also be concluded that, referring to the outage probability of direct links, as the ratio of $\Omega_{s,d}$ to $\Omega_{s,r}$ is fixed, with the increase of $\Omega_{r,d}$, outage probabilities of optimized power allocation system are more likely to drop below those of the direct link only case, as the total power budget increases.

In Fig. 2, $\Omega_{s,d} : \Omega_{s,r} : \Omega_{r,d}$ is set to 0.5 : 0.1 : 0.1, 0.5 : 0.1 : 0.5, 0.5 : 0.1 : 1, 0.5 : 0.1 : 5 and 0.5 : 0.1 : 1000, respectively, with $\Omega_{s,d} = 0.5$. With the increase of $\Omega_{r,d}$, the outage probability of the system will be increased, and ultimately reach the upper limit with the increase of $\Omega_{r,d}$.

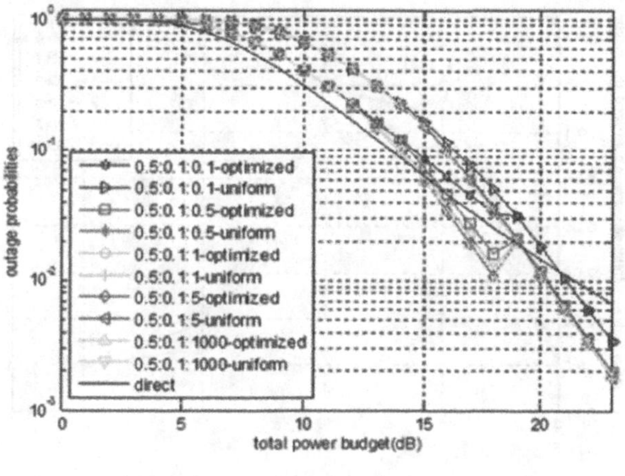

Fig. 2. Outage performances when $\Omega_{sd} > \Omega_{sr}$.

In Fig. 3, also with the same $\Omega_{s,d}$ value, $\Omega_{s,d} : \Omega_{s,r} : \Omega_{r,d}$ is set to $0.5 : 0.1 : 5$, $0.5 : 1 : 5$ and $0.5 : 5 : 5$, respectively. We can see that, when the ratio of $\Omega_{s,d}$ and $\Omega_{s,r}$ increases, the outage probability improvements get less obvious with high $\Omega_{s,r}$.

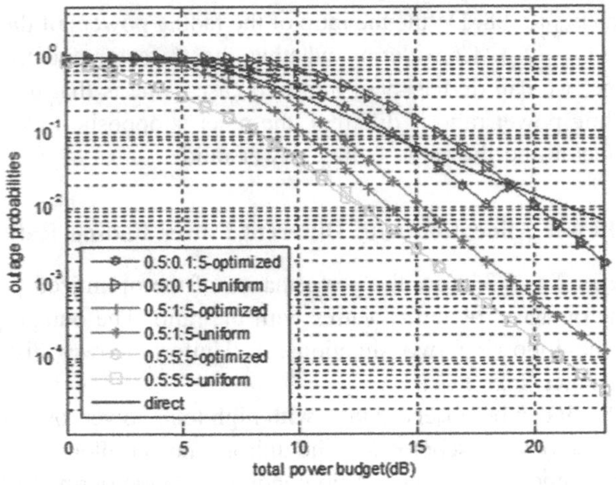

Fig. 3. Outage performances with different power fading ratios.

5 Optimal Power Allocation with Different Rician K- Factors

Set $\Omega_{s,d} : \Omega_{s,r} : \Omega_{r,d} = 0.5 : 1 : 5$. Figure 4 illustrates the outage probability difference of the direct link only case and the optimized power allocation case under different Rician *K*-factors. It is shown that, when the abscissa is small, more LOS improves the outage probability performance. When the abscissa is large, the outage probability differences approach 0, regardless of the *K* values.

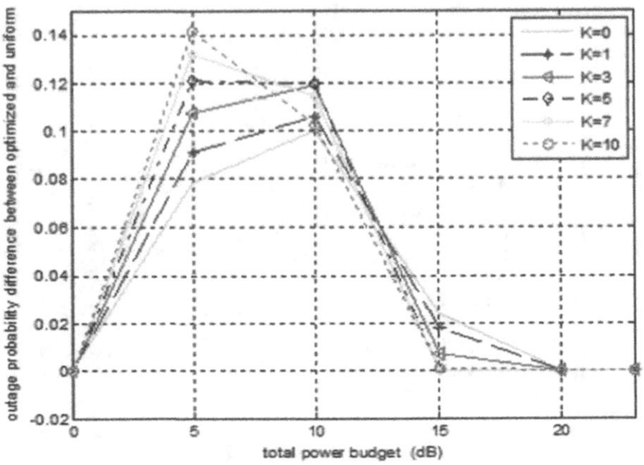

Fig. 4. Outage performance difference with different K-factors.

6 Conclusions

Cooperative communication technology is an effective technology to mitigate fading channels and enhance communication quality. So, it is very necessary to evaluate the performance of the power allocation scheme in such fading environment. We proposed a novel power allocation algorithm in the D-F cooperative communication scenario under different channel fading environments. Through the simulation results, it can be seen that with high total power, outage performances of the optimal power allocation case and the uniform power allocation case tend to be identical under same fading power ratio condition. So it can be seen that the optimal power allocation is not necessary when the total power budget is large. It could also be concluded that, referring to the outage probability of direct links, as the ratio of $\Omega_{s,d}$ to $\Omega_{s,r}$ is fixed, with the increase of $\Omega_{r,d}$, outage probabilities of optimized power allocation system are more likely to drop below those of the direct link only case, as the total power budget increases.

Acknowledgement. The paper is sponsored by National Natural Science Foundation of China (No. 91538104; No. 91438205).

References

1. Laneman, J., Tse, D.N.C., Wornell, G.W.: Cooperative diversity in wireless networks: efficient protocols and outage behavior. IEEE Trans. Inf. Theory **50**(12), 3062–3080 (2004)
2. Wei, G.Z., Ping, W., Qiang, L.F.: Multiuser diversity performance evaluation of 4G cooperative relay cellular network. In: Proceedings of the 15th APCC, pp. 322–325 (2009)
3. Luo, J., Blum, R.S., Cimini, L.J., Greenstein, L.J., Haimovich, A.M.: Decode-and–forward cooperative diversity with power allocation in wireless networks. IEEE Trans. Wirel. Commun. **6**(3), 793–799 (2007)
4. Lin, Q., Na, S.M., Rui, L.L., De, S.J.: Relay selection and power allocation scheme for cellular network using cooperative diversity. In: 2010 International Workshop on DBTA, pp. 1–5 (2010)
5. Jain, N., Dongariya, A., Verma, A.: Comparative study of different types of relay selection scheme for cooperative wireless communication. In: 2017 International Conference on Information, Communication, Instrumentation and Control (ICICIC), Indore, pp. 1–4 (2017)
6. Alkhayyat, A., Sadkhan, S.B.: Bandwidth efficiency analysis of cooperative communication with reactive relay selection. In: 2018 International Conference on Engineering Technology and their Applications (IICETA), Al-Najaf, pp. 77–80 (2018)
7. Simon, M.K., Alouini, M.S.: Digital Communication Over Fading Channels, 2nd edn. Wiley, New York (2005)
8. Oh, H., Nam, H.: Design of non-linearity preprocessor in cooperative diversity systems over rayleigh fading channel and impulsive noise. In: 2016 IEEE Radio and Wireless Symposium (RWS), Austin, TX, pp. 223–225 (2016)
9. Rardin, R.L.: Optimization in Operations Research. Prentice-Hall, Englewood Cliffs. NJ (1998)

Optimal Resource Optimization for Cluster-Based Energy-Efficient Cognitive IoT

Xin Liu[1](✉), Min Jia[2], and Zhenyu Na[3]

[1] School of Information and Communication Engineering, Dalian University of Technology, Dalian 116024, China
liuxinstar1984@dlut.edu.cn

[2] School of Electronics and Information Engineering, Harbin Institute of Technology, Harbin 150080, China
jiamin@hit.edu.cn

[3] School of Information Science and Technology, Dalian Maritime University, Dalian 116026, China
nazhenyu@dlmu.edu.cn

Abstract. In this paper, a cluster-based energy-efficient Cognitive Internet of Things (CIoT) is proposed, which can harvest the radio frequency (RF) energy of the primary user (PU) to supply energy consumption of spectrum sensing. A joint optimization problem of time and node is presented to maximize the spectrum access probability of the CIoT. The simulations show that there are optimal resource allocations to improve both spectrum efficiency and energy efficiency of CIoT.

Keywords: CIoT · Energy harvesting · Cluster · Joint optimization

1 Introduction

Cognitive radio (CR) has been proposed to improve the utilization of the finite spectrum resources through using the idle spectrum of primary user (PU) by chance. However, the interference brought to the PU has to be avoided through spectrum sensing, which may find the presence of the PU by detecting the received signal [1]. Energy detection is used to measure the strength of the received signal, and the presence of the PU can be decided if the signal strength is above a presettled threshold. However, energy detection performance can be decreased when the received signal to noise ratio (SNR) is very low [2]. Cooperative spectrum sensing can be used to improve spectrum sensing performance in fading and shadowing channel, which can obtain a final decision on the presence of the PU by combining local sensing results from multiple CR users locating at different sensing areas [3].

Listen-before-talk mode has been proposed to improve spectrum access of the CR and avoid bringing interference to the PU by dividing the frame structure into sensing slot and transmission slot, in which the detection result in the

M. Jia et al. (Eds.): WiSATS 2019, LNICST 281, pp. 532–540, 2019.
https://doi.org/10.1007/978-3-030-19156-6_50

sensing slot decides the CR status in the transmission slot [4]. It has been proven that there is a sensing-throughput tradeoff in CR, i.e., an optimal sensing time can be achieved to maximize the throughput of the CR. An optimization of cooperative spectrum sensing is proposed to decrease cooperative overhead through obtaining the jointly optimal sensing time and number of cooperative users [5]. Since the CR has the function of sensing spectrum environment, the CR user can be seen as a sensor, which may be applied in sensor network and Internet of Things (IoT) [6]. IoT has been used to connect the things with the Internet through information sensing devices such as radio frequency identification (RFID), which can automatically and intelligently collect, transmit and process information in order to realize the scientific management of the networks. IoT is widely applied in intelligent transportation, environmental protection, government work, public safety, safe home, industrial monitoring and environmental monitoring etc., which has improved system efficiency and reduced human intervention of the network [7]. However, the shortage of spectrum resources has limited the development of the IoT greatly [8]. Currently, cognitive IoT (CIoT) combining with CR is proposed to provide flexible and dynamic spectrum access and expand available spectrum of the IoT. However, the spectrum sensing of the CIoT may consume some time and energy, thus decreasing both transmission time and transmission power [9].

Energy harvesting has been recently proposed to collect radio frequency (RF) energy of wireless signals by converting AC signal to DC voltage using a rectifier circuit. The RF energy is stored in a rechargeable battery to supply system operations, thus, energy harvesting can be seen as an effective method to realize energy-efficient communications [10]. Hence, in this paper we have proposed a cluster-based energy-efficient CIoT which can harvest the RF energy of the PU signal while performing spectrum sensing.

2 System Model

We consider a CIoT constituting of N nodes and a PU network covering L sub-channels. The IoT is divided into D clusters and each cluster has $S = N/D$ nodes. Each cluster selects a cluster head to manage the nodes within the cluster. As shown in Fig. 1, the frame structure of the CIoT is divided into sensing slot and transmission slot, and the CIoT can communicate only when the absence of the PU has been detected in the channel. In the traditional CIoT, the nodes can only sense the PU using the stored battery energy, which decrease the transmission performance due to great sensing energy consumption. However, the proposed cluster-based energy-efficient CIoT has the function of energy harvesting, which can harvest the RF energy of the PU signal to supply energy consumption of spectrum sensing, and each cluster can perform either cooperative spectrum sensing or energy harvesting within sensing slot, as shown in Fig. 2.

Suppose there are K clusters to sense the PU and $D - K$ clusters to harvest energy. The nodes of each sensing cluster sense the PU by energy detection with the sampling number M and send their energy statistics to the cluster head

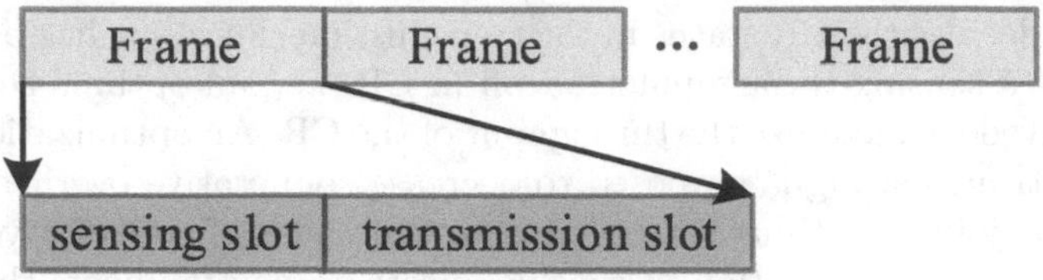

Fig. 1. Frame structure of CIoT.

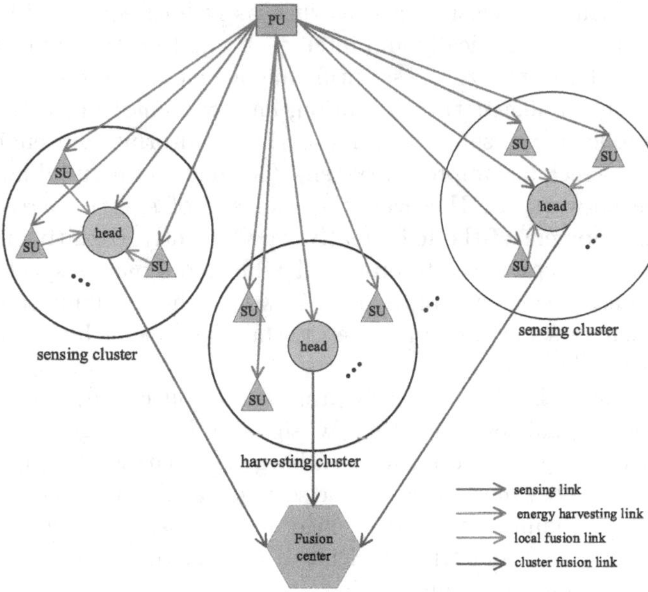

Fig. 2. Network structure of CIoT.

that makes a 1-bit decision by comparing the average accumulated statistic to a threshold λ. Probabilities of false alarm and detection at the cluster head i for $i = 1, 2, ..., K$ are given by [5]

$$P_i^f = Q\left(\left(\frac{\lambda}{\sigma^2} - 1\right)\sqrt{SM}\right) \tag{1}$$

$$P_i^d = Q\left(\left(\frac{\lambda}{\sigma^2} - \gamma - 1\right)\sqrt{\frac{SM}{(\gamma+1)^2}}\right) \tag{2}$$

where the function $Q(x)$ is defined by

$$Q(x) = \frac{1}{\sqrt{2\pi}}\int_x^{+\infty} \exp\left(-\frac{\omega^2}{2}\right) \mathbf{d}\omega \tag{3}$$

All the sensing cluster heads send local 1-bit decisions to the fusion center that makes a final decision on the presence of the PU by combining these

1-bit decisions using OR rule [3]. The cooperative probabilities of false alarm and detection are given by

$$Q_f = 1 - (1 - P_i^f)^K \tag{4}$$

$$Q_d = 1 - (1 - P_i^d)^K \tag{5}$$

From (5), with a given Q_d, P_i^d is obtained as follows

$$P_i^d = 1 - (1 - Q_d)^{\frac{1}{K}} \tag{6}$$

From (2), sensing threshold is calculated as follows

$$\lambda = \left(\frac{Q^{-1}\left(1 - (1 - Q_d)^{\frac{1}{K}}\right)}{\sqrt{SM}} + 1 \right) (\gamma + 1)\sigma^2 \tag{7}$$

Substituting (7) to (1) and (4), Q_f is deduced as follows

$$Q_f = 1 - \left(1 - Q(Q^{-1}(P_i^d)(\gamma + 1) + \gamma\sqrt{SM})\right)^K \tag{8}$$

Suppose the frame time is T, the local sensing time of each node is t_s, and the sensing information reporting time of cluster head is t_r. Each cluster head sends sensing information in the allocated time slot to avoid generating transmission conflict. t_r can be set as a constant according to the maximal distance from the cluster head to the fusion center. The reporting time within one cluster can be ignored due to the short transmission distance from node to head. Thus, the average transmission time is given by $t_d = T - t_s - Kt_r$. The number of sampling nodes $M = t_s f_s$ where f_s is sampling frequency. Hence, the average spectrum access probability of the CIoT is given by

$$P_{acc} = \frac{T - t_s - Kt_r}{T}((1 - Q_f)P_{h0} + (1 - Q_d)P_{h1}) \tag{9}$$

where P_{h0} and P_{h1} denote absence and presence of the PU, respectively, which satisfy $P_{h0} + P_{h1} = 1$. With a given Q_d, P_{acc} is rewritten as follows

$$P_{acc} = \frac{T - t_s - Kt_r}{T} \left(\left(1 - Q\left(Q^{-1}\left(1 - (1 - Q_d)^{\frac{1}{K}}\right)(\gamma + 1) + \gamma\sqrt{St_s f_s}\right)\right)^K P_{h0} + (1 - Q_d)P_{h1} \right) \tag{10}$$

The other $D - K$ clusters harvest the RF energy within sensing time t_s. The average aggregate harvested energy of $(D - K)S$ nodes is given by

$$E_H = (D - K)S(p_s h^2 P_{h1} + p_n)t_s \tag{11}$$

where p_s is the PU power, p_n is the noise power and h is the average channel gain from the PU to the CIoT. Suppose the sensing power of each node is p_r and the sensing information reporting power is p_u, the aggregate consumed sensing energy within sensing time is given by

$$E_S = K(Sp_r t_s + p_u t_r) \tag{12}$$

3 Joint Time and Node Optimization

In this paper, we try to maximize the spectrum access probability of the CIoT subject to the constraints that the detection probability Q_d is above the lower bound α and the harvested energy E_H is larger than the consumed sensing energy E_S. The optimization problem is formulated as follows

$$\max_{t_s,K} P_{acc} \tag{13a}$$
$$\text{s.t. } Q_d \geq \alpha \tag{13b}$$
$$E_H \geq E_S \tag{13c}$$
$$t_s + Kt_r \leq T \tag{13d}$$

which is hard to be solved directly. The optimization problem can be solved using the alternating direction optimization (ADO).

3.1 Sensing Time Optimization

Firstly, fixing K, Eq. (13) becomes a convex optimization problem about τ, which is described as follows

$$\max_{t_s} P_{acc} = \frac{\hat{T} - t_s}{T}\left(\left(1 - Q(\Phi + \Psi\sqrt{t_s})\right)^K P_{h0} + (1 - Q_d)P_{h1}\right) \tag{14a}$$
$$\text{s.t. } Q_d \geq \alpha \tag{14b}$$
$$E_H \geq E_S \tag{14c}$$
$$0 \leq t_s \leq \hat{T} \tag{14d}$$

where $\hat{T} = T - Kt_r$, $\Phi = Q^{-1}\left(1 - (1 - Q_d)^{\frac{1}{K}}\right)(\gamma + 1)$ and $\Psi = \gamma\sqrt{Sf_s}$. Since $Q(x)$ is a monotonically decreasing function, Φ decreases with the increase of Q_d. Hence, P_{acc} decreases with the increase of Q_d, which indicates that P_{acc} can achieve the maximal value only when $Q_d = \alpha$. With $E_H \geq E_s$, we can obtain $t_s \geq t_s^{min}$. t_s^{min} is given by

$$t_s^{min} = \frac{p_u t_r}{S\left(\left(\frac{D}{K} - 1\right)(p_s h^2 p_{h1} + p_n) - p_r\right)} \tag{15}$$

where $(D - K)(p_s h^2 p_{h1} + p_n) - Kp_r > 0$ must be guaranteed where we can get $K < \frac{D(p_s h^2 p_{h1} + p_n)}{p_s h^2 p_{h1} + p_n + p_r}$. Hence, the initial value of K should be chosen within the range from 1 to $\left\lceil \frac{D(p_s h^2 p_{h1} + p_n)}{p_s h^2 p_{h1} + p_n + p_r} \right\rceil$. Then the optimization problem (13) is rewritten as follows

$$\max_{t_s} P_{acc} = \frac{\hat{T} - t_s}{T}\left(\left(1 - Q(\Phi + \Psi\sqrt{t_s})\right)^K P_{h0} + (1 - \alpha)P_{h1}\right) \tag{16a}$$
$$\text{s.t. } t_s^{min} \leq t_s \leq \hat{T} \tag{16b}$$

t_s^* can be achieved using the Newton iterative method that is described in Algorithm 1.

Algorithm 1. Sensing time optimization.

Input: $i = 0$, $t_s^{(i)} \in [t_s^{min}, \hat{T}]$ and estimation error δ;
while $|t_s^{(i)} - t_s^{(i-1)}| > \delta$ **do**
  set $t_s^{(i+1)} = t_s^{(i)} - \frac{\nabla P_{acc}\left(t_s^{(i)}\right)}{\nabla^2 P_{acc}\left(t_s^{(i)}\right)}$
  set $i = i + 1$;
end while
Output: $t_s^* = t_s^{(i)}$.

3.2 IoT Node Optimization

Fixing t_s, the optimization problem (13) about K is rewritten as follows

$$\max_{t_s} P_{acc} = t_r \frac{\tilde{T} - K}{T} (G(K) P_{h0} + (1 - \alpha) P_{h1}) \tag{17a}$$

$$\text{s.t. } 0 \le K \le \tilde{T} \tag{17b}$$

where $\tilde{T} = \frac{T - t_s}{t_r}$, $G(K) = \left(1 - Q(\Phi + \Psi\sqrt{t_s})\right)^K$. From $E_H \ge E_S$, we can get that

$$K \le \frac{SDt_s(P_s h^2 p_{h1} + p_n)}{S(p_s h^2 p_{h1} + p_n + p_r)t_s + p_u t_r} \tag{18}$$

The optimal K^* can be achieved using the enumeration method, which is described as follows

$$K^* = \underset{K=1,2,\ldots,K^{max}}{\operatorname{argmax}} \; P_{acc}(K) \tag{19}$$

We optimize t_s and K alternatively until both of them are convergent. The joint optimization algorithm of t_s and K is described as Algorithm 2.

Algorithm 2. Joint optimization algorithm.

Input: $i = 0$, $t_s^{(i)}$ and $K^{(i)}$;
while any of t_s and K is not convergent or the maximal iteration number has been reached **do**
  fixing $t_s = t_s^{(i)}$, optimize K using (19) and set $K^{(i+1)} = K^*$;
  fixing $K = K^{(i+1)}$, optimize t_s using Algorithm 1 and set $t_s^{(i+1)} = t_s^*$;
  set $i = i + 1$;
end while
Output: $t_s^* = t_s^{(i)}$ and $K^* = K^{(i)}$.

4 Simulations and Discussions

The simulation parameters are set as follows. The absence and presence probabilities of the PU $P_{h0} = P_{h1} = 0.5$, the frame time $T = 10$ ms, the reporting time $t_r = 0.05$ ms, the number of IoT nodes $N = 150$, the number of clusters $D = 30$, the sampling frequency $f_s = 100$ KHz, the PU power $p_s = 1$W, the noise power $p_n = 0.01$ W, the sensing power $p_r = 0.1$ W and the information reporting power $p_u = 0.1$ W. Moreover, the channels obey the Rayleigh distributions (Fig. 3).

It has been indicated that there is an optimal set of sensing time t_s and number of sensing clusters K that maximizes the spectrum access probability of the CIoT. When $t_s = 0.5$ ms and $K = 12$, the maximal $P_{acc} = 0.3952$. Figure 4 shows P_{acc} changing with t_s when $K = [1, 10, 20]$. It is seen that P_{acc} firstly improves and then decreases as t_s increases, which has proven the convex optimization of (14). P_{acc} improves due to the increased spectrum sensing performance but decreases because of the decreased spectrum access time, thus, there is a tradeoff between sensing time and spectrum access. The relationship between spectrum access and energy harvesting is shown in Fig. 5. We can see that P_{acc} firstly improves but then drops rapidly with the increase of harvested energy E_H. Because small E_H can supply the energy used for spectrum access, but large E_H may consume great spectrum resource such as time and nodes. Hence, there is a tradeoff between spectrum access and energy harvesting.

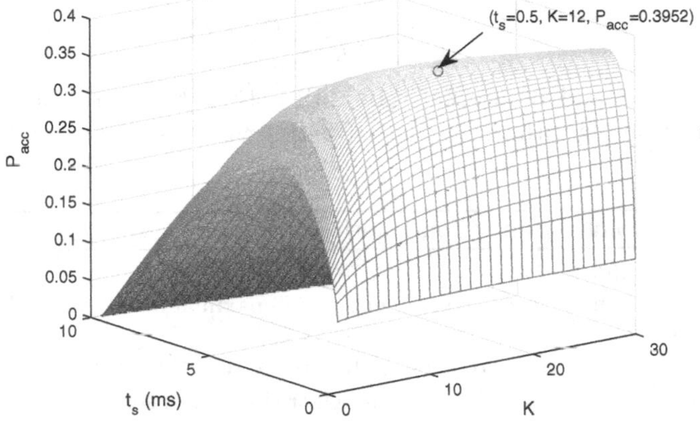

Fig. 3. Spectrum access probability changing jointly with local sensing time and the number of sensing clusters.

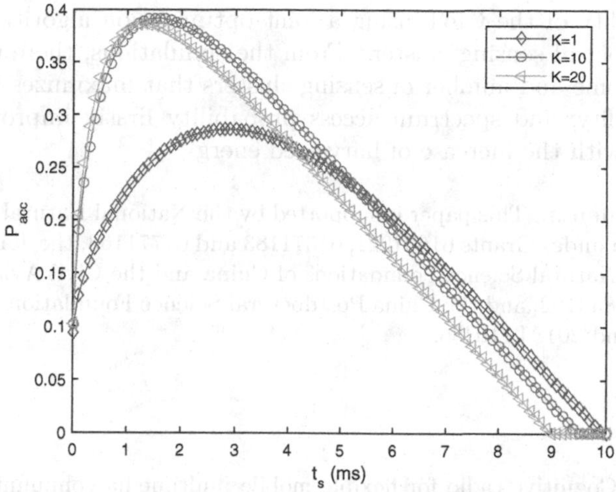

Fig. 4. Spectrum access probability changing with local sensing time.

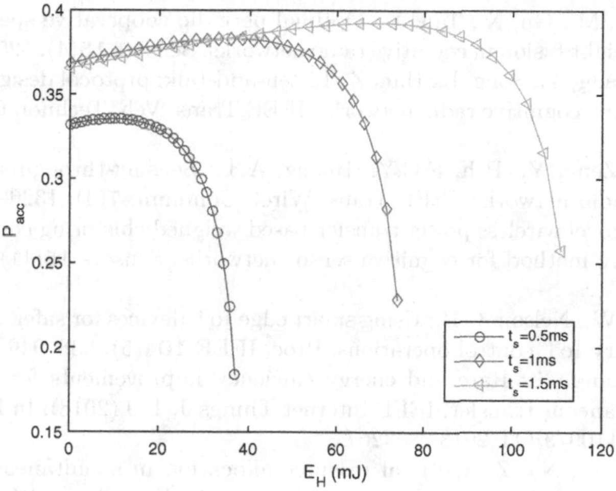

Fig. 5. Spectrum access probability changing with harvested energy.

5 Conclusions

In this paper, a cluster-based energy-efficient CIoT is proposed to improve both spectrum efficiency and energy efficiency, which can harvest the RF energy of the PU while performing spectrum sensing. The frame structure of the CIoT is divided into sensing slot and transmission slot. In the sensing slot, some clusters detect the PU while the other clusters harvest the RF energy, and the harvested energy is used to supply the consumption of spectrum sensing for guaranteeing transmission energy in the transmission slot. We try to maximize the spectrum access probability of the CIoT using a joint optimization algorithm of sensing time and number of sensing clusters. From the simulations, there is an optimal set of sensing time and number of sensing clusters that maximizes the spectrum access probability, and spectrum access probability firstly improves but then drops rapidly with the increase of harvested energy.

Acknowledgements. This paper is supported by the National Natural Science Foundations of China under Grants 61601221, 61671183 and 61771163, the Joint Foundation of the National Natural Science Foundations of China and the Civil Aviation of China under Grant U1833102, and the China Postdoctoral Science Foundations under Grants 2015M580425 and 2018T110496.

References

1. Mitola, J.: Cognitive radio for flexible mobile multimedia communications. Mob. Netw. Appl. **6**(5), 435–441 (2001)
2. Shen, J., Liu, S., Wang, Y.: Robust energy detection in cognitive radio. IET Commun. **3**(6), 1016–1023 (2009)
3. Liu, X., Jia, M., Gu, X., Tan, X.: Optimal periodic cooperative spectrum sensing based on weight fusion in cognitive radio networks. Sensors **13**(4), 5251–5272 (2013)
4. Liao, Y., Wang, T., Song, L., Han, Z.: Listen-and-talk: protocol design and analysis for full-duplex cognitive radio networks. IEEE Trans. Veh. Technol. **66**(1), 656–667 (2017)
5. Liang, Y., Zeng, Y., Peh, E.C.Y., Hoang, A.T.: Sensing-throughput tradeoff for cognitive radio networks. IEEE Trans. Wirel. Commun. **7**(4), 1326–1337 (2008)
6. Liu, X.: A novel wireless power transfer-based weighed clustering cooperative spectrum sensing method for cognitive sensor networks. Sensors **15**(11), 27760–27782 (2015)
7. Condry, M.W., Nelson, C.B.: Using smart edge IoT devices for safer, rapid response with industry IoT control operations. Proc. IEEE **104**(5), 938–946 (2016)
8. Liu, X., Zhang, X.: Rate and energy efficiency improvements for 5G-based IoT with simultaneous transfer. IEEE Internet Things J. 1–9 (2018). In Press. https://doi.org/10.1109/JIOT.2018.2863267
9. Liu, X., Li, F., Na, Z.: Optimal resource allocation in simultaneous cooperative spectrum sensing and energy harvesting for multichannel cognitive radio. IEEE Access **5**, 3801–3812 (2017)
10. Liu, X., Jia, M., Na, Z., Lu, W., Li, F.: Multi-modal cooperative spectrum sensing based on dempster-shafer fusion in 5G-based cognitive radio. IEEE Access **6**, 199–208 (2018)

Successive-Parallel Interference Cancellation Multi-user Detection Algorithm for MUSA Uplink

Shaochuan Wu(✉), Rundong Zuo, Wenbing Zhang, and Yanwu Song

School of Electronics and Information Engineering,
Harbin Institute of Technology, Harbin, China
{scwu,zwbgxy1973}@hit.edu.cn, rd_zuo@163.com, jamie.song95@gmail.com

Abstract. With the approaching of Internet of Things (IoT), non-orthogonal multiple access technology was proposed in the fifth generation (5G) mobile communication system to improve the system capacity and meet the needs of massive connectivity. Multi-User Shared Access (MUSA) technology is a non-orthogonal multiple access technology of code domain. MUSA receiver adopts multi-user detection algorithm, mainly using interference cancellation based on linear detection. This paper proposes the successive-parallel interference cancellation multi-user detection algorithm for the shortage of typical multi-user detection algorithms of MUSA uplink receiver, and gives the comparison results of the proposed algorithm and typical algorithms. Compared with parallel interference cancellation detection algorithm, the proposed algorithm improves the detection performance greatly. Compared with successive interference cancellation detection algorithm, the proposed algorithm reduces the processing time delay effectively.

Keywords: Multi-User Shared Access · Multi-user detection · Interference cancellation · Time delay

1 Introduction

At this stage, due to the increasing needs of users, as well as the rapid development of Mobile Internet and Internet of Things (IoT), the traditional orthogonal multiple access technology [1] is difficult to meet the enormous demand. Orthogonal technology can effectively avoid multi-access interference (MAI), and design complexity of receiver is low. Therefore, the 4G and previous communication systems adopt orthogonal scheme mainly. However, because orthogonal technology requires different resources to be allocated to different users and different users' resources can not overlap each other, the spectrum utilization is not high enough to meet the huge demand of 5G system [2].

This work was supported by the National Science Foundation of China with Grant 61671173.

M. Jia et al. (Eds.): WiSATS 2019, LNICST 281, pp. 541–551, 2019.
https://doi.org/10.1007/978-3-030-19156-6_51

Therefore, non-orthogonal multiple access technology [3] is proposed in 5G wireless system, which is mainly realized in power domain and code domain. The power domain non-orthogonal multiple access (NOMA) scheme [4] was proposed by NTT DOCOMO, where users data are multiplexed in the non-orthogonal manner in power domain and different transmit power is allocated to different users according to different channel conditions. Sparse Code Multiple Access (SCMA) technology [5] and Multi-User Shared Access (MUSA) technology [6] were proposed by HUAWEI Technology and ZTE Corporation as code domain non-orthogonal multiple access technologies, respectively. SCMA technology [7] replaces the QAM modulation and Low Density Signature (LDS) spread spectrum with a multi-dimensional codebook, providing shaping gain and spreading gain. MUSA technology [8,9] spreads user data through non-orthogonal spreading code sequence, and adopts interference cancellation technology at receiver. The technical difficulty and major breakthrough of MUSA is multi-user detection algorithm of receiver. Researchers have done some research, proposing the parallel interference cancellation detection scheme and the two-successive interference cancellation detection scheme. The two schemes reduce computational complexity and processing time delay, but the detection performance declines as well. Pattern Division Multiple Access (PDMA) technology [10] proposed by Datang Telecom Technology is a non-orthogonal multiple access technique adopting PDMA pattern that defines the mapping of transmitted data to a resource group which can consist of time and frequency resources.

Multi-user detection algorithms mainly adopt linear detection algorithm and non-linear detection algorithm. Linear detection [11] is multiplying the received signal directly with the linear operator, including zero forcing (ZF) detection algorithm and minimum mean square error (MMSE) detection algorithm. The detection scheme is simple, but detection performance is poor because of the effect of noise amplification. Non-linear detection [12] mainly means interference cancellation algorithms, which mainly include successive interference cancellation (SIC) detection algorithm and parallel interference cancellation (PIC) detection algorithm. The difference between interference cancellation technology and traditional detection algorithm is that the other users data are regarded as the interference of the detected user data rather than noise in interference cancellation technology. Then the detected user data can be restored by detecting, reconstructing and eliminating other users' data. In the traditional CDMA system, there will be MAI if orthogonality of the code sequences between users can not be guaranteed, so multi-user detection algorithm is widely used [13].

This paper focuses on the research of multi-user detection algorithm for MUSA uplink receiver. This paper proposes the successive-parallel multi-user detection algorithm for the shortage of typical multi-user detection algorithms of MUSA uplink receiver. The proposed algorithm improves the detection performance greatly comparing with parallel interference cancellation detection algorithm and reduces the processing time delay effectively comparing with successive interference cancellation detection algorithm.

The rest of this paper is organized as follows. In Sect. 2, the previous work is introduced including system model and basic concepts of MUSA uplink. Section 3 introduces multi-user detection algorithms including typical multi-user detection algorithms and the proposed multi-user detection algorithm, and Sect. 4 presents comparison results and the performance analysis of multi-user detection algorithms. Finally, conclusions are drawn in Sect. 5.

2 Previous Work

MUSA is a non-orthogonal multiple access technology proposed in 5G system to meet the increasing demand. It can realize grant-free access with a large number of users simultaneously, and is very suitable for IoT. The basic model and concepts of MUSA are introduced in this part.

2.1 Basic Model of MUSA Uplink

MUSA is a NOMA technology based on the complex spreading code sequence, and its uplink access model is shown in Fig. 1. In the transmitter, each user first gets the own modulation data through encoding and constellation mapping. Then each user spreads own modulation data through the spreading code sequence selected randomly. Thus all users' data can be transmitted over a multi-user shared channel and different users data can occupy the same time-frequency resource. In the receiver, the received data is processed first by linear module to get the initial estimation of users' data. Then the detected user eliminates MAI through the interference cancellation module. Finally we can restore the original data for each user through demodulation mapping and decoding.

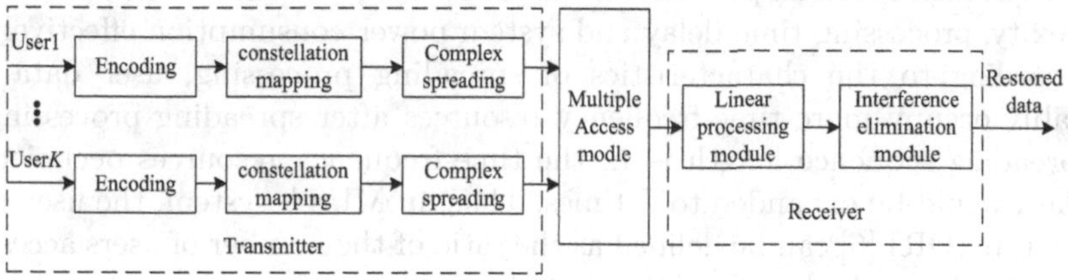

Fig. 1. MUSA uplink access model.

MUSA can be regard as an improvement scheme of CDMA technology. The difference is that MUSA can achieve system overload at transmitter with low cross-correlation complex spreading code sequence. Namely, the number of users accessing at the same time is greater than the length of spreading code sequence. And the spreading code sequences of users need not to be orthogonal.

According to the MUSA uplink access model, each user randomly selects spreading code sequence, then spreads the modulation data to superimposed transmit. The receiving signal after Additive White Gaussian Noise (AWGN) channel can be expressed as

$$\boldsymbol{R} = \sum_{k=1}^{K} \boldsymbol{H}_k \bullet \hat{\boldsymbol{S}}_k + \boldsymbol{N} = \sum_{k=1}^{K} \boldsymbol{H}_k \bullet (\boldsymbol{W}_k \boldsymbol{S}_k) + \boldsymbol{N} \tag{1}$$

where, K is the number of access users. $\hat{\boldsymbol{S}}_k$ and $\boldsymbol{S}_k$ are the spread data and transmitting modulated data, respectively. $\boldsymbol{H}_k$ is channel coefficient and $\boldsymbol{W}_k$ is spreading code sequence randomly selected by user k. $\boldsymbol{N}$ is AWGN, and the symbol "•" represents the multiplication of corresponding position elements of matrices.

Through further deduction, (1) can be written as

$$\boldsymbol{R} = \sum_{k=1}^{K} (\boldsymbol{H}_k \bullet \boldsymbol{W}_k) \boldsymbol{S}_k + \boldsymbol{N} = \sum_{k=1}^{K} \boldsymbol{F}_k \boldsymbol{S}_k + \boldsymbol{N} \tag{2}$$

where $\boldsymbol{F}_k$ is defined as the equivalent channel coefficient matrix. Each column of $\boldsymbol{F}_k$ is the result of $\boldsymbol{H}_k$ multiplying corresponding location elements of the column of $\boldsymbol{W}_k$, and symbol "•" represents the multiplication of $\boldsymbol{H}_k$ and corresponding position elements of every column of $\boldsymbol{W}_k$.

2.2 Complex Spreading Code

The MUSA uplink utilizes complex multivariate code sequences [6] as spreading sequences. The cross-correlation of the sequences is low due to the design with real part and imaginary part even though the length of the code sequence is short. Using complex multivariate code sequence as spreading sequences not only satisfies the high overload performance of the system, but also reduces processing complexity, processing time delay and system power consumption effectively.

According to the characteristics of spreading processing, user data will inevitably occupy more time-frequency resources after spreading processing. If the spreading sequence length is L, the time-frequency resources occupied by user data would be expanded to L times. Thus, in MUSA system, the user overloading rate (OR) [6] can be defined as the ratio of the number of users accessing simultaneously to the length of the spreading sequence.

$$\mathrm{OR} = \frac{K}{L} \tag{3}$$

3 Multi-user Detection Algorithm

Complex spreading sequences assigned to each user in MUSA system are non-orthogonal to each other, so there will be MAI at the receiver. Therefore, it is necessary to adopt multi-user detection algorithm to get the original data of each user.

3.1 Typical Multi-user Detection Algorithm

Three existing typical multi-user detection algorithms of MUSA include MMSE-SIC detection algorithm, MMSE-PIC detection algorithm and the two-successive interference cancellation (MMSE-2SIC) detection algorithm.

Linear processing module of MMSE-SIC multi-user detection algorithm and MMSE-PIC detection algorithm adopt MMSE detection, and interference cancellation module adopt separately successive interference cancellation parallel interference cancellation. The detection performance of MMSE-SIC algorithm is better, but the computational complexity and processing time delay is higher than MMSE-PIC algorithm.

To overcome the high processing time delay of MMSE-SIC algorithm, MMSE-2SIC multi-user detection algorithm was proposed. Its linear processing module adopts MMSE detection, but the interference cancellation module adapts two-successive interference cancellation. The two-successive interference cancellation first calculates the SINR of each user and sorts the users according their SINR. Then the two largest SINR users are selected to detect. This scheme reduces the processing time delay, but the detection performance is worse as well. Next parts mainly introduce the proposed successive-parallel multi-user detection algorithm in this paper.

3.2 Successive-Parallel Multi-user Detection Algorithm

Each iteration of MMSE-PIC detection algorithm needs to detect all users for MMSE detection and eliminate MAI produced by all other users outside themselves. The structure is complex and the performance is poor due to serious MAI. If the strong signal can be detected, reconstructed and eliminated before PIC processing that is equivalent to remove the severe MAI, the data of the rest users would get better detection performance through PIC detection. The essential idea is to detect the users with strong signal through SIC detection firstly, then detect the users with weak signal through PIC detection. That is named as successive-parallel interference cancellation (MMSE-SPIC) multi-user detection algorithm.

The algorithm eliminates the data of users with strong signal, that reduces MAI between users in MUSA uplink receiver and improves the detection performance of users with weak signal. Furthermore, remaining users don't need too many iterations and updates. Its detection performance gets better and processing time delay still is small. The process flow of MMSE-SPIC detection algorithm is shown in Fig. 2.

According to the process flow of Fig. 2, concrete processing steps of MMSE-SPIC detection algorithm is shown in Algorithm 1. In this paper, Cyclic Redundancy Check is used to judge whether the decoding is correct or not.

In SIC processing of Algorithm 1, $\hat{\boldsymbol{\omega}}^n$, $\boldsymbol{R}^n$ and $\boldsymbol{y}^n$ represent MMSE detection coefficient, the receiving signal and the MMSE detecting result in the n-th detection, respectively. $\hat{\boldsymbol{\omega}}^n$ and $\boldsymbol{R}^n$ will be updated when the n-th detection is completed. $\boldsymbol{y}_l^n$ is the portion of $\boldsymbol{R}^n$ involving l, and $\tilde{\boldsymbol{S}}_l$ is the restored signal of user l. Moreover, $\boldsymbol{R}^1 = \boldsymbol{R} = \sum_{k=1}^{K} \boldsymbol{F}_k \boldsymbol{S}_k + \boldsymbol{N}$. In PIC detection, $\hat{\boldsymbol{\omega}}^{K_1}$ is the MMSE detection coefficient for PIC detection, which will not be updated. $\boldsymbol{R}^n_{k_2}$ represents the receiving signal for user k_2 in the n-th iteration, and $\boldsymbol{y}^n_{k_2}$ represents the portion of $\boldsymbol{y}^n$ involving user k_2. $\tilde{\boldsymbol{S}}^n_{k_2}$ is the restored signal for user k_2 in the n-th iteration. Moreover, $K_1 + K_2 = K$.

Algorithm 1. MMSE-SPIC detection algorithm

Require: Channel matrices $\boldsymbol{H}$; Spreading sequence matrices $\boldsymbol{W}$; Received signals $\boldsymbol{R} = \sum_{k=1}^{K} \boldsymbol{H}_k \bullet (\boldsymbol{W}_k \boldsymbol{S}_k) + \boldsymbol{N}$; SINR threshold value M_1; PIC iteration times N;

Ensure: Reconstructed signals $\tilde{\boldsymbol{S}}_k$;

1: STEP1 (Initialization)

2: Equivalent channel matrices $\boldsymbol{F}_k = \boldsymbol{H}_k \bullet \boldsymbol{W}_k$; Received signals $\boldsymbol{R} = \sum_{k=1}^{K} \boldsymbol{F}_k \boldsymbol{S}_k + \boldsymbol{N}$;
MMSE detection coefficient $\boldsymbol{\omega} = \left(\boldsymbol{H}^H \boldsymbol{H} + \sigma^2 \boldsymbol{I}\right)^{-1} \boldsymbol{H}^H$, $\hat{\boldsymbol{\omega}} = \left(\boldsymbol{F}^H \boldsymbol{F} + \sigma^2 \boldsymbol{I}\right)^{-1} \boldsymbol{F}^H$;

3: SINR calculation $\mathrm{SINR}_k = \frac{\|\boldsymbol{F}_k \boldsymbol{\omega}_k\|^2}{\|\boldsymbol{F}_k\|^2 \sum_{k=1}^{K} \|\boldsymbol{\omega}_k\|^2 + \boldsymbol{N}_k}$;

4: STEP2 (SIC processing)

5: All SIC users K_1, $K_1 = \{k | \mathrm{SINR}_k \geqslant M_1, k \in K\}$;

6: **for** $n = 1 : \mathrm{length}\,(K_1)$ **do**

7: (Choose the detected user)

8: Choose user l, meets $\mathrm{SINR}_l = \max_{i \in K_1} \mathrm{SINR}_i$;

9: (MMSE detection) $\boldsymbol{y}^n = \hat{\boldsymbol{\omega}}^n \boldsymbol{R}^n$;

10: (Demodulation&Decoding) $\tilde{\boldsymbol{S}}_l = (\mathrm{Dem\&Dec})\, \boldsymbol{y}^n_l$;

11: (Update)

12: **if** Decoding correct **then**

13: $\boldsymbol{R}^n = \boldsymbol{R}^{n-1} - \boldsymbol{F}_l \tilde{\boldsymbol{S}}_l$;

14: **end if**

15: **end for**

16: All users with correct decoding L;

17: (Updating) $\boldsymbol{R}^{K_1} = \boldsymbol{R}^1 - \sum_{m \in L} \boldsymbol{F}_m \tilde{\boldsymbol{S}}_m$;

18: STEP3 (PIC detection)

19: All PIC users K_2, $K_2 = \{k | \mathrm{SINR}_k < M_1, k \in K\}$;

20: **for** $n = 1 : N$ **do**

21: (MMSE detection) $\boldsymbol{y}^n = \hat{\boldsymbol{\omega}}^{K_1} \boldsymbol{R}^n_{k_2}$;

22: (Demodulation&Decoding) $\tilde{\boldsymbol{S}}^n_{k_2} = (\mathrm{Dem\&Dec})\, \boldsymbol{y}^n_{k_2}$;

23: All users with correct decoding L;

24: (Update) $\boldsymbol{R}^n_{k_2} = \boldsymbol{R}^{K_1} - \sum_{m \in L, m \neq k_2} \boldsymbol{F}_m \tilde{\boldsymbol{S}}_m$;

25: **end for**

26: $\tilde{\boldsymbol{S}}_{k_2} = \tilde{\boldsymbol{S}}^N_{k_2}$;

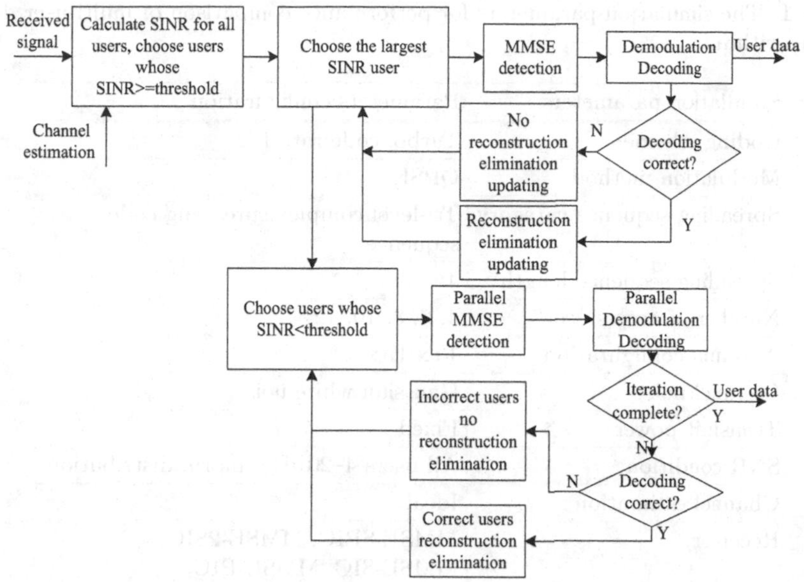

Fig. 2. MMSE-SPIC processing flow.

4 Simulation Results

The proposed multi-user detection algorithm and the three existing typical multi-user detection algorithms will be compared in this part. The simulation parameters [6] are shown in Table 1, and the relationships of average block error rate (BLER) and user overload rate of different algorithms are shown in Fig. 3.

From the simulation result of Fig. 3, the conclusion can be concluded that the detection performance of MMSE-SIC detection algorithm is the best and MMSE-PIC detection algorithm is the worst. That is consistent with theoretical result. About the two rest multi-user detection algorithms, results of the two algorithms are different in different range of users' overload rate.

When the user overload rate is low, the BLER of MMSE-SPIC detection algorithm is lower in the range of 100%–180%. For example, when the user overload rate is 125%, the average BLER is 1.0×10^{-2} for MMSE-2SIC and 2.5×10^{-3} for MMSE-SPIC. When the user overload rate is high, the BLER of MMSE-2SIC detection algorithm is lower in 180%–300%. For example, when the user overload rate is 200%, the average BLER detection is 6.0×10^{-2} for MMSE-SPIC and 4.0×10^{-2} for MMSE-2SIC.

For a small number of access users, MMSE-SPIC detection algorithm firstly detects the users with strong signal through SIC detection, then the remaining few users are for PIC detection. The number of remaining users is small and MAI is weak, so the detection performance is good. When the number of access users is large, the remaining number of users for MMSE-SPIC is large and MAI is strong, so the detection performance becomes poor.

Table 1. The simulation parameters for performance comparison of multi-user detection algorithm.

Simulation parameters	Parameters configuration
Coding scheme	Turbo, code rate 1/2
Modulation method	QPSK
Spreading sequence category	Tri-level complex spreading code sequence
Spreading sequence length	4
Number of access user	4, 6, 8, 10, 12
Antenna configuration	1Tx,1Rx
Channel noise	Gaussian white noise
Transmit power	Fixed
SNR condition	All users 4–20 dB uniform distribution
Channel estimation	Ideal
Receiver	MMSE-SPIC, MMSE-2SIC, MMSE-SIC, MMSE-PIC

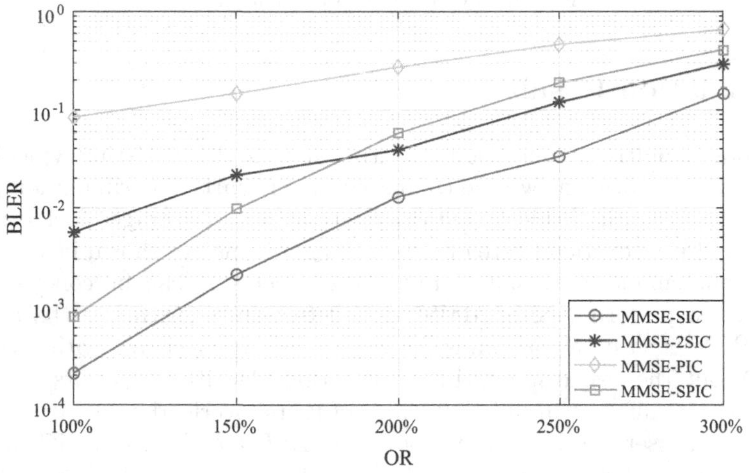

Fig. 3. Performance comparison for multi-user detection algorithms.

According to above description about the proposed algorithm, the choice of SINR threshold value will affect the detection performance of the proposed algorithm. Therefore relevant simulation results are provided in Fig. 4. In this simulation, the overload rate is set to 150% or 200% and that is the number of access users is 6 or 8. The other parameter configuration is similar to Table 1.

Figure 4 shows the impact of the choice of SINR threshold value on BLER in MMSE-SPIC detection algorithm. As can be seen from the curves, BLER

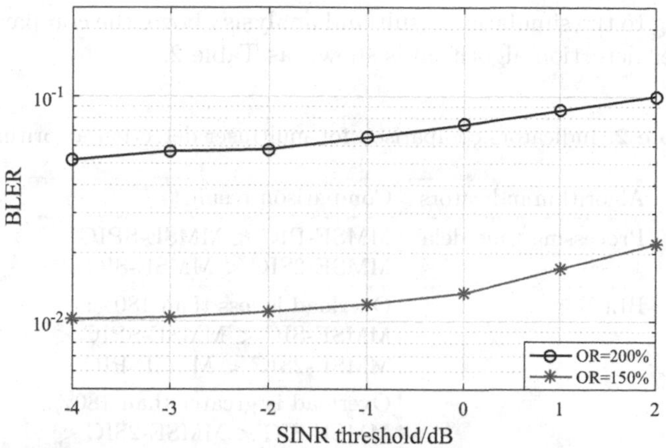

Fig. 4. Impact of the choice of SINR threshold value on BLER.

becomes higher and higher with the increase of SINR threshold. This is because the higher the SINR threshold, the less the number of users doing SIC detection. Thus the more serious the MAI, the worse the performance of the system. If SINR threshold is too high to no user reaching the SINR threshold, all users would do PIC detection. If SINR threshold is too low to all users reaching the SINR threshold value, all users would do SIC detection. System performance is the better when lower overload rate, but processing time delay will be higher because of more users doing SIC detection.

In addition, it can be seen from the curves that the relationship between SINR threshold and BLER is analogous when the overload rate is 150% and 200%. Therefore, considering time delay and detection performance, -2dB is selected as the SINR threshold value of MMSE-SPIC detection algorithm in this paper.

The following is the analysis of the processing time delay of several multi-user detection algorithms. According to the processing flow of detection algorithms, assume that the processing time for SINR calculating and sorting, MMSE detection, demodulation and decoding and reconstruction and elimination are τ_1, τ_2, τ_3, and τ_4, respectively. Thus it is easy to get the processing time delay of MMSE-SIC detection. That is $\tau_{\mathrm{SIC}} = \sum_{i=1}^{K} \tau_{1i} + K(\tau_2 + \tau_3 + \tau_4)$, where K is the number of access users and τ_{1i} is the τ_1 for the ith time detection. The processing time delay of MMSE-PIC detection is $\tau_{\mathrm{PIC}} = N(\tau_2 + \tau_3 + \tau_4)$, where N is the iteration times, $N < K$. The processing time delay of MMSE-2SIC detection is $\tau_{\mathrm{2SIC}} = \sum_{i=1}^{K/2} \tau_{1i} + \frac{K}{2}(\tau_2 + \tau_3 + \tau_4)$. The processing time delay of MMSE-SPIC detection is $\tau_{\mathrm{SPIC}} = \tau_{11} + K_1(\tau_2 + \tau_3 + \tau_4) + N_1(\tau_2 + \tau_3 + \tau_4)$, where N_1 is the iteration times, $N_1 \ll K$, and K_1 is the number of users for SIC detection. Thus we can draw that $\tau_{\mathrm{SIC}} > \tau_{\mathrm{2SIC}} \approx \tau_{\mathrm{SPIC}} > \tau_{\mathrm{PIC}}$.

According to the simulation result and analysis above, the comparison results for multi-user detection algorithm is shown as Table 2.

Table 2. Indicators comparison for multiuser detection algorithm.

Algorithm indicators	Comparison result
Processing time delay	MMSE-PIC < MMSE-SPIC ≈ MMSE-2SIC < MMSE-SIC
BLER	Overload is less than 180%: MMSE-SIC < MMSE-SPIC < MMSE-2SIC < MMSE-PIC Overload is greater than 180%: MMSE-SIC < MMSE-2SIC < MMSE-SPIC < MMSE-PIC

5 Conclusion

As a code domain non-orthogonal multiple access technology, MUSA can effectively improve spectral efficiency and enhance system capacity, and is suitable for IoT services in 5G communication system.

This paper mainly studies the multi-user detection algorithms for MUSA uplink receiver. The successive-parallel interference cancellation multi-user detection algorithm is proposed to overcome the shortage of the typical algorithms. Compared with MMSE-PIC multi-user detection algorithm, the proposed MMSE-SPIC detection algorithm improves detection performance well and ensures low processing time delay in addition. Compared with MMSE-SIC multi-user detection algorithm, MMSE-SPIC detection algorithm effectively reduces processing time delay and ensure good detection performance simultaneously. Moreover, MMSE-SPIC detection algorithm can achieve better detection performance than MMSE-2SIC detection algorithm under the condition that overload rate is below 180%, and the detection performance is acceptable when overload rate more than 180%.

In the future, we can try to combine MUSA with power domain NOMA technology or MIMO technology to further enhance system capacity.

References

1. Wang, P., Xiao, J., Li, P.: Comparison of orthogonal and non-orthogonal approaches to future wireless cellular systems. IEEE Veh. Technol. Mag. **1**(3), 4–11 (2006)
2. Andrews, J.G., et al.: What will 5G be? IEEE J. Sel. Areas Commun. **32**(6), 1065–1082 (2014)
3. Boccardi, F., Heath, R.W., Lozano, A., Marzetta, T.L., Popovski, P.: Five disruptive technology directions for 5G. IEEE Commun. Mag. **52**(2), 74–80 (2014)

4. Benjebbour, A., Saito, Y., Kishiyama, Y., Li, A., Harada, A., Nakamura, T.: Concept and practical considerations of non-orthogonal multiple access (NOMA) for future radio access. In: 2013 International Symposium on Intelligent Signal Processing and Communications Systems (ISPACS), pp. 770–774. IEEE (2013)
5. Nikopour, H., Baligh, H.: Sparse code multiple access. In: 2013 IEEE 24th International Symposium on Personal Indoor and Mobile Radio Communications (PIMRC), pp. 332–336. IEEE (2013)
6. Yuan, Z., Yu, G., Li, W., Yuan, Y., Wang, X., Xu, J.: Multi-user shared access for internet of things. In: 2016 IEEE 83rd Vehicular Technology Conference (VTC Spring), pp. 1–5. IEEE (2016)
7. Yu, L., Lei, X., Fan, P., Chen, D.: An optimized design of SCMA codebook based on star-QAM signaling constellations. In: 2015 International Conference on Wireless Communications Signal Processing (WCSP), pp. 1–5, October 2015
8. Tao, Y., Liu, L., Liu, S., Zhang, Z.: A survey: several technologies of non-orthogonal transmission for 5G. China Commun. **12**(10), 1–15 (2015)
9. Wang, B., Wang, K., Lu, Z., Xie, T., Quan, J.: Comparison study of non-orthogonal multiple access schemes for 5G. In: 2015 IEEE International Symposium on Broadband Multimedia Systems and Broadcasting, pp. 1–5, June 2015
10. Chen, S., Ren, B., Gao, Q., Kang, S., Sun, S., Niu, K.: Pattern division multiple access (PDMA) - a novel nonorthogonal multiple access for fifth-generation radio networks. IEEE Trans. Veh. Technol. **66**(4), 3185–3196 (2017)
11. Lupas, R., Verdu, S.: Linear multiuser detectors for synchronous code-division multiple-access channels. IEEE Trans. Inf. Theory **35**(1), 123–136 (1989)
12. Patel, P., Holtzman, J.: Performance comparison of a DS/CDMA system using a successive interference cancellation (IC) scheme and a parallel IC scheme under fading. In: IEEE International Conference on Communications, ICC 1994, SUPERCOMM/ICC 1994, Conference Record, 'Serving Humanity Through Communications', vol. 1, pp. 510–514, May 1994
13. Deepthy, G.S., Susan, R.J.: Analysis of successive interference cancellation in CDMA systems. In: 2012 Second International Conference on Advanced Computing Communication Technologies, pp. 481–485, January 2012

Enhancing Capture Effect over LEO Satellite Within the Framework of Contention Resolution ALOHA

Zhicheng Qu[1,2], Gengxin Zhang[1,2(✉)], Haotong Cao[1,2], and Jidong Xie[1,2]

[1] College of Telecommunications and Information Engineering, NUPT, Nanjing, China
{1015010132,zgx,1015010309,feng}@njupt.edu.cn
[2] TNNERC, NUPT, Nanjing, China

Abstract. Contention resolution diversity slotted ALOHA (CRDSA) with packet repetition and iterative interference cancellation (IIC) has been proven that achieves 48% improvement in terms of throughput than pure slotted ALOHA which merely has a theoretical throughput upper bound of 0.36. So far, optimizations of such random access scheme have been proposed in the literature called irregular repetition slotted ALOHA (IRSA) and coded slotted ALOHA (CSA) which both targeted the collision channel model. In this paper, the environment of LEO satellite communication and capture effect at the satellite receiver are considered. Meanwhile, due to the inherent propagation feature of LEO satellite, capture effect can be enhanced through separating LEO footprint into districts. Under a setting of finite frame length, this separating scheme is analyzed via Monte Carlo simulation combining with optimized power control. Numerical results are provided, which prove the stability of proposed scheme when channel load exceeding 1.

Keywords: Capture effect · Internet of things · LEO satellite · Power diversity · Random access

1 Introduction

Satellite communication, especially for LEO satellite, has a growing capability for numerous kinds of applications including internet access, supervisory control and data acquisition (SCADA), and internet of things (IoT) [1]. Under this background, a high efficient medium access control (MAC) scheme is needed for ensuring communication quality. Random access (RA) schemes, as their nature of avoiding signalling overhead and providing short transmission latencies, have become a candidate for MAC in satellite communication.

Initiating with the ALOHA scheme proposed by Abramson [2] in 1970, which has a maximum expected throughput of 0.18, various evolutional RA protocols

Supported by National Science Foundation of China under Grant No. 91738201 and No. 61801445.

M. Jia et al. (Eds.): WiSATS 2019, LNICST 281, pp. 552–561, 2019.
https://doi.org/10.1007/978-3-030-19156-6_52

have been published in literature. Slotted ALOHA (SA) [3] introduced the concept of frame and slot into pure ALOHA, and the theoretical maximum throughput of SA has reached 0.36. Furthermore, an improvement of SA called diversity slotted ALOHA (DSA) [4] with packet repetition has been proposed. Under the condition of light traffic load, DSA has performance improvement in transmission delays w.r.t. SA. Contention resolution ALOHA (CRA), an epoch-making enhanced kind of DSA beginning with contention resolution diversity slotted ALOHA (CRDSA) [5], has been proposed with two novel approaches: (1) each packet replica has a pointer directing to the other replicas; (2) receiver uses iterative interference cancellation (IIC). Liva adopted the knowledge of bipartite graphs to describe the transmitting and IIC process of CRDSA. Meanwhile, in [6], the author proposed a novel scheme with irregular packet repetition degree (i.e., each packet may choose different numbers of replicas under a chosen distribution) called irregular repetition slotted ALOHA (IRSA), which can achieve maximum throughput of 0.97 for large frames whereas for CRDSA the value is 0.55. Additionally, a ALOHA-based scheme with the combination of packet erasure correcting codes and IIC called coded slotted ALOHA (CSA) [7] can asymptotically reach the ultimate throughput for collision channel model.

Collision channel model, however, is far from the practical channel situation due to the assumption that no transmission suffered from colliding can be recovered. In common fading channel model, capture effect [8] caused by fading-oriented power variations ensures successful decoding of the sufficiently strong signal even under colliding. Apparently, the LEO satellite channel suffers from fading and shadowing, and the channel state dramatically varies with the elevation angle. In [9], the modeling of LEO satellite channel and the method for analyzing capture probability using SA scheme was presented.

In this paper, we extend the analysis of capture effect in LEO satellite channel within the CRA framework. First, within the capture model of threshold, we derive the expression of capture probability over LEO satellite channel. Next, we intend to enhance the inherent capture effect of LEO satellite system by separating the footprint into districts according to elevation angle α. Among those districts, an optimized power control mechanism is proposed in order to increase the power differential at receiver as well as the capture probability. Finally, the mechanism is investigated within finite frame length via simulations. It is shown that the proposed mechanism indeed enhance the inherent capture effect of LEO satellite communication, and optimize the system performance of throughput.

The paper is organized as follows. Section 2 introduces the system model. Section 3 focuses on expression of capture probabilities for LEO satellite channel. Section 4 presents a ring separating scheme combining with optimized power control among different rings. Section 5 shows the numerical results. Section 6 concludes the paper.

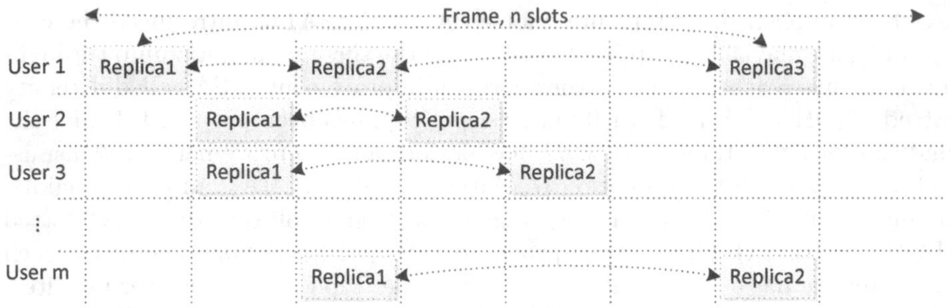

Fig. 1. CRDSA/IRSA scheme.

2 System Model

2.1 Access Protocol and Graph-Based Presentation

On brief overview, the MAC frames have duration of T_f that contain n slots with duration of $T_s = T_f/n$, and each packet transmission can only last for one slot. The normalized channel traffic load G is defined as

$$G = \frac{m}{n} \tag{1}$$

where m is a finite number of users transmitting in a chosen frame. Channel throughput T is a function of G and packet loss rate P_L. Within the framework of CRA, each user choose a repetition degree d independently from a predefined probability mass function (p.m.f) $\{\Lambda_d\}$ and randomly picks up d slots in a frame to transmit d replicas. CRDSA, however, is a special case of CRA that each user has the same repetition degree, which means $\Lambda_d = 1$ for the predefined degree d. Additionally, it is assumed that each replica of the same user contains the whole locating information of the other d-1 replicas. The diagram of CRA protocol is shown in Fig. 1. In [6], the author introduced a bipartite graph-based presentation of CRA scheme. As depicted in Fig. 2, a bipartite graph $\mathcal{G} = \{U, S, E\}$ can fully represent a MAC frame of CRA. $\mathcal{G}$ contains a set U of m user nodes, and a set S of n slot nodes in a frame, and a set E of edges representing each transmitted replica. An edge connects an user node $u_k \in B$ with a slot node $s_j \in S$ iif user k transmits a replica in slot j. Meanwhile, the IIC process of CRA is also presented in Fig. 2. The dashed edge represents a replica transmitted in a collision-free slot so that the other edge connected with the same user node can be removed. After one iteration, the receiver will find another collision-free slot node and repeat the IIC process until meeting the end condition.

The concept of *node-* and *edge-perspective degree distribution* is useful for further analysis. Polynomial representation of user-node and slot-node degree distribution are $\Lambda(x) = \sum_{d=2}^{d_{\max}} \Lambda_d x^d$ and $\Psi(x) = \sum_{c=0}^{m} \Psi_c x^c$, respectively. Λ_d (Ψ_c) denotes the probability that an user node (slot node) possessing d (c)

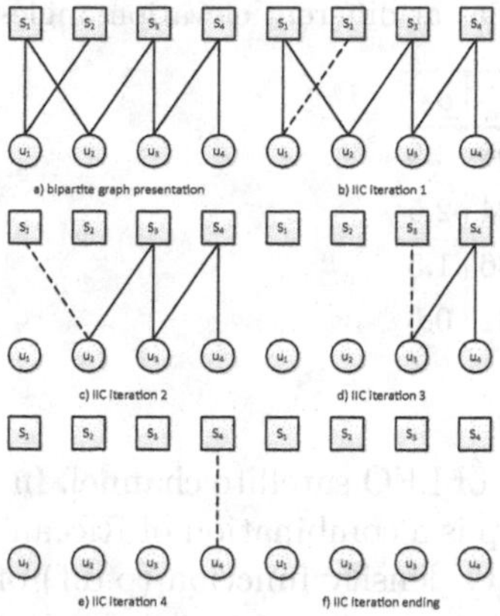

Fig. 2. Bipartite graph-based presentation of CRA.

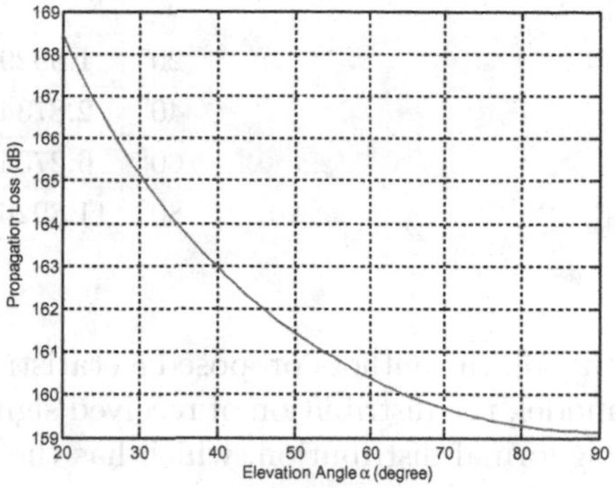

Fig. 3. Free space loss corresponding to α.

edges. As mentioned before, $\{\Lambda_d\}$ is fully controlled by the system while Ψ_c is determined by the traffic load G

$$\Psi_c = \binom{m}{c}\left(\frac{G/R}{m}\right)^c\left(1-\frac{G/R}{m}\right)^{m-c} \tag{2}$$

where R is the scheme rate defined as the inverse of average repetition degree

$$R = \frac{1}{\bar{d}} = \frac{1}{\sum_{d=2}^{d_{\max}} d\Lambda_d}. \tag{3}$$

Similarly, edge-perspective degree distribution can be defined as the p.m.f $\{\lambda_d\}_{d=2}^{d_{\max}}$ and $\{\psi_c\}_{c=0}^{m}$. λ_d is the probability that an edge is linked to a *d-degree* user node, and likewise ψ_c is the probability that an edge is linked to a *c-degree* slot node. Easily, the corresponding polynomial representation of the two distributions are $\lambda(x) = \sum_{d=2}^{d_{\max}} \lambda_d x^{d-1}$ and $\psi(x) = \sum_{c=0}^{m} \psi_c x^{c-1}$. Note that $\lambda(x) = \Lambda'(x)/\Lambda'(1)$ and $\psi(x) = \Psi'(x)/\Psi'(1)$.

2.2 LEO Channel Model

Free space loss is considered as the most important attenuation in LEO channel, and it is calculated as

$$L_{FS} = 32.45 + 20\lg(D) + 20\lg(f) \tag{4}$$

where D is the link distance in kilometers and f is the operating frequency in Mega Hertz. Assuming the LEO orbit altitude is 900 km and operating frequency is 2400 MHz, the free space loss corresponding to α is depicted in Fig. 3.

Table 1. Coefficient values for empirical formulas at different elevation angles

α	K	μ	σ
20°	1.6929	−0.73508	3.5
40°	2.8734	−0.16524	2.5
60°	6.2734	−0.09636	1.5
80°	11.8926	−0.00332	0.5

In [10], the authors proposed a statistical model of LEO satellite channel. In this model, the distribution of received signal envelop is a combination of Ricean and lognormal distribution, which has the probability density function (p.d.f) of

$$f_P(p) = \int_0^\infty f(p|S) f_S(S)\, dS \tag{5}$$

where $f(p|S)$ is a Rice p.d.f under a certain shadowing S

$$\begin{aligned} f(p|S) = 2(K+1)\frac{p}{S^2}\exp\left(-(K+1)\frac{p^2}{S^2} - K\right) \\ \cdot I_0\left(2\frac{p}{S}\sqrt{K(K+1)}\right) \end{aligned} \tag{6}$$

and $f_S(S)$ is a lognormal distribution that S follows

$$f_S(S) = \frac{1}{\sqrt{2\pi}\sigma S}\exp\left(-\frac{1}{2}\left(\frac{\ln S - \mu}{\sigma}\right)^2\right). \tag{7}$$

In (5) and (6), $I_0(\cdot)$ is the zero order modified Bessel function, K is the Rice factor, μ and σ are the mean and the variance of the associated normal variate, respectively. To be noticed, K, μ and σ are associated with α between 20° and 80° degree through empirical formulas

$$\begin{aligned} K(\alpha) &= K_0 + K_1\alpha + K_2\alpha^2 \\ \mu(\alpha) &= \mu_0 + \mu_1\alpha + \mu_2\alpha^2 + \mu_3\alpha^3 \\ \sigma(\alpha) &= \sigma_0 + \sigma_1\alpha \end{aligned} \tag{8}$$

and the empirical value of the three coefficients are listed in Table 1.

3 Capture Probabilities

In this framework, the receiver can discriminate between empty slots and busy slots. The probability that replica i in slot j is successfully recovered is called capture probability. Under threshold-based capture model, signal to interference and noise ratio SINR is the determining factor of capture probability. When the

SINR of replica i exceeds a certain threshold r_{th}, it is considered to be captured, i.e.,

$$\Pr\{\text{replica } i \text{ is caputured}\} = \begin{cases} 1, \ SINR_i \geqslant r_{th} \\ 0, \ \text{otherwise} \end{cases} \tag{9}$$

In (8), $SINR_i$ is defined as follows

$$SINR_i = \frac{P_{ij}}{N + \sum_{m \neq i} P_{mj}} \tag{10}$$

where P_{ij} is the receiving power of i-th packet, and $\sum_{m \neq i} P_{mj}$ denotes the total power of rest packets in slot j.

On graph viewing, at a specific time during the decoding process of a MAC frame, a slot node j may have a node degree of d. To be noticed, after perfect inter-slot and intra-slot (capture) SIC, d is not greater than the original node degree of d_j. Now, we randomly choose one packet from the d packets and call it the reference packet (RP). Meanwhile, the probability that RP is successfully recovered merely through intra-slot SIC is denoted as $C(d,t)$, where $1 \le t \le r$ is the iteration step after the beginning of decoding and in any step prior to t RP cannot be recovered. The total probability $C(d)$ of successfully recovering RP is

$$C(d) = \sum_{t=1}^{d} C(d,t) \tag{11}$$

During intra-slot SIC process, all packets are categorized into two groups in the rule of power. Packets in the first group with stronger power than RP are arranged in a descending order by their powers (i.e., $P_1 \geqslant P_2 \geqslant \cdots \geqslant P_{t-1}$), and the rest packets in the second group are not arranged. Under such arrangement, the probability that at least t packets successfully recovered is denoted by

$$\rho(t) = \Pr\{SINR_1 \geqslant r_{th}, \cdots, SINR_t \geqslant r_{th}\}$$

and $\rho(t)$ is calculated as follows

$$\rho(t) = \int_0^{\infty} dp_r \cdots \int_0^{\infty} dp_{t+1} \times \int_{r_{th}\left(N+\sum_{i=t+1}^{r} p_i\right)}^{\infty} dp_t$$
$$\times \cdots \times \int_{r_{th}\left(N+\sum_{i=2}^{r} p_i\right)}^{\infty} dp_1 f_P(p_r) \cdots f_P(p_1) \tag{12}$$

Moreover, there are $\frac{(d-1)!}{(d-t)!}$ arrangements that RP is not in the first group. Therefore, we have

$$C(d,t) = \frac{(d-1)!}{(d-t)!}\rho(t) \tag{13}$$

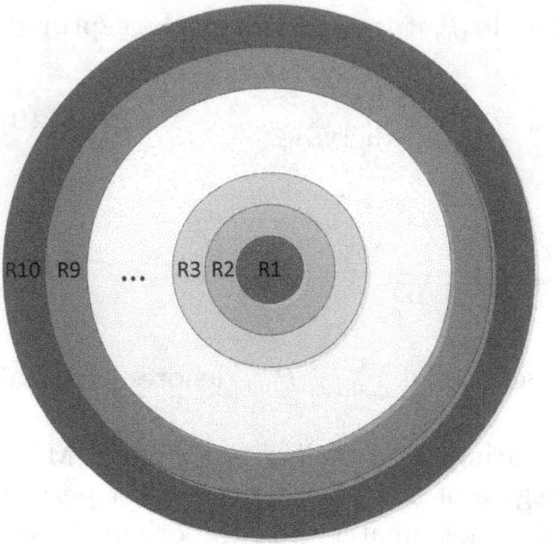

Fig. 4. Ring separating of LEO footprint.

Table 2. Characteristics of each ring

Ring index	Minimum α	Corresponding propagation loss (dB)
1	20.3°	168.3341
2	23.6°	167.0903
3	27.4°	165.8801
4	31.7°	164.7281
5	36.7°	163.6105
6	42.7°	162.5124
7	49.7°	161.4924
8	58.0°	160.5707
9	67.7°	159.8143
10	78.5°	159.3152

In [6], an analysis of SIC convergence was proposed. For a degree-r user node, q is the probability that an connecting edge carries no erasure message, and each other $r-1$ edges have been revealed via previous SIC steps with the probability of $1-l$. Obviously, $q = l^{r-1}$. Similarly, in a degree-c slot node, we have $1-l = (1-q)^{c-1}$ or $l = 1-(1-q)^{c-1}$. Therefore, the average erasure probability of an edge during the k-th iteration is

$$q_k = \sum_r \lambda_r q_k^{(r)} = \sum_r \lambda_r d l_{k-1}^{r-1} \tag{14}$$

and

$$l_k = \sum_c \psi_c l_k^{(c)} \tag{15}$$

Taking $C(d,t)$ into consideration, $l_k^{(c)}$ can be expressed as

$$l_k^{(c)} = 1 - \sum_{d=1}^{c} C(d) \binom{c-1}{d-1} q_k^{d-1} (1-q_k)^{c-d} \tag{16}$$

where $\binom{c-1}{d-1} q_k^{d-1} (1-q_k)^{c-d}$ is the probability that the chosen slot node's degree drops to d. Combining with the edge-perspective degree distribution in Sect. 2.1, where $\psi_c = \exp\{-G/R\}(G/R)^{c-1}/(c-1)!$ when $m \to \infty$ and G/R is constant, l_k corresponds to

$$l_k = 1 - e^{-\frac{G}{R}} \sum_{c=1}^{\infty} \left(\frac{G}{R}\right)^{c-1} \sum_{d=1}^{c} \frac{C(d)}{(d-1)!} q_k^{d-1} (1-q_k)^{c-d} \tag{17}$$

By combining (14) and (16) with the initial value $q_0 = 1$, a density evolution recursion [11] can be exploited to express the asymptotic performance of proposed scheme. However, since the channel fading and free space loss vary from α, there cannot be a exact expression of $C(d)$ through mathematical analysis. Hence, in Sect. 5, we take advantage of Monte Carlo simulation to provide numerical results of the scheme.

4 Enhancing Capture Effect with Ring Separating and Power Control

As an inherent phenomenon in LEO channel, power imbalance is inevitable at the receiver caused by fading and propagation loss that requests system design of higher link margin to compensate. This flaw, however, can be utilized in raising throughput performance via capture effect demonstrated in Sect. 3. In general, all users within a LEO satellite footprint have the same opportunity to transmit their packets, and the corresponding capture effect is called natural capture effect without any control mechanism. As mentioned before, the essence of capture effect is the power differential of receiving packets, which caused by varying propagation loss and fading corresponding to α. To enhance capture effect, an efficient way is to enlarge power differential by exploiting features of LEO satellite communication.

On the contrary to terrestrial cellular communication, in LEO satellite communication, users' irregular movements are replaced by the deterministic satellite orbit movement, which can be precisely predicted by the users. In order to enlarge power differential at receiver, the whole LEO footprint can be separated into different rings according to the value of elevation angle α. Obviously, for inclining LEO satellite orbit, this separation will lead no priority to any user. As shown in Sect. 2.2, the propagation loss and the mean value of fading are in a descending order as α increasing. Assuming a footprint is separated into M rings, where each ring has a allowable transmitting probability $P_i (1 \leq i \leq M)$. Under the circumstance that $P_i = 0$, user belongs to ring i is closed and forbidden transmitting. To be noticed, natural capture effect is achieved by setting all P_i equally. In order to enhance capture effect, i.e. reaching sufficient power differential, the rings which suffer medium propagation loss and fading will be shut down (i.e, corresponding $P_m = 0$) while rings of the strongest and lowest attenuation remain fully available with corresponding $P_i = 1$ $(i \neq m)$. By changing P_i, system will be adaptive to various kinds of traffic and be more efficient. For further enlarging the receiving power differential, a simple method is to add extra power to the rings that suffer the lowest propagation loss and fading.

5 Numerical Results

For example, Fig. 4. shows that a footprint (with altitude h = 900 km and $\alpha \geq 20°$) is equally separated into 10 rings. Meanwhile, the minimum elevation angle and propagation loss of each ring is presented in Table 2. For sufficient power differential (e.g., 6 dB), the allowable transmitting rings will be Ring No.

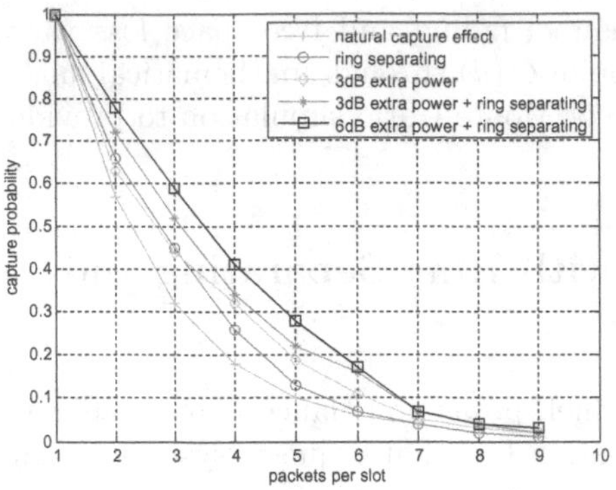

Fig. 5. Capture probability under different schemes.

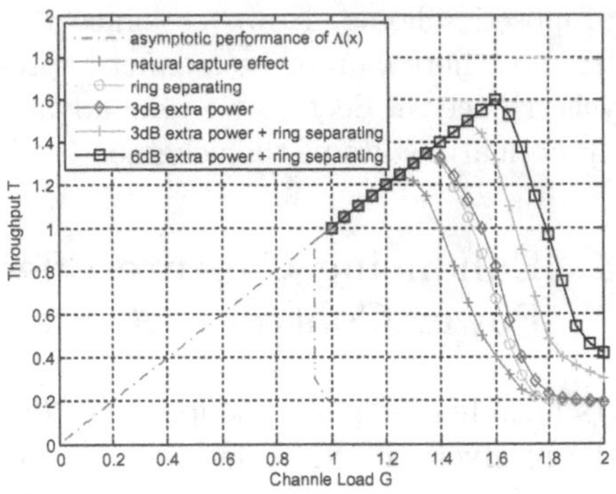

Fig. 6. Throughput performance versus channel load.

1, 2, 9 and 10. We tested the capture probability of the strongest packets and the throughput performance through Monte Carlo simulations under assumption of (1) all users are uniformly distributed in the footprint; (2) capture probability of the strongest packet is (9). Meanwhile, for practical consideration, i.e. limiting the number of pointers in the packet header, the user-node degree distribution is set to $\Lambda(x) = 0.5x^2 + 0.28x^3 + 0.22x^8$, which has a theoretical throughput threshold $G^* = 0.938$ under collision channel model [6]. The other system parameters are set that frame length $n = 200$ slots, $r_{th} = 6$ dB, iteration times $I_{max} = 20$. Figure 5 illustrates the capture probability of the strongest packet. As expected, ring separating scheme raises capture probability of 10% averagely comparing to natural capture. Combining ring separating and extra power compensation (6 dB), the performance is almost 2 times better than natural capture. In Fig. 6, system throughput, defined as the average recovered packets per slot, versus channel traffic load G is provided. The blue dash line is the asymptotic performance of IRSA with the selected user-node degree distribution. By taking capture effect into consideration, all circumstances exhibit peak throughput exceeding 1 [packet/slot], which is the strict upper bound under collision channel. Natural capture can achieve the throughput of 1.26 [packet/slot] while ring separating scheme is able to reach 1.34 [packet/slot] and the stable operating range (i.e., the maximum traffic load that leads to a 20% drop of peak throughput) extend to $G_{sta} = 1.5$, i.e., 60% of gain comparing to the original $G_{sta} = 0.94$. Moreover, within the stable operating range, pure ring separating scheme has a similar performance to that of 3 dB extra power. Similarly, by combining ring separating scheme and extra power compensation (e.g., 3 dB and 6 dB), the peak throughput can reach 1.49 and 1.61 [packet/slot]. Additionally, corresponding gains on stable operating range are 72% and 90%, respectively.

6 Conclusions

The analysis of contention resolution ALOHA over a LEO fading channel, assuming capture effect, is presented in this paper. We provide the expression of capture probability of a reference packet with intra-slot SIC. The closed form approximation, however, is unable to be derived due to LEO channel's fading characteristic, which is a set of PDFs corresponding to α. In addition, we presented a ring separation of LEO footprint combining with power control mechanism in order to enhance capture effect and rasing the system efficiency. Numerical results show that merely taking capture effect into consideration can provide stable performance for channel load values well above 1 [packet/slot]. In a finite frame length with 200 slots, the peak throughput reaches 1.6 [packet/slot] by combining ring separating and power control.

References

1. Qu, Z., Zhang, G., Cao, H., Xie, J.: LEO satellite constellation for internet of things. IEEE Access **5**, 18391–18401 (2017)
2. Abramson, N.: The ALOHA system: another alternative for computer communications. In: 17–19 November 1970, Fall Joint Computer Conference, pp. 281–285 (1970)
3. Okada, H., Igarashi, Y., Nakanishi, Y.: Analysis and application of framed ALOHA channel in satellite packet switching networks - FADRA method. Electron. Commun. Japan **60**, 72–80 (1977)
4. Choudhury, G., Rappaport, S.: Diversity ALOHA - a random access scheme for satellite communications. IEEE Trans. Commun. **31**(3), 450–457 (1983)
5. Casini, E., De Gaudenzi, R., Del Rio Herrero, O.: Contention resolution diversity slotted ALOHA (CRDSA): an enhanced random access schemefor satellite access packet networks. IEEE Trans. Wirel. Commun. **6**(4), 1408–1419 (2007)
6. Liva, G.: Graph-based analysis and optimization of contention resolution diversity slotted ALOHA. IEEE Trans. Commun. **59**(2), 477–487 (2011)
7. Paolini, E., Liva, G., Chiani, M.: Coded slotted ALOHA: a graph-based method for uncoordinated multiple access. IEEE Trans. Inf. Theory **61**(12), 6815–6832 (2015)
8. Zorzi, M., Rao, R.R.: Capture and retransmission control in mobile radio. IEEE J. Sel. Areas Commun. **12**(8), 1289–1298 (1994)
9. Ren, W., Ward, J., Hodgart, S., Sweeting, M.: Modelling of capture effect and analysis in LEO satellite channel. In: 2000 IEEE International Conference on Communications, ICC 2000, vol. 1, pp. 124–128 (2000)
10. Corazza, G.E., Vatalaro, F.: A statistical model for land mobile satellite channels and its application to nongeostationary orbit systems. IEEE Trans. Veh. Technol. **43**(3), 738–742 (1994)
11. Richardson, T., Urbanke, R.: Modern Coding Theory. Cambridge University Press, Cambridge (2008)

The Low Complexity Multi-user Detection Algorithms for Uplink SCMA System

Jingjing Wu, Shaochuan Wu(✉), Rundong Zuo, and Wenbin Zhang

School of Electronics and Information Engineering, Harbin Institute of Technology, Harbin, China
hitwujingjing@163.com, {scwu,zwbgxy1973}@hit.edu.cn, rd_zuo@163.com

Abstract. 5G research gradually focus on non-orthogonal multiple access technology, owing to huge traffic, more mobile terminals, and explosive growth of throughput capacity in recent years. Sparse code multiple access (SCMA) is a multi-dimensional codebook-based non-orthogonal multiplexing technique proposed to address the above requirements. This paper investigates the Message Passing Algorithm (MPA) in the receiver of SCMA and proposes two multi-user detection algorithms with low computational complexity in uplink. Improved Variable Message Passing Algorithm (IVMPA) reduces computational complexity compared to Variable Message Passing Algorithm (VMPA) by changing the users iteration order. Incomplete Iterative Message Passing Algorithm (IIMPA) is proposed to reduce the number of iteration for users with high signal-to-noise ratio (SNR) and reduces computational complexity compared to MPA.

Keywords: SCMA · Multi-user detection · Message Passing Algorithm · Complexity

1 Introduction

SCMA is a sparse code multiple access technology [1], which is similar to the Low Density Signature (LDS) system. LDS as a special case in Code Division Multiple Access (CDMA), its codewords are obtained through spreading Quadrature Amplitude Modulation (QAM) symbols with the low density characteristic sequences [2]. Compared with LDS, SCMA can also improve the spectrum efficiency under the premise of obtaining the low density spread spectrum gain and the moderate complexity of demodulation.

In SCMA uplink, the bit stream of each user is first mapped to N-dimensional complex constellation, and then the constellation is mapped into a K-dimensional sparse codeword. The codeword contains N non-zero elements and $N < K$. Each

This work was supported by the National Science Foundation of China with Grant 61671173.

M. Jia et al. (Eds.): WiSATS 2019, LNICST 281, pp. 562–575, 2019.
https://doi.org/10.1007/978-3-030-19156-6_53

SCMA layer or user holds its own codebook and the codebook includes more than one codeword [3]. In order to improve the spectrum efficiency, multiple users are multiplexed on the same resource block [4,5]. The size of constellation and the length of codeword of users who are overloaded on the same resource is uniform.

Although SCMA can improve the spectrum efficiency remarkably, the multi-user detection algorithm needs to be considered because of multiple users multiplexing on the same resource. SCMA adopting Message Passing Algorithm (MPA) algorithm for multi-user detection. However the detection complexity of MPA is high and the high complexity will directly affect system performance such as time delay and design complicacy of receiver. In order to reduce the complexity of detection algorithm, reference [6] put forward a detection scheme that combines codebook and receiver. The scheme minimizes the complexity of SCMA uplink network detection based on codebook design and implementation of codebook distribution scheme. The technology firstly uses a two-party coordinative search to design a cost-effective algorithm, which determines the mapping matrix and the codebook allocation scheme. Based on the designed mapping matrix, this scheme utilizes the characteristics of SCMA multidimensional modulation to design the parent constellation and users' codebook to reduce the detection complexity.

A low-complexity multi-user detection algorithm based on List-Spherical Decoding (LSD) was proposed in [7]. The LSD algorithm only considers the codewords within a sphere and avoids a detailed search of all possible codcbook groups. The LSD algorithm first sets up the depth-first search tree algorithm and proposes several methods for updating the access nodes to rcduce the size of thc search tree. The LSD is used to set the retrieved users and codeword range before MPA detcction for avoiding the crgodic search detection in the receiver. The simulation results show that the scheme is nearly close to ML detection performance and greatly reduces the decoding complexity. Reference [8] proposed the Log-Message Passing Algorithm (Log-MPA) and compared Log-MPA with traditional MPA in details. The effect of message passing iterations times in Log-MPA decoding on system performance was also investigated. The simulation results show that the Log-MPA algorithm has better performance and lower hardware implementation complexity than MPA. Simulation and board-level verification results show that the performance of Log-MPA is close to MPA. Therefore the Log-MPA decoder can achieve a balance between performance and complexity.

This paper investigates the Message Passing Algorithm (MPA) in the receiver and proposes two multi-user detection algorithms with low computational complexity in uplink. The proposed Improved Variable Message Passing Algorithm (IVMPA) changes the users iteration order based on Variable Message Passing Algorithm (VMPA) and thus reducing computational complexity in the receiver. The another proposed multi-user detection algorithm is Incomplete Iterative Message Passing Algorithm (IIMPA) that reduces the number of iterations for some users with high signal-to-noise ratio (SNR) and thus reducing computational complexity compared to MPA.

The rest of this paper is organized as follows. Section 2 is devoted to introduce the system model. In Sect. 3, the multi-user detection algorithms in the receiver are provided. The simulation results and complexity analysis are given in Sect. 4. The final conclusions are in Sect. 5.

2 Previous Work

In uplink, each user holds an own codebook. Input data of multiple users is mapped to multi-dimensional codewords based the codebooks of users, and then overload and send the codewords on the K OFDMA subcarriers. After receiving the codewords overlapping on the subcarriers, the receiver can demodulate the data of each user utilizing the sparsity of the SCMA codewords through multi-user detection scheme with a certain complexity.

2.1 Basic Model of SCMA Uplink

Assume that the codewords of J users are transmitted with K resources and reach the same receiver at a time slot, the received signal can be described as

$$y = \sum_{u=1}^{J} \sqrt{p_u} diag(h_u) x_u + n \tag{1}$$

where x_u is a column vector of K dimension representing the codeword of user u, and the received signal y is also a column vector of K dimension. p_u and h_u represent the received power and the channel vectors on K OFDMA resources of user u, respectively. $diag(h_u)$ represents diagonal matrix and n is Additive White Gaussian Noise (AWGN).

Figure 1 shows the process that six users transmit data on four resource blocks to the base station for receiving and demodulating. The detailed communication process is that each 2bit binary data of each user is mapped to a high dimensional complex codeword which contains two non-zero elements, and the codewords of six users are reused on the four resource blocks by sparse codewords. The receiver adopts MPA multi-user detection algorithm to detect and demodulate received data. The idea of MPA algorithm is to update the user's message probability according to the initial codewords information, channel state and noise power, and then output codewords information when the iteration reaches a certain number of times. In uplink, the time slot synchronization needs to be guaranteed, and the slot synchronization part is similar to the LTE system.

The J codewords that are mapped from the J codebooks are overloaded and overlapped on K resources, and the overload rate is defined as

$$\lambda = \frac{J}{K} \tag{2}$$

Changing the number of codebooks J and the length of codewords K can achieve different overload rates. Normally, the value of λ will be greater than 1.

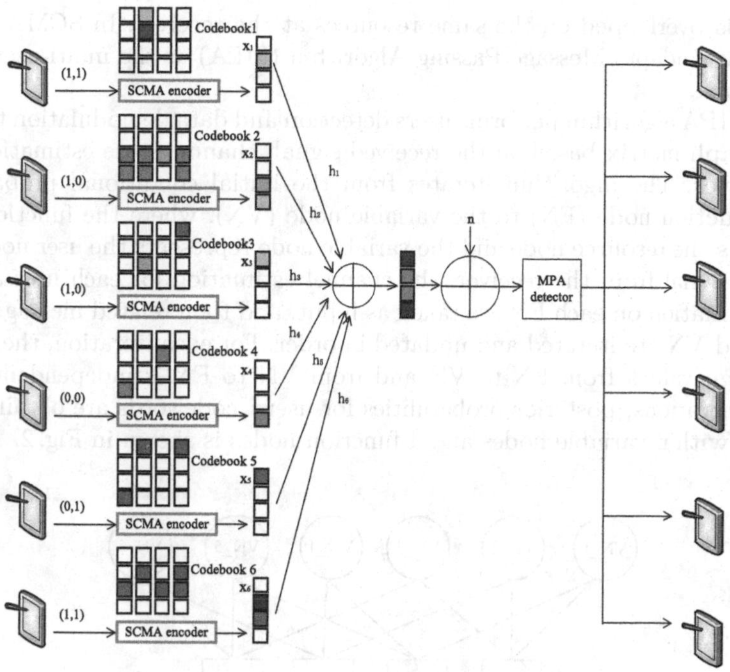

Fig. 1. The SCMA uplink model.

2.2 Design of SCMA Codebook

The codebook design of SCMA includes two parts, the design of factor map matrix and the generation of multidimensional constellation. The factor graph matrix represents the occupancy of each user on the resource blocks, whose sparsity determines the sparsity of SCMA codewords and also shows the users overload on the resources. The multidimensional constellation determines the mapping relationship between users data and the complex constellation. The distribution of points in the constellation determines the relationship between non-zero codewords of different users and the performance of demodulation.

3 The Multi-user Detection Algorithms

This section introduces several multi-user detection algorithms, including the existing detection algorithms and the detection algorithms proposed in this paper.

3.1 The Original Algorithm

In non-orthogonal transmission, the received signal at the receiver includes multiple users' symbols, which makes it difficult to separate and demodulate users' codewords overlapped on the same resources at the receiver. In SCMA uplink, the receiver adapts Message Passing Algorithm (MPA) as the multi-user detection scheme.

The MPA algorithm performs users detection and data demodulation through factor graph matrix based on the received signal, channel state estimation, and noise power. The algorithm iterates from the initial conditional probabilities of the function node (FN) to the variable node (VN), where the function node represents the resource node and the variable node represents the user node. The received signal from the receiver, the channel estimation for each user and the noise estimation on each FN are taken as input, and then related message values of FN and VN are iterated and updated in order. For each iteration, the update of message values from FN to VN and from VN to FN is independent. After enough iterations, posterior probabilities for users' codewords are obtained. An example with 6 variable nodes and 4 function nodes is shown in Fig. 2.

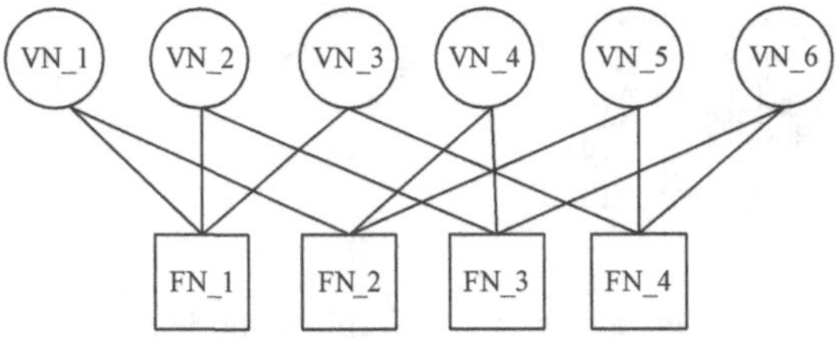

Fig. 2. Factor graph representation of an SCMA system with VN = 6, FN = 4.

Each iteration of detector has two steps. The first step is that message values from FNs to VNs are calculated based on the received signal, channel state and noise power. All FNs to VNs message values are updated in parallel. The function node k to variable node j message values can be written as

$$M^{t}_{c_k \to u_j}(x_j) = \sum_{x_j} \left\{ \begin{array}{l} \frac{1}{\sqrt{2\pi}\sigma} \exp\left(-\frac{1}{2\sigma^2} \left\| y_k - \sum_{v \in \xi_k} h_{k,v} x_{k,v} \right\|^2 \right) \cdot \\ \prod_{l \in \xi_k / \{j\}} M^{t-1}_{u_k \to c_l}(x_j) \end{array} \right\} \tag{3}$$

where t is the current number of iterative, ξ_k represents the index of 1 in the k-th row of the factor graph matrix. When all FNs to VNs message values have updated, this iteration will take the second step.

The second step is the update of message values from FNs to VNs. Similarly, the VN to FN message values depend on the other connected function nodes. Utilizing the output of the first step, the variable node j to the function node k

message values can be written as

$$M^t_{u_j \to c_k}(x_j) = \prod_{m \in \varsigma_j / \{k\}} M^t_{c_m \to u_j}(x_j) \tag{4}$$

where ς_j is the index of 1 in the j-th column of the factor graph matrix. When the number of iterations reaches the pre-set maximum value, the output of MPA detector which is the estimation of users' codewords can be expressed as

$$Q(x_j) = \prod_{k \in \varsigma_j} M^{t_{\max}}_{c_k \to u_j}(x_j) \tag{5}$$

Through above methods, the data of multi-user can be demodulated and separated.

3.2 The Variable MPA Algorithm

In above algorithm, the iterative model is parallel where VNs to FNs message values can be updated until all FNs to VNs message values complete the update. This mode wastes some useful message values to a certain extent. The change in the internal iteration update structure can speed up message values convergence. After each user's FN to VN message values updating the relevant VNs to FNs message values will update. This mode ensures the real-time performance of the iteration and update, and avoids the waste of the message values. The formula can be changed as follows

$$M^t_{c_k \to u_j}(x_j) = \sum_{x_j} \left\{ \begin{array}{l} \frac{1}{\sqrt{2\pi}\sigma} \exp\left(-\frac{1}{2\sigma^2} \left\| y_k - \sum_{v \in \xi_k} h_{k,v} x_{k,v} \right\|^2 \right) \\ \times \prod_{\substack{if(l>j),\\ l \in \xi_k / \{j\}}} M^{t-1}_{u_k \to c_l}(x_j) \prod_{\substack{if(l<j),\\ l \in \xi_k / \{j\}}} M^t_{u_k \to c_l}(x_j) \end{array} \right\} \tag{6}$$

$$M^t_{u_j \to c_k}(x_j) = \prod_{\substack{if(m<j),\\ m \in \varsigma_j / \{k\}}} M^t_{c_m \to u_j}(x_j) \prod_{\substack{if(m>j),\\ m \in \varsigma_j / \{k\}}} M^{t-1}_{c_m \to u_j}(x_j) \tag{7}$$

3.3 The Improved Variable MPA Algorithm

In uplink, the path from each user path to the base station is different and therefore users' data experience different fading conditions, which may be large-scale fading or small-scale fading. Although the transmission power of all users sharing the same resource blocks is equal, users experiencing different fading conditions results in different receiving signal-to-noise ratios (SNR). Therefore, situations where some users' signal power is in the advantage or disadvantage of receiving signal will appear. VNs and FNs message values of users with high received signal power have obviously higher reliability, and message values of users with low signal power is less reliable. In this case, if users with high SNR can preferentially enter the iteration loop, the performance of the multi-user detection can be improved.

Before iteration, the users are sorted according to the received SNR from largest to smallest. The calculation formula can be described as

$$\mathrm{SNR}_i = \frac{p_i|h_i|^2}{\sigma^2} \tag{8}$$

where, $H = (h_1, \cdots, h_J)$ is the channel gain matrix, and $h_j\,(j = 1, \cdots, J)$ represents a column vector with size K (K OFDMA subcarriers).

According to the SNR, IVMPA scheme gets the users' iteration order. Based the sorted users order, the algorithm updates the message values of FNs and VNs in order to take full advantage of more reliable information. The new formula can be described as

$$M^t_{c_k \to u_j}(x_j) = \sum_{x_j} \left\{ \begin{array}{l} \dfrac{1}{\sqrt{2\pi}\sigma} \exp\left(-\dfrac{1}{2\sigma^2} \left\| y_k - \sum\limits_{v \in \xi_k} h_{k,v} x_{k,v} \right\|^2 \right) \\ \times \prod\limits_{\substack{k=order(a) \\ l=order(b) \\ a<b}} M^{t-1}_{u_k \to c_l}(x_j) \prod\limits_{\substack{k=order(a) \\ l=order(b) \\ a>b}} M^t_{u_k \to c_l}(x_j) \end{array} \right\} \tag{9}$$

$$M^t_{u_j \to c_k}(x_j) = \prod_{\substack{j=order(a) \\ m=order(b) \\ a>b}} M^t_{c_m \to u_j}(x_j) \prod_{\substack{j=order(a) \\ m=order(b) \\ a<b}} M^{t-1}_{c_m \to u_j}(x_j) \tag{10}$$

According to the preset user update sequence, FN to VNs and VN to FN message values of each user are updated in turn. For each FN-VN pair currently iteration, if $M_{c_k \to u_j}(x_j)$ is updated, the same FN-VN pair soft information $M_{u_j \to c_k}(x_j)$ is immediately updated so that each updated soft message value can enter the next iteration update in time, thereby accelerating the convergence speed. After a user's all soft message values are updated, update the next user. When all users are updated, the detector will start next iteration same as before. The specific process is shown in Algorithm 1.

Algorithm 1. The IVMPA Algorithm

Require: F, σ^2, $t_{\max}$, t_0, H;
Initialization: $M^0_{c_k \to u_j}(x_j) = \frac{1}{M}$;
if $t \leqslant t_0$ **then**
    for all u_j ($j = order(i), i = 1, \cdots, J$) **do**
        conduct equation (9);
        conduct equation (10);
    end for
end if
if $t = t_{\max}$ **then**
    $Q(x_j) = \prod\limits_{k \in \varsigma_j} M^{t_{\max}}_{c_k \to u_j}(x_j)$;
    $X_j = \max Q(x_j) = \max \prod\limits_{k \in \varsigma_j} M^{t_{\max}}_{c_k \to u_j}(x_j)$;
end if

3.4 The Incomplete Iterative MPA Algorithm

In uplink, each user experiences different fading conditions, and the received SNR at the receiver is not equal. The users with high received SNR has relatively higher reliability and the iterative convergence of soft information is faster than other users. Based on the above basis, an Incomplete Iterative MPA Algorithm (IIMPA) is proposed to enable users with high received SNR to stop the iterations early, and the remaining users continue to iterate until obtaining the codewords information of all users. Because some users stop the iterations in advance, the incomplete iterative algorithm can reduce the demodulation complexity and delay to some extent.

Based on the received SNR, a set of users Ψ_1 for partial iterations and a set of all iterative users Ψ_2 are defined. And the number of iterations for the partial iterative users is set in advance, assuming that the size of Ψ_1 is *num*. At the initial iteration, the algorithm iteratively updates the soft information values of FNs to VNs and VNs to FNs for all users. The process can be described as shown in (3) and (4).

When the initial number of iterations $iter_1$ is reached, the users of Ψ_1 soft information are no longer updated, and the users of Ψ_2 continue to perform the remaining number of iterations until the maximum number of iterations $t_{\max}$ is reached. The specific process is shown in Algorithm 2. The soft information of FNs to VNs and VNs to FNs can be written as

$$M^t_{c_k \to u_j}(x_j) = \sum_{x_j} \left\{ \begin{array}{l} \dfrac{1}{\sqrt{2\pi}\sigma} \exp\left(-\dfrac{1}{2\sigma^2} \left\| y_k - \sum\limits_{v \in \xi_k} h_{k,v} x_{k,v} \right\|^2 \right) \\ \cdot \prod\limits_{l \in \Psi_2 / \{j\}} M^{t-1}_{u_k \to c_l}(x_j) \prod\limits_{l \in \Psi_1} M^{t_0}_{u_k \to c_l}(x_j) \end{array} \right\} \quad (11)$$

Algorithm 2. The IIMPA Algorithm

Require: F, σ^2, $t_{\max}$, $iter_1$, H;
  Initialization: $M^0_{c_k \to u_j}(x_j) = \frac{1}{M}$;
if $t \leqslant iter_1$ **then**
  conduct equation (3);
  conduct equation (4);
end if
for all u_j ($j = order(i), i = 1, \cdots, J$) **do**
  conduct equation (9);
  conduct equation (10);
end for
if $t = iter_1$ **then**
  for $u_j \in \Psi_1$ **do**
    $Q(x_j) = \prod_{k \in \varsigma_j} M^{iter_1}_{c_k \to u_j}(x_j)$;
    $X_j = \max Q(x_j)$;
  end for
end if
if $t > iter_1$ **then**
  for $u_j \in \Psi_2$ **do**
    conduct equation (11);
    conduct equation (12);
  end for
end if
for $u_j \in \Psi_2$ **do**
  $X_j = \max \prod_{k \in \varsigma_j} M^{t_{\max}}_{c_k \to u_j}(x_j)$;
end for

$$M^t_{u_j \to c_l}(x_j) = \prod_{m \in \Psi_2/\{k\}} M^t_{c_m \to u_j}(x_j) \prod_{m \in \Psi_1} M^{t_0}_{c_m \to u_j}(x_j) \tag{12}$$

4 Numerical Results and Analysis

In this section, we will first simulate the bit error rate (BER) performance of the multi-user detection algorithms in SCMA uplink, and then compare the algorithm complexity and demodulation delay. The codebooks of SCMA layers are designed based on the principles reported in [9]. The dimension of SCMA codewords is 4 with 2 non-zero elements. The number of SCMA layers is 6 shared with 4 OFDMA subcarriers. The transmitted signals from SCMA layers have equal powers. All simulations are performed in Rayleigh channel.

4.1 BER Performances of Detection Algorithms

Figure 3 shows that the BER performance comparison between MPA, VMPA, and IVMPA with 1 iteration and 3 iterations in SCMA uplink with Rayleigh channel. The horizontal axis of Fig. 5 is the per bit energy to noise energy ratio, which is equal to each layer. In Rayleigh channel, when the receiver iteration times is 1 and the ratio less than 4, three algorithms seem to have near performance. That is because the influence of the noise power on the demodulation performance is greater than the influence of the order change of the internal iteration. When the ratio more than 6, IVMPA has a significant performance gain over VMPA and MPA algorithms. When the ratio is greater than 8 dB, the IVMPA algorithm obtains about 2 dB performance gain compared to the VMPA algorithm, and the IVMPA algorithm obtains about 5 dB performance gain compared to the MPA algorithm. The reason is that the order of iteration becomes the main factors affecting system performance compared to the smaller noise power. When the number of iterations is 3, the difference in BER performance between three algorithms is very small. The conclusion is that the IVMPA algorithm obtains obvious performance gains when fewer iterations.

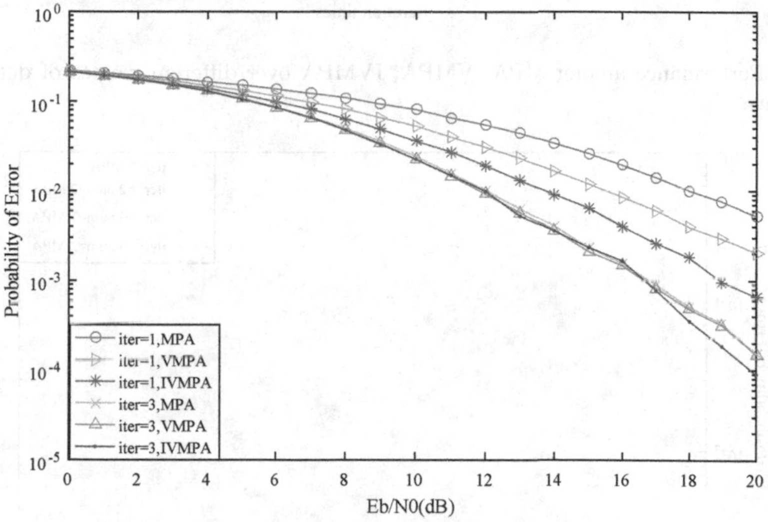

Fig. 3. Performance comparison between MPA, VMPA, and IVMPA with 1 iteration and 3 iterations in uplink with Rayleigh channel.

Figure 4 shows the comparison of convergence speed of MPA, VMPA, and IVMPA algorithms. With the increase of bit-to-noise ratio, the difference between three algorithms is more obvious. That is because the noise power at low SNR greatly affects the performance, and the influence of the iteration times on performance is submerged. When the number of iterations is 2, the BER of IVMPA is almost equal that the number of iterations is 4 of VMPA and MPA algorithm. When the number of iterations are 5, the BER of three algorithms is basically similar. The conclusion is that the IVMPA algorithm can reduce the number of iterations at the expense of very little performance. In other words, the IVMPA algorithm can achieve convergence faster.

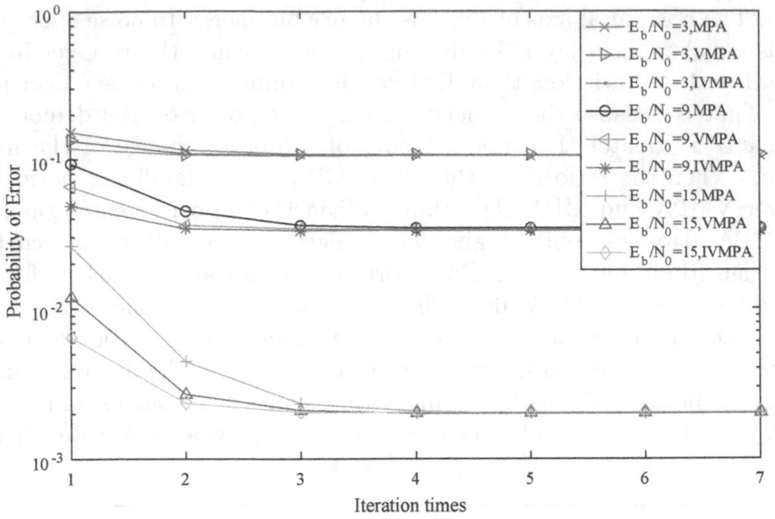

Fig. 4. Performance among MPA, VMPA, IVMPA over different ranges of detection iterations.

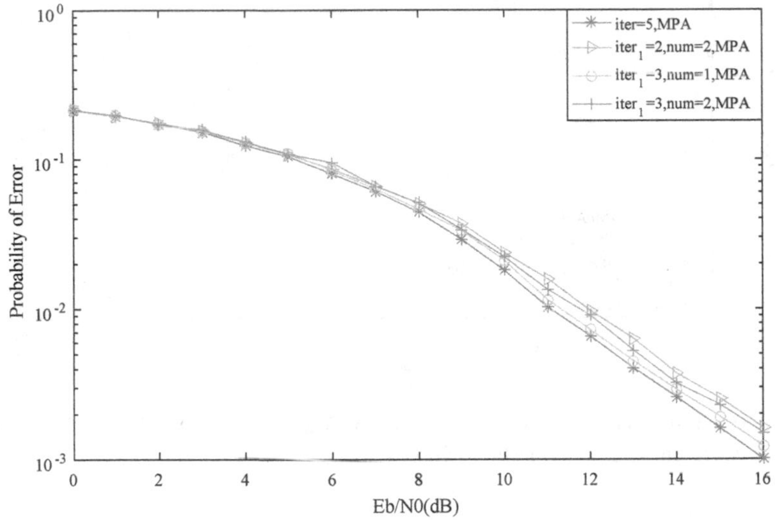

Fig. 5. Performance between IIMPA and MPA algorithm.

Figure 5 shows that the performance comparison between IIMPA and MPA algorithms. From Fig. 7, it can be seen that BER performance of IIMPA algorithm gradually decreases along with the size of users set $iter_1$ increases under the same conditions. When the number of partially iteration users does not change, the link performance decreases along with the value decreases. The reasons for this phenomenon are given as follows. Firstly, the soft information of users who have stopped iteration early has not yet converged. Obviously, the fewer the number of iterations, the worse the reliability of the message value. Secondly, the unreliable soft information will affect the convergence speed of the remaining users.

4.2 The Complexity of Detection Algorithms

The computational complexity of multiplication in MPA detection is described as

$$Mul_{MPA} = [(d_f - 1)\, M^{d_f} d_v J + (d_v - 1)\, M d_f K] I_T \tag{13}$$

The computational complexity of addition can be obtained from

$$Add_{MPA} = M d_f d_v J I_T \tag{14}$$

$Exp_{MPA} = M^{d_f} J I_T$ is the complexity of index in MPA detector. M is the size of SCMA codebooks. I_T is the iterations in detector. d_f is the number of layers sharing one subcarrier. d_v is the number of subcarriers used by one layer. J is the amount of layers. The computational complexity of received SNR is proportional to the number of users, defined as Mul_{SNR}. When users' transmit power is equal, the SNR of each user is proportional to the channel gain. In this case, the relative size of the received SNR can be replaced by the value of the channel gain value. $Mul_{SNR} = 6N$ and $Add_{SNR} = 2N - 1$. When the SCMA codeword is sparse, the computational complexity is relatively low.

It can be seen from the above formulas that the complexity of the detection algorithms is linear with the number of iterations. And It is obvious that reducing the number of iterations can greatly reduce the computational complexity in the receiver.

The delay analysis among three algorithms are as follows.

The time required for MPA algorithm through the demodulation process can be described as

$$\tau_{MPA} = \left\{ \begin{array}{l} \tau_{Mul} \cdot [(d_f - 1)\, M^{d_f} d_v J + (d_v - 1)\, M d_f K] \\ + M d_f d_v J \cdot \tau_{Add} + M^{d_f} J \cdot \tau_{Exp} \end{array} \right\} \cdot I_T \tag{15}$$

τ_{Mul} is multiplication delay, τ_{Add} is addition delay, τ_{Exp} is index delay. It can be seen that the total delay is proportional to detector iteration times I_T. Then, The IVMPA algorithm compared to MPA algorithm and VMPA algorithm, the receiver processing delay reduced $\frac{1}{2}\tau_{MPA} - \tau_{order}$ and $\frac{1}{3}\tau_{MPA} - \tau_{order}$, respectively.

Based on the above simulation and analysis results, the IVMPA algorithm can reduce the number of detection iterations and computational complexity and processing delay at the expense of a small amount of system performance.

The computational complexity analysis of IIMPA algorithm is as follow.

When $num = 1$, the multiplication can be described as

$$\begin{aligned} &Mul_{num=1} = \\ &\left[(d_f - 1) M^{d_f} d_v J + (d_v - 1) M d_f K\right] (I_T - iter_1) + \\ &\begin{bmatrix} \left((d_f - 1) M^{d_f} (K - d_v) d_f + (d_f - 2) M^{d_f - 1}\right) \\ d_v (d_f - 1) + (d_v - 1) M d_v (J - 1) \end{bmatrix} iter_1 \end{aligned} \tag{16}$$

and the addition is

$$\begin{aligned} &Add_{num=1} = \\ &M^{d_f} d_v J (I_T - iter_1) + \\ &\left(M^{d_f} (K - d_v) d_f + M^{d_f - 1}\right) d_v (d_f - 1) iter_1 \end{aligned} \tag{17}$$

the computational complexity of index can be written as

$$\begin{aligned} &Exp = \\ &M^{d_f} J \cdot iter_1 + M^{d_f - 1} (MJ - M + 1) \cdot (I_T - iter_1) \end{aligned} \tag{18}$$

According to above formulas, we can conclude that IIMPA can reduce the computational complexity in some extent. With the increase of partial iteration users, the complexity and delay decrease, while its performance also decreases. It can reach a balance between performance and the complexity of detector.

5 Conclusion

Two low complexity algorithms are proposed to reduce the detector computational complexity and demodulation delay. In SCMA uplink, it is complex for the receiver to separate and demodulate users' data with multiplexing technology. Based on the original algorithm, IVMPA adds the user sort strategy before the iteration, which can take full advantage of high reliability users information. This feature provides the IVMPA algorithm to reduce the iteration times and bring about low complexity and delay. IIMPA reduces the computational complexity by terminating some users' iteration in advance. A balance between user performance and computational complexity is achieved by selecting the appropriate number of iterations and the number of partial iterations users.

References

1. Nikopour, H., Baligh, H.: Sparse code multiple access. In: 2013 IEEE 24th Annual International Symposium on Personal, Indoor, and Mobile Radio Communications (PIMRC), pp. 332–336, September 2013
2. van de Beek, J., Popovic, B.M.: Multiple access with low-density signatures. In: GLOBECOM 2009–2009 IEEE Global Telecommunications Conference, pp. 1–6, November 2009

3. Bayesteh, A., Yi, E., Nikopour, H., Baligh, H.: Blind detection of SCMA for uplink grant-free multiple-access. In: 2014 11th International Symposium on Wireless Communications Systems (ISWCS), pp. 853–857, August 2014
4. Zhang, S., Xu, X., Lu, L., Wu, Y., He, G., Chen, Y.: Sparse code multiple access: an energy efficient uplink approach for 5G wireless systems. In: 2014 IEEE Global Communications Conference, pp. 4782–4787, December 2014
5. Nikopour, H., et al.: SCMA for downlink multiple access of 5G wireless networks. In: 2014 IEEE Global Communications Conference, pp. 3940–3945, December 2014
6. Zhang, L., Xiao, P., Zafar, A., Quddus, A.U., Tafazolli, R.: FBMC system: an insight into doubly dispersive channel impact. IEEE Trans. Veh. Technol. **66**(5), 3942–3956 (2017)
7. Zhai, D., Sheng, M., Wang, X., Li, J.: Joint codebook design and assignment for detection complexity minimization in uplink SCMA networks. In: 2016 IEEE 84th Vehicular Technology Conference (VTC-Fall), pp. 1–5, September 2016
8. Wei, F., Chen, W.: Low complexity iterative receiver design for sparse code multiple access. IEEE Trans. Commun. **65**(2), 621–634 (2017)
9. Taherzadeh, M., Nikopour, H., Bayesteh, A., Baligh, H.: SCMA codebook design. In 2014 IEEE 80th Vehicular Technology Conference (VTC2014-Fall), pp. 1–5, September 2014

On Minimizing Decoding Complexity for Binary Linear Network Codes

Jian Wang(✉), Kui Xu, Xiaoqin Yang, Lihua Chen, Wei Xie, and Jianhui Xu

Army Engineering University of PLA, Nanjing 210007, China
farfly217@163.com, lgdxxukui@126.com, 15261856573@139.com, clhtyue@163.com, edifier77@163.com, xujianhui900118@163.com

Abstract. The typical method adopted in the decoding of linear network codes is Gaussian Elimination (GE), which enjoys extreme low policy complexity in determining actions, i.e., the XORing operation executed upon the decoding matrix and the coded packets. However, the amount of the total required actions is quite large, which makes the overall decoding complexity high. In this paper, we consider the problem of minimizing the decoding complexity of binary linear network codes. We formulate the decoding problem into a special shortest path problem where the weight of each edge consists of: (1) a const weight due to the execution of the action; (2) a variable weight due to the adopted policy in determining the action. The policy is formulated as an optimization problem that minimizes a particular objective function by enumerating over a certain action set. Since finding the optimal policy is intractable, we optimize the policy in dual directions. At one hand, we guarantee the objective function and the action set are similar to the optimal policy that minimizes const weight summation; at the other hand, we guarantee that the objective function have simple structure and the action set is small, so that the variable weight summation is also small. Simulation results demonstrate that our proposed policy can significantly reduce the decoding complexity compared with existing methods.

Keywords: Binary linear network codes · Decoding complexity

1 Introduction

In an erasure broadcast channel, a sender needs to send N packets reliably to M receivers. In each transmission, each receiver either receives a packet exactly or experiences an erasure. For this problem, linear network codes [1] has been demonstrated as a promising solution, where each coded packet is the linear combination of the N source packets over the finite field $GF(q)$. We refer to the coefficients of the linear combination as the encoding vector. A coded packet is

This work is supported by Jiangsu Province Natural Science Foundation (BK20160079), National Natural Science Foundation of China (No. 61671472, No. 61501511, No. 61771486).

M. Jia et al. (Eds.): WiSATS 2019, LNICST 281, pp. 576–586, 2019.
https://doi.org/10.1007/978-3-030-19156-6_54

said to be *innovative* to a receiver if its encoding vector is not in the subspace spanned by the encoding vectors of packets already received. Once a receiver has collected N innovative packets, the N source packets can be recovered through decoding.

Linear network codes can be generated with or without feedback. LT codes [2], Raptor codes [3] and Random Linear Network Codes (RLNC) [4] can be used without feedback. For these codes, coded packets are with certain probabilities to be innovative. With feedback, the design of the coded packets are more targeted [5,6]. It is indicated in [5] that an innovative packet to all receivers can always be found if $q \geq M$. As a result, the *completion time*, measured in terms of the number of packet transmissions, is minimized. For a broadcast system, to obtain a near optimal completion time performance, the above condition can be further relaxed, i.e., it is unnecessary for each coded packet to be innovative to all receivers. We only need to make sure the coded packet is innovative to the receivers with least innovative packets. The simulation results in [6] demonstrate that almost optimal completion time performance can be obtained with $q = 2$.

The excellent performance of linear network codes encourages researchers to consider its practicality. In particular, decoding complexity is an important issue, as mobile devices typically have low computation speed and limited energy. Despite of its excellent completion time performance, it is quite nature to consider adopting $q = 2$, i.e., to generate network codes over the finite field $GF(2)$, due to two obvious benefits. First, the adoption of $GF(2)$ avoids the complex multiplication calculations over the finite field. In traditional RLNC, at most $\frac{N^3}{3} + N^2L$ addition calculations and $\frac{N^3}{3} + N^2L$ multiplication calculations over $GF(q)$ are required with Gaussian Elimination (GE) decoding, where L denotes the length of the packets. Since multiplication calculations are much more complex than addition calculations, $GF(2)$ has incomparable advantage in reducing decoding complexity. Second, $GF(2)$ naturally lead to the sparsity of encoding vectors, which can obviously reduce decoding complexity. In traditional RLNC, each coded packet is the linear combination of all source packets. One important way to reduce the decoding complexity of RLNC is to introduce sparse encoding, i.e., to courage coded packets to contain less source packets [7].

The decoding of binary linear network codes is equivalent to solving sparse linear equations over $GF(2)$ as well as implementing corresponding packets addition. Matrix-free methods such as Wiedemann's coordinate recurrence algorithm [8] and the Lanczos algorithm [9] have smaller complexity compared with GE based method, but the superiority can only be realized when N is large and L is small. However, in practice, N is dozens while L is several thousands or even ten thousands, that means, $N \ll L$. As a result, GE based methods are more suitable for the decoding of binary linear network codes. As far as we know, only few GE based algorithms [6,10–12] have been designed, and the decoding problem had not been formally addressed. In this paper, we address the problem of minimizing the decoding complexity of binary network codes using GE based method. The contributions can be summarized as follows.

First, we formally formulate the decoding problem of binary linear network codes into a special shortest path problem, where all possible states of the decoding matrix together with the coded packets are vertices, and a two-way directed edge between a pair of vertices exists if there is a certain row-adding action can lead to the transformation between them. In traditional shortest path problems, the weight of each edge is fixed, thus to find the path with shortest path is equivalent to finding a sequence of actions that lead to the path with minimum weight summation. However, in our formulated problem, the weight of a edge is related to the adopted policy. In particular, the weight of a edge consists of two components, i.e., a const weight due to the execution of the action upon the decoding matrix as well as the corresponding coded packets, and a variable weight due to the application of the policy in determining the action. In this case, to solve the problem is in fact to find the optimal policy, so that the weight summation, i.e., the addition of the const weight summation and the variable weight summation, can be minimized.

Second, we formulate the optimality equation in terms of the const weight summation and show that the optimal const weight summation function is intractable, which demonstrates that the optimal policy in terms of the weight summation is also intractable. To obtain a good policy, we optimize the policy in dual directions, at one hand, we grasp the main monotonic characteristic of the optimal const weight summation function to make sure the objective function has similar characteristic, and action set contain important actions; at the other hand, we guarantee that the objective function is with simple structure and the cardinality of the action set is small.

Finally, we conduct simulations of our proposed policy for decoding. Simulation results demonstrate that compared with existing decoding methods, our proposed policy can significantly reduce the overall decoding complexity.

2 Decoding Problem Formulation

Consider a broadcasting scenario where a sender wants to deliver N source packets $\{\mathbf{p}_n\}_{n=1}^N$ to multiple receivers. Each source packet contains L bits. A transmitted packet is generated as the linear combination of a subset of all source packets over the finite field $GF(2)$. By convenience, we use an N-dimensional vector called *encoding vector* to present a coded packet, where the n-th source packet is contained in the coded packet if the n-th element of encoding vector equals 1, otherwise the n-th element equals 0. After collecting N innovative coded packets $\{\mathbf{q}_n\}_{n=1}^N$, each receiver maintains a full-rank binary $N \times N$ *decoding matrix* $\mathbf{S}$ with n-th row being the encoding vector of $\mathbf{q}_n$. A sequence of row-adding actions upon the decoding matrix over $GF(2)$ together with bitwise adding actions upon the corresponding coded packets over $GF(2)$ are executed until each row (or column) of the decoding matrix contains only one non-zero element, and all source packets are recovered. Since the row-adding actions upon the decoding matrix and the bitwise addition actions upon the coded packets are implemented simultaneously, throughout the paper, we only mention the row-adding actions for simplicity.

We add a subscript to $\mathbf{S}$ to represent the row-adding action procedure. In particular, we assume that T row-adding actions are required, and the initial decoding matrix and the target decoding matrix are denoted as $\mathbf{S}_1$ and $\mathbf{S}_{T+1}$ respectively. For a particular $\mathbf{S}_t, 1 \leq t \leq T$, a row-adding action $u_t = (i_{\mathbf{S}_t}, j_{\mathbf{S}_t})$ can be selected from the action set

$$\mathcal{U} = \{(i,j)|i,j \in [N] = \{1,2,\cdots,N\}, i \neq j\}.$$

After executing u_t, the decoding matrix is transformed from $\mathbf{S}_t$ to $\mathbf{S}_{t+1}$. In particular, we have

$$\mathbf{S}_{t+1}^{(m,n)} = \begin{cases} \mathbf{S}_t^{(i_{\mathbf{S}_t},n)} \oplus \mathbf{S}_t^{(j_{\mathbf{S}_t},n)} & m = j_{\mathbf{S}_t} \\ \mathbf{S}_t^{(m,n)} & m \in [M] \backslash \{j_{\mathbf{S}_t}\} \end{cases}$$

where $\mathbf{S}_t^{(m,n)}$ denotes the element in m-th row and n-th column of $\mathbf{S}_t$, and $\oplus$ denotes the adding operation over $GF(2)$. For the purpose of emphasizing the action u_t applied at $\mathbf{S}_t$, we also use $\mathbf{S}_{u_t}$ interchangeably with $\mathbf{S}_{t+1}$. Figure 1 illustrates the decoding procedure given an initial decoding matrix.

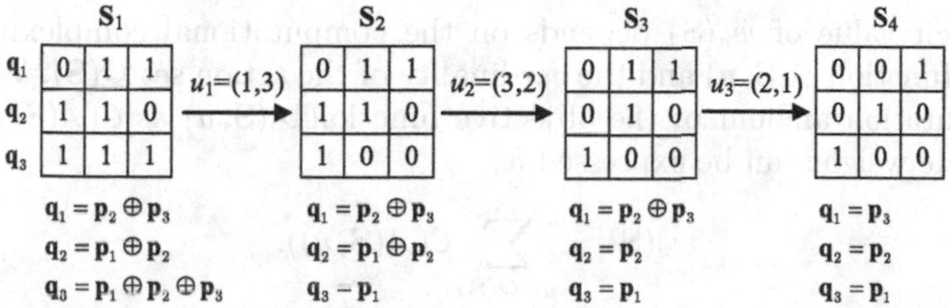

Fig. 1. An illustration of the decoding procedure given an initial decoding matrix $\mathbf{S}_1$.

According to the decoding procedure at each receiver, a directed graph $\mathcal{G} = (\mathcal{V}, \mathcal{E})$ can be constructed, where $\mathcal{V}$ is the set of the vertices corresponding to all possible states of the decoding matrix, and $\mathcal{E}$ is the set of edges that describes the adjacency relations of different vertices. In particular, the edge from $\mathbf{S}$ to $\mathbf{S}'$ exists if $\exists u \in \mathcal{U}$ so that $\mathbf{S}$ is transformed into $\mathbf{S}'$ after executing u, i.e., $\mathbf{S}' = \mathbf{S}_u$. Given an arbitrary initial vertex $\mathbf{S}_1$, we need to find a path to a target vertex, so that the weight summation of the path is minimized. A vertex is said to be a target vertex if each row (or column) of the corresponding decoding matrix contains only one non-zero element, and the set of all target vertices is denoted as $\mathcal{V}_T$. The weight summation of a path refers to the summation of weights of edges in this path.

In traditional shortest path problems, each edge has a fixed weight, thus to find the shortest path is in fact to find a best action sequence. However, in this decoding problem, the weight of each edge consists of two components. The first weight component is a const weight due to the execution of the action upon the decoding matrix and the coded packets. Since the action executed upon the decoding matrix and the coded packets is the binary addition of a pair of N-dimensional vectors and a pair of L bit data sequence respectively, it can simply be expressed as

$$w_c(\mathbf{S}) = N + L \tag{1}$$

and the basic operation is integer addition. The second weight component is a variable weight $w_v(\mathbf{S})$ due to the execution of the policy in determining the action. The definition of a policy is presented as follows.

Definition 1. *A policy $\mu : \mathcal{V}\backslash\mathcal{V}_T \rightarrow \mathcal{U}$ is defined as a function that maps an arbitrary vertex $\boldsymbol{S} \in \mathcal{V}\backslash\mathcal{V}_T$ into a particular action $u \in \mathcal{U}$, that is $u = \mu(\boldsymbol{S})$. Note that the shortest path problem is deterministic, when the initial vertex $\boldsymbol{S}_1$ is determined, a policy will lead to a sequence of actions, i.e., $u_1, u_2, \cdots$.*

Since the available actions are discrete and the effectiveness of actions are non-smooth, a policy can only be constructed as the enumeration over a certain action set $\mathcal{Q}(\mathbf{S}) \subseteq \mathcal{U}$ in minimizing a certain objective function $\mathcal{A}(\mathbf{S}, u)$, that is

$$\mu : \arg\min_{u \in \mathcal{Q}(\mathbf{S})} \mathcal{A}(\mathbf{S}, u). \tag{2}$$

The explicit value of $w_v(\mathbf{S})$ depends on the computational complexity of the objective function $\mathcal{A}(\mathbf{S}, u)$ and the cardinality of the action set $\mathcal{Q}(\mathbf{S})$. We denote the computation amount of the objective function $\mathcal{A}(\mathbf{S}, u)$ as $\mathcal{C}(\mathcal{A}(\mathbf{S}, u))$, thus the variable weight can be expressed as

$$w_v(\mathbf{S}) = \sum_{u \in \mathcal{Q}(\mathbf{S})} \mathcal{C}(\mathcal{A}(\mathbf{S}, u)). \tag{3}$$

We assume that for a particular policy μ, the length of the path is T_μ, thus the decoding problem can be formulated as finding the optimal policy μ^*, i.e., to design $\mathcal{A}(\mathbf{S}, u)$ and $\mathcal{Q}(\mathbf{S})$ so that the weight summation can be minimized, that is,

$$\arg\min_{\mu} V_\mu(\mathbf{S}_1) = \sum_{t=1}^{T_\mu} [w_c(\mathbf{S}_t) + w_v(\mathbf{S}_t)]. \tag{4}$$

3 Policy Optimization

$V_\mu(\mathbf{S}_1)$ can be divided into two parts, i.e., the const weight summation $V_\mu^c(\mathbf{S}_1) = \sum_{t=1}^{T_\mu} w_c(\mathbf{S}_t)$ and the variable weight summation $V_\mu^v(\mathbf{S}_1) = \sum_{t=1}^{T_\mu} w_v(\mathbf{S}_t)$. The const weight summation is the unavoidable cost in solving the shortest path problem. It refers to the costs of executing the actions following a path, which can be regarded as the theoretical lower bound of the weight summation. Since $w_c(\mathbf{S}_t)$ is const, $V_\mu^c(\mathbf{S}_1)$ is linearly proportional to T_μ, thus to minimize $V_\mu^c(\mathbf{S}_1)$ is in fact to minimize T_μ. While the variable weight summation refers to the extra cost that is produced in the procedure of determining the path, which can be minimized, or even eliminated by adopting simple algorithm such as GE algorithm. To minimize $V_{\mu}^{v}(\mathbf{S}_1)$, we need to minimize the variable weight $w_v(\mathbf{S})$ and the path length T_{μ} simultaneously. Thus, in order to minimize $V_{\mu}(\mathbf{S}_1)$, we should minimize $w_v(\mathbf{S})$ and T_{μ} simultaneously.

Unfortunately, minimizing $w_v(\mathbf{S})$ and minimizing T_{μ} are contradicted with each other. According to (3), the computational complexity of $w_v(\mathbf{S})$ is linearly proportional to the cardinality of $\mathcal{Q}(\mathbf{S})$, i.e., $|\mathcal{Q}(\mathbf{S})|$, and the computational amount of $\mathcal{A}(\mathbf{S}, u)$. Thus to minimize $w_v(\mathbf{S})$, we should make $\mathcal{A}(\mathbf{S}, u)$ as simple as possible and the cardinality of $\mathcal{Q}(\mathbf{S})$ as small as possible. Specially, if $\mathcal{A}(\mathbf{S}, u) = 1$ or $|\mathcal{Q}(\mathbf{S})| = 1$, we have $w_v(\mathbf{S}) = 0$. However, an obvious fact is that the more simple structure $\mathcal{A}(\mathbf{S}, u)$ and $\mathcal{Q}(\mathbf{S})$ have, the more likely that the produced actions are close to random selection, thus the longer the length of the path will be. Due to this reason, we can image that GE algorithm which enjoys zero variable weight will suffer from the a long path.

Tn order to minimize T_{μ}, we should guarantee policy μ has similar property with the optimal policy μ_c^* that can minimize $V_{\mu}^{c}(\mathbf{S}_1)$. Note that the optimality equations in terms of $V_{\mu_c^*}^{c}(\mathbf{S}_t)$ can be constructed as

$$V_{\mu_c^*}^{c}(\mathbf{S}_t) = \min_{u_t \in \mathcal{U}} \left[V_{\mu_c^*}^{c}(\mathbf{S}_{u_t}) + w_c(\mathbf{S}_t) \right], t \in [T_{\mu_c^*}]. \tag{5}$$

Thus policy μ_c^* can be expressed as

$$\mu_c^* : \arg\min_{u \in \mathcal{U}} V_{\mu_c^*}^{c}(\mathbf{S}_u). \tag{6}$$

Obviously, to achieve minimum T_{μ}, we should set $\mathcal{A}(\mathbf{S}, u) = V_{\mu_c^*}^{c}(\mathbf{S}_u)$ and $\mathcal{Q}(\mathbf{S}) = \mathcal{U}$. Since there exists a one-to-one correspondence between $\mathbf{S}$ and an N^2-dimensional binary vector, $V_{\mu_c^*}^{c}(\mathbf{S}_u)$ is in fact a pseudo-Boolean function [15], which can be expressed as

$$V_{\mu_c^*}^{c}(\mathbf{S}_u) = \sum_{\mathcal{P} \subseteq \{(m,n) | m \in [N], n \in [N]\}} a_{\mathcal{P}} \prod_{(m,n) \in \mathcal{P}} \mathbf{S}_u^{(m,n)}. \tag{7}$$

Even if we can determine all the coefficients $a_{\mathcal{P}}$, the computation of $V_{\mu_c^*}^{c}(\cdot)$ are with exponential complexity. Consequently, $w_v(\mathbf{S})$ becomes large.

Due to the contradiction demonstrated as above, the optimization over the policy can be implemented by balancing the simplicity and similarity to μ_c^*. At one hand, we should make sure that the expression of $\mathcal{A}(\mathbf{S}, u)$ is simple and the cardinality of $\mathcal{Q}(\mathbf{S})$ is small, thus the variable weight $w_v(\mathbf{S})$ becomes small. At the other hand, the adopted $\mathcal{A}(\mathbf{S}, u)$ should grasp the main characteristics of $V_{\mu_c^*}^{c}(\mathbf{S}_u)$ and $\mathcal{Q}(\mathbf{S})$ should contain the best actions in $\mathcal{U}$ that can minimize $V_{\mu_c^*}^{c}(\mathbf{S}_u)$, so that T_{μ} can be minimized.

3.1 Objective Function Determination

To guarantee the effectiveness of the objective function, $\mathcal{A}(\mathbf{S}, u)$ should reflect the main characteristic of $V_{\mu_c^*}^{c}(\mathbf{S})$, at the same time, it should have simple structure. As presented by (7), $V_{\mu_c^*}^{c}(\mathbf{S}_u)$ is a multilinear function in 0–1 variables, an effective method of simplifying it is to adopt its linear terms as the objective function, i.e.,

$$\mathcal{A}(\mathbf{S}, u) = \sum_{m\in[N],n\in[N]} a_{(m,n)}\mathbf{S}_u^{(m,n)} \tag{8}$$

where $u = (i_{\mathbf{S}}, j_{\mathbf{S}})$ and

$$\mathbf{S}_u^{(m,n)} = \begin{cases} \mathbf{S}^{(i_{\mathbf{S}},n)} \oplus \mathbf{S}^{(j_{\mathbf{S}},n)} & m = j_{\mathbf{S}} \\ \mathbf{S}^{(m,n)} & m \in [M]\backslash\{j_{\mathbf{S}}\} \end{cases} \tag{9}$$

When we set $a_{(m,n)} = 1$, the objective function represents the number of remaining non-zero elements after executing action u. In this situation, minimizing the objective function is equivalent to maximizing the number of the eliminated non-zero elements. Note that our target is to reduce the number of non-zero element to N as quickly as possible, this objective function is positively related to our target. From the perspective of dynamic programming [14], the objective function with $a_{(m,n)} = 1$ can be regarded as the myopia policy, meaning that it only selects the action that can maximize the number of the eliminated non-zero elements, despite of the risk that successor vertex may not have good actions. The existence of coefficients $a_{m,n}$ is to allocate priorities to different elements, so that we can achieve a tradeoff of between the short-term interest (maximizing the number of the eliminated non-zero elements) and the long-term interest (transforming to the vertices that are more likely to have actions that can eliminate more non-zero elements). The following theorem gives us insight in designing $a_{(m,n)}$.

Theorem 1. *When the number of non-zero elements is fixed, a vertex with a larger variance of feature components is expected to eliminate more non-zero elements with a randomly selected action.*

Proof. We assume two vertices $\mathbf{S}$, $\mathbf{S}'$ that have same number of non-zero elements. Their feature vectors are expressed as $\boldsymbol{\phi}_{\mathbf{S}} = [\boldsymbol{\phi}_{\mathbf{S}}^{(1)}, \cdots, \boldsymbol{\phi}_{\mathbf{S}}^{(n)}, \cdots, \boldsymbol{\phi}_{\mathbf{S}}^{(N)}]$ and $\boldsymbol{\phi}_{\mathbf{S}'} = [\boldsymbol{\phi}_{\mathbf{S}'}^{(1)}, \cdots, \boldsymbol{\phi}_{\mathbf{S}'}^{(n)}, \cdots, \boldsymbol{\phi}_{\mathbf{S}'}^{(N)}]$ respectively, with $\sum_{n=1}^{N} \boldsymbol{\phi}_{\mathbf{S}}^{(n)} = \sum_{n=1}^{N} \boldsymbol{\phi}_{\mathbf{S}'}^{(n)} = K$. Without loss of generality, we assume that the variance of $\boldsymbol{\phi}_{\mathbf{S}}$ is smaller than $\boldsymbol{\phi}_{\mathbf{S}'}$, i.e.,

$$\sum_{n=1}^{N} \left(\boldsymbol{\phi}_{\mathbf{S}}^{(n)} - \frac{K}{N}\right)^2 < \sum_{n=1}^{N} \left(\boldsymbol{\phi}_{\mathbf{S}'}^{(n)} - \frac{K}{N}\right)^2$$

which can be further simplified as

$$\sum_{n=1}^{N} \boldsymbol{\phi}_{\mathbf{S}}^{(n)2} < \sum_{n=1}^{N} \boldsymbol{\phi}_{\mathbf{S}'}^{(n)2}. \tag{10}$$

When a random action is selected, the expected eliminated non-zero element in n-th column of $\mathbf{S}$ is

$$\frac{\binom{\phi_{\mathbf{S}}^{(n)}}{2} - \phi_{\mathbf{S}}^{(n)}(N - \phi_{\mathbf{S}}^{(n)})}{\binom{N}{2}} = \frac{3\phi_{\mathbf{S}}^{(n)2} - (2N+1)\phi_{\mathbf{S}}^{(n)}}{N(N-1)}$$

and the expected number of the eliminated non-zero elements in $\mathbf{S}$ is

$$E_{\mathbf{S}} = \sum_{n=1}^{N} \frac{3\phi_{\mathbf{S}}^{(n)2} - (2N+1)\phi_{\mathbf{S}}^{(n)}}{N(N-1)} = \sum_{n=1}^{N} \frac{3\phi_{\mathbf{S}}^{(n)2}}{N(N-1)} - \frac{(2N+1)K}{N(N-1)}.$$

Similarly, the expected number of the eliminated non-zero elements in $\mathbf{S}'$ is

$$E_{\mathbf{S}'} = \sum_{n=1}^{N} \frac{3\phi_{\mathbf{S}'}^{(n)2}}{N(N-1)} - \frac{(2N+1)K}{N(N-1)}.$$

According to (10), we conclude that $E_{\mathbf{S}} < E_{\mathbf{S}'}$. The theorem is proved. □

According to Theorem 3, when we allocate higher priorities to the non-zero elements corresponding to small feature components, i.e., set $a_{(m,n)}$ negative to $\phi_{\mathbf{S}}^{(n)}$, we are more likely to transform into a better successor vertex, and a shorter path can be achieved.

Note that only the elements in $j_{\mathbf{S}}$-th row of $\mathbf{S}$ changes after executing u, we can ignore the common expression components in (9), and (9) can be simplified as

$$\begin{aligned}\mathcal{A}(\mathbf{S}, u) &= \sum_{m\in[N], n\in[N]} a_{(m,n)} \mathbf{S}_u^{(m,n)} - \sum_{m\in[N], n\in[N]} a_{(m,n)} \mathbf{S}^{(m,n)} \\ &= \sum_{n\in[N]} a_{(j_{\mathbf{S}},n)} \left[\mathbf{S}_u^{(j_{\mathbf{S}},n)} - \mathbf{S}^{(j_{\mathbf{S}},n)}\right].\end{aligned} \tag{11}$$

3.2 Action Set Determination

The purpose of designing the action set is to select a small subset of actions from the whole action set $\mathcal{U}$, with the guarantee that the effectiveness of best action selected from the subset is not too far from the best action selected from $\mathcal{U}$ in minimizing $V_{\mu_c^*}^c(\mathbf{S}_u)$. Note that the purpose of executing an action is to eliminate non-zero elements, thus the basic requirement for an action to be effective is that at least one non-zero element is changed to zero. Accordingly, we can naturally construct in total N basic action sets according to the position of the changed non-zero element. In particular, the n-th basic action set $\mathcal{C}_n$ can be constructed as

$$\mathcal{C}_n = \{(i,j) | \mathbf{S}^{(i,n)} = \mathbf{S}^{(j,n)} = 1, i, j \in [N]\} \tag{12}$$

Obviously, any action selected from $\mathcal{C}_n$ can lead to the elimination of a non-zero element in n-th column of $\mathbf{S}$. As a result, the action set $\mathcal{Q}(\mathbf{S})$ should be selected as an subset of $\cup_{n=1}^{N}\mathcal{C}_n$, i.e., $\mathcal{Q}(\mathbf{S}) \subseteq \cup_{n=1}^{N}\mathcal{C}_n$.

For the purpose of limiting the cardinality of $\mathcal{Q}(\mathbf{S})$, it is quite nature to select one basic action set as $\mathcal{Q}(\mathbf{S})$. We can easily prove that an random action selected from all N basic action set can eliminate a same number of non-zero elements on average. However, according to Theorem 1, the non-zero elements corresponding to smaller feature components play more important roles than those corresponding to larger feature components, the basic action set $\mathcal{C}_{\bar{\pi}^{(1)}}$ can best minimize the objective function, where $\bar{\pi}_{\mathbf{S}}$ is the index sequence of feature components sorted from smallest to largest and $\bar{\pi}_{\mathbf{S}}^{(1)}$ is the first index in $\bar{\pi}_{\mathbf{S}}$ As a result, we set

$$\mathcal{Q}(\mathbf{S}) = \mathcal{C}_{\bar{\pi}_{\mathbf{S}}^{(1)}} \tag{13}$$

4 Simulations

In this section, we demonstrate the effectiveness of our designed policy through simulations compared with existing algorithms:

- *PSD* algorithm proposed in [6], which is equivalent to the GE algorithm in the viewpoint of computational complexity.
- *SVD-NC* algorithm proposed in [12], which uses singular value decomposition to easily obtain the inverse of the decoding matrix and obtain the source packets through multiplying the inverse of the decoding matrix by the coded packets.
- *DC-DBS* algorithm proposed in [10], which is a variant GE algorithm with two improvements, i.e., density check is adopted to make sure when row-adding operation is executed the row with less non-zero elements is added to the row with more non-zero elements, delayed backwards substitution is adopted to make sure non-zero elements are not created in backwards substitution.
- *Sparse-NC* algorithm proposed in [11], where a reorder mechanism is proposed for the decoding matrix, so that density check and delayed backwards substitution is achieved.

We set $a_{(m,n)} = 1, \forall m, n \in [N]$. Although this setting may lead to some performance loss in terms of const weight summation, it can avoid complex calculations, such that variable weight can be maintained in a low level. We assume $L = 10000$, which is typical value for the length of data packets. Figures 1 and 2 depict the comparison of different decoding algorithms versus N in terms of the const weight summation $V_{\mu}^{c}(\mathbf{S}_1)$ and the weight summation $V_{\mu}(\mathbf{S}_1)$ respectively. As seen, in both figures, our proposed algorithm achieves best performance among the five algorithms. The comparison results demonstrate that the variable weight summation has been well limited though policy optimization, and is suitable to be applied in the decoding of network codes. In practical situation, N can not be ignored compared with L, that means, the variable weight summation can be a significant component of the weight summation (Fig. 3).

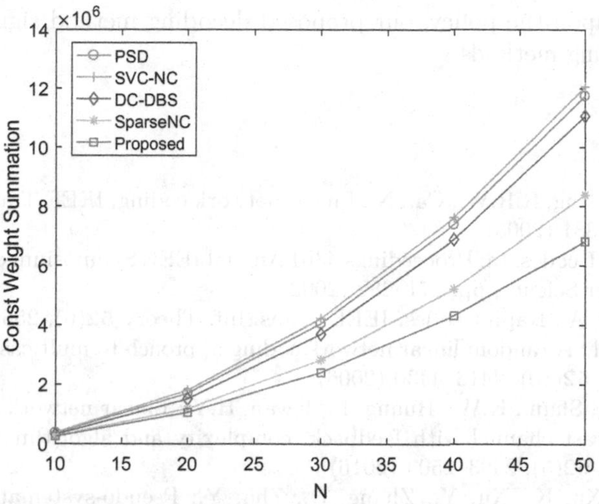

Fig. 2. Comparisons of different algorithms in terms of T_μ versus N. $\rho = 0.5, L = \infty$.

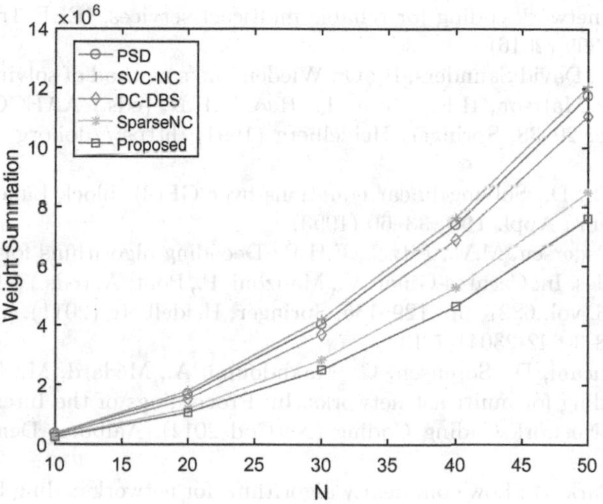

Fig. 3. Comparisons of different algorithms in terms of T_μ versus N. $\rho = 0.5, L = \infty$.

5 Conclusion

In this paper, we focus on minimizing the decoding complexity of binary network codes. Traditional Gaussian elimination method fail to optimize the decoding procedure and suffers from a large decoding complexity. We formulate the decoding problem into a special shortest path problem where the weight of each edge consists of: (1) a const weight due to the execution of the action; (2) a variable weight due to the adopted policy in determining the action. Through optimization upon the policy, our proposed decoding method significantly outperforms existing methods.

References

1. Li, S.-Y., Yeung, R.R.W., Cai, N.: Linear network coding. IEEE Trans. Inf. Theory **49**(2), 371–381 (2003)
2. Luby, M.: LT codes. In: Proceedings 43rd Annual IEEE Symposium on Foundations of Computer Science, pp. 271–282 (2002)
3. Shokrollahi, A.: Raptor codes. IEEE Trans. Inf. Theory **52**(6), 2551–2567 (2006)
4. Ho, T., et al.: A random linear network coding approach to multicast. IEEE Trans. Inf. Theory **52**(10), 4413–4430 (2006)
5. Sung, C.W., Shum, K.W., Huang, L., Kwan, H.Y.: Linear network coding for erasure broadcast channel with feedback: complexity and algorithms. IEEE Trans. Inf. Theory **62**(5), 2493–2503 (2016)
6. Wang, J., Xu, K., Xu, Y., Zhang, D., Zhu, Y.: Pseudo-systematic decoding of hybrid instantly decodable network code for wireless broadcasting. IEEE Wirel. Commun. Lett. **7**, 840–843 (2018)
7. Tassi, A., Chatzigeorgiou, I., Lucani, D.E.: Analysis and optimization of sparse random linear network coding for reliable multicast services. IEEE Trans. Commun. **64**(1), 285–299 (2016)
8. Kaltofen, E., David Saunders, B.: On Wiedemann's method of solving sparse linear systems. In: Mattson, H.F., Mora, T., Rao, T.R.N. (eds.) AAECC 1991. LNCS, vol. 539, pp. 29–38. Springer, Heidelberg (1991). https://doi.org/10.1007/3-540-54522-0_93
9. Coppersmith, D.: Solving linear equations over GF(2): block Lanczos algorithm. Linear Algebra Appl. **192**, 33–60 (1993)
10. Heide, J., Pedersen, M.V., Fitzek, F.H.P.: Decoding algorithms for random linear network codes. In: Casares-Giner, V., Manzoni, P., Pont, A. (eds.) NETWORKING 2011. LNCS, vol. 6827, pp. 129–136. Springer, Heidelberg (2011). https://doi.org/10.1007/978-3-642-23041-7_13
11. Feizi, S., Lucani, D., Sørensen, C., Makhdoumi, A., Médard, M.: Tunable sparse network coding for multicast networks. In: Proceedings of the International Symposium on Network Coding Coding (NetCod 2014), Aalborg, Denmark, pp. 1–6 (2014)
12. Kwon, J., Park, H.: Low complexity algorithms for network coding based on singular value decomposition. In: IEEE 2016 Eighth International Conference on Ubiquitous and Future Networks (ICUFN), pp. 641–643 (2016)
13. Sorour, S., Valaee, S.: Completion delay minimization for instantly decodable network codes. IEEE/ACM Trans. Netw. (TON) **23**, 1553–1567 (2015)
14. Bellman, R.: Dynamic programming and lagrange multipliers. Proc. Natl. Acad. Sci. **42**, 767–769 (1956)
15. Hammer, P.L., Rudeanu, S.: Boolean Methods in Operations Research and Related Areas, vol. 7. Springer, Heidelberg (2012). https://doi.org/10.1007/978-3-642-85823-9

A Passive Direction Finding Algorithm Based on Baselines Selected from Phased Array

Jingtao Ma(✉), Siyue Sun, Guang Liang, Songling Lv, and Xinglong Jiang

Shanghai Engineering Center for Microsatellites, Shanghai, China
majingtao1017@163.com

Abstract. In view of the increasing scale and poor concealment of existing electronic reconnaissance satellites, this paper proposes a passive direction finding algorithm based on baseline selection of communication load phased array. The algorithm performs direction finding by selecting part of array elements in the phased array to form a two-dimensional interferometer. Then the direction finding result of interferometer is used as the basis to determine the spatial domain search range of the MUSIC algorithm. Finally the fast and high precision estimation of elevation angle and azimuth angle is completed by MUSIC algorithm. The algorithm can realize fast and high-precision direction finding under communication concealment. At the same time, multi-scale direction finding results can guide the beamforming of phased array and enhance the communication. This algorithm provides a new solution for the integrated payload of miniaturized concealed electronic reconnaissance and communication.

Keywords: Electronic reconnaissance · Phased array · Direction finding of interferometer · Communication enhancement · Integrated payload

1 Introduction

In the existing passive direction finding algorithms [1], the passive direction finding algorithm based on large phased array [2–5] can improve the direction finding accuracy and anti-interference ability of electronic reconnaissance satellites [6–8]. However, the increasing scale of reconnaissance antennas further increases the economic cost and cycle cost of satellite research and development. In the meantime, the electronic reconnaissance satellites based on large antennas have poor concealment and invulnerability.

According to the above analysis, our country's electronic reconnaissance satellites have the development needs for multi-functionality, practicability, wide adaptability, and concealed anti-destruction. Aiming at the problem of poor concealment, high R&D cost and long period caused by large-scale antennas, there is a need for a novel algorithm to achieve covert and efficient electronic reconnaissance. The algorithm is based on the wide application of phased array antennas in communication satellites. Phased array elements of the communication payload are selected to form an interferometer [9, 10] to achieve fast estimation of target angles and complete reconnaissance tasks under

M. Jia et al. (Eds.): WiSATS 2019, LNICST 281, pp. 587–595, 2019.
https://doi.org/10.1007/978-3-030-19156-6_55

communication concealment. Based on this, according to the task needs, the interferometer direction finding result can be used as priori information, and the spatial search range is narrowed, which can reduce the calculation of spatial spectrum estimation and achieve fast and accurate estimation of the target position. At the same time, the interferometer and spatial spectrum estimation provide angle information of multi-scale resolution, which can guide beamforming and enhance communication. A new solution is provided for a flexible integrated payload system with communication and reconnaissance.

This paper is organized as follow: Firstly, the passive direction finding algorithm based on baselines selected from phased array is introduced in Sect. 2, followed by simulation results in Sect. 3. Finally, conclusions are drawn in Sect. 4.

2 Direction Finding Algorithm Based on Baselines Selected from Phased Array

2.1 Introduction of the Algorithm

The phased array is arranged as shown in Fig. 1, which is a 5 × 5 square array. Six of the array elements are selected to form four baselines. That is, array element 3 and 8, array element 14 and 15 form a two-dimensional short baseline, respectively. Array element 3 and 23, and array element 11 and 15 form a two-dimensional long baseline, respectively.

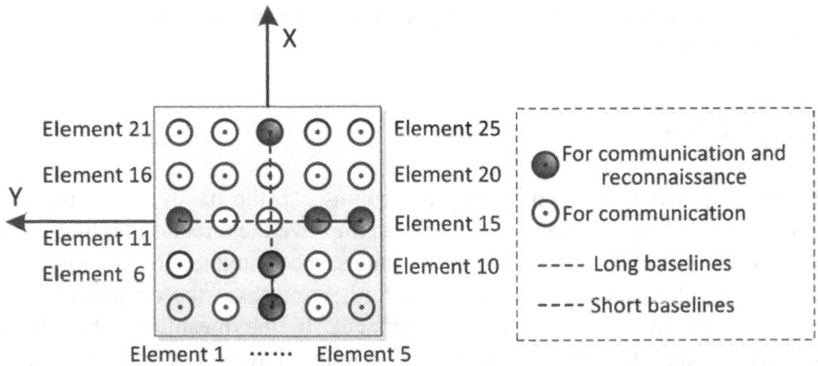

Fig. 1. Arrangement of array and selection of baselines

We define the central array element of the phased array, i.e., the array element 13 as the phase reference point and a Cartesian coordinate system is established. So the short baseline formed by the array element 3 and 8 on the x-axis can obtain the unambiguous phase difference corresponding to the baseline:

$$\Delta\varphi_{3-8} = \frac{2\pi}{\lambda} D_{3-8} \sin\theta \cdot \cos\varphi = \frac{2\pi}{\lambda} d \sin\theta \cdot \cos\varphi \tag{1}$$

Since the element interval is less than half wavelength, the phase difference between the array element 3 and the array element 8 is within the main value section (−π, +π). And the measurement result of phase $\Delta\varphi'_{3-8}$ obtained by the phase detector is also located in the main value section, which indicates that the phase difference corresponding to the short baseline does not include phase multi-valued ambiguity, i.e.:

$$\Delta\varphi_{3-8} = \Delta\varphi'_{3-8} = \frac{2\pi}{\lambda} d \sin\theta \cdot \cos\varphi \tag{2}$$

The short baseline formed by element 15 and 14 on the y-axis gives the unambiguous phase difference corresponding to the baseline:

$$\Delta\varphi_{15-14} = \frac{2\pi}{\lambda} D_{15-14} \sin\theta \cdot \sin\varphi = \frac{2\pi}{\lambda} d \sin\theta \cdot \sin\varphi \tag{3}$$

Similarly, the phase difference corresponding to the short baseline does not include the multi-valued ambiguity. That is, it satisfies:

$$\Delta\varphi_{15-14} = \Delta\varphi'_{15-14} = \frac{2\pi}{\lambda} d \sin\theta \cdot \sin\varphi \tag{4}$$

Where $\Delta\varphi'_{15-14}$ is obtained by the phase detector.

Estimation of elevation $\hat{\theta}_0$ and azimuth angle $\hat{\varphi}_0$ can be obtained from Eqs. (2) and (4).

$$\hat{\varphi}_0 = \arctan\left(\frac{\Delta\varphi'_{15-14}}{\Delta\varphi'_{3-8}}\right) \tag{5}$$

$$\hat{\theta}_0 = \arcsin\left(\frac{\lambda\sqrt{(\Delta\varphi'_{3-8})^2 + (\Delta\varphi'_{15-14})^2}}{2\pi d}\right) \tag{6}$$

The elevation and azimuth estimates obtained with short baselines often do not meet the requirement for accuracy. To reduce the error of direction finding, the length of baseline should be increased as much as possible to increase the baseline to wavelength ratio. Therefore, the two-dimensional angles can be estimated again in combination with the phase difference corresponding to the long baseline, and the highly accurate angle measurement is obtained.

$\hat{\theta}_0$ and $\hat{\varphi}_0$ are used to search for the fuzzy numbers p and q of the phase difference corresponding to the two-dimensional long baseline. Each set of fuzzy numbers (p, q) can calculate a set of corresponding angle estimates. And the closest angle values to $\hat{\theta}_0$ and $\hat{\varphi}_0$ are the target's direction of arrival, which are denoted by $\hat{\theta}_1$, $\hat{\varphi}_1$. Unambiguous and higher precision elevation and azimuth estimates are achieved.

The long baseline formed by the array element 23 and 3 on the x-axis gives the phase difference corresponding to the baseline:

$$\Delta\varphi_{23-3} = \frac{2\pi}{\lambda} D_{23-3} \sin\theta \cdot \cos\varphi = -\frac{2\pi}{\lambda} 4d \sin\theta \cdot \cos\varphi \tag{7}$$

The interval between the array element 23 and the array element 3 is greater than half a wavelength, so the corresponding phase difference has the following relationship with the phase measurement result of the phase detector:

$$\Delta\varphi_{23-3} = \Delta\varphi'_{23-3} + p \cdot 2\pi \tag{8}$$

Where $\Delta\varphi_{23-3}$ is the phase difference corresponding to the long baseline, $\Delta\varphi'_{23-3}$ is the phase measurement result of the phase detector, and p is the full-cycle ambiguous multiple.

Combining Eqs. (7) and (8), we get:

$$-\frac{2\pi}{\lambda} 4d \sin\theta \cdot \cos\varphi = \Delta\varphi'_{23-3} + p \cdot 2\pi \tag{9}$$

Further organizing the above formula, it can be expressed as follows:

$$p = -\frac{4d}{\lambda} \sin\theta \cdot \cos\varphi - \frac{\Delta\varphi'_{23-3}}{2\pi} \tag{10}$$

By performing the inequality operation on the Eq. (10), the search range of p can be obtained. The maximum and minimum values of p are expressed as follows:

$$p_{\min} = -\frac{4d}{\lambda} - \frac{\Delta\varphi'_{23-3}}{2\pi} \quad p_{\max} = \frac{4d}{\lambda} - \frac{\Delta\varphi'_{23-3}}{2\pi} \tag{11}$$

It is known that the measurement value of phase difference is located at $(-\pi, +\pi)$, and the above formulas are rounded to obtain the range of p:

$$p \in [\mathrm{ceil}(-\frac{4d}{\lambda}), \mathrm{floor}(\frac{4d}{\lambda})] \tag{12}$$

Where p is an integer, ceil() means rounding towards positive infinity, and floor() means rounding towards negative infinity.

Similarly, the long baseline formed by the array element 11 and 15 on the y-axis can obtain the phase difference corresponding to the baseline:

$$\Delta\varphi_{11-15} = \frac{2\pi}{\lambda} D_{11-15} \sin\theta \cdot \sin\varphi = -\frac{2\pi}{\lambda} 4d \sin\theta \cdot \sin\varphi \tag{13}$$

The interval between the array element 11 and the array element 15 is greater than half a wavelength, and the corresponding phase difference has the following relationship with the phase measurement result of the phase detector:

$$\Delta\varphi_{11-15} = \Delta\varphi'_{11-15} + q \cdot 2\pi \tag{14}$$

Where $\Delta\varphi_{11-15}$ is the phase difference corresponding to the long baseline, $\Delta\varphi'_{11-15}$ is the phase measurement result of the phase detector, and q is the full-cycle ambiguous multiple.

Combining Eqs. (13) and (14), we get:

$$-\frac{2\pi}{\lambda} 4d \sin\theta \cdot \sin\varphi = \Delta\varphi'_{11-15} + q \cdot 2\pi \tag{15}$$

Further organizing the above formula, it can be expressed as follows:

$$q = -\frac{4d}{\lambda} \sin\theta \cdot \sin\varphi - \frac{\Delta\varphi'_{11-15}}{2\pi} \tag{16}$$

By performing the inequality operation on the Eq. (16), the search range of q can be obtained. The maximum and minimum values of q are expressed as follows:

$$q_{\min} = -\frac{4d}{\lambda} - \frac{\Delta\varphi'_{11-15}}{2\pi} \quad q_{\max} = \frac{4d}{\lambda} - \frac{\Delta\varphi'_{11-15}}{2\pi} \tag{17}$$

It is known that the phase difference measurement value is located at $(-\pi, +\pi)$, and the above formulas are rounded to obtain the range of q:

$$q \in [\text{ceil}(-\frac{4d}{\lambda}), \text{floor}(\frac{4d}{\lambda})] \tag{18}$$

Where q is an integer, ceil() means rounding towards positive infinity, and floor() means rounding towards negative infinity.

Bring the possible value of p into Eq. (9) and the possible value of q into Eq. (15), we can calculate a set of corresponding estimates. The closest angle values to $\hat{\theta}_0$ and $\hat{\varphi}_0$ are the target's direction of arrival.

When the above-mentioned direction finding method based on interferometer still has insufficient angular resolution and the direction finding accuracy does not meet the actual demand, the array antenna can be used to achieve high resolution spatial spectrum estimation. The MUSIC algorithm is the most classic high-resolution DOA estimation algorithm. Its core idea is to decompose the signal and noise subspaces of the covariance matrix of received data. Then according to the intersection feature between the signal and the noise subspaces, a cost function can be constructed to estimate the angles. However, in practical applications, its complex matrix calculation and huge computational complexity make it very hard to apply to the existing practical systems. And there are fewer effective applications on small and medium-sized arrays.

The direction finding accuracy of the MUSIC algorithm is related to the step size of the search. In the case of sufficiently high SNR, the smaller the step size, the higher the accuracy. However, the smaller the step size is selected, the greater the computational complexity on the satellite. The method utilizes the two-dimensional long and short baseline interferometer to provide a priori information, which can significantly reduce the spatial search range of the MUSIC algorithm. The method makes it possible to adopt a smaller search step size, and improves the direction finding accuracy while reducing the computation load. The fast and accurate estimates of the angles are implemented.

The search range determined for the MUSIC's spatial spectrum estimation is as follows:

$$\theta_{search} = \left[\hat{\theta}_1 - \Delta\theta, \hat{\theta}_1 + \Delta\theta\right] \tag{19}$$

$$\varphi_{search} = [\hat{\varphi}_1 - \Delta\varphi, \hat{\varphi}_1 + \Delta\varphi] \tag{20}$$

Thus, the spectral expression of MUSIC is

$$P_{MUSIC}(\theta_{search}, \varphi_{search}) = \frac{1}{a(\theta_{search}, \varphi_{search})^H \cdot U_N \cdot U_N^H \cdot a(\theta_{search}, \varphi_{search})} \tag{21}$$

Where U_N is the noise subspace, $a(\theta_{search}, \varphi_{search})$ is the steering vector, and $(\cdot)^H$ denotes conjugate transpose. The two-dimensional angles corresponding to the peak are the elevation and azimuth of the target.

2.2 Algorithm Flow

The flow of passive direction finding algorithm based on baseline selected from phased array is as follows:

(1) Selecting part of array elements in the phased array to form a two-dimensional interferometer with long and short baselines;
(2) Obtaining the elementary direction finding results and by two-dimensional interferometer;
(3) Using direction finding result of interferometer as the basis to determine the spatial domain search range of the MUSIC algorithm;
(4) Completing the fast and high precision estimation of elevation angle and azimuth angle by MUSIC algorithm;
(5) Multi-scale direction finding results can guide the beamforming of phased array and enhance the communication.

3 Simulation Analysis

Parameter Setting: Carrier frequency, Fc = 3 GHz. Elevation angle = 10.04°. Azimuth angle = 15.07°. Element interval, d = λ/2. Length of long baseline = 4d. Length of short baseline = d. SNR = 10:5:40.

3.1 Direction Finding Results of Short Baselines

It can be seen from Fig. 2 that the estimation errors of angles are quite large when solving the angles only with short baselines.

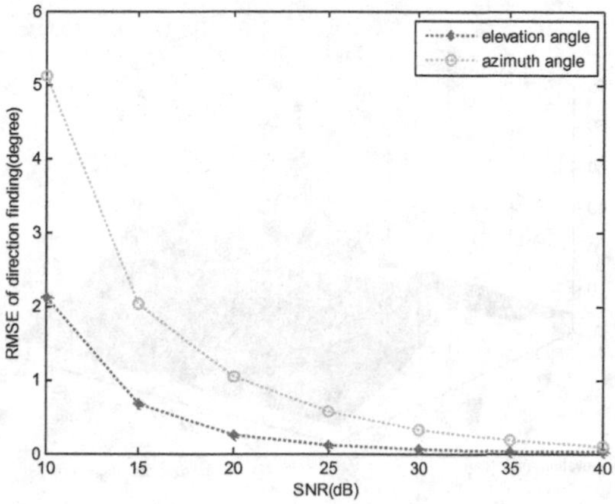

Fig. 2. Direction-finding RMSEs by two-dimensional short baselines versus SNR

3.2 Direction Finding Results of Combining Long and Short Baseline

It can be seen from Fig. 3 that the estimation errors of angles can be reduced after combining long baseline to solve the angles.

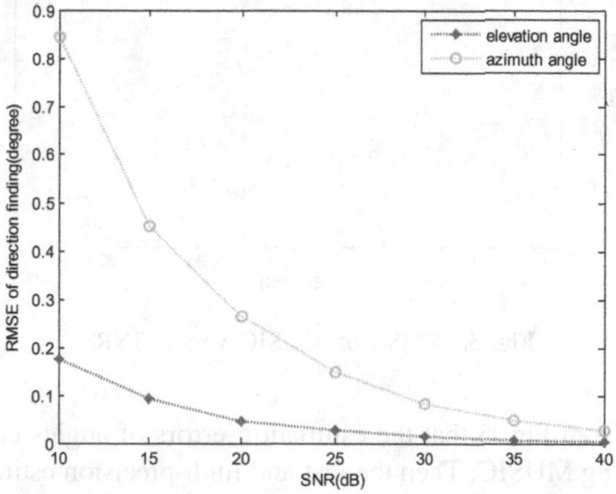

Fig. 3. Direction-finding RMSEs by two-dimensional long and short baselines versus SNR

3.3 Direction Finding Results of MUSIC

As can be seen from the above Fig. 4, the two-dimensional angle estimates are: elevation angle = 10.04°, azimuth angle = 15.07°.

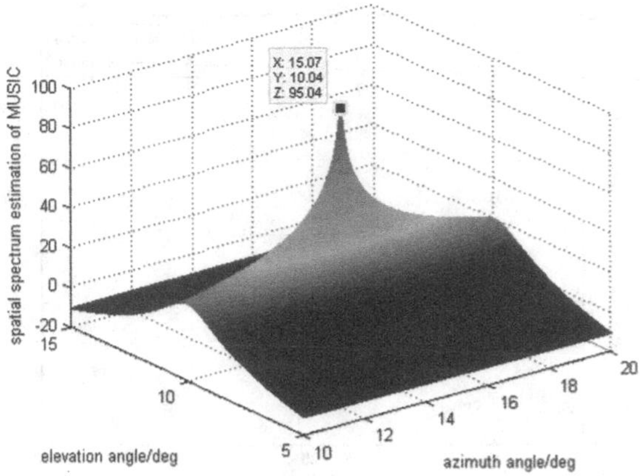

Fig. 4. Direction-finding of MUSIC based on interferometer (SNR = 40 dB)

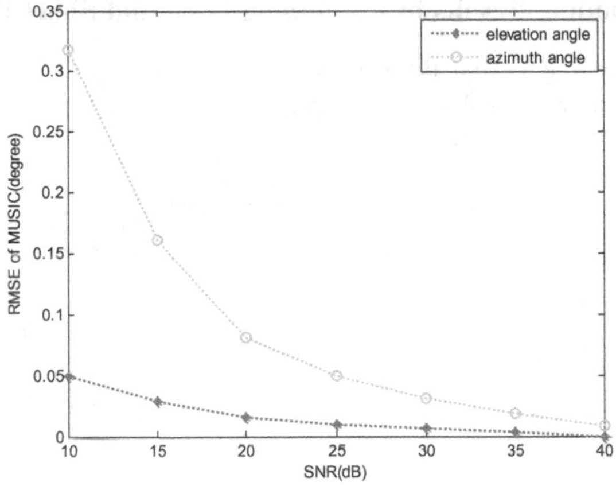

Fig. 5. RMSE of MUSIC versus SNR

It can be seen from Fig. 5 that the estimation errors of angles can be significantly reduced after utilizing MUSIC. Then the fast and high-precision estimates of angles are completed by MUSIC based on interferometer.

4 Conclusion

The algorithm utilizes the array elements of the communication load' phased array to complete direction finding based on the interferometer, which narrows the range of MUSIC spectral search. The fast and accurate estimation of the target' angle and the efficient electronic reconnaissance under the communication' concealment can be realized. In the meantime, the two-scale results of direction finding based on the interferometer and MUSIC method can guide the beamforming of the phased array, which can realize the enhancement of communication with the ground station, and design a flexible payload integrated with communication and electronic reconnaissance.

Acknowledgments. This work was partly supported by National Nature Science Foundation Program of China (No. 61601295), Shanghai Sailing Program (16YF1411000), National Key R&D Program of China (2017YFB0502902) and Autonomous Deployment Program of IAMC (ZZBS17DZ01).

References

1. Zhang, P.: Passive Detection System and its Key Technology. Huazhong University of Science and Technology, 05 January 2012. A Thesis for the Degree of Doctor. (in Chinese)
2. Shaofei, M., Jiansheng, S., Qi, Y., Wei, X.: Analysis of detection capabilities of LEO reconnaissance satellite constellation based on coverage performance. J. Syst. Eng. Electron. **29**(1), 98–104 (2018)
3. Vendik, O.G., Kozlov, D.S.: Phased antenna array with a sidelobe cancellation for suppression of jamming. IEEE Antennas Wirel. Propag. Lett. **11**(8), 648–650 (2012)
4. Buckley, R.H.: Some aspects of the use of photonics in large sensor manifolds. In: Proceedings 2000 IEEE International Conference on Phased Array Systems and Technology (Cat. No.00TH8510), Dana Point, CA, pp. 341–344 (2000)
5. Mingzhi, L., Gang, S., Ling, P.W.: Electron reconnaissance satellite intercepting multifunction phased array radar model. In: 2012 Second International Conference on Instrumentation, Measurement, Computer, Communication and Control, Harbin, pp. 1132–1135 (2012)
6. Guo, F., Fan, Y., Zhou, Y., Xhou, C., Li, Q.: A prospect of space electronic reconnaissance technology. In: Space Electronic Reconnaissance: Localization Theories and Methods. Wiley (2014)
7. Guo, F., Fan, Y., Zhou, Y., Xhou, C., Li, Q.: Introduction to space electronic reconnaissance geolocation. In: Space Electronic Reconnaissance: Localization Theories and Methods. Wiley (2014)
8. Cheng, S., Chen, J., Shen, L.-C., Lv, Y.: A two-level resource organization and optimization framework via optimization and agent negotiation for multi-satellite reconnaissance and surveillance system. In: 2010 the 2nd International Conference on Computer and Automation Engineering (ICCAE), Singapore, pp. 397–401 (2010)
9. Cao, F., Liu, Q.: Analysis on ability of dual-baseline interferometer to resolve angular ambiguities. Aerosp. Electron. Warfare **29**(3), 24–25 (2013). (in Chinese)
10. Lawall, J., Howard, L., Deslattes, R.D., Wu, C.-M.: Multiple interferometer for real-time position control. In: Conference on Lasers and Electro-Optics (CLEO 2000). Technical Digest. Postconference Edition. TOPS (IEEE Cat. No.00CH37088), San Francisco, CA, USA, vol. 39, p. 569 (2000)

DOA Estimation for Coherent and Incoherent Targets with Co-prime MIMO Array

Yong Jia[(✉)], Chao Yan, Chuan Chen, Bin Duo, Xiaoling Zhong, Yong Guo, and Shiying Yin

College of Information Science and Technology, Chengdu University of Technology, Chengdu, China
jiayong2014@cdut.edu.cn

Abstract. In this paper, we consider the problem of DOA estimation for a mix of incoherent and coherent targets by using the monostatic co-prime MIMO array with N sparse transmitting sensors and $2M-1$ sparse receiving sensors. The co-prime MIMO array generates a non-redundant and uniform sub sum co-array with $\mathrm{O}(MN)$ contiguous sensors using only $\mathrm{O}(M+N)$ physical sensors. Based on the concept of sum co-array equivalence, we can obtain different configurations of virtual MIMO arrays with $\mathrm{O}(MN)$ contiguous virtual sensors, and then construct the corresponding virtual data matrices, which provides different tradeoffs between the number of resolvable targets and the maximum number of mutually coherent targets that can be resolved. On the basis of the virtual data matrix and the conventional DOA estimation approaches such as MUSIC, $\mathrm{O}(MN)$ mixed coherent and incoherent targets can be resolved only with $\mathrm{O}(M+N)$ physical sensors, namely the number of resovable targets exceeds the limitation of the number of physical sensors. Finally, simulation results demonstrate the effectiveness of the proposed DOA estimation method with the monostatic co-prime MIMO array in the presence of both the coherent and incoherent targets.

Keywords: DOA estimation · Coherent and incoherent targets · Monostatic MIMO array · Co-prime array

1 Introduction

The co-prime geometry consists of a combination of two sparse uniform linear subarrays whose sensor numbers and inter-sensor spacings depend on two co-prime integers and which was presented firstly to be used in the only-receiving array, implementing DOA estimation for far-field distributed incoherent targets

Supported by National Natural Science Foundation of China under Grant 61501062, 41574136 and 41304117, and Scientific Research Foundation of the Science and Technology Department of Sichuan Province under Grant 2018GZ0454.

M. Jia et al. (Eds.): WiSATS 2019, LNICST 281, pp. 596–607, 2019.
https://doi.org/10.1007/978-3-030-19156-6_56

[2–4,8–10,13–16]. The most attracted point of the receiving co-prime array is a uniform sub-coarray in the associated difference co-array with much more contiguous co-array sensors than physical sensors and the fundamental spacing of half a wavelength, which is capable of providing a dramatic promotion in the degrees-of-freedom and hence can resolve significantly more incoherent targets than the number of physical sensors. That is because the number of the identifiable incoherent targets is determined directly by the sensor number of the difference co-array instead of the co-prime passive array [6].

However, in the case of coherent targets as encountered in multi-path propagation, the DOA estimation methods in [2–4,8–10,13–16] are not feasible because of non-zero cross correlation between two coherent targets. Based on the researches in [7,17], the active transmitting and receiving array, namely monostatic MIMO array can be used to identify a mix of coherent and incoherent targets, and the numbers of receiving sensors and transmitting sensors determine respectively the numbers of the total targets and coherent targets which can be identified. Recently, the co-prime geometry was introduced to the monostatic MIMO array with three different transmitting and receiving configurations for the active DOA estimation of coherent and incoherent targets [1,5]. Specifically, a sparse reconstruction method was proposed for the vectorized covariance matrix of the emulated sum co-array observations from the original data measurements of co-prime MIMO array. Moreover, a new scheme to implement active DOA estimation of coherent and incoherent targets was designed for the co-prime MIMO array in [11], where the DOAs of the incoherent targets were first estimated using subspace-based methods, whereas those of the coherent targets were resolved using Bayesian compressive sensing.

In this paper, we consider the most basic configuration of co-prime MIMO array, namely the first subarray is employed to transmit and the other is for receiving. Obviously, the original data matrix is unable to be used directly for the active DOA estimation because the uniform and sparse spatial sampling from the receiving subarray results in the spectrum aliasing. To address the aliasing problem, inspired by [10], we need to find a desired virtual MIMO array with the receiving inter-sensor spacing of half a wavelength which has the same sum co-array with the co-prime MIMO array. As the sum co-array determines the collected original data matrix of the co-prime array, it can be rearranged to construct the original data matrix of the virtual MIMO array named virtual data matrix which can be utilized to estimate the DOAs of the coherent and incoherent targets.

For a monostatic co-prime MIMO array including N transmitters and $2M-1$ receivers (M and N is two co-prime numbers and M is assumed to be less than N), there is a non-redundant and uniform sub sum co-array with $MN+M-1$ contiguous sensors and the spacing of half a wavelength, which makes it easy to search for a desired virtual MIMO array with the receiving inter-sensor spacing of half a wavelength. In light of $MN+M-1$ co-array sensors, the virtual MIMO array consists of $MN+M$ virtual sensors at most, which is capable of obtaining the DOAs of $O(MN)$ targets from only $O(M+N)$ physical sensors of the co-prime MIMO array. Moreover, we can get multiple different configurations of virtual MIMO arrays with the identical sum co-array, which provide different numbers of tradeoffs between the total number of the resolvable targets and the largest number of mutually coherent targets that can be identified.

2 Methodology

2.1 Signal Model of Monostatic Co-prime MIMO Array

Assume M and N are coprime numbers and M is less than N. A monostatic co-prime MIMO array is shown in Fig. 1, including N transmitters and $2M-1$ receivers whose positions are given by the set

$$\begin{aligned} P_t &= \{Mnd;\ n = 0, 1, \cdots, N-1\} \\ P_r &= \{Nmd;\ m = 1, 2, \cdots, 2M-1\} \end{aligned} \tag{1}$$

where d is a fundamental spacing defined as half one wavelength of transmitting narrowband signal to avoid spatial aliasing. It is clear that the co-prime MIMO array is subjected to uniformly sparse transmitting and sparse sampling.

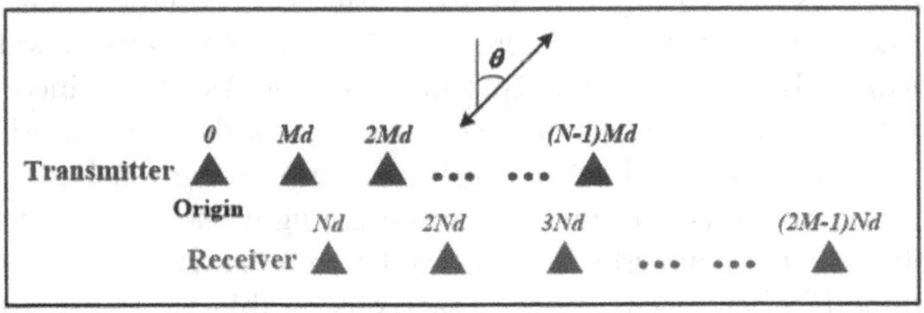

Fig. 1. Geometry of monostatic co-prime MIMO array.

Assume that a mix of targets with L incoherent targets and K coherent targets are located at far-field of the array. For simplification, the incoherent targets are ordered from 1 to L and the coherent targets are ordered from $L+1$ to $L+K$. A narrowband signal is individually transmitted by each of the N transmitters to illuminate these targets, and the reflectivity of all targets is collected by all $2M-1$ receivers to form an $(2M-1)$-by-N natural data matrix modeled as

$$\begin{aligned} \mathbf{X} &= \mathbf{S} + \mathbf{N} \\ &= \left[\sum_{k=1}^{L+K} \bar{s}_{k,n} \cdot \exp\left[jk_0 (r_m + t_n) \sin\theta_k \right] + \bar{n}_{m,n} \right]_{m,n} \\ &= \left[\sum_{k=1}^{L+K} \bar{s}_{k,n} \cdot \exp\left\{ jk_0 \left[mNd + (n-1)Md \right] \sin\theta_k \right\} + \bar{n}_{m,n} \right]_{m,n} \\ & \quad m = 1, 2, \cdots, 2M-1;\ n = 1, 2, \cdots, N \end{aligned} \tag{2}$$

where the (m,n)th entry is the complex reflectivity amplitude measured by the mth receiver when the nth transmitter is applied to illuminate. Moreover, $k_0 = 2\pi/\lambda$ is the wavenumber of the emitted narrowband signal. t_n and r_m are the positions of nth transmitter and mth receiver. θ_k is the DOA of the kth targets. The noise $\bar{n}_{m,n}$ is assumed to be zero mean, temporally and spatially white, and uncorrelated from the targets. The complex reflectivity amplitude $\bar{s}_{k,n}$ can be defined as

$$\bar{s}_{k,n} = \begin{cases} \alpha_k e^{j\beta_{k,n}}, & k = 1, 2, \cdots, L \\ \alpha_k e^{j\beta_n}, & k = L+1, L+2, \cdots, L+K \end{cases} \tag{3}$$

where α_k is a constant complex amplitude and $\beta_{k,n}$ is a random phase for L incoherent targets and N illuminations. However, the random phase β_n is common to all K coherent targets on the nth illumination.

In this case, we express the correlation of target reflectivity as follows.

$$E\left[\bar{s}_{k,n}\bar{s}^*_{k',n'}\right] = \begin{cases} \alpha_k\alpha^*_{k'}E\left[e^{j(\beta_n-\beta_{n'})}\right], & (k, k' = L+1, L+2, \cdots, L+K \\ \alpha_k^2 E\left[e^{j(\beta_{k,n}-\beta_{k,n'})}\right], & (k, k' = 1, 2, \cdots, L \text{ and } k = k') \\ 0, & \text{(otherwise)} \end{cases} \tag{4}$$

In this paper, we consider a simplified scene where the reflectivity of each target is completely coherent during N transmissions, namely $E\left[e^{j(\beta_n-\beta_{n'})}\right] = 1$ and $E\left[e^{j(\beta_{k,n}-\beta_{k,n'})}\right] = 1$.

2.2 Sum Coarray of Co-prime MIMO Array

Based on the $(2M-1)$-by-N natural data matrix of the co-prime MIMO array, we can obtain an $(2M-1)$-by-$(2M-1)$ covariance matrix, but which cannot be used to resolve the targets due to the spectrum aliasing caused by the sparse sampling.

Clearly, the phases of the original data in (2) are determined by the sum of the transceiver positions, namely the sensor position of the sum co-array of the co-prime MIMO array. That is to say, the original data matrix is dependent on the sum co-array directly. Herein, we can search for a desired virtual MIMO array whose sum co-array is identical to that of the co-prime MIMO array, and then construct the associated virtual data matrix by rearranging the original data matrix. Finally, we can use the virtual data matrix to estimate the DOAs.

In order to search for a desired virtual MIMO array being sum-coarray equivalent with the co-prime MIMO array, we first need to exploit the characteristic of the sum co-array of the co-prime MIMO array. The sum co-array of the co-prime array in Fig. 1 is given by Fig. 2.

Due to the co-prime relationship, each transceiver pair forms a unique sensor of the sum co-array. In other words, the co-prime MIMO array is non-redundant from the point of view of the sum co-array. More interesting is that as shown in Fig. 2, the sum co-array can be divided into three sub-coarrays, namely two non-uniform sub-coarrays and a uniform sub-coarray with the fundamental inter-sensor spacing of d. For the uniform sub-coarray, $MN+M-1$ sensors are located

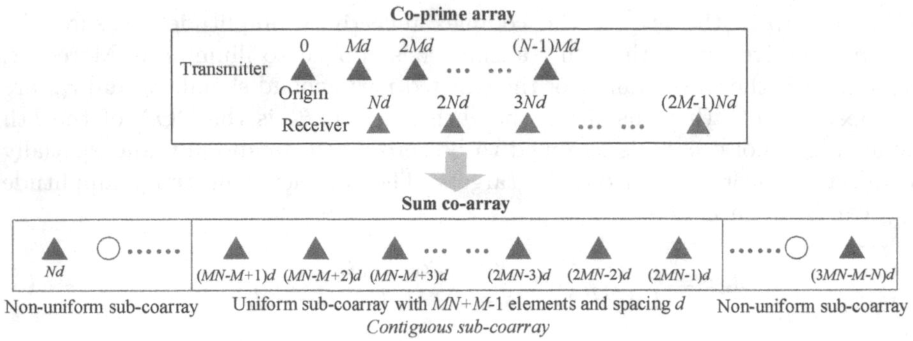

Fig. 2. Geometry of sum co-array of the monostatic co-prime MIMO array.

contiguously from the position $(MN-M+1)d$ to $(2MN-1)d$ with the spacing of d. Therefore, we refer to the uniform sub-coarray with the fundamental inter-sensor spacing as the contiguous sub-coarray as well.

2.3 Searching for Virtual MIMO Array

First the contiguous sub-coarray with $MN+M-1$ sensors and spacing d is chosen as the reference sum co-array due to the convenience in determining a desired virtual MIMO array with the receiver spacing of d avoiding the problem of spectrum aliasing.

The locations of $MN+M-1$ contiguous sensors can be written as the set

$$P_c = \{(MN-M+q)\,d;\ q=1,2,\cdots,MN+M-1\} \tag{5}$$

Assume a desired virtual MIMO array with A transmitters and B receivers is given by

$$\begin{aligned} P_{v,t} &= \{(x_t+\alpha_i i)\,d;\ i=1,2,\cdots,A\} \\ P_{v,r} &= \{(x_r+j)\,d;\ j=1,2,\cdots,B\} \end{aligned} \tag{6}$$

where the spacing of receiving array is fundamental spacing d to avoid spectrum aliasing, while the transmitter spacing is a variable positive integer α_i times d.

The virtual MIMO array is narrowly sum co-array equivalent with the co-prime MIMO array if

$$\begin{aligned} & x_t+\alpha_i i+x_r+j = MN-M+Q, \\ & \forall i\in[1,2,\cdots,A],\ j\in[1,2,\cdots,B],\ Q\in[1,2,\cdots,MN+M-1] \end{aligned} \tag{7}$$

Therefore, the sum co-array of the virtual MIMO array is identical to the contiguous sub-coarray of the co-prime MIMO array.

In order to use the definition of sum co-array equivalence, the numbers of virtual transmitters and receivers should be determined firstly by the number of targets to be identified. This is based on the point that there must be at least as many transmitters as coherent targets and the numbers of receivers must be less than the total number of incoherent and coherent targets. For example, for M_1 targets with M_2 coherent targets ($M_1 \geq M_2$), the virtual MIMO array has to consist of at least M_2 transmitters and M_1 receivers. Then a desired virtual MIMO array can be acquired readily.

Now we give a special example of finding the virtual MIMO array under the condition of $\alpha_i = 1$ and sum coarray equivalence. In this case, a virtual MIMO array including the maximum sensors can be obtained, meaning the maximum number of identifiable targets. The virtual MIMO array can be found by solving the simple optimization problem

$$\begin{cases} x_t + A + x_r + B = 2MN - 1 \\ x_t = b \end{cases} \quad \text{subject to } A + B = MN + M \tag{8}$$

where b can be set as an arbitrary integer. As a result, the positions of the virtual transmit/receive sensors can be expressed as

$$\begin{aligned} P'_{v,t} &= \{(b+i)\, d;\ i = 1, 2, \cdots, MN + M - B\} \\ P'_{v,r} &= \{(MN - M - b - 1 + j)\, d;\ j = 1, 2, \cdots, B\} \end{aligned} \tag{9}$$

As A and B are variables, we can obtain multiple virtual MIMO arrays with different numbers of transmitters and receivers, achieving great flexibility to select a desired virtual MIMO array to satisfy the identification for a different numbers of targets.

2.4 Construction of Virtual Data Matrix

For each desired virtual MIMO array, the virtual data matrix can be constructed by rearranging the original data matrix of the co-prime MIMO array through the following two steps.

First, $MN + M - 1$ distinct data units corresponding to the uniform sub-coarray are extracted from the original data matrix to constitute co-array data vector as

$$\begin{aligned} X_c &= \left[x_{c1}, x_{c2}, \cdots, x_{c(MN+M-1)}\right]^T \\ &= \left[\sum_{k=1}^{L+K} \bar{s}_k \cdot \exp\{jk_0(MN - M + q)d \sin\theta_k\} + \bar{n}_q\right]_q^T \\ & q = 1, 2, \cdots, MN + M - 1 \end{aligned} \tag{10}$$

which is identical to the standard model for passive array processing, with sensors located on the $MN + M - 1$ positions of contiguous sub-coarray.

Then one or multiple sensor positions of the virtual data matrix are filled with the corresponding sensor of the co-array data vector. These sensors are coupled with the same sum co-array position. After repeating this operation for all other sensors, a filled virtual data matrix is obtained. For example, the B-by-$(MN + M - B)$ virtual data matrix of the virtual MIMO array in (10) is constructed as

$$\begin{aligned}\mathbf{X}_v &= [X_c(1), X_c(2), \cdots, X_c(MN+M-B)] \\ &= \left[x_{ck}, x_{c(1+k)}, \cdots, x_{c(B-1+k)}\right]_k^T, \\ k &= 1, 2, \cdots, MN+M-B\end{aligned} \tag{11}$$

2.5 Calculation of MUSIC Spectrum

From a desired B-by-A virtual data matrix, we can obtain a B-by-B virtual covariance matrix, which has been proved to be of the same rank with the number of targets when the number of receivers is more than the number of targets and the transmitters is at least as many as the coherent targets.

Consequently, the MUSIC approach in [12] is performed on the virtual covariance to acquire the DOA spectrum lines of the incoherent and coherent targets, given by

$$CP_{music} = \frac{1}{\bar{v}(\theta)^H \mathbf{U_N} \mathbf{U_N^H} \bar{v}(\theta)} \tag{12}$$

where $\mathbf{U_N}$ is noise subspace composed of the eigenvectors from eigenvalue decomposition of virtual data matrix, and $\bar{v}(\theta) = [1, e^{j\pi \sin\theta}, e^{j2\pi \sin\theta}, \cdots, e^{j(B-1)\pi \sin\theta}]^T$ is the same with the manifold vector of uniform linear receiver array with B sensors. As a result, the DOA spectrum lines of at most B-1 targets including A coherent targets are acquired in the case of $A < B$, while B-1 targets weather coherent or incoherent can be identified at most as $A \geq B$. Considering A and B are associated with the $MN + M - 1$ coarray sensors, in other words, we can estimate the DOAs of $O(MN)$ targets based on the co-prime MIMO array only including $O(M + N)$ physical sensors.

It is worthy that in the case of $A \geq B$, the number of total resolvable coherent and incoherent targets is $B - 1$ that is less than A. That is to say, the A degree-of-freedom for coherent targets is not utilized completely. Therefore, in the searching for a desired virtual MIMO array, the number of virtual transmitters is demanded to be less than the number of virtual receivers in general, making the total degree-of-freedom from the virtual transceivers serve for the DOA estimation of coherent and incoherent targets.

3 MATLAB Simulation Results and Analyses

A monostatic co-prime MIMO array with $N = 4$ transmitters and $2M - 1 = 5$ receivers is chosen in the MATLAB simulations as shown in the subfigure (a) of Fig. 3. For simplification, the fundamental spacing d of half one wavelength is set up as 1. White Gaussian noise with 10 dB signal-to-noise ratio (SNR) and 2000 snapshots is applied for the array noise and the covariance estimation. A 5-by-4 original data matrix is generated and then a 5-by-5 covariance matrix can be calculated to perform MUSIC directly. As shown in Fig. 4, the problem of spectrum aliasing appears in the direct MUSIC spectrum due to the sparse

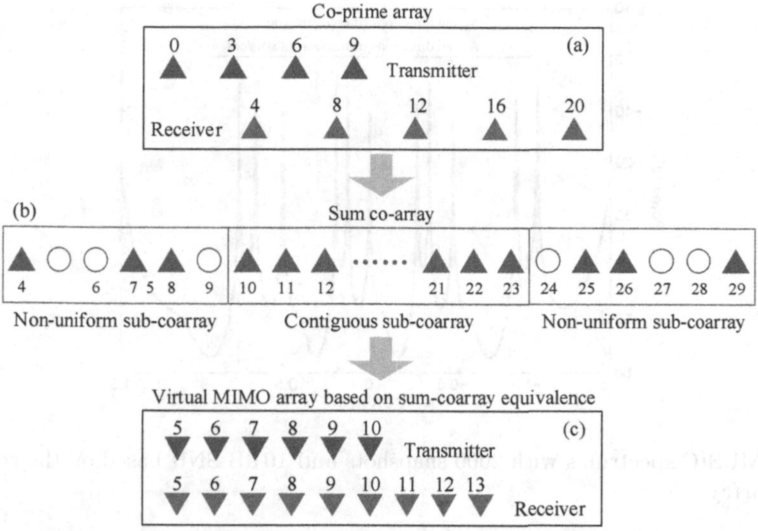

Fig. 3. Geometries of co-prime MIMO array with $M = 3$ and $N = 4$, the corresponding sum co-array and virtual MIMO array based on sum co-array equivalence.

sampling of 2 times one wavelength, which makes it impossible to identify the deployed 4 four targets including 3 coherent targets.

For this co-prime MIMO array, as shown in the subfigure (b) of Fig. 3, a contiguous sub sum co-array is composed of 14 sensors located from $MN - M + 1 = 10$ to $2MN - 1 = 23$ with the inter-sensor spacing of half one wavelength. Therefore, based on the defined sum co-array equivalence, we seek out a virtual MIMO array shown in the subfigure (c) of Fig. 3, consisting of 6 transmitters at [5, 6, 7, 8, 9, 10] and 9 receivers at [5, 6, 7, 8, 9, 10, 11, 12, 13]. Accordingly, 9-by-6 virtual data matrix and 9-by-9 virtual covariance matrix are acquired. Thus 8 targets with 6 coherent targets can be identified at most. As shown in Fig. 5, the spectrum aliasing is disappeared due to the sampling space of half one wavelength. Under the conditions of 10 dB SNR and 2000 snapshots, 8 targets including 6 coherent targets are identified accurately in Fig. 5. Obviously, the numbers of identifiable coherent targets and all targets exceed the number limitations of physical transmitting and receiving sensors respectively.

Finally, we evaluate the flexibility of DOA estimation by searching for different configurations of virtual MIMO array based on the sum co-array equivalence. Figure 6 reveals another two virtual MIMO arrays whose sum co-arrays are the same with the contiguous sub sum co-array. On the one hand, the virtual MIMO array 3 consists of the most seven transmitters when the transmitter number is smaller than the receiver number, which means the maximum identifiable coherent targets. In this case, all seven coherent targets without incoherent targets

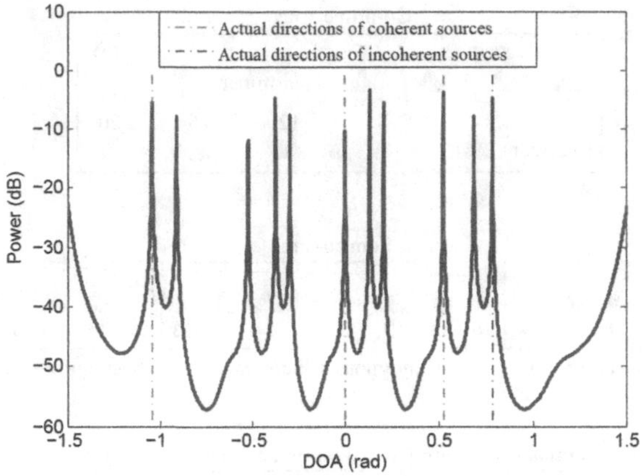

Fig. 4. MUSIC spectrums with 2000 snapshots and 10 dB SNR based on the co-prime MIMO array.

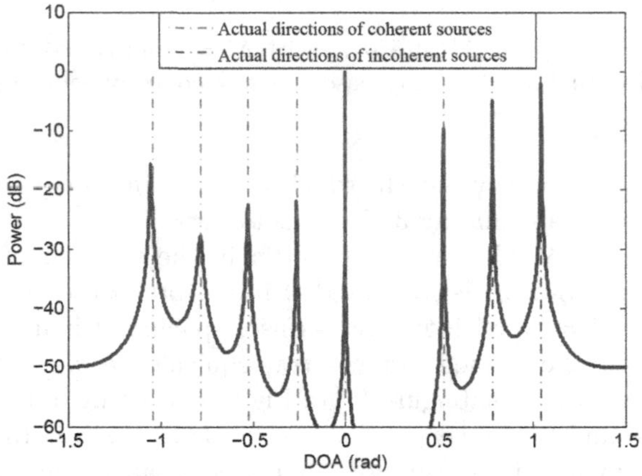

Fig. 5. MUSIC spectrums with 2000 snapshots and 10 dB SNR based on the virtual MIMO array with sum co-array equivalence.

can be resolved as shown in Fig. 7(a). On the other hand, the virtual MIMO array 4 only has two transmitters which can be used to estimate two coherent targets. In other words, the number of resolvable coherent targets reaches the lower limit. However, the most thirteen receivers brings about the maximum resolvable number of twelve for the total of coherent and incoherent targets. Figure 7(b) demonstrates twelve targets with two coherent targets are identified successfully.

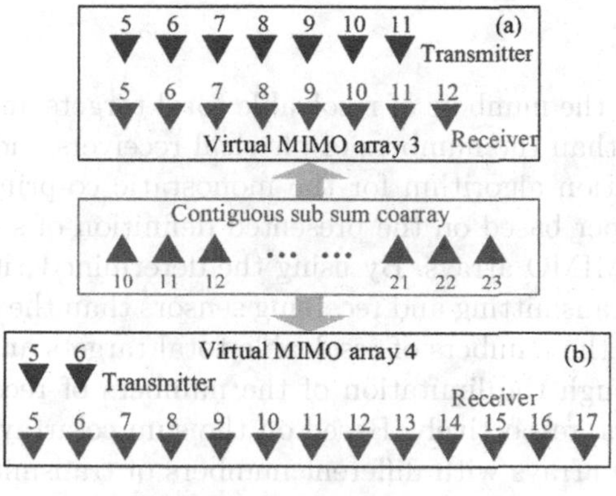

Fig. 6. Geometries of two virtual MIMO arrays based on sum co-array equivalence.

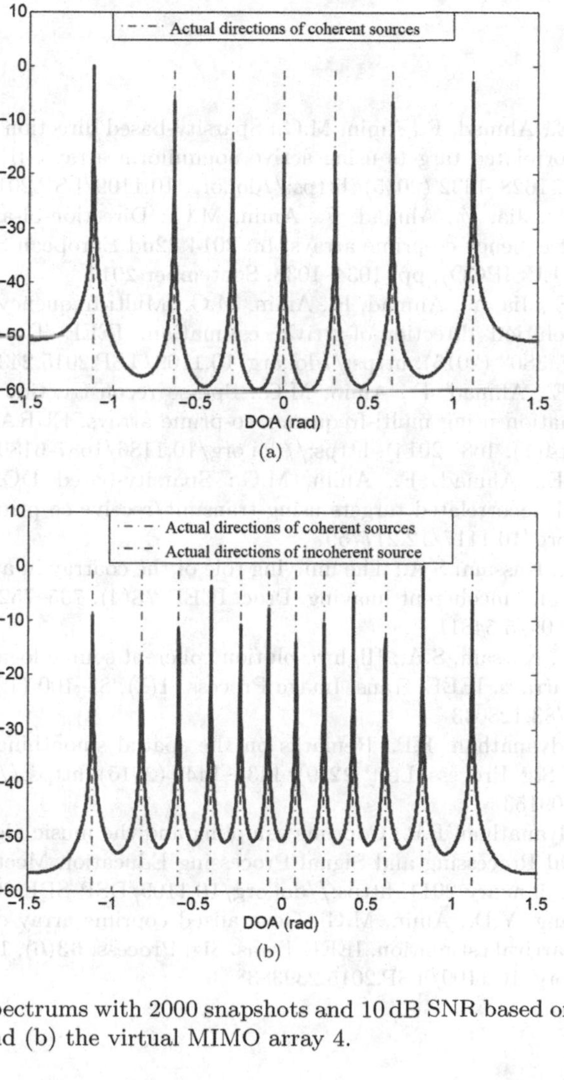

Fig. 7. MUSIC spectrums with 2000 snapshots and 10 dB SNR based on (a) the virtual MIMO array 3 and (b) the virtual MIMO array 4.

4 Conclusion

In order to increase the numbers of resolvable total targets and therein coherent targets to be more than the numbers of physical receivers and transmitters, the active DOA estimation algorithm for the monostatic co-prime MIMO array is designed in this paper based on the presented definition of sum co-array equivalence and virtual MIMO arrays. By using the determined virtual MIMO array with more virtual transmitting and receiving sensors than the physical sensors in the co-prime array, the numbers of resolvable total targets and therein coherent targets breaks through the limitation of the numbers of receiving sensors and transmitting sensors, respectively. Based on the sum co-array equivalence, multiple virtual MIMO arrays with different numbers of transmitters and receivers can be obtained. Therefore, a desired virtual MIMO array can be selected flexibly to meet one specific demand of target identification.

References

1. BouDaher, E., Ahmad, F., Amin, M.G.: Sparsity-based direction finding of coherent and uncorrelated targets using active nonuniform arrays. IEEE Sig. Process. Lett. **22**(10), 1628–1632 (2015). https://doi.org/10.1109/LSP.2015.2417807
2. BouDaher, E., Jia, Y., Ahmad, F., Amin, M.G.: Direction-of-arrival estimation using multi-frequency co-prime arrays. In: 2014 22nd European Signal Processing Conference (EUSIPCO), pp. 1034–1038, September 2014
3. BouDaher, E., Jia, Y., Ahmad, F., Amin, M.G.: Multi-frequency co-prime arrays for high-resolution direction-of-arrival estimation. IEEE Trans. Sig. Process. **63**(14), 3797–3808 (2015). https://doi.org/10.1109/TSP.2015.2432734
4. BouDaher, E., Ahmad, F., Amin, M.G.: Sparse reconstruction for direction-of-arrival estimation using multi-frequency co-prime arrays. EURASIP J. Adv. Sig. Process. **2014**(1), 168 (2014). https://doi.org/10.1186/1687-6180-2014-168
5. BouDaher, E., Ahmad, F., Amin, M.G.: Sparsity-based DOA estimation of coherent and uncorrelated targets using transmit/receive co-prime arrays (2015). https://doi.org/10.1117/12.2177597
6. Hoctor, R.T., Kassam, S.A.: The unifying role of the coarray in aperture synthesis for coherent and incoherent imaging. Proc. IEEE **78**(4), 735–752 (1990). https://doi.org/10.1109/5.54811
7. Hoctor, R.T., Kassam, S.A.: High resolution coherent source location using transmit/receive arrays. IEEE Trans. Image Process. **1**(1), 88–100 (1992). https://doi.org/10.1109/83.128033
8. Liu, C., Vaidyanathan, P.P.: Remarks on the spatial smoothing step in coarray music. IEEE Sig. Process. Lett. **22**(9), 1438–1442 (2015). https://doi.org/10.1109/LSP.2015.2409153
9. Pal, P., Vaidyanathan, P.P.: Coprime sampling and the music algorithm. In: 2011 Digital Signal Processing and Signal Processing Education Meeting (DSP/SPE), pp. 289–294, January 2011. https://doi.org/10.1109/DSP-SPE.2011.5739227
10. Qin, S., Zhang, Y.D., Amin, M.G.: Generalized coprime array configurations for direction-of-arrival estimation. IEEE Trans. Sig. Process. **63**(6), 1377–1390 (2015). https://doi.org/10.1109/TSP.2015.2393838

11. Qin, S., Zhang, Y.D., Amin, M.G.: Doa estimation of mixed coherent and uncorrelated targets exploiting coprime mimo radar. Digit. Sig. Process. **61**, 26–34 (2017). https://doi.org/10.1016/j.dsp.2016.06.006. Special Issue on Coprime Sampling and Arrays
12. Schmidt, R.: Multiple emitter location and signal parameter estimation. IEEE Trans. Antennas Propag. **34**(3), 276–280 (1986). https://doi.org/10.1109/TAP.1986.1143830
13. Tan, Z., Eldar, Y.C., Nehorai, A.: Direction of arrival estimation using co-prime arrays: a super resolution viewpoint. IEEE Trans. Sig. Process. **62**(21), 5565–5576 (2014). https://doi.org/10.1109/TSP.2014.2354316
14. Vaidyanathan, P.P., Pal, P.: Sparse sensing with coprime arrays. In: 2010 Conference Record of the Forty Fourth Asilomar Conference on Signals, Systems and Computers, pp. 1405–1409, November 2010. https://doi.org/10.1109/ACSSC.2010.5757766
15. Vaidyanathan, P.P., Pal, P.: Sparse sensing with co-prime samplers and arrays. IEEE Trans. Sig. Process. **59**(2), 573–586 (2011). https://doi.org/10.1109/TSP.2010.2089682
16. Vaidyanathan, P.P., Pal, P.: Theory of sparse coprime sensing in multiple dimensions. IEEE Trans. Sig. Process. **59**(8), 3592–3608 (2011). https://doi.org/10.1109/TSP.2011.2135348
17. Wang, X., Wang, W., Liu, J., Li, X., Wang, J.: A sparse representation scheme for angle estimation in monostatic mimo radar. Signal Processing **104**, 258–263 (2014). https://doi.org/10.1016/j.sigpro.2014.04.007

DOA Estimation for Coherent and Incoherent Sources Based on Co-prime Array

Yong Jia(✉), Zehua Li, Chao Yan, Bin Duo, Xiaoling Zhong, Yong Guo, and Shiying Yin

College of Information Science and Technology, Chengdu University of Technology, Chengdu, China
jiayong2014@cdut.edu.cn

Abstract. In this paper, a DOA estimation method based on co-prime array is proposed to resolve the coherent and incoherent hybrid sources. Firstly, with respect to the difference co-array of co-prime array, the desired units with corresponding contiguous intervals in the correlation matrix are extracted and rearranged into an augmented correlation matrix. Then we decorrelate the augmented correlation matrix by reconstructing matrix algorithm, forward spatial smoothing and forward-backward spatial smoothing algorithm. Finally, through MUSIC spatial spectrum searching on the basic of the decorrelated correlation matrix, DOA estimation towards sources is obtained. The simulation results show that the proposed method can achieve DOA estimation of the coherent and incoherent hybrid sources with more number than physical array. Through comparison, it can be concluded that the reconstructing matrix algorithm obtains a larger number of distinguishable sources and the error performance of which is better under low SNR. However, the spatial smoothing algorithms have a better estimation error performance in the case of low snapshot.

Keywords: DOA estimation · Co-prime array · Coherent and incoherent sources · Difference co-array

1 Introduction

Direction-of-arrival (DOA) estimation is one of the main part of the array signal processing area, which is widely used in mobile communications, radar, sonar detection, wireless navigation and so on. Uniform linear array (ULA) is adopted by traditional DOA estimation algorithms in general, such as the multiple signal

Supported by National Natural Science Foundation of China under Grant 61501062, 41574136 and 41304117, Scientific Research Foundation of the Science and Technology Department of Sichuan Province under Grant 2018GZ0454, and Student Innovation Entrepreneurship Training Program of SiChuan Province under Grant DCXM089.

M. Jia et al. (Eds.): WiSATS 2019, LNICST 281, pp. 608–619, 2019.
https://doi.org/10.1007/978-3-030-19156-6_57

classification (MUSIC) algorithm [11]. However, the number of resolvable sources is limited by the number of physical elements. Therefore, sparse arrays are been introduced, such as co-prime array [9], nested array [8], minimum redundancy array [7].

Most of the existing DOA estimation algorithms based on co-prime array are against incoherent sources from the point of view of difference co-array [1–6, 9, 10, 12–14]. For example, making use of the one-to-one correspondence between the position of co-array elements and the correlative intervals, the units of correlation matrix are vectorized to be an equivalent single snapshot coherent signal. By spatial smoothing, spatial spectrum of incoherent DOA is obtained [9, 10, 14]. Because of the larger number of elements in difference co-array than the physical elements in co-prime array, the number of resolvable sources can be broken through the limit of physical elements of co-prime array. However, these kind of algorithms are only flexible in dealing with incoherent sources, which is invalid for coherent sources owing to the non-zero cross correlation between two coherent sources.

In this paper, we propose an algorithm to estimate coherent and incoherent sources based on co-prime array. Firstly, with respect to the difference co-array of co-prime array, we extract the corresponding units from the correlation matrix to form an augmented correlation matrix. Then the decorrelation is performed on the augmented correlation matrix by using spatial smoothing method and reconstructing matrix method. Finally, through MUSIC spatial spectrum searching on the decorrelated correlation matrix, DOA estimation towards a mix of scattered sources is implemented. The simulation results show that the proposed algorithm can estimate the coherent and incoherent sources whose number is larger than physical arrays. Furthermore, we compare the performance of reconstructing matrix method, forward spatial smoothing method, and forward and backward spatial smoothing method under the condition of eliminating coherence. The results demonstrate that reconstructing matrix method archives a larger number of DOA estimation, and the error performance of which is better under low signal-to-noise ratio (SNR). Nevertheless, the spatial smoothing algorithm has a better estimation error performance in the case of low snapshot.

2 Signal Model with Coherent and Incoherent Sources for Co-prime Array

A co-prime array consists of two sparse physical arrays as depicted in Fig. 1, where one having N sensors positioned at $\{Mnd_0,\ 0 \leq n \leq N-1\}$, and the other comprising M sensors with positions $\{Nmd_0,\ 0 \leq m \leq 2M-1\}$, M and N being co-prime integers and d_0 being the interval of two adjacent elements and equal to one-half wavelength.

Based on the model of co-prime array above, assume that a mix of scattered sources with L incoherent sources and K coherent sources are located at far field of the array. For simplification, the incoherent sources are ordered from 1 to L and the coherent sources are ordered from $L+1$ to $L+K$. The power of

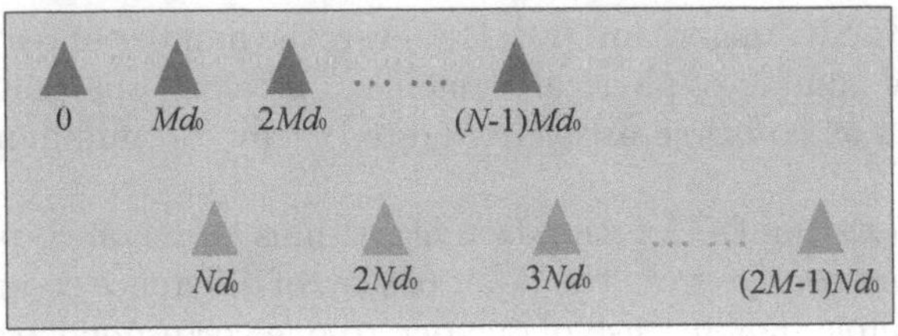

Fig. 1. The model of co-prime array.

$L+K$ sources are $\sigma_1^2(w_0), \sigma_2^2(w_0), \cdots, \sigma_L^2(w_0), \cdots \sigma_{L+K}^2(w_0)$ with directions $[\theta_1, \theta_2, \cdots \theta_L, \cdots \theta_{L+K}]$. Assuming that the sources are uncorrelated and the noise is spatially and temporally white. The power of noise is $\sigma_n^2(w_0)$. Assume that the sources and noise are independent. The received data vector at frequency w_0 can be expressed as

$$X(w_0) = A(w_0) S(w_0) + N(w_0) \tag{1}$$

where $S(w_0) = [s_1(w_0), s_2(w_0), \cdots s_L(w_0), \cdots s_{L+\mathrm{K}}(w_0)]^T$ is the source signal vector at w_0, $N(w_0)$ is the corresponding noise vector, $A(w_0)$ is the array manifold matrix at w_0, and the superscript $(\cdot)^T$ denotes matrix transpose. The $(i,j)\,th$ unit of the manifold matrix can be expressed as

$$[A(w_0)]_{i,j} = e^{jk_0 x_i \sin(\theta_j)}, i = 1, 2, \cdots, N+2M-1; j = 1, 2, \cdots, L, \ldots L+K \tag{2}$$

where x_i is the location of the ith physical sensor of the array, θ_j is the DOA of the jth source, and $k_0 = w_0/c$ is the wavenumber at w_0 with c being the speed of propagation in free space.

3 DOA Estimation for Coherent and Incoherent Sources

3.1 Calculation of Correlation Matrix

According to (1), the correlation matrix with $L+K$ sources is as follows

$$R_{\mathrm{xx}} = E\left\{X(w_0) X^H(w_0)\right\} \tag{3}$$

where the superscript $(\cdot)^H$ denotes Hermitian operation, and $E\{\cdot\}$ denotes the statistical expectation operator. In practice, (3) is replaced by sample averaging.

Here, the cross-correlation coefficient is defined as

$$\rho_{mn} = E\left\{s_m(w_0) s_n^*(w_0)\right\}, L+1 \le m, n \le L+K, m \ne n \tag{4}$$

Based on (2) and (4), the units with correlative interval p in correlation matrix can be expressed as

$$r(p) = \sum_{l=1}^{L+K} \sigma_l^2 e^{jk_0 p d_0 \sin(\theta_l)} + \sum_{m=L+1}^{L+K} \sum_{n=L+1}^{L+K} \rho_{mn} e^{jk_0(x_i \sin(\theta_m) - x_{i'} \sin(\theta_n))} + \sigma_n^2 \delta(p) \tag{5}$$

where pd_0 is the position difference of two physical array sensors located at x_i and $x_{i'}$. This indicates that the phase of desired first terms in correlation units for DOA estimation are uniquely determined by the positions of difference co-array. The second cross-terms between two coherent sources in correlation units are regarded as interferences which will be removed by the subsequent decorrelation operation.

3.2 The Model of Difference Co-array

The difference co-array of the co-prime array in Fig. 1 is shown in Fig. 2. The element positions of the difference co-array form the set as

$$S(w_0) = \{\pm (Mnd_0 - Nmd_0)\}, 0 \le n \le N-1, 0 \le m \le 2M-1 \quad (6)$$

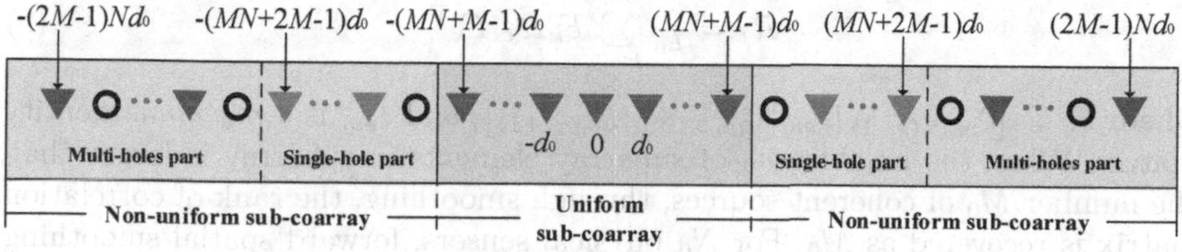

Fig. 2. The model of difference co-array.

As shown in Fig. 2, we can see that the difference co-array extends from $-N(2M-1)d_0$ to $N(2M-1)d_0$ and has a contiguous set of elements between $-(MN+M-1)d_0$ and $(MN+M-1)d_0$ with the inter-element spacing of d_0. The other positions of difference co-array are discontinuous and have holes.

3.3 Correlation Matrix Augmentation

As for the continuous elements from $-(MN+M-1)d_0$ to $(MN+M-1)d_0$ in difference co-array, the correlation units with corresponding correlative interval $-(MN+M-1)$ to $(MN+M-1)$ are extracted from correlation matrix to form a vector as

$$[r(-MN-M+1), r(-MN-M+2), \cdots, r(MN+M-1)] \quad (7)$$

Then these correlation units in (7) are rearranged into an $(MN+M) \times (MN+M)$ augmented correlation matrix as

$$R_{xx} = \begin{pmatrix} r(0) & r(1) & \cdots & r(MN+M-1) \\ r(-1) & r(0) & \cdots & r(MN+M-2) \\ \vdots & \vdots & \ddots & \vdots \\ r(-MN-M+1) & r(-MN-M+2) & \cdots & r(0) \end{pmatrix} \quad (8)$$

Obviously, the augmented correlation matrix is equivalent to that of a uniform array with $MN+M$ physical elements and inter-element spacing of d_0.

3.4 Decorrelation of Augmented Correlation Matrix

In the case of existing coherent sources, the augmented correlation matrix R_{xx} suffers from the phenomenon of rank defect, which attributes to the failure of DOA estimation with eigenvalue decomposition, such as MUSIC algorithm. The key to solve the rank defect is to perform decorrelation about the augmented correlation matrix. The general decorrelation algorithms include spatial smoothing algorithm and reconstructing matrix algorithm.

Forward spatial smoothing algorithm is an effective algorithm to decorrelate coherence of sources. The main method of which is to divide the uniform linear physical array of N_0 elements into L_0 interlaced subarrays where the number of elements in each subarray is $m_0 = N_0 - L_0 + 1$. Therefore, the decorrelation can be realized by averaging the correlation matrices of all subarrays, and then a $m_0 \times m_0$ smoothed correlation matrix can be expressed as

$$R_f = \frac{1}{L_0} \sum_{k=1}^{L_0} F_k R_{\mathrm{xx}} F_k{}^T \tag{9}$$

where $F_k = \left[0_{m_0 \times (k-1)} \left| I_{m_0} \right| 0_{m_0 \times (N_0 - k - m_0 + 1)}\right]$, and I_{m_0} is a $m_0 \times m_0$ identity matrix. When the number m_0 of subarray elements in subarray is larger than the number M_0 of coherent sources, through smoothing, the rank of correlation matrix is recovered as M_0. For N_0 physical sensors, forward spatial smoothing algorithm can achieve the decorrelation of $N_0/2$ coherent sources. The principle of backward spatial smoothing algorithm is similar to that of forward spatial smoothing. The distinction is that the dividing of physical array starting from the last element.

At the basis of rotation invariance of ULA, the forward and backward spatial smoothing algorithm deal with the correlation matrix by forward smoothing and backward smoothing at the same time. The smoothed correlation matrix is formed as

$$R_{fb} = \frac{1}{2L_0} \sum_{k=1}^{L_0} F_k \left(R_{\mathrm{xx}} + J R_{\mathrm{xx}}^* J\right) F_k^T \tag{10}$$

where J is permutation matrix with dimension N_0, whose value of units in back-diagonal is 1 and others are 0. For N_0 physical elements, forward and backward spatial smoothing algorithm can achieve a decorrelation of $3N_0/2$ coherent sources.

The decorrelating coherence of spatial smoothing algorithm is on the premise of sacrificing the degrees-of-freedom of DOA estimation, namely the reduction of resolvable sources. The reconstructing matrix algorithm is a better choice to guarantee the degrees-of-freedom and decorrelation at the same time.

Based on the reconstructing matrix algorithm, the correlation units in (7) can also be rearranged into another $(MN+M) \times (MN+M)$ augmented correlation matrix as

$$R_{Toeplitz} = \begin{pmatrix} r(0) & r(1) & \cdots & r(MN+M-1) \\ 0 & r(0) & \cdots & r(MN+M-2) \\ \vdots & \vdots & \ddots & \vdots \\ 0 & 0 & \cdots & r(0) \end{pmatrix} \tag{11}$$

The reconstructed correlation matrix $R_{Toeplitz}$ is an upper triangular matrix which is a full rank matrix regardless of the relativity among sources. Then the matrix $R_{Toeplitz}$ is processed as

$$R'_{Toeplitz} = J_M R^*_{Toeplitz} J_M \tag{12}$$

where J_M is a $(MN + M) \times (MN + M)$ permutation matrix just as J in (10). Finally, the desired correlation matrix is generated by $R'_{xx} = (R_{Toeplitz} + R'_{Toeplitz})/2$, which can be used to realize DOA estimation of at most $MN+M-1$ coherent sources more than physical elements of co-prime array.

3.5 Utilizing the Holes

The DOA estimation algorithm above based on difference co-array of co-prime array utilizes only the contiguous co-array elements, abandoning all the discontinuous ones, namely the degrees-of-freedom is $MN + M - 1$. This unexploited discontinuous co-array elements mean the loss of degrees-of-freedom. In order to make the best of all degrees-of-freedom from the difference co-array, the correlation units corresponding to these holes in co-array can be regarded as with zero. In this case, the dimension of reconstructed correlation matrix R'_{xx} can be extended from $MN + M$ to $(2M - 1)N + 1$. Therefore, the degrees-of-freedom of DOA estimation is raised to $(2M - 1)N$. In other words, at most $(2M - 1)N$ sources can be resolved.

4 Simulation and Performance Analysis

4.1 Simulation of DOA Estimation

Based on Fig. 1, a co-prime array with $M = 2$ and $N = 3$, including $2M+N-1 = 6$ physical sensors is applied in the simulation. The inter-element spacing of d_0 is set as 1. The element positions of two sub-array is $\{0, 2, 4\}$ and $\{3, 6, 9\}$, respectively. Furthermore, based on (6), the contiguous elements in difference co-array is from $-(MN+M-1) = -7$ to $MN+M-1 = 7$. Through reconstructing matrix algorithm, a reconstructed correlation matrix of 8×8 is obtained. Based on MUSIC algorithm, 7 coherent sources can be estimated at most. A mix of 3 coherent and 4 incoherent sources are simulated with a total of 2000 snapshots and SNR of 0 dB. The result of DOA estimation is shown in Fig. 3. The vertical dashed and dotted lines in the figure indicate the true DOAs of the sources of coherent and incoherent sources. As expected, the DOAs of all 7 sources are accurately estimated.

For further study, all elements of difference co-array including discontinuous elements from $-(2M-1)N = -9$ to $(2M-1)N = 9$ are utilized by filling the correlation units corresponding to the hole in $-(MN+M) = -8$ and $MN+M = 8$ with 0. Under the condition of 2000 snapshots and 0 dB SNR, Fig. 4 provides the DOA estimation result of 4 coherent and 5 incoherent sources. Obviously, all 9 sources are resolved accurately, which demonstrates the improvement of

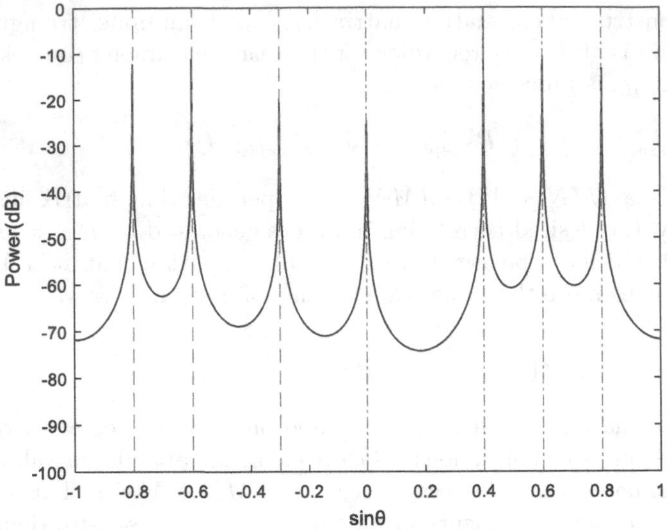

Fig. 3. DOA estimation of 3 coherent sources and 4 incoherent sources.

resolvable sources by using these discontinuous co-array elements. Considering the worst condition that all the sources are coherent, the following simulations are performed to compare the performance of forward spatial smoothing algorithm, forward and backward spatial smoothing algorithm and reconstructing matrix algorithm in maximum number of DOA estimation. More specifically, three groups of simulations are carried out under the conditions of 3, 4 and 5 coherent sources, respectively. Besides, only the contiguous co-array elements are considered in the following simulations. The simulation results are given in Figs. 5, 6 and 7, where the vertical lines indicate the true DOAs.

It can be seen from Figs. 5 and 6 that reconstructing matrix and spatial smoothing algorithm can both estimate the sources correctly. As shown in Fig. 7, when the number of coherent sources increases to 5, forward spatial smoothing algorithm has lost efficacy. Furthermore, in the case of 7 coherent sources, only the reconstructing matrix algorithm still stays correct estimation, which means the superiority in resolvable ability of reconstructing matrix algorithm (Fig. 8).

4.2 Performance Analysis

In this section, the error performance comparison of three decorrelation algorithms is provided by 500 Monte Carlo trials on the basis of 4 coherent sources. The root-mean-square error (RMSE) of DOA estimation for 4 coherent sources is calculated as

$$RMSE = \frac{1}{4}\sum_{k=1}^{4}\sqrt{\frac{1}{500}\sum_{j=1}^{500}\left(\hat{\theta}_{jk} - \theta_k\right)^2} \tag{13}$$

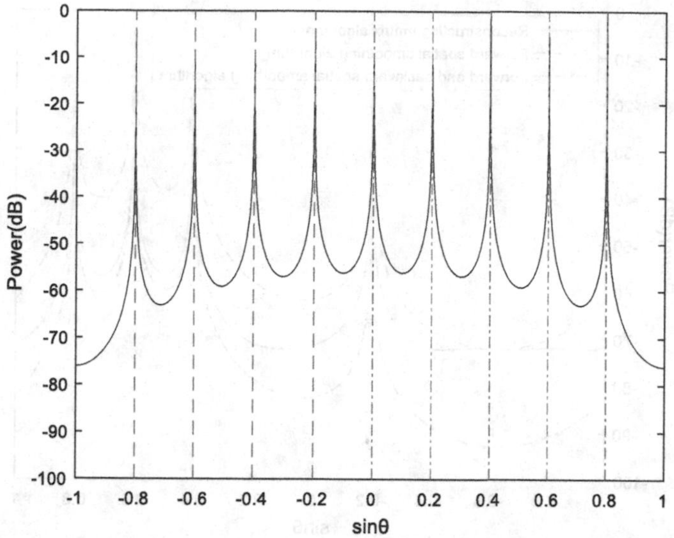

Fig. 4. DOA estimation of 4 coherent sources and 5 incoherent sources.

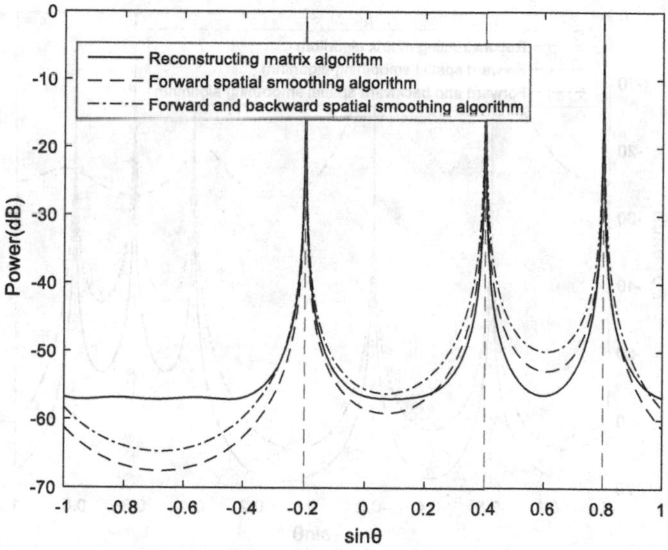

Fig. 5. DOA estimation of three algorithms under 3 coherent sources.

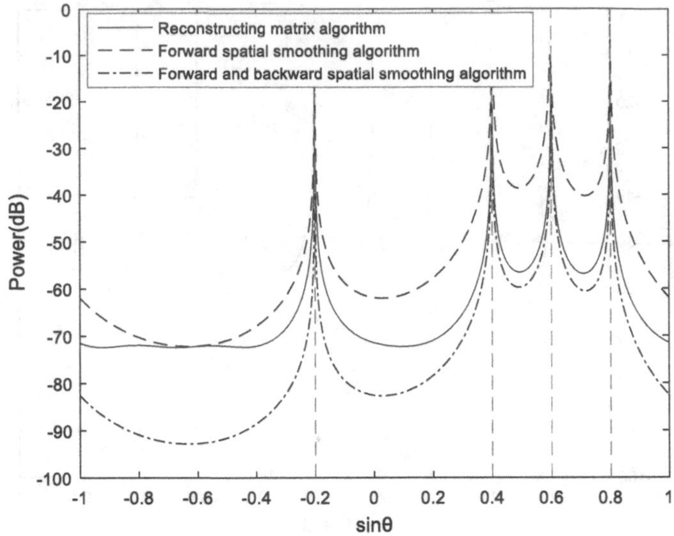

Fig. 6. DOA estimation of three algorithms under 4 coherent sources.

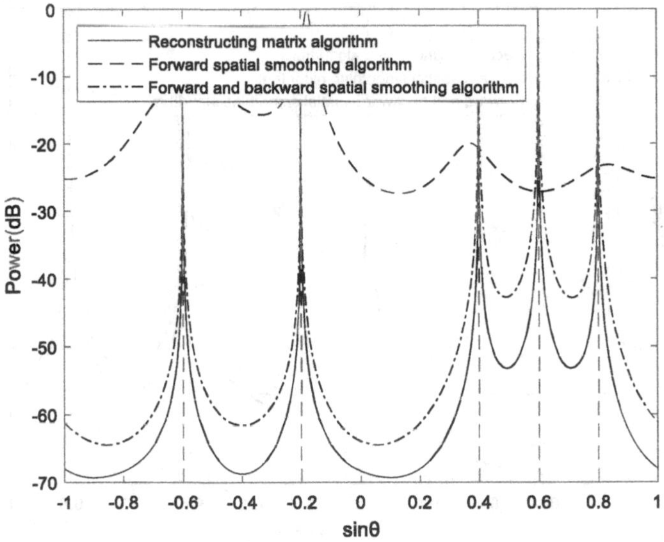

Fig. 7. DOA estimation of three algorithms under 5 coherent sources.

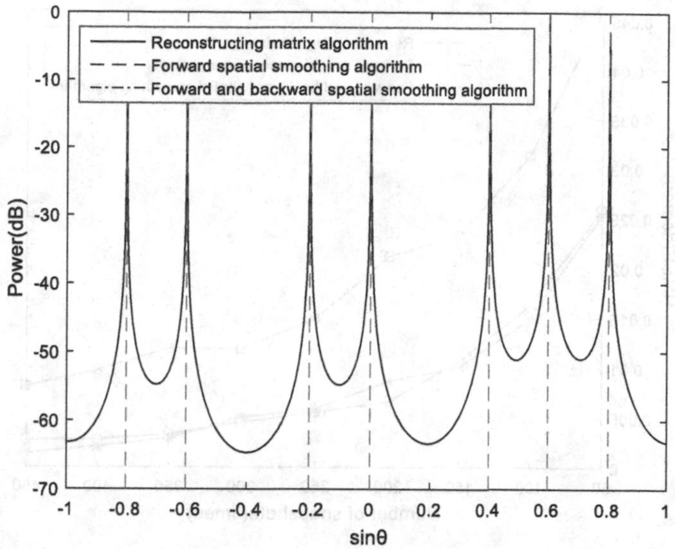

Fig. 8. DOA estimation of three algorithms under 7 coherent sources.

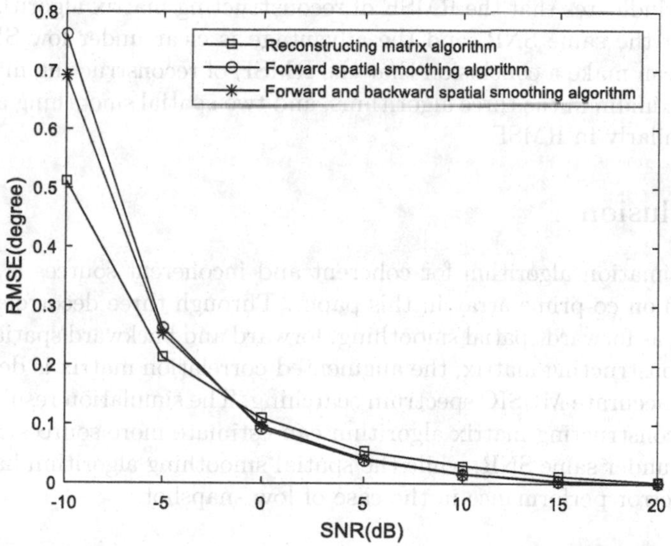

Fig. 9. Performance of three algorithms under different SNRs.

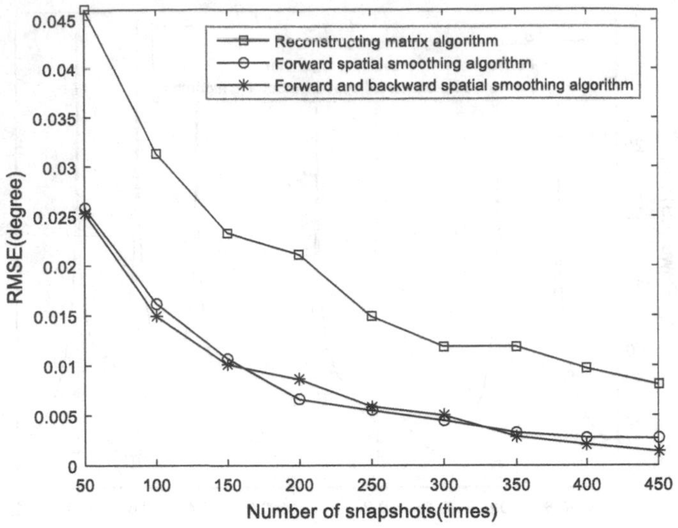

Fig. 10. Performance of three algorithms under different numbers of snapshots.

where θ_k is the true DOA and $\hat{\theta}_j k$ is the estimated DOA.

Figure 9 indicates that the RMSE of reconstructing matrix algorithm is minimum under the same SNR, and the advantage is clear under low SNR. From Fig. 10, we can make a conclusion that the RMSE of reconstructing matrix algorithm is maximum in the three algorithms, and two spatial smoothing algorithms perform similarly in RMSE.

5 Conclusion

A DOA estimation algorithm for coherent and incoherent sources is been proposed based on co-prime array in this paper. Through three decorrelation algorithms such as forward spatial smoothing, forward and backward spatial smoothing and reconstructing matrix, the augmented correlation matrix is decorrelated to serve for accurate MUSIC spectrum searching. The simulation results indicate that the reconstructing matrix algorithm can estimate more sources and have a lower error under same SNR, while the spatial smoothing algorithm has a better estimation error performance in the case of low snapshot.

References

1. BouDaher, E., Ahmad, F., Amin, M.: Sparse reconstruction for direction-of-arrival estimation using multi-frequency co-prime arrays. EURASIP J. Adv. Sig. Process **168**, 1–11 (2014)
2. BouDaher, E., Jia, Y., Ahmad, F., Amin, M.G.: Multi-frequency co-prime arrays for high-resolution direction-of-arrival estimation. IEEE Trans. Sig. Process. **63**(14), 3797–3808 (2015)

3. Boudaher, E., Jia, Y., Ahmad, F., Amin, M.G.: Direction-of-arrival estimation using multi-frequency co-prime arrays. In: 22nd European Signal Processing Conference, pp. 1034–1038 (2014)
4. Bush, D., Xiang, N.: Broadband implementation of coprime linear microphone arrays for direction of arrival estimation. J. Acoust. Soc. Am. **138**(1), 447–456 (2015)
5. Bush, D.R., Xiang, N., Summers, J.E.: Experimental investigations on coprime microphone arrays for direction-of-arrival estimation. J. Acoust. Soc. Am. **136**(4), 2214 (2014)
6. Liu, C.L., Vaidyanathan, P.P.: Remarks on the spatial smoothing step in coarray music. IEEE Sig. Process. Lett. **22**(9), 1438–1442 (2015)
7. Moffet, A.: Minimum-redundancy linear arrays. IEEE Trans. Antennas Propag. **16**(2), 172–175 (1968)
8. Pal, P., Vaidyanathan, P.P.: Nested arrays: a novel approach to array processing with enhanced degrees of freedom. IEEE Trans. Sig. Process. **58**(8), 4167–4181 (2010)
9. Pal, P., Vaidyanathan, P.P.: Coprime sampling and the music algorithm. In: 2011 Digital Signal Processing and Signal Processing Education Meeting, pp. 289–294 (2011)
10. Qin, S., Zhang, Y.D., Amin, M.G.: Generalized coprime array configurations for direction-of-arrival estimation. IEEE Trans. Sig. Process. **63**(6), 1377–1390 (2015)
11. Schmidt, R.O.: Multiple emitter location and signal parameter estimation. IEEE Trans. Antennas Propag. **34**(3), 276–280 (1986)
12. Shen, Q., Liu, W., Cui, W., Wu, S., Zhang, Y.D., Amin, M.G.: Low-complexity direction-of-arrival estimation based on wideband co-prime arrays. IEEE/ACM Trans. Audio Speech Lang. Process. **23**(9), 1445–1453 (2015)
13. Tan, Z., Eldar, Y.C., Nehorai, A.: Direction of arrival estimation using co-prime arrays: a super resolution viewpoint. IEEE Trans. Sign. Process. **62**(21), 5565–5576 (2014)
14. Vaidyanathan, P.P., Pal, P.: Sparse sensing with co-prime samplers and arrays. IEEE Trans. Sig. Process. **59**(2), 573–586 (2011)

Through-the-Wall Radar Imaging Based on Deep Learning

Kaimin Wang[1], Jiang Qian[1,2(✉)], Shaoyin Huang[1], Yong Wang[1,3,4], Xiaobo Yang[2], and Bin Duo[5]

[1] School of Resources and Environment, UESTC, Chengdu 611731, Sichuan, China
jqian@uestc.edu.cn

[2] School of Information and Communication Engineering, UESTC, Chengdu 611731, Sichuan, China

[3] Department of Geography, Planning, and Environment, East Carolina University, Greenville, NC 27858, USA

[4] Institute of Remote Sensing Big Data, Big Data Research Center, UESTC, Chengdu 611731, Sichuan, China

[5] College of Information Science and Technology, Chengdu University of Technology, Chengdu, China

Abstract. High resolution image can be obtained with backprojection (BP) algorithm, but at the same time, significant grating lobes will be brought in radar image and reduce the quality of image. This paper presents a through-the-wall radar (TWR) imaging method based on deep learning to improve the quality of radar image. A convolutional neural network was designed for TWR imaging, the radar image can be obtained as the output of neural network. The simulation and real data experiments demonstrate the effectiveness of proposed method.

Keywords: Through-the-wall radar imaging · Convolutional neural network (CNN)

1 Introduction

To obtain high range and azimuth resolutions, the backprojection (BP) algorithm is employed to through-the -wall radar imaging. However, the process of energy integration will bring in grating lobes. Significant grating lobes may increase false alarms or even submerge the weak target near a strong target [4], and may effect the later process, such as target detection and identification. Thus, it is necessary to propose a new radar imaging method. Deep learning has been successfully employed to tackle several image tasks such as target detection

This work was supported in part by the National Natural Science Foundation of China under Grant 61401077 and the China Postdoctoral Science Foundation under Grant 2015M580784. This work was also supported by Sichuan Science and Technology Program under Grant 2019YFG0099.

M. Jia et al. (Eds.): WiSATS 2019, LNICST 281, pp. 620–627, 2019.
https://doi.org/10.1007/978-3-030-19156-6_58

and show better performance than traditional methods. In radar imaging community, the complex valued convolutional neural network (CCNN) has achieved a good result in enhancing radar imaging [2]. Neural network can learn features of images from training data, then it will optimize weights to be adaptive to training data. Finally, a trained model is obtained after many iterations, and can be employed to solve specific problem. In order to solve the problem of through-the-wall radar imaging performance, a new imaging method is proposed. Firstly, through-the-wall radar signal model and BP algorithm are analyzed, then we can generate training data via the signal model. Secondly, neural network are designed for through wall radar imaging. Finally, the trained neural network can be employed to obtain a better image than the image generated by BP algorithm. Simulation and real experimental results show that grating lobes are suppressed and the quality of image is improved.

2 Signal Model and BP Algorithm

2.1 Signal Model

For through wall radar, we analyze the signal model with one transmitter and N receivers. The position of antennas can be found in Fig. 1, where T is transmitter and Ri ($i = 1, 2, \ldots, N$) is receivers.

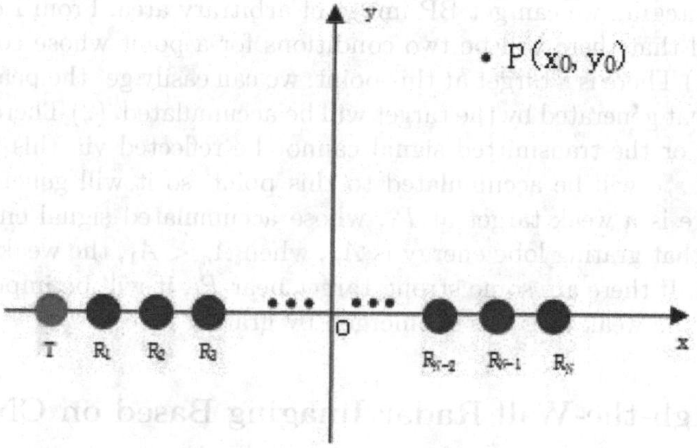

Fig. 1. Geometry of the scenario.

For through-the-wall radar, the transmitted signal can be expressed as follows:

$$s(t) = a(t) \exp(j2\pi f_c t) \tag{1}$$

where $a(t)$ is the waveform of transmitted signal, t is fast time, and f_c denotes carrier frequency. The echo signal can be written as

$$s_r(t_m, t) = a(t - t_m) \exp[j2\pi f_c (t - t_m)] \tag{2}$$

where t_m is the delay of transmitted signal and echo signal that can be written as follow

$$t_m = \frac{\sqrt{(x_0-x_m)^2-(y_0-y_m)^2}-\sqrt{(x_0-x_t)^2-(y_0-y_t)^2}}{c} \tag{3}$$

where (x_0, y_0) is coordinate of arbitrary point's, (x_m, y_m) is the mth $(m = 1, 2, \ldots, N)$ receiver's coordinate, and (x_m, y_m) is the transmitter's coordinate.

2.2 BP Algorithm

Before employ BP algorithm, demodulation and range compression should be done. For different transmitted signal, there are different methods to complete this process. For example, we can use a matched filtering implement range compression of linear frequency modulated (LFM) signal by operation of convolution. After range compression, we get the time domain signal as follows [3]

$$s_{rc}(t_m, t) = sinc\left[B\left(t - t_m\right)\right] \exp\left(-j2\pi f_c t_m\right) \tag{4}$$

where B is the bandwidth of transmitted signal. Then, the range compression signal can be projected onto Cartesian grids to form a through wall radar image which can be given by following integral [1,5]

$$I\left(x_0, y_0\right) = \int s_{rc}\left(t_m, t\right)|_{t=t_m} \exp\left(j2\pi f_c t_m\right) dt_m \tag{5}$$

Via BP integral, we can get BP image of arbitrary area. From Eqs. 4 and 5, we can found that there will be two conditions for a point whose coordinate is $P_1(x_1, y_1)$: (1) There is a target at this point, we can easily get the peak energy of echo signal that generated by the target will be accumulated. (2) There is nothing at this point or the transmitted signal cannot be reflected via this point, then side lobes of $s_r c$ will be accumulated to this point, so it will generate grating lobes. If there is a weak target at P_1, whose accumulated signal energy is A_1, and assume that grating lobe energy is A_n, when $A_n < A_1$, the weak target will be defocused. If there are some strong target near P_1, it will be impossible that $A_n > A_1$, so the weak target is submerged by grating lobes.

3 Through-the-Wall Radar Imaging Based on CNN

In order to get through-the-wall radar image with high performance, we design a CNN to enhance imaging. The network structure can be found in Fig. 2.

First, the echo signal data input into the network, to get an initial image, we designed a fully connected layer which is achieved by BP algorithm. After getting a BP image, the absolute value image of BP image input into the next layer.

For generation of training data, we can define the expected target function as [2]:

$$O(x, y) = p(x, y) * |o(x, y)| \tag{6}$$

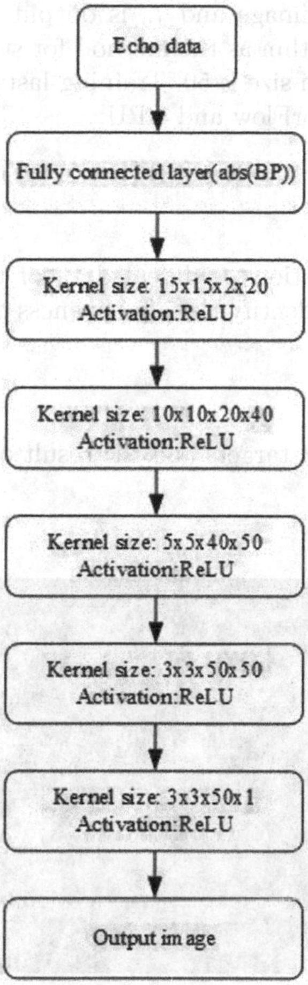

Fig. 2. Network structure.

where "*" represents operation of convolution, $o(x, y)$ is the scattering coefficients of target and $p(x, y)$ is ideal point spread function (PSF), which can be written as

$$p(x, y) = \exp\left(-\frac{x^2}{\sigma_x^2} - \frac{y^2}{\sigma_y^2}\right) \tag{7}$$

where σ_x, σ_y control the width of $p(x, y)$. To get high resolution image, the values of them are 0.012, 0.012 respectively.

We generate 10000 sets of reference images which include 4 12 points of random coordinates (x, y) within a square area by 6 and $o(x, y) = 1$. Then generate corresponding echo data as training data. The loss function is defined as:

$$E = \sum (O - f_o)^2 \tag{8}$$

where O denotes reference image and f_o is output image of neural networks. We employ the Adam algorithm as the method for stochastic optimization. The learning rate is 10e−4, batch size is 50. Training lasts for 10 epochs. Our implementation is based on TensorFlow and CPU.

4 Experiments

In this section, both simulations and real data of through-the-wall radar are presented and analyzed to identify the effectiveness of the proposed methods.

4.1 Simulation

For simulation data, we set 4 targets and the result of BP imaging can be found in Fig. 3.

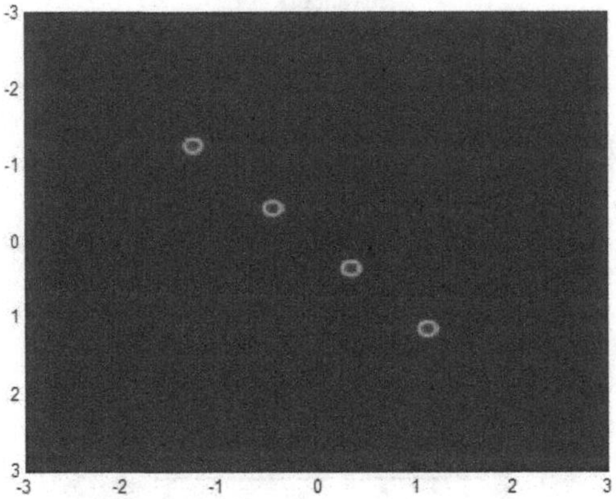

Fig. 3. The result of BP imaging.

From Fig. 3, we found that the energy focus on the positions we set. Nevertheless the grating lobes degrade the quality of image. Near the target position, grating lobes energy cannot be ignored. When training neural network, the reference image is shown in Fig. 4.

It is clear that in the reference image the energy only focuses on the target position. During the training phase, the neural network will refine the weight matrix which can make, the output image close to this reference image. After training, the output image of neural network is presented in Fig. 5.

It is shown that the image quality of the output image is improved comparing to the BP image. The energy of grating lobes is decreased, and the energy focuses on the target.

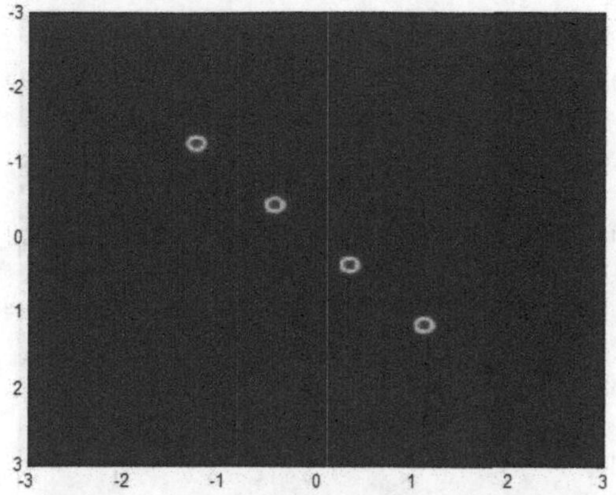

Fig. 4. Reference image.

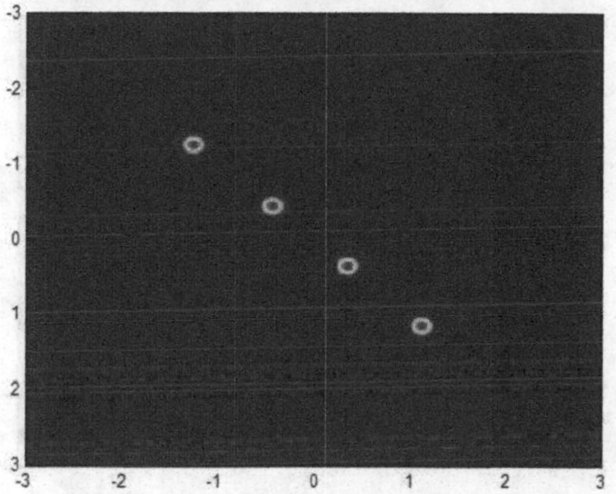

Fig. 5. The output image of neural network.

4.2 Real Data Experiment

The experiment scenario is a target behind wall and the radar antennas are placed at the another side. The BP image is shown in Fig. 6.

The quality of BP image is not good because of grating lobes. After putting echo data into the neural networks, we obtain the output image shown in Fig. 7.

The image quality has been improved significantly comparing to BP image, it is useful for following work such as target detection and identification.

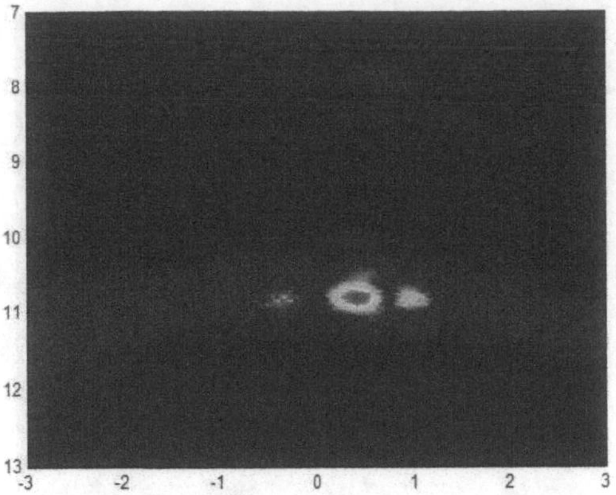

Fig. 6. BP image of real data.

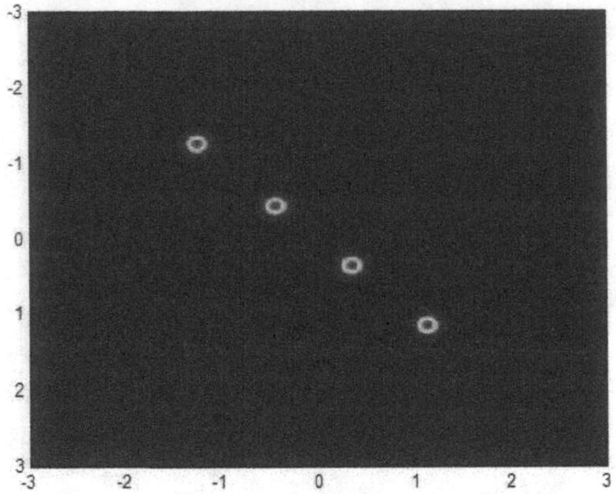

Fig. 7. The output image of neural network of real data.

5 Conclusion

A novel and effective neural network based through-the-wall radar imaging algorithm is proposed. Radar signal model and BP imaging algorithm are analyzed firstly. Then combining with CNN, we design the structure of neural networks. Finally, we obtain quality improved radar image with CNN. We believe neural network will bring more benefits to radar imaging in the future.

References

1. Desai, M.D., Jenkins, W.K.: Convolution backprojection image reconstruction for spotlight mode synthetic aperture radar. IEEE Trans. Image Process. **1**(4), 505–517 (1992). https://doi.org/10.1109/83.199920
2. Gao, J., Deng, B., Qin, Y., Wang, H., Li, X.: Enhanced radar imaging using a complex-valued convolutional neural network. IEEE Geosci. Remote Sens. Lett. **16**(1), 35–39 (2019). https://doi.org/10.1109/LGRS.2018.2866567
3. Huang, C., Qian, J., Wang, Y., Jia, Y.: Coherent integration with backprojected images for near field moving target. In: 2016 IEEE Radar Conference, RadarConf, pp. 1–4, May 2016. https://doi.org/10.1109/RADAR.2016.7485211
4. Song, Y., Zhu, J., Hu, J., Jin, T., Zhou, Z.: Grating lobes suppression for ultra-wideband MIMO radar imaging. In: 2017 3rd IEEE International Conference on Computer and Communications, ICCC, pp. 957–961, December 2017. https://doi.org/10.1109/CompComm.2017.8322685
5. Zhou, S., Yang, L., Zhao, L., Bi, G.: Quasi-polar-based FFBP algorithm for miniature UAV SAR imaging without navigational data. IEEE Trans. Geosci. Remote Sens. **55**(12), 7053–7065 (2017). https://doi.org/10.1109/TGRS.2017.2739133

A High Precision Indoor Cooperative Localization Scheme Based on UWB Signals

Guofu Yong, Zhuoran Cai(✉), and Hao Dong

Shandong Institute of Space Electronic Technology, Yantai 264670, China
yong.guofu@163.com, qingdaogancai@126.com, donghao00513@163.com

Abstract. High precision localization is a kind of promising technology in industry and everyday life. In this paper, ultra-wide band (UWB) signals are employed to make use of its high time resolution to obtain high precision ranging results. In dense multipath indoor environment, an entropy based first path detection is proposed to take advantage of the essential features of noise and UWB signals. Furthermore, when the number of anchor nodes is less than three, some of the indoor users are employed as auxiliary anchor nodes to obtain high precision localization result. The lease square error method is employed to get the localization result. Simulation results show that the entropy based first path detection algorithm can get the ranging result in a high accuracy. Besides, when there are not enough anchor nodes, the proposed cooperative localization scheme can help localization with high precision.

Keywords: Entropy · First path detection · Ultra-wide band (UWB) · Cooperative localization

1 Introduction

Indoor environment is beyond the coverage of GPS. Due to the high-temporal resolution and good obstacle-penetration capabilities of ultra-wide band (UWB) signals, UWB technique has the capability of high precision ranging, which makes it a strong enabler for indoor localization applications [1]. Therefore, UWB is seen as the potential technique for high-definition situation-aware applications such as equipment and personnel tracking, control of home appliances and a large set of emerging wireless sensor networks applications.

For UWB signals, time of arrival (TOA) based ranging can take full advantage of its large bandwidth and time-delay resolution [3]. However, in dense multipath indoor environments, there exists non-line-of-sight (NLOS) conditions [2]. In this case, the first path is not always the strongest path. Thus it is difficult to detect the TOA of first path. This phenomenon severely degrades the ranging and localization performances.

M. Jia et al. (Eds.): WiSATS 2019, LNICST 281, pp. 628–636, 2019.
https://doi.org/10.1007/978-3-030-19156-6_59

To address this problem, many approaches were proposed to obtain high accuracy first path detection results, such as maximum energy selection (MES), MES searching-back (MES-SB), coherent detection and some threshold-crossing-based methods (TC) [4]. In MES methods, the received signal block with the maximum energy is considered as the firs path. Thus the accuracy of first path detection mainly bases on the length of block. Furthermore, there is a delay between the first path and the path with maximum energy in NLOS conditions, which results in a biased estimation. In TC methods, the energy block which first exceeds the threshold is regarded as the first path. Therefore, the key of TC methods is to set a appropriate threshold. Besides, the mathematical models of ranging was also analyzed to improve the accuracy [5]. These methods depends on prior information. High computational complexity also makes them hard to deploy in real time applications. In recent years, information theory based approaches were proposed to exploit the difference of entropy of random noise and known UWB ranging pulse [6,7]. These approaches can achieve high precision even in NLOS conditions.

In this paper, due to the difference of entropy of random noise and known UWB ranging pulse, an entropy based first path detection method is analyzed to obtain high accuracy ranging results. Besides, when the number of anchor nodes is not sufficient, some of the indoor users with known location are employed as auxiliary anchor nodes. In this way, sufficient reference nodes are available to achieve high precision localization results. Simulation results show that the proposed approach has high localization precision.

The rest of the paper is organized as follows. Section 2 presents the signal model of indoor UWB systems. The cooperative localization framework is introduced in Sect. 3, simulations and discussions are given in Sect. 4. Finally the paper is concluded in Sect. 5.

2 Signal Model of Indoor UWB System

The most often used UWB pulse signal is Gaussian pulse waveform and its derivatives in various orders. For example, the second order derivative of Gaussian pulse can be written as

$$s(t) = \left(1 - 4\pi \left(\frac{t - t_d}{\tau_m}\right)^2\right) \exp\left(-2\pi \left(\frac{t - t_d}{\tau_m}\right)\right), \tag{1}$$

where t_d is the pulse center and τ_m is the pulse shape parameter.

In this paper, we consider the high precision localization application of UWB systems in indoor environments. Therefore, channel model of CM1 and CM2 in IEEE 802.15.4a are considered, which are LOS of indoor residential (7–20 m) and NLOS of indoor residential (7–20 m), respectively. The channel model described in IEEE 802.15.4a is a modified classical Saleh-Valenzuela model, in which the paths of UWB signals arrive in clusters. the channel impulse response of this kind of multi-path multi-cluster UWB channel can be expressed as

$$h(t) = \sum_{l=0}^{L}\sum_{k=0}^{K} \alpha_{k,l} \exp{(j\phi_{k,l})}\delta(t-T_l-\tau_{k,l}), \tag{2}$$

where $\alpha_{k,l}$ is the gain factor of kth multipath component in the lth cluster. T_l is the time delay of lth cluster, $\tau_{k,l}$ is the time delay of kth multipath component in the lth cluster. $\phi_{k,l}$ denotes the signal phase of kth multipath component in the lth cluster, which is uniformly distributed in $[0, 2\pi)$. L and K are the number of clusters and paths, respectively.

For given transmitted signal waveform $s(t)$ and the channel impulse response $h(t)$, the received signal can be expressed as

$$\begin{aligned} r(t) &= s(t) * h(t) + n(t) \\ &= \sum_{l=0}^{L}\sum_{k=0}^{K} \alpha_{k,l} \exp{(j\phi_{k,l})} s(t-T_l-\tau_{k,l}) + n(t), \end{aligned} \tag{3}$$

where $n(t)$ is the additive white Gaussian noise (AWGN).

3 Indoor Cooperative Localization Framework

3.1 Cooperative Localization Model

Consider a UWB-based indoor localization system, which adopts the round-trip time-of-flight (RTOF) measurement for ranging. We assume M stationary anchor nodes with known locations and N indoor users with localization requirements in an indoor region. In this system, indoor users sends a certain UWB pulse waveform to the anchors nodes, each anchor node responses with a UWB pulse signal. Then the indoor user can calculate the distances from these anchor nodes. Thereby, the position of indoor user can be calculated. The system is shown in Fig. 1.

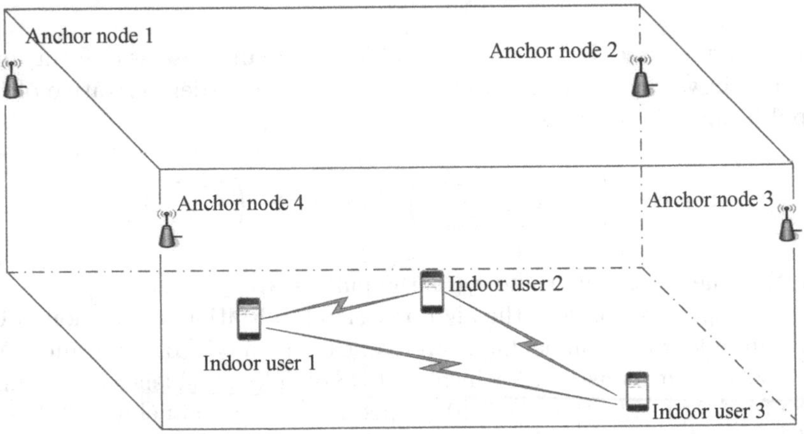

Fig. 1. Illustration of the indoor localization system (4 anchor nodes and 3 indoor users).

However, due to long distance or severe blockage, the communication link between indoor user and the anchor nodes can not always be established effectively. In an indoor localization system show by Fig. 1, if indoor user 3 can not get the response pulse from some of the anchor node (e.g., anchor node 1 and 4 can not received the ranging request from indoor user 3), then only 2 anchor node are employed to locate indoor user 3. In a three-dimension environment, at least 3 anchor nodes are required to get the position of an indoor user. Therefore, a cooperative localization scheme is proposed to locate the indoor user when the number of anchor nodes is not sufficient. Firstly, indoor user 1 and user 2 can get their position by employing the 4 anchor nodes. Then indoor user 3 can send a ranging request to user 1 and user 2 to get the distance between them. In this way, indoor user 1 and user 2 are employed as auxiliary anchor nodes. At last, 5 anchor nodes are available to get the position of indoor user 3.

3.2 Entropy Based TOA Estimation for UWB Ranging

To obtain the position of indoor users, the first step is to estimate the distances between indoor user and these anchor nodes. An entropy based TOA estimation method is proposed to get these distances. The essential difference of noise and UWB signals can be effectively reflected by the entropy. As is known, AWGN is a kind of random signals at the receiver, whereas UWB pulse waveform is a known signal. Therefore, the first path (FP) at the receiver can be precisely estimated by detecting the dramatic decreasing of entropy of the received signals. The procedure of entropy based TOA estimation is shown in Fig. 2.

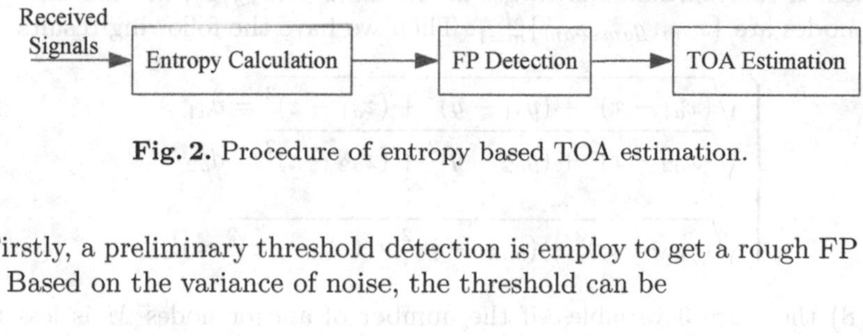

Fig. 2. Procedure of entropy based TOA estimation.

Firstly, a preliminary threshold detection is employ to get a rough FP detection. Based on the variance of noise, the threshold can be

$$\eta = \alpha\sigma, \tag{4}$$

where σ and α denote the standard deviation of noise and the constant factor for threshold adjustment, respectively.

Then, the received signals can be expressed as $\mathbf{R}$, the size of $\mathbf{R}$ is $N \times K$, where N is the number of frames of the received signal, K is the number of samples per frame. Thus $\mathbf{R_{n,k}}$ is the kth sample of nth frame. By preliminary threshold detection, the following result can be obtained

$$\mathbf{U}_{n,k} = \begin{cases} 1 & if \quad \mathbf{R}_{n,k} > \eta \\ 0 & else \end{cases}. \tag{5}$$

where $\mathbf{U}$ is a matrix with the same size of $\mathbf{R}$.

For the kth sample, the sample before the kth index in all frames is regarded as a new sequence, and the subset $\mathbf{\Phi}_k = \{l_n\}$ can expressed as

$$l_n = \arg\max_m m\,, \qquad (6)$$
$$s.t. \quad (a) \quad \mathbf{U}_{n,m} = 1;$$
$$(b) \quad m < k.$$

Then, we get the subsets $\mathbf{\Phi}_k$ of the received signals. We let e_i be the ith non-repetitive element in $\mathbf{\Phi}_k$. Therefore, the entropy is given by

$$E_k = -\sum_{i=1}^{I} (p_i/K) \log_b (p_i/K), \qquad (7)$$

where p_i denotes the occurrence frequency of e_i.

In the view of information theory, the largest entropy will be achieved when all non-repetitive elements occur with the same frequency, namely, random distribution. However, for the desired signals, the corresponding entropies are relatively small, because these samples exceed threshold in most cases. In this way, the distances between nodes in this network can be obtained.

3.3 Cooperative Localization

Based on the obtained ranging results, the position of target indoor user can be estimated. If the coordinate of target indoor user is (x, y, z), the coordinates of anchor nodes are $\{x_{am}, y_{am}, z_{am}\}_{m=1}^{M}$. Then we have the following results

$$\begin{cases} \sqrt{(x_{a1}-x)^2+(y_{a1}-y)^2+(z_{a1}-z)^2} = d_{a1} \\ \sqrt{(x_{a2}-x)^2+(y_{a2}-y)^2+(z_{a2}-z)^2} = d_{a2} \\ \cdots \\ \sqrt{(x_{aM}-x)^2+(y_{aM}-y)^2+(z_{aM}-z)^2} = d_{aM} \end{cases} . \qquad (8)$$

In (8) there are 3 variables, if the number of anchor nodes M is less than 3, the position of target user can not be estimated precisely. Therefore, in this paper some of the indoor users are employed as auxiliary anchor nodes, their coordinates are $\{x_{un}, y_{un}, z_{un}\}_{n=1}^{N-1}$, then we have

$$\begin{cases} \sqrt{(x_{u1}-x)^2+(y_{u1}-y)^2+(z_{u1}-z)^2} = d_{u1} \\ \sqrt{(x_{u2}-x)^2+(y_{u2}-y)^2+(z_{u2}-z)^2} = d_{u2} \\ \cdots \\ \sqrt{(x_{u(N-1)}-x)^2+(y_{u(N-1)}-y)^2+(z_{u(N-1)}-z)^2} = d_{u(N-1)} \end{cases} . \qquad (9)$$

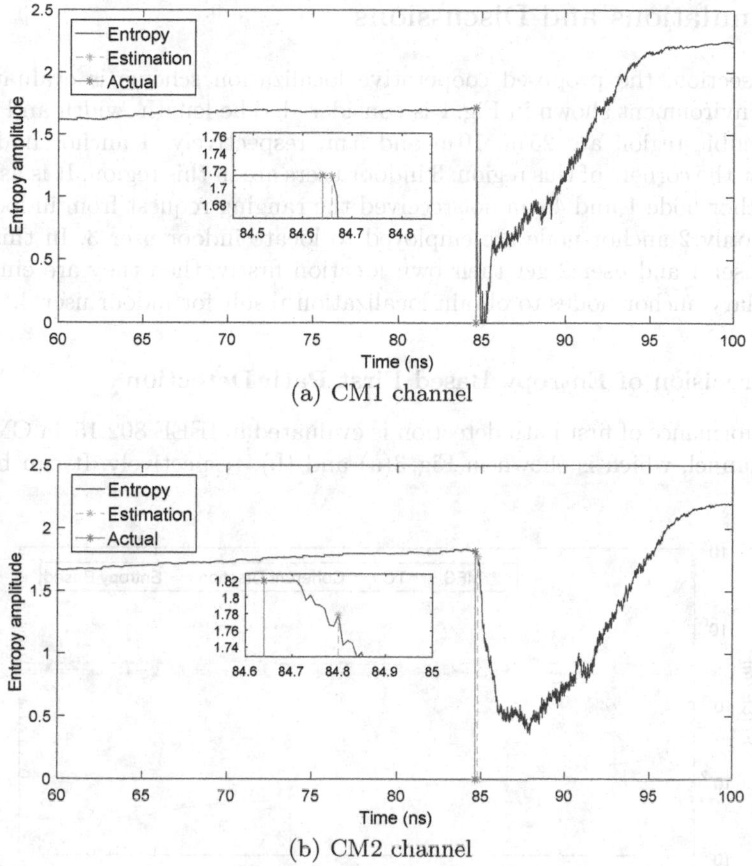

Fig. 3. Entropy based first path detection.

The position of target indoor user can be obtained by solving the following minimum optimization problem

$$\min\left(\sum_{m=1}^{M}\left|\sqrt{(x-x_{am})^2+(y-y_{am})^2+(z-z_{am})^2}-\hat{d}_{am}\right| + \sum_{n=1}^{N-1}\left|\sqrt{(x-x_{un})^2+(y-y_{un})^2+(z-z_{un})^2}-\hat{d}_{un}\right|\right), \tag{10}$$

where $\hat{d}_{am}$ and $\hat{d}_{un}$ are the estimation of d_{am} and d_{un}, respectively. In this paper, the least square error (LSE) estimator is employed to solve (10).

4 Simulations and Discussions

In this section, the proposed cooperative localization scheme is evaluated. A indoor environment shown in Fig. 1 is considered. The length, width and height of this cubic region are 25 m, 10 m and 5 m, respectively. 4 anchor nodes are placed at the corners of this region. 3 indoor users are in this region. It is assumed that anchor node 1 and 4 can not received the ranging request from indoor user 3, then only 2 anchor node are employed to locate indoor user 3. In this case, indoor user 1 and user 2 get their own location firstly, then they are employed as auxiliary anchor nodes to obtain localization result for indoor user 3.

4.1 Precision of Entropy Based First Path Detection

The performance of first path detection is evaluated in IEEE 802.15.4a CM1 and CM2 channel, which is shown in Fig. 3(a) and (b), respectively. It can be seen

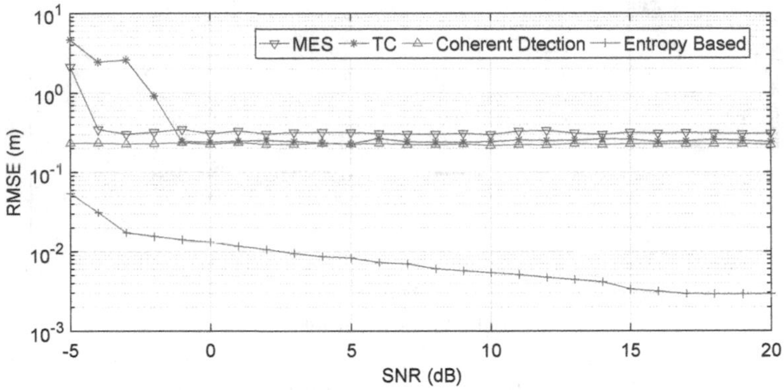

(a) CM1 channel

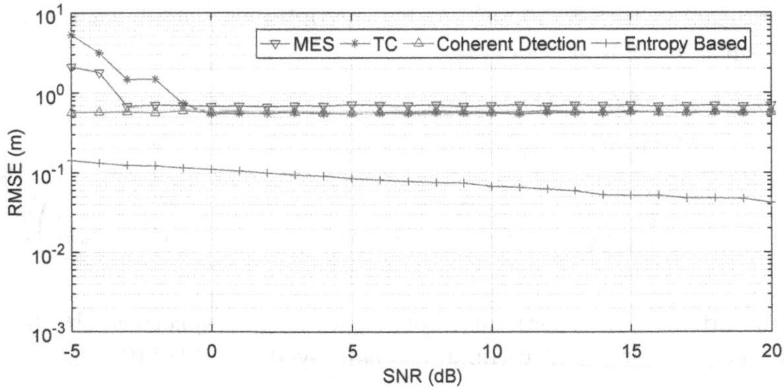

(b) CM2 channel

Fig. 4. Localization accuracy comparison in RMSE.

from Fig. 3 that the entropy amplitude has a significant decline when the first path of UWB arrives. This is because for random noise, the entropy altitude has a high value, whereas the UWB signals are known signals at the receiver, thus it has a very low entropy. When the SNR of received signal is 20 dB, the TOA estimation errors in CM1 and CM2 channel are 0.06 ns and 0.14 ns, respectively.

4.2 Precision of Cooperative Localization

The precision of the proposed cooperative localization scheme is also evaluated by comparing with existing approaches. The ranging results obtained by MES, TC, coherent detection, as well as the proposed entropy based method are employed to get the location of indoor user 3 by solving Eq. (10) through least square error method. The results are shown in Fig. 4. It shows that the root mean square error (RMSE) of localization decreases when the SNR of received signal increases. The proposed entropy based cooperative localization scheme always has a better performance than existing approaches. In CM1 channel, which is a LOS channel, the RMSE is less than 1 cm when SNR is higher than 5 dB. In CM2 channel, which is a NLOS channel, The RMSE is less than 10 cm when SNR is higher than 5 dB. This is because in NLOS channel, the energy of first path is too weak to be precisely detected.

5 Conclusions

In this paper, a cooperative localization scheme is proposed for high precision localization applications in indoor environments. The differences between random noise and known UWB signal are exploited by calculating the entropy of received signal to obtain a high accuracy TOA estimation result. Besides, when the number of anchor nodes is not sufficient, we propose a cooperative localization method, where the indoor users with known locations are employed as auxiliary anchor nodes to obtain localization result for the target indoor user. Performance evaluation results show that the proposed cooperative localization scheme can achieve high accuracy localization results in both LOS and NLOS conditions. Hence, the proposed cooperative localization scheme can be a promising solution for high precision localization requirements in indoor harsh environments.

References

1. Angelis, G.D., Moschitta, A., Carbone, P.: Positioning techniques in indoor environments based on stochastic modeling of UWB round-trip-time measurements. IEEE Trans. Intell. Transp. Syst. **17**(8), 2272–2281 (2016)
2. Dardari, D., Conti, A., Ferner, U., et al.: Ranging with ultrawide bandwidth signals in multipath environments. Proc. IEEE **97**(2), 404–426 (2009)
3. Lee, J.Y., Scholtz, R.A.: Ranging in a dense multipath environment using an UWB radio link. Proc. IEEE J. Sel. Areas Commun. **20**(9), 1677–1683 (2002)

4. Guvenc, I., Sahinoglu, Z.: Threshold selection for UWB TOA estimation based on kurtosis analysis. Commun. Lett. IEEE **9**(12), 1025–1027 (2005)
5. Bartoletti, S., Dai, W., Conti, A., et al.: A mathematical model for wideband ranging. IEEE J. Sel. Top. Signal Process. **9**(2), 216–228 (2015)
6. Yin, Z., Cui, K., Wu, Z., et al.: Entropy-based TOA estimation and SVM-based ranging error mitigation in UWB ranging systems. Sensors **15**(5), 11701–11724 (2015)
7. Yin, Z., Jiang, X., Yang, Z., et al.: WUB-IP: a high-precision UWB positioning scheme for indoor multiuser applications. IEEE Syst. J. **PP**(99), 1–10 (2018)

Over the Air Test Method for Beidou Intelligent Terminals

Qinjuan Zhang[1(✉)], Na Wang[1], Xun Dai[1], Shijiao Zhang[2], and Xiaochen Chen[1]

[1] China Telecommunication Technology Labs (CTTL), Beijing, People's Republic of China
zhangqinjuan@caict.ac.cn
[2] Hydsoft Co., LTD., Beijing, People's Republic of China

Abstract. The number of Beidou intelligent terminal is dramatically increasing recently. Only during 2017, there have been More than 200 mobile communication terminals supporting BDS applied for telecom equipment access to network license. It's important to evaluate the Beidou antenna performance of these intelligent terminals but currently there is neither specification nor common methods. Over-The-Air (OTA) test evaluates three-dimension (3D) radiated antenna performance in anechoic chamber to approach the real user experience. In this paper, an over the air test method for Beidou intelligent terminal is proposed, including standalone mode and communication assisted mode. The test scenarios and test procedures for radiated 3D Carrier-to-Noise (C/N0) pattern measurement and radiated sensitivity measurement are described. An over the air test system is developed in China Telecommunication Technology Lab (CTTL) and a number of intelligent terminals supporting Beidou are tested. The results indicate that although large numbers of terminals are claimed supporting Beidou, its Beidou antenna performance is relatively poor and when Global Position System (GPS) is not available, Beidou positioning cannot meet the user requirements currently. Thus, it is urgent to standardize the Beidou OTA technical requirements and test methods of intelligent terminals.

Keywords: Beidou navigation satellite system (BDS) · Assisted-Beidou navigation satellite system (A-BDS) · Intelligent terminal · Over the air test (OTA test)

1 Introduction

The OTA test can evaluate 3D radiated antenna performance of terminals with full anechoic chamber which can simulate the effects of the operators by testing the antenna performance under different statuses such as free space, hand and head phantom. So, OTA test is crucial for evaluating navigation and positioning terminals' performance since it indicates the real user experience.

Recently, the number of Beidou intelligent terminal is dramatically increasing. Only during 2017, there have been More than 200 mobile communication terminals supporting BDS applied for telecom equipment access to network license. It's important to test their Beidou antenna performance. CTIA OTA test plan [1] version

M. Jia et al. (Eds.): WiSATS 2019, LNICST 281, pp. 637–647, 2019.
https://doi.org/10.1007/978-3-030-19156-6_60

3.7 defines the GPS and GLONASS standalone OTA test method; A-GPS and A-GLONASS OTA test method has already been defined in version prior, which is evaluated by Total Isotropic Sensitivity (TIS), Upper Hemisphere Isotropic Sensitivity (UHIS) and Partial Isotropic GNSS Sensitivity (PIGS) to measure the 3D radiated receiving sensitivity performance. While as for Beidou OTA test method, it hasn't been defined in CTIA specification. 3GPP technical specification 37.571.1 [2] defines A-GNSS radio frequency (RF) conducted test methods including AGPS, A-BDS and A-GLONASS; however, the test cases only evaluate conducted RF performance not including antenna performance. Meanwhile, Ref. [3] only includes network assisted mode doesn't consider standalone mode. In the 17 standards issued by China satellite navigation system office, standard [3] mainly focuses on GNSS antenna performance test, but it only includes Voltage Standing Wave Ratio (VSWR), noise coefficient, gain and other parameters of circular polarization antenna itself, not involves the antenna sensitivity of the entire Beidou equipment. In [4], the RF conducted performance test methods and test system of the Beidou terminals are introduced, including standalone mode and the network assisted mode. (The mainly difference between standalone BDS and A-BDS is that, assistant data including time, ephemeris, almanac and approximate position can be supplied by network for A-BDS mode. The BDS intelligent terminals in the market now can only support standalone mode.)

In a word, currently there is neither Beidou OTA test specification nor common method for A-BDS mode and standalone BDS mode. Considering the current situation, a Beidou antenna OTA performance test method, including the standalone mode and network assisted mode, is proposed in this paper and a test system is developed according to the proposed method, based on which a large amount of Beidou intelligent terminals are tested.

2 System Architecture

The BDS antenna performance can be test in full anechoic chamber as shown in Figs. 1 and 2 for standalone mode and network assisted mode respectively. BDS standalone system mainly includes satellite signal simulator and communication antenna. For network assisted mode, there should be a mobile network simulator additionally. The satellite signal simulator is used to simulate the satellite navigation signal, satellite orbit, atmospheric delay error and user trajectory, while the mobile network simulator is used to simulate the base station signal and send the network assisted information.

For network assisted mode, the communication between the equipment under test (EUT) and system to collect measurement data, such as positioning results and C/N0 information, is via signaling protocol defined in corresponding cellular technologies, e.g. RRLP in GSM, RRC in WCDMA, LPP in LTE or IP connection in SUPL. For standalone mode, those signaling protocols in control plane and IP connection in user plane are not applicable, so the information needs to be transmitted by other way. In order to simply the design and implementation to support different types of EUTs, the communication protocol is defined to be running on TCP/IP transport layer in our system as currently discussed in CTIA version 3.7. The information loopback method is the principal matter to be solved for standalone mode. Two methods are used in

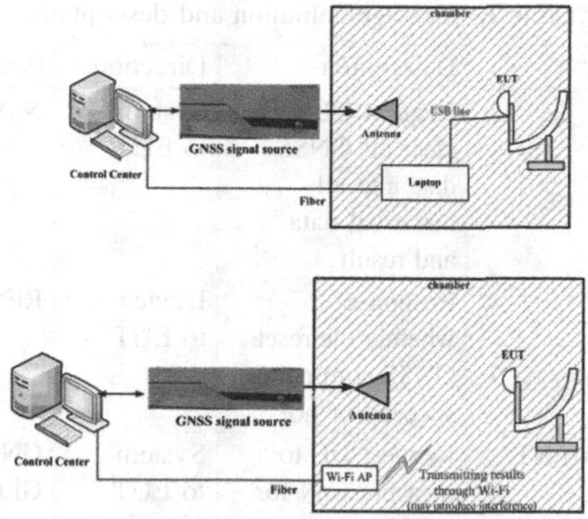

Fig. 1. Standalone BDS OTA test system

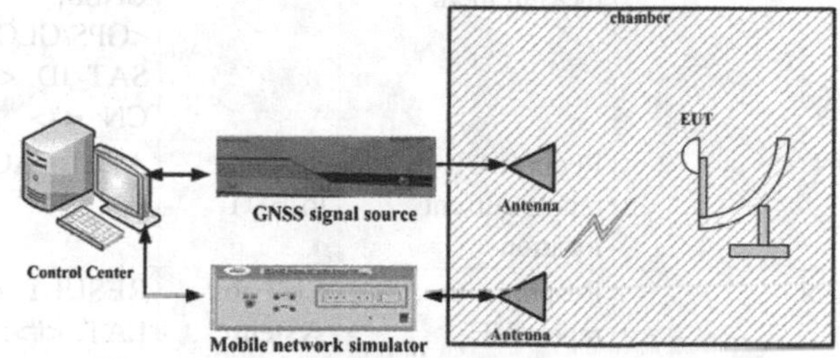

Fig. 2. A-BDS OTA test system

CTTL lab, one is USB-optical fiber, in which a laptop is placed in the chamber to collect information from the EUT and transmit it to the control center through fiber. The other is Wi-Fi, in which a Wi-Fi Access Point (AP) is placed in the chamber to loopback the information.

The TCP/IP protocol is request/response based. According to the test procedure, the system sends request to EUT and EUT acts based on the command and provides response to the system. The format of the request/response message is defined as follows:

<Message ID><PARAM1 ID>:<PARAM1 VALUE>;

<PARAM2 ID>:<PARAM2 VALUE>;

<PARAMN ID>:<PARAMN VALUE><CR><LF>

There are 6 messages needed to enable standalone GNSS performance test as being discussed in CTIA. They are REQ_RESET_GNSS, RESP_RESET_GNSS, REQ_CN_MEASUREMENT, RESP_CN_MEASUREMENT, REQ_LCOATION and RESP_LOCATION. The detailed definition and description of each message is in Table 1.

Table 1. Message definition and description.

Message ID	Description	Direction	Parameters & values
REQ_RESET_GNSS	Request UE to clear all GNSS data and all historical data and result	System to EUT	N/A
RESP_RESET_GNSS	Response whether the reset GNSS command succeed or not	Device to EUT	RESULT: <OK/FAIL>
REQ_CN_MEASUREMENT	Request UE to measure C/N for GNSS	System to EUT	GNSS: <GPS/GPS, GLONASS>; ACCURACY: <H/M/L>
RESP_CN_MEASUREMENT	Response to report C/N measurement	EUT to system	RESULT: <OK/FAIL>; TOTAL: <#>; GNSS: <GPS/GLONASS/BDS>; SAT_ID: <#>; CN: <#>
REQ_LOCATION	Request UE to report current location	System to EUT	ACCURACY: <H/M/L>
RESP_LOCATION	Response to report UE location	EUT to system	RESULT: <OK/FAIL>; LAT: <#>; LONG: <#>; ALT: <#>

3 Test Method

The Beidou antenna test will determine the Total Isotropic Sensitivity, the Upper Hemisphere Isotropic Sensitivity (theta = 0 to 90°) and the Partial Isotropic GNSS Sensitivity (theta = 0 to 120°) of the Beidou terminals. This test can be applied to UE-based and UE-assisted A-BDS and standalone BDS devices. The test conditions are the same as that specified in [5]. The test procedure consists of the following measurements:

- Radiated 3D C/N0 pattern measurement
- Radiated sensitivity measurement.

3.1 Radiated 3D C/N0 Pattern Measurement

Devices supporting UE-assisted A-BDS can perform this section; however, devices supporting UE-based A-BDS only may not be able to perform this section. If a device supports both methods, then the radiated 3D C/N0 pattern measurement may be limited to UE-assisted A-BDS. The 3D C/N0 pattern will then be used for determining the radiated BDS performance for both UE-assisted and UE-based A-BDS. If a device only supports UE-based A-BDS then the C/N0 data shall be stored in the EUT's internal memory or to enable UE-assisted A-BDS or some other test mode to perform the radiated 3D C/N0 pattern measurement. For standalone BDS, C/N0 pattern can be loopback by means of USB-optical fiber or Wi-Fi as shown in Fig. 1.

The pattern data shall be determined by averaging C/N0 measurement of all visible Beidou satellites for each measurement at each point on the sphere. The Beidou satellite simulator shall provide the number of satellites specified herein and each satellite vehicle shall be at the same power. The C/N0 pattern data should be obtained in tracking mode and shall be linearized by the linearization method described in Sect. 3.2.2.

The Beidou satellite simulator shall implement Scenario #1 as defined in 3GPP TS 37.571-5 section 6.2.1.2.1 subclause 7, which shall be reset before the initial satellites become invisible. The scenario parameters shall be set as required in section 7.2 subtest 9 of 3GPP TS 37.571-1, as shown in Table 2, except that random errors for the UE locations and location alternating requirement shall not be implemented. Meanwhile for standalone mode EUT response time is longer, e.g. 120 s. C/N0 pattern test is performed on all supported channels. Moreover, in order to save battery power, a lower transmission power is used that is at least10 dB lower than the maximum transmission power.

Table 2. C/N0 pattern test parameters.

Parameters	Settings
Number of satellites	6
HDOP range	1.4–2.1
Propagation conditions	AWGN
Time assistance (for A-BDS only)	±2 s
Signal power	−133 dBm

3.2 Radiated Sensitivity Measurement

3.2.1 EIS

The radiated A-BDS and standalone BDS sensitivity search shall be performed at the position/polarization where the peak C/N0 value was obtained in the upper hemisphere. The EUT's receiver sensitivity will be the minimum Beidou signal level that results in a passing result for the applicable A-BDS/standalone BDS sensitivity test specified herein. The maximum sensitivity search step size shall be no more than 0.5 dB when the satellite vehicle power level is near the sensitivity level. The BDS satellite simulator shall implement GNSS Scenario #1 as defined in 3GPP TS 37.571-5 [6] section 6.2.1.2.1 for 3GPP TS 37.571-1 [2] subclause 7, sub-test 9 as Table 3, except that random errors for the UE locations and alternating location requirement shall not be implemented. The scenario shall be reset before the initial satellites become invisible. Sensitivity test will be conducted in capture mode, which means the sensitivity is acquisition sensitivity.

Note that the satellite power levels for the sensitivity test are such that there will be one satellite, which transmits 9 dB higher than the other satellites. The reported sensitivity level will be based on the power of the weaker satellites. The 1 dB test tolerance or test parameter relaxation for the absolute BDS signal level in C.2.1 in 3GPP TS 37.571-1 shall not be used in reporting the sensitivity measurement results.

Table 3. C/N0 pattern test parameters.

Test parameter description	Test parameter settings
Number of satellites	6
HDOP range	1.4–2.1
Propagation conditions	AWGN
Time assistance for A-BDS mode	Coarse, ±2 s
EUT response time	120.3 s for standalone BDS mode 20.3 s for A-BDS mode
Success rate	45 successful fixes with the necessary accuracy out of 50 attempts (90%) for standalone BDS mode 95 successful fixes with the necessary accuracy out of 100 attempts (95%) for A-BDS mode
Position accuracy	101.3 m

3.2.2 Linearization

The C/N0 pattern measurements shall be linearized as follows. The peak value in the C/N0 pattern shall be determined from the data collected in Sect. 3.1. Re-position the EUT to the location with the maximum C/N0 measurement of the upper hemisphere. Measurements shall be made at a maximum of 1 dB steps from the peak C/N0 value in Sect. 3.1 to at least 10 dB below. These C/N0 measurements along with the corresponding signal level shall be used to linearize the pattern data collected in Sect. 3.1 such that every pattern data corresponds to a signal level. The linearization can be accomplished through piecewise linear method as shown in Fig. 3. C/N0 data that falls within the utilized step size shall be linearly interpolated, while C/N0 data that falls outside of the data set shall be linearized to a line that is extended using the same slope as linearization at the edge of the data set. By linearization, the 3D isotropic sensitivity can be calculated by C/N0 pattern.

We take two examples to illustrate the piecewise linear procedure. It is assumed that the best sensitivity on the peak point of the C/N0 pattern on the upper hemisphere is −154 dBm with C/N0 = 47. The corresponding relationship between the satellite power and C/N0 is as shown in Table 4. Suppose that we need to calculate the sensitivity of a point (target point 1) with C/N0 = 27. From Table 4, the power corresponding to C/N0 = 27 is −147 dBm, while the power corresponding to C/N0 = 47 is −126 dBm, which is 21 dB higher than that of target point 1. So that the sensitivity difference between the two points should also be 21 dB. Then the sensitivity of target

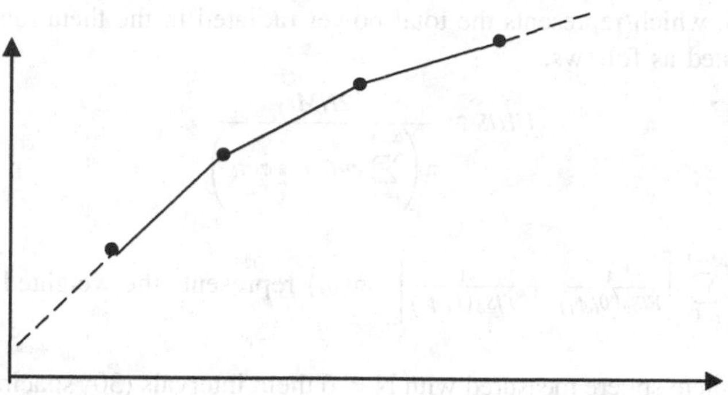

Fig. 3. Piecewise linear method

point 1 should be −133 dBm, 21 dB higher than −154 dBm. Suppose that we want to calculate the sensitivity of a point (target point 2) with C/N0 42.5. From Table 1, the powers corresponding to 42 and 43 are −132 dBm and −131 dBm respectively. With piecewise linear the power corresponding to C/N0 = 42.5 should be −131.5 dBm, while the power corresponding to C/N0 = 47 is −126 dBm which is 5.5 dB higher than that of target point 2. Then the sensitivity of target point 2 should be −148.5 dBm, also 5.5 dB higher than −154 dBm.

Table 4. Relationship between satellite signal power and C/N0.

Power	−125	−126	−127	−128	−129	−130	−131	−132	−133	−134
C/N_0	48	47	46.5	45	45	44	43	42	41	40
Power	−135	−136	−137	−138	−139	−140	−141	−142	−143	−144
C/N_0	39	38	37	36	35	34	33	32	31	30
Power	−145	−146	−147	−148	−149	−150	−151	−152	−153	−154
C/N_0	29	27.8	27	26	25	23.5	23	22	20.5	19.5

3.2.3 Sensitivity Calculation

According to linearization in Sect. 3.2.2, isotropic sensitivity of every point on the sphere is obtained, from which the TIS, UHIS and PIGS of the EUT can be calculated by formula 1–3.

For a complete sphere measured with N theta intervals and M phi intervals, both with even angular spacing, the TIS is calculated as follows.

$$TIS \cong \frac{2NM}{\pi \sum_{i=2}^{4} \sum_{j=0}^{M-1} \left[\frac{1}{EIS_{\theta}(\theta_i, \varphi_j)} + \frac{1}{EIS_{\varphi}(\theta_i, \varphi_j)} \right] \sin(\theta_i)} \quad (1)$$

where EIS is the radiated effective isotropic sensitivity measured or calculated by linearization at each direction and polarization.

The UHIS, which represents the total power radiated in the theta range from 0 to 90°, is calculated as follows.

$$UHIS \cong \frac{2NM}{\pi\left(\sum_{i=1}^{\frac{N}{2}-1} cut_i + \frac{1}{2} cut_{\frac{N}{2}}\right)} \tag{2}$$

where $cut_i \cong \sum_{j=0}^{M-1}\left[\frac{1}{EIS_\theta(\theta_i,\phi_j)} + \frac{1}{EIS_\phi(\theta_i,\phi_j)}\right]\sin(\theta_i)$ represents the weighted sum of each conical cut.

For a complete sphere measured with N = 6 theta intervals (30° spacing) and M phi intervals, both with even angular spacing, the PIGS, which represents the total power radiated in the theta range from 0 to 120° is calculated as follows:

$$PIGS \cong \frac{2NM}{\pi\left(\sum_{i=1}^{\frac{N}{2}} cut_i + \frac{1}{2} cut_{\frac{N}{2}+1}\right)} \tag{3}$$

where: $cut_i \cong \sum_{j=0}^{M-1}\left[\frac{1}{EIS_\theta(\theta_i,\phi_j)} + \frac{1}{EIS_\phi(\theta_i,\phi_j)}\right]\sin(\theta_i)$ represents the weighted sum of each conical cut.

4 Results

We developed a Beidou OTA test software used in control center according to the interface in Sect. 2 and the procedure in Sect. 3, with screen shot as Fig. 4.

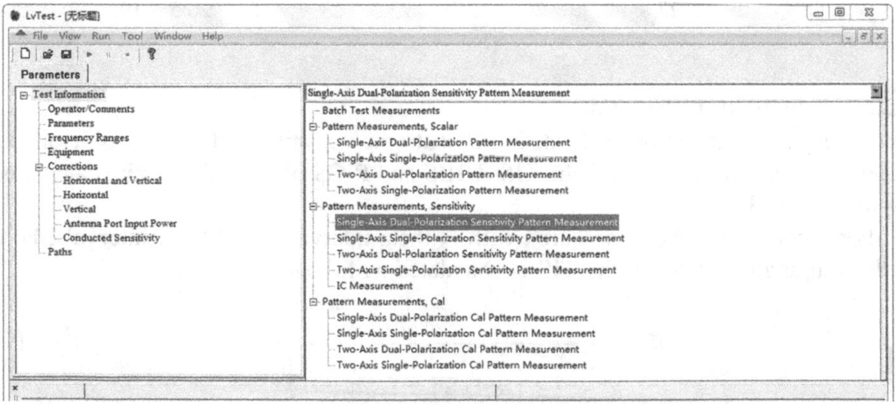

Fig. 4. Beidou OTA software

For standalone BDS, two applications based on android and windows phone platform respectively are developed to loop back standalone BDS information. In our system, two methods are used, one using USB to optical fiber; the other using Wi-Fi, both through TCP/IP protocol, as shown in Fig. 1. For USB method, we developed a customized box with size 20 × 15 × 2.5 cm to replace the laptop, which can be put under absorbing materials to avoid interference (Fig. 5).

Fig. 5. Customized box to transmit data to control center

The entire Beidou OTA test system is developed based on ETS AMS 8600 chamber. The NSS8000 satellite simulator from National University of Defense Technology is used (Fig. 6).

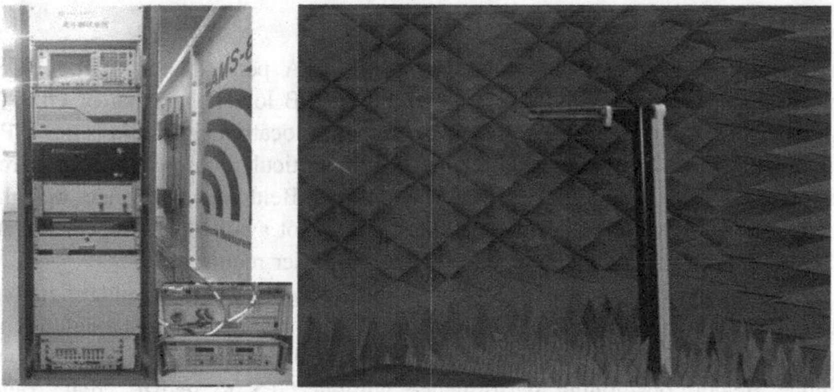

Fig. 6. Beidou OTA test system based on 8600 chamber

From the intelligent terminals declared supporting BDS in market, all of which only support standalone BDS, we choose 17 terminals and test their standalone BDS OTA performance. For these 17 terminals, the sensitivity results are shown in Figs. 7 and 8.

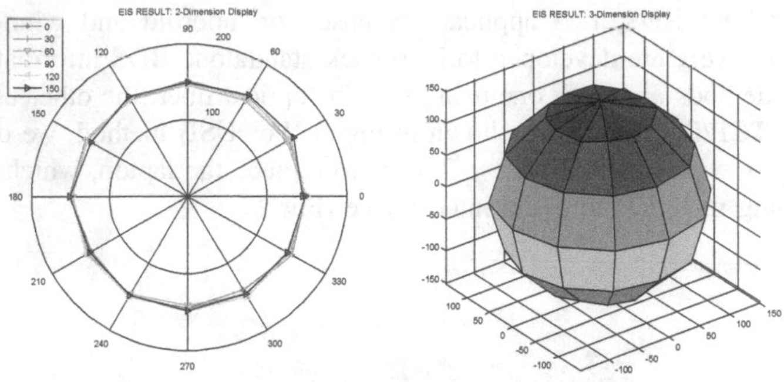

Fig. 7. 3D isotropic sensitivity

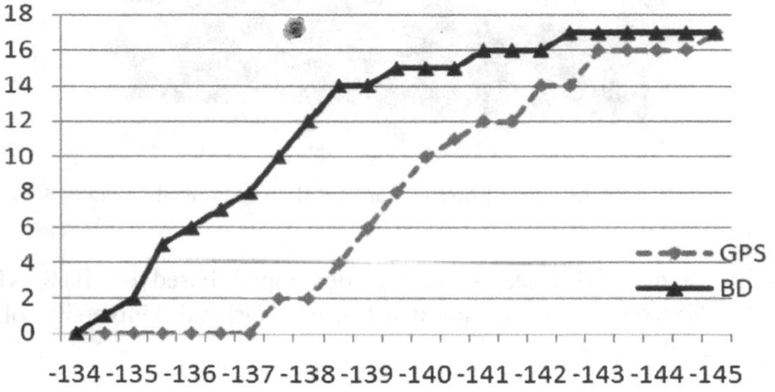

Fig. 8. GPS/BDS TIS results

From the results, we found that the overall OTA performance of the BDS is relatively poor compared to GPS, which is about 3 dB lower than that of GPS. The design principle of the majority of intelligent terminals location algorithm is that GPS is the main method while Beidou is supplemented. In particular, chip channel resource is allocated to GPS satellite in priority, which led to poor Beidou performance. In sight of national security and user experience, when GPS is not available, Beidou navigation and positioning must also be able to meet the basic user requirements.

In view of the current situation, it is urgent to speed up the standardization of Beidou navigation and positioning for intelligent terminals, including standalone mode and assisted mode. Moreover, considering the actual problem, it is also urgent to guarantee Beidou positioning performance without GPS to realize “real” Beidou positioning.

5 Conclusion

This paper introduces a Beidou OTA performance testing method for intelligent terminals, which can reflect 3D antenna sensitivity performance of the terminals. According to the proposed method, a test system is developed based on which 100 Beidou intelligent terminals are tested. Results show that most of them only support Beidou and GPS dual constellation positioning while only a small number of them support Beidou standalone positioning without GPS but their performance is relatively poor. Thus, it is urgent to speed up the standardization of Beidou navigation positioning for intelligent terminals and promote "real" Beidou positioning at current situation.

References

1. CTIA 3.5.2: Test plan for wireless device over-the-air performance (2015)
2. GPP TS 37.571-1 User Equipment (UE) conformance specification for UE positioning; part 1: conformance test specification (2015)
3. BD 420004-2015: Performance requirements and test methods for BeiDou/Global Navigation Satellite Systems (GNSS) navigation antenna (2015)
4. Zhang, Q., Li, M., Wang, N., et al.: Research on test method of Beidou two civil equipment. Modern Sci. Technol. Telecommun. **44**(7), 18–22 (2014)
5. YD/T 1484 measurement method for radiated RF power and receiver performance of wireless device (2013)
6. GPP TS 37.571-5 User Equipment (UE) conformance specification for UE positioning; part 5: test scenarios and assistance data (2015)

Research on Intelligent Wireless Channel Allocation in HAPS 5G System Based on Reinforcement Learning

Zhou Wu, Ming-xiang Guan(✉), Yingjie Cui, Xuemei Cao, Le Wang, Jianfeng Ye, and Bao Peng

Shenzhen Institute of Information Technology, Shenzhen 518029, Guangdong, China
gmx2020@126.com

Abstract. An intelligent wireless channel allocation algorithm for HAPS 5G systems based on reinforcement learning was proposed. Q-learning reinforcement learning algorithm and the back-propagation neural network were combined, which made HAPS 5G systems autonomous learn according to the environment and allocate channel resources of the system efficiently.

Keywords: High altitude platform system · Reinforcement learning · Artificial intelligence

1 Introduction

The future 5G network will be an intelligent system with multi-service, multi-access technology and multi-level coverage [1–3]. The purpose of development of HAPS is to provide supplementary wireless services for ground stations and satellites. The application of 5G key technologies in HAPS communication systems has many outstanding advantages.

A wireless dynamic channel allocation algorithm for HAPS communication based on distance decision is proposed, which guarantees the quality of service of all kinds of services and maximizes the resource utilization ratio of high altitude platform communication in reference [4]. Aiming at the problem of horizontal swing caused by stratospheric crosswind on high-altitude platforms, a channel allocation algorithm combining channel reservation with handoff queuing is proposed to solve the problem of handoff between cellular for the ground calling users to continue to obtain reliable services in reference [5]. The algorithm takes full account of the service level requirements of different types of user terminals, differentiates the priority of user terminals, and queues the handoff callers on the basis of channel reservation from the point of view of reducing the handover failure rate.

This paper proposes an intelligent wireless channel allocation algorithm for HAPS 5G communication systems based on reinforcement learning, which adopts Q-learning reinforcement learning algorithm in artificial intelligence algorithm and combines back-propagation neural network to enable HAPS 5G communication system to learn

M. Jia et al. (Eds.): WiSATS 2019, LNICST 281, pp. 648–655, 2019.
https://doi.org/10.1007/978-3-030-19156-6_61

independently according to environment, intelligently according to channel load and blocking condition. The channel resources are allocated effectively in the system.

2 Q-Learning Reinforcement Learning Algorithm

Q-learning is one of the most famous algorithms in the field of reinforcement learning. It learns how to choose the next action (a) by perceiving reward and punishment (r). The detailed algorithm steps are as follows:

1. for each state s and action a, the initialization table Q (s, a) is 0.
2. observe the current state s;
3. Repeat it all the time.
   (1) select an action a and execute it.
   (2) receive an immediate return of r;
   (3) observe the new state s', and update the table item Q according to the following form:

$$Q(s,a) = r(s,a) + \gamma * \max Q(s',a'), s = s' \quad (1)$$

This paper proposes an intelligent wireless channel allocation algorithm based on reinforcement learning for HAPS 5G communication system, which uses Q-learning reinforcement learning algorithm in artificial intelligence algorithm and combines back-propagation neural network to enable the HAPS 5G communication system to learn independently according to the environment and intelligently according to the channel, load and blocking. Agents perceive the state information in the channel environment through continuous interaction with the channel environment, learn from the environment state to the action mapping, and use the back-propagation neural network for learning training, use the neural network instead of the Q value table, and train the network with each Q update as a training example to update the evaluation function, and repeat cycle iteration until convergence condition is satisfied, then stop learning.

3 Intelligent Wireless Channel Allocation Algorithm Based on Q-Learning Reinforcement Learning

The channel assignment problem of HAPS 5G communication system is solved based on Q-learning reinforcement learning algorithm. The channel assignment problem is modeled as a Markov process, which generates an instantaneous return value at each step of learning, and the state converges at the end of learning. Therefore, in order to realize the algorithm modeling, the instantaneous return value R, channel state S and channel assignment action A must be determined.

(1) Instantaneous return valuc R

The following principles must be satisfied for intelligent channel allocation:

(a) in the case of existing channel resources, all channels are allocated and the fairness principle is satisfied.
(b) the channel allocation satisfies the outage rate and the minimum principle of GoS (Grade of Service).
(c) channel assignment satisfies the minimum principle of blocking rate.

Therefore, the instantaneous return value of the intelligent channel allocation algorithm is designed to achieve convergence according to the above principles:

- if the a, b and c principles are met, the instantaneous return value of the channel assignment is R = 10.
- if we only meet the a and b principles and do not meet the c principles, then R = 7;
- if we only meet the a and c principles and do not meet the b principles, then R = 5;
- if we only meet the a Principle and do not meet the b and c principles, then R = 3;
- if we do not meet the a principles and satisfy only b and c principles, then R = 0;
- if three principles are not satisfied, then R = −10.

(2) Channel state S

Channel state represents the quality of the channel and the usage of the channel and the idleness of the channel in each period of time before the channel is allocated. The state set of the current allocated channel can be known through the channel state information.

The channel allocated by the intelligent channel assignment algorithm at the same time must meet the following requirements:

(a) Free channel resources;

The number of channels provided by the system is greater than the sum of the peak number of channels needed by each cell in a cluster to satisfy its respective service levels. In this case, the user's demand does not reach the system capacity, so only a certain number of channels need to be allocated to each cell to meet the demand, and the remaining number of channels can be set as a dynamic allocation part, so the enhancements learning algorithm can be used to allocate the free channel.

(b) Scheduling time does not conflict;

In the training phase, a conflicting coefficient is obtained by recording the channel in which a conflict occurs at a certain scheduling time. After the training phase is over, a channel conflict distribution table can be obtained. The conflict coefficient of non conflict scheduling time is 0, and the more conflict time, the greater the conflict coefficient.

(c) Channel quality

According to the channel estimation, the channel quality of the idle channel can be divided into three levels according to the channel quality from high to low:

The best channel quality = 10;
The qualifying channel quality = 5;
The worst channel quality = 0;

(d) GoS (Grade of Service)

According to the requirement of GoS, the priority of channel assignment can be divided into the following 4 categories:

Emergency business level, Level = 100;
High priority business level, Level = 50;
Medium priority business level, Level = 30;
Low priority business level, Level = 10.

(3) Channel assignment action A

Channel allocation action is to select which channel to allocate among the free channel resources, and it also needs to reflect the service level information.

We use a 5-bit binary representation in which the lowest bit denotes whether the channel is allocated, if allocated, is 1, otherwise 0. The 2nd and 3rd bits represent the channel quality, with the best quality is 10, the qualifying quality is 01, and the worst quality is 00, 11 reserved. The 4th and 5th bits are the service level, the emergency service is 11, the high priority is 10, the middle priority is 01, and the low priority is 00.

In this way, we discretize the channel state into the above four variables, the total number of channels is N. So the channel state table of the intelligent channel allocation device contains 4 * N elements, called channel state mode matrix.

The learning process will converge only if each idle channel state and allocation action are used indefinitely and frequently because of the complex and changeable wireless channel environment and the variety of wireless services and the mobility and uncertainty of users. In the 5G era, there will be a large number of traffic connections, and the state-action pair of channel assignment problem will be a huge state space. It is difficult to search such a huge space in practice and it is almost impossible to get all the state-action Q-value tables. So in this case, in order to make the reinforcement learning algorithm achieve the desired effect, we choose to use the back propagation neural network to quickly obtain the estimate of Q value. The neural network is used to replace the Q value table, and every Q update is used as a training example to train the network. When training the intelligent channel assignment BP network, we can quantify the channel state S and take it as the first input of the neural network. Then the neural network finally outputs an estimate of Q value, and compares this Q value with the Q value obtained from the previous learning, and trains the BP network to get the expected Q value.

Intelligent channel allocation BP network is divided into three layers, the number of input layer units is 4 * N channel state. The third layer output layer is only one and the number of hidden layer neural units is chosen 32. All levels of neurons form a fully interconnected connection and hidden layer is S-shaped transfer function and output layer is linear transfer function.

The initial weight matrix of BP network in this paper is:

$$W^2 = 4 * N * 32, W^3 = 32 * 1 \quad b^2 = 1 * 32, b^3 = 1 * 1$$

Initial weights are chosen randomly in (0,1) to avoid possible saddle points without leaving the flat area of the performance surface.

A lot of training data will be generated during our continuous training in the system. Although these data are not the best strategy for dealing with the environment at that time, it is the experience gained by interacting with the environment that is very helpful to our training system. So we set up a replay_buffer to save new interactive data to overwrite the old data, and each time randomly take a batch from the replay_buffer to train our system.

Each record in replay_buffer contains the following:

(a) state; the channel status of the current device;
(b) action: the behavior of our agent in the current state;
(c) reward: the profit from the environment after agent has made the choice behavior;
(d) next_state: the next state that the agent transferred after the agent has made the choice behavior;
(e) done: the flag to indicate if the training is ok.

4 Performance Comparison and Analysis

4.1 Establishment of Simulation Environment

Next, we will simulate the algorithm in this paper to verify the performance of the algorithm. The simulation model used in this article is shown in Fig. 1. Using a typical 4-platform 32-channel model, the simulation area consists of seven cellular cells, each of which is hexagonal in size, and the seven cells studied are all located in the inner ring area covered by four high-altitude communication platforms. The antenna gain mode meets the ITU standard for high-altitude platform communication. It is assumed that the mobile users distribute uniformly throughout the service area and the antenna of the mobile users points to the high-altitude platforms they access without bias. The transmitting power of each mobile user is the same. The propagation environment obeys the law of free space link loss. We analyze the network performance using the intelligent channel allocation algorithm in a mixed service environment. We choose several business scenarios from the main application scenarios of 5G:

(1) Traffic 1: cloud AR/VR business. VR/AR requires a large number of data transmission. The quality of the channel determines the quality of VR/AR video data transmission. 5G network needs to allocate the corresponding quality level of the channel based on different types of AR/VR services and different environments;
(2) Traffic 2: Vehicle networking business. It includes traditional cars, remote control driving and unmanned autopilot. Vehicle life cycle maintenance, sensor data packets, etc. require secure, reliable, low latency and high broadband connections, which are essential in highways and dense cities. 5G network needs to assign the corresponding quality level and service priority channel according to different types of vehicles in different environments.
(3) Traffic 3: voice business. There are still a large number of voice services in 5G network. 5G network needs to allocate a large number of voice services optimally in the case of channel collision and sudden emergence of high priority services.

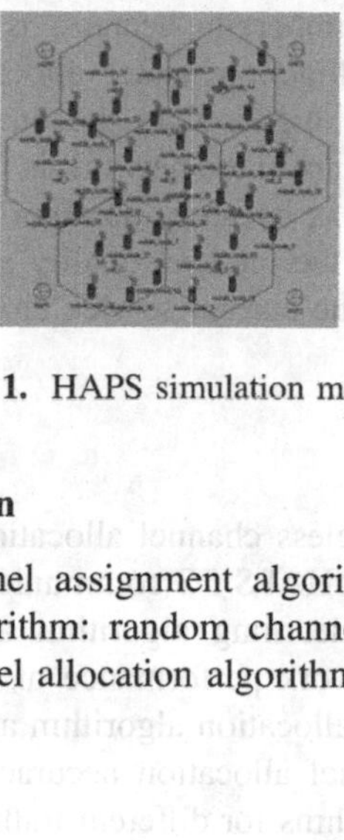

Fig. 1. HAPS simulation model

4.2 Performance Comparison

We choose two classical channel assignment algorithms in HAPS communication system as the comparison algorithm: random channel allocation algorithm [6] and Worst channel acceptable channel allocation algorithm [7].

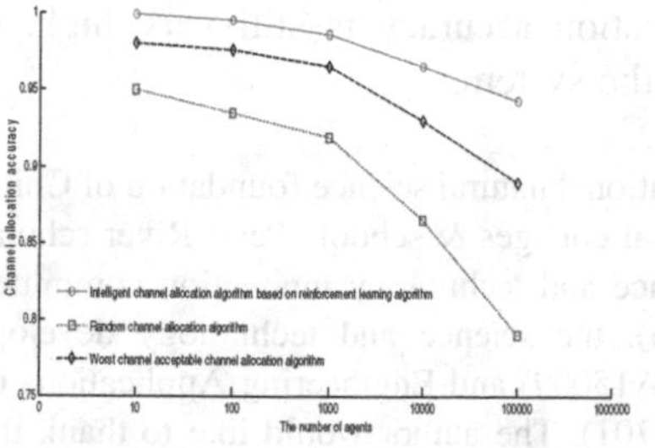

Fig. 2. Channel allocation accuracy of traffic 1

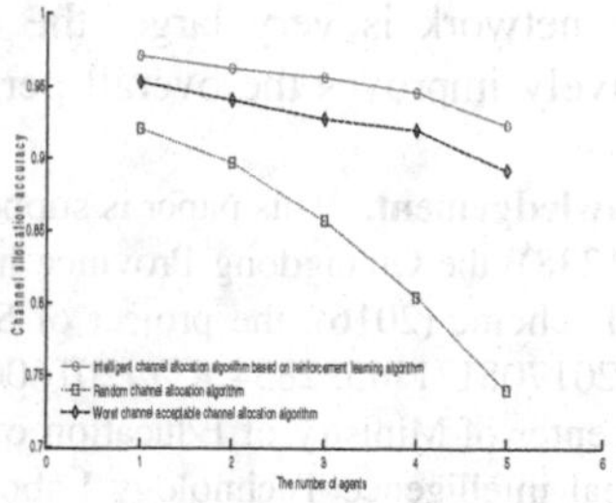

Fig. 3. Channel allocation accuracy of traffic 2

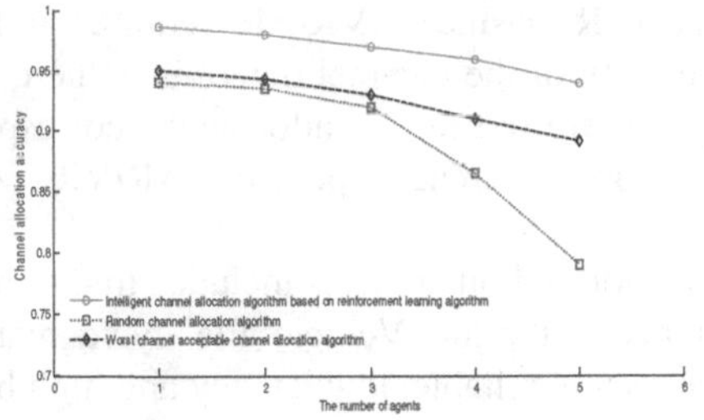

Fig. 4. Channel allocation accuracy of traffic 3

Figures 2, 3 and 4 show the channel allocation accuracy of traffic 1, traffic 2 and traffic 3 under three channel resource allocation algorithms respectively. As it can be seen from Figs. 2, 3 and 4, the channel allocation accuracy of the three channel resource allocation algorithms decreases with the increase of the number of agents in the network, especially for the random channel allocation algorithm, when the number of agents increases to a certain number, the decrease is especially obvious. The channel allocation accuracy of the intelligent channel allocation algorithm based on reinforcement learning algorithm is higher than the other two algorithms for different traffic. Even if the number of agents in the network is very large, the channel allocation accuracy is still very high. This is because the algorithm can dynamically adjust the channel allocation according to the channel quality and priority of different services and select the best channel for the current service channel quality and service level.

5 Conclusions

In this paper, an intelligent wireless channel allocation algorithm based on the reinforcement learning algorithm for HAPS 5G communication system is proposed, which uses Q-learning reinforcement learning algorithm and combines back-propagation neural network. Finally the network performance of the proposed algorithm is compared with the random channel allocation algorithm and the worst acceptable channel allocation algorithm. The channel allocation accuracy of the proposed algorithm is higher than the other two algorithms for different traffic. Even if the number of agents in the network is very large, the channel allocation accuracy is still very high. It effectively improves the overall performance of the system.

Acknowledgement. This paper is supported by the national natural science foundation of China (61401288), the Guangdong Province higher vocational colleges & schools Pearl River scholar funded scheme (2016), the project of Shenzhen science and technology innovation committee (JCYJ20170817114522834,JCYJ20160608151239996), the science and technology development center of Ministry of Education of China (2017A15009) and Engineering Applications of Artificial intelligence Technology Laboratory (PT201701). The author would like to thank the editor and the anonymous reviewers for their contributions that enriched the final paper.

References

1. Cao, Z., Zhao, X., Soares, F.M.: 38-GHz millimeter wave beam steered fiber wireless systems for 5G indoor coverage: architectures, devices, and links. IEEE J. Quantum Electron. **53**(1), 1–9 (2017)
2. Yuan, Y., Zhao, X.: 5G: vision, scenarios and enabling technologies. ZTE Commun. **13**(1), 69–79 (2015)
3. Cid, E.L., Táboas, M.P., Sánchez, M.G.: Microcellular radio channel characterization at 60GHz for 5G communications. IEEE Antennas Wirel. Propag. Lett. **16**(99), 1–4 (2017)
4. Guan, M., Guo, Q., Gu, X.: A dynamic wireless channel allocation algorithm in HAPS communication based on distance verdict. Electron. J. **41**(1), 18–23 (2013)
5. Jiang, J., Zhang, B., Guo, D., Ye, Z.: A channel assigning algorithm for platform displacement model in HAPS communication system. Telecommun. Eng. **55**(8), 906–912 (2015)
6. Grace, D., Spillard, C., Thornton, J., Tozer, T.C.: Channel assignment strategies for high altitude platform spot-beam architecture. In: The 13th IEEE International Symposium on Personal, Indoor and Mobile Radio Communications, vol. 9, pp. 1586–1590 (2002)
7. Pace, P., Aloi, G., De Rango, F.: An integrated satellite-HAP-terrestrial system architecture: resources allocation and traffic management issues. In: IEEE 59th Vehicular Technology Conference, vol. 5, pp. 2872–2875 (2004)

Shielding Effectiveness Improvement Method of Optoelectronic Instrumental Windows Utilizing Transparent Mesh PET Film

Cao Kai(✉), Kairang Wang, and Changwen Liu

Beijing Institute of Radio Metrology and Measurement, Beijing 100854, People's Republic of China
caokai13579@126.com

Abstract. In order to improve shielding effectiveness of optoelectronic instrumental windows, a filtering method is proposed using a transparent mesh PET film consisting of flexible PET film and conductive mesh film. And then an analysis model is built based on optical characteristic transfer-matrix theory of multi-layer optical films. Simulation and analysis indicate that shielding effectiveness can be improved by optimizing thickness of flexible PET films to make corresponding quarter-wavelength frequency move to low one in frequency-band of 10–20 GHz. Optimization results show that shielding effectiveness of optimized optoelectronic instrumental windows utilizing a transparent mesh PET film is higher than 16.8 dB by optimizing the thickness of a flexible PET film of 200 μm. So it can be concluded that the proposed filtering method utilizing a transparent mesh PET film can be used to improve shielding effectiveness of optoelectronic instrumental windows.

Keywords: Filtering method · Shielding effectiveness · Transparent mesh PET film · Optoelectronic instrumental window · Optimization

1 Introduction

With increasing electromagnetic interference and information leakage, optoelectronic instrumental windows require both high optical transparence and desired electromagnetic interference shielding against low-frequency (rf/microwave) interference [1–3]. Conductive metal mesh has been widely used as filters for microwave and optical signals and attracted much attention from the research community due to its capability of high transmitting optical signals and strong shielding against electromagnetic interference at the same time [4–6]. In order to obtain strong electromagnetic shielding, a filtering method for existing optoelectronic instrumental windows is presented using a transparent mesh PET (polyethylene terephthalate) film consisting of a flexible PET film and conductive metal mesh fabricated on PET film. And then a corresponding theoretical analysis model of the proposed high transparent multi-layer mesh films is built based on optical characteristic transfer-matrix theory of multi-layer optical film systems. Simulation and analysis indicate that the electromagnetic shielding effectiveness of optoelectronic measurement instrumental windows utilizing high

M. Jia et al. (Eds.): WiSATS 2019, LNICST 281, pp. 656–660, 2019.
https://doi.org/10.1007/978-3-030-19156-6_62

transparent multi-layer mesh Films can be improved effectively by optimizing the thickness of the transparent flexible PET optical films to make the corresponding quarter-wavelength frequencies move to low ones in the frequency-band of 10–20 GHz. Optimization design results show that the electromagnetic shielding effectiveness of the optimized optoelectronic measurement instrumental windows utilizing high transparent multi-layer mesh films is higher than 16.8 dB by optimizing the thickness of the high transparent flexibel PET films of 200 μm in the frequency-band of 10–20 GHz. So it can be concluded that the proposed filtering method utilizing high transparent multi-layer mesh films can be used to effectively improve electromagnetic shielding effectiveness of optical windows of optoelectronic measurement instruments.

2 Filtering Method

Traditional filtering structure for optical window of electromagnetic shielding consists of a metallic mesh coating deposited on a quartz glass as shown in Fig. 1. The mesh optical window has an advantage of high optical transparency and strong electromagnetic shielding performance. But its electromagnetic shielding decreases as frequency increases. So it is necessary to design a filtering structure to improve electromagnetic shielding performance over interference microwave frequency band.

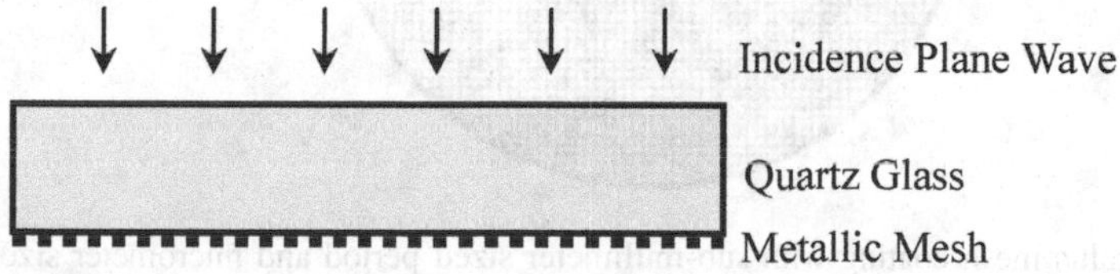

Fig. 1. Traditional filtering structure for optoelectronic instrumental window utilizing a metallic mesh on quartz glass.

In order to improve shielding effectiveness, a filtering method is proposed using a transparent mesh PET film covered on optoelectronic instrumental windows. As shown in Fig. 2, a transparent mesh PET film consists of a flexible PET film and conductive metal mesh fabricated on a PET film.

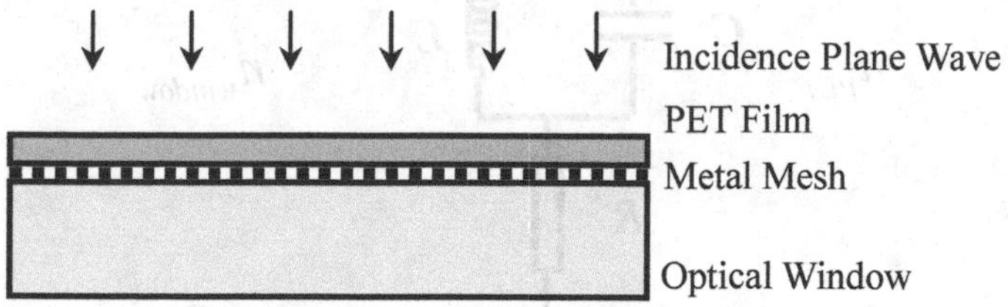

Fig. 2. Filtering structure for optoelectronic instrumental window utilizing a transparent mesh PET film.

3 Model and Optimization

The presented filtering structure of optoelectronic instrumental mesh PET windows is a three-layer film, and can be modeled based on transfer-matrix theory of multi-layer optical films [7–12]. An theoretical analysis model of the presented filtering structure of optoelectronic instrumental windows is built.

As shown in Fig. 3, metallic mesh coating consists of sub-millimeter sized period and micrometer size linewidth.

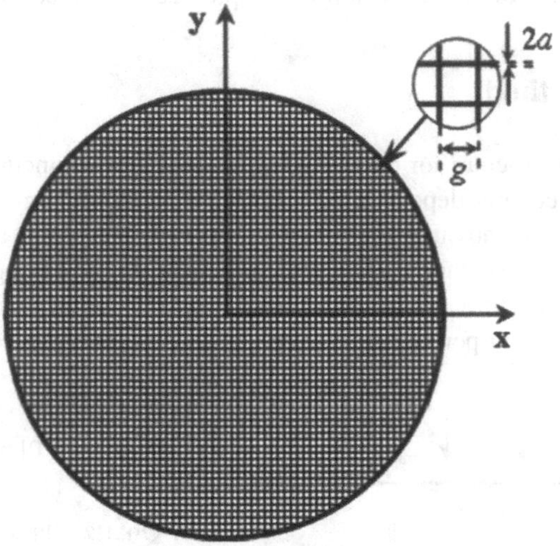

Fig. 3. Metallic mesh coating with sub-millimeter sized period and micrometer size linewidth.

As shown in Fig. 4, the presented filtering structure of optoelectronic instrumental windows is a three-layer film system, so it can be modeled based on optical characteristic transfer-matrix theory of multi-layer optical film systems.

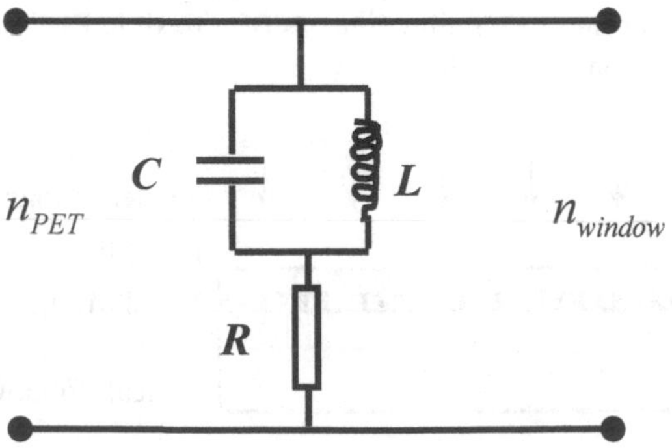

Fig. 4. Equivalent circuit model of transparent mesh PET optical window

Firstly, the transfer-matrix of conductive mesh is shown below:

$$M_{mesh} = \begin{bmatrix} A_m & B_m \\ C_m & D_m \end{bmatrix} = \begin{bmatrix} 1 & 0 \\ (R_m/Z_0 + jX_m/Z_0)^{-1} & 1 \end{bmatrix} \quad (1)$$

where *Rm* and *Xm* are the equivalent impedance and admittance of conductive mesh respectively. Z_0 is impedance of free space. Then the transfer-matrix of PET film and window substrate can be obtained based on optical film theory:

$$M_{PET(window)} = \begin{bmatrix} A & B \\ C & D \end{bmatrix} = \begin{bmatrix} \cos(2\pi nd/\lambda) & -\frac{i\sin(2\pi nd/\lambda)}{cn\varepsilon_o} \\ -icn\varepsilon_o \sin(2\pi nd/\lambda) & \cos(2\pi nd/\lambda) \end{bmatrix} \quad (2)$$

where ε_0 is dielectric constant of free space, *c* is light speed, λ is wavelength of incidence wave, *n* and *d* are refractive index and thickness of PET or window.

So the transfer-matrix of the presented three-layer film filtering structure of optoelectronic instrumental windows can be expressed:

$$M = M_{PET} M_{mesh} M_{window} = \begin{bmatrix} A & B \\ C & D \end{bmatrix} \quad (3)$$

The electromagnetic shielding effectiveness (SE) is given by:

$$SE(dB) = -20\log\left|\frac{A\eta_0 + B\eta_0^2 - C - D\eta_0}{A\eta_0 + B\eta_0^2 + C + D\eta_0}\right| \quad (4)$$

Shielding effectiveness of optoelectronic instrumental mesh PET film windows with different thickness of PET film is analyzed and shown in Fig. 5. The thickness of window substrate is 5 mm, mesh linewidth and period are 2 μm and 250 μm respectively.

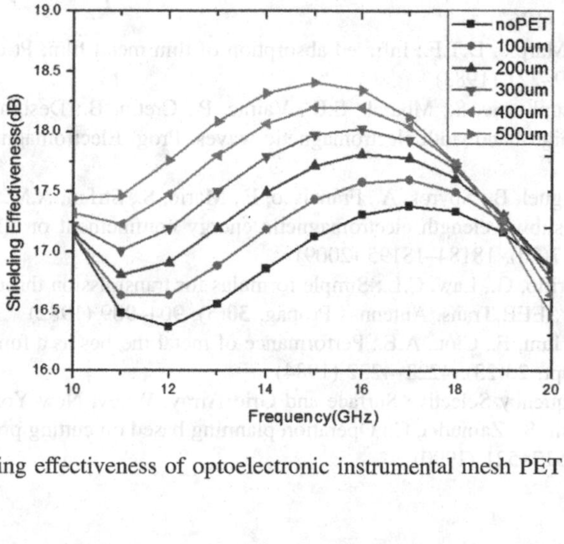

Fig. 5. Shielding effectiveness of optoelectronic instrumental mesh PET film windows.

It can be seen from Fig. 5 that simulation results indicate that shielding effectiveness of optoelectronic instrumental mesh PET film windows can be improved by optimizing the thickness of a transparent flexible PET film to make corresponding quarter-wavelength frequencies move to low ones in frequency-band of 10–20 GHz. Optimization results show that shielding effectiveness of the optimized mesh PET film window is higher than 16.8 dB by optimizing the thickness of a transparent flexible PET film of 200 μm.

4 Conclusion

A filtering method for existing optoelectronic instrumental window is presented using a transparent mesh PET film consisting of a flexible PET film and conductive metal mesh fabricated on PET film to obtain strong electromagnetic shielding. Theoretical analysis and optimization results show that shielding effectiveness of the optimized optoelectronic instrumental mesh PET film window is higher than 16.8 dB by optimizing the thickness of the flexible PET films of 200 μm. So it can be concluded that the proposed filtering method utilizing a transparent mesh PET film can be used to effectively improve shielding effectiveness of optoelectronic instrumental windows.

References

1. Kohin, M., Wein, S.J., Traylor, J.D., Chase, R.C., Chapman, J.E.: Analysis and design of transparent conductive coatings and filters. Opt. Eng. **132**(5), 911–925 (1993)
2. Liu, Y.M., Tan, J.B., Liu, J.: Use of a genetic algorithm with a penalty strategy to optimize optical communication window mesh. J. Opt. A: Pure Appl. Opt. **11**, 045403 (2009)
3. Tan, J.B., Liu, Y.M.: Optimization of optical communication window mesh through full-wave analysis of periodic mesh. Opt. Commun. **281**, 4835–4839 (2008)
4. Saremi, M.S., Nourian, M., Mirsalehi, M.M., Keshmiri, S.H.: Design of multilayer polarizing beam splitters using genetic algorithm. Opt. Commun. **233**, 57–59 (2004)
5. Ulrich, R.: Far-infrared properties of metallic mesh and its complementary structure. Infrared Phys. **7**, 37–55 (1967)
6. Mahan, G.D., Marple, D.T.F.: Infrared absorption of thin metal film: Pt on Si. Appl. Phys. Lett. **42**(3), 219–221 (1983)
7. Baron, B.T., Euphrasie, S., Mbarek, S.B., Vairac, P., Cretin, B.: Design of metallic mesh absorbers for high bandwidth electromagnetic waves. Prog. Electromagn. Res. **8**, 135–147 (2009)
8. Miguel, N., Miguel, B., Spyros, A., Francisco, F., Mario, S., Strfan, A.M.: Broadband spoof plasmons and subwavelength electromagnetic energy confinement on ultrathin metafilms. Opt. Express **17**(20), 18184–18195 (2009)
9. Lee, S.W., Zarrillo, G., Law, C.L.: Simple formulas for transmission through periodic metal grids or plates. IEEE Trans. Antennas Propag. **30**(5), 904–909 (1982)
10. Herbert, P.M., Jam, F., Ciou, A.E.: Performance of metal meshes as a function of incidence angle. Appl. Opt. **23**(23), 4228–4232 (1984)
11. Wu, T.K.: Frequency Selective Surface and Grid Array. Wiley, New York (1995)
12. Tlusty, J., Smith, S., Zamudia, C.: Operation planning based on cutting process model. Ann. CIRP **39**(12), 517–521 (1990)

Author Index

Printed in the United States
By Bookmasters